To my mother and fat
Miroslava and Frank K

MODERNITY AND POWER

FRANK NINKOVICH

MODERNITY
AND
POWER

◦◊·◦◊·◦◊◦

A History of the Domino Theory
in the Twentieth Century

THE UNIVERSITY OF CHICAGO PRESS
Chicago & London

FRANK NINKOVICH is professor of history at St. John's University in New York City. He is the author of *The Diplomacy of Ideas: U.S. Foreign Policy and Cultural Relations, 1938–1950,* and *Germany and the United States: The Transformation of the German Question since 1945.*

The University of Chicago Press, Chicago 60637
The University of Chicago Press, Ltd., London
© 1994 by The University of Chicago
All rights reserved. Published 1994
Printed in the United States of America
03 02 01 00 99 98 97 96 95 94   1 2 3 4 5

ISBN: 0-226-58650-2 (cloth)
0-226-58651-0 (paper)

Library of Congress Cataloging-in-Publication Data

Ninkovich, Frank A., 1944–
    Modernity and power : a history of the domino theory in the
twentieth century / Frank Ninkovich.
        p.   cm.
    Includes bibliographical references and index.
    1. World politics—20th century.   2. United States—Foreign
relations—20th century.   I. Title.
D453.N56   1994
327'.09'04—dc20   94-5733
                                                                        CIP

This book is printed on acid-free paper.

CONTENTS

Acknowledgments IX

Introduction XI

1 Roosevelt and Taft: The Emergence of Civilization
as Policy Principle 1

2 Woodrow Wilson and the Historical Necessity of Idealism 37

3 Herbert Hoover: Culture versus Civilization 69

4 Franklin D. Roosevelt: The Halfway Wilsonian 99

5 Wilsonian Problems: George F. Kennan and the Definition
of the Cold War 133

6 Wilsonian Solutions: Toward a New Language of Power 166

7 Eisenhower's Symbolic Cold War 203

8 John F. Kennedy and the Impossibility of Realism 241

9 Lyndon Johnson and the Crisis of World Opinion 276

Conclusion 312

Abbreviations Used Frequently in the Notes 321

Notes 323

Index 409

ACKNOWLEDGMENTS

T HE WORK OF HISTORIANS would be impossible without the collaboration of professional archivists. The following individuals stand out most prominently in my memory for valuable assistance rendered: at the Truman Library, Irwin Mueller and Liz Safly; at the Hoover Library, Bob Wood, Dwight Miller, Cora Pedersen, and Shirley Sondergard; at the Lyndon B. Johnson Library, David Humphrey. While in Austin, Walt W. Rostow was gracious enough to grant me an interview. At Princeton's Seeley G. Mudd Library, Jean Holliday was unfailingly helpful. The list would be much longer were it not for the fact that, in some cases, my archival visits were of the hit-and-run variety in which I did not have time to develop closer relationships.

I would like also to thank some friends who provided encouragement and advice at opportune moments. To Dorothy Jones, who over the years has listened to various of my musings and responded with reasoned judgments, sound advice, and encouragement, I shall always be grateful. Hugh De Santis has never failed to make himself available for talks which, whether highly theoretical or hopelessly mundane, were always stimulating. Akira Iriye, as always, has been there when I needed him. On more occasions than I would like to recall, Warren Cohen and Lawrence Kaplan dutifully wrote letters of recommendation to various funding bodies. John Milton Cooper, Jr., too, was generous enough to listen to my ideas and go to bat for me. Thanks are also due to all my colleagues in diplomatic history. The writing of history is of necessity a solitary pursuit, but it would not be possible at all were it not for the stimulating community of discourse created and fostered by the profession.

I would also like to acknowledge with gratitude various institutions that, over the years, made possible the completion of this study. A fellowship from the National Endowment for the Humanities allowed me to take a year away from teaching to begin this study. Subsequently, travel grants from the Harry S. Truman Library and the Lyndon B. Johnson Library helped defray costs of research. St. John's University granted me a semester's leave with pay to fill a then-becalmed manuscript with new wind.

A portion of chapter 1 was published some years ago in different form in *Diplomatic History*. Thanks are due to its editor, Michael Hogan, for graciously allowing me to include portions of that essay in this work.

Appreciation is also due to Doug Mitchell, General Editor at the University of Chicago Press, for his receptiveness to a manuscript that I feared would be greeted with considerable skepticism. Happily, I could not have asked for a more sympathetic and understanding editor. Carol Saller of the University of Chicago Press deserves a medal for painstakingly unearthing errors of every variety imaginable.

As always, my wife, Carol, has put up with all my eccentricities and showed a matter-of-fact confidence in my ability to see this work through to completion. This work is dedicated to my parents, who taught me the most important things.

INTRODUCTION

I N TRYING TO IMPART to his listeners a sense of how to think about
foreign policy, Dean Acheson once said that "one must begin, if one is
to be truthful, with the most obvious of platitudes . . . a truth which
one has taken for granted."[1] This book about American internationalism in
the twentieth century centers on the career of such a platitude: the belief that
the United States could be secure, as a polity and a society, only within the
nurturing environment of a liberal world civilization. It would seem that
platitudes are, by definition, so obvious as to be analytically useless. But the
most puzzling phenomena in this world are precisely the ones we take for
granted. This is certainly the case within the scholarly disciplines, where the
foundational concepts that are the tools for unearthing new knowledge—
power in political science, culture in anthropology, truth in philosophy, fact
in history—themselves prove to be quite problematic as new subatomic levels
continue to be discovered, explored, and colonized by the larger world of
understanding. For the American statesmen in this study, civilization was no
less foundational and no less problematic.

When American statesmen in the first half of the twentieth century measured other nations by the yardstick of civilization, their point of reference
was modernization. Of course, the term "modernization," which is of mid–
twentieth century vintage, was not yet in the language, but the oft-used word
"civilization" was close enough in meaning to be its conceptual parent.[2]
Like modernization, civilization suggested a sweeping contrast between past
and present in which an industrially based modern way of life had ushered in
an institutionally profound, globe-girdling transformation that stood without
historical parallel. More specifically, it subsumed many of the analytical
concepts that would later become mainstays of social scientific modernization
theory. Among other things, it assumed that modernity was characterized by
a legal-rational outlook dominated by science, the professionalization and

bureaucratization of institutions, and, not least, the emergence of a global division of labor as a result of the workings of the market economy.

Because civilization was, at the time, less a sociological than a historical concept, it was, like all historical outlooks, an unstable mixture of fact and value.[3] Though later weeded out by social scientists, unabashedly value-loaded terms such as peace, prosperity, and the inexorable global advance of Christianity and democracy seemed at the time vital ingredients in the complex formula for "progress" synthesized in the experimental laboratory of Western history. Such terms suggest a self-congratulatory smugness that was indeed present in much of the rhetoric of the time, but thoughtful types realized that civilization also had a problematic side to it, perhaps best summarized by what one author has called "the shock of the new."[4] The fin-de-siècle progressive historical sensibility was keenly aware that the modern present was so new and different that traditional beliefs were inadequate as guides to contemporary behavior. Walter Lippmann captured perfectly this sense of credal flux when he wrote about the need for modern industrial societies to "substitute purpose for tradition" and to "treat life not as something given but as something to be shaped."[5]

New facts, new values—all of this was highly unsettling and problematic. Civilization was grounded in the indisputably revolutionary social and cultural consequences of industrialism, of course, but the facts tended to become fuzzy and indeterminate once one attempted to go beyond broad outline in describing what was happening to society, either nationally or internationally. And then, even if the facts of what civilization was doing to the world had been absolutely transparent, objective knowledge could still not have been alchemized into policy, for as Alasdair MacIntyre has pointed out, "questions of ends are questions of values, and on values reason is silent."[6] Despite the self-confident and ostensibly scientific demeanor of much social analysis of this period, then, the modern outlook was in fact beset by doubt and uncertainty as to the nature of the civilizational process and its trajectory.

This apprehensiveness was reflected in thinking about U.S. foreign policy. It was a commonplace at the turn of the century that the United States, as an inexorable part of the civilizational process, was becoming a world power. For some, the seductive charms of power opened up a terrifying prospect in which the United States would lose the virtue derived from chaste separation from the Old World. Because they saw the workings of power as a historical constant, traditionalists fearful of America's absorption into a global milieu of power would have agreed with Paul Ricoeur's comment that "power does not have much of a history."[7] However, if one starts with what Anthony Giddens has called a "discontinuist interpretation of modern history,"[8] as did most of the protagonists of this story, this traditional view of power seems to distort modern realities. For those who thought in civilizational terms, few assumed that this process of absorption meant that the United States would need to adopt traditional Old World values and methods. Far from entering a static and stable order, it seemed apparent that the United States was being drawn instead into a system that was itself undergoing a dramatic metamorphosis in which foreign-policy problems were drastically different from those encountered in the past.[9]

For American statesmen, convinced that "the change to change"[10] extended also to international relations, power most definitely did have a history, one that was entering a dramatic new phase. Even had it wanted to, the United States could not have become a traditional kind of power, because its entrance onto the stage of world politics was being forced by a modernization process that was simultaneously revising the dramatic conventions of power politics. These changes were not uniformly for the better. While the new global environment in which the United States found itself certainly held extraordinary promise, it also proved to be mined with unprecedented perils. Indeed, it soon enough became clear that the continued reliance upon power in traditional forms as the keystone of international politics had become too dangerous, given the recent emergence of a runaway capacity for self-destruction whose devastating effects were compounded by the universalizing effects of geographic contraction. Thus the historicization of power, its modernization, made impossible any resort to traditional realism.

One of the features of being modern, or postmodern, is that we are ambivalent about progress. We no longer take progress on faith because we recognize that there exist no extrahistorical patterns to guide the overall direction of what is a high-risk historical process in which the benefits of modernity are always shadowed by extraordinary dangers. Just as our sense of history is permeated with doubt and relativism, so too American statesmen were well aware that they were operating without benefit of the reassuring presence of a guiding Providence.[11] This sense of rootlessness and contingency was accompanied by the realization that history could "crash," a possibility given ever-greater plausibility by the political catastrophes that darkened the century. American policymakers took it for granted that civilization, if not taken in hand and redirected, contained within itself ironic possibilities for self-immolation. Far from being utopian idealists, then, they fully shared the twentieth century's discontents.

The novelty of the problem of power in a modern context evoked a correspondingly novel concern with world opinion as a solution. In their own way, American statesmen were just as much participants in the conceptual revolution of modernity as were avant-garde artists, litterateurs, and musicians. They understood that modernity implied a revolutionary break with traditional social structures and cultural forms.[12] This association of civilization with radical modernity helps to explain why the principles and practice of American foreign policy as it developed in the course of the century were so different from those prescribed by traditional manuals of power politics.[13] If Providence or natural balances no longer sufficed as workaday expedients, policymakers understood that power could not, as in the past, simply be opposed to power without bringing down upon the world the most frightful consequences. Therefore, a reliance on some form of world opinion, a conceptual harnessing of structural forces with built-in runaway tendencies, emerged as the only possible solution to peculiarly modern problems of international relations.

Common to all the statesmen in this study—even to an isolationist like Herbert Hoover—was the conviction that structural interdependence required some form of transcultural understanding if it was to hold together. Inasmuch as this study deals with what Clifford Geertz has called "local knowledge," it should be made clear at the outset that it is not a study of world opinion as such but an investigation of the American conception of world opinion, a conception that was necessarily limited by the peculiarities of time and place. It is, of course, arguable whether terms like "civilization" and "world opinion" have any objective standing in foreign affairs, but they mattered if only because American policymakers believed that they did. Indeed, much of American foreign policy in the twentieth century, which is marked by an obsession with credibility and a neglect of the traditional realist concern for matching means with ends, is inexplicable unless one recognizes that the preoccupation with world opinion seemed an unavoidable solution to certain novel geopolitical problems.[14] With internationalism thus defined as a set of beliefs about the importance of beliefs, it should not be surprising that the content of their policies, which featured ideas about culture, civilization, ideology, and symbolism, was very close to the core intellectual concerns of modernity.

This novel way of thinking about foreign affairs corresponded to the general shift that has taken place in the twentieth century away from a correspondence theory of truth that stresses the tight connection between words and things to one emphasizing meaningful coherence as a test of validity. By this new conception, the national interest—that is, the values in which policy was grounded—would no longer be determined by concrete criteria like tangible military threats, an immediate calculus of economic gain or loss, or a nationalistic concern for maintaining prestige. Instead, international events would be graded for importance on the basis of their impact upon civilizational beliefs, whose continued coherence and solidarity was the key to checking a slide into global chaos. Interests, formerly "hard," material, and national, became by this new standard soft, symbolic, and international. The efficacy of American policy would therefore be determined by the degree of conviction that a belief system could command. This symbolic approach to the management of power, I will argue, provides the key to explaining otherwise puzzling elements of cold-war policy, especially its preoccupation with what I have called symbolic interventionism.

Apart from the substantive practical solutions, the analytical method inherent in the American approach to foreign policy was also quite modern in a sense that has yet to receive adequate recognition. The modern view of human understanding as an active process of interpretation and construction of reality is a fair approximation of what American policymakers were doing.[15] They acted on the basis of a historical interpretation that provided one possible explanation of events that were shot through with what one anthropologist has called "theoretically absolute indeterminacy."[16] Statesmen "read" the international environment as if it were a text, but for much of the twentieth century a condition obtained which was the opposite of dyslexia: incoherence inhered in the text rather than in the minds of the readers. Since the global environment of the 1920s and 1930s was so confusing and indeterminate, conceptual order could not emerge solely from mastery of objective details or by the application of traditional recipes. It had to be supplied imaginatively by statesmen. With traditional definitions of national interest no longer of much use, events were necessarily overlaid by a template of historical interpretation which helped statesmen to construct reality.[17] Given the impossibility of applying scientific or objectivist approaches to knowledge to international relations, historical understanding, inexact as it was, was the only available tool for making sense of the world.

To emphasize the centrality of historical interpretation and symbolism in no way implies that American policy was somehow divorced from reality (although its rejection of traditional "realism" is another matter). Nor, for that matter was the historical interpretation of international modernization, an empirically verifiable process with national and international dimensions, merely an ideological "reflection" or distortion of events. Because, as David Carr has put it, "narrative activity is a constitutive part of action, and not just an embellishment,"[18] the larger historical ideas of statesmen were just as much a part of reality as the "objective" circumstances that they were presumably "about." Historical interpretation was not something that they imposed upon events, but an important feature of lived experience that was subject to pragmatic tests of truth in the laboratory of policy experience.[19]

The translation of this conceptual revolution into practical policy occupies much of this book, and that is where the domino theory comes in.

Though it is not immediately obvious, the domino theory encapsulates the central foreign-policy presuppositions of this new way of thinking. The domino theory is a metaphor, a word-picture that explains one process by identifying it with another. A picture is often worth a thousand words of description, but Hegel was closer to the mark in his contention that words provide a higher order of conceptual knowledge than sensuous pictures or images. Metaphors as verbal pictures are deceptively simple ways of achieving understanding. As George Lakoff and Mark Johnson suggest, they organize "a whole system of concepts with respect to one another,"[20] while for Max Black "every metaphor is the tip of a submerged model."[21] Assuming, therefore, that metaphors are deceptive in their simplicity, and that they both organize and conceal linguistic concepts, it is possible to "unpack" the propositions that lie beneath the figurative image of toppling dominoes. In this case, not too much thought is required to tease out the domino metaphor's propositional content.

First, the metaphor implies the absence of a homeostatic, self-regulating system. Translated into strategic terms, it suggests the lack of a self-equilibrating balance of power. Second, the geopolitical analogue of closely spaced dominoes is a view of the world organized as a tightly linked system. Third, the horizontal domino image can also be translated into a vertical military dimension whose main feature is open-ended and uncontrollable escalation. Fourth, whether the chain reaction starts in the center or in the remotest, farthest end of the chain, and however circuitous the patterns and alignments, once the disturbance begins, the last domino, that is, the United States, will fall. Fifth, and least obviously, if the chain reaction cannot stop itself, it must be checked by a force capable of analyzing the domino process and subverting its dynamics.

These various propositions were first elaborated, though hardly in such abstract and systematic form, by Woodrow Wilson during World War I, not long after America's entry into the war. Far from being a slave to the idealistic worldview with which he has been so closely identified, Wilson was making strategic arguments that very much resembled the interventionist rationales offered up in the late 1930s and during the cold war, arguments that came to be embodied in the domino theory. By tracing the cold war's geopolitical genealogy to Wilsonianism more directly and convincingly than has been done heretofore, I hope not only to show how the domino theory emerged and matured, but to demonstrate why its ideas were so compelling to American statesmen. John Lewis Gaddis once wrote, with his usual perceptiveness, that the Vietnam War "was fought for geopolitical reasons that remain obscure to this day."[22] Perhaps it will seem less obscure as a result of the intellectual odyssey described by this work.

By tracing the changing relationships of the propositions to one another once their historical birth date has been established—in this case World War I rather than Munich or the Truman Doctrine—I hope to tell a more complex story that goes beyond the mere repetitive cataloging of episodes that feature domino-related metaphors such as the rotten apple spoiling the barrel, bandwagon effect, landslide, cork in the bottle, finger in the dike, and so on.[23] Perhaps some light will be shed on other cold-war explanatory terms— bipolarity, Manicheanism, zero-sum game, for example—that are guilty of a similar metaphorical reductionism. I hope to show that the underlying system of propositions governing the thinking of policymakers was far more complex, indeterminate, and logically precarious.

Put somewhat differently, this book deals with what Ernest May, in a seminal essay, called the "axioms" underlying foreign-policy calculations by showing how these axioms came into being and how they changed over time.[24] In order to convey a better understanding of the context from which the strategic sensibility behind the domino theory emerged, it seemed advisable to start my discussion of modernity and civilization with Theodore Roosevelt at the turn of the century, though obviously it could be taken farther back still. The most manageable way of handling the topic was to limit my story only to major American statesmen and to an interpretation of their relative contributions. I realize that the policy process is far more complex than is suggested by this biographical approach, but there seemed little alternative to deliberate simplification by personification if I was to tell the story at all. Besides, if the old heroic framework of history still has any mileage left in it, it is likely to be found in diplomatic history.

The ideological trajectory of these axioms as they evolved over the decades conforms to a pattern that has been well outlined in the social scientific literature on social movements. Though it may seem that ideas are the most volatile and unpredictable of human creations—especially for intellectuals who tend to use and discard them like toys—ideologies are actually much like institutions in their life cycles and duration. The systems of ideas that govern our political sensibilities tend to go through a cycle of creative articulation, preliminary organization, and attainment of power, only to be followed by a period of self-contradiction and perhaps even decay as a result of having to deal with the complexities of power inevitably encountered once enthroned. In a very rough way, the typical careers of ideologies tend to correspond to the patterns of institutional creation and decline, which is why the study of ideology is generally associated with the sociology of knowledge—ideas and social action go hand in hand.[25]

In keeping with this general schema, the first part of this book deals with the gestation and birth of these Wilsonian strategic premises, their slow growth in the quarter century following America's rejection of the Versailles Treaty, and their sudden leap into responsible adulthood in the 1940s. Once the domino theory's underlying propositions were internalized or "sedimented" as axioms by policymakers, they did not remain buried, chemically inert, under metaphorical topsoil. There was, to be sure, little change in how problems were defined, but the same was not true for solutions, where considerable innovation took place. As new constellations of problems emerged, the policy applications of domino thinking generated a maze of contradictions and paradoxes that required constant reconsideration. Consequently, the second half of the book focuses on the various solutions posed to the basic problem of stopping a domino reaction or, better yet, preventing it from starting in the first place, once policymakers began to get feedback from their application of domino-based policy.

Although this shift from conceptualization to implementation has made it necessary for me to pay closer attention to specific policy issues in the second half of the book, I do not pretend to deal comprehensively with the various crises touched upon. Other historians have analyzed them in far more detail than I could ever hope to, while still others have already outlined the larger narrative that I will be adopting in a very unoriginal way.[26] Inasmuch as this is a work of reinterpretation rather than a synthesis of the existing literature, I have felt the obligation to ground it in primary sources. For this reason, and because an already lengthy work would have become longer still, I have chosen not to cite in any great detail the enormous secondary literature on U.S. foreign relations. It is because these primary sources are available only through the 1960s that the work ends with the Johnson administration. Though I trust that the Vietnam War does mark a natural stopping point, as the conclusion suggests, the story could, in principle, easily enough be extended to the present. One of the benefits of doing research in the various archival repositories was that I came to appreciate how deeply some of my colleagues have gone into topics whose surface I was only skimming. Fortunately, that kind of mastery is not crucial to my story, which seeks merely to trace in a general way the civilizational logic of policymaking in this century.

I

ROOSEVELT AND TAFT: THE EMERGENCE OF CIVILIZATION AS POLICY PRINCIPLE

THEODORE ROOSEVELT: CHARACTER, CULTURE, AND CIVILIZATION

VIRGINIA WOOLF ONCE WROTE THAT "on or about December 1910, human character changed."[1] Cultural transformations can hardly be dated with such outrageous precision, but she had a point nevertheless: the end of the first decade of the twentieth century does seem as good a point in time as any to mark the advent of modernism, a cultural revolution that introduced complex and radically new ways of seeing the world.[2] Though this upheaval is normally associated with epochal breakthroughs in the arts and sciences, an analogous intellectual transformation was taking place at about the same time in the high culture of American foreign policy. The most obvious indication of such a conceptual revolution was the nearly total reversal in the American image of Great Britain, Germany, Russia, China, and Japan. Within the space of a few years, Britain and China, once held in low repute, were suddenly bathed in a more flattering light, while Wilhelmine Germany, czarist Russia, and Meiji Japan came to appear as suspicious and untrustworthy powers.[3]

Although the specific twists and turns of U.S. relations with all these nations certainly help to account for these changes of viewpoint, the near simultaneity of their occurrence cannot be explained solely by tracing the impact of discrete events. More important than particular circumstances in accounting for these reversals of outlook was the general transformation of the historical frame from which Americans viewed the world.[4] The turnabout in perception from benign to sinister or vice-versa was, in each instance, based on judgments concerning the degree of modernity of the nations in question. The new favorites, those that rose in American opinion, were closely identified with the virtues of civilization, while those that declined came up short by that measure.

The first president to make a conscious and consistent effort to situate American foreign policy within this civilizational frame was Theodore Roosevelt. He was the first modern president in foreign affairs because he was the first to deal with the implications of modernity. His originality lay in his historical interpretation of America's place in the modern world, in his effort to make sense of the nation's expanding interests, and in his attempts to make policies that were consistent with that formulation. Unfortunately, Roosevelt's remarkable personality has tended to obscure the true nature of his historical significance. Personality and policy have been so closely intertwined in our image of the man that we continue to see Roosevelt as a caveman in drag, as if we knew that his feminine protestations of principle failed miserably to conceal the hairy masculinity beneath. Given this psychological reductionism, we have tended to interpret his foreign policy as a direct extension of his overpowering personality. According to Howard K. Beale's classic judgment, Roosevelt "saw world events and policies in terms of power. He was intrigued with power, with the problems of power, and with rivalries of power."[5]

However, those who knew him well realized that his diplomacy was not a reflex of his emotional urges. Elihu Root, who served successively as secretary of war and secretary of state under the Rough Rider, recalled Roosevelt as measuring "each international question against the background of those tendencies through which civilization develops and along which particular civilizations advance or decline." In thought and action alike, his belief in civilization was the key to what Lewis Einstein, among the more perceptive Roosevelt-watchers, has called "the reasoned philosophy of his conduct." Rather than the impulsive troglodyte wielding the big stick, it was the cultured Roosevelt employing interpretive reason who heralded the emergence of the modern American presidency in foreign affairs. Far more than temperament, it was Roosevelt's understanding of history that, besides putting some badly needed rouge of erudition on his rough image, dictated how he conceived of his nation's global destiny.[6]

In contrast to his meager physiognomic endowments as a youth, Roosevelt was naturally blessed (or cursed, depending on one's point of view) with an unusually muscular historical sensibility. How many other college seniors have begun to write something as consequential as *The History of the Naval War of 1812,* the multivolume work he began while still at Harvard? His numerous historical works, most notably *The Naval War of 1812* and *The Winning of the West,* eventually gained him well-deserved recognition as president of the American Historical Association. We do not know what moved him to write history—that is a question most historians would have trouble answering for themselves—but it is obvious that the cultivation of an understanding of history mattered deeply to Roosevelt.

What role did history play in Roosevelt's foreign policy? At first glance, the answer seems fairly straightforward. With William Jennings Bryan playing the naive Jefferson to Roosevelt's heroic Hamilton, historical debate resembled a shadow play that illuminated the eternally recurring confrontations of timeless issues and protagonists. For those who, like Roosevelt, were of the neo-Federalist persuasion, the need for a strong, efficient central government seemed even more compelling during the Progressive Era than during the early national period. Because, according to Roosevelt, wise statesmanship depended on an "adherence to the principles and policies under which this nation was built up and in accordance with which it must go on," policy could not afford to drift away from its mooring in past experience. The Federalist heroes were also models of strength and energy. Their unrefined but basic character traits, occasionally termed the "barbarian virtues" by Roosevelt, seemed no less indispensable to preserving the republic from decay in his day than during the critical formative period of American history. In foreign affairs, the Federalists' manly willingness to accept the use of force as a regrettable but necessary occasional instrument of national policy continued to provide meaningful inspiration.[7]

While character was the grain of sand around which the pearl of civilization developed, it was only a means for pursuing larger ends that had to be historically conceived and understood. For Roosevelt, history was not concretely given by the past, nor was it a mass of objective facts painstakingly assembled, witness his condescending attitude toward the detailed, fact-grubbing, "scientific history" that predominated among the newly established professionals in the universities. Instead, history as written by the masters was an imaginative art form that contained the usual elements of literary craft: heroic protagonists, moral struggle, and clear plot development. Imagination helped to vivify personalities and illuminate details, but it was also indispensable to grasping the large contours of plot necessary to any compelling interpretation.[8]

This visionary historical frame was also quite essential to foreign policy. "When we say that the great historian must be a man of imagination," Roosevelt maintained, "we use the word as we use it when we say that the great statesman must be a man of imagination." Statesmanship demanded above all vision, sympathetic insight into a future shaped by flux and change, lest one fall victim to "that complete and brutal indifference to futurity" of which Tocqueville had warned. The dynamism of civilization called for a forward-looking historical frame, on the horizon of which one glimpsed the reconciliation of American and global destinies. Roosevelt believed that difficulties would most likely arise from "a serious indifference to, and inability to grasp, the future on the part of our people as a whole." "We are all peering into the future," he wrote in 1895, "to try to forecast the action of the great dumb forces set in motion by the stupendous industrial revolution which has taken place in this century." Tradition mattered, but the lessons of the past and an empirical grasp of nineteenth-century developments needed to be recontextualized by a convincing historical reading of America's place in the emerging global era.[9]

Although professional historians had not yet gotten around to the study of world history, Roosevelt had no doubts that he was up to the intellectual demands of understanding contemporary global currents. Indeed, if one were to draw up a "cosmopolitanism index" in the manner of social scientists, Roosevelt's numbers would go off the scale. It was this cosmopolitan cast of mind that most set him apart from the ancestral heroes and the myth of two worlds that heretofore had dominated American historical thought. True, the Founding Fathers had also been members of a transnational cosmopolitan elite, but their foreign-policy legacy only wound up reinforcing the "provincial" cast of mind that Roosevelt gleefully ridiculed. It was positively naive to think that America occupied a historical niche unto itself. "Frowning or hopeful, every man of leadership in any line of thought or effort must look beyond the limits of his own country," he insisted. Attempting to smash the Old World–New World dichotomy that Americans took as an article of national faith, he argued: "The differences between these 'new' American and these 'old' European nations are not as great as those which separate the 'new' nations from one another, and the 'old' nations one from another."[10]

As a result of this modernist cast of thought, some basic assumptions of Federalist foreign policy—a regional-hemispheric approach to international politics, a classical political orientation to foreign relations, and a timeless view of history as a repository of eternal truths about human nature—were supplanted or seriously modified by Roosevelt's evolutionist ideas. In his Romanes Lecture of 1910, he asserted, in good modernist fashion, that "the present civilization can be compared to nothing that has gone before. It is literally a world movement." The perception of the globe's unity in space and time was crucial, for it obliterated the geographical, cultural, and temporal distinctions that gave life to the historical myth of old and new worlds. Henceforth one would have to conceptualize the national interest from the standpoint of the unity of global processes rather than from the particularist frame with which statecraft had traditionally been more comfortable.[11]

No doubt many would have considered this to be a hopelessly abstract theoretical issue, but Roosevelt was convinced that the global expansion of civilization had "more vital consequences than any other to the future of the race and of the world." Should the United States fail to come to terms with this ecumenical trend and its implications, he feared that the nation would "become so isolated from the struggles of the rest of the world, and so immersed in our material prosperity, so that we shall become genuinely effete." Given civilization's global compass, the implication was unmistakable: henceforth integration into the mainstream of world history must be the guiding theme of American statesmanship. This meant, obviously, that the United States needed to modernize its diplomacy to fit new global circumstances.[12]

The most striking international feature of triumphant Western "civilization" was imperialism. With the reputation for national power coming to depend increasingly on a nation's stature as a world power, the fulfillment of nationalist ambition would therefore have to come via some form of internationalism, which, in practical terms, meant imperialism. Roosevelt's endless references to civilization now seem curiously archaic, primarily because they were closely related to his apologetics for an imperialism that, in retrospect, is viewed with embarrassment. Yet it was precisely in the phenomenon of imperialism that Roosevelt and many other Progressives saw an opportunity for the successful reconciliation of American and global destinies. Throughout his presidency, if not afterward, Roosevelt's historical vision was satisfied by fitting the novelty of modern imperialism into a traditional strategic frame of reference.[13]

This was hardly an easy task. The United States was already a world power at the time Theodore Roosevelt became president in 1901, but it was a world power without a global program. Having been catapulted to imperial prominence suddenly in the Spanish-American War of 1898, America's conquests had come more easily than their justification. The impassioned but inconclusive debate on annexing the Philippines only aggravated the intellectual confusion besetting the country. Though the annexation went through, just barely, as a party measure, America had become a world power in spite of herself, a nation with imperial status but no settled sense of its imperial role, buffeted by powerful forces within and without that cried out for explanation.

For many younger Americans, imperialism was an attractive gateway to modernity that seemed to open onto an entirely new road in international politics, one in which the stubbornly persistent stain of European power politics would finally be removed by the cleansing action of a universal modernizing process. Imperialism appeared to be the agent of a new international order in which Old World *Machtpolitik* was giving way to a universal, modern, and more benign system in which the United States could feel comfortably at home. According to Herbert Croly, better known as a theoretician of domestic progressivism, it remained as unthinkable as ever that the United States should seek to become a European power, but at the same time it seemed foreordained that "Europe, the United States, Japan, and China must all eventually take their places in a world system." From this viewpoint America's rise to world power, far from Europeanizing its foreign policy, coincided with the creation, through the agency of imperialism, of a new and radically global matrix for diplomacy. Rather than America becoming Europeanized by its rise to world power, both America and the Continent would be globalized.[14]

Although the colonial scramble may have seemed to some as nothing more than the projection of squalid European politics onto a world stage, many Progressives saw it differently. For one thing, because imperialism featured as major actors non-European nations with interests, values, and traditions different from Europe's, it had the makings of a world system which was qualitatively far different from the narrower concerns of the European balance of power. Moreover, even if the newcomers were excluded from consideration, the imperialist lineups did not match the European rosters. Indeed, the rapid formation and dissolution of imperialist alignments led students of the subject like Paul Reinsch to predict that imperialism would spell the end of fixed alliances in favor of "kaleidoscopic change." Rather than overflowing its banks onto a global flood plain, therefore, the European system seemed destined to remain confined to the Continent. As England was discovering, the balance of power was a limiting factor in the ability to pursue worldwide interests; overseas attachments were hostage to European events, and vice-versa.[15]

While the diplomacy of imperialism seemed to herald a harmonious new brand of world politics among the great powers, its powerful developmental rationale added to its historical appeal. Prominent among the concepts used by Roosevelt to highlight this side of imperial expansion was the clichéd evolutionary idea, of Enlightenment origin, that cultures progressed from savagery to barbarism to civilization. However deficient this concept may seem from today's more relativist and pluralist standpoint, this trichotomy—with vital intermediate gradations, as we shall see—was nevertheless the accepted scientific yardstick of the time for gauging cultural development. Inasmuch as innovation and progress were seldom generated spontaneously by individual cultures, it seemed incumbent upon the civilized races to transplant the seeds of civilization where they had failed to germinate of their own accord. "It is our duty toward the people living in barbarism to see that they are freed from their chains, and we can free them only by destroying barbarism itself," Roosevelt argued. Consequently, to tolerate liberation movements and leave peoples like the Filipinos to their own devices would constitute "an international crime."[16]

His fascination with racial and cultural struggle has suggested to more than one observer that Roosevelt surveyed "the great sweep of history from a social Darwinian frame of reference," when in fact his biological evolutionary views never strayed onto the adjoining, but quite clearly marked, intellectual property of Social Darwinism. Darwinism for Roosevelt remained a biological theory from which it was wholly inappropriate to draw the kind of analogical evolutionary inferences found in Social Darwinism. Pointing to the common failure to make such distinctions, he complained that "the trouble about Darwinism is that people confound it with evolution." This criticism was made from a Lamarckian perspective, which happened to be the prevailing scientific outlook of his day. Affirming the heart of Lamarckian doctrine, he maintained that "society progresses, the improvement being due mainly to the transmission of culturally acquired characters."[17]

Unlike many of his out-and-out racist contemporaries, Roosevelt saw no reason why all people could not eventually become civilized. Evolution, after all, was a ladder, not a greased pole. He could and did advert constantly to racial differences, often in depreciatory or contemptuous terms, and he certainly believed in genetic inferiority, but his Lamarckianism always left open the possibility of gradual improvement. Granted, this was a period of confused thinking about race and culture, when one writer could even refer seriously to the "Anglican race." But in its scientific assumptions and political conclusions, Roosevelt's position was clearly far removed from what one historian has described as "a mystique of white supremacy supported by the Darwinian concept of the survival of the fittest."[18]

Because cultural evolution's developmental logic superseded and contradicted the purely organic laws of nature, Roosevelt also rejected the conflict model of social change associated with the purely sociological variants of Social Darwinism. "The rivalry of natural selection is but one of the features in progress," he maintained, going on to argue that "progress is made in spite of it." Thus cultural evolution, the growth of civilization with its progressive strengthening of law and order, transcended Darwinian struggle, be it man against nature or man versus man. As the global expression of cultural evolution, civilization brought order worldwide through the spread of morality and the reinforcement of virtue, whereas the anarchic Darwinian vision promised only intermittent, despotically enforced peace in an endless, chaotic chain of conflict. Though law and order in the domestic sense was lacking, nevertheless Roosevelt felt that the imperatives of civilized existence were compellingly at work in international society.[19]

Imperialism made eminently good sense from all the elements of Roosevelt's worldview, for it assured the nation's status as one of civilization's leading disseminators, helped ease the United States into the flow of civilization by contributing to world order, and harmonized the progressive yearning for order, cooperation, and rationality with the continued exercise of the primal manly virtues. There were economic arguments to be made on behalf of empire, of course, but Roosevelt the antimaterialist always preferred to focus on the spiritual rewards. America's greatness in the coming centuries would be determined largely by the degree to which it would contribute to sustaining the forward momentum of Anglo-Saxon values which Roosevelt placed at the cutting edge of history. Besides quickening the subject peoples, imperial conquests would have a tonic effect on the already civilized, for nations, like individuals, also needed to lead strenuous lives. "The masterful instinct which alone can make a race great" could be perpetuated only through the Lamarckian law of exercise.[20]

Law and order, too, would be served because Roosevelt believed that "warlike intervention by the civilized powers would contribute directly to the peace of the world." There was, he maintained, "a real analogy between the use of force in international and the use of force in national matters," though the absence of a sovereign international authority obviously meant that the analogy could not be pushed too far. Still, a civilizing imperialism, one which assured that "each part of the world should be prosperous and well-policed," seemed to offer a functional substitute for civil order. Typically, Roosevelt took this imperialist bromide to a provocative extreme when he claimed that "every expansion of a great civilized power means a victory for law, order, and righteousness" and that peace would come to the world only through "the warlike power of a civilized people."[21]

However fanciful, given the technological gap, this "struggle" between civilization and barbarism was more than cant. As president, Roosevelt's focus was clearly on North-South relations. If, as he believed, the civilized powers were capable of maintaining peace among themselves, then the road to world peace lay through imperialism pursued *à outrance*. To his credit, he was unafraid to pursue this logic to its limits by suggesting that, once the external dangers to civilization were well in hand, the advanced nations might at that point seriously consider the possibility of disarmament. According to Roosevelt: "If China became civilized like Japan, if the Turkish Empire were abolished, and all of uncivilized Africa and Asia held by England or France or Russia and Germany, then I believe we should be within sight of a time when a general international agreement could be made by which armies and navies could be reduced so as to meet merely the needs of internal and international police work."

The process of global pacification initially envisioned by Roosevelt is difficult, indeed impossible, to reconcile with the idea, often attributed to him, that there existed an uneasy world balance of power. Quite to the contrary, his optimistic imperialist internationalism presupposed the absence of fundamental conflicts of interest among the civilized powers.[22]

TRADITION AND CIVILIZATION: THE IMPOSSIBLE BALANCING ACT

Roosevelt was no radical modernizer. In its strategic essentials, his differential ordering of priorities by region—domination in the Caribbean, balance of power in East Asia, and nonentanglement in Europe—hardly qualifies as an example of modern globalism. Indeed, if conceived only in terms of power, it was actually nonmodern, for it continued to divide the world into watertight strategic compartments much as Hamilton had done in Federalist 11. However, this rather dowdy strategic fabric was updated rather ingeniously by the addition of Roosevelt's flamboyant rhetoric of civilization and stitched seamlessly into his modish diplomacy of imperialism.

To the extent that the "world movement" did contain possibilities for collisions between the United States and the great powers, Roosevelt was quite anxious to avoid them while maintaining America's favored geographical position. Once he became a responsible national politician, imperialism as a practical matter assumed more problematic dimensions. Roosevelt no less than other members of the foreign-policy elite expressed alarm at an insatiable European expansionist appetite which, having already swallowed up Africa and much of Asia, needed only to reach Central and South America before attaining its natural limits. The situation seemed loaded with possibilities for conflict between America's historically acquired rights in the form of the Monroe Doctrine and Roosevelt's faith in the progressive flow of world historical currents.

The Venezuela crisis of 1895, in which the British appeared to be seeking to expand their Guiana colony at the expense of Venezuela, touched off warning bells in Roosevelt's mind. In a letter to the *Harvard Crimson,* he argued that acquiescence before such expansion would mean "the Monroe Doctrine has no real existence." To tolerate such European aggrandizement in the Americas would constitute "abject surrender of our principles." The strident American response, almost instinctive in its assertion of territoriality, he saw as being "based on national self-interest" and was "meant to uphold our interests in the teeth of the formidable Old World powers." Roosevelt professed also to be "fully alive to the danger from Japan." Because American interests were "as great in the Pacific as in the Atlantic, in the Hawaiian islands as in the West Indies,'' he thought it a ''horrible failure'' and ''colossal crime'' when the Cleveland administration in 1893 cravenly failed to follow through with the annexation of Hawaii.[23]

Roosevelt was quick to find firm traditional footing for his position, taking his stand on the Monroe Doctrine. The ''cardinal feature of American foreign policy,'' he called it, never ceasing to emphasize its sacredness or the soundness of its historically validated insights. In an 1896 magazine article, he defined its central thrust as ''forbidding European encroachment on American soil.'' A few years later, at the height of the Cuban crisis, Roosevelt vowed to ''treat as cause for war any effort by a European power to get as much as a fresh foothold of any kind on American soil.'' Here in full throat was the ''carnal larynx'' discerned by Richard Hofstadter, apparently roaring out of inherited territorial instinct at the scent of civilization's imperial approach.[24]

But Roosevelt was less interested in preserving a bygone regional world order than in reconciling the American tradition of diplomacy to the new world system. The Hamiltonian conception of a world divided into four politically isolated spheres could easily have been translated into analogously exclusive imperial spheres of influence, but Roosevelt had no difficulty in accepting European commercial and cultural influence in the Caribbean region so long as the political integrity of the doctrine remained intact. Too rigid an exclusionary position would not only contradict his universalism, it might also antagonize the Old World's powers rather than insulate the United States from them. Thus he was quite willing to have the United States serve as the fiduciary for European economic interests in the region.

Strictly speaking, the Roosevelt Corollary, if one takes a corollary to be a logical inference from axiomatic premises, was no corollary at all. Whereas the Monroe Doctrine had assumed a wall of separation between Europe and America, with two entirely different systems of domestic governance and foreign relations, the Roosevelt Corollary assumed a global process, epitomized by the Anglo-American rapprochement, in which those differences had narrowed considerably or disappeared altogether. As Herbert Croly argued, ''The emancipated and nationalized European states of today, so far from being essentially antagonistic to the American democratic nation, are constantly tending towards a condition which invites closer and more fruitful association with the United States.'' Roosevelt's assertion of an ''international police power'' in the Caribbean was made in the lingua franca of civilization, not in the tongue of Monrovian particularism.[25]

Although he took his stand on tradition, Roosevelt was fairly candid (for a politician) about the need to modernize the doctrine. It could not remain in a ''fossilized'' condition, he argued; ''either it must be abandoned or modified to meet the changing needs of national life." To make the doctrine "a living entity," it ought "not to be justified by precedent merely, but by the needs of the nation and the true interests of Western civilization." With the mention of civilization's "interests," it became clear that the refurbishment of the doctrine was quite extensive. Indeed, in Roosevelt's hands the doctrine was reincarnated rather than resurrected.[26]

Roosevelt's "corollary" was not totally discontinuous. The assertion of American power had the traditional aim of preventing Europe's politics from washing over to the Western Hemisphere, to prevent the worst case of the balance-of-power principle from becoming the basis of the nation's regional diplomacy. As Roosevelt put it, "We do not wish to bring ourselves to a position where we shall have to emulate the European system of enormous armies." To that extent, at least, hemispheric separation still existed. Whether or not the same was true of the associated principle of nonentanglement in European affairs was, given Roosevelt's internationalist logic, open to question, but it was a question that did not yet demand an answer.[27]

If American primacy in the Caribbean rested on propinquity and tradition, Roosevelt was quite prepared to acknowledge the same principles at work in Asia. As he confided to his German friend Speck von Sternburg, he wished that "the same policy could be pursued in China" as in the Caribbean, but by some other power. This was a view he would never abandon. Unlike many naval officers, who tended to give equal weight to the Monroe Doctrine and the Open Door policy as "genuine national commitments," it was always clear to Roosevelt that the Open Door depended always on a favorable imperialist environment in which primary responsibility fell to nations with regional historical interests far more compelling than America's recently asserted commercial and cultural ambitions in East Asia. In policy terms, this implied, as a basic assumption of Roosevelt's Far Eastern diplomacy, that China and the Open Door were not worth fighting over.[28]

Moreover, Roosevelt, unlike many of his countrymen, had little interest in seeing the United States cast in a major eleemosynary role. Initially, he hoped that the great powers would "act in concert and once for all put China in a position where she has to behave," but he soon came to prefer a single controlling hand. Gauging East Asian developments more from the "visionary standpoint" of civilization than from American commercial interests, Russia seemed at first to be the natural imperial power in the region. At one point, Roosevelt expressed the wish that "Russia could grow fast enough in civilization to make it possible to cooperate with her and let her have her way in working up Slav civilization in her part of Asia." More realistically, though, he felt that Russia was likely to develop, at least for the time being, "on lines that run directly counter to what we are accustomed to consider as progress.'' Once such fears came to override his hopes, the implicitly anti-Russian policy pursued by Secretary of State John Hay began to seem more attractive.[29]

At the other end of the East Asian teeter-totter sat Japan. Russia's loss of historical weight in Roosevelt's esteem was initially offset by a growing appreciation of the magnitude of Japanese achievements in development and warfare, especially of ''the wonderful military spirit'' which he associated with the Samurai tradition. Arguments predicting an inevitable racial collision were brushed aside with the contention that the Japanese would make ''desirable additions'' to the ranks of the civilized powers. If treated fairly, he felt that Japan would ''play her part honorably and well in the world's work of the twentieth century.''[30]

Partly as a consequence of this growing admiration, but also as a result of the impression that it was promoting ''the policy to which we are already committed,'' Japan replaced Russia in Roosevelt's mind as the preferred imperial overseer for East Asia. Roosevelt was not referring solely to Japan's ostensible support of the Open Door principle. As he wrote to Hay, ''The Japs have played our game because they have played the game of civilized mankind.'' Consequently, once the Russo-Japanese War broke out in 1904 over conflicting interests in Korea, there was little doubt as to which side Roosevelt would cheer on to victory. A few years later he recalled what ''a hideous thing'' it would have been ''for Russia to triumph under leadership such as she then had—a hideous thing for the world and for the Russian people.''[31]

But soon enough he developed doubts about the wisdom of unchallenged Japanese hegemony in East Asia, doubts which were cast in cultural terms. He had originally hoped Japan would ''develop herself, and seek to develop China, along paths which would make the first and possibly the second great civilized powers.'' Industrial modernization and military efficiency would pose no threat because Japan would absorb Western values; it would ''almost necessarily mean that this nation has itself become civilized in the process; and we shall then simply be dealing with another civilized nation of non-aryan blood.''[32]

However, the overbearing behavior evinced by Japan's military successes led him to question whether this evolution was in fact taking place in Japan: ''I wish I were certain that the Japanese down at bottom did not lump Russians, English, Americans, Germans, all of us, simply as white devils inferior to themselves not only in what they regard as the essentials of civilization, but in courage and forethought, and to be treated politely only so long as would enable the Japanese to take advantage of our national jealousies, and beat us in turn.'' Aware that Japan's victory might stoke its chauvinism and set the stage for a future conflict with the United States, he contented himself with the hope that Japanese aggressiveness was "only a passing phase." Once it had passed through its militant stage, Japan would "feel a desire to enter more and more into the circle of the great civilized nations as one of their number." But that day seemed far off in the future. For the nearer term, Roosevelt modified his initially unqualified enthusiasm for a Japanese triumph with the more equivocal opinion that neither Russia nor Japan should become dominant in Northeast Asia.[33]

Because this latter view was at the heart of his mediation effort at the Portsmouth negotiations, it has been argued that "the key to an understanding of Roosevelt's role in peacemaking is found in his concept of *Realpolitik.*" True, Roosevelt felt that Russia's and Japan's "geographical area of friction should not be eliminated" following the war, but the issue was conceived in cultural terms as a "Slav peril vs. a yellow peril." If neither Japan nor Russia was yet worthy of civilized stewardship, a balance of power would have to do as second best, but that approach clearly had its drawbacks. Years later Roosevelt would write with regret that "there is war in China precisely because there has been no Asiatic Monroe Doctrine." In any event, a policy of balance of power presumes some willingness to exert power in maintaining the balance, a commitment Roosevelt never seriously contemplated for the United States in East Asia in the event that some inhospitable power threatened to attain regional hegemony. His mediation, he wrote to Root, had been conducted "on an exclusively altruistic basis." Taking care to retract America's claws on regional power issues, the major dispute with Japan turned out to be over immigration, which hinged instead on "the great fact of difference in race." Appropriately enough, this dispute was settled in civilized fashion with a "gentleman's agreement."[34]

The acid test of Roosevelt's commitment to civilization, and that of all twentieth-century American statesmen for that matter, came in his dealings with Europe. Both the rhetoric of civilization and traditional American interests marked Europe as the region where the United States should be least active politically. According to evolutionary logic, Europe should have been the most peaceful of all areas because, according to Roosevelt, the growth of peacefulness had been "confined strictly to those [nations] that are civilized." Amity among the great powers depended on a growing cultural empathy without which the arbitration of disputes would be unthinkable. Indeed, arbitration was itself emblematic of civilized status. Although highly critical of legal utopians who anticipated the imminent triumph of international law, Roosevelt was a strong advocate of "the policy of minimizing the chances of war among civilized peoples, of multiplying the methods and chances of honorably avoiding war in the event of controversy." It was no sudden aberration, therefore, when in his Nobel Peace Prize address he broached the possibility of a League of Peace, which would prevent war among the civilized powers and exercise an "international police power" over less advanced nations.[35]

There was, of course, much more to it than that, as Roosevelt would have been the first to point out. Not everything could be arbitrated. "Nations may, and often must, have conflicting interests," he recognized, "and in the present age patriotism stands a good deal ahead of cosmopolitanism." Then, too, the three-stage image of civilization was too simple, for even the civilized nations were at different stages of development. Not that they were making no progress. As he put it in a letter to Cecil Spring Rice in 1897: "[The Russians] are below the Germans just as the Germans are below us . . . [but] we are all treading the same path, some faster, some slower; and though the Russian started farther behind, yet he has traveled that path very much further and faster since the days of Ivan the Terrible than our people have traveled it since the days of Elizabeth." Still, for the time being, nations like Germany and Russia had advanced only to an intermediate stage between barbarism and civilization which he termed "military despotism." As proof, Roosevelt pointed to Germany's callow "attitude toward war," pejoratively termed "the Bismarck attitude," which was characteristic of a phase "in the progress of civilization England and America have now outgrown."[36]

These notable gaps between the civilized nations could conceivably have consequences both for the European balance and for the United States. As he wrote to Root in 1900, a disaster to the British Empire would soon force the United States to come "face to face with the question of either abandoning the Monroe Doctrine and submitting to the acquisition of American territory by some great European military power, or going to war." But the idea of the United States as a balancer of last resort in Europe acting as a backstop for the British was alien to the Rooseveltian philosophy. To begin with, he had no vocabulary with which to describe conflicts of interest solely in amoral balance-of-power terms. Power as the *ultima ratio* was by definition barbaric and opposed to the interests of civilization. For all his panegyrics about war, he advocated only just wars, to be fought, in a strict Augustinian sense, as "a means to an end—righteousness." Because war for the balance of power was devoid of the moral justification that was central to all of Roosevelt's international dealings, for him to have accepted the notion of a world balance of power would have required that he totally recast his ideological framework.[37]

And even if he had thought differently, the weight of tradition would have prevented him from swerving too sharply. Public opinion, Roosevelt realized, was so thoroughly sedimented that it ruled out meddling in European affairs. As he put it: "It would be well nigh impossible, even if it were not highly undesirable, for this country to engage with another country to carry out any policy save one which has become the inherited tradition of the country, like the Monroe Doctrine." The Roosevelt Corollary had stretched the doctrine to its limits, but intervention in Europe, even when the balance of power broke down, would have made total nonsense of it by requiring the abandonment of the doctrine in order to preserve it.[38]

But if intervention in Europe remained taboo from a power political standpoint, it was hardly unthinkable when considered from the quite different frame of civilization. Writing in 1904 to Jacob Gould Schurman, Roosevelt had agreed that "the Monroe Doctrine should not be pushed to such an extreme as to warrant our interference with the affairs of other nations." This statement assumed a favorable civilizational context. When civilization was threatened, however, his interpretation of the Monroe Doctrine changed to fit civilizational requirements. The full extent of his revisionism only became evident in 1914 following the outbreak of war in Europe, when, in an apparently complete turnabout, he insisted to Andrew D. White that "the Monroe Doctrine has nothing whatever to do, and never has had anything to do with the question of avoiding entangling alliances in the Eastern Hemisphere."[39]

The explanation for Roosevelt's eventual flip-flop on the world war is traceable to his civilizational creed. Though his first inclination had been to stand by and await a peace of exhaustion, such an outcome, no matter how sensible in balance-of-power terms, would not have produced a peace of righteousness. Thus long before a collapse of the balance of power was threatened by the total triumph of one of the coalitions, or even before it became clear that American interests would be severely harmed by submarine warfare, Roosevelt took his interventionist stand in response to an issue that disturbed many cosmopolitan sensibilities: the German invasion of Belgium, launched to put the Schlieffen Plan into effect. Taking umbrage at the brutalities and injustices being inflicted on that tiny nation had little to do with calculations of power, realpolitik, or a strategic threat to the United States. Unburdening himself to one of his many British friends, he explained that "in a really tremendous world struggle, with a great moral issue involved, neutrality does not serve righteousness, for to be neutral between right and wrong is to serve wrong." Whereas Britain stood "for humanity, for mankind," Germany's atrocious behavior marked it as a despotism, civilization's enemy in a war which was "in its essence one between militarism and democracy."[40]

Roosevelt's interventionism, by pointing out that civilized values were universally applicable and not just a rationalization for taming the natives on the periphery, certainly showed the seriousness of his internationalism, which turned out to be far more moralistic than that of Woodrow Wilson—for all his moralizing, Wilson, as we shall see, did at least articulate a geostrategic rationale for intervening in Europe. But Roosevelt's turnabout also showed how poorly he had grounded his historical outlook in the two caissons of tradition and modernity. His position on the war undermined the traditional underpinnings on which his diplomacy had been erected and, by exposing his internationalism to full view for the first time, also revealed how historically impoverished and inconsistent it really was. In both respects, his modernity was built on a historical foundation incapable of supporting it.

Unfortunately, all the components of Roosevelt's cosmopolitanism—his historicism, his globalism, his belief in the growing supersession of power by culture, even his belief in civilization as an ultimately moral process— proved to be quite incompatible with the precepts he had once trotted out to justify his foreign policy. Though modernizing in intent, his ideology had at one time accurately reflected and rationalized traditional American interests, but going to war for the rights of Belgium and civilization far exceeded the regional role outlined in Roosevelt's neo-Federalist vision of global order. In the end, historicism superseded historical tradition, and righteousness took precedence over the concern with specifically American rights. Quite simply, his policy had outgrown its historical roots.

Roosevelt's attitude toward World War I showed that the kind of history that mattered to him in his conduct of foreign affairs was not the variety that we normally conceive of as having a limiting, conservative effect. That kind of history, history as inherited values, history as policies sanctified by tradi- tion, history as precedent, history as *past*—all that was secondary. History of this kind had been employed by him as a rhetorical device for rationalizing and justifying policy departures from tradition. In his attitude toward World War I, the neo-Federalism that had once informed his policies was revealed for what it was, a view of history as it is perhaps best understood by most Americans—as something that no longer matters.

But did Roosevelt, then, having rejected tradition, at least have a clear sense of the present or an accurate presentiment of the future? Not really, for his conception of civilization as it worked itself out in the face of a brutal reality turned out to be, in a number of significant respects, an unacceptable, sociologically shallow, and unsatisfying interpretation of the modernization of international relations. The problem was most immediately apparent in his understanding of the Great War's implications for civilization. His metaphor of an international *posse comitatus* arrayed against a wrongdoing Germany, although it suggested a raw but fundamentally just frontier legality, also pointed to an indefinite period of frontier lawlessness at a time when many felt that frontierlike conditions could no longer be tolerated. His unblinking advocacy of unprecedented bloodshed on behalf of a civilization that seemed unworthy of the name was symptomatic of his blindness to what others in this century have increasingly come to dread as the ultimate, tragic irony of history: that an indomitable will-to-power, disguised as virtue, would lead to civilization's destruction.[41]

But then, the war for Roosevelt was devoid of apocalyptic meaning. "I do not agree with you," he informed Arthur Lee, "when you speak of this as the last war for civilization." His was an idealism without a utopia, in which history was a staging of Zeno's paradox, a race in which mankind as Achilles could never overtake the tortoise of civilization. He could rally the faithful to do battle for the Lord at Armageddon in domestic politics, but in the international arena his summons to arms held out the prospect only of more wars, a seemingly endless series of struggles for the survival of the more civilized that were scarcely distinguishable from the Darwinian struggles of the past. Although he had earlier talked optimistically about the likelihood of peace at the civilized core, he accepted its absence with a remarkable equanimity. This high tolerance for conflict would lead some to suspect, wrongly, that for Roosevelt the barbarian virtues were ends in themselves when actually it was more complicated than that. The truth was, he could not sanction an internationalism based on power, but neither could he imagine one without it.[42]

The bleak and unsatisfying view of the modernized future implied in Roosevelt's view of the Great War was accompanied by shortcomings in his understanding of the global modernization process. Roosevelt's conception of civilization and his vision of history studiously ignored the growing interdependence produced by the vast impersonal forces of modernization. Because he was unable to see civilization as the growth of a reticulated world society, Roosevelt's thought was missing the structural understanding of military and economic interdependence that would inform the thought of all his twentieth-century successors in office. His hypertrophied internationalist moralism existed conceptually within an underdeveloped international body. If this recalls the imbalance between the combative character and puny physique of Roosevelt's adolescence, that is only an ironic reflection on the fact that his was not a mature internationalism.

It was no secret that Roosevelt was not an internationalist in any significant economic sense. As Speaker of the House "Uncle Joe" Cannon confirmed, Roosevelt "rather despised trade" and could summon little enthusiasm for grappling with commercial issues. Roosevelt took only grudging note of the industrial revolution as a factor in global modernization. Moreover, his political sociology of modernization was quite unimaginative, his later advocacy of intervention in Europe consisting of heavy servings of moralism in preference to geostrategic nouvelle cuisine. If there were any new strategic consequences implied in modernization, apart from variations on basic Federalist themes, Roosevelt's diplomacy had been calculated to avert them. The central point is that Roosevelt was not really keen about thinking through the implications of the central processes of modernization: economic development, political and strategic interdependence, and the emergence of global ideologies. His head sided with modernity, but his heart beat with the ancients.[43]

If Roosevelt's understanding of the sociology of modernization was weak and only half-formed, his sense of its ideology was inconsistent and even idiosyncratic. His classical republicanism was difficult to reconcile with modern liberalism's marketplace values and its attachment to selfish individualism. To the extent that he believed republican character to be a microcosm of national character, he was indeed something of an anachronism, a primitive, as his immediate successors sensed. All his paeans to civilization notwithstanding, Roosevelt was deeply ambivalent about the process and always wary of its corrosive potential. Civilization was a constant struggle for improvement that was rooted in virtuous individual character and purchased by heroic achievement, a struggle in which the renewal of "virtue" was continually threatened rather than automatically guaranteed by commercial and industrial expansion.

His republican ideology was even less applicable to modernization as an international process. As we shall see, the conception of civilization as it took form in twentieth-century American foreign policy would feature a belief in the functional necessity of an international collective conscience or superego, an effective world opinion, which would serve as counterpart and antidote to the structural dangers generated by growing interdependence. But Roosevelt's understanding of value and interest was rooted in an essentialist view of culture in which it was impossible to base pubic policy on anything beyond national character. If character was defined in terms of a tight individual and cultural nexus, there was no room for any meaningful spiritual counterpart to global society. If the main factor behind the spread and consolidation of empires was culturally grounded military valor, that preoccupation with cultural particularity practically assured that Roosevelt could not think in terms of the primacy of the whole, much less consider shaping foreign policy on the basis of global requirements. Consequently, he was only too happy to apportion imperial responsibilities on the basis of traditional geographic distributions of power that corresponded roughly to what nations thought of as their "essential" security interests.

For all his marvelous historical gifts, then, Roosevelt found it impossible to go beyond moralizing and confront the basic conditions of modernity. His traditional policies could not support his moralistic internationalism, while the view of history in which the latter was grounded was incapable of surviving on its own. In the end, the epitaph on his tombstone, "Keep your eyes on the stars and your feet on the ground," stands as an unwitting reproach to his inability to do either. For his successors, therefore, his conceptually spread-eagled ideology of civilization held little attraction. Because his outlook abandoned the past while at the same time it badly misinterpreted the modernizing present, it left Roosevelt only with an unconvincing and unappealing picture of the future that found few takers. Their more consistently modern approach to the historical possibilities of foreign policy would be more solidly anchored to America's liberal heritage, with its faith in the beneficent working of market processes and institutional structures supported by world opinion.

The Roosevelt revolution in foreign policy was cosmetic, an attempt to make the sagging face of federalism more attractive to those who might otherwise be seduced by newer, more dangerous doctrines, but it could not reverse the onset of ideological old age. Stripped of its gaudy makeup, his diplomacy revealed the old regional distribution of global power which Americans had long taken for granted and the narrow nationalist assumptions underlying traditional diplomatic practice. Roosevelt's novelty resided in his willingness to accept imperialism as a fact of modern international life and to seek an American role in the constellation of colonial powers. But Roosevelt sidestepped the more important question of relations between the developed nations. If imperialism was merely a symptom of potent new forces that were erupting and transforming the global environment, then Roosevelt's policies, no matter how flamboyant or dramatic, simply begged the question of adapting to radical change.

Roosevelt's diplomacy marked the effective culmination of a cultural tradition, one which he himself in his later years would abandon without having anything solid to put in its place. Having erected a new structure on an existing foundation, he could rest content for having achieved during the period of his presidency a masterful reconciliation of tradition and modernity in his hemispheric policy. An ideology must first be joined to a cultural tradition before it can hope to be effective, but in Roosevelt's case, his views always reflected more his unique temperament than historical wisdom, however defined. Far from pointing the way to America's international future, then, Roosevelt's foreign policy was idiosyncratic and nonfoundational.[44] He was at best a transitional figure, an antimodern modernizer, the first modern American president and the last traditional American statesman.

WILLIAM HOWARD TAFT: TAKING MODERNIZATION SERIOUSLY

Unlikely as it seems, the genial and often phlegmatic William Howard Taft was far more of a globalist and activist in his foreign policy than his dynamo of a predecessor. Taft's presidency marks the beginning of modern American internationalism in at least three respects. It assumed that contemporary diplomacy was radically different from the power politics of the past as a result of the global modernization process; it began to break down the regional view on which United States foreign policy had traditionally been based; and it introduced world opinion as a device for the management of critical diplomatic problems—a theme that would, in one form or another, become the leitmotif of American diplomacy for the remainder of the century. Whereas Roosevelt's policies were shot through with tensions and contradictions which would make them unsuitable for subsequent statesmen, Taft's sensitivity to the emergence of global currents made his diplomacy far more relevant to dealing with twentieth-century conditions.

Under Roosevelt, Taft had been the perfect subordinate, a self-effacing adjutant who was closely tied to Roosevelt's foreign policies. Yet, as it turned out, Taft and Roosevelt had very different ideas about the meaning of modern world history. Early on, Taft appeared to echo the Rooseveltian theme of globalism, as in his Cincinnati acceptance speech in which he stated that "we are a world power and cannot help it." But Taft's definition of world power was quite different from Roosevelt's. While it postulated "an influence throughout the world," for Taft world power was wielded for "the betterment of mankind, for the uplifting of our unfortunate fellow-creatures, for the maintenance of peace, for the encouragement of trade, for the promotion of morality and civilization." Similarly, for his secretary of state, Philander Knox, the United States had "honestly won rank as a world power in the movement for universal peace."[45]

Taft's irenic definition of world power, which consciously or not echoed the Spencerian view of civilization as a progress from militarism to industrialism, seems less odd in the light of his bitter critique of Roosevelt's attitude toward force and war. What actually set the men at odds was their radically opposed historical sensibilities. The difference between the two was, as historians have noted, in no small measure the difference between the peaceful bourgeois and the traditional warrior, a distinction that quite rightly suggests the existence of a wide gulf between the two men's conceptions of modernity.

Roosevelt seemed quite content to treat imperialism as a symbol, to the point of dropping it when it became inconvenient, whereas Taft was determined to go behind the trappings to address the foreign-policy substance of modernization. Roosevelt's civilization was veneer only; Taft's, solid hardwood. Taft believed that civilization had already progressed to the point that the use of military power was, in most respects, no longer necessary. Because individual swashbuckling was being overtaken by impersonal social forces, Roosevelt's obsession with war and personal heroism was, therefore, patently out of touch with the times and, by that token, unrealistic.[46]

For Taft, to ignore the workings of trade, which was only the extensive side of the intensive revolution of industrialism, was to blind oneself to the mainspring of modern world history. It was axiomatic and "doubtless true that trade and trade extension are the foundation in practical life of most advances in civilization." Taft's belief that "modern diplomacy is commercial," an assertion which lay at the heart of his "dollar diplomacy," echoed contemporary commercial thinking. But it was explicitly premised on the fact of structural interdependence brought about by global modernization, which he assumed was bound to have a transforming impact on traditional values and power patterns.[47]

Roosevelt's classical republicanism was not the only possible view of what America was all about. As the State Department's Willard Straight tried to explain, dollar diplomacy was a reflection of the nation's new economic power and of the status derived from that power. It was "a logical manifestation of our national growth, and of the rightful assumption by the United States of a more important place at the council table of nations." Commercial diplomacy, then, instead of threatening the national character, was simply being faithful to the nation's new industrial identity. Since America had changed, so too would its foreign policy, leaving in the process little room for archaic Rooseveltian notions of "character."[48]

Moreover, the values behind dollar diplomacy need not be peculiarly American. Where Roosevelt stressed national character, Taft gave primacy of place to a transcultural liberal ideology, which was not only a worldview in its global frame of reference but seemed likely to become a universal creed thanks to cultural diffusion. This ideology grew out of the interests generated by the global web of commerce and was a by-product of the advanced level of development shared by many societies. Put another way, Roosevelt's fascination with the psychology of power ignored its international sociology as well as the sociology of knowledge, the necessary conditioning of beliefs in conformity with changing social patterns, that accompanied it. In a brief discussion of international currents, Walter Lippmann complained that "we were always a little too late for the facts." With his eye fixed on the transforming power of socioeconomic forces, Taft believed the time had come to align ideological values with sociological fact, to coordinate consciousness and structure.[49]

All this talk of promoting commerce left the administration vulnerable to accusations of materialism. Indeed, "dollar diplomacy" was used as a rhetorical brush by Democrats and Progressives to paint a picture of Taft's diplomacy as a servant of big business and monopoly capital. Obviously, this grated, especially as the reductionism of the critics did nothing at all to convey the complex global sensibility behind dollar diplomacy that far transcended a concern for special interests. "The popular conception of a capitalist is a creature without a conscience or a soul," Knox complained, insisting to the contrary that "the American capitalist has both and has them developed to an unusual degree." Smarting at suggestions that dollar diplomacy was simply the reflexive expression of special interests, Knox felt obliged to deliver a speech on "the spirit of American diplomacy" which, as he explained to his subordinate, Huntington Wilson, would "bring out its altruism and unselfishness." It would show that Taft's foreign policy was not simply a diplomacy of sharp elbows designed to push the United States to the fore in the international scramble for economic advantage.[50]

According to Knox, the global nexus of commerce was going beyond nationalism to stimulate a new sense of community and an awareness of the "solidarity of human interest." Arguing that the ideological tendency of modernity was "manifestly toward international unity," Knox spoke rhapsodically of "the identity of interest and the oneness of the world." On the assumption that commercial contact bred understanding, he even went so far as to maintain that "the common interest of the nations is being recognized as superior to their special interests." In a talk delivered before the American Asiatic Association in Yokohama, Japan, Knox claimed to discern "a decided impulse towards social coordination that must become a real cosmic force." From this perspective, dollar diplomacy was simply the attempt to take advantage of "the remarkable progress and great effectiveness of international cooperation within the last few decades as compared with earlier times."[51]

Although this growth of cooperation was grounded in the growing complexity of the global division of labor, it was equally the product of the workings of an international public opinion. "Does it not rest," Knox asked rhetorically, "upon the practically simultaneous operation of the common mind and the conscience of the world upon common knowledge? . . . Instantaneous world communication is very modern. Ribs of steel and nerves of wire . . . have enabled [nations] sharing a common knowledge, animated by a common conscience, to take common and contemporaneous action while the need is yet fresh . . . Each nation instantaneously feels the compulsion of the public opinion of all nations." This world opinion, given its roots in international structural realities, was by its very nature conducive to global harmony.[52]

American internationalism has always been anticultural in its bias. According to Taft, for example, "the progress of Christian civilization is the elimination of the difference between the conscience of the individual and the conscience of the nation." The attenuation of nationalism meant that the new global consciousness would be characterized by a rejection of blind custom in favor of a growing attachment to the anticultural values of freedom inscribed in liberal ideology. Even so, there was still a long way to go. Taft acknowledged that "we have not reached the millennium where the mere expression of opinion is going to accomplish everything," and many of his earlier speeches as president reflected a Rooseveltian awareness of the necessity for national power "to put ourselves in a position where we can uphold our dignity and uphold our opinion in favor of international morality." But the assumptions behind his diplomacy made it clear that this kind of power was clearly vestigial or atavistic in a Schumpeterian sense and that it would be difficult to imagine circumstances under which it might be exercised.[53]

For those critics of dollar diplomacy who argued that an assertive policy of commercial promotion was bound to embroil the United States in serious conflicts of interest with other great powers, Taft had a simple rejoinder. The slogan "dollars not bullets" guaranteed, in large print, that the Taft administration's diplomacy would not be political in the Clausewitzian sense. Although dollar diplomacy was certainly undertaken as an exercise of American influence, economic action was, as Max Weber pointed out, in the last analysis "a *peaceful* exercise of power." Thus Taft could insist quite seriously that "there is nothing inconsistent in the promotion of peaceful relations and the promotion of trade relations." The pursuit of economic interest was undertaken from the standpoint of a more inclusive historical frame in which a liberal and international capitalist society was the inherently peaceful successor to the aggressive militarist practices inherited from feudal times.[54]

All this might have amounted to little more than gaseous rhetoric had not the Taft administration attempted to reduce it to diplomatic practice. In the Caribbean region, there was not much to distinguish Taft's diplomacy from that of his predecessor. America may have entered a career as a world power, but its global policies turned on a stationary Caribbean hub. Nevertheless, some attention was paid to the causes as well as to the symptoms of revolutionary unrest in the region. In this regard, at least, the rhetoric of dollar diplomacy was consistent, involving the "same principle" in Latin America as in the Far East. The Monroe Doctrine, Knox acknowledged, was frankly interventionist, but if so, "the most effective way to escape the

logical consequences of the Monroe Doctrine is to help them help themselves.'' Because those annoying revolving-door revolutions were incubated
by unsettled conditions, the situation could improve only with "the material
benefits realized from financial regeneration.'' The issue, then, was not solely
power, or the desire to forestall European interventions, but "reform.'' "True
stability,'' Knox understood, was "best established not by military but by
economic and social forces.'' Of course, the Taft administration had no real
understanding of how to develop the region—nor, for that matter, did anyone
else—but its appreciation of the need for development was genuine enough.[55]

Whatever its regional shortcomings, the universalistic assumptions of
dollar diplomacy meant that its true test would have to come at some distance
from the Western Hemisphere. The best example of dollar diplomacy in
operation, as well as the most misunderstood, came in the Far East, where
managing the volatile diplomacy of imperialism was important as a test case
of the viability of civilized cooperation. From Taft's perspective, the possibility of conflict among great powers was greatest when they were dragged into
tangential disputes. As he pointed out in his presidential message of 3 December 1912, "only the failure of small nations to maintain internal stability
could affect the peace of the world.''[56]

In pursuing dollar diplomacy in China, Taft relied on a communal conception of imperialism. Whereas Roosevelt had sought to cut the imperial
division of labor among the great powers to the pattern of their traditional
power interests, Taft started with the assumption that there existed among
them from the beginning a broadly based community of interest. Indeed,
Taft's policy bore more than a superficial resemblance to what Marxist theo-
rist Karl Kautsky called "ultraimperialism,'' an approach which envisioned
"the common exploitation of the world by internationally united finance
capital in place of the mutual rivalries of national finance capital.'' Substitute
"development'' for "exploitation'' and you have a fair description of the
rationale behind Taft's China diplomacy.[57]

Upon assuming the presidency, Taft made clear that he was "anxious
to encourage the Oriental trade and to have a man at Peking who understood
its importance.'' As Knox wrote the chairman of the Senate Committee on
Appropriations, "With the results of intense internal development all countries are now turning their attention more earnestly to foreign trade.'' The
maturation of the American economy, especially with the emergence of im-
pressively concentrated finance capital at the turn of the century, appeared
to coincide happily with the imminent takeoff of the Chinese economy. Knox
claimed to discern "almost boundless commercial opportunities in the [Chi-
nese] empire,'' an area which was "preeminently adapted for American enterprise.''[58]

Statements like these suggested that the Taft administration's China policy was dominated by a narrow bottom-line mentality. But it was well aware, as the modest trade statistics made clear, that any significant payoff could come only in the future as the consequence of successful Chinese development. Commerce was the end, but it presupposed a China developed enough to absorb foreign imports. Only with investments which stimulated industrial growth would the commercial opportunities be forthcoming. American investment, coupled with America's dominant role in the westernization of China, would strengthen China and thus assure the viability of American investment. In short, the key to the success of the Open Door policy was the modernization of China. Contrasted with the Rooseveltian image of cultural narcosis and decay, or what one writer termed "a fossilized representative of an antique system, physically active but mentally inert," was the emerging image of a young China, rousing from a centuries-old slumber and rubbing the sand of the past from its eyes.[59]

The Taft administration coincided with the golden age of American religious and cultural influence in China. It was a period in which a groundswell of interest emerged in the evangelization and modernization of the Middle Kingdom, fueled by the belief that the United States was destined to lead the Chinese to the promised land of democracy and modern industrial society. Taft was particularly taken with the secular educational side of the American missionary presence, waxing warmly enthusiastic about its potential. Referring to the recent abolition of the hidebound examination system, during his Shanghai visit in 1907 he had expressed pleasure in the knowledge that "the education of the Chinese in America has had much to do with the present steps toward reform begun by the government in China." Back home early the next year, he expressed his enthusiasm for missions "from the standpoint of political, governmental advancement, the advancement of modern civilization": "China is looking forward to progress. China is to be guided by whom? It is to be guided by the young Christian students and scholars that either learn English or some foreign language at home or are sent abroad to be instructed, and who come back and whose words are listened to by those who exercise influence at the head of the government. Therefore it is that these frontier posts of civilization are so much more important than the mere numerical count of converts seems to make them." Of course, the missionary effort was all the more welcome for its salutary moral influence. Missionaries would "embody the real morality" of the nation and act as a wholesome counterbalance to the seamier side of relations.[60]

Consequently, during the Taft administration the modernization of China became for the first time a formal part of U.S. diplomatic strategy, whereupon it would remain a prominent feature of American Far Eastern policy, this despite the bumbling usually associated with Taft's dollar diplomacy. Modernization was not only an idealistic end of American policy, but a process to be nurtured. Two things had changed since the 1890s to warrant taking this new course. First was the accelerating pace of change within China. As Knox noted in a letter to H. M. Hoyt in 1909, "The development of China had not progressed to such an extent at the time the doctrine of the 'Open Door' was promulgated as to make it much more than a theory for harmonious action." Changed, too, was America's conception of its role. The Open Door had been articulated at a time when the United States viewed itself as an outsider in relation to the activities of the European powers, but "civilization" called for a *cooperative* approach to modernization. As Knox had noted, the structural facts of the global economy had "caused nations to see that their interests were similar and interdependent and that a like policy is necessary as well for the expansion as for the protection of their interests."[61]

As the opening move in demonstrating America's new global influence and expanding commercial opportunity, Taft decided to become a party crasher by joining the European consortium which had been organized for the purpose of providing capital for the completion of the so-called Hukuang railroad, a line running between Beijing and Canton. After Taft wrote to the Chinese prince regent to express his "intense personal interest in making the use of American capital in the development of China," the United States was admitted to the imperialists' inner sanctum. Taft considered it "quite a diplomatic victory" and the public opinion of the country concurred. The *Washington Post* noted with satisfaction that prior to this event the United States had "stood politely by and the others have pressed through without so much as a backward look to see if the doorkeeper were following."[62]

According to Knox, the greater significance of American admission to the consortium was that it had been "opposed by the great powers of Europe who have always held a monopoly of such financial plans and that in spite of this opposition the United States has won and thereby secured a political prestige in China which is virtually paramount." The United States now had "a substantial interest in the development of China," one which gave it "more than a moral right to have a voice in all questions affecting China's welfare." Being a member of the club was, however, but a first step toward accomplishing larger modernizing objectives. The forging of common financial ties meant, as Taft's message to Congress put it, that it was "to the interest of all alike to join in maintaining the political integrity of China and to unite in sympathetic and practical cooperation for the peaceful development of the Chinese Empire." The gambit defused what Knox saw as the "greatest danger" in China, that arising from "disagreements among the great western nations."[63]

As Knox later admitted, the American entry into the consortium, while important in itself, was "but the first step in a new phase of the traditional policy of the United States in China and with special reference to Manchuria." It was the opening move in a game whose immediate object was to break the Japanese railroad monopoly in Manchuria. Knox's way of defusing the situation was to propose that all the Manchurian railways be neutralized by an international syndicate which would then manage railway development in China until the Chinese were themselves in a position to take charge. Knox's neutralization proposal has usually been viewed as disastrous for the Taft administration because it brought together the Japanese and the Russians, heretofore bitter regional rivals, in a new spheres-of-influence agreement.[64]

The larger purpose of neutralization was to remove development from the framework of a competitive diplomacy of imperialism. According to one State Department memo, the proposal had a host of advantages. It would "ensure the effectiveness of the Open Door policy, facilitate trade and commerce equally to all nations, help to maintain equilibrium in the Far East, and be a great step toward the securing of peace from and in that quarter for at least a sufficient time to allow for some other means to arise which would further prevent war." Knox believed that the proposal would ultimately attract even the two aggressive imperialist powers in the region for whom it seemed to have no appeal whatever. For Russia, participation provided "a dignified escape from the acute situation likely to confront Russia in Manchuria." With everyone else aboard, Knox expected to "smoke out" Japan. If, as Knox believed, Japan was fearful of being left as the odd man out, the joint solution would "doubtless bring them to a more sober condition of mind and make them less dangerous."[65]

Unfortunately for the administration, the scheme backfired and ever since has been held up as an example of muddle-headed American diplomacy. A policy that was supposed to defuse the old diplomacy of imperialism seemed only to entrench it even more deeply. Criticizing the policy to his superior in terms that would later seem the common sense of the matter, old China hand W. W. Rockhill argued that "nothing could, in my opinion, be more dangerous for the peace of the Far East and the normal development of our interests in that region than an arrangement between Japan and Russia . . . the result of which might be the practical dividing of Manchuria between the two powers."[66]

Apart from some references to "maladroit diplomacy," public opinion at the time was by no means so unfavorable, but the episode contributed mightily to the falling out between Roosevelt and Taft that ended in the Rough Rider's renegade Bull Moose candidacy for the presidency in 1912. Roosevelt had already scolded Knox early in 1909 about the importance of

maintaining good relations with Japan, but the Manchurian proposal excited
Roosevelt's worst fears and prompted him to lecture his former pupils about
the need to avoid a war with Japan over China or Manchuria. Roosevelt
informed Knox bluntly that Japan's primary interests lay in Korea and Manchuria, to which Japan was necessarily very sensitive, and reminded him that
Japan was face-to-face with Russia, a great power "with rankling memories
of injury." Accordingly, Japan's position on the mainland had to be judged
"on the actual facts of the case, and not by mere study of treaties." As for
the Chinese, they were "weak, lacked cohesion, and were unreliable." It
would be folly, therefore, for the United States to get in the way of what he
conceived to be "the inevitable movement of the Japanese in Manchuria."[67]

Roosevelt's spirited chalk-talk on Far Eastern diplomacy was undoubtedly prompted by a question that has lain in the back of historians' minds
ever since: What kind of dilettantism prompted the Taft administration to
think that such a harebrained proposal had the slightest chance of success?
The adamant response by Taft and Knox to Roosevelt's broadside is instructive, as is their subsequent approach to China diplomacy. From their perspective they continued to see it as not only a worthy effort, but one which paid
great dividends. In other words, they viewed it as a success! Actually, Taft
agreed wholeheartedly about the need to avoid war with Japan, but whereas
for Roosevelt the solution lay in greater caution, for Taft it lay in a more
active Far Eastern policy which would promote cooperation rather than help-
lessly concede the idea that great-power interests in China were incompatible.
In contrast to Roosevelt's easy dismissal of the Open Door policy, Taft
bridled at the notion of "tacitly and by insensible degrees and gradual acquiescence" allowing it to become "a pious fraud." At the very least, American
policy had the effect of "clearing the atmosphere" and allowed it to see
where the other nations stood.[68]

In a suggested reply to Roosevelt written by Knox, the argument was
put in terms of world opinion. "The Japanese government is certainly not
indifferent to world opinion," Knox argued, "and it is much better that we
should try to bring Japan's policy in China up to the level of ours, where we
may differ, than to lower our policy to the level of hers." Taft still held out
hope for a change of heart by the British, which would be vital to forcing
Japan's hand. But even if that did not come to pass, he felt it "much better
for us to stand consistently by our principles even though we fail in getting
them generally adopted."[69]

But that did not mean that the administration was willing to fight about
the Open Door as a matter of principle. If, as one historian has remarked,
"the Taft administration embarked on an ambitious program in China without
immediate effective naval force to back it up," it was because it did not see

force as instrumental to its policies. As William Braisted has argued, even at the point where relations with Japan became most touchy, "Taft never allowed the Manchurian episode or rumblings from elsewhere to shake his conviction that war between Japan and the United States was entirely unlikely." The truth was, it made little sense to see China as an arena of conflict. As one memorandum put it: "It is not presumed that the United States would ever resort to war, either alone or in combination with other powers, to insure the integrity of China's territory, nor does it seem that our commercial interests would warrant or require a resort to war for their protection. The obvious way to prevent such a contingency is to encourage and assist China to become strong enough to protect herself."

As for the Japanese, Taft had written, even before becoming president: "What under heavens do we want to fight Japan for? What do they want to fight us for?" He urged that talk of war "should be stamped on at every opportunity." Taft's policy in the Far East must therefore be viewed in the overall irenic thrust of dollar diplomacy. Though he was certainly far more alive to the commercial threat from Japan, it was with a sense of proportion befitting a good capitalist. Knox confirmed this antimercantilist sentiment shortly after the conclusion of the 1911 commercial treaty with Japan, when he said that "the keenest competitors in business may yet be the firmest friends."[70]

Roosevelt need not have worried about the administration's sense of diplomatic *mesure*. Knox had already indicated in 1909 that "I don't want to see this China business to [*sic*] become disproportional," which of course it had, at least in the press. Knox seemed to understand at the time, arguing that "we are not to undertake a quixotically altruistic task for China's benefit" and emphasized instead the commercial value to the United States. As for antagonizing Japan, Taft later informed Roosevelt that the United States had "carefully refrained from going beyond the natural and proper steps to promote our own competitive interests in that region." Indeed, he suggested a few months later that Roosevelt was being carried away by his imagination, especially as the new treaty of commerce and friendship with Japan had put the United States "on the best possible basis with that country, and there is nothing she would less like than a controversy with us at present."[71]

While the Manchurian proposal was decidedly a failure, it did not end in a debacle. Whatever the temporary importance attached to Manchuria, it was, after all, only peripheral to the central problem of China's destiny. According to Lewis Einstein, a young diplomat stationed in Beijing who had been a favorite of Roosevelt's, "The critical problem [was], not how to save Manchuria, but how to save China." Given the dangers of greatpower competition, Einstein suggested, "a concert of power is as necessary at Peking as at Constantinople.'' The analogy to the decaying Ottoman empire was striking, but not altogether accurate, as Einstein himself was quick to point out. China was less the sick man of Asia than a slumbering giant, waiting to be roused and rejuvenated in an oriental equivalent of the Western renaissance. And instead of the great powers standing watchfully over China's inert body, like a group of competing morticians, the Open Door in Taft's conception was a means whereby modern Western commercial and cultural techniques would restore China to health.[72]

Should a Chinese system along these lines be created, Einstein felt that it might ''restrict existing encroachments within their present limits and retard the process of absorption so as to afford her a chance to stand on her own feet.'' In another memo to Knox, Einstein predicted that ''if ever China is again able to assert its own, it will not be long before Japan and Russia find their position to be untenable.'' Writing to Taft from Beijing, Bishop J. E. Bashford argued that a policy of great-power cooperation, even if reduced to a system of mutual frustration that left China to modernize on its own, by minimizing foreign domination would be ''the ideal solution of the Far Eastern problem.'' And that is basically what emerged. While the Japanese retained their preeminent position in Manchuria, for the rest of China the consortium system managed to preserve Chinese sovereignty while allowing time for the much desired modernization of the country.[73]

The issue of cooperation took on some urgency in 1910 when the Chinese government raised the question of a new currency loan. The creation of a six-power consortium was hardly satisfactory to all concerned. The Chinese, who had been hoping to use the Americans as a counterweight to the other, more predatory China powers, were sorely disappointed at seeing the United States become a member. Moreover, American policy had the unanticipated effect of contributing to the toppling of the ancien régime. While no currency loan was ever made, the long delayed Hukuang railway loan did finally go through, only to stimulate such resentment against foreign domination of China that it contributed greatly to the revolution against the Ching dynasty.[74]

Yet, from the long view, events were proceeding, if not exactly on track, in line with the ineluctable timetable of progressive history. With the advent to power of revolutionary republicans under Dr. Sun Yat-sen, the lifting of the dead weight of corrupt imperial institutions seemed so greatly to lighten China's load on its path to modernity that the administration had reason to exult. According to a speech in Knox's files, the ''awakening'' of China was the result of two causes, for which the United States deserved its share of credit: ''her contact with the modern world, and the increase of her knowledge of the true God.'' He called for a further action on behalf of ''the redemption of a race.''[75]

Following the declaration of the Chinese Republic in 1912, the administration expanded its cooperative approach to the modernization of China by agreeing to the formation in June of a new Six-Power Consortium. The grouping included, at the insistence of Britain and France, their Japanese and Russian allies and acknowledged their spheres of influence in Manchuria and Mongolia. What seemed to some a headlong retreat by Knox struck others as a brilliant tactical stroke that rescued the substance of China policy. The *Washington Post* described the Six-Power Consortium as "the most striking diplomatic achievement and international financing event of the 20th century." The end result would be cooperation until China was "firmly established and has carefully mobilized its inherent strength." "The way these loans have been handled," said R. S. Miller reassuringly to Knox, "is strictly in line with your neutralization policy." Indeed, near the end of his term as secretary, Knox allowed himself the dangerous luxury of describing the new consortium as "a great factor making for permanent world peace, so far as the Great Powers are concerned."[76]

This was not a forced shift to a cooperative policy, as some historians have contended; rather, it was a continuation of the policy of seeking an end to great-power exclusivity in China. By sacrificing the limb to assure the health of the tree, the administration was betting that the setbacks to the Open Door in Manchuria would be only temporary. As a later State Department memo argued it, a policy of cooperation within the eighteen provinces proper "was really indirectly aiding China in working out its own salvation in such outlying districts as Manchuria, where it seems necessary to leave China to work out its own salvation if the six power concert is to be preserved." Thus, according to Einstein, the United States, "instead of stirring up the waters of the Manchurian problem," was now focused on the "greater question" of China. The consortium offered "a rational plan for the development of China along lines of mutual benefit and without placing any one power in a position of predominant authority."[77]

The consortium technique would be abandoned by the new Wilson administration early in 1913, presumably because it was imperialistic and because the American group's domination by large Wall Street bankers violated Wilson's petit bourgeois mentality. Knox called the withdrawal a "fiasco," but Wilson in the end would go back to the consortium approach, since the principle of unanimity by which it operated at least forestalled lone-wolf diplomacy in China. The consortium was a choral group without songs to sing, but at least it saved its members from cacophony. It is hard to see what alternatives existed. Since American aspirations for China were commercial and cultural, and not power political, a straightforwardly aggressive approach would have run up against serious strategic difficulties, not to mention problems with American public opinion. On the other hand, leaving China to the other powers would mean acquiescing in spheres of influence that would have effectively nullified America's commercial and cultural ambitions. Indeed, the cooperative developmental logic of the Taft administration's policies was so compelling that it would be picked up in the early 1920s as the centerpiece of the Harding administration's China policy.[78]

The distinguishing feature of Taftian diplomacy was its realization that it was useless to speak about the modernization of diplomacy at all unless it applied first of all to relations in the center among the great powers. Because dollar diplomacy presumed growing harmony among the core states, it was intended to apply even to Europe; indeed, especially to Europe. Thus the "great jewel" of his administration, according to Taft, was a series of far-reaching arbitration treaties among the major powers. In a speech to the American Peace and Arbitration League meeting in New York on 22 March 1910, Taft startled his audience by stating that he saw no reason in principle why "matters of national honor" could not be submitted to arbitral tribunals for final decision. In effect, this meant that nations would bind themselves in advance to abjure war over matters once defined as vital national interests. Surprised and heartened by the enthusiastic public response, Taft suggested treaties of arbitration to deal with all "justiciable" questions, that is, questions which could be settled by the application of legal principles. Should the governments disagree as to whether an issue was in fact susceptible of justiciable treatment, it would be taken up by a six-man panel which, if five members agreed, could then refer it to an arbitral tribunal for final settlement. By the end of the year, the British and French governments responded favorably in principle to an American proposal and by August 1911 the novel arbitration treaties had been negotiated.[79]

The treaties reflected the prevailing conviction that war between certain nations was scarcely conceivable. Taft thought he saw aborning a "real increase in the brotherhood of man" and a yearning among peoples "for some sort of a temple of justice in which kings and nations may be parties." He perceived also a growing community of sentiment among the great powers, a civilizational core around which he proposed to wind the legal armature of his treaties. Far from celebrating prematurely a fictitious unanimity that no one believed yet existed, he hoped to use the treaties as a means of creating that unity by providing a compelling example to powers not yet convinced of the importance of the new international climate of opinion.[80]

The Taft years coincided with the heyday of the American peace movement, which was at this time largely an elitist, upper-class affair supported liberally by money from the new philanthropic foundations that sprang up like exotic flowers from the manure pile of robber baron fortunes. Men like

Nicholas Murray Butler, president of Columbia University and mover and shaker in such organizations as the Carnegie Endowment for International Peace and the American Association for International Conciliation, believed that there was in process of formation a cosmopolitan "international mind" among the elites of the world's developed nations which could not help but soon find political expression.

It was a movement with which Taft was largely in sympathy. Although Carnegie was under the impression that the move toward unqualified arbitration "was like most extremely great things, quite easy," Taft's attempts to win passage of the treaties ran into a number of roadblocks. Not surprisingly, one of the more formidable barricades was manned by Roosevelt, who objected loudly to their sweeping character. To Roosevelt, some issues, indeed the most important ones, implied primordial civic attachments that by their very nature could not be arbitrated. Arbitration meant compromise, and a fundamental national interest was by definition not compromisable.[81]

For Taft, this limited view of arbitration was not much of an improvement over traditional attitudes toward international relations in which national power was the final arbiter of national destinies. Taft realized that the connection between war and vital interests was no longer so simple. He believed along with Norman Angell that nations could no longer afford war. Then too, continuing to define interests from a national framework when the structure of interests was obviously global was a logical contradiction that guaranteed the kind of conflict that arbitration was supposed to avoid. Thus, in order for arbitration to be effective, it had to be unqualified. "We can not make omelets without breaking eggs," Taft argued while on the stump for his treaties. "We cannot submit international questions to arbitration without the prospect of losing . . . if we are going into the arbitration game, if I may call it such, we must play through to the end, and we must take our hard knocks with equanimity."[82]

Following the signature of the treaties with Great Britain and France in August 1911, Taft envisioned the inclusion of Germany, Russia, the Netherlands, Norway, and Sweden in the arbitral club. "Perhaps, we may after a while induce Japan to come in," he hoped. As Taft later noted, the real point with Britain and France was never the arbitration of fundamental matters, for between the United States and those nations "it was hardly conceivable . . . that any issue could arise which would not be settled by arbitration." The treaties mattered "only as an encouragement to other nations in the settlement of their differences." He knew full well that many nations, if left to themselves, were hardly likely to cultivate the arbitrating frame of mind. Such statements indicated an awareness that arbitration was at best a means to improvement rather than an end.[83]

Those who believed that the treaties betrayed a utopian sensibility and a failure to recognize the deep-seated flaws of international society missed the point. For Taft, the arbitration treaties were not an ideal solution. Taft's true love was an international court backed by world opinion that would dispense impartial justice on the basis of legal principles without regard for national sensibilities. He never assumed for a moment that a utopian state of civilization had arrived which the treaties would reflect and codify. Instead, he sought to take practical piecemeal measures in the hope of modifying the present unsatisfactory international system in which a few powerful nations persisted in acting according to the old rules. In this project he hoped to build upon a sturdy Anglo-Saxon foundation. As Knox put it in 1909: "It is an indication of the favorable prospects for the realization of the aspirations for universal peace and arbitration of international differences that the nations best equipped for the maintenance of their claims with force are among the first to propose their peaceful adjudication."[84] In this case, power and principle appeared to coincide.

Unfortunately, the British connection cut both ways. While it appealed to those who sensed that the two nations were heading down the same civilized path, and while it helped defuse the potential of the Anglo-Japanese alliance, it carried geopolitical freight which many were not prepared to accept. Some accused the president of dragging the United States into an alliance with Great Britain and France. Foreign Minister Sir Edward Grey, for one, did not hesitate to conceal his hopes that this might in fact occur. Anticipating an approach that would be taken up by the League of Nations in the 1920s in the Geneva Protocol, he hoped for a de facto alliance in which two parties with a treaty of arbitration would probably agree to "join with each other in any case in which one had a quarrel with a third Power by which arbitration was refused." While this argument would gain in attractiveness over time, it was too advanced for the Taft administration.[85]

Whatever their far-reaching geopolitical consequences, it was their domestic import that defeated the treaties. Here Roosevelt was not the main problem, for the Senate was far more skeptical than he on this matter. Taft believed that the criterion of "justiciability," in combination with the safeguards contained in the voting provisions of the treaty, provided ample protection for American interests. He also attempted to appease the Senate by providing assurances as to the inviolability of the Monroe Doctrine. However, to allow a body other than the Senate to decide what was arbitrable would take an important power out of that jealous body's hands, as Roosevelt's close friend, Senator Lodge, accurately noted. Once submitted to the upper chamber for ratification, the predictable avalanche of criticisms buried whatever meaning the treaties possessed. For a variety of reasons—opposition on grounds of principle, domestic politics, and fear of abdicating its constitutional role in the treaty-making process—the Senate first bent out of place and weakened the frame of the treaty and then, to assure that this political kite would never leave the ground, added a long tail of reservations on immigration, issues of territorial integrity, U.S. debts, and the Monroe Doctrine.[86]

Questions of tactical bumbling by the administration aside, at bottom the Senate's action reflected its distrust of world public opinion as a substitute for traditional community sentiment. The primitive senatorial dentistry having rendered the treaties toothless, Taft finally decided against proceeding with ratification. But the treaties remained close to his heart and he always regretted his inability to put them through. In his final postmortem, Taft chalked the failure up to historical reasons. Writing to Knox, he remarked: "you and I seemed to be a little in advance."[87]

As THIS CHAPTER SUGGESTS, the basic alternatives of American internationalism in the twentieth century are not to be discerned by choosing from a line-up consisting of the usual suspects; instead of Roosevelt and Wilson, the comparison between Taft and Roosevelt is more appropriate, for they are the ones who articulated the two extreme possibilities in the American adjustment to "civilization." Their dispute over the nature of modernization sheds light on why it is so odd that in the pages of history Roosevelt has been depicted as a man of prudence and Taft as the reckless adventurer. Roosevelt's traditionalism gave the appearance of cautiousness, whereas Taft's sincere attachment to a diplomacy of modernization implied a need for diplomatic engagement. For Roosevelt, interdependence was dangerous. By bringing the great powers into close proximity, it created situations that could easily produce clashes of interest which could be resolved in the only way that issues of this kind were ever settled: through war. Taft, however, saw contact and interaction on a global plane as being historically inevitable and nonthreatening to boot. The modern world was so different from anything encountered before that a reliance on tradition and the premodern heroic framework of diplomacy was the greatest obstacle to clear thinking in foreign affairs.

Taft's diplomacy was, in retrospect, simple-minded and naive in its expectations of great-power harmony. To its enduring credit, however, it recognized that historical change was producing international conditions with which traditional diplomacy, both European and American, could not possibly cope. In pursuit of novel approaches to a rapidly modernizing world, the Taft administration also pioneered a number of themes that would be picked up by his immediate successor, Woodrow Wilson. Though Wilson would scorn dollar diplomacy as materialistic, he too would place great emphasis on economic internationalism and, even more so than Taft, would rely on world opinion to cement international cooperation.

Wilson would be a more thoroughgoing internationalist yet, for he would deal with a dimension missing from the diplomacy of his predecessors: an internationalism of power. If there was one structural element of the modern international environment that did not fall within Taft's historical interpretation, or within Roosevelt's for that matter, it was the possibility that interdependence had created a fundamentally new strategic environment in which a war among the European powers could inexorably involve the United States. Roosevelt's imperialism and Taft's dollar diplomacy had moved significantly beyond nineteenth-century isolationism, but they nevertheless remained quite traditional in their refusal to contemplate power political involvements in Europe and Asia. Roosevelt had been concerned with the dangers of internationalism, Taft with its opportunities. But for Wilson, the New World held marvelous possibilities at the same time that it also revealed hitherto unimaginable dangers. It was this combination of promise and peril, the understanding that the obverse side of modern solidarity was chaos, that would produce the conceptual revolution of Wilsonianism.

2

WOODROW WILSON AND THE HISTORICAL NECESSITY OF IDEALISM

WOODROW WILSON'S REPUTATION as the father of modern American internationalism is something of a puzzle. In politics, patriarchal stature is usually awarded to those who create enduring policies or institutions, yet in Wilson's case any assessment of his historical legacy that takes as its guide the landmarks of his diplomacy cannot avoid the embarrassing conclusion that his influence was short-lived. To be sure, Wilson did set a precedent for intervening in Europe, but his reasons for doing so were based on a traditional attachment to international law and neutral rights that has had little meaning for succeeding generations. As George Kennan accurately noted in 1951, "Looking backward today on these endless disputes between our government and the belligerents over neutral rights, it seems hard to understand how we could have attached so much importance to them."[1]

This verdict of long-run irrelevance seems equally applicable to Wilson's idealistic postwar policies. The half-life of America's enthusiasm for collective security lasted barely a generation and decayed so rapidly thereafter that American internationalism bore scant resemblance to his vision of a world order based on the League of Nations. Despite the continuing poignancy of his personal tragedy, it has become increasingly difficult with the passage of time to enter sympathetically into a frame of mind that came to seem, in view of what followed, almost as quixotic as the mentality behind the Children's Crusade. Even from a post–cold war perspective, the road traveled to that point had not been mapped out by Wilson. The United Nations, it might be argued, owed much to Wilson, but, as I will argue, it was designed to deal with a very different kind of world than the one Wilson had in mind when he conceived of the League of Nations. Because his vision of a world freed from the curse of power politics seems to bear no practical relation to the power-obsessed century that followed, Wilson seems a hopelessly distant and exotic historical figure, a stranger to both his time and to ours.[2]

Nevertheless, our intuitive sense of Wilson's centrality to the story of twentieth-century American internationalism is correct: he did lay the foundations of modern American foreign policy. However, to get to the enduring significance of the man one needs to look past his saintly aura and explore the lesser-known dark side of his thought, a side whose somber understanding of the modern implications of power grounded solidly what otherwise appears to be an idealism rooted in nothing but thin air. His policies, whose idealism as we shall see was very limited in any case, were more the product of his understanding of historical necessity than of utopian impulse. And while his preachments emphasized global community, his political creed was not the product of a missionary determination to impose abstract metaphysical ideals.

Wilson was the kind of liberal, as described by Richard Rorty, whose "sense of human solidarity is based on a sense of common danger."[3] At the height of his powers, he became obsessed with defining that unprecedented universal danger and drawing the appropriate conclusions for human solidarity. The eventual collapse of the League of Nations marked the failure of Wilson's practical policy suggestions, but the compelling strategic vision that had made the league necessary in the first place would in due time become the common sense of the matter to American statesmen, as would the logic of Wilson's solidarist approach to dealing with them. This stereoscopic insight, his simultaneous view of problem and solution, gave to Wilson's historical world image a realistic depth of perspective that succeeding generations of policymakers could not improve upon. Wilson's historical understanding, not his practical policy intelligence, provides the basis for his claim to patriarchal stature.

FROM IMPERIALISM TO BALANCE OF POWER

Like most statesmen, Wilson's basic ideas about international relations were formed prior to attaining high office. Although his wartime views on collective security were to some extent improvised responses to events, they were equally the product of predisposition, the result of nearly two decades of intelligent reflection on foreign affairs in his earlier careers as a political scientist and university president. Wilson's internationalism, like Roosevelt's, was to a large extent a product of a historical sensibility far more expansive than the localist frame from which his fellow citizens approached foreign affairs. As part of the general reorientation of conceptual categories of time and space then taking place in the Western world, Wilson came increasingly to interpret events abroad in modern terms from "a genuinely world-historical framework of action and experience.'' From 1900 onward (at which time he already judged the world to be ''a single vicinage; each part had become neighbor to all the rest''), he preached constantly of the end of isolation and of the need to formulate a new American sense of purpose for the overseas task that lay ahead.[4]

For Wilson, American imperialism was, as the Munich crisis would be for those of another time, the formative historical experience of his generation. The worldwide expansion of power afforded cause for optimism because it allowed the European powers, accustomed to the fetid atmosphere and cramped living conditions of the continental balance of power, to breathe in the fresh air of the global countryside. In contrast to the Leninist image of a shrunken capitalist world suddenly too small to accommodate the growth of monopoly capital, Americans saw plenty of elbow room in an expansive global arena where, according to Herbert Croly, ''the restless and adventurous members of a national body can have their fling without dangerous consequences.'' For Paul Reinsch, there was a field ''vast enough for the exercise of all the energies of civilization,'' while Wilson saw colonies as ''a frontier on which to turn loose the colts of the race.'' With a spatial logic reminiscent of Madison's Federalist 10, competing national interests, which if confined to a smaller sphere would have led to a struggle for mastery, were assimilated smoothly and harmlessly into a capacious world system. This salutary expansion of the arena of international politics, accompanied by changes in the internal structure of European nations, made possible hitherto unthinkable cooperation. A democratizing world had learned ''self control'' since the French Revolution, Wilson believed.[5]

However, things got hazy very quickly after that; unlike Munich and its aftermath, there were no immediate ''lessons'' of empire that came as a sudden epiphany. At this point in time, American images of Germany, Japan, Russia, and China were only beginning their slow but dramatic turnabout and were not sufficiently well-defined even in outline to form a coherent new intellectual portrait of the world. Thus while the events surrounding the Spanish-American War were as dramatic as any in the experience of American foreign relations since the War of 1812, the context in which they were played out was not. The contrast between concrete action and fuzzy purpose forced Wilson to ponder the geopolitical implications of his nation's colonial spree.

Wilson was not overly enthusiastic about imperialism, but he accepted it as an inevitable sequel to America's history of continuous frontier expansion and, since it coincided with America's maturation as a nation, he welcomed it as a way for America to fall into step with the march of world history. Despite his overall approval of the process, however, some important historical discontinuities provided cause for concern. The problem was that colonial expansion, "although as natural, as inevitable, as characteristic as the old, showed a radical difference in character and seemed likely to change everything that had gone before." Wilson was not referring here to the question of governing alien peoples which agitated so many of his contemporaries, but to the diplomatic implications of empire.[6]

The war was a rite of passage, but Wilson was intelligent enough to realize that there was no clear sense of what it was a passage *to*. Enthusiastic imperialism, to his mind, had been "largely a question of brawn and courage." In other words, imperialism as a policy had been an impulsive, almost libidinous happening, without being channeled beforehand by politically sublimated ends. While Rooseveltian swashbuckling had sufficed for purposes of warfare, Wilson understood that "a far finer sense of diplomacy and statecraft" was needed to transform imperialism's raw impulses into creative policy. The sober second thoughts that Americans gave to the career of empire at the very point of embarking upon it was proof of Wilson's suspicion that no settled national policy lay behind it. But his insight into the shortcomings of impulsive imperialism was a negative critique only, while his call for an intelligently formulated national interest merely begged the question of what constituted the national interest in the first place. As he well knew, without constructive policy recommendations, declarations of this kind were mere velleities with little applicability to real world problems.[7]

It was obvious that the United States was becoming a world power, one of those nations, as defined by Archibald Cary Coolidge in *America as a World Power,* which were "directly interested in all parts of the world and whose voices must be listened to everywhere." There was no blinking the fact, he realized, that America had "come out of her days of adolescence and preparation" and had "taken her place among the powers of the world," a "leader" and "pacemaker in the wide field of foreign affairs." But this too was a commonplace of his time that said nothing about America's national interest. That was not the half of it, for the question of expediency inherent in any conception of national interest, "itself infinitely hard to settle," was complicated by the problem of "moral obligation." "What *ought* we to do?" he asked himself, obviously perplexed.[8]

Part of the answer, the most obvious part to Wilson, lay in a British-American colonial stewardship in which the two leading Anglo-Saxon nations would dutifully "moderate the process in the interests of liberty." Wilson was an ardent Anglophile who had shuddered at the thought of the United States and Great Britain, "the two kindred nations which stood together at the front of the world's progress," going to war during the brief but highly charged Venezuela crisis of 1895. In 1901 he declared that "it is only now that, in the crucial conflict for Christendom, we stand before the world in policy as well as in race alongside of England.'' In succeeding years, Wilson continued to express his faith in the political and ideological solidarity of the English-speaking peoples.[9]

With the forces of light thus defined in terms of a common heritage of democratic ideals, the autocratic forces of darkness lurking in the shadows—Germany and Russia—were easily identified. But a narrowly Anglo-Saxonist imperialism was loaded with possibilities for conflict and would have held little attraction for progressives like Wilson had it not been counterbalanced by ideological themes that stressed commercial and cultural dynamics as factors promoting a well-nigh inevitable great-power harmony. Expanding on the already trite liberal theme that global civilization was characterized by functional interdependence, in 1907 Wilson noted that the world had been ''drawn into a common market,'' from which he concluded that ''peace itself becomes a matter of conference and international combination. Cooperation is the law of action in the modern world.'' His 1916 statement that ''an inevitable partnership of interests has been brought upon the nations'' attested to his ongoing attachment to this functionalist credo.[10]

Wilson saw progress in cultural terms, too, as travel, diplomacy, and the common heritage of the English-speaking peoples were knitting the world together in ''international understandings.'' But while an interdependence created by global market forces certainly contributed to the creation of inter-cultural understanding, the successful operation of those structural processes making for global cohesion was itself dependent upon the existence of a prior understanding of their desirability. Given the unavoidable fact of involvement in this new era of interdependence, Wilson was bothered by the intellectual pitfalls of ''isolation and provincialism.'' In his days as a much sought-after public speaker, he sought to convince his audiences of the need to readjust their thinking by hammering away at the need for a cosmopolitan awareness that transcended mere local knowledge. He liked to clinch his argument with the assertion, to which he attached great weight even while violating it in his personal life, that fear and hatred were the products of ignorance. ''[I] can't hate a man I know,'' he insisted.[11]

If all went well, the twentieth century would see a peaceful expansion of commerce, ''a world mastered, if not united, by the power of armed fleets patrolling it from end to end, in the interests of peace and European and American trade.'' The transforming effects of this peaceful commercial and cultural expansion would inevitably work their way from periphery to center. ''Now it is the Philippines and Alaska,'' Wilson predicted in 1906. ''Soon it will be the shore of Asia, and then Autocratic Europe shall hear us knocking at their back door, demanding admittance for American ideas, customs, and arts." Eventually, colonized and colonizers alike would be transformed as the imperialist tail, though it began as an appendage of continental politics, would one day wag the dog of European statecraft. The continental balance of power, once the diplomatic fulcrum of the world, would itself be dislodged by the imperatives of global cooperation.[12]

Viewed in this light, American imperialism, far from registering American entry into a global Darwinian struggle, was a means of radically transforming world politics for the better that was wholly consistent with the domestic reformism of the Progressive movement. However much John Hay, that world-weary secretary of state, may have thought talk of America's preeminent moral position in China to be mere "flap-doodle," Wilson saw America as "a sort of pure air blowing in world politics, destroying illusions and cleaning places of morbid miasmatic gases." Much like a chemical catalyst, the United States would be able to promote salutary change without endangering the purity of its virtuous first principles.[13]

This optimistic vision of global great-power cooperation could not, admittedly, pass muster as a policy because it emphasized ends to the total neglect of means. But if Wilson did not have a fully developed agenda for America's role in world politics, it was not for lack of effort in trying to articulate one. America's imperial expansion, he recognized, had brought it into "international relationships which had to be defined and which called for the best statesmanship." Stating the obvious was one thing and defining these new relationships quite another, yet Wilson was never at a loss for a method. Convinced that the historian was "a sort of prophet," he believed that both the problem and its solution could be clarified only by historical interpretation.[14]

For Wilson, history was a three-dimensional exercise in which the study of the past should both furnish "object-lessons for the present" and prefigure the future. He was in spirit one of the Progressive "New Historians" for whom historical understanding prepared the ground for change and for whom policy tightly corseted by tradition was giving way to policy historically imagined. For example, in 1914 he maintained that "no man can look at the past, of the history of this world, without seeing a vision of the future of this world." This faith in history's capacity to meaningfully structure contemporary national experience, which was central to Wilson's conception of historical scholarship, carried over into his attempts to use history as a template for charting American policy.[15]

Unfortunately, the historical auguries were themselves vague, as America's international future meshed only inconclusively with Wilson's sense of national development. American history, he recognized at the turn of the century, had been "brought at last into perspective, to be seen as what it is, an integral portion of the general history of civilization." As one who approached history in literary terms of narrative, centuries were the "dramatic unit" of American history. Within this scheme of emplotment, Wilson depicted the seventeenth century as a century of colonization; the eighteenth, as a century of war, "to clear the stage"; the nineteenth, as a century of nation-making; and the twentieth, as "a century of ———?"[16]

Although he could not fill in the blank, at least America's starring global role stood out with utter clarity. Already in 1905 Wilson had no doubts as to his nation's destiny: "I suppose that in our hearts we know that we shall rule the world," he said. Notwithstanding this sense of grand anticipation, Wilson was waiting for events to clarify his ideals by defining the concrete possibilities of political action. Despite his repeated invocations of the need for "insight and vision," and his belief that these were most likely to be supplied by a reinterpretation of traditional American ideals under the leadership of a reinvigorated presidency, his views and homiletic urgings were, in fact, shot through with uncertainty.[17]

Try as he might, he could not imagine the what and the how of a modern foreign policy that went beyond Roosevelt's neo-Federalist approach to "civilization" and Taft's economic universalism. Momentous change there would inevitably be, but in the prewar decade the articulation of its particulars was impossible. Wilson admitted to being unsure, along with everyone else, of "what we will find over the big curve" and, for all his attempts to lift the veil of the future, he acknowledged freely that "we have for the nonce no clear purpose or programme." All he could offer for the time being was "pieces of the imaginative conception that America has had of her destiny in the world."[18]

Wilson attributed the inability to frame concrete policies to the complex and still ambiguous onslaught of modernity. "Even rectitude of intention waits on enlightenment, purpose on knowledge," he said in 1909, in attempting to explain the muddled and confused thought of his day. "The light of creeds and codes is slow to penetrate the nebulous mass of our present social structure, which is changing but not yet formed. The saving health of moral sanity among the nations of the earth waits, as usual, upon the thought and purposes of the individuals who compose them." The problem in the fin-de-siècle period was that the American community had "not yet awakened to a common consciousness." This consciousness would have to evolve in the light of further developments before policy could be shaped, and Wilson could only wonder as to when this crystallization would take place and what it held in store. New ideas would have to be precipitated out of the centrifuge of events.[19]

As a good historian and Progressive, Wilson relied on facts to help shape his judgments, but the march of events proved to be so slow in providing them that the long-awaited clarification would not arrive until the war. And when at last it did come, it took an unexpected and quite confusing turn that forced Wilson to abandon his long-held view of imperialism as the central fact of modern world politics. Imperialism and its attendant process of civilized expansion turned out to have been a false trail, blocked by the landslide of the Great War from reaching the historically appointed destination of great-power harmony. Once the war's larger meaning became evident to Wilson, his globalist outlook shifted away from its original positive focus—empire having been discredited by virtue of its contribution to starting the war—and brought to center stage a problem to which he had hitherto paid scant attention: the historical significance of the European balance of power. Instead of changing the world from the outside in, it would have to be done from the inside out; and instead of a feeling of liberating spaciousness to the world system, the tight web of interdependence would ensnare and limit all nations.

THE END OF THE EUROPEAN BALANCE:
IMPLICATIONS FOR WORLD POLITICS

Wilson's views on the balance of power were not fully formed until mid-1917, following American entry into the war and the decision to send an expeditionary force to France. By that time, he had come to the conclusion that the European balance had been so critically wounded by the Great War that, even if it should survive, it could never recover fully enough to resume its traditional task of assuring European stability and Western expansion. Wilson's assessment of the condition of the European power balance was not, as is often assumed, merely the knee-jerk reflex of a liberal ideologue. Like most Americans, he detested its amorality, aristocratic elitism, and reliance upon power as the last word in international life, but these culturally inherited instincts do not go very far toward explaining a sophisticated Wilsonian outlook that far transcended simple moralistic idealism. For all his inbred antipathy to the balance of power, Wilson's crusading ideals were based on a hardheaded reading of history that, far from being cause for unalloyed joy in Wilson's liberal heart, envisioned unprecedented dangers that required a dramatic new conception of diplomacy. Wilson had always assumed, as a matter of liberal optimism, that the balance of power was fated for extinction, but the war brought home to him the unexpectedly dismal understanding of just how perilous its permanent demise could be to the international environment.[20]

Wilson's outlook had very little to do, at least on a conscious level, with religious belief or missionary impulse. Aware that such a connection could

easily enough be made, quite early in his academic career he had considered
and rejected the view that history was an expression of Providence. "Society
does not know any other world," he insisted. "It must save itself in this
world." For politics, the implications of this viewpoint were clearly secular:
"Therefore I believe that the social ethic is a utilitarian ethic, not an absolute
one; that it is what you may accomplish by agreement, and not by an abstract
process of right and wrong." While he was, unquestionably, deeply religious,
he did not believe that the personal certainties of faith could be translated
into political truths or that the existence of a divine plan mitigated the responsibility or capability for directing one's destiny.[21]

Always realizing the need to give Caesar his due, Wilson was careful
not to confuse faith with politics. In 1903, he belittled the tendency to make
transcendent claims for temporal pursuits by pointing out that "the destiny
of a nation is in this world, not the next. Here shall our nation rise or fall,
grow or decline." Sixteen years later at the Paris Peace Conference, he was
still arguing that "religious teaching hadn't found a practical solution for the
troubles of the world and states and they must have some one to give them
practical relief for their distress." Given this self-imposed boundary between
the sacred and the profane, to inject religion into Wilson's worldview is not
merely extraneous, it is a definite hindrance to understanding his diplomacy
and its contagious appeal among those who did not share his religious convic-
tions. His politics of salvation were wholly secular.[22]

Wilson's idealism has also been overrated. Wilson was no mystic, nor,
with his lifelong interest in practical politics and effective leadership, was he
a dreamer. Typical were his remarks to a postwar audience: "There is nothing
I respect so much as a fact," he told them. "The real difficulty in all political
affairs is to know whether you can translate your theories into facts or not."
He resented having his views labeled as "academic" when he knew that
diplomacy, like all politics, rested on a recognition of hard facts. In his
early years he had dutifully read and assimilated his Machiavelli, and early
recommended *The Prince* to "sentimental men" as a work which "would
cause the scales to fall from their eyes, in their view of the world of politics."
Even in so basic a text of his "idealism" as his immortal "Peace without
Victory" address of 22 January 1917, he took care to point out to a joint
session of Congress that his head was not in the clouds. "I wish frankly to
uncover realities," he insisted. At a meeting of the Council of Ten in Paris,
he noted that "he had been accused of being a hopeless idealist, but as a
matter of fact he never accepted an ideal until he could see its practical
application." Similarly, when discussing his ambitious postwar program in
1918 he insisted that he was not chasing will-o'-the-wisps, but instead was
"trying to work out a purely scientific proposition 'What will stay put?'"

In the balance between what is and what ought to be, Wilson gave political pride of place to existing realities.[23]

Wilson was also thoroughly familiar with the concept of balance of power, whose uncomplicated essentials he grasped readily enough, but there were plenty of reasons apart from idealistic arguments for him to disdain it. For one thing, he did not view the balance of power as an immutable natural law which human beings, and nations, ignored at their peril, with no hope whatsoever of changing it. He believed instead that "human choice enters into the laws of the state, whereas from natural laws that choice is altogether excluded; they are dominated by fixed necessity." Raised in the reform Darwinist climate of the late nineteenth century, the world of politics for Wilson was not a mine field seeded with mechanical laws, ready to explode on contact at the tread of foolhardy politicians. Since the balance of power was a human, that is to say historical, creation, it was subject to change like anything else historical.[24]

Then too, there was no American tradition of raison d'état, which was, after all, part of a European cultural patrimony not passed down to Americans. If the classical balance depended on a "common ground of culture in the European states," as the historian Edward Gulick has pointed out, that common ground was noticeably absent from the American cultural tradition and, for that matter, from the East Asian as well. Nor, in terms of political ecology, had Americans been forced to adapt their thinking to its logic. Indeed, much of American foreign policy, as was evident from the works of Alexander Hamilton and the preachments of the Monroe Doctrine, was prelapsarian, intent upon preventing the original sin of a balance of power from being committed in North America. A century of free security had not made it necessary, and, to the extent that the United States had exercised power upon others it was largely in the Caribbean region, where the American position was increasingly hegemonic as the nineteenth century wore on. Finally, Wilson's early analysis of imperialism had led him to believe, along with other Progressives of his generation, that the cooperative imperatives of the global modernizing process, of which imperialism was so spectacular a symptom, would ultimately subvert the spirit of competitive nationalism which was the soul of realpolitik.[25]

The European balance of power would not remain offstage in American diplomatic thought much longer, however, for the Great War highlighted its central role in the historical crisis through which the world was passing. To start with, the unparalleled destructiveness and revolutionary social chaos unleashed by the war, whose costs far exceeded any conceivable benefits attainable by victory, brought home to Wilson the self-defeating nature of modern war as an institutional device for settling differences among the great powers. Moreover, the failure of his attempt to maintain American neutrality and the emergence of *world* war meant that the European balance of power as a geographically self-contained and self-regulating mechanism was extinct. Great-power wars were now global, because interdependence was more than economic; indeed, the globe was like a dry forest that could easily be set ablaze even by sparks struck from small conflicts. Last, and most important for Wilson, the chance that Europe might come to be dominated by a single great power, while itself no historical novelty, raised the further possibility that this power, taking advantage of economic interdependence and equipped with modern military technology, could use its continental resources to build a position of global hegemony perilous to the United States.

Wilson's gradual articulation of these ideas and his formulation of policies to deal with them would constitute a sharp break with the traditional historical world image. There were no indications from the outset that such an epochal change was imminent; indeed, the situation, as he spelled it out in the neutrality period from 1914 to 1917, seemed quite familiar. America's national honor and its ability to defend its neutral rights under international law, paramount concerns of American diplomacy since the earliest days of the republic, were being challenged once again, this time by German submarine warfare. In the aftermath of the U-boat sinkings of the *Lusitania* and the *Arabic* in 1915, Wilson resorted to the time-honored language of national interest and prestige to describe American concerns. "What America is bound to fight for when the time comes is nothing less than her self-respect," he argued. He continued to minimize the military threat through the middle of 1916. With the exception of the German challenge to neutral rights, he maintained that the United States had "very little to gain or to lose" and certainly "nothing to fear" from the struggle in Europe.[26]

Wilson envisioned the possibility of a German drive for world domination from the opening days of World War I, but the idea of a global threat, which would become central to American foreign policy in the twentieth century, was not fully appreciated until after the United States entered the war. The public expression of this danger, and its entry into the political vocabulary of American statesmanship, was delayed by Wilson's hopes for neutral mediation and by the existence of a seemingly unbreakable military stalemate in Europe that minimized any danger to the Americas. Thus throughout the period of neutrality Wilson denied the existence of a military threat to the United States, a belief he backed by his stubborn opposition to calls for military preparedness. As he saw it, he would not "turn America into a military camp" when there was "no reason to fear that from any quarter our independence or the integrity of our territory is threatened." Even when political pressure forced him to propose measures for limited preparedness in January 1916, he continued to deny the existence of a strategic peril. "We are not thinking of invasion of the territory of the United States," he said. "That is not what is making us anxious . . . certainly not."[27]

Privately, however, the hypothetical possibilities were more worrisome than he let on, for Wilson and his advisers were apprehensive, from the very beginning, about the security threat that could arise in the event of a German victory. In a series of well-known ruminations, Wilson quickly adopted as his own the view of his intimate adviser and alter ego, Colonel Edward M. House, that a German triumph would mean "the unspeakable tyranny of militarism for generations to come." The effect of a British and French collapse on the Continent, Wilson believed, would threaten America to its very core, for it would "change the course of our civilization and make the United States a military nation." This he repeated to the British ambassador in Washington, Sir Cecil Spring Rice, and again in 1915, when he told House that "if Germany and her militaristic ideas were to win, the obligation upon us was stronger than ever."[28]

An Entente triumph seemed benign by comparison. For example, Wilson told an interviewer in December 1914 that "I cannot see now that it would greatly hurt the interests of the United States if either France or Russia or Great Britain should finally dictate the settlement." Fortifying this strategic conviction was Wilson's well-known Anglophilism, an ideological partiality for Britain that stood out even more strongly when set against his view of Germany (which prided itself on being the land of *Kultur*) as "essentially selfish and lacking spirituality." Given his values, this was the worst thing he could possibly say about a nation.[29]

A similar mixture of ideological and strategic calculations led a number of Wilson's advisers to advocate the abandonment of neutrality. House, who believed that "our hopes, our aspirations and our sympathies are closely woven with the democracies of France and England," by 1916 favored making war on Germany, though he was careful not to press the argument too aggressively on his prickly, neutrality-minded president. Secretary of State Robert Lansing, a strong-minded man with little influence in shaping Wilson's views, had already formed similar conclusions by August 1915. Hoping to take advantage of Wilson's peacemaking ambitions, Lansing urged belligerency, ostensibly as a means of assuring a moderate settlement, but his basic motive was the fear that a German triumph would see the Reich "turn upon us as its next obstacle to imperial rule over the world."[30]

Although Wilson's views on Germany generally resembled those of his advisers, their fears for the national security at this point must have seemed overblown in view of the apparently unbreakable military stalemate. Intervention was doubly questionable in light of his belief that nonbelligerency was essential to mediating the conflict, an objective that loomed ever larger in his neutrality policy. Still, despite Wilson's insistence on only the most noble justifications for making war, his rigid defense of American interests and neutral rights, no matter how idealistically phrased in terms of international law, was pushing the nation toward the war's vortex for essentially the same nationalistic motives for which he criticized the European powers. Neutral rights and prestige were, after all, selfish ideas. Wilson's dissatisfaction with the narrowness of international law was evident in his postwar complaint that "you could not mention to any other government anything that concerned it unless you could prove that your own interests were involved."[31]

The point was not merely to defend international law, but to change it. Thus instead of standing warily aside from the struggle with one hand on his wallet and the other on his pistol, Wilson sought to position himself above the battle and look at the war with a scholar's analytical eye, "from the point of view of the rest of the world." His was a detachment born of a larger commitment to rebuilding a seriously flawed system of international relations. He could be emotionally moved by the slaughter then taking place in Europe but, unlike his advisers, he would not be politically deflected by the passions being generated by the conflict. Indeed, the more grave the war became for neutrals and belligerents alike, the more convinced he became of the need for high-minded mediation. Wilson's mediation scheme was based on the optimistic assumption that the bloodletting had given birth to a common interest in peace among the belligerents that, if properly nurtured by him, could become the basis for a restructured postwar order. With Wilson continuing to view the United States as only an indirectly interested party, his worries about neutral rights were akin to dealing with the light fallout of volcanic ash from distant European eruptions.[32]

At this point, Wilson's thinking had yet to come to terms with the momentous geopolitical implications of the war as a power struggle. Considered purely from the point of view of its intracontinental role, however, the balance of power already struck him as being obsolete. He had concluded by 1916 that, with Europe committing suicide as a result of its reliance on unlimited military means to regulate its affairs, thus making a mockery of the means-ends calculus that brought on the war, the balance of power was a shibboleth. As radical journalist John Reed explained following an interview with the president in 1914, Wilson opposed the war "not primarily because it is bloody or cruel, but because it no longer accomplishes its purpose." In the same vein, when preparing his peace note of November 1916, he wrote that "the big outstanding thing to be remembered by all nations was the utter uselessness of the utter sacrifices made." As a human institution, war was supposed to be instrumental, a useful means for achieving desirable national ends, but this war was consuming the very societies it was supposed to preserve and strengthen.[33]

In addition to the immediate havoc wreaked upon European society, nothing would be settled by the war. Whatever the verdict of arms for the Entente—win, lose, or draw—the future looked uniformly dismal. While the stalemate may have seemed at first sight to some observers to be an excellent illustration of the effectiveness of the balance of power, Wilson thought otherwise. Only if it served to demonstrate the futility of the system, a conviction that he had once hoped the belligerents would come to on their own, was a deadlock desirable; otherwise, it would only bring yet another war. A peace with victory, even an Entente victory, would also break down eventually because of its effect on victors and vanquished alike. "One Sedan brings on another, and victory is an intoxicant that fires the national brain and leaves a craving for more," he maintained. And, of course, for the embittered loser, the revanchism unleashed by an unjust settlement would only produce "more wars."[34]

Given the intolerable costs of its self-perpetuating cycle of self-defeating violence, the inherent instability of the balance of power could no longer be tolerated. In a brilliant address at the Free Trade Hall on 30 December 1918, Wilson argued that "interest does not bind men together. Interest separates men, for the moment there is the slightest departure from the nice adjustment of interests jealousies begin to spring up." As a matter of logic, the balance of power was self-contradictory precisely because it was "determined by the unstable equilibrium of competing interests." Wilson made this plain enough in an address to the Italian Parliament: "We know that there cannot be another balance of power. That has been tried and found wanting, for the best of all reasons that it does not stay balanced inside itself, and a weight which does not hold together cannot constitute a makeweight in the affairs of men."[35]

Despite the graphic horrors of the struggle raging in Europe, Wilson's critique at this time resembled the traditional liberal view of the balance of power as a recipe for war. That is, it was treated pretty much as a pernicious abstraction that would have caused little concern had its breakdown been localized within Europe. Once his neutrality policy had collapsed, however, the future of the balance of power became a matter of life and death. Though submarine warfare was the casus belli, once involved, Wilson saw American participation as inevitable and not as the result of some accidental "incidents," which, if more adroitly handled thorough diplomacy, might have preserved the peace.

In his second inaugural address Wilson confessed the error of his earlier posture toward the war—a momentous admission for one so intellectually prideful—saying now that "to be indifferent or independent of it was out of the question." A few months later he went even further and asserted "with a clear conscience about the war that it was necessary that we should enter it. It was inevitable that we should enter it." Only after the war did Wilson admit openly that "America did not at first see the full meaning of the war which has just ended," but by that time he had gone a long way toward putting the failed neutrality experiment and its obsolete rationales behind him by articulating his new understanding of what was really at stake. He would spell it out even more clearly to the Senate following his return from the peace conference: "It was not an accident or a matter of sudden choice that we are no longer isolated and devoted to a policy which has only our own interest and advantage for its object." This was of utmost importance: for Wilson was saying that the country had passed a historical point of no return in which the defense of neutral rights no longer made sense because in the modern world structural conditions had made neutrality impossible.[36]

"The facts of the world have changed," Wilson stated in 1919. Specifically, he had come to understand that in the modern era European great-power wars were necessarily world wars. Wilson was not alone in this belief. Léon Bourgeois of France, with whom Wilson frequently locked horns in Paris, nevertheless agreed fully that "henceforth no local conflict can be confined to some one part of the world." Sir Halford Mackinder, widely conceded to be the founder of modern geopolitics, described the process in much the same terms in a book published in 1919. He compared modern global crises to the volcanic explosion at Krakatoa, which generated shock waves that circled the globe. Relying more on analogy than on an appraisal of social dynamics to make his point, he nevertheless argued that "that, in the ultimate analysis, is why every considerable state was bound to be drawn into the recent war." The meaning of the war by this time went far beyond traditional American concerns like the defense of neutral rights or disinterested service to Europe to assume world-historical significance. World wars implied global stakes. World War I was a global conflict as a result of an inexorable process of historical development in which not simply the European balance but the future of the entire international environment was at issue.[37]

In mid-1917, after the United States had become a belligerent as a result of the submarine crisis and the seriousness of the precarious military situation on the western front had sunk in, Wilson began to stress these new perils. With American entry into the war, Wilson's worst fears concerning the German danger, once kept to himself, suddenly leaped to the forefront in his explanations of the war's meaning. Whereas formerly he had shown little interest in the war's origins and focused only on its side-effects upon neutral commerce, the causes and direct consequences of military aggression and the fate of the European balance now became abiding concerns. As the immediate possibilities narrowed down to peace or victory, he drew an alarming—and in retrospect very familiar—picture of what was at stake, a picture that had little to do with the by now passé issue of freedom of the seas. Now he claimed that America and its partners were fighting "a vast military establishment" which had "secretly planned to dominate the world." Henceforth the specter of world conquest was repeatedly conjured up. In 1918, he insisted that "everything will go by the board if we don't win." America's timely entry into the war "prevented a catastrophe that might have overwhelmed the world," he told a postwar audience in Paris.[38]

Wilson suggested that Germany had been well on the way to world mastery through peaceful economic methods when the Prussian warlords decided to take the more direct and violent route. He pointed to Germany's program of eastward expansion through Europe and Central Asia, the so-called *Mitteleuropa* scheme, in which the object was "to throw a broad belt of German power and political control across the very center of Europe and beyond the Mediterranean into the heart of Asia." Following the consolidation of this "empire of force" the Germans would "erect an empire of gain and commercial supremacy." Once German power was "inserted into the heart of the world," he argued that "her power can disturb the world as long as she keeps it." By controlling the world's central trade routes, Germany would "dominate the world itself."[39]

From that point, Germany's powerful economic base and strategic location would set the stage for a final showdown for world power. "That programme once carried out," Wilson warned, "America and all who care or dare to stand with her must arm and prepare themselves to contest the mastery of the world." Though Wilson sensed the wild improbability of it all, especially as there were no German plans to invade the United States, he could not deny the logic of Germany's behavior. "The whole thing is preposterous and impossible, and yet is not that what the whole course and action of the German armies has meant wherever they have moved?" he asked. Indeed, this seems to be exactly what some of the more extreme German expansionists had in mind. Attempting to shift attention away from the issue of neutral rights, Wilson continued to focus on the theme of world conquest as the basic justification for American belligerency. Following his return from Paris, he told reporters in July 1919 that the war "had brought home to all of the people of the United States exactly what the war itself meant in its original effort on the part of Germany to overwhelm the world."[40]

By filling in the details of a hazy, worst-case strategic script originally unworthy of presidential action, Wilson became a forceful exponent of what would become the domino theory's nightmare scenario: a vision of a chain of events that begins with a localized and seemingly insignificant incident which then mushrooms into a decisive global struggle on whose outcome hinges the survival of America's liberal institutions. The cheek-by-jowl politics of modernity made not only European war, but conflict of any kind potentially cataclysmic. In a letter to John St. Loe Strachey, Wilson described the new world as one in which "any quarrel, however small, however limited the questions it involves, may again, if carried to the point of war, kindle a flame throughout the world." With no regional balances to serve as firebreaks, a world without collective security would be a macrocosm of the Balkan tinderbox—in effect, a domino world. Others had already defined the German peril in similar terms, but it was Wilson alone who would weave the assumptions underlying these fears into an audacious new synthesis.[41]

How serious was this talk of world conquest? One expects, in time of war, to hear superheated rhetoric that demonizes the enemy and exaggerates their evil designs, but in this case everything points to the conclusion that Wilson's alarums were not contrived. For one thing, the menace as Wilson defined it was less Germany's capacity for world conquest, which was at best questionable, than the grave side-effects of measures that would have been necessary to prevent it, in effect Prussianizing the country and turning it into a garrison state. By arguing that the threat was "not the aggression of any great nation but the aggression of a system," he was distinguishing between the aggressor and the novel structural danger. Indeed, just being in the position to brandish a threat of this kind implied possession of the capacity to transform the geopolitical environment and reverse the course of history, to cut off the oxygen without which American society, and liberal institutions generally, would asphyxiate. The capability derived from continental hegemony, combined with the aggressive intentions embodied in Germany's militarist institutions, posed an intolerable new kind of danger.[42]

This shift away from the defense of neutral rights to fending off German domination of Europe and, by extension, the world system was underlined by a momentous, and wholly unanticipated, change in military strategy. The American military during the years of neutrality had based their war plans on the threat of an invasion of the Western Hemisphere, one that might materialize *after* this war. This hemispheric-mindedness was quite traditional. But the decision to send an expeditionary force to the Continent, the necessity of which became evident only following the U.S. declaration of war in April 1917, signaled a historic change of outlook. A war fought for neutral rights ought logically to have been a naval war, one in which the punishment fit the crime. But by mid-1917, especially in the aftermath of the disastrous French-conceived Nivelle offensive, the possibility emerged that the United

States and the Allies might lose, which in turn raised the novel kind of threat to American security articulated by Wilson that had not been contemplated by convention-bound military thinkers. Thus, even though the French and British military planners had initially intended to assign the United States to the menial backstage job of outfitter, the new global stakes made necessary a starring continental role for American ground forces. Not everyone got the message, of course. "You're not actually going to send troops there, are you?" said one congressman, obviously aghast, as the magnitude of American involvement became apparent.[43]

It was not simply the self-defeating violence that repelled Wilson, or the threat to the liberal world environment, but also the poisonous vapors of revolution spewed out by the war in its latter stages. Radicalism born of desperation was the child of war in the modern age and the stakes were nothing less than the preservation of liberal civilization: "Either we are going to guarantee civilization or we are going to abandon it," he told an audience in Salt Lake City. Just as war had been globalized, the world had become a single ideological disease pool that allowed the United States to be infected by contagions from abroad. He warned another audience that "everywhere, even in the United States, there is an antagonism toward the ordered processes of government. We feel the evil influence on this side of the Atlantic, and on the other side of the Atlantic every public man knows that it is knocking at the door of his government."[44]

Once set in motion, then, modern war set in train tragic self-destructive processes. The new global threat, while wearing German dress in this case, was rooted in factors far more fundamental than specific national failings. It was the result of a structural transformation in the world's political environment caused by the historic passing away of the European balance of power as the central fact of global politics. Wilson's original hostility to the balance of power as an immoral and senseless system was pretty much academic; after all, it was European business. But this breakdown of the European equilibrium was different. In the past, the system had functioned not only despite, but because of, its repeated breakdowns; but this collapse would have to be the last because the world could not afford any more. The balance and the stakes were now global in scope. America's participation in the war to fend off German domination served as conclusive proof that new, and supremely threatening, global dynamics had taken over.[45]

A balance that could not be limited in any way was no balance at all. If its breakdown led to wholesale and ruinously expensive slaughter, if its violence spread to global dimensions, if it spewed out revolutionary upheavals, and if its wars threatened the world system itself, the image of prudence, rationality, and mathematical calculation associated with the term "balance" was totally unmerited. For Wilson, then, the problem with the old realism was that it was not realistic enough in its failure to take account of modern geopolitical facts. The balance of power had not fallen by force of idealistic arguments; rather, it had undermined itself through the very logic of power that was its raison d'être and by the inability of its practitioners to understand its self-subverting nature. There was only one possible conclusion to be drawn: "There must be something substituted for the balance of power."[46]

From a pragmatic standpoint, what no longer worked was no longer diplomatically true. To draw upon inapplicable lessons of the past by resuscitating the balance of power would only set the stage for yet another, this time apocalyptic, reenactment of his generation's folly in a new war that was likely to be far more destructive. Because one could neither reform nor recreate what history had effectively destroyed, Wilson felt emboldened to "predict with absolute certainty that within another generation there will be another world war if the nations of the world do not concert the method by which to prevent it." Given the current state of exhaustion, it would not come soon, but unless the appropriate steps were taken, he insisted that "the next time will come; it will come while this generation is living, and the children will be sacrificed upon the altar of that war." In a prophesy that has yet to be invalidated, he predicted that "it will be the last war. Humanity will never suffer another, if humanity survives." "What the Germans used were toys as compared with what would be used in the next war," he predicted. Given the patently suicidal character of modern war and its certain proliferation across the globe, any regional system of balanced jealousies could only break down and result in "not mere conflict but cataclysm."[47]

With much justification, therefore, Wilson did not view himself as conducting an idealistic quest to reform the existing system. Like most liberals, he did not turn a blind eye to power. Indeed, Wilson's talk about making "the world safe for democracy" implied the existence of a peril, whereas seeking to democratize the globe out of democratic zealotry did not. To rebut charges of meddling messianism Wilson pointed out that while at Paris "some of the most cynical men I have ever had to deal with" agreed on the necessity of creating the League of Nations. The problem, however, was that the threat visualized by Wilson, not having the immediacy of a cocked pistol, did not generate the cultural equivalent of an instinctual response. Since the United States had no direct, reflexive stake in what happened on the Continent, an understanding of the danger to the United States posed by events there required a considerable capacity for abstract thought.[48]

Wilson understood that the old balance of power was the logical counterpart, in international relations, to the economic belief in the automatic benevolence of the Invisible Hand whose regulative logic operated to enforce a benign outcome on unbridled competition, thereby making possible the continued progress of civilization. But the war demonstrated that power competition could no longer be allowed to operate unfettered in the expectation that "equilibrium" would be magically restored. While balance had in the past operated invisibly in the background as the medium in which foreign affairs were conducted, the war had shoved it to the foreground and rendered it problematic.

A mechanism formerly entrusted with maintaining equilibrium that now led inexorably to ecological transformation could no longer be entrusted with the godlike power to control international relations. Global integration had resulted in ecological simplification, a reduction in the number and variety of regional and local political systems, and it also brought about a magnified vulnerability to disturbance attendant to such simplifications. Epochal system transformation was in prospect; the only question was whether it would be a global system dominated by an atavistic power or a system controlled in the interests of liberal development.

WORLD OPINION

The war not only highlighted the problem but revealed a solution: the substitution of world opinion for the balance of power. The Wilsonian remedy would be idealistic in this sense: if structural interactions and power relationships left to their own devices failed to produce a rational outcome from the standpoint of civilization's needs, then, as befitted the progressive mentality, the solution would have to be sought in the realm of mind and rational control. Wilson's awareness of the potentially catastrophic implications of the structural modernization and integration of the globe thus pointed him in the direction of searching for a collective conscience that would perform in a rational manner the task once performed by the balance of power's superhuman Cunning of Reason. As former president Taft reported, Wilson believed that only collective security could "stop the spread of a local war into a general conflagration." Liberal internationalism could not survive by entrusting the future to the combustible mixture of transnational structures and nationalist mentalities.[49]

This emphasis on mind was entirely consistent with a Progressive historical sensibility, shared fully by Wilson, in which it was possible to see reality in the most sordid terms and yet to arrive at an optimistic solution. The choice, as Wilson conceived it, was not between collective security or a balance of power. The knowledge that geopolitical space had been compressed to a globally explosive density was, after all, the basic lesson learned from the futile attempt to maintain neutrality. One was left with the choice of either world opinion or the universal horrors of the domino world created by the historical obsolescence of the balance of power, which was really not much of a choice at all. If one insists on calling his solution idealistic, it was an idealism commensurate with the unthinkable horrors of the problem it addressed.[50]

It was only with America's entry into the war that all the historical pieces fell into place in such a way that the "plot [was] written plain upon every scene and every act of the great tragedy." Wilson saw the war take on "positive and well defined purposes which we did not determine and which we cannot alter." Now, finally, he felt able to gaze into the future, beyond a war whose coming he was already heralding in 1914 as "the dawn of a new age." In an interview at the close of the neutrality period, Wilson revealed that he had "tried to look at this war ten years ahead, to be a historian at the same time I was an actor." No longer did he complain of obstructed vision.[51]

As he looked beyond the chaos of the moment, the death throes of the balance of power gave a powerful assist to the definition of that very same public opinion which previously had been unformed. In the course of the war Wilson came to believe that "the common will of mankind [had] been substituted for the particular purposes of individual states." With the consciousness of the public growing daily "more and more unclouded," world opinion, which he believed to be "the mistress of the world," was finally coming into its own.[52]

But just what was world opinion, anyhow? Wilson's deification of world opinion has most often been equated with his faith in the global triumph of the political institutions of democracy. While this is accurate in a superficial sense, his confidence in world opinion was more complex than the image of an ingenuous democratic universalism suggests. Actually, his conception of world opinion referred more to the workings of societies than to their political forms. As a liberal, he was a believer in the primacy of the private sphere. As a historian, he was interested in understanding what would later come to be known as social history: "not so much in what happened as in what underlay the happening; not so much in the tides as in the silent forces that underlay them." When he complained that past diplomacy had erred in "thinking of the relations of governments and forgetting the relations of peoples," he had this sociocultural dimension in mind.[53]

In the first place, and most obviously, world opinion assumed the existence of a structural interdependence among societies. In his persistent attacks on provincialism, Wilson started with the common internationalist thesis of interdependence, arguing that modern man had managed "to make a world that cannot be taken to pieces." But while he dutifully stressed the underlying importance of mechanical processes, he knew that the complex articulation of a global *Gesellschaft,* an international society without a corresponding sense of community, was wholly inadequate to the tasks he had in mind. A functional internationalism lacking sentiment, even if accompanied by a cosmopolitan awareness of transnational linkages, was incapable of going beyond the kind of business logic that appeared to characterize the interest-driven dollar diplomacy of his Republican predecessor in office. Interdependence alone offered no miracle cure, for it was, after all, the macroscopic cause of the German danger. "The only thing that will hold the world steady," Wilson concluded, "is this same silent, all-powerful opinion of mankind."[54]

Whatever Wilson's confidence in his genius for persuasion, building a new order on the foundations of world public opinion was not something that he undertook with breathless enthusiasm. The task, as he gravely told the Italian Parliament, was "no less colossal than this, to set up a new international psychology." And this, he realized, presupposed the premature harvesting of fruit that, under normal conditions, would require much more time to ripen fully. When in the first month of the war House tried to convince him of the strength of world public opinion, Wilson's first reaction had been that "reforms of this sort came too slowly, and he did not have a hopeful outlook." Nevertheless, as the war progressed, he convinced himself that the basis for peace, "the essential basis of endurance—the psychological basis," actually existed.[55]

In time, Wilson came to believe that the war itself had created the necessary consciousness. Wilson was no Hegelian, but to his mind wars certainly represented the triumph or defeat of great ideas. The universal yearning for peace, Wilson made clear, was the product of the war's unprecedented destructiveness. As its immense implications became apparent, it seemed to create "a great compulsion of the common conscience" which made it possible to obey "the mandates of humanity." Like the Civil War, this global conflict was forging unity out of chaos. And just as the Napoleonic wars were succeeded by "a great intellectual and spiritual renaissance," Wilson expected the same of the Great War's aftermath. The war, he predicted, was "going to oblige every man to know that he lives in a new age, and that he has got to live, not according to the traditions of the past, but according to the necessities of the present and the prophesies of the future." The pattern of history seemed so clear as to be incontrovertible, so powerful that statesmen "must follow the clarified common thought or be broken."[56]

The sober reflection behind Wilson's belief in the war's power to transform received ideas comes across all the more strongly when one considers that it had to be accommodated to his Burkean cultural conservatism. For

Wilson, world opinion was no contrived substitute for the balance of power on the order of William James's moral equivalent of war. To impose some abstract, rationalist design on the world would have run contrary to his long-held historical conservatism, from which he derived the fundamental principle that laws, and by extension treaties, were "more or less successful generalizations of political experience." Under no circumstances could "the rule of historical continuity" be violated. Besides being a body of principles, law, he felt, was "an active force, for whatever a whole community accepts is necessarily a ruling element." Therefore, according to Wilson, a social reformer "never proposes as laws those which do not represent the universal sentiments" because that would be tantamount to "social immorality" and a violation of "the law of progress." All this was made clear in some after-dinner remarks in Paris in May 1919, in which he said that "you cannot throw off the habits of society that have bound us in the past. You cannot throw off the habits of society any more than you can throw off the habits of the individual immediately. They must be slowly got rid of, or, rather, they must be slowly altered."[57]

Because ideals had to be socially embodied, reforms were founded "not in law, but in conscience"—this as in "collective conscience." National affairs and the political functions of the state, he felt, were "not conducted upon reasoned opinion," but as part of "a great organic process of the human mind." As a result, the greatest political ideas were not the result of individual genius, but were instead taken "out of the air." If politically significant public opinion was the reflection of an "organic and common life," its accurate gauging required a conservative appreciation of basic cultural values.[58]

But with so many radically differing cultural traditions, how could one hope ever to reconcile conflicting cultural viewpoints? The answer lay in Wilson's view of the constitutive feature of mankind: human nature. In one of his talks during his Princeton years, he admitted to always opening his classes with a quotation, taken from Burke, that "institutions must be adjusted to human nature," which he referred to as "a common legal conscience in mankind or more generally as "a common pulse in us all." From at least the time that he wrote *The State* in 1889, Wilson believed that customs could be altered by war. This war, he made clear, was "going to strip human nature naked" and force people "to stand face to face without any sort of disguise, without any sort of attempt to hoodwink one another." To the Gridiron Club in 1917 he revealed his belief in this acceleration and intensification of mutual understanding: "We are all human beings of like sort. But we never felt it before as we feel it now." Like a blast furnace eliminating slag, the war was burning off the impurities of local tradition that formerly had corrupted and divided mankind. With the destruction of traditional mentalities, the construction of genuinely human values was for the first time becoming politically feasible.[59]

Human nature, however, was also a property of primitive peoples with limited horizons, among whom warfare was a common practice. It was a lowest common denominator when, as Wilson realized, the trick was "to make a society instead of a set of barbarians out of the governments of the world." The task, in Wilson's mind, was to build a global community on the basis of the human potential for universal civilization rather than to recover some simple preternatural harmony. Employing as his measure of civilized progress the argument of Walter Bagehot's *Physics and Politics,* which traced the transition from the rule of arbitrary power to an "age of discussion," Wilson believed that the people, who after the Napoleonic wars were "speechless and unorganized and without the means of self-expression," were "wide awake now." The destructiveness of war and the constructive possibilities of democracy had moved in slowly converging historical lines that finally intersected at the Wilsonian moment. Roused from its age-old slumber, a newly awakened world opinion heralded the arrival of that long-awaited point in history in which politics and culture finally reflected, rather than obstructed, the yearnings of human nature. The war was thus a salubrious plague; it yielded the serum that made possible inoculation against its recurrence.[60]

Whereas the politics of the modernization process had perplexed him throughout his pre-presidential years, the pieces of the historical puzzle had finally come together to form a picture of the war as an epochal struggle in which "the past and present are in deadly grapple." Wilson described the Central Powers as anachronisms whose governments were "clothed with the strange trappings and the primitive authority of an age that is altogether alien and hostile to our own." His claim that the enemy leadership lived "in a world dead and gone" was indicative of the confidence he placed in his hard-won understanding of the new historical realities.[61]

The political translation of these social, cultural, and historical developments into a new world order that abolished the possibility of great-power war, far from being a product of tallying voter preferences through democratic processes, required a special kind of international understanding on the part of very special statesmen. It is true that for Wilson, public opinion in foreign policy was not, as it would later come to be conceived, elite opinion. Quite the contrary. If, as he believed, wars were the product of jealousies and intrigues "among nations where small groups control, rather than the great body of opinion," then peace could not come "so long as the destinies of men are determined by small groups who make selfish choices of their own.''[62]

But while he believed in the common people, he felt no need to take the public pulse with regularity. His hostility to populism in the 1890s had already shown his lack of faith in the direct, unmediated expression of mass opinion. While some reformers of his time preferred to educate public opinion, Wilson saw instead a need for ''interpretation . . . the kind of vision which sees beneath the surface into the real needs and motives and sympathies of mankind.'' Brushing aside the simplistic principle of *vox populi vox dei,* he defined democracy as ''an insight into the essential relationship of men to each other.'' Statesmanship involved bringing to the surface and verbalizing what people were prepared to believe, could they but articulate their ideas.[63]

In a revealing evening conversation during the opening stages of the Paris Peace Conference, Wilson argued that there existed ''a latent consciousness of world ideals, new ones, which may have come about without the whole body of the people being conscious of them.'' It was the statesman's function, from which he derived his authority, to give practical expression to this ''inarticulate consciousness,'' to give voice to the spirit of the age. Wilson had earlier intimated the power which flowed from this discursive capacity to crystallize thought. ''Those who weave together the thought and the ideals and the conceptions of mankind also weave together its action,'' he said to a group of missionaries in May 1916. In trying to explain how he wove these ideas together, Wilson resorted to his experience as a historian who, as a student of American history and thought, ''had saturated himself in it.'' American opinion, because of the ethnic diversity of the population, was for Wilson a reliable barometer of world sentiment. Pressed as to how he derived his insights into peoples' psyches, he claimed to have pieced them together ''as one should a mosaic.'' That ability to interpret and synthesize was of the essence of statesmanship.[64]

Unlike the Bolsheviks, who pretended to be able to divine ''objective class consciousness'' by reading the text of history, this as a rationalization for elite control, Wilson was a political artist trying to define a new sensibility out of the half-formed intellectual tendencies of his time. Because the currents of history swirled about in confusing and even contradictory patterns, and because an understanding of immediate interests did not necessarily open a window of understanding to more encompassing political realities, creative interpretation was indispensable. Thus, Wilson was quite consciously relying on the same ''keen poetical sensibility'' that he believed had been the key to Gladstone's genius for choosing policies that anticipated and fostered the long-term liberal trajectory of history. As a man who had at one time seriously entertained literary ambitions and believed that "we live by poetry and not by prose," his faith in progress depended on imaginative historical interpretation and the ability to shape action accordingly. After all, Wilson did firmly believe that there was "something about the poet which makes him the best interpreter, not only of life, but of national purpose." Enduring peace would be the product of a collective acceptance of his interpretation.[65]

Although Wilson's faith in world opinion may have looked like millennarianism to many—and to insist that the controlling reality of world politics not only ought to be but *had* to be the discursive powers of mankind was indeed saying quite a lot—it was not really idealistic or utopian in its expectations. World opinion at its purest implied, to use Jurgen Habermas's phrase, "unconstrained communication." But this kind of world, one based exclusively on reasoned conversation, was far more idyllic than the one Wilson had in mind. Wilson realized that communication was dependent, among other things, on levels of development, race, culture, ideology, and, despite his talk of a league composed of democracies, differing political systems and traditions. Inasmuch as these well-entrenched barriers to the emergence of a global culture were in no immediate danger of being breached, Wilson's view of world opinion was forced of necessity to be quite limited and even ideologically conservative. It was less than truly global, too. Since the war was basically a Euro-American struggle, he believed that its psychological impact was confined largely to the peoples of the West who, by virtue of the tragic wisdom derived from searing wartime experience, now shared a single, simple truth: the unthinkability of war as an institution in a modern world system.[66]

Because Wilson understood that the end of the war would not bring frictionless cooperation among nations, his focus was on immediate dangers to be avoided rather than on the realization of a utopia. Indeed, the League of Nations project assumed that occasions for sin in the form of war-threatening disputes among the great powers would recur in the future even with the installation of a new global regime based on world opinion. That was why "restraint upon the passions of ambitious nations" was necessary. Collective security based on world public opinion, then, did not envision a utopia of undistorted communication but something far more limited—a new language of power that relied, as had the old, upon the sanction of force.[67]

Even in this limited sense, Wilson knew full well that the reign of public opinion was in no way inevitable, an understanding which lent an air of fragility to his progressive understanding that history had no script. What if statesmen failed to interpret properly the lessons of history or to intuit the needs of the common human conscience? And what if the system of collective security failed to take root? With the balance of power gone forever, and in the absence of a system of collective security, Wilson saw another world war ignited by the unquenched passions still afoot. Fear, then, just as much as trust, was the basis of world opinion, a fear rooted in a common recognition of sociological truism: the intolerability of war among the major powers and the realization of its virtual inevitability if structural forces were given their head. Collective security was thus the product of collective insecurity, an equation more Hobbesian than Lockean in character.[68]

Faith in progress, like all faith, is a victory over doubt. Since the turn of the century Wilson had been disturbed at the slowness of public opinion to find its voice, and many of his speeches had been clouded with a sense of uneasiness over the future that carried over into his postwar statements. For example, in 1900 he complained of an unmistakable "reaction against democracy," and concluded that mankind faced "a peril of reactionary revolution." He saw the war in the same apocalyptic terms, as a struggle which would "determine the history of the world . . . for more than a century to come." Whatever its outcome, and it was not necessarily beneficent, the change would be "fundamental and tremendous."[69]

It was, sadly, entirely conceivable that history might careen toward the abyss; indeed, Wilson feared that the war would "throw the world back three or four centuries." When he insisted that the danger of his time was "nothing less than an unsettlement of the foundations of our civilization," he was talking about history hurtling wildly off the tracks, about force and blind custom turning back the gradual ascendancy of discussion over force in human affairs. It was wholly in character when, at the moment of triumph, just before departing for the peace conference, Wilson turned Cassandra by reminding Americans that "the past is secure, but the future is doubtful." The world could only "look forward to something like a generation of doubt and disorder" unless his interpretation was generally accepted.[70]

History could be a source of inspired change for the better, but it was also susceptible to mindless repetition. Emphasizing the latter in his public appeals for passage of the treaty, Wilson warned his audiences that "the past is only a prediction of the future, and all this terrible thing that your brothers and husbands and sweethearts have been through may have to be gone through with again." Given the passions and hatreds of the day, unless the League of Nations were made a going concern, a rematch would take place "just as soon as the most ambitious nations can recover from the financial stress of the war."[71]

No innocent abroad when it came to an understanding of European power factors, Wilson anticipated the geopolitical problems raised by the creation of weak new states in central and eastern Europe. Not only did he believe that the war had doomed the Continent's balance of power, he also realized that the treaty, partly through his doing, had not fashioned a new one. While it had crippled Germany in many ways, still the treaty had left it as the strongest power in central Europe. At the peace conference, Wilson expressed concern "whether sufficient thought had been given towards ensuring the safety of those regions against further German aggression." If the new states set up by the peace conference were forced to shift for themselves by a league crippled at birth, then the Germans could, "at their leisure, by intriguing, by every subtle process of which they are master, accomplish what they could not accomplish by arms, and we will have abandoned the people whom we redeemed." Wilson thus pleaded with his country not to "set weak peoples up in independence and then leave them to be preyed upon."[72]

The fear of Germany may have been uppermost in people's minds, as it was in Wilson's when he said that "this was a war to make similar wars impossible," but the League of Nations was supposed to be able to deal with any great power that stepped out of line. The problems did not need to originate in Europe, moreover. In April 1919, he reminded his colleagues on the Council of Four at Paris that "in the future, the greatest dangers for the world can arise in the Pacific." He likened the situation developing in the Far East to "sparks hidden under a bed of leaves, which smolder gradually for months and grow little by little, invisible, until the moment when, suddenly, those great forest fires explode, as we sometimes see in America." That was why he was so careful to placate Japan, despite what appeared to be its unreasonable demands in China, since Japan's refusal to ratify could have meant from the start an ineffectual world opinion "and a return to the old 'balance of power' system in the world—on a scale greater than ever."[73]

In practical terms, then, this meant maintaining the wartime alliance. With the exception of Germany, which he anticipated would become a member following a period of probation, the league was composed of the "great fighting nations of the world." "The most fatal thing that could happen," he told the American delegation in June 1919, "would be that sharp lines of division should be drawn among the Allied and Associated Powers." Wilson was concerned first and foremost "to perpetuate this combination of the great powers of the world in the maintenance of justice." To be sure, this continuation of the alliance had the drawback, as pointed out by Elihu Root and others, of freezing a status quo favorable to the victorious powers, thereby making difficult any peaceful change. But for Wilson the immediate problem was less one of accommodating changes brought about by structural transformations than of guarding against desires for change rooted in atavistic desires for conquest. One could worry about that constructive kind of change later on; for the time being, it was more important to dam up the destructive impulses that threatened to wash over the globe.[74]

Keeping the Allies on board was necessary to maintaining the solidary front of world opinion, but more important yet was the assurance that America believed unreservedly in the treaty. For Wilson, America was the linchpin of world opinion, "the hope of the world," and U.S. support was "the only sufficient guarantee to the peace of the world." Without whole-hearted American backing, the "unthinkable" would happen. The treaty, said Wilson, would be "nothing but a modern scrap of paper." "Think of the picture," he exhorted his audiences, "think of the utter blackness that would fall on the world." Wilson was convinced that American commitment to the covenant was the only cement capable of binding together the new world order because America was "the only country in the world whose leadership and guidance will be accepted." The other powers, if left to themselves, were bound to falter. Just as U.S. military might had tipped the scales during the war, only an unreserved American commitment to Article X—the pledge by league members to resist aggression— would provide the necessary psychological underpinning for the new world order.[75]

This emphasis on the indispensability of the U.S. role in the new world order was a reflection of Wilson's conservatism on the issue of world opinion, for if the United States could not provide the league's center of gravity, who could? Only the United States, with its power and freedom from local preju-dices and entanglements, had the credentials adequate to fill the position of carrier of the internationalist idea. In his recognition that a global ideology could be sustained only through the support of a hegemonic power capable of acting on a holistic view of international issues, Wilson also displayed a conservative appreciation of the connection between ideology and power. The key, then, to maintaining the solidarity of the international conscience against war was the credibility of the American commitment to propping up world opinion. That was why Wilson was so adamant against reservations on Article X, which he described as "the kingpin of the whole structure." Without it, the league would be "only a debating society, and I would not be interested in a debating society," he said pointedly. Reservations of any kind to the treaty were distasteful to him because of his belief that they could generate an orgy of revision, but reservations to Article X would "change the entire meaning of the Treaty and exempt the United States from all responsibility for the preservation of peace."[76]

If America were not absolutely serious about enforcing Article X, then, as Bernard Baruch concluded many years later, "America's signature on the Covenant would have been, at best, a meaningless scrawl on an empty sheet of paper." "Nothing less depends upon this decision," Wilson said in his final address at Pueblo, Colorado, before being felled by the stroke that would also paralyze his ability to lead, "nothing less than the liberation and salvation of the world." When he talked about rejecting the treaty and "breaking the heart of the world," the metaphor referred ultimately to the wave of violence that would wash over the globe if America turned down the role of mainstay of the new system. As for the danger in helping the world, Wilson's reply was simple: "It would be fatal to us not to help it."[77]

DESPITE HIS SUPERB RHETORICAL GIFTS, Wilson failed to persuade his country of the validity of his ideas. It is unlikely that he could ever have done so, given the basic intractability of the very public opinion that he claimed to be able to read and shape into a common consciousness. Archibald Cary Coolidge was on the mark when he noted in 1920 "how transitory public opinion is these days in even the most important questions." For the time being, he concluded, Americans "do not want to have anything to do with the league as it is." Although the historical consensus is that a compromise could have obtained passage of the treaty and admission of the United States into the league, Wilson's insistence on the absolute credibility of the American commitment to Article X was something that the country was clearly not primed to accept. Wilson meant to make American exceptionalism an argument on behalf of joining the league, not realizing that it could equally well be used as an argument against U.S. membership. Withal, Wilson's thinking was strategically too pessimistic and culturally too optimistic for his times. His insights would take another generation to sink in, and even then his successors would never feel completely comfortable with the reliability of the public's support for the new internationalism.[78]

Indicative of this problem was the way in which Wilson argued the case for the league. In the main, he relied upon idealistic rhetoric on the assumption that this was the straightest route to the hearts of the electorate. As we shall see, this idealistic mode of presentation would continue to shadow public expositions of the domino theory during the cold war. As for the geostrategic Wilsonian message emphasized here, it is questionable whether Americans would have accepted it even if they had understood it fully. His conceptual breakthrough could not be sustained because it outran its logistical support. Having taken care to sell the war in traditional terms of national honor and selfless idealism, his geopolitical arguments, if pressed too hard, would probably have strained credulity. In defining the threat, Wilson was very much a man ahead of his time whose resort to prophesy was an indication that he was preaching a doctrine that was still foreign to American political discourse. Thus the war was viewed as a "crusade," a religiously inspired quest for the grail of world peace, and not as the decisive geopolitical moment that Wilson conceived it to be.

Moreover, there is a question as to how fully formed and logically developed all these ideas were even in Wilson's mind. They were most assuredly present, but Wilson had a penchant for relying excessively on metaphor to put across his points. Take, for example, the way in which he described America's entry into the war: "So the fire burned in Europe, until it spread and spread like a great forest conflagration, and every free nation was at last aroused; saw the danger, saw the fearful sparks blowing over, carried by the winds of passion and likely to lodge in their own dear countries and destroy their own free homes." The image of flames leaping the oceans captured in economical and striking fashion the novelty of the situation that Wilson was trying to impress upon others, but the very vividness of the verbal portrait acted as a barrier to a discursive understanding of the strategic details of his argument. Wilson's rhetoric was intended to conceptualize, to bring a clear and consistent pattern of historical interpretation to a war whose larger meaning remained unclear to many, but the message could have been clearer had it been delivered with more matter and less art.[79]

Even then, it is unlikely that he could have successfully put across the message. Wilson occupied the presidency at a time when the structure of international relations was undergoing a revolutionary transformation whose implications were by no means self-evident. If the historical situation had been as clear-cut as Wilson saw it, there would have been no alternative to going into the league on his terms. The liberals would not have been disillusioned and the traditional isolationists would have been knocked out of action and sent to the political sidelines. For the time being, however, Americans felt uncomfortable with Wilson's strategic internationalism. What with the huge gap between neutral rights as the casus belli and the historical-strategic arguments underlying collective security that should have been used to join the conflict and cement the peace, the world war was so confusing and inconclusive an experience for many Americans that they could hardly be expected to reverse their deep-seated foreign-policy habits so swiftly. Wilsonian ideology would later become "sedimented" as part of the seemingly natural order of American political culture, but only after hard experience had demonstrated to everyone's satisfaction that his assessment was accurate.

Although neither his analysis of the novel character of the modern world crisis nor his radical prescriptions for dealing with it were immediately accepted by the American people, the scattered seeds would sprout later, but only after having been so altered genetically that Wilson, had he lived, might have denied he was a Wilsonian. The Wilsonian vision in its full amplitude oscillated between the promise of secular redemption through collective security and the peril of damnation in another world conflagration. Wilson's successors after World War II would find themselves living in a world that conformed to the grim picture that he had drawn, yet one in which the war's successful outcome allowed no second chance for creating Wilson's utopia. With collective security discredited and the United Nations immobilized from its inception, only the bleak residue of his world image remained as the working capital inherited by America's cold-war statesmen. Theirs would be a world of Wilsonian problems without Wilsonian answers. Thus Wilson's image of mankind at the crossroads lived on, as his successors found themselves as he had, teetering precariously on the knife's edge between the fear of totalitarian world domination and the equally chilling fear of fighting a world war in the effort to prevent it. This sense of danger was fully as necessary to Wilson's idealistic program as it would be to the tough-minded diplomacy of his descendants.

Woodrow Wilson was the founding father of modern American internationalism because he was the first to articulate the fundamental principles underlying the domino theory. His emphasis on the threat to the world's political environment, on the historical obsolescence of the European balance of power, on the macro implications of micro conflicts, on the global character of modern war and the revolutionary dangers arising therefrom—all these issues would reappear with much greater urgency in the future. Not only do all the basic domino themes appear for the first time in coherent form in his thought, they proceed from a grim historical appraisal of uniquely modern geopolitical realities not usually associated with a man we continue to see as the incarnation of idealism. And, as we shall see, these same ideas were also capable of generating solutions based on world opinion quite different from the kind Wilson had in mind when he promoted his beloved League of Nations. In this way, his thought prefigured the hard-boiled mentality that would dominate American diplomacy in the cold-war era.

Because of its mixed historical sensibility, Wilsonianism was a secular theodicy and thereby far more complex than a onesided emphasis on utopian idealism would have it. Americans have preferred to recall his idealism, either to praise, disown, or unmask it, but it was actually the dark side of the Wilsonian picture of the world, the negative for which the positive image was never developed, that they inherited. The utopian granules of his world picture were rather quickly washed away, but the somber underlying images remained clearly fixed in cold-war assumptions about the structure of the modern world. Wilson as founder of a secular religion may have been a false prophet, but in his capacity as definer of evil, Americans remained his spiritual children.

3

HERBERT HOOVER: CULTURE
VERSUS CIVILIZATION

ALTHOUGH 200-PROOF WILSONIANISM was dead, the Republican administrations of the 1920s were soon enough serving up a denatured alternative. Their less potent, nonpolitical brew of internationalism included the promotion of trade and investment, disarmament, the Open Door, and, as the centerpiece of their policies, a reliance on world opinion to bind the system together. The centrality of world opinion was evident in the two major policy initiatives of the decade, the Washington treaties of 1922 and the Kellogg-Briand Pact of 1928, each of which relied heavily on the assumption that fear of international opprobrium was sufficient to prevent miscreant nations from stepping out of line. In East Asia, the Four Power Pact radically dismantled the balance of power and replaced it with nothing more than an agreement to consult together in the event of a threat to regional stability in the Pacific. This belief in what diplomat Hugh Gibson called "a state of mind, the psychology of peace" was also a conspicuous feature of the Kellogg-Briand Pact, or Pact of Paris, which committed its signatories to the principle that war was illegal, but without obligating them in any way to punish violators. Even a lesser initiative like the Dawes Plan, which propped up the German economy and eased the reparations crisis, was pitched to "the public conscience of the world" in the conviction, as Charles Dawes put it, that "public sentiment will overthrow any Government opposing it."[1]

This institutionalization of the belief that developed nations were unwilling to be perceived as disturbers of global tranquility marked an expansion in scale of the optimistic dollar diplomacy of the Taft administration, with its emphasis on great-power harmony and the principle of unanimity. Although it is clear in retrospect that policymakers were naive to invest so much hope in this sort of world opinion, they were not so foolish as to believe that it had any deterrent power—world opinion was resorted to only because of the belief that the traditional sanctions of force were unnecessary in the first place. This sunny and benign internationalism and its diplomacy without commitment, with its painless pledges to abide by the status quo while blithely ignoring the likelihood of its disruption, was conceivable only in the absence of the kind of fear that Wilson had assumed would provide the driving force behind a politically potent world opinion. To the extent that its millennial side made possible this return of optimism, Wilsonianism was its own worst enemy. Wilson's depiction of the war as a struggle against atavistic regimes tethered to a bygone era meant that the only significant obstacle to the renewed advance of the inherently benign process of civilization appeared to have been removed with the defeat of the Central Powers. Ironically, Wilsonianism was unlikely to take root unless the very foundations of civilization came to be viewed as problematic.[2]

Nevertheless, there was some serious and more realistic thinking going on in the 1920s about the forces of international modernization that departed significantly from the feckless optimism of mainstream Republican policy. This reexamination of internationalism paralleled the more complex understanding of modernity that emerged in the 1920s with the addition, among other things, of disturbing irrational components like Freudian depth psychology and an anthropological relativism that stressed the role of the irrational in human nature while defining mankind in terms of cultural uniqueness. The decade also saw a political and ideological reaction against Enlightenment rationalism and liberalism, most dramatically in the growth of fascism, but doubts about once-sacred dogmas were perturbing introspective liberal thinkers as well.

This recoil often took the form of agonized second thoughts about the "great transformation" that had revolutionized societies from within and without, often at great human cost, by allowing powerful market forces to work their will on the assumption that unalloyed progress would be the net result. Wilsonianism started with the premise that the resulting global integration was inevitable and desirable, but in the 1920s a number of theorists and statesmen began either to reject it outright or, at a minimum, sought to limit the capacity of the rapidly encroaching global environment to engulf and swallow up traditional, and still sacred, forms of social life. From the standpoint of a reflexive, self-conscious modernity, the danger of radical disruption came not from external sources like atavistic remnants of feudalism, but from flaws inherent in the very process of modernization that tended to be identified all too uncritically with the march of progress. In the mind of a thoughtful statesman like Herbert Hoover, modernity was so problematic as to cast into serious doubt the clichéd view of modern history as a salutary process of global integration and evolution toward democratic institutions.[3]

Hoover believed that Wilsonianism was based on an unwarranted nineteenth-century liberal optimism about internationalism. If Wilson saw a strategic dark side to modernity, Hoover was every bit as alarmist about the sociocultural underpinnings that internationalists typically relied upon to undergird their optimism. While other Republicans abandoned Wilson's strategic integrationism and went back to nurturing the fraternal twins of commerce and culture, Hoover's understanding of the commercial and cultural implications of global modernization was far more ambivalent—and more realistic—than the views of his contemporaries and predecessors. Hoover understood that the realities of interdependence cut both ways, that the compression of space and time that brought peoples closer together in enforced contact was not necessarily conducive to harmony, and that global modernization contained within itself the potential for economic chaos and social revolution. He was sensitive, moreover, to existing cultural differences that could not easily be bridged and attuned as well to modernizing forces that made for even greater cultural diversity. This commercial, cultural, and ideological realism would be as fully necessary to future American statesmen as would be the strategic legacy of Wilsonianism, for the simple reason that without it an understanding of the kinds of perils that Wilson had descried would have been quite superficial.

AMERICANISM AS INTERNATIONAL PHILANTHROPY

The emergence of Hoover's deep appreciation of cultural uniqueness was very much a product of his extensive international experience as a fabulously successful mining engineer. Following his graduation from Stanford in 1895, Hoover set out on a global odyssey that, between 1902 and 1908 alone, had him circling the globe five times. He traveled so much, in fact, that he spent about two years of his life aboard ship. Many of his hours on the high seas were taken up in reading, as Hoover took care to mine for the ideas and customs of the exotic lands whose mineral riches he was about to exploit. On his way to China, for example, he sailed "with a full batch of reading of all the standard books on Chinese life and customs."[4]

Hoover was so fascinated by the differences of race and culture he encountered in his travels that, as a young mining engineer in Australia, he began to acquire what his biographer called "an extraordinary education in cultural anthropology." The raw frontier mining towns of western Australia, with their mixed immigrant communities thrown hard against populations of aboriginal Australians, introduced Hoover to new worlds in which, as he recalled, in a phrase that captured the essence of his outlook, "history became a reality and America a contrast." Although he observed with much interest the behavior of paleolithic tribesmen, more instructive still to Hoover were the culturally based variations between so-called civilized peoples. For example, he noted that Australian workers accomplished "about two-thirds the amount of work of a California miner, and only about 40 per cent more than the Kaffirs of the Rand." These traits were not simply accidents of cultural upbringing, but, according to the Lamarckian science that Hoover imbibed at Stanford, were products of blood inheritance. Although Hoover was, for his time, a liberal on the subject of race, the conclusions he drew from his first-hand observations were pessimistic about the capacity of non-Europeans to catch up with the West. Whereas Lamarckians like Theodore Roosevelt played up the potential for civilization, Hoover saw only a vast gap unlikely to be closed any time soon.[5]

Far from making him a citizen of the world, Hoover's wanderings from mine to mine accentuated his belief in American uniqueness and superiority. All this travel, living no more than three months in a single place, was, as Hoover recalled, "a dog's life." As his homesickness increased, his views of foreign peoples and customs lost any semblance of anthropological detachment and became frankly judgmental. His friend Ray Lyman Wilbur recalled that Hoover was "of such a strong American type that he found difficulty in getting on with some of the foreigners." He could be scornful of the Arabs, but his view of civilized Englishmen seemed even more harsh, verging at times on Anglophobia. He was irritated by the reserve and snobbishness of the "Willie Boys," as he called them, by their cautious business habits, and their jealousy at his success. His often stormy business dealings in London stoked his sense of Americanism to the point that he became known around town as "Hail Columbia Hoover" and "star spangled Hoover." Not surprisingly, homecomings to the "enchantment in the air and hills of California" were increasingly invested with an almost mystical significance. Hoover's discomfiting experiences led him to conclude by 1912 that "the American is always an alien abroad. He can never assimilate." Instead of lending a universalist cast to his view of the world, then, his exposure to foreign peoples reinforced his sense of difference and of America's geographical and historical distinctiveness. This strong exceptionalist bent would have a significant bearing on his views of international relations in the 1920s and 1930s.[6]

Hoover's view of America's special place in history would become fully apparent in the course of the world war. Prior to its outbreak, he had taken only a casual interest in European diplomacy. His views were somewhat on the cynical side, as is evident from his 1910 comment that "I have never before heard so much talk of peace, nor seen so many men buckling on their side-arms." He listened to the pacifist arguments of his friend, Stanford president David Starr Jordan, only to reject them because he could not swallow their underlying assumption: the growth of a common human sentiment.

According to Hoover, "History and modern evidence showed certain currents of nationalism which undermined the whole hypothesis on which such propaganda is based." Thus, when the war erupted, he harbored no utopian hopes. "What the realization of such a war may be one can only stutter at," he wrote, venturing only the gloomy prediction that there were "seven years of considerable privation" in the offing."[7]

In August 1914, Hoover was at the point of returning at long last to the United States following the spectacular odyssey in which he had made his fortune. The war delayed his homecoming but advanced his plans to enter public service by giving him the opportunity to display for a global audience the administrative talents he had honed during his career as an organizer of far-flung mining enterprises. These skills were so remarkable that, by war's end, he was being acclaimed as "the one man who can organize anything." Hoover first attracted widespread public attention when he put together a committee of American businessmen to aid Americans stranded in Europe by the war. Shortly thereafter, a much larger task was dumped in his lap: the feeding of Belgium, a nation of seven million people victimized by a struggle of wills between Great Britain and Germany over British blockade practices. It was a pivotal experience that defined for Hoover the meaning of America's relationship to Europe as a neutral power and established the possibilities—and the limits—of world opinion.[8]

Both powers denied any obligation to feed Belgium, which was largely dependent on imported foodstuffs, on the grounds that it was the other's responsibility. Conceivably, if neither side had flinched in this game of "chicken," the result would have been to starve a nation of innocents. Hoover stepped in and managed to organize, through his Commission for the Relief of Belgium (CRB), a system of victualing the country which proved acceptable to all concerned. Although he stressed the moral obligation of doing so to the two belligerents, they assented to relief operations out of political motives. For the British, Belgian relief legitimized a blockade unpopular with neutral nations, while sympathy for the Belgians and the brutal image of the German occupation seemed likely to translate into sympathy for the British cause. The Germans, for their part, by permitting the distribution of relief supplies, eased the burden on their overstrained agricultural resources and spared themselves the odium of having a nation starve under their administration.[9]

The American ambassador to Belgium, Brand Whitlock, misleadingly described the story of the CRB as "a romance" in which Hoover's role was one of "great idealism." On the surface, it seemed simply a matter of some individual Americans acting privately out of a long tradition of benevolence. According to Hoover, the CRB appealed to "the natural philanthropy of the

American people, our wealth and abundance, our admiration for these people.'' In actuality, though, the CRB's combination of humanitarianism and high politics embodied in many ways the ambitious new sense of neutrality that Wilson was then articulating as his country's distinctive attitude toward foreign affairs. The feeding of Belgium fit perfectly the progressive profile of being above the political battle while requiring at the same time an intimate involvement with the belligerents in an attempt to change their behavior. Hoover, like Wilson, was concerned to demonstrate in his handling of the CRB ''that neutrality need not be a mere barren negation'' and he did it so effectively that he was soon acclaimed by his intimates as ''the only living neutral.'' Thanks in large part to this parallelism in their views on the positive possibilities of neutrality, by 1916 Hoover considered the president to be ''a very great man.''[10]

Hoover believed that Belgian relief was made possible not by his managerial skills or by the self-interest of the belligerents, but by world public opinion. Brandishing his ''club of public opinion,'' Hoover pressed his concerns in the conviction that the belligerent nation which refused to go along with Belgian relief would ''have to carry the brand of Cain as their murderers.'' To apply this kind of pressure, he sought ''to create the widest possible feeling, both in the belligerent and in neutral countries, as to the rights of the Belgian population'' by publicizing the issue as thoroughly as possible. The fear of negative publicity would force the two parties, even though understandably preoccupied with the brutal logic of war, to look at their responsibilities from an ''enlightened position.'' But the body of opinion that counted most for Hoover was American public opinion, because only America's status as a powerful neutral, underwritten by popular support for the nation's high ideals, assured a respectful hearing in London and Berlin.[11]

Hoover's harsh reaction to German submarine tactics provided yet another parallel with Wilsonian neutrality. The torpedoing of the *Lusitania* in particular on 6 May 1915 threw Hoover into an anti-German rage. The sinking roused many Americans to a fighting fury, but it struck especially close to home for Hoover since he had often used that very ship to cross the Atlantic and his wife, Lou Henry Hoover, had just missed booking passage on the ill-fated liner's last voyage. Indicting the entire German people rather than the authoritarian leadership for this crime, he concluded, in a letter to a friend, that ''some of these days the civilized world has got to fight these people to the finish.''[12]

Hoover soon reverted to his traditional isolationist view of strategy, however, and, like many others back home, began to argue that the logical course of action was military preparedness. The main point at issue, he concluded, was the defense of neutral rights: ''Unless America today takes a strong lead in the vindication of the rights of neutrals and the upholding and enforcement of international agreements, the world will have slipped back two hundred years into barbarism.'' His traditionalist logic was evident in his belief that unless the United States stood firm on neutral rights, America "would, in the long run, seriously jeopardize the whole of our independence from encroachment from Europe.'' Smarting at Wilson's suggestion that the United States was "too proud to fight,'' Hoover urged the president to adopt a stance which would include both a tough reiteration of neutral rights, "a strong line of constructive character,'' and the articulation of high ideals as an antidote to the German emphasis on *Kultur*.[13]

Although initially pessimistic about the possibility of staying out of war following the issuance of Wilson's stern note to Germany, by August Hoover was telling Colonel House that, barring any further incidents, "the situation with the United States could drift along without actual break.'' After his pugnacious earlier memos, Hoover reverted to a more level-headed neutrality and, following the satisfactory conclusion to the *Lusitania* exchanges, even congratulated Wilson for having avoided "an infinite disaster to the American people.''[14]

Once the resumption of unrestricted submarine warfare early in 1917 made it clear that America would become a belligerent, Hoover was relieved that Americans no longer needed to remain "silent witnesses of the character of the forces dominating this war.'' Despite the nation's participation, his view of the United States as being perched on an aerie far above the low-level concerns of the European combatants led him to advocate separating the nation from the European war effort. Like many others in the opening months of American belligerency, Hoover saw no strategic point to military intervention in Europe. Rather than outfit an expeditionary force, he favored allowing the European allies to raise American recruits for their armies, which would permit the United States to build up a large defensive force in the meantime. Anticipating considerable disagreement at the peace conference between the United States and the Allies, he argued that "our weight in the accomplishment of our ideals will be greatly in proportion to the strength which we can throw into the scale.'' The American contribution ought to be at a level more fundamental than troops or military hardware. "The prime service of our Country in this war is ships and food,'' he argued. "We must send to our Allies more wheat, [etc.] . . . if their men are to fight.'' Though Wilson decided otherwise, this difference of opinion did not prevent Hoover's absorption into the war cabinet as food administrator, in which capacity he performed with his customary brilliance.[15]

Hoover was second only to the president in stature among the Americans present at the Paris Peace Conference. It was here that their differences, submerged during the war, surfaced and built toward a subsequent break between the two men. Wilson's approach to World War I hovered, he later said, "in an idealistic stratosphere far above the earthly ground upon which the war was being fought." Wilson was obsessed with the ethereal problem of putting an end to war, whereas Hoover was concerned with handling its far more pressing revolutionary consequences. As the de facto economic dictator of Europe, heading what he called the "second intervention" that provided food relief pending the restoration of Europe's ability to feed herself, Hoover found himself at the margins of the political horse-trading. But the postwar chaos provided him with an opportunity to use his by now familiar humanitarian means to deal with what, to his mind, were more fundamental issues. It was in this elemental war against hunger and social chaos that Hoover's functional brand of internationalism began to chafe against what seemed to him the empty abstractions of geopolitics and the "incompetence" of the politicians.[16]

Hoover found much to object to in the policies of the Allied statesmen. The blockade of Germany, which was maintained in full force after the armistice with an eye to assuring Germany's signature of the treaty, seemed, apart from its inherent inhumanity, stupidly calculated to delay the restoration of economic order in Europe and was fueling the spread of bolshevism besides. "Famine breeds anarchy," he said, "anarchy is infectious, the infections of such a cess-pool will jeopardize France and Britain, [and] will yet spread to the United States." German industrial output was considered essential to world production, and it stood to reason that the Germans could not be expected to work on empty stomachs. In the absence of robust economic growth, there was little point to demanding significant reparations, since an anemic Germany could hardly be expected to be a steady blood donor. The long view also suggested the need for more lenient treatment of Germany. "We and our children must live with these seventy million Germans," Hoover reminded others, insisting that "no matter how deeply we may feel at the present moment, our vision must stretch over the next hundred years and we must now write into history such acts as will stand creditably in the minds of our children."[17]

While the content of the treaty was objectionable, its form was even more difficult for Hoover to swallow. Especially irritating were Allied attempts to harness America's abundant resources to their own political purposes. Judged by the criterion of economic efficiency, the inclusion of the United States in their cartel-like schemes reminded him of an organization which "wants to hold the skilled laborer down to the level of the inefficient and unskilled man." The United States should not become a close economic partner of the Europeans; rather, it ought to act as regulator and balancer of the world economy. As he had put it on the eve of the Armistice, "we must nurse Europe back to industry and self-support and we must ourselves avoid entanglement in the process."[18]

Hoover responded no less harshly to the idea of entanglement on the political level, especially to the possibility of American participation in the various enforcement commissions being set up by the treaty. The prospect of being ensnared in organizations that the United States could not control filled him with horror. Because the American viewpoint was "essentially different," he warned Wilson that membership would have the effect "of dragging the United States into every political and economic question in Europe and constantly endeavoring to secure pledges of economic and political support from us in return for our agreeing to matters which we consider for their common good, where we have no interest."

In an impassioned memorandum that articulated what would become the constants of his subsequent isolationism, Hoover poured out his doubts about postwar political involvement. "I have no doubt," he told Wilson, "that if we could undertake to police the world and had the wisdom of statesmanship to see its gradual social evolution, that we would be making a great contribution to civilization, but I am certain that the American people are not prepared for any such measure." Instead, the United States was "the one great moral reserve in the world today." If peace were not concluded on the basis of the fourteen points, he advocated withdrawal from Europe "lock, stock, and barrel." Consistent with his humanitarian internationalism, however, Hoover was careful to add that "we should lend to the whole world our economic and moral strength, or the world will swim in a sea of misery and disaster worse than the dark ages."[19]

Swallowing his disappointment at the treaty's unsavory political features, Hoover fought the good fight on behalf of the League of Nations following his return from Paris. He recited some familiar lines from the Wilsonian text when he argued that the balance of power, a system "born of armies and navies, aristocracies, autocracies, and reactionaries generally," would soon be replaced with "a piece of machinery with such authority that the balance of power could be abandoned as a relic of the middle ages." Hoover sounded very Wilsonian, too, when he talked about world public opinion and its potential for revolutionizing the way the powers went about their business. The league, Hoover maintained, was "an organization of the moral sense of the civilized states." It was an institution "representing the public opinion of the world." Speaking to the student body at Stanford in October 1919, he sounded the entire litany of Wilsonian themes pertaining to civilization and public opinion. The league came "from the heart and mind of the world," he said. "With the stimulation of the world conscience . . . if aggression were undertaken, the public opinion of the world would come to be enlightened and the aggressor could be made an outcast from the society of civilized nations."[20]

If the league project failed, the likelihood, at a minimum, was rearmament for the United States. "A peace without us means more Army and Navy for us," he predicted. Without a league and its promotion of disarmament, he foresaw the need for crushing taxes in order to "enter a race of preparedness and build up a military caste of our own." Europe would undoubtedly "break into further wars of races, classes, and combinations" and, at that point, history would repeat itself. Maintaining an old-fashioned arm's-length neutrality seemed hardly feasible, since America had "already experienced the impossibility of maintaining neutrality with self-respect and safety." And even if the United States did manage somehow to keep out, it would unquestionably suffer "fearful economic losses." Hoover told the students, "If we believe we can see our neighbors return to another thirty years war through the breakdown of this treaty, and we still maintain our progress, it is the egotism of insanity." The end result of this process would be to "take civilization back to the middle ages."[21]

This elaboration of the consequences of not joining the league sounded very Wilsonian at the time, but at heart it was not, because it took for granted the existence of historical continuity on two basic points: the European balance of power and America's continuing detachment from Europe. The war was not an accidental and nearly fatal misstep that occurred just before the summit of civilization had been reached; rather, the European balance of power was a tradition whose underlying causes were as powerfully entrenched as ever. As Hoover put it, the war "was not just a fortuitous incident apart from the whole inheritance of Europe" but a product of "age-old hates, rivalries, and imperialisms." And there was absolutely no way of uprooting these deep-seated causes of conflict. Whatever the consequences for the United States of turmoil in Europe, and Hoover always readily acknowledged that they were enormous, the danger was not a radical transformation of the world environment of the kind that Wilson had outlined, but—however different in degree—a threat to American neutrality and independence that the age-old system would continue to pose.[22]

If Europe was unchanged in its strategic essentials, it followed that no transfiguration of American policy was called for. The U.S. contribution to the League of Nations could be effective only if it were a logical outgrowth of the tradition of neutrality. Departing from Wilson's strategic conception of America's role in the league, Hoover argued that Europe needed not American military power, but instead "our economic and moral weight, our idealism, and our disinterested sense of justice." He would later express more directly the view of most Americans that the United States had no vital strategic stake in the continental struggle by insisting that the war had been fought for idealistic reasons. The United States, he recalled, was "the only nation since the Crusades to fight other peoples' battles at her own gigantic loss." Given the certainty of continued strife in Europe, Article X was but a blank check for endless American involvement in Europe's power politics. The danger to neutral rights from continuing European turmoil was formidable enough; it would be compounded many times over by ongoing and intimate American involvement in the Continent's affairs.[23]

As Wilson dug in his heels on Article X, Hoover finally declared his affiliation with the Republican party and shifted from unreserved support of Wilson to backing the treaty with reservations, thereby minimizing its geopolitical aspects. His downplaying of security issues had already been made apparent in Paris. As Hoover put it in a memo to Wilson on 5 June 1919, "To me, from an American point of view, we have been fighting aristocracy and militarism, and it has been destroyed. I feel the paramount issues now are to secure stability of government in Europe." All the talk about the league's political functions therefore struck him as missing the main point of concluding a peace. Hoover now insisted that "what is of most importance is that many of the articles in the League are 'good' articles, such as disarmament, arbitration, and international health." Whatever the treaty's shortcomings, its expeditious passage would at least revive the circulatory system of the international economy and check the economic and social chaos which otherwise might overwhelm all.[24]

By this time, Hoover viewed the treaty quite prosaically as something necessary to getting on with the world's work. The centerpiece of modernization, after all, was industrialization, a process that needed to be resumed as quickly as possible by focusing on reconstruction. "The dominating fact of this last century," he would later say, "has been economic development. And it continues today as the force which dominates the whole spiritual, social and political life of our country and the world." The most likely inoculation against another war would come not from the political provisions of the treaty, but from the restoration of production and prosperity. Hoover thus emphasized those aspects of the league which contributed most directly to promoting economic recovery while downplaying its security role. Making collective security the sticking point made little sense when the most important task was to assure the long-term functioning of the world economic system. It was irresponsible for the world to be "engrossed in a talkfest" when what it really needed was to go back to work. Fed up with Wilson's stubborn insistence on ratification on his terms only, in 1920 Hoover accused the administration of having "obstinately held up the peace of the world for eighteen months.'' It was indicative of his complete lack of empathy for strategic Wilsonianism that Hoover later described Wilson's resistance to reservations in the treaty as "pathological" in nature.[25]

ECONOMIC INTERDEPENDENCE VS. CULTURAL UNIQUENESS

With the defeat of the treaty in the Senate in 1920, the Republican Harding administration was free to define its own variant of internationalism. And Hoover, for one, realized quite early that a new definition of foreign policy was necessary in a rapidly changing world. In 1921, he asserted that "we have abandoned our natural isolation, but we have yet to settle the basis of our new relationship.'' His stand on the war and the treaty had been based pretty much on the traditional strategic conception grounded in the long-standing doctrine of neutral rights. If anything, his wartime experience confirmed the continuing validity of the fundamentals of that outlook, but he realized nevertheless that it needed to be updated. From the 1920s onward, therefore, he would articulate the essentials of a new worldview based on his understanding of two key dimensions of modernity: the global division of labor, and cultural particularism. He would see positive and negative sides to each, but ultimately it was the unstable historical relationship between these two factors that set well-defined limits to what a new foreign policy could hope to achieve.[26]

The importance of business was axiomatic to the acolytes of the New Era. Civilization, for Hoover and the Republican administrations of the 1920s, was defined largely in economic terms as a world society bound together by the cords of commerce and an increasingly specialized division of labor. The flavor of the decade comes across best in a 1928 remark of a retiring consul, who said flatly that "as diplomatic functions today are mainly economic, this places the Department of Commerce in control of the substance of diplomacy, and leaves the State Department with social relationships.'' Concurring with this view, Hoover concluded that "the political issues in the United States during the next 10 or 15 years will be predominantly economic as the world has entered upon a period when economic themes have risen to the level of emotion.'' So powerful was this fixation on economic development that even Hoover's lively interest in promoting disarmament was prompted more by the economic benefits it would bring than by the military dangers it would remove.

But Hoover paid far more attention to the downside of interdependence than his optimistic Republican colleagues. Instead of taking for granted the existence of an economic harmony of interests, he was concerned primarily with the shaky structure of the international economy and the ideological implications of its malfunctioning. Although he pooh-poohed talk of a strategic threat, he did take very seriously the possibility of a collapse of the world system due to a breakdown of the economic processes that had created it. As the era of totalitarianism dawned, Hoover was quite sensitive to the possibility that failures of the international market economy might stimulate the growth and spread of antidemocratic transnational ideologies. Moreover, while Taft had counted confidently on the emergence of an international conscience to hold things together, Hoover was a skeptic about world opinion, becoming more and more convinced over time that the growing integration of the globe presented a serious threat to traditional cultural values.[27]

Whatever his doubts about the process, no American statesman prior to Hoover had ever made so compelling a case for the realities of economic interdependence. Indeed, few others were as well-equipped as Hoover by background to understand in practical terms the ligaments of finance and trade that bound the modern world economy together. In the 1920s, at any rate, he believed that "the whole structure of our advancing civilization would crumble and the great mass of mankind would travel backwards if the foreign trade of the world were to cease." This was so because the world had "come to a condition of economic dependence upon which no nation can morally or physically survive continued isolation." By 1927, he was still arguing that "the world has now grown into absolute interdependence," and, as his subsequent internationalist interpretation of the Great Depression showed, he saw the American economy entangled in a global web of economic filaments.[28]

America no longer needed to export to retire its debt, yet selling abroad was necessary as a way of venting domestic surpluses while "vast quantities of imports" from Europe were needed "in payment of interest and capital which we have already invested in Europe." The nation also needed access to raw materials. Moreover, the solutions to many domestic problems, "such as the size of our armament, reduction in taxation, and the prevention of agricultural and industrial depression and consequent unemployment, [were] dependent upon stability abroad and upon our access to the world's markets." In 1926, he argued that "notwithstanding progress made in American foreign trade during the past decade," trade expansion was "essential to continued economic stability in this country." Consequently, during his tenure as commerce secretary under Harding and Coolidge, Hoover continued vigorously to promote commercial expansion abroad.[29]

Given the need for a healthy world economy, resolving the problems of reconstruction required an ecumenical view. "If we are to maintain a market for our commodities abroad and to maintain our own sources of supply of materials essential to our welfare," Hoover explained, "we must be interested in the welfare of other states." In practical terms, this meant a healthy Europe. "If America and the other countries of the world are to prosper, if civilization is to go forward rather than backward," he reasoned, "Europe must get on her feet." Should Europe fail to recover its export capacity and standard of living, the United States would inexorably be "dragged down to meet her standards." If America refused to help revive Europe's economy, it was conceivable that the Continent might become "an economic slave of the Western Hemisphere," in which case "war would be the only emancipator." In practice, Hoover's economic policies seemed to be guided by the principle that what was good for the American economy was good for the world, if one is to judge by his insistence on high tariffs, his political acquiescence in allowing intergovernmental debts to hang like a sword of Damocles over the world economy, and his apparent double standard regarding the Open Door. But here as elsewhere, Hoover believed that the United States, as the locomotive of the world economy and hence the key to global prosperity, could not be judged by ordinary standards.[30]

Hoover did refer with pride to America's self-sufficiency and pointed to the fact that the United States depended on foreign trade for only a small fraction of its economic transactions. But since it was so dependent on the international economy for its well-being, the United States could not rationally choose isolation so long as the system was functioning. Hoover raised the abstract possibility of doing so, but he made it clear that this was not a serious option. "If we are going to isolate ourselves and isolate ourselves thoroughly and absolutely and suffer all the consequences, it is a logical thing to do," he reasoned, but he concluded that "there is no isolation if we are going to attempt to maintain relationship with the rest of the world." The United States could either make its contribution to "the common gift of civilization" or "degenerate economically and morally."[31]

The fact that Hoover raised the possibility of autarchy at all, however, is an indication of the tentativeness of internationalism in the 1920s. As the next decade's passion for economic nationalism would demonstrate, the degree of economic reticulation was not far enough advanced at that point to rule out a return to autarchy as a practical alternative for most great powers. In the 1930s, with world trade having shrunk to minimal levels, protectionism rampant, and the world economy coming to resemble partially overlapping spheres rather than a densely interlaced Jackson Pollock painting, the choice in favor of withdrawal and economic nationalism would be more easily made.

The potential effects of economic chaos extended well beyond matters of national income, for modern internationalism posed yet another danger: the spread of totalitarian ideologies. Ideologies, and not world opinion or an international mind, were the real intellectual by-products of global industrialization. If a healthy world economy required the universalization of a technocratic functional rationality, it stood to reason that the opposite also held true: its breakdown could give rise to widespread dysfunctional beliefs. Hoover was among the first to recognize that radical ideology had the potential to serve as a dangerous ersatz form of world opinion because of its capacity to traverse frontiers. Hoover's emphasis on global economic recovery, which for a time fueled his enthusiasm for the League of Nations and for a quick political settlement, was to a large extent motivated by his fear of bolshevism and its impact on Europe and the United States.

He had already warned Wilson in June 1919 at the windup of the peace conference that "after peace, the greatest outstanding situation in the world insistent for solution . . . is Russia." Socialism had nothing whatever to do with progress; it was, on the contrary, a thoroughly antimodern doctrine that was well-suited to appeal to the "denseness of ignorance and superstition" of the Russian people. Bolshevism's success, he argued, was a consequence not of rational considerations, but of the emotional extremes produced by social chaos. Socialism did not emerge necessarily out of the contradictions of capitalism, but it did feed off failures of the market system that were a result of political and managerial shortsightedness. Although Hoover was convinced that in the end bolshevism would collapse from its inherent economic ineptitude, the hatreds and irrational power politics of Europe had allowed it to become a potentially serious threat to the West and to an America then in the grip of a Red Scare.[32]

Bolshevism presented a number of concrete dangers. There was, in the first place, an outside chance that it might become a left-wing incarnation of the autocratic militarism that the United States had just vanquished—a "Bolshevik militarism." In the spring of 1919, Hoover worried briefly about the Bolsheviks undertaking "large military crusades in an attempt to impose their doctrines on other defenseless people," though he soon fell in with Wilson's view that backward Russia was incapable of militant expansion. But even if bolshevism had been militarily dangerous, military means would have been inappropriate to dealing with it because, strictly speaking, its origins were not political. In this Hoover was also in accord with Wilson, who believed that using military force against communism was akin to using a broom to sweep back the ocean.[33]

Rather than involve the United States in "a ten year military entanglement in Europe" that "threaten[ed] to pull us from our national ideals," a remedy better fitted to the disease was to provide food relief to the famine-stricken and politically volatile regions of eastern Europe and Soviet Russia. With revolutionary fevers running high in Europe, American aid was designed to "give the world a little time to cool off." As one of Hoover's lieutenants in eastern Europe put it, "Bread is mightier than the sword." Over the long term, the only sensible course in dealing with deep-rooted historical problems was to rely on the historical inevitability of a Thermidorean reaction. Ideologies, Hoover believed, were like meteors that were fated to burn themselves out as they journeyed into the atmosphere of political reality, but they could not be shot down in midair.[34]

Unfortunately, bolshevism was not simply a European concern. Hoover feared that Bolshevik ideology had the capacity, if economic stabilization and growth were not achieved, to subvert the foundations of the international economy and the American social system. Again and again, he resorted to the disease metaphor to describe socialism: "Bolshevism spreads like a disease, must run its course of destruction, and is no respecter of national boundaries." Given the interdependence of the world economy and the economic shock waves sure to result from the disruptions attending radicalization in Europe, the United States was bound to be affected, first by economic decline and then by radicalism at home. Hoover believed that in the modern era, with the stimulus of rapid communications, "social forces are rapid in their penetration and social diseases are quick in universal infection." Shortly after the war, it seemed evident that "if Europe is plunged into economic chaos, America, too, will have economic demoralization." If economic instability continued, Hoover predicted "a period of the most utter disintegration" of the American social fabric. "Every wind that blows carries to our shores an infection of racial discontent from this great ferment," he warned. "Every convulsion there has an economic reaction upon our own people."[35]

As the postwar economic outlook improved, the ideological specter began to fade. Even though the Leninist regime had consolidated power by 1922, Hoover was convinced, according to one report, that within five years there would be no more bolshevism in Russia. By mid-decade, Hoover saw bolshevism as among the "new, although lesser, forces of malevolence that brewed from the cauldron of the war." By 1927 he pronounced the socialist experiment a failure and, seeing the New Economic Policy (NEP) as a harbinger of the USSR's capitalist future, asserted that "the pendulum is swinging back." Hewing to his doctrine of relying on national instincts, he maintained that "Russia must work out her own political and economic system." All this seemed to confirm his initial judgment that "Russia must find herself" and that the ideology would have to "burn itself out in the hearts of the people." At that point, bolshevism would then swing toward the right and "find the point of stabilization based on racial instincts." The consolidation of the Stalinist regime only caused Hoover to push back the date of bolshevism's ultimate collapse. Ultimately, the problem of Communist ideology and its spread lay in the realm of economics and not of geopolitics, which is how cold-war statesmen would have preferred to view it in the late 1940s.[36]

This concern with the spread of socialist lifeboat economics in a capsizing world economy points to the second major area of Hoover's foreign-policy thought: his desire to avert the contamination of American cultural values. Commercial and cultural internationalism are often joined conceptually at the hip, sometimes with cultural relations being viewed as a way of promoting commercial expansion and sometimes the other way around, but Hoover's views were quite distinctive and unusually perceptive in their refusal to view the two as complementaries. Quite the contrary, the division of labor, domestic and foreign, by virtue of its power to effect radical social change, seemed more likely to generate a crisis of cultural values. They did not so much automatically go together as require skillful synthesis and reconciliation.

Whatever their complexity, economic problems were, in principle anyway, straightforwardly objective in character. They could be addressed through technical means by resort to facts, numbers, science, and technology, all of which figured heavily in the progressivism by which Hoover made his reputation as a political engineer. But these kinds of "scientific" considerations, however important, merely scratched the surface and did not touch upon more fundamental issues of values. Hoover believed that "we must go far deeper than the superficials of our political and economic structure, for these are but the products of our social philosophy." National life was "something more than aggregations of groups of producers and consumers and capitalists." For all his emphasis on the social facts, on economic processes and their ideological implications, Hoover was no economic reductionist. One could infer as much from his refusal to see a global strategic matrix as a necessary outcome of economic interdependence, but it was all the more evident in his preoccupation with the centrality of cultural values and his understanding that "social life is organic and not mechanical." Coping successfully with economic dislocation and ideological ferment, at least at the national level, demanded more than technocratic virtuosity.[37]

Economic processes were steered by cultural values. In other words, institutional configurations would have to be shaped by a concern for national identity and character that was, in its way, every bit as compelling as Roosevelt's neorepublican preoccupation with virtue had been. More precisely, Hoover believed in a tight fit between culture and ideology. He believed that "five or six great social philosophies are at struggle in the world for ascendancy" and argued that "some of these ideas are perhaps more adapted to one race than another." As he put it somewhat later: "No nation can introduce a new social philosophy or a new culture alien to its growth without moral and spiritual chaos.'' Inasmuch as his analysis of the pathologies of the modern world pointed to the need for an alteration of economic doctrine and ideology fitted to America's peculiar needs, this point was far from academic for Hoover. Just pointing at the dangers of radicalization without having a positive alternative ready to hand would do little in itself to blunt socialism's mass appeal. ''A definite American substitute is needed lest the disintegrating theories of Europe infect more of our own people,'' he said. Solutions required ''sure judgment guided by the adherence to national ideals.''[38]

Hoover's musings on these problems were articulated in his slender volume, published in 1922, *American Individualism*. Like many Europeans during the 1920s, Hoover sensed a civilizational malaise in the air and a spiritual pessimism that was a response to the growth of industrial civilization and a liberalism turned sour. Hoover was frankly frightened by the regimentation of the war, which he hoped would be only temporary. If continued, ''through the crushing of individual action and its inequities [it] would, if for no other reason, destroy the foundations of our civilization.'' Hoover was willing to grant the possibility that radical revolutions might be salutary for some European nations, but he insisted that ''it does not follow that such philosophies have any place with us.'' Eschewing mechanical questions, he hoped to find a *via media* between fascism and Marxism by pinpointing ''the social forces that will sustain economic progress.'' The book attempted to reconcile the tensions between the structural gigantism of the modern era and the continuing need for individual initiative, between selfishness and altruism, between democracy and elitism, by reformulating and adapting traditional American ideals to new historical conditions. With his typical realism, Hoover believed that large-scale economic organization and big government were here to stay, requiring the adoption of his ''voluntarist'' version of corporatism in which individualism remained ''the sole source of progress.''[39]

American Individualism referred not only to the qualities of individual personality but to the uniqueness of American national character. Individualism was as much a culturally instilled trait as it was a product of personal character formation. In a foreword to a volume entitled *America and the New Era*, Hoover argued that ''America is a distinctive social personality, and personality is characterized by a peculiar reaction to problems, a unique way of doing things. The war revealed this individual note.'' Therefore the solutions to the difficulties of modernity should come organically from within. If culture needed defending, it would have to be the source of its own salvation. As he put it elsewhere: ''The solution must be found on national instincts and the normal development of national institutions.'' A new ideology had to be found "by Americans, in a practical way, based upon American ideas, on American philosophy of life." Should Americans fail to come up with an indigenous solution, the worst of all evils would befall the country: "The Europeanization of the United States."[40]

Hoover did not believe that internationalism was all of a piece. Implicit in this view was the assumption, later to become central to his isolationism, that America had successfully escaped European history and had good reason to fear the confluence of their historical streams. While admittedly the world had grown closer together as a social organism, historical development had also produced the cultural differentiation that accounted for American exceptionalism. The mere fact that the modernizing nations were having the same general experience of industrialization did not mean that they would respond identically to it. Apart from the unity imposed by functional specialization, the global division of labor also produced a segmentary differentiation. The fertile soil of modernity supported many different kinds of vegetation that competed for space by adapting to different habitats and niches. America was the clearest example of this process of individuation. "We have grown far apart from Europe," Hoover said after the war. "We lead Europe in every social and moral aspect by fifty years." Although he referred in 1919 to "our sister civilization in Europe," his emphasis shifted increasingly to the enormous historical and cultural gap between the United States and the Continent, the two having "drifted farther and farther apart over 300 years."[41]

Hoover would henceforth take a particularist approach based on the reality of cultural and racial uniqueness and historical particularism. Whereas Wilson and many other Progressives believed that the New and Old Worlds were beginning to converge culturally, Hoover's experience had convinced him of "the enormous distance that we of America have grown from Europe in the century and a half of our national existence, in our outlook on life, our relation to our neighbors and our social and political ideals." In the absence of a common Hobbesian strategic danger, these underlying cultural and racial differences could not be bridged by appealing to a universal conscience. Since foreign relations were rooted not in the ambitions of autocratic elites but in divergent and often conflicting cultural realities, Hoover believed that "no international agreement is immutable" and that "the forces which run through peoples are infinitely more powerful than any written document"—especially internationalist documents with universalist principles. For that matter, thoroughgoing internationalism in the economic sphere was impossible for the same reason as in the political sphere: the absence of intercultural solidarity.[42]

Just as market forces did not automatically make for harmony, neither were they ultimately responsible for conflict. Hoover believed, as he wrote in 1915, that there were "ambitions inherent in races." The peacemaking effort in Paris had failed because of "a collision of civilizations" in which "the idealism of the Western world was in clash with deep forces in Europe with its racial *mores* and the grim necessities of these twenty-six races." As he recalled so grimly in his *Ordeal of Woodrow Wilson,* "In the blood of many of the delegations at Versailles were the genes of a thousand years of hate and distrust, bred of religious and racial persecution and domination by other races." Wilson viewed Article X as the symbol of a solidary world opinion which, if mobilized, would obviate the new strategic threat of world war and world domination. For Hoover, exactly the reverse was true: the imaginary quality of Wilson's threat was complemented by the total inability to do anything about it even if it were true.[43]

What remained of internationalism once Hoover had stripped away Wilson's strategic globalism and his collective solutions were the realities of economic interdependence and cultural uniqueness. This minimalist internationalism—Taft's dollar diplomacy minus an international conscience—acknowledged the existence of an international division of labor and the desirability, on functional grounds, of international cooperation, but little else besides. The degree of economic integration that had been attained was still so modest and precarious that the solidarist Wilsonian interpretation of history was scarcely worth entertaining. Because the point of no return had not yet been reached, the fundamental question as to whether the United States had entered the stream of global history was still open. Seeing international society pulled together by growing functional interdependence and simultaneously separated by a growing sense of cultural distinctiveness, Hoover tried to fashion a foreign policy on the basis of a quite different historical interpretation: one which saw a world headed in two different directions. He wanted the best of both worlds out of his foreign policy, of course, but he was quite prepared to accept the worst.[44]

Apart from his understanding of the globe's economic reticulation, Hoover's internationalism was basically a primordial humanitarianism informed by elemental sympathy and charity in the face of human suffering and calamity. He believed Americans to be a peaceful people, yet with his "black view of human nature" and his cultural particularism,[45] it was obvious that the growing unification of the world could not be matched by a corresponding convergence in the realm of values, at least not in any future worth worrying about. Calamity, far from being the great teacher leading the world to unity, was simply a confirmation of the enduring human condition. Rejecting the possibility of any transcultural harmony apart from that which was functionally imposed, Hoover was a humanitarian who did not believe in mankind.

WORLD OPINION AS MORAL STANDARD

If Hoover's lack of civilizational optimism could tolerate only an arm's-length cooperation with Europe, his bifurcated internationalism manifested itself even more clearly in his approach to East Asia. Just as East Asia had been a convenient proving ground for the Taft administration's new globalism, the crisis that broke out in September 1931 with the Japanese conquest of Manchuria and the subsequent dismemberment of China through the creation of a puppet state of Manchukuo provided a stage for the clear articulation of Hoover's internationalism. The United States responded to this challenge to the treaty structure erected during the 1920s by invoking the novel Hoover-Stimson doctrine, which denied the legality of annexations accomplished through force, a position that was adopted shortly thereafter by the League of Nations. The doctrine was very much shaped by the president, but not before a test of wills with his secretary of state, Henry Stimson, in which their two contrasting interpretations of international history were pitted against one another.

The difference of opinion appeared at first to revolve around the quite manageable secondary issue of means rather than ends. As Stimson wrote in his diaries, "on the rights and wrongs of the situation [Hoover] is just as strong as anybody could want him . . . the only difference is when he comes to method." The president and his secretary of state agreed on many elements of the situation: the Jekyll and Hyde character of Japanese diplomacy, the immorality and illegality of their behavior, the danger to the entire postwar treaty structure and not simply to the status quo in the Far East, the necessity of avoiding war, and the importance of world public opinion. But this apparent harmony of judgment concealed important disagreements on just what the danger was and on the role of world public opinion in dealing with it.[46]

Hoover's reaction was shaped by a first-hand familiarity with China and the Far East matched by few other American leaders. According to his friend and secretary of the interior, Ray Lyman Wilbur, it was Hoover's "oriental experience" that guided his formulation of American policy in the crisis. He had lived in China for a number of years at the turn of the century as the director of the Kaiping coal mines, a period in his life when his interest in Chinese culture was strong enough to justify taking Chinese lessons for two hours a day. At the siege of Tientsin during the antiforeign Boxer Rebellion of 1900, Hoover responded with typical energy and efficiency by organizing the defense of the port city. Hoover thus possessed far greater hands-on experience and expertise in China and had a deeper understanding of the relationship between business and politics in that region than any American statesman before or since.[47]

Hoover was alternately amused and repelled by the Chinese way of life. On the one hand, China could be "great fun" and the exotic Chinese seen as "one great joke." At the same time complaints about backwardness, ignorance, superstition, inefficiency, graft, procrastination, duplicity, lack of Western-style morality—the entire catalog of Western criticisms of China's ways—can be found in Hoover's letters home. By the time of the Boxer Rebellion, his wife noted that Hoover "was more or less convinced that all Chinamen ought to be done away with on general principles." Following the completion of his stint in China, she recalled that they turned their backs on China "with much relief." Nevertheless, his enmity never went so far as to make him a sinophobe. Hoover and his wife always recognized the "element of real grievance" in the Chinese case against the West and appreciated the force of Chinese nationalism and its roots in the resentment of foreign exploitation. Moreover, Hoover was impressed by the Chinese capacity for hard work and by the depth of Chinese civilization, enough so as to become a serious student of Chinese history and a collector of works about China in European languages.[48]

Hoover's hardheaded and unsentimental view of China led him to reject the commercial and cultural premises underlying the Open Door policy. Opportunities for trade and development were almost nil, given China's lack of an exportable surplus, its overwhelmingly agricultural character, and, as he put it, "some kind of kink in the Chinese mind which does not adapt itself well to western methods of administrative organization." For those who trumpeted the benefits of China's cheap labor, he pointed to the countervailing disadvantages of "simply appalling and universal dishonesty of the working classes, the racial slowness, and the low average intelligence," not to speak of administrative incapacity, traits which made it unlikely that China would soon come up to Western standards of productivity. Judging Chinese labor the same way he did mines—on the basis of a comparative international standard of efficiency—China would always come up short. But then, Hoover viewed the entire Far East as an economic backwater.[49]

Hoover trained the same skeptical eye on visions of democratic reform. In the first volume of his *Memoirs,* in a section written in the 1910s, he downplayed the chances of democracy in China, the best to be hoped for being a "democratic oligarchy" which would serve until that distant day when the achievement of mass literacy, the ground of democracy, would allow China to abandon its backward political ways. In addition, democracy could emerge only in conjunction with economic development. Democracy was "a western concept which requires the same form of administrative machinery as we have developed for production and distribution." Hoover did not wish to disparage "a great race," but he warned enthusiastic western-izers that "China is not going to be made occidental."[50]

All told, Chinese civilization was in extreme disrepair. The mere thought of the imminent modernization of China set to racing the pulses of many Americans who saw in the Middle Kingdom fertile soil for the growth of industrialization, democracy, and Christianity, but Hoover's view of China's potential was distinctly downbeat. He believed, as one interlocutor recalled, that "China had had it. Its culture had passed its zenith and in decay did not recover." As for the fears on the part of some that a modernized China would present more danger than opportunity to Western manufacturers, these were but "a phantasma in the occidental mind." With China's promise lying in a distant future, America's stake in that country had to be viewed as a small but highly speculative investment, to be written off without regret if it failed to pan out.[51]

Unburdened by Wilson's geopolitical fears or Taft's view of the Open Door as the symbol of the new world order, Hoover looked to local cultural and historical forces to explain the Sino-Japanese conflict. He contended that China's massive size and the inertia of its civilization "always had succeeded and would succeed in throwing off the efforts of other nations like Japan to penetrate it and dominate it." He was also confident that "no matter what the Japanese did to China the passive resistance and superior number of Chinese would ultimately either absorb or overwhelm Japan." In his memoirs Hoover predicted that "no matter what Japan does in time they will not Japanify China and if they stay long enough they will be absorbed or expelled by the Chinese." By taking the long and regional view of China's eventual triumph, he refused to interpret events there as a geopolitical crisis. A re-gional political system, like an independent suspension in an automobile, prevented shocks from being transmitted throughout the global chassis.[52]

Stimson's view of the Far East's importance differed in a number of fundamental respects. Thanks to his experience as governor-general of the Philippines, he, too, fancied himself a Far Eastern expert. But whereas Hoo-ver's first-hand experience with the treaty port system had left a lasting cynicism about Western altruism in China, Stimson was a firm believer in the white man's westernizing burden. He lamented his chief's failure to appreciate the "real nobility" of the Open Door policy as contrasted with "all those lurking forces of selfishness and cynicism which are grouped behind the idea that China cannot amount to anything anyhow and therefore why not do what we want with her." He believed, moreover, in America's modernizing mission in China, in "the hold which our attitude has upon China and the confidence which China has in us." What was taking place in China was therefore a matter of concern to the United States because it was taking place "in our part of the world."[53]

But even if China had not been in America's part of the world, the Manchurian issue would still have been important because of its bearing on larger global issues. Just as their differences regarding China's potential for modernization and closeness to the United States were the fruit of divergent historical and cultural assumptions, so too the Manchuria crisis was a symbol of vastly differing interpretations of the political and military consequences of Japanese military expansionism. For the first few months of the crisis, Japan's position as a bulwark against bolshevism in Asia and its status as America's largest trading partner in the Far East led the administration to follow a restrained approach in the hope of buttressing moderate politicians within Japan against the military extremists. Hoover even expressed some sympathy for the Japanese case, suggesting that there were some very real grievances behind its action. But as Japan pressed still farther into China, Stimson reassessed his view of the crisis by casting it into a global Wilsonian mold, thereby setting the stage for a major policy disagreement with the president.[54]

At the heart of their policy struggle was a disagreement over what was then still a relatively minor aspect of the Wilsonian worldview, one that Wilson mentioned on only a few occasions: the belief that distant local conflicts had the potential for spreading into global war. As Far Eastern Chief Stanley K. Hornbeck later restated this Wilsonian theme, it was no longer possible for nations to engage in war without seriously affecting the well-being of other nations. In the seamless fabric of modern interdependence, there existed "a general interest and a general concern in which the right of the whole group, and therefore of any of its members, to object to disturbances of the peace and above all to exert themselves to prevent war is inherent." He concluded: "Disturb this fabric at any point and you produce disturbances throughout its entirety." For other neo-Wilsonians, like James T. Shotwell, the consequences were more far-ranging still. According to Shotwell, a modern understanding demanded "a new appreciation of the fact that any major event taking place in distant corners of the world, for which the United States has no initial responsibility whatever, is almost sure to involve this country sooner or later." It was this argument that Stimson employed in December 1931 when he warned the president that "Japan was setting on foot a possible war with China which might spread to the entire world."[55]

Stimson would later argue the point at greater length in an April 1933

Foreign Affairs article. In this piece, he asserted that the Great War marked, among the industrial nations of the world, "a definite turning point in the evolution of public opinion in respect to war," a change that was "predicated upon definite economic and evolutionary facts." One of these facts was an economic interdependence that made nations "much more vulnerable to war," an interdependence that was "irrevocable." The combination of destructive military technology and economic interdependence had demonstrated that modern civilization was "too fragile to endure the stress of modern war as a function of recognized international policy." While statesmen in the developed nations fully appreciated this equation—or so he thought—Stimson argued that the less civilized areas were "occupied by races and tribes of men" who were "not so much incommoded by war as we are." Hornbeck also recognized that "the conceptions of many peoples and of many states have not yet attained the lofty heights which are represented in the thought of those nations which have been primarily responsible for the conclusion of these treaties." The ideal of peace was, therefore, "an ideal of a few Occidental states."[56]

This combination of local volatility and global combustibility meant that the whole world had come to resemble the Balkan powder keg. According to Stimson, "Economic inter-connection had already so far developed that war anywhere in the world, even among those nations whose economic and social organization is less complicated, is always a danger to the rest of civilization. It is like a prairie fire; and a war once started in any portion of the earth is likely to envelop the whole. Nowhere can war be neglected as entirely innocuous to the rest of the world." This much was clear to Stimson and would remain so throughout the decade. Seeking historical parallels, he compared Hoover's inaction to the futility of Wilson's attempt to maintain neutrality. And, anticipating what had become clear only retrospectively to Wilson in 1917, he confided to his diary the belief that it was "almost impossible that there should not be an armed clash between two such different civilizations."[57]

This kind of strategic sensibility was completely absent from the president's thinking. Whatever the immorality of Japanese behavior—and Hoover was willing to acknowledge that morality in international life was sometimes a matter of timing—he saw no fundamental threat of the kind conjured up by Stimson. Hoover never took seriously the Wilsonian strategic argument concerning the inadmissibility of another war, the circumstances likely to cause it, or the means of preventing it. Although he was quite clear on the global linkages between economics, ideology, and politics, he resolutely refused to draw internationalist political conclusions. While Stimson thought in terms of a global "prairie fire," a Hooverian pyrogenic metaphor would have seen conflicts of this kind as akin to forest fires, natural phenomena which would have to burn themselves out before regenerative processes could set in. From this perspective, the Asian conflict, however serious, was not a full-blown cataclysm, for it was not at all clear to Hoover how war would result from leaving the situation alone. Since the Japanese did "not imperil the freedom of the American people, the economic or moral future of our people," Hoover did "not propose ever to sacrifice American life for anything short of this."[58]

Modern war was a calamity, to be sure, but American participation would be a greater disaster still. To tamper with these "smoldering fires" would be to risk precisely the prairie fire that Stimson so greatly feared. Hoover "pointed out strongly the folly of getting into a war with Japan on this subject; that such a war could not be localized or kept within bounds, and that it would mean the landing of forces in the Far East which we had no reason or sense in doing." Nor was he convinced that sanctions would pour water on the situation, for the Japanese were hardly likely to cave in to such pressure without a fight. The pro-Japanese under secretary of state, William Castle, knew his man. Hoover, he said, would never go to war for the integrity of China, because he "saw the fallacy of burning down the house in order to destroy one pernicious book in the library." The key to keeping conflicts local was, by not intervening, to allow natural regional balances to do their work. Thus, while Hoover believed that it might take the Chinese as long as fifty years to expel the invaders, he insisted that "for us to risk destroying our civilization, already in sufficient dangers, to speed this period up to seven years, was not particularly inviting."[59]

It boiled down to a question of which kind of war posed a greater danger to the United States: an interventionist war or an East Asian war. Clearly, in Hoover's diagnosis, the globalist cure was worse than the regional disease. Even if the East Asian conflict were to spread, American involvement was out of the question. Hoover was fond of telling foreign diplomats that, from the view of the man in the street, the United States, after 150 years of isolation, had entered the Great War and spent forty billion dollars, only to be faced with massive chaos, whose effects as president he was still trying to clean up. As he said in 1920, "Another war will mean the dissolution of society." For Hoover, a greater danger to the United States already existed in the form of the Great Depression, whose international origins took first call on the energies of the nation's statesmen. Thus a war to vindicate internationalism could only wreck what little of it there was. Summing up his strategic isolationism, "he said he would fight for Continental United States as far as anybody, but he would not fight for Asia."[60]

Hoover understood, along with Under Secretary Castle, that unless war was prevented, "all the treaties of peace, the Kellogg Pact and all that sort of thing becomes very futile." But it was not as if those treaties mattered all that much in the first place. Reminded by Stimson of this challenge to the treaty structure, Hoover on one occasion referred to it as "scraps of paper" while on another he argued that "it may be a case of having outstripped the progress of the world in taking too high a position." This absence of faith in high-minded treaties was complemented by a disdain for the potential of international organization. As he stated at the time and afterward, he "had no confidence in the league," which even as a purely European organization suffered from impotence. Internationalism was ultimately an abstraction, an idea not worth fighting or dying for.[61]

Stimson and Hoover eventually compromised on the nonrecognition policy as a way of handling the situation. Whatever their differences, they agreed that the rejection of collective security had left American world policy "to rest solely upon treaties with the sanction of public opinion alone." They agreed, too, that world opinion could be employed as an instrument of power. As State Department hard-liner Stanley Hornbeck noted, there were "many kinds of force: the force of public opinion, the force of money, the force of arms, et cetera," but in a situation like the Manchurian crisis, "the deciding factor [was] that of force—in some form or forms." Viewed in this light, the Hoover-Stimson doctrine was quite clearly new, rhetorically barbed, and much more activist than doing nothing at all. The United States was departing from its traditional isolationist pattern of merely setting an example by venturing to define a new standard which other nations, through international law, were urged to adopt as their own. By rejecting the argument that might makes right, it was setting Japan on notice that its actions could no longer be legitimized under the legal umbrella of the existing international regime.[62]

But there was a world of difference as to how the two men construed the significance of that opinion. Hoover and Stimson had agreed on a principled solution to a problem whose underlying meaning continued to divide them. For Stimson, the problem was not only to "put the situation morally in its right place,"[63] but to force a reversal of the Japanese program, which "would be a tremendous loss to the higher motives and the higher policies if Japan gets away with this." Stimson had tried cooperation with the League of Nations in the hope that "this great demonstration of solidarity . . . against any war in Manchuria" would do the trick. After failing in an attempt to concert action with a noticeably reluctant Great Britain, he fell back on the hope that nonrecognition would have "a very potent effect." As if to convince himself that such a tack could actually succeed, he adverted constantly to Japan's backpedaling in the aftermath of the Twenty-One Demands episode, and to the Shantung dispute, and in addition held up (in a classic case of present-day wishes distorting memories of the past) the effectiveness of world opinion in halting the brief Sino-Soviet border war of 1929. Given this history of Japanese behavior, he was counting on the "moral consciousness of a thoughtful nation" which had previously shown itself sensitive to the logic of internationalism.[64]

But the refusal to provide any legal cover for Japanese conquests amounted to a reliance on the same force that had failed to prevent the crisis in the first place: international public opinion. As American policy went to its self-imposed limits of nonrecognition and as it became clear that the Japanese would not be deterred by moral declarations, Stimson began to entertain the prospect of taking more forceful measures. He was thrown "a little bit nearer my old view that we haven't yet reached the stage where we can dispense with police force." Defining the issue as one of power in which the avoidance of global war dictated the use of preemptive force by the civilized nations, Stimson was quite willing to press for an economic boycott of Japan and even to employ military bluff in the hope of getting Japan to back down, only to be confounded by Hoover's public disavowal of such options.[65]

Hoover refused to go any farther because he saw the doctrine mainly as an expression of principled disapprobation by the United States. Guided by his nominalist cultural beliefs and the cautionary experience of the Great War, Hoover refused to move beyond moral reprobation. For Woodrow Wilson, America's activist and committed *will* was essential to the effectiveness of world opinion, but Hoover much preferred America's detached moral example. In this respect, Hoover's internationalism had not strayed far from its economic and humanitarian roots. America's role in preserving peace, he had once said, "must be different from that of the other great nations of the world." Given geographic security, freedom from entanglement in the balance of power, and American disinterestedness, the United States could provide "a different and in many ways a more effective service to peace." He would emphasize public opinion, but from the same exceptionalist standpoint with which he had used it as a "club" during his administration of Belgian relief. The use of that club had always presumed a desire on the part of the belligerents to avoid being hit by it. If, however, they were willing to absorb the blow, that is where the matter would end. Hoover thus advocated a universal moral solution to what was, in his mind, a local political problem.[66]

Although this meant, in the end, that the Kellogg-Briand Pact and the Nine-Power Treaty—indeed the entire 1920s treaty system—were not in fact the expression of a functioning international culture of shame, Hoover nevertheless took pride in the nonrecognition doctrine and continued to insist that it was his creation and not Stimson's, less from any expectation that it would have any appreciable effect on the situation in the Far East than from its demonstration that America had reached this level of civilized maturity. The doctrine was like a beam of light cutting through the dense fog of a storm-tossed world. Confident that the United States, in its separate historical anchorage, could ride out any gales in its New World haven, Hoover was content to let world opinion develop without forcing it. As he put it in his memoirs, this was not isolationism, but the expression of "a belief that somewhere, somehow, there must be an abiding sanctuary for law and a sanctuary for civilization." However, sanctuary suggested the leadership of the monastery, itself a symbol of spiritual withdrawal from a troubled world, as a way of preserving civilization until that distant time when global society had been pacified. Hoover was definitely interested in "the importance of retaining the leadership of public opinion," but it was a detached and withdrawn kind of moral leadership in which the American role was to serve as a role model, not to lead by hands-on involvement.[67]

If the dispute between Hoover and Stimson proves anything, it shows how shallowly rooted were Wilson's geostrategic arguments. It was understood that the whole episode was symbolic, of course, but there was no sense of precisely how it was so. Manchuria was an alarm, but it triggered no reflexive determination to respond. It was like a fire bell that set the fire department to debating whether to answer the alarm and fight the fire or to let the blaze burn itself out, ending with an agreement that pyromania was, in principle, reprehensible. These hopelessly incompatible responses indicated how little agreed were American statesmen in their mental pictures of the course of international history. Hoover showed that the degree of indeterminacy was far greater and that the possibilities for choice afforded by internationalism were far more complex than Wilson's either/or formulation had made them out to be.

Even in the late 1930s, when the situation would appear far more threatening, Hoover still found it possible to choose nonintervention. Fearing the consequences of military involvement more than any harm that might come from abstention, he unflinchingly chose the latter. America alone, even if cut off from its Old World past, was preferable to an intervention doomed to make matters even worse. He even jettisoned all his former arguments on behalf of interdependence. For, when all was considered, fundamental values were far more important to him than the risk of contamination posed by a modernity gone off the rails.

From today's perspective, Hoover comes across as something of a diplomatic dinosaur, but that is far from true. While he rejected all the strategic elements of Wilsonian internationalism—Wilson's belief in the end of the European balance of power, the specter of a global takeover, the structural imperatives that could suck the United States into another global war with obscure beginnings—future statesmen would have to come to grips with his particularist sense of culture and his understanding of the cataclysmic potential of economic collapse and the ideological perils that accompanied it. Whereas Wilson concentrated on portraying the strategic foreground, Hoover showed that the sociocultural background was every bit as worthy of abiding concern, thereby adding considerable depth and complexity to what had been essentially a two-dimensional Wilsonian picture of the world. With his more sensitive appreciation of the tension between the structural and the psychological forces underlying modernity, Hoover contributed as much to the internationalist legacy as did Wilson—not least in his understanding of why matters would most likely get out of hand in the future. After Hoover, civilization would become as much the problem as the solution and Stimson's distinction between civilized and uncivilized states would henceforth disappear from the calculations, and the vocabularies, of American statesmen.

Most important, Hoover's outlook contributed to a de-idealization of world opinion. No longer would American statesmen, in dealing with the structural problems of world politics, be able to contemplate recruiting a world opinion from the growing ranks of democratic westernized nations in a progressive world civilization. Instead, they would be more closely attuned to Hoover's understanding that world opinion did not have any universal social or cultural embodiment as a result of the modernization process. So while time would eventually vindicate Wilson's strategic prophecies, given the gap between structural interdependence and the increasingly obvious absence of the cohesive intercultural beliefs needed to tie them together, the medicine of world opinion in its overpowering Wilsonian dosage would never again be prescribed as a serious policy option by American statesmen. Global cohesion would have to be anchored almost exclusively in fear rather than trust, around power and ideology rather than idealism. That fear was itself quite problematic. It could, as the 1930s would apparently show, become the basis for an attitude of appeasement that could pave the way for global domination. Or it could become the rather brittle clay for shaping a world opinion resistant to intimidation. American policy in future would have to work between these two extremes.

4

FRANKLIN D. ROOSEVELT: THE HALFWAY WILSONIAN

BY RENOUNCING INTERVENTIONISM in the Western Hemisphere while getting involved militarily everywhere else, Franklin D. Roosevelt completely reversed the traditional pattern of U.S. foreign relations. Unfortunately, while the peaks of this policy upheaval readily strike the eye, its conceptual base remains shrouded by a dense layer of mist. This foggy patch in our knowledge is attributable partly to the inscrutable character of this sphinxlike figure who, for all his conviviality and charm, concealed his innermost thoughts in chambers unlikely ever to be opened by historical archaeologists. His secretiveness, coupled with a tendency to move in startling zigs and zags, not to mention his unembarrassed espousal of contradictory principles and policies, has left the organizing principles of his diplomacy shrouded in mystery. As a result, our historical snapshots of the man show him in wildly contrasting poses and outfits: here as nationalist or internationalist, there as realist or idealist, elsewhere as isolationist or interventionist.

Some of the mystery can be dispelled by viewing FDR's foreign-policy thought as a transitional phase in the evolution of Wilsonian ideology. While there is little doubt about Wilson's enormous influence on Roosevelt's internationalism, it was not the pure Wilsonian gospel that the new president preached. The isolationist temper of the times and the need to attend to the Great Depression at home by resorting to economically nationalist expedients would have prevented a full-blown revival of the old-time religion in any case, but it was an anti-utopian reading of global history more than domestic political factors that accounted for Roosevelt's substantial revision of the Wilsonian worldview. In keeping with his congenital inability to take ideologies seriously, FDR was a partial Wilsonian who, over the course of his presidency, shifted from the bright to the dark side, from a fixation with   99 universalist rhetoric to a concern with military outcomes, from concentration on utopian solutions to pragmatic absorption in the problem.[1]

FDR's diplomacy started with ritual invocations of world opinion and ended by coping on an ad hoc basis with geopolitical nightmares. With his assumption of the presidency in 1933, the idea of civilization as a closely integrated functional community tied together by world opinion reemerged in the rhetoric and practice of American foreign policy. Reflecting this preoccupation with Wilsonian solutions, the rhetoric of the New Deal consistently stressed, until the eve of World War II, the priority of the spiritual values of civilization. But by the late 1930s, as the meager results of his sermonizing led him to conclude that world opinion was ineffective, FDR's attention and rhetoric shifted to the geopolitical problems first adumbrated by Wilson. From this point on, FDR would do more than any other American statesman in this century to anchor the principle of the geopolitical unity of the world into the bedrock of American political culture. By so doing, he was largely responsible for a transformation of Wilsonianism that made it descriptively more convincing—and, at the same time, prescriptively more problematic— for his successors.

THE ASCENDANCY OF SPIRIT

The record of Roosevelt's intellectual development from childhood to the time he assumed the presidency leaves little room for doubt that his internationalism took for granted the complementarity of social processes and human values. Like his illustrious cousin Theodore, Franklin received an aristocratic upbringing that taught him to view events overseas as significant. As a young man he traveled frequently to the Continent and received an education that stressed language training, including French, German, Greek, and Latin. Stamp collecting taught him geography and sparked an interest in what he later termed ethnology, while an interest in the sea and sailing primed him to accept the navalist theories of Alfred Thayer Mahan. Personal inclination was backed by strong academic encouragement. His first adviser at Harvard was Archibald Cary Coolidge, one of the first twentieth-century intellectuals to perceive the United States as a world power, with whom he remained on cordial terms following graduation.[2]

Roosevelt's early views on international relations were hand-me-downs from his mentors, cousin Theodore and Woodrow Wilson, which he wore unashamedly and sometimes in incongruous combinations. Not surprisingly, they featured contradictory points of view. On the one hand, he expressed the characteristically facile optimism in history as an onward-and-upward progress of liberty that was second nature to much of the fin-de-siècle generation. In a 1912 speech reviewing the meaning of the past thousand years of history, for example, he was at no loss to find a bright guiding thread, arguing that "taking the nations as a whole today, in Europe and in America, the liberty of the individual has been accomplished." In typical Progressive or new-liberal fashion, he looked forward to new advances in the "liberty of the community."[3]

This sunny outlook was eclipsed during his tenure as assistant secretary of the navy in the Wilson administration, when his comments took on a belligerent nationalist edge that recalled the brash aggressiveness of the younger TR of the 1890s. Like his cousin, he emphasized efficiency and virtue, his wartime speeches echoing the republican jeremiads about sheltered comfort and selfish individualism. Convinced that the war was an occasion for testing and honing the national character, FDR appeared at times to regret the comparative safety from which the United States fought the war. "The war does not touch our shores as yet," he is reported as saying in July 1917. "I sometimes think that if it did it ought to be a blessing in disguise, to awaken that spirit in us without which the task of the army and navy will be in vain."[4]

Many of his private comments reflected the public impatience of his cousin with the cautious policies of the Wilson administration. There was a similarity in their man-of-action dismissiveness of the weak and, in their view, effeminate, neutrality policy of the president. The European war, far from occurring on another planet, portended all sorts of serious difficulties for his country, problems that could be met only through preparedness, efficiency, planning, and foresight, themes that he repeated time and again. The American people, he believed, were no further advanced than "kindergarten" in their understanding of such momentous issues. Never in doubt about where his sympathies lay, he would periodically charge into the office of his superior, the avuncular secretary of the navy Josephus Daniels, to demand that "we've got to get into this war." And once the United States had become a belligerent, FDR clearly revelled in his duties, only wishing that they could have been weightier.[5]

His strategic outlook on world affairs borrowed heavily from Mahanian naval doctrine and traditional conceptions of neutrality that stressed the need to defend the nation's commercial and imperial interests abroad. Without trade, he believed that "you would have economic death in this country before long." At this point, Roosevelt had dropped his earlier talk about the common democratic values of a global civilization. Quite the contrary, because there were "a great many nations and a great many peoples with different ideals and different thoughts, some that seem hopelessly irreconcilable," the abolition of war was, at the time, inconceivable. He was quick to ridicule the "soft mush about everlasting peace which so many statesmen are handing out to a gullible public" and dismissed, rather perfunctorily, the faith of those like his chief, Daniels, who believed "in human nature and civilization and similar idealistic nonsense."[6]

Like all eclipses, this one was brief, and by war's end the rays of Wilsonianism began to suffuse his rhetoric. As he stated in his vice-presidential acceptance speech, in a phrase that directly contradicted Hoover's perspective, it was now "impossible to be in the world and not of it." Once the struggle for ratification of the treaty was joined, FDR made it clear that the League of Nations' primary function was to prevent another great-power crisis from exploding into a world war. "If Germany, say ten years hence, should look for her revenge and attempt to form an alliance with Japan or Russia, or both," he maintained, "the knowledge that automatically the whole world would be leagued against her would be sufficient to prevent war without firing a shot." Echoing the prophecies made by Wilson a year earlier, he also foresaw disaster in the event of a U.S. refusal to join the league. "We can look forward in the war that must inevitably come to methods far more terrible than anything we have yet seen," he predicted. "If the world war showed anything," he wrote for the *Harvard Advocate,* "it showed the American people the futility of imagining that they could live in snug contentment their own lives in their own way while the rest of the world burned in the conflagration of war across the ocean."[7]

But peril and promise were, in the Wilsonian scheme of things, directly related. Earlier in the year, in a speech at the Harvard Union, FDR reaffirmed his belief in civilization and progress as a process that, despite occasional steps backward, was "continuing to go up." That is why his Wilsonian rhetoric could emphasize the necessity of placing world opinion and morality firmly in charge of all aspects of international life. "The whole theory of the League," he explained, "rests upon a meeting of the minds of the civilized nations after full and frank discussion." He also stated his relativist conviction, essential to the Wilsonian perception of global modernity as ushering in a radically different kind of geopolitics, that many of the supposed lessons of history, even those taught by the reputedly timeless examples set by Washington and Lincoln, were of little help in an era in which unfamiliar dangers made necessary novel solutions. "None of the previous generation, even, can understand the problems that we are facing," he argued.[8]

As the 1920s proved, when he became one of the custodians of the Wilsonian flame, FDR's recitations of the Wilsonian creed were not simply the remarks of a communicant automatically, but without deep conviction, mouthing the catechism out of a sense of duty. In addition to serving as a trustee of the Woodrow Wilson Foundation, FDR was serious enough about propagating the gospel to draft a modified version of the League of Nations Covenant that he hoped would bypass objections to American membership. Whereas earlier he had been an advocate of honing the national character through war, perhaps as a result of the physical ordeal he underwent after contracting polio in 1921, a more tempered view emerged in which war was no longer an object of almost boyish relish. Forsaking his old enthusiasms, FDR complained in 1922 that "people are still thinking in terms of war rather than in terms of trying to remove the causes of war." Nationalism, he had concluded, was dominated by considerations of "face, honor, and all other fool things."[9]

Throughout the decade, FDR tried to promote a broader perspective on international affairs. "What is mostly suffered from in this country today is provincialism," he wrote to the editor of a farm journal. "We look on a world picture, not a gallery of national representations," he argued in a Harvard Phi Beta Kappa address. "The civilization trend covers all continents, not Europe alone." Even China, he noted on another occasion, had "torn loose from ancient traditions in this vast world movement for better things." In one of his few attempts to limn a picture of historical development in broad strokes, FDR asserted that the trend line of history was not only upward, but that science, technology, and economic progress made inevitable "the unification of mankind": "Isolation of individual nations will be as difficult in this future as would be the isolation of New England or the South today. The same laws of the history of progress apply. First, the self-sufficient small community, then the grouping of several communities, then the nation, then alliances between nations, and now a permanent congress of nations."[10]

FDR's thinking in the 1910s had focused on the inevitable conflicts of interest that arose between competitive nationalisms, but in the 1920s he stressed the emergence of a common global civilization whose economic wiring was channeled by spiritual conduit. While he readily acknowledged that economic ties were "forcing the issue," he refused to let his analysis rest solely on the foundation of economic exchange. He did not forget economic realities—full-fledged isolation would inevitably bring "hard times"—but he refused to reduce his analysis of internationalism to a "materialist" stress on economic forces which would have meant accepting, in his eyes, the Republican "dollars and cents point of view" of international relations. Thanks to the Republican party's purely economic emphasis on functional interdependence, he complained, the United States had "lost our leadership of the moral forces of mankind." His preferred alternative was a vision of service to a mankind which was at heart one. "True service will not come until all the world recognizes all the rest of the world as one big family," he insisted. Echoing Wilson's oft-repeated line, he asserted that "there is much truth in the thought that one cannot hate a person whom one knows." Contrary to materialist definitions of interests, he was convinced that "as in the relations between individuals, so the attitude and spirit are controlling factors in the affairs of nations."[11]

Since international problems and their solutions originated in the realm of spirit, Wilson's message, especially the new internationalist temper that undergirded Wilsonianism optimism, was more relevant than ever. "The more spiritual attitude gains ground every day and year that passes," he wrote to the *Baltimore Sun* in 1923. It was "a new phase of civilization" that lay back of "the constantly increasing demand that there shall be no more war." In an article outlining the basics of a Democratic foreign policy, FDR called for the acceptance of "not only certain facts but many new principles of a higher law, a new and better standard in international relations." He pointed out with some pride, as well as with evident regret, that Wilson the prophet had greater standing outside America than at home. "The world of thought outside America gives him far greater recognition today than we do here," he wrote to John Spargo in 1923. A few years later, he wrote to Viscount Robert Cecil, the British father of the League of Nations, to urge that "the general spirit which underlies the League and the World Court should be kept alive." This cosmopolitan vision provided a deep structure of historical conviction to what otherwise might have been construed as convenient partisan assaults on Republican foreign policy.[12]

CIVILIZATION WITHOUT POWER

Upon taking over the presidency in 1933, FDR continued to emphasize a communitarian approach on the assumption that world public opinion and common civilizational values could make a difference. American leadership in molding world opinion was more than a ritual act of homage to Wilson, however, because to FDR's mind the climate of foreign relations in both Europe and the Far East as the New Deal got under way was extraordinarily gloomy. Indeed, one is struck by the premonitory fears in the president's world picture at that time. Looking at the Far East, FDR "admitted the possibility of war and said flatly that it might be better to have it now than later" and saw at the same time "a very strong possibility of war with Germany." FDR waited for a new dawn, but the horizon grew no brighter over time. By 1936, Roosevelt believed the world to be "in the last days of the period of peace before a long chaos." The following year, he warned that "the patient will die of the 'armament disease' in a few years unless a major operation is performed." Though he was convinced that the crisis of world liberalism was temporary, it was not clear that the democracies could ride out the storm. If modern war intervened, it could "drag civilization to a level from which world-wide recovery may be all but impossible."[13]

The early New Deal charted a nationalist course toward economic recovery, but FDR's underlying internationalism was made explicit in his espousal of world opinion in a speech before the Woodrow Wilson Foundation in December 1933. In his best Wilsonian tone, he insisted that "the old policies, the old alliances, the old combinations and balances of power have proved themselves inadequate for the preservation of world peace." Taking up an idea first suggested by journalist Walter Lippmann, FDR began to argue that "only eight percent of the world population, made up of the Germans and the Japanese, seem to be blocking an otherwise unanimous desire" for peace and disarmament." Even this optimistic arithmetic exaggerated the scope of the problem, which originated "not in the world population but in the political leaders of the population." It followed that "we could get a world accord on world peace immediately if the people of the world could speak for themselves," if only the obstructionist minority could "do their own thinking and not be so finely led." The problem lay in the criminality of a few, not in some endemic anarchy caused by the incommensurability of cultural values among peoples. Totalitarianism was in many ways a modern phenomenon, but in its blockage of popular sentiments it was nothing more than a historical addendum to authoritarianism.[14]

This assumption that there existed a vast buried pool of international concord underlying all the artificial nationalist boundaries on the surface helps account for the unabashedly preachy style of FDR's administration in the 1930s. "It is only through constant education and the stressing of the ideals of peace that those who still seek imperialism can be brought in line with the majority," he insisted. FDR was well aware that in the modern era the ability to control the flow of information made it difficult for his message to get through. As he confessed to his Wilsonian ambassador to Germany, William E. Dodd, "The theory of Woodrow Wilson that one can appeal to the citizens over the head of the government is no longer tenable, for the reason that the dissemination of news—real news . . . is no longer possible." "Racial isolation," he believed, an isolation that was being artificially promoted and enforced by despotic governments, contributed to nationalist antagonisms.[15]

FDR often wondered whether he was swimming against the tide. Writing to his ambassador in Warsaw in 1934, he put it this way: "The chief problem is, of course, whether the marching of the general spirit of things is heading consciously or sub-consciously toward an idea of the extension of boundaries." Whether or not the *Weltgeist* was heading in the wrong direction, there seemed few alternatives to sermonizing. As his assistant secretary of state reported, FDR "said that he hated to preach, but that there was not much else that could be done." Despite repeated disappointments, he continued stubbornly to proclaim "the eventual effectiveness of preaching and preaching again."[16]

Had FDR wanted to do more than talk, the isolationist political climate of the 1930s would have restrained him from going beyond Hoover's view of the United States as a role model. At best, he was limited to influencing events through indirect political action, by practicing what he preached. "I do not know that the United States can save civilization," he said, "but at least by our example we can make people think and give them the opportunity of saving themselves." After a shaky start in Cuba, Roosevelt's hemispheric policy quickly put behind it the military interventionism of the past, a telling indication of how far he had come from cousin Theodore's viewpoint. The Good Neighbor Policy, besides being a modern expression of America's traditional regionalism, was intended also to have universal implications. Peace everywhere, not only in the Western Hemisphere, depended "upon the acceptance of the principle and practice of the good neighbor," or, put otherwise, the Golden Rule. By setting up the United States as a paragon of virtue, his fondest hope for the policy was to see "some moral repercussions in Europe."[17]

Roosevelt did more than sample a thimbleful of isolationism in the mid 1930s—he drank deeply of it by proclaiming publicly and privately that American policy in the event of a European conflict would be neutrality. In a portion of his 1936 message to Congress that could have been written by Hoover, he made clear the American position should war break out overseas: "The United States and the rest of the Americas can play but one role: through a well-ordered neutrality to do naught to encourage the contest, through adequate defense to save ourselves from embroilment and attack, and through example and all legitimate encouragement and assistance to persuade other nations to return to the days of peace and good-will." Writing in response to a pessimistic forecast by Columbia University President Nicholas Murray Butler, FDR came up with the same prescription: "If a calamity such as you foresee should fall upon mankind, we must make sure that this Nation shall not become involved."[18]

Roosevelt's isolationism was quite genuine, but it was also misleading because it was fitted into an unusual context. By mid-decade, foreign-policy debate had become obsessed with the issue of neutrality. Wilson had believed in 1919 that freedom of the seas was a dead issue because in the next conflict there would be no neutrals, but Americans failed to agree. In the mid-1930s, the only significant foreign-policy question was: What kind of neutrality? Beneath the surface of the apparent consensus on staying out of another

European war, the meaning of neutrality was by no means self-evident. In fact, the concept was taken up by widely opposed groups and redefined to suit their interpretations of the world. During the 1930s three quite different interpretations of neutrality vied for dominance: the old nationalist tradition of neutral rights, the self-abnegating view of the new isolationists, and the positive internationalist version favored by the president. The logical possibilities ranged across a continuum that involved cooperation and collective security at one end (though at a far remove from Europe), complete isolation at another, and classical neutral rights in the middle.[19]

These perspectives were at issue in the maneuvering over those legislative landmarks of the 1930s, the Neutrality Acts. The battle began in 1934 with the introduction of legislation by the administration designed to promote a positive version of neutrality in which the president would have the power to align U.S. policy with League of Nations sanctions by declaring discretionary embargoes. In its original form, the measure implied the existence of a world community capable of taking effective action against aggression, one with which the United States could coordinate its policies. Explaining its purport to Dodd in Berlin, FDR said, "The crux of the matter lies in the deep question of allowing some discretion to the executive." By a piece of legislative jiujitsu, this internationalist measure was turned against itself when the final bill directed the president to apply the arms embargo impartially against all the warring parties.[20]

Ironically, the isolationist Neutrality Acts did eventually contribute to a revival of internationalism, though hardly in the way Roosevelt expected. In rewriting legislation designed to prevent American intervention in a European war on the pattern of 1917—by embargoing arms shipments, banning loans to belligerents, and prohibiting passenger travel on belligerent vessels— Congress jettisoned the traditional view of neutral rights which was premised on the indispensability of trade and which assumed the continued functioning of a market system in time of war. This view was so deeply ingrained that America had gone to war, not only in 1917, but in 1812 and nearly on several other occasions, to uphold the principle. By abandoning the kind of nationalism that had been a major contributory factor to the treaty debacle in 1920—especially the nationalist determination to uphold with force if necessary the right to trade without outside dictation—in favor of what FDR called the "peace at any price" theory, the Neutrality Acts struck at the heart of the old isolationist tradition. The willingness to relinquish such rights meant, as FDR correctly understood, that the old international law had "completely disappeared."[21]

Congressional intent was clear, but one wonders whether the lawmakers were aware of the conceptual significance of their handiwork. For in rejecting the idea of nationalism in an interdependent world, they were implicitly accepting—by doing everything they could to avoid it—Wilson's argument that war in the modern era was indeed likely to take on global proportions. To be sure, the bills provided only for an arms embargo and not a total cutoff of trade, but by renouncing the sanctity of the principle of neutral rights they also rejected, at least by implication, the traditional assumption upon which neutral rights were based: that there existed an economic interdependence among nations from which it was intolerable to be cut off. The bills were devoid of any conception of national interest whatsoever, except perhaps for the absolute need to avoid war. The Neutrality Acts may have been a flight from internationalism, but they were at the same time also a flight from nationalism, a repudiation of what not very long ago had been considered a sacred touchstone of national existence.[22]

It was this rejection of the nationalist past from fear of an internationalist future that made the Neutrality Acts, in one sense, a quite modern phenomenon. Because harking to the "lessons of the past" learned during World War I required a break with foreign-policy tradition, the new isolationism was historically ungrounded; indeed, the mere fact that the meaning of isolationism had to be debated meant that it had lost its former axiomatic status. As historian Charles Beard understood, this meant that a new conception of America's world role was necessary, one that began with a blank sheet of paper and articulated a new view of history on the assumption that the old views were played out. "Horrible as the thought may be for simple minds," he wrote of an isolationist stance in *The Devil Theory of War,* "it is a fact that such a policy, indeed every large public policy, is *an interpretation of history*—past, in the making, and to be made."[23]

Whereas American isolation in the past had meant being in the world but not of it, the last-gasp version of the 1930s viewed America as being a separate historical entity entirely. This kind of isolationism, FDR recognized, was based on the belief that "if the civilization of Europe is about to destroy itself through internal strife, it might just as well go ahead and do it and that the United States can stand idly by." Despite the attempts of Beard and a few others to draw a new world picture complete with all the autarchic details, no new view of history as compelling as the old was in sight. Having abandoned both tradition and internationalist modernity, the historical rootlessness of isolationism made extremely precarious its ideological survival.[24]

Thanks in part to this absence of a coherent worldview, the difficulties in fixing isolationism's historical longitude exacerbated problems of determining its contemporary political latitude. As Manfred Jonas has demonstrated, the isolationist coalition included as varied a collection of bedfellows as one could hope to find. Their willingness to suspend normal ideological animosities in the interest of remaining at peace resembled a wartime suspension of politics as usual. But this common revulsion against internationalism was united only by a negative, which meant that any positive political expressions could not be politically developed. Quite unintentionally, then, the isolationism of the 1930s, by virtue of its sheer negativity, was helpful to internationalism, for once it had been invalidated on the practical level, there was no ideological line of defense left to fall back upon. The net result was that isolationist and internationalist intellectual compounds were refined into their most simplified forms, without the possibility of a return to the old intermediate position on neutral rights.[25]

However shaky their historical vision and however politically empty, the isolationists had a better claim to the title of realists, given their reliance on concrete and immediately understandable rationales for going to war. The argument of Joseph P. Kennedy—"If we had to fight to protect our lives we would do better fighting in our own back yard"—was both more traditional and far more insightful as to what would trigger a public response than the abstract and hypothetical world-historical rationales being pressed by the internationalists. Isolationists like Hoover were also concerned about possible transformations of the national polity, only in their case the primary danger was the presidential dictatorship and centralization likely to arise from involvement in a war. Here they could point to World War I as an example of the statist pitfalls of modern war, whereas the internationalists could rely only on conjecture.

Pure isolation may have been historically ungrounded, but the Wilsonian brand of internationalism, because of its counterintuitive and interpretive character, also lacked a solid footing in tradition. Both perspectives, because of their rejection of the past and their heavy reliance on interpretation of events whose historical meaning was unclear, were essentially wagers on the future. It is too much to suggest, as Selig Adler has done, that the Neutrality Acts promoted the outbreak of the war that eventually dragged the country in—the fate of the world hardly hung in the balance on this legislation—but they did assure that the country's entry into the war would not be on the basis of issues that had pulled it into the last conflict. World War II would be a repeat for many Europeans; not so for Americans, for whom involvement would take place along lines entirely different from those in the first war.[26]

If FDR's assumptions about the global danger of aggressive expansionism in the modern world were correct, then the hollowness of the assumptions behind the Neutrality Acts could not help but become manifest eventually in the laboratory of experience. But while the emergence of the new-style isolationism left a turn to internationalism as the only surviving alternative, the about-face would not take the form of a return to Wilsonian collective security. As the events of the late 1930s forced the isolationist tide to recede from its high water mark, they also led FDR to trade in his former reliance on world opinion for a new emphasis on the strategic dimension of Wilsonian thought. The change was not immediate. With the darkening of the international sky in 1937 and 1938 as a result of the Sino-Japanese War and the looming crisis over Czechoslovakia, his rhetoric shifted in the direction of more specifically delineating the kinds of dangers that these events posed and exploring concrete measures to ward them off. Although his Wilsonian initiatives continued to presuppose the desirability of community action, they would be only way-stations to the complete abandonment of reliance on world opinion.

FDR's most telling Wilsonian foray of 1937 was his famous "Quarantine Speech," delivered in November. The address was notable because FDR avoided the usual abstract rhetoric about war being inimical to the United States and talked instead in concrete terms about expansion as a quest for world domination that ran "the risk of plunging the whole world into war." In Stimsonian fashion, he described war as a contagion that was able to "engulf states and peoples remote from the original scene of hostilities." In FDR's disease metaphor, the chain of infection, if left untreated, would not burn itself out until it had radically affected the health of the global body politic. The balance of power in the past had been an endemic malady that mankind could live with; modern power, however, had epidemic implications that made necessary communal medical intervention.[27]

This proposal to quarantine fascist expansionism traded heavily on the idea of world opinion. Quarantine, which suggested a communal imposition of ostracism, was of course very closely connected conceptually with the sanction of nonintercourse which was a linchpin of collective security as embodied in Article XVI of the league covenant. Still wedded to the Wilsonian framework of the 90 percent–10 percent theory, FDR based his position on the existence of a "solidarity and interdependence about the modern world, both technically and morally." Putting threat and solution together, he wrote to one of his ambassadors that "we cannot stop the spread of Fascism unless world opinion realizes its ultimate dangers." Writing afterward to his old Groton schoolmaster, Endicott Peabody, he predicted "a growing response to the ideal that when a few nations fail to maintain certain fundamental rules of conduct, the most practical and most peaceful thing to do in the long run is to 'quarantine' them."[28]

Recognizing that the employment of world opinion as a club was increasingly problematic, the administration also considered using it as a carrot in the form of economic appeasement. The most serious scheme, hatched in the mind of Under Secretary of State Sumner Welles, looked to the convening of a world economic conference, which, like the Congress of Berlin in the late 1870s, would settle the outstanding issues of the day. On the assumption that the aggressor nations were "have-nots" looking for economic security, Welles hoped that the conference could eliminate the economic motives for aggression by guaranteeing equal access to markets and raw materials throughout the world, increasing the volume of world trade by lowering trade barriers, and strengthening international law. Writing in a Wilsonian vein, Welles thought this desirable "from the standpoint of world psychology" because "the mere fact that the nations of the world today could by concerted action agree upon anything of vital importance would in itself be a material step forward." Assistant Secretary Adolf Berle identified the Wilsonian-communitarian roots of this proposal when he noted to his diary: "Of course, this is nothing more than the kind of thing which the League of Nations did except that it is not mortgaged to maintaining the status quo."[29]

Roosevelt gave the go-ahead to Welles's scheme despite his reservations about economic measures alone as "a pretty weak reed for Europe to lean on" because they did not go to the root of the problem. In its failure to address the problem of armaments, which was itself symptomatic of deeper problems of nationalism, militarism, and power politics, the proposal was not Wilsonian enough. As he wrote to Mussolini in 1937: "All of these efforts, even if they are joined by additional nations, and even if a greater total of world trade results in the coming years, will not prove a completely effective guarantee of international peace if world armament among the nations continues on its present scale." Trade liberalization—"simplification" he liked to call it—had to go "hand in hand" with disarmament. Economic poultices could only slow the progress of the disease, which was still likely to be fatal if its internal symptoms were not addressed. And this, of course, required a will to peace.[30]

Even so, for the time being, FDR welcomed the principle of appeasement. In an April press conference, he admitted that the United States had "urged the promotion of peace through the finding of means for economic appeasement," and he would soon back the idea on the political plane as well during the Munich crisis. Perhaps the most interesting thing about Munich, given the emphasis placed upon it in the postwar period, is how little impact it made at the time. Like all watersheds, it requires a very long perspective from both sides of the time continuum to realize its centrality. Disguising Munich's ultimate significance was the fact that there was nothing inherently inconsistent about appeasement with FDR's previous ideas, for the very idea of appeasement was rooted in the communitarian belief that disputes could be resolved by discussion and consensus, rather than through power. Indeed, since force was illicit under the League of Nations as a way of producing change, appeasement was the only logical remaining alternative.[31]

This seemed to be FDR's view of the episode, at least at first. Once the Munich bargain had been sealed, Roosevelt gave vent to his optimism that, if nothing else, it had awakened the old Wilsonian fear among world opinion. Writing to Canadian Prime Minister W. L. Mackenzie King, he pointed out the silver lining: "We have had before our eyes tangible proof, if proof were needed that the people of the world have a clear realization of what a general European war would mean and that those who work for the peaceful solution of international problems have the overwhelming support of their fellowmen." The recent war scare, the vertiginous experience of looking over the precipice, had "created a worldwide passion for peace" which was "more universal now than at any previous time." It was understandable, therefore, that he could afterward write that he was "not a bit upset over the final result."[32]

It was only with the conclusive failure of the Munich accords to fulfill these larger expectations that FDR realized that the remedy for greed was not charity. The *Kristallnacht* pogrom of November, nominally a domestic incident, had enormous geopolitical implications for FDR because it demonstrated the futility of relying on common values. "I could scarcely believe that such things could occur in a twentieth century civilization," he said in rueful amazement. This new understanding that, in the absence of shared values, agreements like Munich were only self-defeating became increasingly pronounced in FDR's thinking from this point. Typical was his 1940 criticism of continuing hopes among Republicans for the appeasement of Hitler, views which he characterized as "based on the materialism in which they view not only themselves but their country." That criticism reflected not so much a belief that "materialistic" agreements reached through diplomatic horse-trading were undesirable, but a conviction that, by themselves, they were unworkable. From this point on, FDR's sociocultural views would be much closer to Hoover's than to Wilson's, but not so his strategic perspective.[33]

POWER WITHOUT CIVILIZATION

By late 1938 FDR had begun to recognize the sterility of continued appeals to world public opinion. The failure of the League of Nations to halt the Italians in Ethiopia or the Japanese in China had already led him to conclude that the organization had been "destroyed" and started him thinking about what would happen should world opinion prove a total failure. In his 1939 message to Congress, he confessed ruefully that words had been "futile." He might have had himself in mind when he said that "during these eight years many of our people clung to the hope that the innate decency of mankind would protect the unprepared who showed their innate trust in mankind. Today we are all wiser—and sadder.'' As he abandoned hope in world opinion as an effective force, FDR began in compensation to emphasize in earnest the other side of his Wilsonianism, the side he would have preferred not to évoke. He abandoned communitarianism in favor of coping with the Wilsonian nightmare world. Having exhausted and jettisoned one of his Wilsonian fuel tanks, he would rely henceforth completely on the other.[34]

Roosevelt's glum view of international affairs began with the fact that he did not talk about or rely upon the European balance of power. Indeed, his fears were based on the conviction that it had disappeared. Nor did FDR's new thinking on international relations assume that a balance of power would be the ''natural'' result of international competition. By 1939, as summed up by his friend and ambassador to the USSR, Joseph Davies, there was ''neither collective security nor a balance of power to secure peace and the civilization of Europe.'' True, there was a concern with Britain's survival, but that was grounded in the fear that the European balance was passé. After May 1940, FDR felt unable to count on the survival of Great Britain because the Nazi regime was determined to place its continued existence in doubt, thus making a mockery of Britain's former role as continental balancer of last resort. If Britain fell or struck a deal with Hitler, what then? Following the failure of his peace propaganda, FDR began to answer that question by emphasizing, in terms reminiscent of Wilson's warnings some twenty years earlier, the global implications of modern war.[35]

FDR is responsible for articulating and explaining in detailed fashion strategic assumptions that previously had received only metaphorical expression. Although he tended to exaggerate America's military vulnerability in order to offset the bunker mentality of the isolationists, his arguments about the perils facing the country were, like Wilson's, based less on a belief in the existence of a direct military threat to the United States than on the fear that a combined assault of the Axis powers might lead to a strangulating constriction of the open world environment. FDR understood that it was not immediate dangers that needed to be taken into account, as in traditional realpolitik, but the danger to the international milieu, whose transformation by the dictatorships would have made the world unlivable for the United States. Finding himself faced with the prospect of living in a neighborhood in which homeowners would have to arm to the teeth and barricade themselves within their houses to protect themselves from local thugs, FDR decided that that kind of neighborhood would not be worth living in. Better to address the causes of sociopathy in the first place.[36]

Although FDR liked to talk in terms of ''real world forces come into conflict," the continental dominance of Germany and the aggressiveness of the regime made it necessary for him to base planning on what Rexford Tugwell called "an interpretation of intentions." This appreciation of events necessarily entailed a good deal of speculation and interpretation and also involved rejecting the logic of advisers like William C. Bullitt, who insisted that there was "no basis of policy more unreal or disastrous than the apprehension of remote future dangers." Disregarding such advice, FDR chose instead to treat with utmost seriousness what he called "potentialities for the future." After sketching his worst-case scenario one day to Assistant Secretary Berle, Roosevelt acknowledged that this was a "possibility only, but a possibility no far-sighted statesman could afford to permit." It was his obligation as president "to warn the American people that they, too, should think of possible ultimate results in Europe and the Far East" and of "conceivable consequences." The possibility of a Europe dominated by a single aggressive power with global ambitions and reach, he admitted publicly, was a "pipe dream, but we have to think about pipe dreams."[37]

This need to make policy on the basis of hypothetical worst-case possibilities rather than react, as in the past, to palpable immediate dangers was hardly "realism" in any classical sense, but that was because modernity had changed reality to the point that old truths no longer applied. Much more so than Wilson, Roosevelt was aware that accurate thinking about the contemporary international environment required a reorientation of the basic perceptual forms of space, time, and velocity upon which people depended to gauge international change. The American people, he was convinced, had "much to learn of the 'relativity' of world geography and the rapid annihilation of distance and purely local economics." Indeed, modern technology had resulted in "the annihilation of time and space." Drawing the appropriate conclusions, he wrote Pope Pius XII that "because the people of this nation have come to a realization that time and distance no longer exist in the older sense, they understand that which harms one segment of humanity harms all the rest."[38]

Not only did the new weapons technologies make possible the rapid conquest of much of Europe, they were responsible also for reducing the importance of distance as a military factor. For example, FDR argued that the earth had been "so shrunk by the airplane and the radio that Europe is closer to America today than was one side of these [Great Smokey] mountains to the other side when the pioneers toiled through the primitive forest." In 1938, in the press conference in which he responded to *Kristallnacht*, he pointed out that, thanks in part to the airplane, "any possible attack has been brought infinitely closer than it was 5 years or 20 years or 50 years ago." The "effective timing of defense, and the distant points from which attacks may be launched are completely different from what they were twenty years ago.'' On another occasion, FDR spoke to those Americans in the midwestern heartland who felt themselves far removed from happenings overseas. He explained that Mexico was only seven days away from Germany and, re- counting the experience of the brother of a Chinese friend, he said: ''Let me tell you about Iowa . . . they had wiped out one of the rural communities in the Iowa of China. He never thought it could happen, I never thought it could happen and his brother in Canton never thought it could happen.'' China's ability to Sinify its conquerors over the long term had been reassuring to some, but the prospect of a similar military inundation of the United States put a different perspective on things.[39]

FDR was struck, too, by the remarkable speed with which international developments moved, part of the general ''acceleration of history'' character- istic of modernization, which meant that the United States would not have the luxury of time as it did during World War I. ''Never in my life have I seen things moving in the world with more cross currents or with greater velocity,'' he wrote in 1937 to William Phillips. He marveled at the changes over the course of his lifetime. ''In the old days we used to try at least to think a generation ahead,'' he wrote to a friend, but that kind of leisurely anticipation was no longer possible in a world in which the near-term future had become increasingly uncertain and unpredictable. Now the window of time between the threat and the planning of the actions necessary to forestall it was much smaller. Inasmuch as the velocity of events placed a premium on preparation for any eventuality, FDR was correspondingly critical of what he viewed as shortsightedness. ''There has been a tendency,'' he said, ''on the part of all of us to concentrate too much on the immediate present as it concerns us rather than to think of the ultimate consequences of this collapse of law and order.''[40]

In March 1939, he drew out the implications of the transformation in this imaginative extended metaphor: ''Up to the last summer I was willing to make mental bets that such and such a thing would happen and such and such a thing would not happen. Today, however, I have stopped being a mental bookmaker because so many horses are scratched and so many other horses have become added starters each twenty-four hours that we are not even certain that the trainers, jockeys and spectators may not end up in a 'free-for-all' fight in which the grandstand will be burned down and most of the spectators, horses, trainers and jockeys go to the hospital or the ceme- tery.'' For such a massive sociohistorical process, then, modernity had very little inertia and was remarkably fragile. It could at any moment veer off the mountain road of civilization and plunge toward self-destruction.[41]

Roosevelt's preachments now turned to educating Americans to new "facts of life" which had first emerged during the Great War and which Wilson had tried to lay before the public. "We perceive the danger in a world-wide arena," he said somewhat hopefully in May 1940. Unfortunately, understanding of this kind came slowly. Individuals often experienced conversions that resulted in radical alteration of behavior, but Roosevelt understood that the same was not true of nations, where cultural lag got in the way. "It takes several generations to understand the type of 'fact of life' to which I refer," he wrote to Norman Thomas. "Very few people really came to understand the lessons of the World War—even though twenty years went by . . . The lessons of this war constitute relatively such a complete change from older methods that less than 1% of our people have understood." Most people, he believed, simply had "no conception of what modern war, with or without a declaration of war, involves."[42]

As war in Europe approached, FDR attempted to spell out its practical consequences for the nation and, in so doing, went far beyond Wilson's luridly suggestive wartime stress on *Mitteleuropa.* For one thing, there would be serious economic consequences following a Nazi victory. "If military domination were to keep on expanding," FDR predicted, "the influence of that military aggression would be felt all over the world, for the very simple reason that the aggressor nations would extend their barter system." In that event, the United States had three choices: economic isolation, reducing wages to compete with the low-wage labor of the planned economies, or subsidizing trade and thereby politicizing it. None of these alternatives was very attractive. Citing the disastrous Jeffersonian embargo as incontrovertible evidence against a reclusive policy, he pointed out that "of course the damned thing didn't work. In the first place it was practically unenforceable and, in the second place, the country began to strangle." The nation had put up with serious unemployment and unrest (the contemporary significance of which was all too obvious) and still it drifted into war. "So much for an illustration from history," he concluded.[43]

A competitive policy, on the other hand, would likely put American world trade "at the mercy of the combine," thus jeopardizing the hard-won Good Neighbor policy in Latin America. German control of the Continent would lead to "the most gigantic armament race and the most devastating trade wars in all history." This image depended on the kind of logic used by Free-Soilers and Republicans in the 1850s to describe the fatal dangers posed by the slave power to free labor. Eventually the United States would be surrounded by hostile states and the nightmare the Monroe Doctrine had been designed to avoid, the formation of a balance of power in the Americas, would at last become a dreadful reality. Following Munich, at a White House meeting FDR pointed out that "for the first time since the Holy Alliance in

1818 the United States now faced the possibility of an attack on the Atlantic side in both the Northern and Southern Hemispheres."[44]

But, significantly, these economic doomsday scenarios were only by-products of military expansion. Estimates of the capacity of Hitler's Europe to outproduce the United States took on relevance only on the assumption that his assets would be gained and expanded through conquest. At the time of Munich, the hope was that German policy was limited to incorporating contiguous German-speaking populations into the Reich, but by March 1939 with Hitler's march into Prague and the subsequent dissolution of Czechoslovakia, that interpretation was no longer tenable. As FDR explained at a press conference: "Where there was a limit last autumn, there is no limit today. It makes a very different picture. And, there being no limit today, this new policy may be carried out on an increasing scale in any part of the world. From our point of view such a policy could . . . mean German domination, not only in all the small nations of Europe, but . . . very possibly . . . other continents."[45]

Early in 1939, in a meeting with members of the Senate Military Affairs Committee, FDR outlined, in dominolike terms, the specific sequence of steps which the threat would likely follow: "Now, when there is domination of Europe, the next step, of course, is that all the small nations would drop into the basket of their own accord because it is silly for them to resist." He described a process of "the gradual encirclement of the United States by the removal of first lines of defense" in Europe and the Mediterranean, followed by the employment of economic and military means to dominate a defenseless Africa and South America. In the Pacific, the American line of defense was "a series of islands" which would prevent the Japanese from dominating the entire Pacific, but in the Atlantic, the first line was "the continued existence of a very large group of nations—their continued, independent existence."[46]

Infuriated by press leaks that had him placing America's frontier on the Rhine, FDR called them "utter rubbish" and "deliberate misrepresentation" and insisted that his remarks had been "completely twisted around." In trying to set things right, however, FDR's clarification tended to confirm rather than to repudiate the reports:

> There are certain nations, about thirty or forty strong—perhaps thirty outside this continent—whose continued independent political and military and economic existence and, let us say, their economic independence, the continuance of those three factors, especially the political independence, as long as they have it, it acts as a protection for the democracies of this hemisphere. You see the point? Now, suppose I was to say that the continued independence, in a political and economic sense, of Finland is of tremendous importance to

the safety of the United States. Now, isn't that a very different thing than saying that the frontier of the United States is in Europe?

He added to his list the Baltic States, Holland, Portugal, Belgium, Switzerland, Greece, Egypt, Turkey, and Persia and mentioned that a year earlier he might have added Czechoslovakia "as a link in the American defense against German and Italian aggression in the future." The United States had "a continuing interest in their remaining free and independent," but this, he insisted, was "a very different thing from talking about the frontiers of the United States being on the Rhine."[47]

Although the president was correct in the narrow sense—while the crossing of an American border would automatically be a casus belli, the independence of the nations he had in mind was only of "tremendous importance"—this holistic view of American security could, by taking the next logical step, be used to justify American intervention in distant locales. Interpreted broadly, the American frontier could be everywhere and anywhere. This was indeed universalist rhetoric, but it played up the darker side of the Wilsonian worldview by portraying the democratic nations as lemmings poised collectively to go to their deaths. By so defining American national interests, FDR had taken the United States to the doorstep of the domino theory—although, as we shall see, it would remain for other statesmen to open the door.

Writing to Nicholas Murray Butler in 1939, he insisted that "a policy designed to prevent the outbreak of war anywhere is essentially in accord with our national interests." This assertion not only reiterated the core of Article XI of the league covenant, which stated that war or the threat of war was of concern to every state; in light of the expressed concern for American national security, it went beyond it. In view of the ultimate consequences, it followed that the United States had, in Wilsonian terms, "a vital interest in seeing that world peace is maintained." Putting it a bit differently in one of his fireside chats shortly following the invasion of Poland, FDR urged the American people to "master at the outset a simple but unalterable fact in modern foreign relations. When peace has been broken anywhere, peace of all countries is in danger." American policy, therefore, was vitally interested "to try to prevent any war in any part of the world" because, if successful, it would "not raise certain questions which would be raised if war started."[48]

Even though he received reports in which Hitler purportedly ridiculed having any global ambitions, the administration became increasingly certain that the ultimate threat was world conquest. This alarm bell was sounded many times, but a conversation between Cordell Hull and a skeptical Herbert Hoover held in February 1941 was typical. Hull insisted that the Germans, bent on world conquest, would eventually force South America into their "economic or political axis" as a prelude to attacking the United States. In the 1920s, Charles Beard had mockingly described the world-conquest thesis of World War I as "a story for babes." Nevertheless, here was FDR in a press conference, arguing that "it is a perfectly open and shut thing and, if you have the complete, physical power to do it, you win." Echoing Wilson's self-consciousness about the exaggerated sound of such a scheme, he concluded: "Isn't that right? It sounds like a crazy picture but it is perfectly obvious, it is so sensible."[49]

In any case, given the stakes and the swiftness and decisiveness with which events moved, the United States could not afford to gamble that the world-conquest scenario might be a fiction. One consequence of modernity was that the United States found itself in a high-risk environment in which, as the interventionist Dean Acheson pointed out, "we can be wrong only once." The magnification of risk characteristic of modernity was perhaps most evident in the high stakes of international statesmanship. In the past, statesmen could often afford to be wrong, but in this case there seemed to be no margin for error.[50]

With the conquest of Europe, the raw material resources of Africa, large parts of Asia, and the Australasian islands would come under Axis control, augmenting their power and perhaps cutting off America's access to them. In his 1941 State of the Union address, FDR insisted that it was "immature— and incidentally, untrue—for anyone to brag that an unprepared America, singlehanded, and with one hand tied behind its back, can hold off the entire world." Responding to Joseph P. Kennedy's assertion that he would go down in history either as the greatest president in history or the "greatest horse's ass," FDR added another alternative: 'I may go down as the President of an unimportant country at the end of my term.'"[51]

FDR envisioned a "policy of world domination between Germany, Italy and Japan" based on what amounted to "an offensive and defensive alliance." Although Germany was the "immediate menace," the larger danger stemmed from the coalition of expansionist nations on both ocean flanks. In the late 1930s, the idea began to gain ground, to the point that it became an idée fixe in 1940, that the threat was a coordinated one. As Henry Morgenthau put it to his chief in September 1938: "So well have the aggressor nations mastered the tactics of aggression that a victory in one part of the world is followed by a burst of aggression elsewhere." In the aftermath of the signature of the Tripartite Pact of 1940, FDR described the situation in terms of what subsequently would become known as zero-sum logic. "Today, Japan and Germany and Italy are allies. Whatever any one of them gains or 'wins' is a gain for their side and, conversely, a loss for the other side."[52]

These Rooseveltian strategical musings drew the connection between events in the Pacific and in Europe far more explicitly than did the Stimsonian prairie-fire analogy. The connecting link in the common chain of European and Asian events was Great Britain. But the British, it was clear, had their hands full with Germany, the rise of Japan in the Pacific, and the development of air power which rendered them vulnerable to attack. Saving Britain required preserving the British Empire, which meant protecting British imperial interests in the Far East against Japan. Spiritually mankind was not of a piece, but strategically the world was one.[53]

While the ability of the United States to survive in a world dominated by the expansionist dictatorships was never seriously in question, even by the internationalists, the crucial consideration was the conditions under which it would be forced to survive. A future in which the nation would be continually preoccupied with fending off economic strangulation and military conquest was one in which basic cultural values were at stake. In a speech to the governing board of the Pan American Union, FDR emphasized the necessity of avoiding "an organization of world affairs which permits us no choice but to turn our countries into barracks, unless we are to be the vassals of some conquering empire." "What shall we be defending?" FDR asked in 1940. "We shall be defending a way of life which has given more freedom to the soul and body of man than has ever been realized in the world before." This nonmessianic realization that saving the nation required the salvation of everybody else, that culture and civilization were intertwined, that national identity was tightly linked to a pattern of global history, echoed Wilson's recognition of the same problem when he called for making the world safe for democracy. "Our type of civilization," FDR said, "though saved for a generation by the first World War, is once again a world issue."[54]

By this formulation, the nation's security was being jeopardized in an indirect sense—at issue was not so much the prospect of inclement weather as the effects of a fundamental change in the global climate. Making the point that the United States was incapable of surviving alone as a political culture, in a speech delivered in Canada in 1938, FDR declared that "civilization is not national—it is international." As a matter of logical implication, then, the real danger from isolation was isolation. According to Cordell Hull, "Isolation is not a means to security; it is a fruitful source of insecurity." Whether or not the United States could successfully stay out of the war was thus beside the point. If Germany and Japan succeeded in militarily reorganizing the world system into closed regions, the necessity of creating a "garrison state" would utterly transform the American polity and economy in a totalitarian direction. As Robert W. Tucker has argued, for a great nation "the ultimate expression of security can rarely be found in its physical or economic dimensions, but must instead be found in the moral-psychological—or, if one prefers, the spiritual—dimension.'' In this case, the diamond of American cultural uniqueness could shine only within the setting of a liberal Western civilization.[55]

FDR's aim in educating the public was not to drive home the wisdom of collective security, since by this time collective security's raison d'être of nipping war in the bud was rapidly becoming a wistful memory. With no Wilsonian road map to show the way, the objective was instead to lay the groundwork for some sort of strategic response to the snowballing crisis. Well into 1939, American military planning had reflected the fundamental uncertainty of worldview that drove the ongoing debate between isolationists and internationalists. The Rainbow Plans, drawn up in 1939, were not a table d'hôte menu; rather, they offered an à la carte choice that appealed to policymaking tastes of all kinds. If America's relation to the world was essentially hemispheric, so too could be America's defense. On the other hand, if the threat was global, a worldwide strategy could be cooked up. As Maurice Matloff put it some years later, the diversity of the Rainbow Plans "reflected not only the 'fog' surrounding the intentions and capabilities of potential enemies and friends, but also the uncertainty concerning the future temper and will of the American people.'' By January 1941, a common strategy was worked out with the British and Canadians in the ABC-1 conversations in which it was agreed that Germany, as the greater threat, needed to be disposed of first; but that still left open enormous questions regarding the degree and the timing of American involvement.[56]

Those questions were finally answered by Pearl Harbor. Assuming that FDR did want to enter the war by this time, Pearl Harbor must have come as both a surprise and a relief, and the German decision to declare war four days later must have lifted an even greater burden of anxiety from his shoulders. If one goes by the book, it should not have happened this way, especially as the hard line against Japan that provoked the attack might have ruined the ABC-1 strategy of taking the offensive in the Atlantic and assuming a defensive position in the Pacific. Were it not for Hitler's decision to honor the Tripartite Pact, the nation might have found itself tied down in a war with Japan which, even though it would have been backed to the hilt by the public, would have been the wrong war from the standpoint of grand strategy. But FDR's policies ought not be judged in the light of traditional "realist" standards when it is precisely those kinds of standards that his administration was rejecting. The failure to translate the coherent image of a combined military threat into an effective diplomatic posture and the resultant bumbling into war was due only in part to poor planning and bureaucratic confusion and even less to a devious "back door to war" mentality, for on this matter Wilsonianism had provided some rather vague but still accurate signposts.

Viewed from the inside, this mind-boggling gap between strategy and diplomacy was actually a triumph of Wilsonian holism. Hitler's decision to declare war was not so much a godsend as a vindication of FDR's hard line against Japan and the soundness of the geostrategic perception underlying it that the world crisis was all of a piece, that all doors of aggression opened to global war. Regardless of the clumsy way in which the United States entered the war, then, Pearl Harbor at least had the effect of confirming the perception that the danger facing the United States was solidary in nature. With the involvement in war originating in an area of the world in which the United States had been commercially and culturally interested but strategically remote, events in Europe and Asia were now viewed as being cut from the same bolt of civilizational cloth. It helped, too, in drawing the global connections that the tough line against Japan had enjoyed much broader popular support than FDR's more ambiguous line toward Europe. In future, American strategy in Korea and Vietnam would feature a fundamentally similar view of the relation between part and whole.

The two worldviews contending for dominance in the United States during the 1930s could never have been rationally adjudicated, since each was rational within its own ambit. Worldviews, like everything else, are the children of events, and it was the misfortune of isolationism to contend that the United States could exist securely in a completely insulated world of its own when Pearl Harbor demonstrated otherwise. As conspiracy theorists have recognized, while failing at the same time to understand the nonconspiratorial dynamics behind war with Japan, Pearl Harbor settled the isolationist-interventionist debate with a finality impossible of achievement by resort to rational debate alone. Pearl Harbor was thus not simply a military disaster for the United States. Inasmuch as it did far more serious damage to the idea of two worlds than to American security, it was the best thing that could have happened to American internationalism. Narrowly construed, the desire to show prior knowledge of the attack on Roosevelt's part of the assault centered on the question of presidential abuse of power. More broadly considered, the accusation of conspiracy was a pathetic attempt to reopen a metahistorical question no longer at issue.

THE IMPASSE OF WILSONIANISM

The confusion and the lack of policy guidelines with which the United States came out of the war closed the parentheses on the disorderly way in which it had entered it. In 1942, FDR wrote that he was "a bit appalled by the percentage of people who have no clear idea of what the war is about.'' Actually, by this time the American public reflected fairly well his understanding. As attested by countless B movies in which the Nazi villain at some point revealed his maniacal design by declaring ''Today Europe, tomorrow the world,'' they certainly understood the menace of world conquest in its broadest, if somewhat lurid, terms and they comprehended also the threat to the American way of life posed by an isolated United States. To that extent, the common impression that American soldiers were fighting for motherhood and apple pie was not far off base. If there was a shortcoming in the public mind, it was one that FDR shared: a conceptual inability to draw a convincing image of a postwar order. For the public, it was the bandwagon movement toward Wilsonianism that was at the root of the problem; in the president's case, the reverse was true. His switch to apocalyptic Wilsonianism, with its corollary abandonment of the sunny possibilities of world opinion, left a blank image.[57]

The manner in which FDR approached postwar problems was indicative of his realization that the Wilsonian language of civilized community was inapplicable to the postwar world. All his previous talk about spirit having proved empty, he was faced with the problem of producing the effects of community without its necessary base of neighborly values. Even if he had desired a world order infused with the spirit of collective security, the process of developing and nurturing the coalition against the Axis powers made impossible any rearticulation of a crusading neo-Wilsonian creed. He was forced to recognize the potency of, even to rely upon, the very same divisive forces that had coalesced to ruin Wilson's vision in the 1920s—nationalism, bolshevism, and civilizational differences in the Far East, all of them in their own way ''spiritual''—to help win the war and shape the peace.

By comparison with Wilson's wartime allies, FDR's comrades in arms were a diverse bunch. With the inclusion of China and the Soviet Union as major partners, FDR's world order became more inclusive and universalistic than Wilson's, but by the same token it was rendered less utopian, losing in idealistic focus what it had gained in geographic and ideological breadth. Indeed, civilization had become so problematic that its postwar salvation would have to be assured by expelling some of its former leading members, incorporating noncivilized states, and tolerating its sworn ideological antagonist.

The persistence of nationalism and cultural particularism as a fundamental problem was evident in FDR's treatment of the German problem. Whatever the punitive elements of the Versailles settlement and Wilson's own tendency to harshness, Wilson's cultural internationalism had made it possible to look forward to a reintegration of Germany into the Western community on the assumption that a democratized Germany would in due time assimilate the values of the League of Nations members. But FDR was not so certain that Germans could be reformed. Whether or not his childhood misadventures with German authoritarianism had anything to do with it, it seemed fairly clear that, as one historian has argued, "his anti-German biases were deeper than his abhorrence of Hitler's Nazi dictatorship and military aggression." Many of his advisers, questioning any distinction between the Germans and their leadership, assumed that Hitler was "the florescence of the German people." Typical of this group was Vice President Henry Wallace, who insisted that "those who think that getting rid of Hitler will clear up the situation simply don't know what they are talking about." According to Hull, "This Nazism is down in the German people a thousand miles deep and you have just got to uproot it, and you can't do it by just shooting a few people."[58]

Although Roosevelt complained that "efforts to prove that the Germans have always been barbarians for a thousand years as a nation go a bit too far," it was clear that the problem of German national character was as deeply disturbing to the president as it was to many intellectuals of the day who explained Germany's descent into barbarism in terms of cultural deficiencies. The German problem seemed to be the product of a cultural soil so overgrown with weeds that the tender shoots of democracy could not easily be transplanted. Having agreed on the need to keep the enemy disarmed, Roosevelt commented later in the war that "Germany understands only one kind of language." At the very minimum this emphasis on harshness meant that the lessons of power—the only language that the Germans understood—rather than a merciful reintegrationist philosophy would have to apply.[59]

There were, of course, many liberals within the administration who advocated blending Germany into a prosperous international community on functional grounds. Their contrasting perspective set up the other pole of the debate over soft and hard approaches to the peace. FDR definitely leaned toward harshness, if only to let the Germans know "that this time at least they have definitely lost the war." In August 1944, as the time approached when Allied forces would actually begin their occupation of Germany, FDR's hard-line ideas came out in a number of conversations with his secretary of the treasury, Henry Morgenthau. "We have got to be tough with Germany and I mean the German people not just the Nazis," he said. "We either have to castrate the German people or you have got to treat them in such a manner so they just can't go on reproducing people who want to continue the way they have in the past." A week later, he elaborated: "Too many people here and in England hold to the view that the German people as a whole are not responsible for what has taken place—that only a few Nazi leaders are responsible. That unfortunately is not based on fact.''[60]

Morgenthau's solution to the problem of civilization was to demodernize what had been one of its central components. Eventually, and this would apply with even greater force to Japan, where race seemed to be an even more obtrusive barrier to integration than culture, a combination of long-term control and integrationism would be settled upon, but it was by no means clear at this time how that might be accomplished. It was evident that the German problem and the Soviet problem were interlinked and that postwar planning for Germany would affect the postwar relationship with the Soviet Union. A major argument in favor of a harsh policy toward Germany, which was favored by the public, was that it could act as a powerful cement of continuing allied unity. As an OSS paper, quoting Walter Lippmann's arguments, concluded: "If we can unite together in order to restrain Germany, we can unite Europe, and Europe will bind together the Russians and ourselves. If we cannot agree about Germany, then we shall engender a deep dispute as to whether the Russians or the British-Americans are to draw Germany into their orbit."[61]

Unfortunately, what seemed desirable for Germany, the USSR, and Europe conflicted with the desiderata of sound global policy. A Carthaginian approach based on a long-term occupation and deindustrialization would have severe economic disadvantages for the European and global economies and might conceivably generate the kind of radical unrest on the Continent, from both the left and the right, that had surfaced at the end of the First War. Moreover, the superficially attractive alternative of partition smacked of realpolitik and might seal the division of Europe into Soviet and Western spheres of influence. To what depth Roosevelt did his conceptual spadework on these alternatives and turned them over in his mind is unclear, though they were so obvious that they could not be ignored. Given the unpalatable nature of the options so starkly posed, there was no point in making an immediate choice, for if the future did not present any rosier alternatives, at least it seemed unlikely to pose any bleaker ones. In the case of planning for Germany, therefore, Roosevelt's much criticized procrastination on postwar issues was exceedingly well founded. Once he rescinded his approval of the Morgenthau Plan in the face of sensational press disclosures, FDR went no further for the very good reason that the alternatives were loaded with dynamite. He left the matter at the ill-defined level of "cooperation" with his allies.

In the Far East, racial and cultural differences also worked against a Wilsonian outcome. To keep both the Japanese and British happy, it had been necessary at Versailles to make egregious exceptions to Wilsonian universalism by allowing the diplomacy of imperialism to continue in China and by refusing to grant the declaration of racial equality demanded by the Japanese. But in World War II, China was deemed an important member of the coalition, if only because of the large number of Japanese troops it managed to keep tied down in its interior. Postwar considerations of political balance mattered, too. China's socioeconomic backwardness and chaotic internal politics disqualified it from great-power status by any realistic calculus, but Roosevelt believed that it would be "very useful twenty-five or fifty years hence, even though China cannot contribute much military or naval support for the moment."[62]

FDR's China policy was characterized by a lack of concern for Wilsonian democratic niceties. The president remained reluctant to associate himself with the zeal, common to many liberals of the day, for reforming the Kuomintang. For some Americans, the war provided a heaven-sent opportunity to transform China into the Far East's leading democracy, an ambition that had long underlain America's Open Door policy in the region. There were three basic options: reform; adding the Communist Chinese as members of the anti-Japanese coalition; and continuing to back the corrupt and inefficient regime of Chiang Kai-shek. It is telling that the two latter alternatives, both un-Wilsonian, were the ones most seriously considered by FDR. When it came to a choice between Chiang and General Joseph Stilwell, who wished to reform the corrupt practices of the Kuomintang in the hope of promoting military efficiency against Japan, Roosevelt unambiguously sided with the generalissimo. He had long ago stated his belief that it would take "many years and possibly several revolutions" to reform China because "the new China cannot be built up in a day." There were forces at work that were "almost incomprehensible to us westerners" and he did not believe that "any Western civilization's action can ever affect the people of China very deeply." Thus, FDR's approach to China was deeply tinctured by a belief in cultural differences and influenced by an awareness of regional power realities that Wilson would have preferred to sidestep.[63]

A final obstacle to a Wilsonian solution lay in the problem posed by Communist ideology. The fear of bolshevism that had played such a large role at Versailles receded in the 1920s following the formation of the firebreak *cordon sanitaire* in eastern Europe, giving way to the general expectation that the flames of communism would eventually burn themselves out. However, the unexpected emergence of the USSR as an indispensable member of the Grand Alliance and as a major postwar actor made impossible a similar quarantine approach. To the extent that he could do so, FDR tried to emphasize nonideological points of agreement with the USSR. From the time of recognition in 1933 to the see-no-evil attitude during the show trials and purges and the foresight exercised in making sure that the Soviets would be eligible for Lend-Lease assistance, the president tried to deal with the Soviets from a supraideological standpoint in the recognition that the Nazi threat superseded their ideological differences. From this standpoint, it was obvious, as he told Chiang, that "any attitude which would be harmful to our united effort in winning the war would be unwarranted."[64]

But it was impossible to confine the Soviet problem exclusively to considerations of power and interest. If interests converged, it was in the nature of things that they would in due course differ. Given the imperative of avoiding another war, therefore, some basis of mutual understanding other than power would be necessary. World War II was an ideological war to the extent that it was a conflict between universalist and nationalist "isms," but it required little foresight to realize that victory over the Axis posed dialectical possibilities of division down the road. Consequently, as their wartime contacts with the USSR demonstrated, many Americans displayed an overpowering need to believe that the Soviet regime was undergoing a spiritual metamorphosis. To some extent, undoubtedly, the image of Soviet-American friendship was simply an illusion fostered by wartime propaganda needs, the passing off of a *mariage de convenance* as true love, but even some of the most hard-bitten anti-Soviet diplomats in the State Department came to believe for a time during the war that communism was mellowing. To continue to argue, in light of this fact, that ideology was secondary, would be to insist on the necessity of self-delusion.

Realizing full well the importance of ideology to the postwar era, FDR attempted in a number of ways to minimize the possibility of a falling out with the Soviets. One approach was to argue that, apart from the immediate benefits of Soviet partnership, the long-term dangers of bolshevism were not nearly as menacing as the German threat because the German regime was bent on expansion through conquest while the Soviets were not. Russia had a dictatorship also, in its way every bit as brutal as the German if not more so, yet FDR believed that it was nonexpansionist and, as he noted in a letter to the pope, less dangerous to the freedom of worship on which he placed such great weight. FDR believed that a Soviet repulse of the German invasion would mean "the liberation of Europe from Nazi domination—and at the same time I do not think we need to worry about any possibility of Russian domination."[65] Bolshevism, while more brazenly universal a creed than fascism, was militarily more modest—a fundamental distinction.

As for the ideological differences themselves, he freely admitted that the USSR's cosmopolitan creed was quite unlike the liberal conception he carried inside his head. Their "idea of civilization and human happiness is so totally different from ours," he once remarked. But just as his pragmatism led him to overlook China's authoritarian lapses, too much emphasis on the USSR's obvious democratic shortcomings would also have been counterproductive. As he told John Foster Dulles, he had a fear lest "too much 'idealism' in these matters should lead to a rejection of collaboration as a permanent principle."[66]

But that, too, would be worked out at some point over the horizon. Recalling the comments of Soviet envoy Maxim Litvinoff, who had suggested in 1933 that the two nations had started out at the opposite poles of 0-100 and had converged to the point of 40-60, FDR wondered in 1942 whether "perhaps Litvinoff's thoughts of nine years ago are coming true." According to W. Averell Harriman, FDR believed that the Soviet command model would eventually decentralize, Communist revolutionary fervor would subside, the innate religious feeling of the Russian people would reassert itself, and, "above all, he believed that the intimacies the war had forced upon us could, and should, be used to establish the basis for postwar collaboration." Another hopeful sign was the banking of Soviet ideological fires during the war, symbolized by the shutting down of the Comintern.[67]

It would all work out happily in the end, thanks to what was then called "convergence." The belief in convergence was banal and innocent at the same time that it was a sociologically sophisticated long-term outlook. Convergence assumed a contracting, antientropic ideological universe in which the functional specialization and differentiation of modernity would produce mechanisms of control and a net decrease in disorder. As such, it was a logical outgrowth of the evolutionist paradigm of civilization, with its dual emphasis on the growth of integrative market forces and a corresponding international conscience. Obviously, a pure market approach was of little relevance in the face of the USSR's commitment to a command economy. Yet FDR's internationalism also contained a social welfare dimension, going so far as to envision a global New Deal which went beyond marketplace mores. With an attenuation of Communist ideology, this common vision of governmentally fostered global social justice might suffice to hold together what otherwise could only be a problematic and rocky relationship. If sufficiently plied with the lubricant of American reconstruction aid, Roosevelt thought the Soviets could be trusted to exercise self-restraint until convergence had taken place. But convergence, too, lay in the distant future. Given the reality of the ideological fissure, the only conceivable solution was to stick with the accidental coalition of ideological opposites that had been forged in the heat of the war, a course that many World War I Wilsonians would have viewed as anathema.[68]

In the absence of underlying social, cultural, and ideological harmony,

FDR's solution eventually came down to maintaining good relations among the leaders, personal connections that flowed not out of any natural affinities among the nations, but out of the determination to cooperate as a by-product of the lessons of the war. Historical memory and a common appreciation of new geopolitical realities, rather than historical utopianism, would be the cement of good relations. As Eleanor Roosevelt described it, the conversations between her husband and Stalin "indicated a certain amount of flexibility and encouraged my husband to believe that confidence could be built between the two leaders and that we might at least find a way to live in the world together, each country developing along the lines that seemed best for it." The idea that leaders, rather than peoples, should determine the path of relations was also quite un-Wilsonian, but it seemed the only possible course in a world in which international public opinion was a negligible factor.[69]

Oblivious to the kinds of obstacles that FDR had to face, a powerful current of neo-Wilsonian sentiment swelled within the country as the war progressed. For much of the American public and its political representatives, the war was both a fulfillment of the Wilsonian prophesy and the occasion for a belated, guilt-saturated revival of Wilson's thwarted vision. This element of guilt would be quite important during the cold war as the buttress for the belief that America was responsible for holding world opinion together. But for the moment, with his very different understanding of the world, FDR must have viewed such sentiment as something akin to the Indian ghost dance, a pathetic revivalism in the face of transformed realities. Instead of dampening the enthusiasm, however, he turned it to his advantage by promoting, with the help of the unreconstructed Wilsonian enthusiasm of the otherwise ignored Cordell Hull, the creation of a new United Nations Organization in which the concept of collective security was nowhere to be found. "One merit of such a program," Roosevelt mused, "is that it is totally different from the principles laid down in the Covenant of the League of Nations."[70]

FDR envisioned a regional "police power"—the United States and China would handle Asia, the British and the Russians would police Europe, Britain and Brazil would take Africa, and the United States would take the Western Hemisphere. The term "policemen" was artfully chosen to suggest the operations of friendly neighborhood cops rather than the image of soldiering, which suggested full-fledged war. Not only did this geographical division of labor correspond more closely to the nation's traditional interests, it was assumed that American participation would most likely be on the economic level. As FDR informed John Foster Dulles in 1944, "peace would be preserved by the joint force of the four great powers and . . . there would be economic sanctions as proposed by FDR's Chicago speech. Economic sanctions could be as effective as bombs and were more humane."[71]

Sanctions were not designed to be applied against any of the permanent members of the UNO's security council, however. The power to be exercised by these four quite different policemen was, as FDR informed George Norris, to be "superimposed" or "superassumed." "Superimposed" over what? The answer could only be: over a world without a collective conscience to guide it. Although his Good Neighbor policy was a model for global relationships, FDR realized that the hemispheric settlement, which itself took a long time to accomplish and was still shaky, "was easy in comparison with the task before us in Europe and the Far East." Wilson had preached the existence of a common conscience transcending cultural barriers, but FDR realized early on, in Hooverian fashion, that it would take time to disseminate "the ideals of peace among the very diverse nationalities and national egos of a vast number of separate peoples who, for one reason or another over a thousand years, have divided themselves into a hundred different forms of hate."[72]

The UN, by design and as a matter of political necessity, was far less ambitious than the League of Nations in the problems it was designed to resolve. The league, for all the covenant's haziness with respect to implementation, was at least intended to deal with great-power aggression, through embargo at a minimum and military sanctions at the extreme. Its automatic sanctions, as Wilson argued, were intended to prevent the outbreak of a war like World War I. Council members possessed a veto, to be sure, but they could not vote on the investigation of disputes to which they were party. The UN veto, by contrast, better known at the time as "the principle of unanimity," left no ambiguity whatsoever about the necessity of great-power cooperation if the system was to work. With the airtight veto and absence of automatic sanctions, actions by the security council could be invoked only against lesser powers.

At bottom, then, the UN scheme was actually post-Wilsonian,[73] not because it relied on the major powers, but because of its assumption that relations among those very same powers would be conflict-free. The kinds of dangers that Wilson envisioned, not being solvable by institutional means, were simply leapfrogged by taking for granted, with crossed fingers, the existence of a kind of world that even the league had not thought possible to create any time soon. The creators of the UN played the reel of history on fast-forward in the hope that nothing of significance would be skipped over. All this seems transparently clear in retrospect, but it is nevertheless astonishing to consider how wildly the enthusiastic internationalists and the far fewer geopoliticians in the United States misinterpreted the UN's meaning. The former would insist on the institution performing a job that, by design, it could not do; the latter berated it for ignoring "realities" of realpolitik, when it was precisely those realities that dictated the principle of unanimity in the first place. To put it yet another way, the solution to Wilson's war with war was simply to declare victory in the hope that the Second World War had sown the seeds for resolving the problem.

In contrast to Wilson's richly detailed image of the postwar world, the United States came out of World War II with a blank canvas. The failure of world opinion in the late 1930s had left Roosevelt to grapple with the geopolitical nightmare that Wilson had painted, the domino world that Wilson had seen forming and sought to avoid. FDR was quite certain of the dangers of the modern universalization of power first intuited by Wilson, so much so as to articulate its perils in greater detail than anyone else before or since, but he was unable to go much beyond a circular policy of "cooperation" that was both end and means. While Wilson had envisioned a structural danger that was complemented by a communitarian solution, by the end of the Roosevelt era the idealistic political side of the Wilsonian legacy that counted on the existence of human values rooted in a common civilizing process was so watered down as to make it unrecognizable. Ironically, then, although he did more than anyone else to dethrone isolationism and enshrine the Wilsonian strategic sensibility, FDR also presided over the failure of the Wilsonian dream.

The result of Roosevelt's effort to lay the foundations for a world order based on neither Wilsonian world public opinion nor an international balance of power was that no postwar program addressing the kinds of dangers that Wilson had first discerned and which the United States had just fought to ward off had been formulated. To his credit, Roosevelt had always been quite modest in this regard. For example, as early as 1939 he was confiding to William Allen White that he had no expectations of creating a millennial postwar peace, that at best he wanted to avoid "a patched up temporizing peace which would blow up in our faces in a year or two." In his depictions of the gravity of the world situation, FDR described himself as a "realist," and he continued to berate his isolationist opponents well into the war for their "failure to evaluate the world situation as it really was," but this realism—more accurately, halfway Wilsonianism—was of little help in formulating more than the most obvious and banal postwar plans that sidestepped the truly important issues.[74]

"Cooperation," however vague, was not dictated by FDR's ingrained tendency to temporize and to play things by ear; instead, it was the result of the absence of a score from which to play. With the world immersed in conflict, he found himself in terra incognita, in a kind of world for which Wilson had failed utterly to provide any kind of policy guidance, much as Marx had been of little practical help to the Bolsheviks. Whatever else one might say about Wilsonianism, it was a logically coherent ideological system in which the magnitude of the threat was matched by comprehensiveness of solution. If one retained Wilson's global definition of the threat, as FDR did, it was unclear what an alternative to Wilsonianism would look like without a cohesive international public opinion. Roosevelt was left only with the existence of sin without the certainty of redemption. All he could do was sign his name to the empty canvas in the hope that his reputation for artistic brilliance would stave off criticism of a work in progress.

Roosevelt had undergone a metamorphosis from "Dr. New Deal" to "Dr. Win-the-War," but there were no further transformations in the offing; had he lived, there was no "Dr. Postwar Order" waiting to take over at the war's conclusion. And it is too much to demand that there should have been another change of identity, for Roosevelt was only being faithful to his own standard of realism. This understandable absence of guideposts, itself the product of so much uncertainty, meant that some intermediate form of maintaining world order among the powers, one that bridged the gap between the failed Wilsonianism and the still embryonic United Nations order, would have to be created in the postwar years. Postwar statesmen would build on the strategic Wilsonian foundation that FDR had left them and erect a new structure based on a modified version of world opinion. That order would be called the cold war.

5

WILSONIAN PROBLEMS:
GEORGE F. KENNAN AND THE
DEFINITION OF THE COLD WAR

VIEWED FROM THE STANDPOINT of power politics, the story of World War II and the cold war was a quite conventional and unsurprising tale of a political marriage of convenience whose inevitable collapse was hastened, but not fundamentally caused, by ideological incompatibility. But from the modernist historical frame, in which power was appraised on the basis of its civilizational content, the story line looked rather different. From that vantage point, World War II had been fought to decide whether the world would be functionally whole or segmented into regional empires. Its dialectical successor, the cold war, was a contest between competing forms of internationalism to decide which brand of modernization would hold sway.[1] Besides being the cause of the breakup, ideology was also in large measure responsible for defining the form of the relationship after the break. Following a period of relative optimism, the emergence of the settled conviction that Soviet ideology was inherently malignant triggered a revitalization of strategic Wilsonianism and its grim understanding of the modern world's precarious strategic underpinnings. And that understanding in turn fixed the conceptual boundaries within which U.S. cold-war policy would henceforth operate.

The cold war did not begin with FDR's death. Instead of lurching clumsily and completely from starry-eyed wartime hopes to the opposite extreme of Wilsonian pessimism, policymakers first gave a serious hearing to FDR's case for cooperation with the Kremlin. Of course, there was no direct encounter as such with Roosevelt's ideas about postwar cooperation, since not many people knew what they were and, in any event, his rough sketch had never been translated into a policy blueprint. As it happened, the detailed case for cooperation implicit in FDR's thinking came from a quite surprising source. Roosevelt's basic ideas were architecturally redrafted by George Frost Kennan, a professed realist whose explanation of the connections between ideol- *133* ogy and power furnished the only real alternative to Wilsonian strategic pessimism. The widespread popularity of Kennan's initial conception of the cold war was attributable neither to any sudden mass conversion to the precepts of power politics or to the outbreak of a rabid anti-Sovietism; rather, his ideas made sense at the time because they explained the failure to fulfill euphoric hopes for the United Nations in explicit terms that gave policy substance to the vague emphasis on cooperation transmitted by FDR.

But Kennan's conception of containment, which prescribed a much less confrontational and ambitious foreign policy than the one eventually settled upon, was not destined to last. His definition of ideology and its old-fashioned privileging of power were ultimately too conservative to explain the radical discontinuities between postwar problems and traditional diplomatic concerns. As official Washington came to the conviction that Soviet ideology was more menacing than Kennan had made it appear, thinking within the foreign-policy establishment gravitated to the dark side of Wilsonianism, causing Kennan's star to decline nearly as fast as it had ascended. Once Kennan's moderate interpretation of Soviet intentions was rejected, the Wilsonian strategic sensibility and its accompanying sense of civilizational peril reemerged in full force as the axiomatic core of America's cold-war policy.

FDR AND KENNAN: FROM COOPERATION TO CONTAINMENT

The man heading the ship of state in the postwar period was Harry S. Truman, an old-fashioned Wilsonian from Missouri who, as FDR's last vice president, had been kept pretty much in the dark about FDR's postwar plans. However, his lack of intimacy with FDR did not prevent him from sharing Roosevelt's sensibility toward the Russians or his optimism about postwar cooperation. "To have a reasonably lasting peace the three powers must be able to trust each other and they must themselves honestly want it," he wrote in his diary in May 1945, thereby defining the core of FDR's policy as well as anyone ever has. Like FDR, Truman recoiled at the thought of a peace based on realpolitik, arguing that "with nations, as with people, if you give good will and fair dealing, you stand a better chance to get the same in return. Suspicion of others begets suspicion." To define enemies a priori, to begin with the assumption of conflicting purposes, to assume that international society was at bottom anarchic, all that would be self-defeating. Cooperation was for Truman, as it was for FDR, the *will* to cooperate, the basing of foreign policy on a hard-rock substratum of good intentions rather than on the quicksand of "power realities." Indeed, this determination to get along with the Russians sounded suspiciously similar to what only three years later he would be criticizing as ''the insidious propaganda that peace can be obtained simply by wanting peace.''[2]

An optimistic strain of internationalism was evident in Truman's attribution of Soviet-American differences to linguistic misunderstandings, essentially problems of translation, rather than to unbridgeable differences of worldview. At a press conference late in 1945, he insisted that ''the difficulty, I think is a matter of understanding between us and Russia . . . principally because we don't speak the same language.'' However, in the language that counted, the tongue of diplomatic bargaining, the Soviets had thus far seemed reasonable enough. The point was made in an early meeting with Soviet Foreign Minister Vyacheslav Molotov, who suggested to the new president that ''the three governments had been able to find a common language and that on this basis they had been settling their differences.'' Despite a rough beginning in which Truman's abrasive style contrasted unfavorably with FDR's silkier diplomatic touch, he was still reasonably confident in June 1945 of a harmonious relationship: ''I'm not afraid of Russia. They've always been our friends and I can't see any reason why they shouldn't always be.''[3]

Unfortunately, the developing postwar relationship did not meet the rosy expectations of wartime collective security enthusiasts. As numerous disagreements emerged in rapid succession, though not to the point of a major crisis, the failure of the best of all possible worlds to appear led many to fear for the worst. But while it was quite clear that something was seriously amiss, the rapid decompression and confusion of the immediate postwar period made it difficult to assess the meaning for the long-term diplomatic climate of this sudden outbreak of heavy weather in the relationship. ''The most noticeable thing here at home,'' noted the new army chief of staff, General Dwight D. Eisenhower, ''is the great confusion that seems to prevail in all circles, high and low, both in governmental and in private life.'' Those who suspected that the Soviets would prove to be unfaithful partners could do no better than to suggest the adoption of a quid pro quo approach in the hope of making the Soviets more tractable, but even that kind of thinking, far from being a hard line, differed little from the kind of horse-trading that had seen the alliance through the war.[4]

Only in 1946 did American policymakers come to grips intellectually with the Soviet problem. This was the year which saw alarming developments in the Soviet refusal to evacuate their troops from northern Iran at the appointed time, Winston Churchill's ''Iron Curtain'' speech complaining of the tightening Soviet grip in eastern Europe, diverging approaches to the occupation of Korea, a speech by Stalin that asserted the incompatibility of communism and capitalism and left many observers to draw the inference that the differences would be settled by war, and the failure to implement the Potsdam accords by creating centralized German agencies or a workable arrangement on reparations. These and other ominous problems, though insufficiently clear-cut as a guide to Soviet intentions, suggested that wartime optimism had been overinflated.

At the time, intentions, far more than capabilities, seemed the key variable in predicting the course of relations between the two countries. What were the Soviets up to? What were their motives? As an early postwar analysis of the USSR suggested, the basic problem was "not the objective one of the comparative capabilities of the USSR and any other country or countries, but the subjective conception of the Soviet leaders respecting the relations of the Soviet state with non-Soviet states." Policymakers therefore took special note of Stalin's election speech of February 1946, which brought out of storage the Leninist thesis that capitalist contradictions would inevitably generate conflicts that would embroil the USSR in war. Though an intelligence review highlighted the speech's "stated emphasis on defense rather than aggression," the future nevertheless began to look much more grim in its aftermath. The details of how the two sides would come to blows seemed less important than the positing of unbreachable ideological barriers and the inevitability of conflict, all of which gave the future a self-fulfillingly tragic cast as a matter of ideological design. The cataclysmic implications of a failure to cooperate were obvious to all. As an example, the diplomatic thunderclaps that rolled through the conference creating the UN in San Francisco caused Jan Masaryk, a frustrated Czech delegate, to plead for everyone to "please stop talking of the next world war."[5]

It is difficult to overstate American ignorance of Soviet motives at this time. Not only were Americans hazy about the specifics of Soviet Marxist beliefs, they were even less clear in their understanding of what ideology was and how much importance to attribute to it. In their thinking about ideology, Americans were much less concerned with the content of Soviet Marxism than with the degree to which it was removed from reality. Ideology seemed to be a secular religion, tantamount to fanaticism, that inevitably brought to mind the bloody and intolerant religious wars of the past. As a Pentagon planning group would later argue, peace, which could come only "through the medium of world-wide good will," was unlikely "because the major governments of the world are sharply divided in ideologies and ultimate aims." The belief that cooperation could not survive ideological hostility explains what otherwise seems the hysterical characterization of Stalin's speech by Justice William O. Douglas as a "declaration of World War III."[6]

Through the spring of 1946, intelligence reviews emphasized the dangerous consequences of Moscow's return to zealotry. "Since the end of the war the general tenor of Soviet official statements has indicated at least a partial return to a traditional Marxist thinking about foreign political affairs," said one such document. Another pointed out that the strong Marxist flavor of Soviet foreign policy, which meant that it was "founded upon suspicion," automatically precluded the kind of day-to-day practical cooperation Americans had in mind. Among those worried about Soviet motives, Secretary of the Navy James T. Forrestal cut to the core of American concerns about the Soviet return to ideology. For him, "the fundamental question" in dealing with the USSR was "whether we are dealing with a nation or a religion." Forrestal's question was important because, as one military pamphlet put it, "if the tenets of Marxism and Leninism continue to be the lodestar of Soviet foreign policy, the successful development of such a military instrument [the Red Army] will provide military means for supporting the spread of socialism abroad." By the mid-1940s, bolshevism, sponsored by a temporarily exhausted but still powerful state capable of fortifying its ideological appeal with the radiance of its power, possessed all the building blocks of an ideological success story in the making. Whereas it had once been possible to view bolshevism as an accidental outgrowth of the First War that could safely be ignored once stability had been restored in Europe, its geopolitical significance was past due for reassessment.[7]

An early study commissioned by Forrestal drew the most extreme conclusions from this ideological revival. According to its author, Edward Willett, "Only a cursory reading of Communist sources is needed to convince one that utter destruction of the present capitalistic system is a basic aim of communism." In a bone-chilling declaration that one day would become a working hypothesis for Washington defense strategists, he asserted that "if a true Communist could destroy the United States by pushing a button, he would do so." Although Willett noted Stalin's strong sense of realpolitik and took some comfort in the probability that the ideology was likely to wane in the future, his analysis was unsatisfying in the extreme because it failed to relate principle to practice.

Willett's paper, based solely on the study of Marxist principles, presented no convincing portrayal of the relation between ideology and the interests of the Soviet state, the needs of the Communist party, or the real world of political action. As even Willett admitted, it was "highly improbable that the United States and Russia would ever come to blows over an abstract principle." The best he could do was to put the issue in unsatisfying either/ or form: "We have to deal on the one hand with the seeming certainty of war if Marxian Communism prevails, and on the other hand with the *possibility* of avoiding war if Communism does not prevail." But this was simply to restate Forrestal's question in more sophisticated terms without providing an answer.

The anticapitalist values were clear, but how solidly rooted were they? How were the norms of Soviet behavior related to ideology?

Given the intellectual vacuum, there was a crying need for creative thought in the postwar years that Truman was not equipped, intellectually or temperamentally, to fill, but he was intelligent enough at least to realize his shortcomings. His scoffing response to suggestions that he would be considered a great president was, "You've got to have brains to be a great man." Thus Truman excused himself from playing any role in defining the problem, although as we shall see, the analyses that came out of his bureaucracies fitted nicely the basic worldview which he brought to the presidency. Apart from his Wilsonian predilections, he had no agenda to impose and as a rule went along with the consensus formed by the foreign-policy elite, in most cases allowing all but the most crucial thumbs-up, thumbs-down decisions to be fought out and implemented by his gladiators in the bureaucratic arena. As Clark Clifford later recalled, Truman "*never* got involved in the complexities of the period."[8]

It is within this context of intellectual floundering about and fear of Soviet ideological hostility that George Kennan made his contribution to American statesmanship. Kennan received Russian language training in Berlin in the 1920s and, along the way, absorbed a view of international politics as realpolitik that was based on idealistic-romantic German conceptions of culture and nationality as the irreducible foundations of the nation-state system of international relations. His views were so permeated with this European outlook that even his later neo-isolationism would originate from a Europeanist's shudder at the thought of a bumptious America throwing its weight around rather than in the exceptionalism in which isolationism was usually grounded. His intellectual monkishness also made him a loner within the clubby Foreign Service. Only later would his estrangement from the foreign-policy tradition become evident as he elaborated some of the specifics of containment and found himself increasingly in disagreement with his colleagues. For someone so alienated from the American foreign-policy culture, Kennan was an altogether unlikely candidate for the job of defining the fundamentals of U.S. foreign policy, but he was ideally equipped to interpret Soviet policy to his superiors—which he proceeded to do.[9]

For a time, Kennan was all the rage in Washington. His "long telegram" of February 1946 has been justly hailed as a crucial document for its role in recasting the image of the USSR within the American official mind. His explanation, offered with a literary flair and intellectual force rarely found in State Department documents, enjoyed a remarkable *succès d'estime* because it deflated, with some well-aimed intellectual pinpricks, the balloon of pro-Soviet feeling that had been swollen by wartime euphoria. Its importance lay less in its policy recommendations—which were impossibly vague—than in its elucidation of the relation between nationalism, ideology, and culture in a way that assuaged official Washington's worst fears and reassured it that the Soviet problem was quite manageable. To put it somewhat provocatively, Kennan's "long telegram" and "X" article of the following year articulated in a new and intellectually more rigorous way the approach to cooperation that FDR had never felt able to voice publicly.[10]

As someone who was quite appalled by the "romantic and universalistic concepts with which we emerged from the recent war," Kennan would doubtless have objected strenuously to any suggestion that he was following in FDR's footsteps. But he, like most everyone else, had been taken in by surface appearances. His highly critical view of Roosevelt was based on the mistaken assumption that FDR's support for the UN originated in Wilsonian naivete and that FDR's vision of cooperation with the Russians anticipated having an easy time of it after the war. But, as we have seen, FDR's views, with the exception of his hopes for close personal ties among leaders, were far from being shallow. His view of cooperation assumed the existence of a common language of power upon which satisfactory peaceful relationships could be based pending the convergence of ideological trajectories over the long term.[11]

As it turned out, Kennan would reassure Americans on both scores, confirming with tight reasoning and without glossing over any difficulties the basic assumptions of Rooseveltian diplomacy in a way that FDR never could have done. It was through Kennan that FDR's views on cooperation entered the mainstream of American foreign-policy discourse. Like his fellow Russian expert and friend, Charles Bohlen, Kennan realized that "for the United States, the ideological element of Soviet policy was of vital importance." Knowing full well that Americans were operating from a near-bottomless ignorance in their understanding of communism in the Soviet Union, he understood that "most people, when they go off on this subject, go off the beam on the question of the fundamentals of Russian-American relations, on the question of how the people in Moscow think, what makes them tick, what their psychology is."[12]

Kennan's first major contribution to American diplomacy came in his analysis of Soviet ideology and its relation to foreign policy. There are, at bottom, three faces of ideology, one of them cultural and historical and the other two sociological, that emphasize, respectively, its connections to past, present, and future. It is possible to see ideology as a belief system whose makeup is a function of deep roots in the historical soil from which it sprouts, as a conservative phenomenon that reflects and rationalizes existing institutions and values, or as a radical belief system driven by a utopian imagination totally hostile to a wicked status quo. Every successful ideology incorporates, although in varying degrees, each of these three dimensions. Kennan would play up all three at one time or another in making his case for the tractability of the Soviet problem and his insistence that it could be managed short of war. While the elements of Kennan's hybrid view of ideology were not wholly consistent with one another, his package was nevertheless far more sophisticated than other explanations then making the rounds.

In 1946, Kennan was almost wholly preoccupied in answering the diagnostic question put by Forrestal; his prescriptions for containment at this time as sketched in the long telegram and his subsequent essay as "X" in *Foreign Affairs* ("The Sources of Soviet Conduct") constituted little more than a suggestive afterthought. His analysis of what he termed the Kremlin's "neurotic view of world affairs" began with his understanding of Russian national character, or what we today would call culture, and its implications for Russia's external relations. For Kennan, the Soviet belief in a menacing external world was wholly subjective, an a priori outlook that had "little to do with conditions outside Russia." The Soviet mind did not objectively mirror the world so much as project a distorted image upon it. If the Soviet Union's objective situation and the calculations of power and interest inferrible from that situation were poor guides to understanding its policies, neither would a close reading of Marxist-Leninist dialectics reveal much of use— indeed, Kennan displayed remarkably little interest in the specifics of the Communist creed.[13]

One inescapable explanation for the hostility to the outside world displayed by the Communists was the enduring gravitational pull of Russian cultural tradition. This aspect of Kennan's view of ideology rejected the traditional, Marxist-derived view of ideology as a "reflex" of material interests. Here Kennan was anticipating the philosopher Paul Ricoeur, who argued that the notion of an ideological "reflex," which had to take a symbolic form if it were to be expressed at all, made little sense unless one assumed the prior existence of some symbolic medium. In this case, the symbolic medium to which Marxism was mated was Great Russian cultural tradition, pretty much in the same sense that liberal ideology was historically identified with the American way of life.[14]

To understand the operation of Marxism in Russia, Kennan, who was gifted with a penetrating historical sensibility, believed it was first necessary to see it as part of a larger pattern of historical continuity. Marxist dogma was "a perfect vehicle for [the] sense of insecurity with which Bolsheviks, even more than previous Russian rulers, were afflicted." The letter of Marxism was one thing, but the underlying spirit of Soviet ideology, derived from the nation's traditions, induced the Soviets to behave much as Russians had always behaved. While the present-day feeling of threat was surely neurotic, it had not been so in the past, when the country "had never known a friendly neighbor or indeed any tolerant equilibrium of separate powers, either internal or international." Traditional patterns endured because Russian modernization had been so forced and uneven. As Kennan later described the historical burden of Russia: "Due to the fatal lapses in its speed of development, it had to jump over too many phases to be a wholly balanced and healthy state." Soviet policy was thus but part of "the steady advance of uneasy Russian nationalism, a centuries old movement in which conceptions of offense and defense are inextricably confused." Further embroidering this theme, he told one public audience back home, "We are dealing here not with individual whims but with deep-seated habits of thought and with national characteristics anchored in the experience of centuries." History, with its high coefficient of drag, made communism far less aerodynamic than it appeared to the naked eye.[15]

Kennan did not emphasize the past to the exclusion of the present. The second spur of his analysis had a sociological point of departure, proceeding from what we today would call an "interest theory" of ideology which has some close affinities with the Marxist view. Ideology functioned as "a sort of mental eye or prism through which the Soviet Communists received their impression of what transpires in the outside world" and it dictated "the form in which all discussions of the Kremlin must be presented," but it was hardly the determining factor in shaping Soviet attitudes. "Marxist doctrine [did] not provide the mainspring of Soviet action," Kennan insisted. "That mainspring is something deeper." In a famous phrase, he described Marxism as simply the "fig leaf of their moral and intellectual respectability," underneath which lay the institutional source of shame: "the internal circumstances of Soviet power." Soviet hostility was founded therefore "not in the realities of foreign antagonism but in the necessity of explaining away the maintenance of dictatorial authority at home." The role of ideology was thus reduced in Kennan's formulation to a veil worn by the regime that functioned effectively to conceal the sociology of power from inquisitive outsiders.[16]

Putting the matter in terms quite congenial to interest theorists of American politics, he claimed that "these groups have come to constitute a great vested interest, an interest vested in the basic precariousness of Russia's international position." Driven by a functional-structural need to demonize the outside world, ideology was what one scholar has called a "socially necessary illusion." The Soviet leaders were but "the last of that succession of cruel and wasteful Russian rulers who have relentlessly forced [the] country on to ever new heights of military power in order to guarantee external security of their internally weak regimes." Adroitly turning the Marxist view of ideology against itself, Kennan suggested that, far from being motivated by any regard for the objective truth of history, it was the infrastructural base of power interests that supported the superstructure of ideological beliefs. In the interplay between ideas and action, ideology was, in the final analysis, "a product and not a determinant of social and political reality."[17]

The implications of this pattern of explanation were extraordinarily important. Yes, Kennan was saying, the Soviets were indeed ideologues, but he pushed the analysis a bit further. Because ideology was rooted in historical tradition and institutional structures that justified the continued existence in power of specific interest groups and their policies, Kennan saw it as an inherently conservative phenomenon, whose raison d'être was to justify the status quo. Therefore, to describe the Soviets as ideologues was not to leap to the conclusion that they were wild radicals. Kennan's interpretation of ideology contrasted with what Karl Mannheim called a "utopian" mentality, a messianic outlook which, without any anchorage in tradition or the prudential habits of self-preservation fostered by the ongoing exercise of power, would indeed have been supremely dangerous for the United States. The far more dangerous alternative would have been to face a group of ideologues without any anchorage whatever in past or present, a group of fanatics who had hijacked the apparatus of the Soviet state with utter unconcern for its needs and traditions or for their own survival. Martyrdom had its place in religious creeds, perhaps, but it was not part of communism's allure, whose kingdom was of this world.

By explaining ideology in terms of its fit with the czarist past and its role in legitimizing the totalitarian Soviet power structure, Kennan was minimizing its importance as a factor in Soviet foreign policy. In the larger scheme of things, it was epiphenomenal, a means to the end of preserving the power of the Soviet leadership. However, to downgrade ideology in this sense was not to say that it was specious or inconsequential. Precisely because the Soviet belief system had been grafted onto institutional patterns that had deep cultural-historical roots, it was capable of vigorous growth. Kennan did not believe, as some subsequent commentators have suggested, that the problem facing American foreign policy would have been substantially the same had Russia been governed by a non-Communist but intensely nationalist regime. In fact, he warned against "the pitfall of identifying Soviet foreign policy with Russian national tradition" and warned that this was "no normal clash of national interest."[18]

Kennan tried to leave room in his analysis for the operation of the third face of ideology, but he was never able to draw from it a perspective that harmonized with the first two images. Although the distinctiveness of Leninism certainly lay in its attentiveness to the importance of political power, it seemed somehow too reductionist to portray the Communist hierarchy as a gnostic sect committed secretly to realpolitik. "It may be argued that the Soviet leaders are power-conscious realists whose pretensions to ideology are only a cynical sham," he said on one occasion. "I could not go along with this," he concluded, saying that "it would be a great mistake to underrate the importance of ideology in the official Soviet psychology." He contended that "it would be wrong to think that the Soviet leaders dish out this stuff for the rank and file of the Communists, and do not believe it themselves. The party line is for *everyone* in Russia." In an early draft of the "X" article that would spread his influence to the broader public, he stated that his experience in Russia had convinced him that "the foreign policy of the Soviet leaders is deeply anchored in communist philosophy and doctrine." Because of that, "no one should underrate importance of dogma in Soviet affairs."[19]

At this point, the argument became quite foggy, and Kennan knew it. When it came to assessing the relation between the conservative, interest-centered frontal view of ideology and its utopian profile, Kennan readily acknowledged that there were "few tasks of psychological analysis more difficult than that of tracing the interaction of these two forces." He admitted that "this was a question to which there was no one clear answer," and "looking backwards, he found that in conversations on different occasions he had himself given a diversity of answers to it." Indeed, the record shows frequent contradictions and inconsistencies as he slalomed between the widely spaced poles of his various arguments. On one occasion he went so far as to assert that Soviet leaders "are essentially fanatics. They have been committed from youth, without exception, to a set of ideas which purports to have all the answers to human problems . . . It is one of the characteristics of this faith, as of all militant faiths, that its believers do not question it . . . as fanatics they are not amenable to reasonable argument." On another occasion, he pivoted sharply toward the tradition side of the argument and played up its conservative implications by insisting that "pure Marxism is dead" and that the Soviet leaders were "the heirs to Tsardom" who had "come to think of international relations only in terms of power competition."[20]

On balance, though, the radical explanation clearly took third place. While the Soviet Union may have been "neurotic" and its view of the world internally generated, the basics of Soviet policy were in essence no different than the historically and institutionally grounded policies of all nation states (which he would from time to time criticize with equal vigor as being founded not on external realities but internally generated delusions). Indeed, cultural peculiarities were the basis of the modern nation-state system. It was precisely because nations did not speak the same language that power-based diplomacy had become the lingua franca of international relations. Since cultural differences had always been mediated by power politics, and since the Soviet leadership's basic concern was the survival of their regime, he believed that, given the facts of contemporary international life, the two nations could successfully communicate at that level.

Kennan's emphasis on power was optimistic because of his assurance— the central point of his analysis—that ultimately the Soviets would recognize contemporary power realities for what they were and, consequently, their foreign policy would have a reasonable sense of limits. The United States and the Soviet Union *could* speak a common language which, though not the ecstatic glossolalia envisioned by internationalists, happened to be the only language that existed among nations. Whatever the declaratory goals of Communist dogma, their intentions could be modified by power and relations successfully managed by traditional diplomacy. All things considered, then, the Communist challenge was a dangerous new wrinkle on an ancient theme, but one that was definitely capable of being ironed out.[21]

Kennan told American policymakers what they wanted to hear by answering in the affirmative the question as to whether the United States could continue to get along with the Soviets. In Rooseveltian terms, the Soviets could be induced to cooperate, though obviously in a far less amiable way than FDR, with his faith in personal relationships, had envisioned. But Kennan's more valuable and enduring contribution to American foreign policy came not from the diagnosis, but from his prescription for coping with the problem until it disappeared: containment. In time, there would be a good deal of disagreement over the precise meaning of containment and its practical application, which Kennan first defined in his "X" article as "the adroit and vigilant application of counterforce at a series of constantly shifting geographical and political points." But the disagreements would only surface later, as the United States was faced with a choice between major foreign-policy alternatives. The important feature of containment at this time was not the statement of method, which was poorly and misleadingly specified by Kennan in any case, but the end it envisioned. There was little debate or controversy on this point, which would become a cardinal assumption of American policy.[22]

Containment postulated two phases, the short term and the longer-term future. The burden of the initial phase was to avoid war with the current leadership of the USSR. Although difficulties were bound to arise, Kennan believed that "if situations are properly handled, there need be no prestige-engaging showdowns." If the tactics of containment were adroitly handled, the long-term strategy would take care of itself. If the methods of containment were applied "for a period of time long enough to encompass a respectable portion of the organic process of growth and change in Soviet political life, then they might have a permanent modifying effect on the outlook and habits of Soviet power.'' Following a steady policy of containment, ''a day must come when the realization will dawn in Moscow that a diplomacy aimed at a shattering of power in other states cannot be successful, and I think on the heels of that realization will come the understanding that in this international society of which we form a part today the prosperity of one country is really the prosperity of all.'' The payoff for containment, Kennan believed, would come ''within a reasonable time,'' within five to fifteen years according to various of his estimates, but these forecasts were not to be taken too seriously. The crucial point was that there was ''no time limit for the achievement of our objective under conditions of peace.''[23]

Kennan was arguing that time and history were on the side of the West. The waning of revolutionary fervor was sure to come because the exercise of power and the refractory nature of reality and politics would inevitably produce contradictions that could not be reconciled with the ideology. In time, something would have to give, and inevitably it would be the ideology. If the United States could only hold the line, Kennan anticipated ''the same gradual mellowing of the regime that has come after all revolutions,'' as conservative impulses reasserted themselves. Eventually, an ideological hollowing out would take place until ultimately the emptiness of the regime's belief system became apparent to the Soviet people, thus sapping its legitimacy. Indeed, Kennan believed that already ''the Soviet Government has largely lost the soul of its people.'' It might take a while, then, but Thermidor would come. In an unsent letter to Walter Lippmann, he concluded that ''the Russians will defeat themselves . . . I am willing to let time be the judge.''[24]

This view of the future, which cast the issue in world-historical terms, was not very far removed from the wartime doctrine of convergence. Containment was based on a historical act of faith, albeit a conservative one. As one who viewed change as inevitable yet distrusted progress as painful and disillusioning, Kennan banked on the waning of utopian revolutionary expectations that was the inevitable fate of all millennarian social movements that took power and expected to keep it. As a holding action until convergence took effect, containment would solve the long-term problem as well, though in the conservative anti–New Deal climate of the postwar period the process of ideological transformation was more of a one-way street. A balance of power would thus buy time for the inevitable breakthrough in the ''balance of ideas.''[25]

With the acceptance of the idea of containment, American policy rested on a cornerstone of historical interpretation which, all too often taken for granted, was actually quite remarkable. The belief that history would be the ultimate judge of the cold war seems less a radical leap of faith if it is recognized as simply another way of reformulating the civilizational creed that had long animated American foreign policy. In the long view, it was but a reaffirmation of an abiding conviction that time was on America's side. Had the USSR been thought incapable of modernizing in a democratic direction; had it been believed that communism was riding a swelling tide of history; had there existed ideological self-doubts or presentiments of decay within the United States—at best the country could have looked forward to a cynical future of endless power balancing that was not only different from but worse than traditional realpolitik. Even assuming that that kind of diplomacy could have successfully avoided a war, the cold war would have taken on permanency and, in a serious sense, would have become ideologically pointless. Thus, while Kennan minimized the allure of the future in Soviet thinking, an auspicious view of futurity was indispensable to America's ability to make containment work.

As Kennan realized, the whole point of the policy was that the taming of the Kremlin could "be logically pursued not only in the event of a war but also in time of peace and by peaceful means." This was an understated way of putting the matter. For other Americans, the expectations of eventually restoring freedom to the Soviet bloc and bringing democracy to the Soviet Union were actually "utopian objectives," which, as James B. Conant explained, were "in reality the cold-war objectives in time of peace and the war slogans in time of war." For all of Kennan's emphasis on traditional realism, then, the historical dimension of containment constituted nothing less than a reversal of the formula of foreign policy stated by philosopher of war Karl von Clausewitz: the cold war would be a continuation of war by other means. The success of containment, Kennan believed, would not bring the promised Wilsonian millennium, because the world was "not advancing toward peace and enlightenment and prosperity, certainly not advancing very fast." International society, he believed, was "still an arena of deadly contest and rivalry." But for others, containment seemed an alternate route to the achievement of Wilson's utopia while avoiding yet another war, one that was quite consistent with the long Wilsonian tradition of ostracizing aggressors through quarantines and embargoes in the belief that enforced isolation would eventually bring them to their senses.[26]

Although his ideological diagnosis was often restated in a reductionist form that he would have found unacceptable, Kennan's conservative gloss on Soviet ideology was, for a time, all the rage. In the president's case, Kennan was simply restating what he already believed. Truman believed that Marxism of the Russian variety "isn't communism at all but just police government pure and simple." "There's no socialism in Russia," Truman wrote in his diary on 7 June 1945. He told his daughter following a visit by

Molotov that "really there is no difference between the government which Mr. Molotov represents and the one the Czar represented—or the one Hitler spoke for." Around the time of the Truman Doctrine, he wrote his daughter: "I knew at Potsdam that there is no difference in totalitarian states, call them what you will." In the same vein, he wrote again in 1948 that "a totalitarian state is no different whether you call it Nazi, Fascist, Communist or Franco Spain . . . The oligarchy in Russia is no different from the Czars, Louis XIV, Napoleon, Charles I and Cromwell. It is a Frankenstein dictatorship worse than any of the others, Hitler included."[27]

Many others within the administration also pretended to see through the ideological makeup to the grubby interest-group realities of Soviet political life. Ambassador Walter Bedell Smith in Moscow echoed Kennan's views when he asserted that Soviet policy was "grounded in Czarist history and reinforced by Communist conviction." As Clark Clifford later recalled, "What the Soviet Union was engaged in bore no resemblance to what Karl Marx envisioned as communism." Secretary of State Marshall, professing to be puzzled by Soviet misbehavior, found "at least a partial explanation in the historical characteristics of the Russian Government and its officials through a long period of years and not solely related to the present regime." Under Secretary Dean Acheson held the same view—one of the few to be fairly consistent on this issue over time—to the point of appropriating Kennan's fig-leaf metaphor to describe Soviet ideology. "Without communist ideology Stalin is no different from Peter the Great or Ivan the Terrible," said Acheson. "This communist ideology, even to those who do not believe it, furnishes not only the allies which it has abroad but the essential element of respectability. The Russians cannot drop it." "The center of all Russian thinking is the security of the regime," he maintained.[28]

Kennan's analysis allowed others to work their way through Soviet ideology and to focus on the problem of power. Had the Soviet problem been viewed as simply a matter of ideological antagonism, it could have been treated much as it had been in the 1920s, but it was not communism per se but its use as a tool for the extension of Soviet power that worried American policymakers, as they indicated time and again. American representatives strived in vain to convince the Soviets of this. Ambassador Walter Bedell Smith explained to Stalin in 1946 that the United States "did not oppose Communism because of its Marxian ideology but purely and simply because we had seen repeated instances of Communist minorities coming into power by illegal means and against the will of the majority of the population . . . The US remained convinced that these minority coups d'etat would have been quite impossible without the moral and physical support of the USSR." This meant, as Dean Acheson said in 1947, that the battle was "not one between Communism and something else. That is purely secondary.'' Acheson always argued that preventing the spread of communism was ''a highly inadequate expression of the American attitude.'' Communism was important, to be sure, ''but only as a consequence of a deeper interest.'' It was its exploitation as ''the instrument, and a most insidious and effective instrument, of aggression and foreign domination'' that concerned him and members of the administration. The initial American reductionist view was put in its baldest form by an assistant secretary of state who told Eleanor Roosevelt in an interview that ''the Russians think and act only in terms of strict realism and that we were trying to deal with them on those terms.''[29]

Most everyone connected with the first Truman administration believed that at some point the ideological blaze would burn itself out. Willett, for example, predicted that ''the passage of time might easily mean a movement of Soviet Russia away from Communism and in the direction of Capitalist democracy.'' A 1948 House report, ''The Strategy and Tactics of World Communism,'' even though it assumed Russian national interests to be ''subordinate to the objective of world revolution'' and asserted that Soviet foreign policy ''begins with the assumption of inevitable war,'' nevertheless concluded that communism had been ''degenerating from a great theory of history, and a great dream of human betterment, into a technique for power.'' It noted that ''the strains of experience that contradict the faith have grown and are continuing to grow'' and that ''these weaknesses will be felt over the long pull.'' The power structure was described by others as ''fragile,'' contrary to human nature and the fundamental desires of the Russian people, and the like. Indeed, the very fragility and brittleness of the Soviet power structure made it all the more dangerous. Part of Soviet aggressiveness was, according to the CIA, designed ''to hold together a cracking economic and ideological structure by building up an atmosphere of international crisis.'' Kennan himself thought the Soviets would be most dangerous and would require exceptionally skillful handling at the point at which their empire began to crumble beneath them.[30]

The overwhelmingly favorable reception given to Kennan's ideas was quite deceptive, however, since it played only to a passing mood in Washington. In the space of a few years, the policy elite would shift its support to the more radical estimate of ideology, thereby displacing FDR's and Kennan's relatively moderate views on cooperation and bringing into play the far more sinister Wilsonian strategic image of the postwar world. Kennan's original evaluation of Soviet intentions was made early in 1946, in an atmosphere of disappointment over the failure of utopian expectations to be met, but still at a time before any serious great-power confrontations had occurred. By the second Truman administration, however, as fears of domestic subversion mounted, as the shock of the Soviet A-bomb explosion set in late in 1949, and as the Communists presented numerous challenges and scored major successes abroad, the importance of ideology was revalued upward. By that time, ideology was viewed, more accurately, as an aggressive, self-confident phenomenon which by its very nature could not be skeptical or cautious and which had to risk the deployment of political power in pursuit of its objectives.[31]

By 1949, with the Soviet regime more firmly entrenched in power than ever and seemingly all the bolder for it, the perception was beginning to take hold that the Kremlin's ambitions and its willingness to risk war were greater than originally thought and, inasmuch as violence appeared to be doctrinally embedded in Soviet thought, the global implications of the threat were correspondingly highlighted. An influential essay in *Foreign Affairs* by the anonymous "Historicus" argued that "uncompromisingly revolutionary" theory was central to the Soviets and that "world Communism is the supreme aim, Soviet power the major instrument by which it will be achieved." Increasingly, descriptions of Soviet ideology described it as a "messianic" rather than "passive" force that "spurs the USSR to assist the transformation of the Marxist blueprint into a reality." Kennan's successor as director of the Policy Planning Staff, Paul Nitze, argued that the Soviets, far from mellowing and showing themselves amenable to negotiation, were in fact more inclined to take potentially disastrous risks. Although Nitze minimized the likelihood of the Soviets launching an all-out assault on the West in the near future, they were thought to have "a greater willingness than in the past to undertake a course of action, including a possible use of force in local areas, which might lead to an accidental outbreak of general military conflict. Thus the chance of war through miscalculation is increased."[32]

This new view was codified in April 1950 in NSC 68, an attempt at credal formulation that justified a program of massive rearmament to deter the Soviets from pursuing their alleged design. Like all bureaucratic documents, NSC 68 tried to have it all ways, as for example in its description of the Kremlin as "inescapably militant because it possesses and is possessed by a world-wide revolutionary movement, because it is the inheritor of Russian imperialism and because it is a totalitarian dictatorship"—a blanket definition that covered all three faces of ideology. Nevertheless, the document clearly favored the radical definition of Marxist-Leninism, arguing that the Soviet Union, "unlike previous aspirants to hegemony, is animated by a new fanatic faith, antithetical to our own, and seeks to impose its absolute authority over the rest of the world." One comment on NSC 68 aptly condensed that policy paper's sense of the significance of ideology to the cold war: "What we are really up against is a conflict of basic concepts of which the present and prospective power threat to our security is a product." The Korean War would elevate this interpretation to the status of scriptural truth.[33]

How far Washington had traveled in its thinking on this matter was evident from the reaction to an address delivered in 1951 by Rear Admiral Leslie C. Stevens, a former naval attaché to Moscow. Virtually reversing Kennan's logic, he argued that "motivation by Marxist-Leninist-Stalinist doctrine is predominant" and that "nationalism is used as a tool by the Bolsheviks, whereas the Russians do not use Bolshevism as a tool to secure their ends." For the admiral, this was an important distinction because "the ultimate objective of world control was never an aim of Tsarist Russia, nor has it arisen now merely because Russia has suddenly become strong and formidable." He quoted Lenin to the effect that "a series of the most frightful collisions between the Soviet republic and bourgeois states is inevitable." Thus the ideology, whatever its roots in the past and in the power structure of the present, did provide "a blueprint of the future," a historical vision every bit as compelling to its Communist adherents as the American view of civilization was to U.S. foreign policy. In a note to Harriman that showed no awareness that he was recanting his old views, Truman described the admiral's speech as "about the best statement on Soviet military intentions that I have seen."[34]

By 1952, the Policy Planning Staff had also completely reversed its position. In response to arguments like Bohlen's that "the Stalin regime is interested in maintaining power in Russia entirely for the sake of power and not at all as a base for eventual world revolution," it pointed to "a false dichotomy between power and ideology" and argued that it was "dangerous . . . to assume that Soviet foreign policy encourages tensions abroad only as a contribution to the maintenance of the regime." A hard-core minority of doubters in Washington had been convinced of all this from the beginning, but as Soviet ideology was accorded greater weight in Soviet intentions, policymakers began to assume that the cold war was more dangerous than Kennan had described it and would require correspondingly weightier countermeasures.[35]

This heightened appreciation of ideology as a source of Soviet conduct had an enormous impact on America's cold-war foreign policy. Defining the Soviet problem in terms of Great Russian imperial tradition had, in its own way, been reassuring. Although the USSR was hardly a liberal democracy or a status quo power, it had the indispensable virtue, in Franklin D. Roosevelt's mind, as well as Kennan's, of at least seeming to understand the ultimate consequences of expansionism, all the more so after nearly having been its victim. It was comforting, too, that Soviet communism was viewed as a faith in decline, one, moreover, whose high priests were hardly fanatics but prudent leaders averse to suicidal risk-taking in pursuit of Marxism's nominal global ambitions. As the American view of the Soviet danger grew, however, it evoked the stark Wilsonian strategic vision in its full strength.

Despite the widely accepted view that his "Long Telegram" "firmly fixed the assumptions on which American foreign policy continued to be based for the next two decades,"[36] Kennan played a far more limited role in elaborating the axioms that dominated the thinking of American policymakers during the cold war. While the ultimate ends of containment—shepherding the evolution of the Soviet Union to democracy by barking whenever it tended to stray toward expansionism—were firmly installed as part of the foundation of cold-war policy, Kennan's rather shallow imprint was evident in the consistent rejection of his major policy recommendations from 1948 on. Part of the explanation for the disagreement over containment lies in Kennan's own change of view, beginning in 1948, in which he started to push softer policies toward the Soviets than he had during the hard-line, power political phase of his early postwar thought. But while Kennan's views shifted, so too did official Washington's definition of the cold war. The fault line separating Kennan's "realism" from the administration's viewpoint was visible in their differences over the dark side of Wilsonianism, whose propositions had emerged by 1950 from their formerly questionable status to become the axioms underlying a new foreign-policy consensus.

THE RETURN OF WILSONIANISM

Kennan could only wonder at the sudden militancy in Washington, especially as no objective changes had taken place since the end of the war to affect America's strategic situation. By his accounting, "nothing that recently occurred has altered these essential elements." That was quite true, but Kennan failed to take into account the sea change in American thinking about Soviet intentions. Among other things, his failure to discern what was going on in the official mind was evident in the wrong-headedness of his famous distinction between Soviet intentions and capabilities. Kennan argued that American policymakers were becoming obsessed with Soviet military strength, a fixation that produced an inflation of the much milder threat that an objective analysis of Soviet intentions, the kind of analysis at which he excelled, would suggest. But the preoccupation with Soviet capabilities (which was admittedly quite pronounced) made little sense in the absence of a corresponding concern with Soviet intentions, which had long been the administration's barometer for judging Moscow. Because American analysts had always argued from intentions to outcomes, Soviet military strength seemed all the more dangerous in view of the expansionist designs attributed to the Kremlin. In any case, to draw a hard and fast distinction between intentions and capabilities was suspect, since the two moved in tandem as components of events and would have to be interpreted together. In this case, official Washington did not ignore Soviet intentions; it just interpreted them differently than did Kennan.[37]

Kennan was so accustomed to thinking of Wilsonianism as an idealistic creed without any geostrategic foundation that he was relatively helpless to deal with it when it resurfaced. Believing that he had exorcised the spirit of idealistic Wilsonianism, he found himself fighting a losing battle with its strategic doppelganger. The marginal significance of Kennan's view of containment comes across forcefully when one looks at the policy debates of the late 1940s in which Kennan was opposed to all the basic assumptions of strategic Wilsonianism: that there existed a danger of world conquest; that the European balance of power had collapsed and could not be restored; that peripheral crises could escalate into world wars; and that the solution lay in world opinion. He did agree on the necessity of avoiding a war with the USSR (thereby distancing himself from traditional realpolitik), but his differences over its likelihood and on how best to prevent it stemmed from his rejection of these other elements of Wilsonianism. Thus ironically, in the minds of his fellow policymakers the former realist and hard-liner suddenly began to go soft by erring consistently on the side of unwarranted optimism.[38]

The first major point of disagreement between Kennan and the administration emerged over an issue that Kennan thought he had long ago set to rest in the writings that gained him fame. In contrast to the cautious view of the Kremlin inherent in Kennan's analysis of Communist ideology, the Soviet Union's ultimate ambition was increasingly being defined in terms of world conquest rather than the limited imperialism of Russia. As a preparatory document for NSC 68 put it: "The issues that face us are momentous, involving the fulfillment or destruction not only of the Republic but of civilization itself." This was crucial, especially because the primary concern of internationalists since Wilson's time had been the kind of international environment in which the United States existed. Not surprisingly then, given this strategic mind-set and the seemingly vast reach of Soviet power, the strategic problems confronting the United States took on a familiar cast. Indeed, George Marshall's reflections on the postwar situation from the vantage point of 1949 come close to expressing a sense of déjà vu: "I found the problems from the viewpoint of geographical location and of pressure to be almost identical in many respects with those of the war years. There was the same problem between East and West; the same limitations as to our capabilities; the same pressures at home and abroad, in regard to various areas, and there was the same necessity for a very steady and determined stand in regard to these various problems."[39]

For Dean Acheson, too, Marshall's successor as secretary of state, the underlying problem was exactly the same as that faced in the 1930s. In 1939, Acheson had warned that Axis victories would bring "our internment on this continent and such portion of the one to the south as we can physically control . . . surrounded by hostile camps." In 1950, little seemed to have changed. As he explained to Christian Herter, the Soviets "would like nothing better than to see us standing alone, confronted with the realization that we had no friends outside the hemisphere, thoroughly confused politically and economically." Their aim, he was convinced, was "to detach, one after another, various portions of the free world, so that what is left may have a sense of shrinking and narrowing environment, a sense of the inevitability of their power and ultimate dominion." It was essential, therefore, in Acheson's view, for American policy to "create a world climate, a world condition which at the very least is tolerable to the survival of our national values, and which at the best makes for the flourishing of those values."[40]

By the time of Korea, there was no doubt that the maintenance of this favorable international climate entailed global obligations. As Clark Clifford recalled, "It looked to us at the time that they were engaged in a program of world conquest. . . . It's just about that simple." The assumption of a Soviet design for world conquest quickly became holy writ within a few years and was enshrined as a fundamental axiom in NSC 68: "the complete subversion of the machinery of government and structure of society in the countries of the non-Soviet world and their replacement by an apparatus and structure subservient to and controlled from the Kremlin." The Korean War only reinforced the truth of this revised estimate. "Their *ultimate objective*," said the CIA in late 1950, "is to establish a Communist world controlled by themselves or their successors." Inasmuch as communism was undoubtedly an internationalist creed, its promotion in rank to the status of a driving force in Soviet policy reestablished the threat of world conquest as a fundamental policy concern and once again cast into doubt the progressive view of world history so central to America's self-conception.[41]

For Kennan, his conservative interpretation of Soviet motives matched his long historical view that international politics took place, by definition, in an unfriendly world environment; for other administration policymakers, the environment was precisely the issue. To the argument that Stalin's autarchic program of "Socialism in One Country," reinforced by the czarist legacy of insularity, marked an abandonment of Marxian internationalism, others like CIA Director Hoyt Vandenberg could remind Truman in September

1946, "If it is kept in mind that the ultimate aim of Communism is a Soviet Union of the world, then of course, Communism is possible in *the one* country." In any case, Nazi Germany and Japan had in their own way created closed economic systems without any apparent diminution of expansionist drive. Kennan may have believed that "parallels between Stalinism and Hitlerism were very dangerous," but most American leaders saw little difference between the two in terms of ultimate ambition.[42]

Although Kennan and his comrade-in-arms Charles Bohlen on occasion contributed statements of their own that fed this sense of world-historical danger, at bottom they were never convinced that a Communist world empire was an operational aim of the Kremlin. In the first place, Soviet leaders did not think that way. According to Bohlen, "Stalin, unlike Lenin or Trotsky, would seek to achieve only the maximum feasible extension of the power of the Kremlin." But even if they did harbor such dreams, they were unrealizable. As early as 1946, Kennan had argued that it was "unrealistic to assume that there could be any real possibility of a communist sphere of influence embracing a substantial part of the rest of the world . . . Russia's resources are already severely taxed." Bohlen, too, entered his objections to such a view by arguing that there were inherent limits to Soviet ambitions, but remonstrances of this kind amounted to little more than an ineffective rearguard action.[43]

As the conviction of unlimited Soviet ambition gained ground, so too did the belief that they were willing to run grave risks of war to achieve it, thus activating another by-now primal Wilsonian fear. In 1947, the consensus appeared to be that "the *immediate* Soviet aim may be to progress toward ultimate world domination only so far as methods short of war will permit." While the goal may have existed as a matter of theory, it seemed too remote in time and too detached from immediate Soviet interests and behavior to form the foundation of geopolitical strategy. Yet the growing fixation with Communist doctrine and its talk of the inevitability of war led to a far more frightening conclusion. As Bohlen understood, the belief that the Soviet Union was truly intent on dominating the world carried "the implication that all other considerations are subordinate to this purpose and that great risks would be run for the sake of its achievement." By thus oversimplifying the problem facing the United States, it led "inevitably to the conclusion that war is inevitable."[44]

Kennan fully shared this view. He could only express his "disbelief that the Soviet leaders contemplated launching world conflict by armed force" when to his mind the greater danger of conflict with the Soviets stemmed from their *weakness*. Criticizing the American military's apparent quest for total security, Kennan argued that "if you think in terms of a hot war, almost everything you do in the cold war is wrong." If Americans took literally the doctrine of inevitability of war, the nation's cold-war objectives would be rendered meaningless. From Kennan's point of view, containment was designed to turn the short-term Soviet reluctance to engage in war in pursuit of its objectives into a permanent condition. Despite the admitted ambiguity of his pronouncement in the "X" article, Kennan came to define containment essentially as a political process that minimized the need for a military approach; if it failed, military solutions would be called for, but only then, and in measured amounts. To be sure, containment was designed, as he said in 1946, "to keep the Russians confronted with superior strength," but it had to be implemented "in so friendly and unprovocative a manner that its basic purposes will not be subject to misinterpretation."[45]

However eloquent, Kennan could only play Canute against the rising tide of strategic Wilsonianism. By 1949, the threat of war was ritually embedded in the prefaces of military documents purporting to describe the peril facing the United States. Although in March 1947 the Joint Chiefs of Staff (JCS) had gone on record to declare that "the Soviet Union currently possesses neither the desire nor the resources to conduct a major war" and Marshall was telling the generals a year later that there would be no war, a few years later that seemed highly questionable. Indeed, it was already being questioned within the Pentagon by the Joint Strategic Survey Committee, which announced that "the greatest threat to international peace and security is USSR advancement through aggressive and expansionist measures toward attainment of its ultimate goal of world domination." By the end of 1949, the fear of war was constantly on the minds of the nation's, and the West's, leaders. By August 1950, NSC 73/4 stated flatly that it was "a tenet of communism that war between communist and non-communist countries is inevitable," concluding that this conviction was "a basic premise in the determination of Soviet foreign policy."[46]

Kennan also differed radically with the administration's estimates of the structural causes that threatened the international system and made war a possibility, most passionately so with the growing sense that the European balance of power was beyond rehabilitation. There was little disagreement on the central importance of Europe; that, at least, was a matter of consensus. In Kennan's view, American security depended traditionally on the existence of a Europe composed of "a considerable number of free states subservient to no great power." Should this kind of Europe disappear, the United States would have to make "a basic revision of the whole concept of our international position" and reconcile itself to "a cultural and spiritual loss incalculable in its long-term effects." Modern military technology made possible the extension of control to much larger areas, leaving open "the possibility of

such tremendous economic and political strength from that side as to constitute a real threat to the security of the North American continent.'' Ultimately, one had ''to fall back on something like an instinctive feeling'' that
a pluralist Europe was worth saving. Should the United States fail to preserve
it, Kennan predicted that ''we would have to become for the first time . . . in
our whole history completely cynical in the conduct of our foreign policy.''[47]

The United States was not without some complicity in bringing about
this peril, for in removing one threat to the European balance it had helped
to install another. The United States had trumped the German bid for domination, but ''in so doing we had brought this center [the USSR] into the heart
of Europe.'' ''The tragedy of this last world war,'' Kennan wrote, ''is that
we were not powerful enough to take on both power centers at the same
time, which would have been the rational thing to do; we had to use one to
defeat the other,'' which left the United States with ''a hell of a problem on
our hands to know how to deal with it.'' But the United States had made a
bad situation even worse. In what was his most biting criticism of FDR's
wartime policies, Kennan insisted that the consequence of Roosevelt's naive
policy of cooperation was that the United States had ''tacitly acquiesced, as
part of the whole conclusion of the war, in the Red Army advance into these
countries and in the establishment of Soviet political control.'' The United
States had ''conceded to Russia in effect certain expansions of territory, both
in the Far East and in eastern Europe, which we possibly would not have
conceded in the same way if we had not wished to have Russia as a future
friend.''[48]

This critique set the stage for Kennan's falling out with the administration
over its evolving European policy. Americans, as historian John Lewis Gaddis has pointed out, wished to restore an *independent* Europe, but it was not
immediately clear just what that meant, especially as the issue was not really
argued in balance-of-power terms. Kennan was one of the few to speak this
language bluntly, insisting that ''all in all, our policy must be directed toward
restoring a balance of power in Europe and Asia.'' Despite the self-evident
centrality of the Continent, the United States had been remarkably vague
when it came to discussing its future. FDR at Yalta had talked about the
United States withdrawing within a couple of years, leaving Europe to the
British and the Soviets on the implicit assumption that a workable balance
would emerge. This casual treatment of the issue continued into the postwar
period, when the first inclination was to allow the Europeans time to recover
and sort out their own affairs. Showing more sensitivity to possible accusations of American hegemony than to power factors, Marshall explained in
late 1947 that ''it is certainly not our purpose to exploit the situation by
filling the vacuum with American power,'' for if that were done, ''our policy

would not be directed toward ending European dependency upon this country but toward perpetuating that relationship."[49]

The European Recovery Program was largely restorative in economic terms, therefore, but not very long after its inception it was perceived to be totally inadequate in dealing with the continuing power imbalance, which, if left unaddressed, might subvert European recovery and lead to its communization. Kennan adamantly opposed an American military guarantee for western Europe, which in 1948 became the topic of serious negotiations in Washington with the west European governments. He preferred instead the reestablishment of a balance on the Continent, although one much modified from the past, in which a European federation would act as a counterweight against the Soviet Union and in which Germany would be so thoroughly absorbed that it could present no danger of domination. As Kennan explained to Marshall, "Only such a union holds out any hope of restoring the balance of power in Europe without permitting Germany to become again the dominant power." This basic solution seemed "clear enough."[50]

But such a federation began to seem impossible of achievement without a prior withdrawal of Russian power from central Europe. Thus it would be necessary "to remove Russian influence throughout Europe to an extent which would make it possible for all European countries to lead again an independent national existence." Inasmuch as the United States had tacitly conceded control of eastern and southeastern Europe to the Soviets, there was no question of their withdrawing voluntarily without some powerful inducement. Since Kennan viewed both the Soviet and American presences in the heart of Europe to be unnatural, the necessary first step in restoring Europe as an independent power base was for both superpowers to withdraw from central Europe, thereby making room for a restored European balance under some sort of federal union. All this was premised on the assumption that American policy was directed "toward the eventual peaceful withdrawal of both the United States and the U.S.S.R. from the heart of Europe, and accordingly toward the encouragement of the growth of a third force which can absorb and take over the territory between the two."[51]

The only open diplomatic path to that goal at the time was an agreement on German unification and neutralization, paved by a mutual withdrawal of the superpowers from their central European positions. Kennan's neutralization approach marked a significant change from his thinking as recently as 1947, when he saw a partition of Germany and Europe as the only sensible cold-war approach. At the time he had said: "I hope we won't shrink from carrying out that partition rather than giving the Russians the chance to dominate the whole country." But his thought had shifted rapidly in the direction of viewing the Marshall Plan as a point of departure for negotiations with the Russians, looking to their eventual pullback, following which the western European nations would be free to unite. His conclusion: "A balance will then have been created on the Eurasian continent; and we will have surmounted successfully the greatest political crisis this country has ever faced in world affairs." Whether or not such a negotiated withdrawal was possible at the time was, as even Kennan admitted, a debatable question. Nevertheless, even after the Berlin crisis of 1948 had consolidated opinion against him, Kennan believed that the United States would "still be faced with the old task of maneuvering our Russian friends back where they belong by the political and economic strength of Europe." He hoped to leave "a number of open doors through which the Russians . . . could finally retreat."[52]

Minimizing the Soviet military threat, Kennan argued that containment was supposed to encourage Europeans to resist internal, not external, violence, "to defend the *internal* security of their countries." As he saw it, "the peoples of Western Europe could do away with two-thirds of their own danger if they would face up to the problems of their own communists." While a stiffening of confidence was desirable, Kennan believed that a military pact would also have negative consequences. It would militarize the problem, divert resources from economic recovery, and take attention away from what was essentially a political problem best handled by the west Europeans. And it would, by creating a clear military dividing line through Europe, accentuate the Continent's division and "make it impossible for any of the satellite countries even to contemplate anything in the nature of a gradual withdrawal from Russian domination." It would "tend to fix, and make unchangeable by peaceful means, the present line of east-west division."[53]

Dean Acheson was initially undecided about Germany when he assumed the secretaryship in 1949, but the issue was too closely connected to the imperatives of west European revival and the need for physical security to warrant a gamble. Acheson decided ultimately that "there would be fewer and less painful difficulties by going ahead with the west German government than by attempting to unite Germany first." Because the Allies had already chosen a pass through the mountains, it was too late to turn back before the winter snows set in. Given the perceived intractability of Soviet goals and the powerful conviction of American military leaders and European statesmen that the Continent could not hope any time soon to become a third force, the only possible alternative at the time was the one Kennan wanted to avoid: a Soviet-American balance. As Acheson told the Senate Foreign Relations Committee early in 1950: "you have to realize that at the present time there is a line drawn across Europe which, so far as we can see, looks as though it were permanent." In this conception, a neutral space in which a restored

Europe would be allowed to draw the breath of life and grow was a fantasy. Even Bohlen disagreed with Kennan over the likelihood of the Soviets allowing a neutralist solution to take hold: "The concept of a cushion or neutral zone I think they would consider as in the nature of a tempting prize with which they would play around without as acute fears of the consequences as they would in a non-neutral area."[54]

The Truman administration, swept along by a tide of European opinion eager for American backing and aid, believed that history had demonstrated that Europe was incapable of setting right its own affairs without an American presence. The basic cause of western European instability, a legacy of Franco-German antagonism, was impossible to resolve without an American guarantee, something that the French had long been pleading for. As Acheson told some leading U.S. senators, "It was doubtful that, without some such pact, the French would ever be reconciled to the inevitable diminution of direct allied control over Germany and the progressive reduction of occupation troops; that a pact of this nature would give France a greater sense of security against Germany as well as the Soviet Union." For the Europeans it was only the benevolent American imperialists that made possible the mediation of disputes without which the achievement of integration would have been unthinkable.[55]

Thus the American government was unwilling to risk an approach to the Russians based on mutual disengagement. Although in the abstract most policymakers heartily agreed with Kennan's emphasis on the desirability of a European union,[56] in practice the promotion of a fully united Europe and the undoubted stability it would bring seemed far too chancy to adopt as a near-term policy objective. An American withdrawal would leave behind it only a vacuum filled with uncertainty and weakness. The negotiation of a military alliance, in conjunction with the momentum of policy that was pushing in the direction of a de facto partition of Germany, put an effective end to the first chapter of this story in 1949. To most other policymakers in the administration, Kennan's neutralization proposals were much too dangerous, for in an era of bipolarity there could be no independent European balance in which Europe would be a third force. As Anders Stephanson has pointed out, in this instance it was Kennan, ostensibly a realist, who was pushing utopian proposals.

Given the expanded view of the Soviet danger and the Continent's structural infirmity, American involvement in Europe would need to be far greater than Kennan had first envisioned. He believed that economic recovery and restored self-confidence, coupled with meaningful negotiations with Moscow over mutual withdrawal, would be sufficient to restore the kind of independent existence he envisioned. For others in the administration, the argument for unity assumed the existence of precisely what was most lacking in Europe: confidence. The prevalence of weakness and outright fear meant that the kind of Europe envisioned by Kennan would be worse than the old balance of power. European unity would be an end, but it could not be a means. The ultimate solution would be a united Europe in which the balance of power was totally abolished, and not merely restored, which meant that the Soviet threat would first have to disappear; but until the arrival of that glorious day, some time after the cold war had ended, the United States could not afford to leave Europe to the Europeans.

The argument was thus a historical dispute about one of the basic issues of Wilsonianism. It boiled down to a question of whether the balance would be truly European, or whether it would be an American-maintained balance in Europe. From his Europeanist perspective, Kennan believed that a tolerable European balance could successfully be restored, with a minimal Soviet and American intrusive presence, by getting the Europeans to stand on their own. But the importunities of European leaders for an American guarantee bespoke a sense of insecurity and weak morale that could not be ignored. Moreover, Kennan's argument overlooked the fact that the degree of European solidarity that did exist was elicited only by virtue of the existence of the Soviet threat. If, as he had long maintained, the problem was subjective and psychological, and if the Europeans felt that they needed a military guarantee for reassurance, then any argument opposing such military involvement consigned European thinking to the fuzzy realm of false consciousness. Kennan did not shrink from such a dubious argument. As he put it, "The need for military alliances and rearmament on the part of the Europeans is primarily a *subjective* one, arising in their own minds as a result of their failure to understand correctly their own position." Kennan seemed to believe in "patient, cure thyself," whereas the Europeans had become attached to their physician. But if, as Averell Harriman told a Senate committee, the North Atlantic Pact involved "the deepest of all emotions in men," it made little sense to blame Europe's weakness on the psychological insecurity of Europeans. One could hardly expect to harness that insecurity, which was itself the product of the historic collapse of the European balance, in restoring an independent equilibrium.[57]

Yet another difference emerged between Kennan and the administration as a consequence of the shift to strategic Wilsonianism, this one having to do with the heightened importance attached to the periphery as a result of the collapse of the European balance of power and the globalization of politics. The Wilsonian notion of a global Balkan powder keg, of a world potentially ablaze without regional firebreaks, was the least well developed aspect of Wilsonianism, as was evident from the vague articulation of the problem during the Manchurian crisis. The Japanese threat to the Far East in 1940 had filled in a global picture, but only as a result of its strategic linkage to events in Europe via the threat to the survival of the British Empire. But now the postwar power vacuum in Europe, coupled with decolonization, had produced a vacuum in other areas as well and contributed to a growing feeling that events in obscure regions had the potential to mushroom into crises of global proportions. Though the gap between Kennan and the policy establishment on this issue was not very wide, at least not in the beginning, it proved ultimately to be far more important because the increasing weight being given to events in East Asia portended the emergence of a neo-Wilsonian obsession with world opinion that would be seen by U.S. policymakers as the key to winning the cold war—an approach that would, in the process, contravene the first principles of realist diplomacy.

As a Europe-first type who felt that the United States was greatly overextended, Kennan believed that a heavy American involvement in the Far East would divert attention and resources from more pressing obligations. He could discern no fundamental national interests in China, not even the Open Door policy, which was merely "an expression of our long-range aspirations" incapable of achievement any time soon. Moreover, he argued that China's problems were beyond America's capacity to manage. "China could take all of the national budget we could divert to it for the next 25 years and the problems would be worse at the end of that time than they are today," he said in 1947. It followed that China's destiny was largely in its own hands, its salvation lying "essentially with the Chinese—not with foreigners." Taking a position similar to Hoover's in 1932, Kennan argued that a Communist victory in China would not be an unalloyed disaster to American interests since the Russians would simply "come a cropper on that problem just as everybody else has for hundreds of years." The fall of China would be painful, Kennan believed, but hardly fatal, given that "world realities have greater tolerances than we commonly suppose against ambitious schemes for world domination." The only sensible policy was to let nature take its course until another historical cycle took hold, as it was bound to do. This was, admittedly, a long-term proposition, but there was no short-cut. "The Kremlin waited twenty-five years for the fulfillment of its revolution in China," Kennan noted. "We may have to persevere as long or longer."[58]

Though Kennan's comments gave the impression that the United States was itching to intervene in China, his hands-off approach was actually quite congenial to high-level thinking in Washington until 1950. Contrary to Kennan's belief in the potency of the Open Door myth, the United States had traditionally been chary of translating its commercial and cultural tenets into power political involvement in the region. The American habit of treating

China as a strategic backwater, so evident throughout the 1930s and the war, did not change in the postwar years. By mid-1948, dismay at the successes of Mao Zedong and the People's Liberation Army coexisted with a willingness within the administration to reconcile itself to a Communist triumph, since it seemed too late in any event to rescue Chiang's incompetent regime. Much as American policymakers disliked the prospect of a Communist China, they realized that the fall of the nationalist regime was "only a matter of time" and were quite willing to follow Kennan's advice by waiting for the historical pendulum to complete its long arc. As Acheson told a Senate committee, the cost of any attempt to save Chiang's regime on Formosa would be "far greater than any benefit." The best to be hoped for in the short run was a Titoist China, unmistakably Communist but at least not a pliable instrument of Soviet global strategy.[59]

Apart from tradition, another potent argument on behalf of a lowered profile in the Far East was the Truman administration's initial concern to match resources with objectives. Truman's FY 1950 budget ceiling of 14.4 billion dollars on military spending had forced strategists to define their priorities and focus on defending the areas most important to U.S. security. In 1949, Under Secretary Webb wrote the president of a reevaluation of American foreign policy, "with an idea to reducing our commitments in any areas where this is possible and planning progressive pulling in of our horns as the post-war recovery begins to materialize in other countries." In this kind of reckoning, China came far down the list. According to a CIA review of the world situation made in late 1947, the Far East was "of only third priority" behind Europe and the Middle East in strategic significance. It was simply taken for granted, as Clark Clifford recalled of these early postwar years of policy formulation, that "it was *Western Europe* that really mattered to us at the time." The same consciousness of limits obtained in the dispensing of military assistance, a concern readily apparent in Bob Lovett's caution against "spreading the butter so thin that it would not feed anyone." Not surprisingly, then, the administration was unwilling to invest massively in an attempt to reverse the course of events in China.[60]

Nevertheless, despite the fact that American policymakers had written off China beforehand, the Communist takeover delivered a heavy psychological blow. A draft of NSC 48 of October 1949 admitted frankly that "the extension of Communist authority in China represents a grievous political defeat for us." At a minimum, the Communist victory made clear that the balance in Asia had also been destroyed and highlighted the need to stabilize the rest of the region, a point with which Kennan, who was pushing "straight power concepts," readily agreed. Following the establishment of the People's Republic, Acheson argued that it was better to get American minds off China and concentrate on more important issues in the region, particularly Japan, India, and Indochina. "The real center of our interest in Asia must lie in these other countries," he argued.[61]

A draft of NSC 48/2 in October 1949 argued that "if Japan were added to the communist bloc, the Soviet Asiatic base could become a source of strength capable of tipping the balance of world power dangerously against the United States." But Japan, though hugely important, was never in any immediate jeopardy from the fall of China. Instead of making waves locally, Far Eastern crises were like stones hurled laterally into water that skipped over their initial point of impact to sink eventually in Europe. The global reverberations were evident from the document's assertion that any further Communist successes in the region might set off "a political rout the repercussions of which will be felt throughout the world." The suggestion here seemed to be that in the new world system, the Far East was not only vulnerable but somehow vital as well, something that had not been the case only a few years ago. As PPS/50 stated in 1949, U.S. security and welfare were so "closely bound up with the peace and security of the world community" that "aggression, anywhere, may jeopardize the security of the U.S."[62]

But just how was that true? It was not so much the territorial loss or even the exposure of regional weakness as the unexpected effect on morale resulting from the deep historical attachment to China that bothered many Americans. As John Foster Dulles told Truman in 1950, "Americans had lost confidence as a result of what had happened, particularly in the East," which "made it possible for men like McCarthy to make a deep impression upon the situation and to achieve prominence." This wound inflicted by China on the American psyche would wreak havoc upon U.S. politics over the next decade and push the United States toward a degree of involvement in the region that previously would have seemed unthinkable. But that emotional attachment alone, even with the domestic political firestorms that it generated, would never have been sufficient to warrant such a sea change in policy.[63]

The more important psychological tie-in would come between Far Eastern crises and *world* opinion. Never having been important in itself, except to small groups of sinophiles, China's international value to Americans had always been measured by its symbolic connection to other processes, most notably as the chief illustration of the progressive possibilities of modernization and the operation of a harmonious world opinion. By late 1949, the stage was being set for a reversal of that symbolic role, with China and the Far East now primed to become symbols of the dangers to world opinion.[64] That transformation from good to evil would by itself have done little to change the region's strategic status were it not for the fact that symbolism itself was beginning to take on a new importance in American cold-war policy. For it was precisely at this time that a neo-Wilsonian conception of world opinion, one ascribing global implications to the symbolic aspects of power, made it impossible to play down the consequences of China's fall. The revolutionary character of this new kind of symbolic connection between East and West, which will be taken up in the next chapter, would not become clear until the Korean War, but by late 1949 American thinking was already on the verge of accepting the idea that a world with a seriously weakened European center was, in a very real sense, a world-system without a periphery, a world in which theoretical distinctions of regional priority had remarkably little significance in practice. As if anticipating a basic tenet of postmodernism, the foreign-policy periphery would now become central.

So, despite the initial tendency to minimize the strategic importance of events in China and the desire to dovetail ends with means, the administration would in the end elevate events in the region to global significance. Realists have ever since criticized the recklessness and extravagance of American globalism for violating a basic axiom of prudent policymaking: preventing overextension by tailoring commitments to resources. But the perfect mating of ends and means would have struck policymakers as a utopian solution to what they saw, quite differently, as the unfortunate but unavoidable necessity of confronting problems of global scope with limited means. The American government would remain sensitive throughout the cold war to the nation's limited resources, yet it continued to insist that fitting commitments to capabilities, far from being prudent, would be a luxury it could not afford. Realists worked from the inside out, but the new global sensibility worked from the outside in when defining interests. The costs of dealing with a global threat would be high, but the extreme consequences of a collapse of the open world environment made realism seem like false economy by comparison.

GEORGE KENNAN CONTRIBUTED ENORMOUSLY to his nation's foreign policy by suggesting that ideological differences, however polarized in theory, did not necessarily mean war and by defining the emerging period of tension as a world-historical contest which would culminate in the victory of mainstream Western civilization. Over time, the wisdom of those arguments would become clear. The irony of Kennan's contribution is that he wound up advocating an approach to the Soviet Union that was much closer in spirit and method to the workmanlike relationship envisioned by FDR than to the policies adopted in the name of containment. It is a measure of his misunderstanding of the American foreign-policy culture and its modernist interpretation of civilization that he thought he was attacking Wilsonianism when in fact he was embroidering FDR's views. Those views were congenial for a time, but it must be remembered that even FDR shared Wilson's understanding of the underlying strategic problem of modern world history. Kennan's traditional historical frame, by comparison, had only shallow roots in American policy culture. When optimism waned, Kennan's colleagues in the upper reaches of the administration reverted to what were actually harsher Wilsonian interpretations—of Soviet ambitions, the structural problems of the international environment, and the means necessary to deal with them. As a result of his inability to cope with the power of the Wilsonian historical frame and its strategic axioms, he was shoved to the margins of policy influence.

As the father of containment, Kennan gave American policy a name, which, although a great achievement, brought with it no godlike power of cultural creation—that distinction belonged to Woodrow Wilson and his successors. He was a transitional intellectual figure whose basic ideas on containment remained important but who failed to understand Wilsonianism and the grip it had taken on the American foreign-policy imagination. Far from being the father of containment, then, Kennan was more like a midwife who acted to ease the birth of a policy, which, as it began to mature, was taken by its parents from his hands and shaped according to their values. Because Kennan had always been an outsider, temperamentally, culturally, and institutionally, it was not surprising that he would find his true métier in his postgovernment career as a historian and cold-war critic who promoted an approach to living with the Soviets that resembled what Roosevelt, during the war, probably had in mind.[65]

Neither is it surprising that he would be out of fundamental sympathy with the neo-Wilsonian solution devised to deal with the cold war. Kennan had provided an alternative to Wilsonian optimism, but not to Wilsonian pessimism. Once the Soviet problem had been cast in the neo-Wilsonian strategic mold, it was only a matter of time before the Truman administration settled on world opinion, though in drastically revised form, to deal with the kinds of difficulties that Wilson had first foreseen. There was a certain logical inevitability to this, because Wilson's strategic view of the world formed an intellectual system in which the solution was integrally fitted to the magnitude of the problem. As we shall see, the Wilsonian insight that modern problems of power could not be managed by the traditional resort to power left no other choice.

6

WILSONIAN SOLUTIONS: TOWARD A NEW LANGUAGE OF POWER

A S THE COLD WAR'S strategic problems took on a recognizably Wilsonian profile, the policies shaped to meet them also revealed a strong Wilsonian family resemblance. Because cold-war policymakers fully shared Wilson's belief that traditional methods of power balancing and crisis diplomacy were obsolete and self-defeating, and because the necessity for a noncataclysmic adjustment of differences pending the long-term resolution of the ideological struggle was the very heart of the concept of containment, the Truman administration rejected the failed politics of the past. However, it had no clear idea of what exactly to put in their place. It was evident to most everyone, in quite general and abstract terms, that power could be met only with power, but that only posed the more fundamental problem, for which history provided no reassuring examples, of how to employ that power without starting another major war. Although policymakers sensed from the beginning that the way out lay in some variation on the Wilsonian theme of world opinion, it is a measure of the utter novelty and untraditional character of the situation facing them that their search for a workable solution continued down to the Truman administration's frustrating final days and, beyond that, throughout the cold war. The cold war, by this definition, was simply the ongoing attempt to work out neo-Wilsonian solutions to a nightmarish set of problems first defined by Wilson.[1]

THE NEO-WILSONIAN PROBLEMATIC

The documents of the early cold-war period are full of references to the need to assert a language of power. In mid-1946, for example, Admiral Leahy declared: "The Soviet mentality will recognize only one deterrent to their policy of aggression, and that is force." The U.S. delegation in Bulgaria reported similarly that the Soviets "have respect for but one thing and that is force." Clark Clifford, in an extremely alarmist study that came on the heels of Kennan's analysis, made the same point and went on to recommend a willingness to wage nuclear and biological warfare, if need be, in response to Soviet provocations. Forrestal had decided by early 1947 that the cold war was "a fundamental struggle between our kind of society and the Russians' and that the Russians would not respond to anything but power." And Truman, in his typically down-to-earth manner, asserted that "our friends the Russkies understand only one language—how many divisions have you— actual or potential."[2]

The conventionality of this emphasis on power was, in a way, comforting. Even after the more sinister view of Soviet ideology took hold, administration policymakers continued to believe that, whatever its zealotry, the Soviet leadership's concern for self-preservation would force it to draw back. Had it been otherwise, had Soviet policy been viewed as ideological to the point of fanaticism, had the cold war actually turned into what Arthur Schlesinger, Jr., called a "religious war," then, as one extreme analysis would later conclude, only two courses of action would have been open: "either to bring about an internal collapse of that regime or to destroy it by force of arms." But even Admiral Stevens, in drawing a picture of unlimited Soviet ambition, admitted that the Soviets were not fanatics prepared to commit suicide on behalf of their faith. "The wall against which they will not run their heads now is war with the West," he concluded.[3]

The problem with this analysis was that power was not a language at all, but its opposite, its deliberate employment signaling the inability to settle disputes through discussion. From the Wilsonian perspective, modern power had the fatal drawback of being a means that threatened to vitiate the ends of policy. The conviction that the traditional theory and practice of power politics were responsible for the worst-case possibilities of global war and authoritarian closure of the international system in the modern era was shared even by archetypal power politicians like Winston Churchill. His famed "Iron Curtain" address of 1946, in which he declared that the Soviets respected nothing so much as power, also featured the unnoticed but significant assertion that balance-of-power policies were likely to defeat their own aims. "The old doctrine of a balance of power is unsound," he said in that speech. "We cannot afford, if we can help it, to work on narrow margins, offering temptations to a trial of strength."[4]

By Wilsonian reckoning, power in its modern context was as much problem as solution. General George C. Marshall, for one, recognized that "another major war at worst would destroy the United States; at best would only be won at a terrible cost in blood and treasure." For Dean Acheson, the implications of the increase in destructive potential could not be described simply in terms of differences in degree. "We have arrived at the point in the art of scientific and technical warfare," he said, "where the resort of force will mean the defeat of everybody's foreign policy. It will mean universal destruction." Similarly, General Eisenhower believed that "another war, even if resulting in the complete defeat of the enemy, would bring in its wake such grave disorder, dissatisfaction, and physical destruction of cities and resources, that we would be almost certain to lose that for which we fought—namely, the system of free enterprise and individual liberty, both of which are at the base of our system." Under novel conditions of warfare, as Under Secretary of State Robert Lovett understood, "no nation could expect victory." It would appear, then, that the repudiation of the instrumental Clausewitzian view of war as a continuation of foreign policy had been internalized quite well by top administration policymakers. By this standard, the real significance of the Clifford report's hawkish recommendations concerning the use of force was its unacceptability as a basis for cold-war policy, which was underscored by Truman's decision to recall all existing copies of the document and lock them up, sterilizing them inside the Oval Office safe before their infectious ideas could be transmitted.[5]

Yet the alternative of cooperation on the basis of shared values was ruled out, too. By mid-1949, with intermittent four-power meetings having produced only inconclusive wrangling, the search for a diplomatic meeting of the minds with the Russians had come to seem pointless. If we use E. H. Carr's definition of foreign policy as a process that oscillates between force and appeasement, Americans recoiled from both extremes as a matter of principle. Having rejected the tradition of realpolitik and its repeated breakdowns, Americans were simultaneously on guard against cutting deals lest the use of carrots be interpreted on all sides as appeasement. In the aftermath of Munich, negotiation meant compromise, compromise meant appeasement, and appeasement led, in the end, to war. At best, as NSC 68 argued, any agreements "would reflect present realities and would therefore be unacceptable." Not surprisingly, then, Acheson could tell the UN secretary general, the Senate Committee on Foreign Relations, and everyone who would listen that discussion would not produce solutions. As Thomas Etzold has observed, this rejection of the traditional view of negotiation meant that during the early cold war "there was almost no diplomacy in the old sense."[6]

By rejecting the alternatives of force and appeasement while at the same time despairing of effective international organization or cooperation along the lines suggested by FDR and Kennan, cold-war policymakers no longer had available to them any of the diplomatic tools traditionally used to attain national objectives: realpolitik, collective security, and negotiation. General Douglas MacArthur, of all people, put the American predicament most starkly and precisely in 1945 at the time of Japan's surrender: "Military alliances, balances of power, Leagues of nations, all in turn failed, leaving the only path to be by way of the crucible of war," he said, only to conclude that "the utter destructiveness of war now blocks out this alternative."[7]

Despite the tendency to view cold-war policy as an automatic reflex deriving from the experience of the 1930s, the post-traditional world in which policymakers found themselves, a world of Wilsonian problems without obvious Wilsonian solutions, contained many broad lessons of history but no obvious lessons of the past for policy. Nevertheless, the Wilsonian definition of the problem virtually mandated that policymakers follow a Wilsonian approach, though it proved to be hardly so obvious and straightforward as that in practice. As Acheson confessed in 1949, "Our actions since World War II had not been based on any broad global plan, . . . to the contrary, a great deal of improvisation had been necessary." Indeed, until the Korean War the incrementalism of American policy was a notable example of the kind of ideological change that has been called "creeping transformation."[8]

Collective security as envisioned in Wilson's proposal for the League of Nations had relied on two basic elements: the threat of superior force imposed by the global community in rolling back aggression and, more important, a united world opinion that gave credibility to that force as a way of preventing aggression in the first place. The Truman administration would, over time, come to rely on both. From 1947 on, American policymakers began slowly and haltingly to put together a neo-Wilsonian "language of power" in which overwhelming power backed by collective will was supposed to prevent conflict from snowballing out of control. By 1950, the administration had determined that the building up of "facts" and situations of strength was an indispensable element of policy. Long before it arrived at that understanding, however, it sought to nurture the psychological conditions of solidarity necessary to making a success of containment.[9]

Although no other alternatives seemed available, both elements of this neo-Wilsonian strategy were beset by serious problems. The determination to deal with the Soviets by creating situations of strength, on the basis of what Melvyn Leffler has called "a preponderance of power," was, while obviously indispensable to long-run containment, full of short-run difficulties and imponderables. In the first place, the United States, beset by budgetary worries while driven ideologically to assume commitments that exceeded even its formidable capabilities, never possessed absolute preponderance, even during the heyday of its nuclear monopoly, and as time went on the margin of superiority would grow slimmer. A more serious liability was the absence in the "situations of strength" approach of any clear concept of how to deal with crises that threatened to upset the status quo of containment.

The "facts" that Acheson liked to talk about left ample room for the Soviets to maneuver in pursuit of their ambitions without automatically precipitating the apocalyptic conflict that both sides presumably wanted to avoid. Given all the possibilities for expansion short of full-scale war, the doctrinal ambition of Soviet policy, and the Kremlin's growing willingness to take risks in the full understanding that the United States wanted to avoid war, what was to be done about more ambiguous situations that might, sooner or later, draw the two powers into collision?

Preponderant power rested ultimately on a perceptual foundation because it depended on a credible, determined world opinion to give it effect. The failure of the Wilsonian prototype made all the more vital the creation of a modified version of world opinion capable of preventing another unlimited war. That was, after all, the whole point of containment: power could not actually be used to impose one's will upon the adversary without defeating one's fundamental objectives. Because internationalists had long agreed that war originated "in the minds of men," that is where it would have to be prevented if the cold war was to be truly about the prevention of war. If the cold war was to be fought on psychological and symbolic ground, this meant that a truly discursive and communicative "language of power" would have to be created, one with a literal meaning divorced from the ironic sense usually attached to that phrase. In searching for a way of discouraging Communist advances and convincing the Soviets of the unthinkable folly of getting involved in another war, policymakers gravitated slowly but naturally to a reliance on an ersatz collective security. This neo-Wilsonian attempt to create a rump world opinion was three-pronged, focusing variously on friend, foe, and self.[10]

Although the adoption of this strategy meant, by definition, that the United States could not act alone, the perceived weakness of America's allies put the United States in the position of shoring up a Western morale that seemed always on the brink of collapse. Playing Atlas was all the more difficult because even policymakers were confused about means and wary of the doubtful reliability of a domestic public opinion that seemed not to understand the basic problem. With all these uncertainties, the effective consolidation of world opinion would be, throughout the cold war, more a problematic end than an effective means for American foreign policy. In seeking to frame a strategy that could communicate credible messages to the Soviets, hold together the free world, and maintain a viable domestic foreign-policy consensus, America's cold-war leaders would discover that the contradictions resulting from their policies made it difficult, and in some cases impossible, to strike a satisfactory balance among these three objectives.

The tentativeness of American postwar policy was evident from the sequence in which it evolved. Through mid-1949, the lingering heritage of interwar internationalism gave rise to repeated attempts at bolstering world opinion by preventing the collapse of Western morale, but without attempting to translate it into effective power. The Korean War finally forced the United States to consolidate psychology and power, but, as policymakers discovered, the policies improvised during that crisis were themselves quite unsatisfactory in dealing with the fundamental problems posed by the Wilsonian worldview. With each new initiative designed to demonstrate American commitment, what appear in retrospect to be the landmarks of postwar American policy looked, at the time, more like signposts pointing to roads not yet traveled.

THE SEARCH FOR A LANGUAGE OF POWER

The Truman Doctrine was only the first step toward defining a solution to Wilson's nightmare. If nothing else, the breathtaking speed with which it was formulated certainly demonstrated the sedimentation of Wilson's darker views into the foreign-policy culture. "I don't recall President Truman agonizing through the decision," said Clark Clifford. George Elsey maintained that "it was not something you could sit around and debate for weeks and months." But while the Truman Doctrine was notable for displaying an almost reflexive unanimity on basic policy goals that was not present a decade earlier, at the same time its knee-jerk quality meant that it could not be a closely defined and precisely articulated declaration of policy.[11]

A simmering Communist insurgency in Greece suddenly boiled over and became an American problem when the British served notice that they could no longer keep the lid on in Greece. The American nose for trouble in the region had already been sensitized in August 1946, when the Soviets began to pressure the Turks for joint basing rights in the straits. At that time, Acheson was quick to point out the wider implications of the issue, arguing that "acceding to these demands would be followed next by infiltration and domination of Greece by Russia with the obvious consequences in the Middle East and the obvious threat to line of communications of the British to India." Heeding Acheson's advice to call the Soviet hand, Truman came down in favor of firmness. "We might as well find out whether the Russians were bent on world conquest now as in five or ten years," he said. While that test was met by encouraging the Turks to hold firm and by sending a carrier squadron to the eastern Mediterranean, something more than traditional gunboat diplomacy was required in the Greek crisis.[12]

Assessments of the consequences of the fall of Greece and Turkey made the following spring were nearly unanimous in their predictions of doom should the United States fail to take action. Truman was fond of using a map to point out the historical importance of the Near East as a strategic cross-roads, but it was the symbolic significance of Greece that was uppermost in the administration's thinking. Kennan, whose views were typical in this instance, believed that a passive response would flash a green light to the Soviets, who would certainly "conclude that they have us on the run and we may look for rapid action on their part, designed to complete the collapse of our position on the Eurasian land mass." Besides encouraging the Soviets to probe further, a lack of will in Greece would also have a devastating effect on world opinion in friendly nations. "It is not too much to say," Acheson told the House Foreign Affairs Committee, "that the outcome in Greece and Turkey would be watched with deep concern throughout the vast area from the Dardanelles to the China Sea. It is also being watched with deep interest by the peoples of the west." Thus, while the immediate problem was regional, a perceptual multiplier effect gave it global significance. As a State Department pamphlet describing the purposes of the Greek aid program put it, the overthrow of the Greek government "would have profoundly disturbing psychological effects on many countries throughout the world."[13]

Given these stakes, high State Department officials like Marshall and Acheson were convinced that the nation had arrived at a world-historical juncture. An early draft of Truman's address to Congress reflected this lofty sense of historical occasion. "If there are any forms of government or principles we wish to see survive in this world, it is up to us to see to it that they survive," the document asserted. "For not since ancient times has there been such a polarization of power on this earth. Not since Athens and Sparta, not since Rome and Carthage, has economic and military strength been divided so preponderantly between two states." Ultimately, as Acheson told a group of startled legislators in the White House, the situation came down to "a question of whether . . . three-fourths of the world's territory is to be controlled by the Communists." Far from reflecting a desire to galvanize the American people by exaggerating the threat, administration spokesmen, tormented by the same kind of terrible possibilities described by Wilson during the First World War, were in fact expressing their deepest fears.[14]

In light of the sense of epochal significance surrounding the occasion and the widespread belief that the United States was being faced, in Marshall's words, "with the first crisis of a series which might extend Soviet domination to Europe, the Middle East and Asia," policymakers felt the need for a credal statement as opposed to merely an ad hoc response. Thus, in requesting an appropriation of 400 million dollars to deal with the Greek and Turkish problems, Truman pointed to the ultimate objective of Wilsonianism when he declared American policy to be "the creation of conditions in which we and other nations will be able to work out a way of life free from coercion.'' Stressing the potentially calamitous effect on the open world environment of a demoralized and defeatist world opinion if Greece fell, he warned that "discouragement and possible failure would quickly be the lot of neighboring people" in the Middle East, not to mention the "profound effect" such an event would have in Europe.[15]

Just what was entailed by this commitment to defend the free way of life was left unclear. In justifying this approach, Acheson believed that FDR, in similar circumstances, "would make a statement of global policy, but confine the request for money right now to Greece and Turkey.'' Despite the recognition that similar threats were likely to arise in other parts of the world, he told the Senate Committee on Foreign Relations less than two weeks following Truman's address that any future requests for aid would "have to be considered according to the circumstances in each individual case,'' with no assurance that the United States would automatically adopt measures like those proposed for Greece and Turkey. Moreover, the "global policy" was hardly worldwide in a geographic sense at this time, as was made clear by the administration's reluctance to plunge more deeply into the Chinese civil war.[16]

This disparity between the spectacular nature of the justification and the cautious interpretation of its implications for the future should not have been surprising, since policymakers had barely an inkling of the new kinds of challenges that the nation would be called upon to face or the solutions that would be needed to deal with them. The crucial point for the time being was to affirm the strategic essentials of Wilsonian internationalism and to make clear America's commitment to action. The Truman Doctrine was above all a statement of belief in the activist essence of the Wilsonian creed, a commitment to the idea of commitment. Ever since the rejection of the Treaty of Versailles by the Senate, the litmus test of Wilsonian internationalism had been the nation's commitment to activism in the face of crises abroad. During the interwar years, American presidents had repeatedly talked about aggression anywhere being a matter of concern to the United States, only to couch their declarations in such abstract terms as to make clear that such aggression was really not a matter of vital interest. The Truman Doctrine reversed the Hoover-Stimson approach of erecting only legal and moral roadblocks to aggression by declaring the strategic importance of overseas crises and stating the determination to do something effective about them. In promising not to break the heart of the world again, Truman was concerned to send a message to the Soviets and to reassure a wavering world opinion.[17]

Although the Truman Doctrine was more a diffuse statement of the Wilsonian credo underlying administration thinking than a detailed doctrine, the emphasis on propping up world opinion anticipated the basic concern of its immediate follow-up in Europe, the Marshall Plan. The Truman Doctrine and the Marshall Plan were the Siamese twins of American policy for this period not only because of their close succession in time, but because they were addressed to the same problem: Europe. Since Europe was the key to maintaining an effective world opinion, the administration was concerned primarily with restoring European confidence or at least preventing its collapse. With Europe living under the threatening shadow of the USSR and its growing coven of satellites and also plagued by economic difficulties of the first order, Europe's inability to restore a once formidable export economy betokened more serious problems ahead. Having barely rescued a drowning Continent during World War II, by 1947 anxious policymakers concluded that economic revival would require artificial respiration in the form of direct economic intervention.[18]

As in the Greek crisis, the psychological dimension of the problem was at the heart of administration thinking. In drawing up a plan of American aid to stimulate European recovery, the chief worry of Kennan and other State Department planners was not the Soviet military threat to the Continent, which was considered to be negligible, but the fragile psychic economy of the Europeans. Kennan was convinced that "what is important is not what things actually are but what they seem to be—not the actual shapes of the realities but the shadows which are cast by those shapes upon the minds of men." The real danger was the belief that communism was "the coming thing, the movement of the future--that it is on the make and there is no stopping it." If people saw no hope of being rewarded for working and saving, then western Europe would be tilling the kind of barren economic ground from which the weeds of communism would quickly sprout. Marshall concurred wholeheartedly, arguing that the remedy lay in "restoring the confidence of the European people in the economic future of their own countries and of Europe as a whole."[19]

If one factors out the common emphasis on world opinion, the Marshall Plan was strategically far more ambiguous than the Truman Doctrine. In a moment of excess, Acheson declared that the European Recovery Program had "replaced the long-sought great power leadership as the last best hope for recovery abroad and American security at home." In his inaugural address Truman listed the ERP as one of the mainstays of American foreign policy. Yet the Marshall Plan was hardly a revolutionary departure in American policy—at least in conceptual terms—because it looked more to the past than to the Wilsonian future; conceivably, it would have made good policy sense to undertake it even if there had been no cold war. As Imanuel Wexler has argued, the plan was based on the assumption that "an improvement in Europe's economic health would, in turn, promote long-run political stability and peace on the Continent," an assumption that was rooted in the 1920s faith in the ability of economic means to secure political ends. By following in the wishful Lend-Lease tradition of promising "cheap security," it evaded the question of the future of the European balance of power. What's more, with its congressionally mandated emphasis on promoting European unification, the Marshall Plan could even be sold in isolationist terms as an inexpensive way of keeping the United States *out* of Europe. Its geopolitical ambiguity was further accentuated by a lack of domestic enthusiasm for its passage that mocked the Truman Doctrine's recent emphasis on American will. Indeed, Marshall recalled that "there was so much feeling about further appropriations for Europe, that we knew the whole problem was how to meet that opposition."[20]

The continuing psychological vulnerability of the Continent and the limited value of attempting economic solutions to geopolitical problems were exposed quickly enough in June 1948 when the Soviets shut down all land and water access routes to West Berlin, thereby isolating its population and the allied garrisons in the western sectors. The immediate crisis was provoked by the imposition of a currency reform by the Western powers, but that step was itself the product of the decision taken earlier in the year to include the western zones of occupation in the European Recovery Program. American and Soviet policymakers realized that these measures, by taking German policy far beyond any existing four-power agreements on Germany's status, threatened the breakdown of the quadripartite occupation regime. In turn, the end of allied cooperation in Germany, however limited, posed disturbing questions for the future of Europe and the world.

As the first clear-cut credibility crisis of the postwar era, the blockade featured elements that would be present in all future cold-war confrontations. The dispute over Berlin centered on a strategically marginal area that nevertheless involved the risk of general war as the result of a deep concern with the three faces of credibility. Throughout the crisis, American policymakers sought to send an unambiguous message to the Soviets that would prevent further escalation and bolster German and European morale, all the while displaying an underlying apprehensiveness about the degree to which the United States was actually committed to seeing the cold war through. Still, there were also major differences between Berlin and crises to come that limited its usefulness as a paradigm for handling future confrontations. As a purely European crisis, it lacked the global coloration of subsequent cold-war showdowns. And, for all its seriousness, there was relatively little danger of war in 1948 as policymakers on both sides took care to operate within clearly specified limits.

When the Soviets severed the land access routes, the United States decided quickly to hang on in a position that was patently indefensible. Few outposts were as hopelessly exposed as Berlin, 110 miles deep within the Soviet zone, where the presence of the Western powers depended for access on three slender highway corridors cutting through the Soviet-controlled countryside. The U.S. Army was understandably unenthusiastic about the prospect of having to defend this exposed island, no matter Truman's emphatic statement, "We were going to stay. Period." As one gloomy administration exercise in futurology put it: "Any of the courses predicated on the Western Powers' remaining in Berlin is likely in the long run to prove ineffective. The Western position in the city would increasingly deteriorate, and ultimate Western withdrawal would probably become necessary." Six months into the airlift, the NSC concurred: "Without satisfactory resolution, the Western position in Berlin is untenable in the long run." Nevertheless, if time was the enemy, it was also potentially a friend, for the airlift was essentially a way of buying a plot of time on which to build a diplomatic solution.[21]

Given its strategic irrelevance and the insuperable difficulties in staying on for the long haul, Berlin's importance was almost entirely symbolic. That was hardly an argument against staying, however, for most policymakers sensed that symbolism was central to America's cold-war strategy. Knuckling under to the Russians would send entirely the wrong message and serve to encourage further aggressive acts in other places strategically more important. As Under Secretary of State Lovett explained to a meeting of the National Security Council, "The problem of Berlin must not be looked at solely as a problem in Germany. Account must be taken of Russia and her aims as a whole." In this case, the administration's assessment was supported by domestic public opinion which, in the words of one document, concurred in "the belief that surrender in Berlin would only result in future aggression elsewhere."[22]

Important, too, was the need to send a message of reassurance to the Europeans, lest the confidence bought with Marshall funds be blown away by a sudden gust of demoralization. The American ambassador in London, Lew Douglas, warned that withdrawal from Berlin would have "serious, if not disastrous, consequences in western Germany and throughout western Europe." Morale in West Germany, whose economic revival was fast becoming the key to the recovery of Europe, could not be allowed to collapse as a result of the loss of the symbolic capital city. According to General Lucius Clay, the commander of the American occupation, making the easy decision to retreat now would mean only more difficult choices in the future. "With each retreat we will find ourselves confronted with the same problem but with fewer and fewer allies on our side," he predicted. Similarly, a State

Department analysis saw a withdrawal as "catastrophic," for "in the minds of Europeans retreat would be viewed as an ignominious surrender." Clay's political adviser, Robert Murphy, argued that "our withdrawal, either voluntary or involuntary, would have severe psychological repercussions which would, at this critical stage in the European situation, extend far beyond the boundaries of Berlin and even Germany." Acheson later summed up the perceived stakes: "We couldn't afford to have the Russians win in Berlin; otherwise Europe was down the drain."[23]

The Truman Doctrine and Marshall Plan were examples of American willingness to appropriate money, but Berlin required resolution of an altogether different kind. In the 1930s the Fascist powers, priding themselves on their superior will, were greeted with the rather sorry spectacle of moralizing and hand-wringing from the major democracies. Understandably, then, there were many within the administration, Robert Murphy among the most prominent, who worried about the "strength of determination in Washington to maintain the position." He feared that the strategic liabilities of the situation and the "lack of specific purpose for our presence here may over the long term combine to vitiate US determination to hold fast." Retreat, he told the State Department, "would be tantamount to an acknowledgment of lack of courage to resist Soviet pressure short of war and would amount to a public confession of weakness under pressure." For General Clay, if America did "not believe the issue is cast now, then it never will and communism will run rampant." A few months after leaving office, Dean Acheson, referring to the Berlin blockade crisis, emphasized "the overwhelming importance of winning that struggle. We had to stay in Berlin, and we had to emerge from this trial of will with the Russians still there . . . we had to stay with it, no matter what the consequences might be."[24]

And yet, for all the importance invested in it, the crisis stopped well short of a military confrontation. Ignored was the advice of Winston Churchill to threaten to "raze their cities" if the Soviets did not withdraw from Berlin and eastern Germany. Likewise ignored were the few hawks in the Truman administration, most notably Clay and Murphy, who pressed for a military challenge of the blockade in the belief that the Russians were bluffing. Nuclear-capable B-29 bombers were moved to British bases as a token of American determination, but Clay's proposal to send an armored column of reinforcements down the autobahn was quickly rejected as far too risky. As Marshall said, "We intend to stay in Berlin and we will resist force with force, but not initiate it." Unlike future crises, open talk of military measures was sedulously avoided.[25]

Further diminishing the possibility of war was Washington's understanding that the Soviet move, far from being an expansionist act, was an understandable counter to measures taken by the Western powers in Germany. Secretary of the Army Kenneth Royall acknowledged to Henry Stimson that "the Soviets have some basis for their argument, in view of the tripartite actions we have been forced to take regarding Germany." Even Truman, in the lurid description found in his *Memoirs,* described the crisis as a "counter-attack" by communism. Washington recognized that the Soviets were employing their blockade of the city as a diplomatic tactic, which suggested that some reasonable bargain might yet be struck on the issue of a continued allied presence in the city. The National Security Council, for example, speculated that the purpose of the blockade was "to force the resumption of Four-Power negotiations about Germany under conditions largely favorable to the USSR." Some policymakers, most notably Ambassador Smith in Moscow, thought a deal allowing the Soviets back into Germany might not be a bad idea. As one CIA memo in favor of negotiations put it, "Weighed against a continuation of our present dilemma . . . the gamble would appear to be worthwhile." Though not much hope was invested in them, behind-the-scenes negotiations continued throughout the crisis.[26]

Given the obvious Soviet interest in continuing to have a say in matters affecting the relatively more important western portion of Germany, it seemed unlikely that they would risk war over Berlin. The CIA predicted that the Soviets would "probably use every means short of armed force to compel [the Western] powers to leave the city." And this estimate proved correct. The Soviets harassed the airlift but allowed it to continue, while the Americans chose not to go beyond the airlift as a means of challenging the blockade. Clay himself came around to the point of view that "we can take humiliation and pressure short of war in Berlin without losing face." The JCS, meanwhile, was more worried about who would fire the first shot in the *next* Berlin crisis. A new blockade, they speculated, might feature "a determination to force us out of Berlin by taking any steps to make the airlift abortive, or, perhaps, to bring about a major war issue." The behavior of the two adversaries throughout the crisis thus showed an implicit agreement to use escape roads in the event that the diplomatic brakes failed. Obligingly, in the spring of 1949 the Russians agreed, for their own reasons, to lift the blockade in return for another four-power conclave of foreign ministers.[27]

Nerve-jangling as it was, then, the Berlin crisis never threatened at any point to explode suddenly and unstoppably into war. The airlift was unquestionably a way of showing steadfastness, but it showed at least as much ingenuity in finessing a confrontation as it did a clear resolve to face down the Russians. Its adoption in the first place was a clear signal to Moscow of America's wish to limit the consequences of the crisis and to keep it on a nonmilitary plane. By using the airlift as a way of scrambling to temporary safety on higher ground in the hope that the floodwaters of danger would eventually recede, the United States showed that it preferred above all to avoid making the choice between withdrawal or staying on and fighting. A disgusted Robert Murphy, obsessed with showing unambiguous resolve, thought the airlift proved only that the United States could "keep alive a great city by the use of air transport alone." Despite its surface appearances, the first Berlin crisis displayed a quite limited show of determination, one that stopped far short of making the city the supreme symbol of cold-war policy that it would later become.[28]

The Berlin airlift, coupled with the earlier Communist coup in Czecho-slovakia, was a major factor in inducing the United States to formally aban-don its 150-year-old tradition of political isolation by becoming a signatory to the North Atlantic Treaty. In the wake of 1948's events, it seemed apparent to Washington that the Marshall Plan, despite its great importance, was des-tined to fall short of its aims, as economic confidence was unlikely to take hold in the absence of political security. The North Atlantic Treaty would attempt to add the missing ingredient of political commitment to the Marshall Plan's recipe for shoring up European morale.[29]

Again, the straightforwardly military dimensions of the European prob-lem, though hardly negligible, took second place to psychological factors in the calculations of American statesmen. To all indications, the Russians were relying on methods short of war, primarily political intimidation and subver-sion by use of Communist fifth columns. Nevertheless, given the ideological hostility of the two systems, conflict was possible even if both parties desired to avert a war. As NSC 20/4 pointed out in November 1948, a serious misreading of each other's intentions was always a real possibility. Because incidents arising through miscalculation could balloon beyond control once in progress, a strong show of Western determination seemed necessary in order to prevent them from arising in the first place. Echoing the sentiments of Winston Churchill, Ambassador Douglas in London argued that "we can only deter them by a real show of resolution. Such a determination combined with the re-establishment of Western Europe as a center of power, may lead to a satisfactory settlement."[30]

Following the signature of the Brussels Pact in 1948 and the creation of the Western Union, American policymakers came around to accepting the view of western European statesmen that the psychological vulnerability of the Continent could be lessened by military reassurance that only the United States could provide. While the State Department had anticipated and dis-counted the Czech coup, it could not ignore the implications of that event for creating a defeatist climate of opinion in western Europe. In the view of John Hickerson, the prime mover behind the NATO alliance, the Czech coup had "created widespread fear and a certain bandwagon psychology, particularly in the crucial non-Communist left." He concluded with a call for "a general stiffening of morale in free Europe," which would be achievable only by convincing "non-Communist elements that friendly external force comparable to the threatening external source is available." Marshall soon agreed, and informed Truman that "at least an indication of our willingness to consult on means of stopping further extension of Communist dictatorship in Europe is necessary to stiffen morale in the free countries of Europe." Rapid progress was made in drafting a treaty, which was ready for signature in April 1949.[31]

Whatever its outward resemblance to great-power alliances of the past, the North Atlantic Treaty was not about power in any direct and obvious sense. For one thing, the United States viewed western Europe as a rump segment of world opinion. The relations between members of the NATO alliance, a community of democracies at similar levels of socioeconomic and cultural development among whom war was coming to be conceived as impossible, resembled in miniature what the League of Nations was eventually supposed to become. Acheson described this collective will in Wilsonian terms as being based on "a community of spirit, a community of history, and a community of interest in these Atlantic countries." As the CIA put it in 1949, "Considerations of expedient national interest are not excluded in the relations of the Western powers, but a mutual heritage affords a firmer and more enduring basis of common interest . . . For the United States, the integrity of Western Christendom is essential to the integrity of Western Civilization."[32]

The power political implications of the treaty commitment were also quite vague. With regard to the crucial issue of the future of the European balance of power, for example, the rhetoric surrounding the treaty contained more than mere traces of the continuing belief that Europe was capable of mounting an independent defense. The alliance was still based on the philanthropic principles and precedents of Lend-Lease and the European Recovery Program, in which the Europeans, with American assistance, were expected to rebuild their house while Americans played the role of generous relatives cosigning and guaranteeing the mortgage and even lending the down payment until they got back on their feet. Despite the abandonment of George Washington's caveat against entangling alliances, the signature of the North Atlantic Treaty was a relatively painless and noncontroversial step for American policymakers to take because the American guarantee merely ratified officially what history had already legislated through U.S. intervention in two world wars. What was not clear at the time was that a promise once again to lock the barn door when it was too late was quite different from the far more substantial commitment that would be required of the United States once it became obvious that policy ought to focus on obviating the need for a third intervention.[33]

Even when judged on its own terms as an exercise in morale boosting, the treaty was premised on assumptions that contradicted its stated ends. The large-scale program of arms aid that followed its signing, the Military Assistance Program, was not intended to provide Europe with an objective capacity for self-defence; rather, the idea was to nurture self-confidence and a will to resist Soviet expansionism among west Europeans. As Bob Lovett argued about military aid, "It is the psychological effect, rather than the intrinsic military value, which is of primary importance." However, historian Chester Pach, Jr., has shown that "the extension of arms assistance was a symbolic act; it required frequent repetition, lest the cessation of aid destroy the foreign confidence that the United States had so sedulously tried to nurture." As this analysis suggests, the absence of reciprocity meant that the power of reassurance lay only in the hands of the donor and could not be transferred to the recipient. The Wilsonian conception of world opinion had been premised on the existence of a self-confident core of democracies. But given Europe's chronic sense of psychological weakness and uncertainty, there could never be a *restoration* of European confidence in the traditional sense. Only American power and American commitment could stabilize the Continent.[34]

As a result, this policy of morale building contained a built-in dynamic, not very well understood by policymakers at the time, which tended to pull the country into a deep commitment of indefinite duration. The United States agreed to become the guarantor of European security in the expectation that the American presence would bring stability, security, confidence in the future, resolution of Franco-German differences, and tangible movement toward unity. However, in creating a sense of security the United States would also be undercutting the impulse to unity, which was supposed eventually to produce an independent European balance; at the same time, it would be diminishing the spirit of self-reliance that it wished to encourage among Europeans. As a result, the tendency would be to stretch out indefinitely the period of "empire by invitation," with all the corrosive consequences that result from overstaying one's welcome. There were other potential ironies, as well. As we shall see, once the need for military power became evident, the NATO solution contained within itself destabilizing possibilities that flowed from the need to mortgage itself to German nationalism on the issue of reunification.

The American commitment to NATO also posed some difficulties for morale and world opinion outside Europe. What with Europe's metaphorical status as the "meteorological center" of world politics, it was hoped by some that putting an end to turbulence on the Continent would prevent the outbreak of storms in the rest of the world. But the imputed logic of Soviet behavior suggested a geological metaphor of political isostasy, in which pressure blocked in one place would only result in increased pressure elsewhere. As Moscow chargé Elbridge Durbrow had warned in 1947, "If Europe can indeed be held firm and if we become deeply committed on the continent in the process, we may then see the Kremlin try to direct development and exploitation of what Stalin termed the great 'reserves of the revolution in the colonies and dependent countries.'" The CIA also assumed in July 1949 that with stabilization in Europe "the USSR would direct a greater effort toward the Far East."[35]

While for Europeans the North Atlantic Treaty was, in Acheson's words, "the thing by which they gage their whole degree of security and movement toward security," the administration was beginning to realize that the message to non-European areas might be the reverse of that intended. By traditional realist logic, to concentrate on the security of one area was to make others less secure. Departmental adviser John Foster Dulles followed this line of reasoning in suggesting that the very signature of the NATO treaty, by showing American determination in Europe, lessened American credibility elsewhere. Should the United States "fall back and allow doubtful areas to fall under Soviet communist control," he suggested in a May 1950 memo, many non-European nations would "feel confirmed in the impression, already drawn from the North Atlantic Treaty, that we do not expect to stand firm short of the North Atlantic area."[36]

By the logic of internationalism, then, the commitment to NATO seemed to require greater commitment everywhere else, lest debacles in the Far East rebound and affect the situation in Europe. As Dean Rusk, an assistant secretary of state at the time, put it: "Aggression anywhere—not only in the North Atlantic area, but anywhere—is a matter of the greatest concern to us." Thus, the strengthening of opinion in Europe required greater sensitivity to the effect on opinion of events elsewhere. For policymakers like Acheson, such complexities were simply brushed aside as imponderables or irrelevancies in light of the overriding need to show resolution. "Now, the fact of the matter was that when you took the whole problem, the will to do something was the most essential part of this whole thing," Acheson told a House committee. "History has taught us that the absence of such determination and of its clear statement in advance is gravely dangerous."[37]

Despite Acheson's emphasis on will, the North Atlantic pact failed to achieve the avidly sought-for sense of confidence in the West. The tentativeness of U.S. policy and the failure of its attempts thus far to build up a confident world opinion without power became apparent in late 1949 as a huge cloud of gloom descended upon Washington. The formation of the People's Republic of China in the autumn and the confirmed detonation of the Soviet Union's first nuclear weapon produced a new respect for Soviet might and led rapidly to the conclusion that augmented military power would be necessary to restrain the Soviet bloc. No longer did it seem possible to reinforce the morale of others by economic and political measures without first increasing the military credibility of the United States.

NSC 20 had already asserted that "military superiority was a requisite of containment." Although there was an understanding in mid-1947 that "the USSR at will, could speedily overrun continental Europe, the Near East, northern China, and Korea," the belief for the next two years was that American power was sufficient to deter this worst-case catastrophe. Hewing to this line, in mid-1949 the State Department argued that Soviet war-making capacity was "definitely inferior to that of the Western powers, even without taking account of the atom bomb. So long as this is true, it appears unlikely that the Kremlin will deliberately precipitate a major conflict." But that sense of security and superiority rested largely on the possession of an atomic monopoly which vanished with the Russian detonation of a nuclear device. According to Acheson, "It changed everything, and [Truman] realized it ten seconds after it happened." As he subsequently described the situation: "We haven't got the monopoly of the atomic bomb. This great thing that Churchill says is—has policed the world has disappeared. It doesn't exist anymore. What do you do?"[38]

Though objectively the Kremlin had done nothing new in the way of expansion and the fall of China had long been a foregone conclusion, the mere existence of a Soviet A-bomb, irrespective of quantity or delivery capability, threatened to negate all the psychological initiatives taken in Europe since 1947. The National Security Council had acknowledged in 1948 that whatever "feeling of security" western Europe enjoyed was the result of the U.S. nuclear monopoly, "because the atomic bomb, under American trusteeship, offers the present major counterbalance to the ever-present threat of the Soviet military power." In the absence of a nuclear monopoly, then, it followed that insecurity would reign. Following this bleak reasoning, a CIA review of the world situation at the end of 1949 concluded that "Western European calm in the face of publicity about the new Soviet atomic capability and current Soviet restraint in propaganda do not alter the fact that the USSR will try increasingly to persuade Europeans that the balance of world power has shifted decisively away from the western world." As John Lewis Gaddis has suggested, "World order, and with it American security, had come to depend as much on *perceptions* of the balance of power as on what that balance actually was."[39]

Inevitably, the Soviet A-bomb undermined whatever self-confidence the Americans possessed. Pessimism was the prevailing mood in Washington late in 1949, born of the belief that all the measures taken so far had been half-measures. By 1950 the consensus of opinion within the capital was that containment, as thus far practiced, was failing, with influentials like Bernard Baruch going so far as to assert that "we are losing the cold war." Some intelligence reports indicated that Moscow was planning war in the near future, without waiting for a prefatory crisis of capitalism. In a March 1950 conversation with Congressman Christian Herter, Acheson noted that "during the last six to nine months there had been a trend against us which, if allowed to continue, would lead to a considerable deterioration in our position." The Soviets had "extended their sphere of influence materially in the past several years. They have no intention of stopping and are determined to bring about a situation where we will be confronted by having the rest of the world under their domination." Reinforcing the growing concern within the State Department and the military were reports that Congress, reflecting public opinion, was calling for "some sort of bold action."[40]

Acheson's solution was "to make a colossal effort" at rearmament in order to create what he would later call "real power." Along with the military, he believed that American power would have to be significantly augmented to make war unthinkable to the Soviets. Rejecting Kennan's argument that a militarization of the cold war would lead almost inevitably to conflict, Acheson contended that the Pentagon fully understood that its "war machine" was one "whose objective is that it never be used" and that the generals were in fact "responsive to the thesis that our objective is to prevent war." Since Acheson continued to believe that the Soviets were not militarily-minded, the whole point of a build-up would be psychological. "For the time being the method of force directly applied does not seem to them to be the most propitious," he said, and he wanted to keep it that way.[41]

The decision and the justification for rearmament were set forth in NSC 68, which was issued in April 1950. In a credal prologue, this document systematically pulled together all the various strands of the Wilsonian strategic problematic and the new view of Soviet ideology from the scattered policy declarations of the postwar period. However, it was not the conceptual chart for navigating the cold war that its drafters had hoped it would be. While it marked a step forward in its frank recognition of the need for American power, NSC 68 was also a backward-looking document because it relied on a classical form of deterrence: avoiding war by making credible the threat to go to war. Just as generals were assuming that the next war would be a world war, so too were policymakers resorting to traditional assumptions on how best to avoid it. Despite his advocacy of a military build-up, Policy Planning Staff Director Nitze rejected as too provocative the National Security Resources Board's suggestion for massive civil defense preparations by arguing that "we should concentrate on the things we can do which will help prevent a possible war rather than to proceed on the assumption that a war will occur in the near future." A strong military posture, one capable of mobilizing superior strength against the Soviets, was vital as "an ultimate guarantee of our national security."[42]

By the standards of Wilsonian logic, this kind of situation was precisely the sort that was fated inevitably to break down. It was the knowledge that classical deterrence had always failed in the past that caused people like Robert Oppenheimer to worry, after reviewing the document, that the policy would cause war rather than prevent it. "If one is honest," he said, "the most probable view of the future is that of war, exploding atomic bombs, death, and the end of most freedom." Kennan, too, in criticizing the militarization of American policy, argued that rearmament would defeat its own aims. These kinds of critiques of classical deterrence indicated that NSC 68, far from being a blueprint of the cold war, was actually a document whose outlook, very much rooted in the past, reflected an inability to draw up such a design. Rearmament and classical deterrence may have been necessary as "an indispensable backdrop to the conduct of the policy of containment," but they had little to say about the foreground in which policy would actually have to operate.[43]

NSC 68 assumed that containment consisted of body-building and the striking of impressive muscular poses when in fact it held in store a series of freestyle wrestling matches for which rules had yet to be formulated. The document said little about dealing with smaller symbolic crises whose management would become the central problem of the cold war. Although it cautioned against giving in to "piecemeal aggression," it spoke only vaguely, and with altogether too much bravado, about making "*critical points* which we cannot hold the occasion for a global war of annihilation." Only afterward did Acheson admit ruefully that NSC 68 had missed the point entirely by gearing itself primarily to reversing a perceived trend toward general war. As he recalled in 1953, "our minds had been more heavily on the major point of the danger of an all out war with the USSR, and much . . . of our policy planning . . . was geared into this primary and more fatal risk." The result of this traditional thinking was that when the first major military threat of the postwar period emerged, the United States had no plans to deal with it.[44]

KOREA: NO LESSONS OF THE PAST

The attempt to buoy the European spirit and the decision to create overwhelming American power were basic ingredients of a neo-Wilsonian approach to fighting the cold war, yet 1950 showed that they had not been combined in the proper mixture. For all the variations on a theme of credibility spun out since 1947 by U.S. policymakers, a satisfactory language of power to replace traditional power politics and collective security had not yet been articulated; indeed, in the prevailing gloom of Washington, many policymakers, with their obsessive dread about an imminent all-out war with the Soviet Union, appeared to have little confidence that an alternative language *could* be spoken. Korea marked a crucial turn in the cold war because it finally brought to the forefront of policy attention the central problem of dealing with aggression once it had actually started and of doing so in a way that would prevent the cascade of global calamities so dreaded by Wilsonian thought.

At first, the policy essentials seemed cut and dried. The American response to news of the North Korean invasion was so rapid as if to seem, in Ernest May's term, axiomatic. Describing the initial White House meeting following receipt of news of the North Korean invasion, Philip Jessup recalled, "I don't think there was a question in anyone's mind or that it entered into the discussion that took place—as to whether or not we would stand up . . . I think it was just sort of clear to us, almost without discussion, that we were going to." The swiftness with which Acheson brought the issue before the UN Security Council and the president's vivid recollections of Munich and other diplomatic debacles of the 1930s have reinforced the impression that the decision to intervene was triggered by memories of the past and moved by powerful forces in the collective unconscious.[45]

The well-known account in Truman's *Memoirs* that describes his train of thought while returning to Washington from his Missouri home presents the classic illustration of policy being determined by historical memory:

> In my generation, this was not the first occasion when the strong had attacked the weak. I recalled some earlier instances: Manchuria, Ethiopia, Austria. I remembered how each time that the democracies failed to act it had encouraged the aggressors to keep going ahead. Communism was acting in Korea just as Hitler, Mussolini, and the Japanese had acted ten, fifteen, and twenty years earlier. I felt certain that if South Korea was allowed to fall Communist leaders would be emboldened to override nations closer to our own shores . . . If this

was allowed to go unchallenged it would mean a third world war, just as similar incidents had brought on the second world war.

This accent on the Munich analogy was not simply post facto rationalization. As he wrote at the time to British Prime Minister Attlee, if the Western democracies had stood together in the 1930s, "the whole history of our time would have been different." Citing the "lessons of history," Truman also reminded Congress that "the fateful events of the 1930s, when aggression unopposed bred more aggression and eventually war, were fresh in our memory."[46]

The president was not the only high policymaker determined not to repeat the blunders of the past. Governmental opinion was overwhelmingly in favor of a strong response to the invasion. As MacArthur's acting political adviser in Japan argued, "to sit by while Korea is overrun by unprovoked armed attack would start [a] disastrous chain of events leading most probably to world war." In a telegram to London explaining the American position, Acheson noted that "the tragic history of the 30s demonstrates beyond any doubt that the sole hope of preserving the peace of the world is to halt before they spread initial acts of aggression of this character." Arguing that "the whole future of the free world is at stake," he maintained that the consequences "would be disastrous if the Soviet Union can now establish the proposal that aggression can be a profitable transaction." The embassy in Moscow saw it as a "clear-cut Soviet challenge which . . . US should answer firmly and swiftly." It felt that South Korea's destruction would have "incalculably grave repercussions" in Japan, Southeast Asia, and "other areas as well." The State Department's Office of Intelligence Research suggested that inaction would generate the feeling throughout Asia and elsewhere that "the USSR is advancing invincibly, and there would be a greatly increased impulse to 'get on the bandwagon.' "[47]

The argument from historical memory assumes that the decision to intervene was analogous to a conditioned reflex, an instrumental response triggered automatically by a stimulus as the consequence of a learning process. Yet American policy was not simply a product stamped out mechanically from the analogical die of the Munich syndrome. There were no "lessons of the past" in the repertoire of American policy derived from events of the 1930s because it was never clear exactly what should have been done to prevent Hitler's aggression. The Munich analogy specified only what was not permitted, the only practical injunction deducible from it being a negative—"Thou shalt not appease"—which ruled out any attempts at negotiation. Quite apart from the desirability of Neville Chamberlain and Edouard Daladier, the British and French leaders, showing stiffer backbones, it was far from obvious what FDR ought to or could have done in that situation. In short, the Munich analogy was operationally useless.[48]

The absence of a conditioning process that could have created automatic, habitual responses points to a more fundamental difficulty yet in using the Munich analogy as an explanation for American policy in Korea. It arises from the fact that narrowly empiricist approaches that see learning as a product of external stimuli and reflexive recall do little to explain how the conceptual frameworks necessary to ordering that experience emerged. Historical memory was at work, to be sure, but that memory in itself would have been meaningless without the larger pattern of historical interpretation by which policymakers made sense of it. The memory of Munich was, by itself, quite incapable of providing such a framework. As Henry Stimson's evaluation of the Manchuria crisis of 1931 demonstrated, that framework, traceable back to Woodrow Wilson and his historical interpretation of the new configuration of world politics, owed nothing at all to Munich.[49]

Munich became important only once the outbreak of war had confirmed the folly of appeasement in a way that validated Wilson's bleak prophesies. Thus it was not so much historical memory at work as the cultural sedimentation of the Wilsonian interpretation of history, which gave to Munich a post hoc significance that it did not possess at the time. Munich was important because American statesmen had become predisposed to attribute significance to it thanks to their acceptance of the Wilsonian strategic outlook, not as a result of habit. In other words, Munich was not the paradigm, but its primary historical exemplification. Munich was only a metaphor that stood for a larger pattern of historical understanding. In practical terms, this meant that the grand lessons of history had been learned, but that there was little to draw upon in the way of operative lessons of the past. Policymakers were thus simultaneously possessed by absolute certainty and by confusion. Convinced of Korea's global significance from within the Wilsonian historical frame, they were at the same time confronted by the obscure and contradictory aspects of a historically contingent situation.[50]

The absence of historical signposts to guide administration policy in Korea was evident from its woefully undeveloped logic of deterrence. From all indications, this was *the* test Americans had been anticipating with some dread since 1949. Notes of a Blair House meeting on June 26 reported the president as saying that "he had done everything he could for five years to prevent this kind of situation. Now the situation is here and we must do what we can to meet it." Yet, probably because of the fear that such wars would be uncontrollable, thus spelling the failure of containment, the administration had not developed any well-considered policy for dealing with them. There was a huge gap between the "whether," which was admittedly axiomatic in view of the perceived consequences of failure to respond, and the "how," to which little or no thought had yet been given. Consequently, when the North Korean invasion took place, the administration was forced to improvise decisions on issues of supreme importance.[51]

Because the Wilsonian sensibility provided no clear-cut recipe for dealing with a problem which, in its particulars, was far different from that faced at Munich and which raised different policy questions, there was very little—apart from the commitment to intervene—that was automatic or reflexive about the intervention in Korea. The Korean situation raised a host of completely novel policy issues. One major point of difference with the 1930s was that the United States was clearly dealing in this instance with a surrogate, which complicated matters considerably. The situation was potentially confusing enough for Acheson to have to remind the Senate Committee on Foreign Relations that "the real heart of the problem we face, is the Soviet Union. We must never allow that to be obscured at all." On another occasion, he counseled the committee to "never lose sight of this fact, that is the central motivating power here." The United States had already encountered a similar problem in Europe, where it discovered that the use of subversive fifth columns was both exasperating, because the Soviets could distance themselves from events, and comforting, because the institutional cushion insulated both sides from the dreaded danger of head-to-head confrontation.[52]

Although it was generally assumed that "the Soviet movement is monolithic," as the service secretaries put it, analyses also pointed out that the Soviet reliance on surrogates suggested a desire to avoid war; therefore, any American reaction should, instead of forcing the Russians' hand, permit them to withdraw without losing face. Instead of staring down the aggressors, then, as a strict antiappeasement sensibility would have it, this logic suggested that it would be more prudent to avoid looking them in the eye. Arguing in this vein, the Moscow embassy recommended that direct representations regarding Korea should not be made to the Kremlin because of the danger of engaging its prestige. Fear of Moscow's response was coupled with apprehension at how America's allies might react. Soon after the Chinese Communist intervention in November 1950, Acheson "agreed entirely that we would not, at this time, say the USSR is responsible because we could not do anything about following such a charge against the Soviet Union due to the attitude of our allies."[53]

Novel, too, was the occurrence of the challenge in a remote peninsula in Northeast Asia hitherto of only minor interest to the United States, yet one for which the United States had some direct responsibility and which was fortunately located for purposes of defense. Acheson later recalled that "I don't believe that anybody believed at that time that so much of the fate of the rest of the world was going to arise out of this place." Nevertheless, although Korea was far removed from the United States and outside the critical defensive perimeter outlined publicly by Acheson a few months earlier, the United States got off lightly thanks to the heavy American presence there. The service secretaries emphasized that "there is no other place in the world—except those where Allied troops are present—where we possess military strength in any way comparable to that which was available in Japan for use in Korea." Indeed, General Omar Bradley recognized immediately that Korea "offered as good an occasion for action in drawing the line as anywhere else."[54]

The supranational dimension of the Korean crisis provided yet another contrast to the 1930s. The Korean War was fought under the banner of the United Nations and, as the administration continued to insist, as an exercise in "collective security," a phrase that still possessed a powerful resonance in domestic public opinion. It was ironic indeed that the individual responsible for shunting the Korean problem to the United Nations was Dean Acheson, who ordinarily had little regard for that organization's peacekeeping potential. Apparently the lessons of the NATO treaty, in which Senator Vandenberg's relentless kibitzing heavily emphasized NATO's relationship to the UN, had not been lost on Acheson. A United Nations action made more palatable to a sizeable segment of the American public an intervention which, if conducted nakedly by the United States and a few faint-hearted allies, might otherwise have received only lukewarm support. That the intervention was made possible by the Soviet Union's temporary absence from the Security Council was hardly proof of the organization's effectiveness, but UN involvement nevertheless provided a sneak preview of the kind of cooperation that would have been possible had it been capable of functioning as originally envisioned.

Another new historical wrinkle was added by the understanding that Korea was a civil conflict ensconced within complex regional dynamics nested within a geopolitical struggle. Everyone understood that the division of Korea was artificial. If U.S. officials refused to play up the civil dimensions of the conflict, nevertheless they understood very well that Korea was "a land in which the North and South are as tied together as a pretzel," as Edwin Pauley once put it. While Koreans north and south were obsessed with ending the forced partition of their country, the United States could not help but view Korea through geopolitical lenses. The closest historical analogy for this aspect of the situation, the Spanish civil war, provided no useful strategic insights.[55]

The regional dimension of the Korean invasion and the American response further accentuated the distinctiveness of the Korean situation from previous crises. Whereas the logic dividing Europe between East and West had been quite clear since at least the war's end, the power situation in the Far East was murkily defined. In the past, stability in the Asian and Pacific region had been provided by the European imperial powers and Japan, but Europe's prostration and Japan's defeat had left a vacuum of disorder that would be filled in one way or another. This vacuum, coupled with the success of communism in China, the ideological vulnerability of the region, the emergence of semiautonomous Communist-Nationalist regimes, and, lastly, the cold war in the Far East, brought Asia to the center of policymakers' attention. Though well aware of the region's turbulence, until 1950 American policy lacked a firm sense of its global significance because the image of the world as a global powder keg or macrocosm of the Balkans was the least well articulated aspect of the Wilsonian worldview.[56]

Despite pressures from the Republican right wing for a tougher line against communism in Asia, until the North Korean attack, the administration pursued what was essentially a Hooverian policy of allowing the dust to settle in China. Thanks to Korea, it was forced to confront head-on a central issue of the cold war that it had finessed during the Berlin crisis: the centrality of symbolism and its effect on world opinion. The close connection between symbolism and the Wilsonian strategic problematic would go a long way toward explaining why peripheral sideshows would occupy much of the cold-war limelight in the 1950s and 1960s. Henceforth, the kind of geographic ranking of American priorities that Kennan had in mind—a concern for Europe and Japan, primarily—was impossible to enforce because problems of perception, will, and world opinion could not be geographically localized. The most original aspect of the decision to intervene in Korea, therefore, was the understanding that the stakes were not territorial in any immediate sense, but symbolic chips that could later be cashed in for greater prizes.[57]

The crucial importance of symbolism was so self-evident to most policymakers from the very beginning that they did not question its geopolitical implications—but it was not obvious to all. Thinking along traditional lines, Secretary of Defense Louis Johnson told the Blair House assemblage on 26 June that "Korea is just a symbol . . . It isn't important." No doubt Johnson believed he was speaking the common sense of the matter, inasmuch as Korea to this point had consistently been declared a strategically negligible patch of real estate. Prior to 1950, it had been little more than a king-sized headache to the American military, who time and again defined the peninsula as having no military significance and urged a withdrawal from that troublesome land. This view was enshrined as policy—on paper, at least. Many in the State Department, Kennan included, agreed. In 1948 he argued that "we would have to get out of Korea as gracefully as possible." The dominant sentiment in favor of cutting losses was summed up in 1948 by Bob Lovett, who believed that "we would lose some [face], but this was the best we can expect to do."[58]

Johnson looked at Korea's importance from the standpoint of its value in a world war, in which case Korea would truly have been a strategic backwater. His conception of symbolism was one in which the value of the symbol was directly proportional to the objective importance of the external reality it signified. If strategic assets or interests were tangible, objective, or in some sense quantifiable, then Korea's peripheral status would indeed have rendered it "merely" symbolic and Johnson's point of view would easily have carried the day. However, the unquestioned connection between Korea and the neo-Wilsonian reliance on world opinion as the key to containment amplified the invasion's signals to the point that it seemed imperative to take a stand.

This view of symbolism depended on the modernist understanding that symbols derive their meaning not from any correspondence to an objectively measurable source in reality but from the symbol system in which they are embedded. Symbols thus evoke and represent their symbolic universe—in this case, the neo-Wilsonian interpretation of history that undergirded world opinion. If systems of meaning are constitutive of reality, it follows that a loss of faith in their coherence implies a radical change in how that reality will subsequently be constituted. Much as a rejection of the cross signalizes a renunciation of Christianity, inaction in the face of perceived aggression would have been a repudiation of the very idea of world opinion and the American commitment to buttressing it.[59]

This rejection of the objectivist conception of national interests in favor of a new "political economy of symbolic exchange" did not mean that Korea was simply a subjective matter in which, as some historians would have it, "metaphysical symbolism replaced tangible objectives." Wilsonianism had always been two-dimensional in its understanding of the connection between symbols and structures. For Johnson's colleagues, Korea was important precisely because of the real consequences that would flow from readings of American action or inaction. A weak American response would be translated into beliefs and psychological states of mind that would ultimately affect the security of the Western world. Far more dangerous than the threat of physical conquest was the growing perception of Soviet success, which served to confirm the Communist claim to be riding the wave of history, a perception that could well turn into a self-fulfilling prophecy. The enemy would be emboldened and endangered peoples would read the text of history so as to reconcile themselves to the inevitable. With traditional balancing systems no longer available to check expansion, any defeat might have a lethal demoralizing effect upon nations in the front line of containment. And, not insignificantly for the domestically beleaguered Truman administration, domestic support for American internationalism might dry up quite rapidly following the flash flood of interest in the United Nations. Failure to act would have thrown open to doubt the American commitment to the Wilsonian worldview—the credo in credibility—with the result, as the Moscow embassy suggested, that it would have been necessary to reexamine totally cold-war policy.[60]

Cold-war logic thus reversed the traditional relationship between reality and appearance. Whereas formerly symbolism had been seen as only a form of power, and an inferior one at that, power had now become a servant of symbolism. Because the cold war was psychologically defined as an exercise in maintaining credibility and world opinion, Korea's symbolic stature made all the difference. Driving home the centrality of appearances, Acheson argued at the Blair House meeting that "it was important for us to do something even if the effort were not successful." It was not a case, as has been suggested by some historians who rely on the traditional objectivist criterion, in which "the symbol . . . became mightier than the reality." Nor was it a matter, in Raymond Aron's phrase, of "the growing tendency to substitute symbol for reality in the discrimination of interests and issues." Rather, symbolism was the key to molding and forming reality by maintaining the cohesion of world opinion and faith in liberal civilization that lay at the heart of containment. With its emphasis on a global psychology of power, the American concern for face went much further than that typically attributed to the oriental mind by Westerners.[61]

Even prior to the invasion, the State Department had used Korea's symbolic importance as an argument against the military's desire to withdraw totally from the peninsula. After the occupation ended in 1948, it continued to advocate an American presence because South Korea was an American creation whose collapse would damage American prestige. As early as 1946, Truman's friend and occasional emissary Edwin Pauley had described Korea as "one of the greatest ideological battlegrounds of our time." In making the case for continued economic assistance to Korea, as late as 18 June 1950, Under Secretary James Webb argued that "world opinion was sensitive to the contest between the two powers in the peninsula as a barometer of events." Thanks to the State Department's persistence, economic aid was continued, if somewhat fitfully, and the American diplomatic presence in Korea was formidable. In 1950, the American Embassy in Seoul, with a staff of about two thousand, was the largest in the world, so large that it included a mortuary icebox (capacity five).[62]

Most important of all the novelties facing American policymakers, Korea was the first real test of the viability of the Wilsonian worldview. Settling on the symbolic importance of Korea had been fairly easy inasmuch as cold-war policy had been emphasizing world opinion ever since the time of the Truman Doctrine; framing a response that would send the appropriate messages was far more difficult. For those few individuals within the government who had anticipated this kind of situation, the solution could come only by actually risking war. In 1948, Kennan had been at his most prescient in predicting the need to meet force with force on a limited basis. "We may have to face up to the fact," he said, "that there may be instances where violence somewhere in the world on a limited scale is more desirable than the alternatives, because those alternatives would be [eventual] global wars in which we ourselves would be involved, in which no one would win, and in which all civilization would be dragged down."[63]

More pointedly yet, John Foster Dulles suggested that a "series of disasters" could "probably be prevented if at some doubtful point we take a strong and dramatic stand that shows our confidence and resolution." He was, at this time, seeking an American commitment to defend Chiang Kai-shek's regime on Formosa in the hope of restricting Communist influence to the mainland. He admitted that "a strong stand at Formosa would involve a slightly increased risk of early war," but concluded nevertheless in a rehearsal of his future performances that "sometimes such a risk has to be taken." This kind of talk no doubt seemed wild at the time, but if a convincing display of credibility was in fact a central concern, then it was actually more prudent to take a military stand in a marginal area. In Central Europe it was all too easy to imagine an incident escalating beyond control, whereas clashes on the periphery could more readily be limited to symbolic displays. Assuming that both superpowers understood the dangers of direct confrontation at the center, the margins were a more logical place to do battle.[64]

This new understanding of the importance of the relationship between symbolism and world opinion in turn forced American policymakers to take a leap in the dark with regard to method. *Si vis pacem, para bellum.* "If you want peace, prepare for war," the old maxim went, and that is what the United States, in one form or another, had been leading up to until it finally adopted NSC 68. In Karl von Clausewitz's classical instrumental formulation, if deterrence, power balancing, and diplomacy all failed, then outstanding issues would be settled through war. Some thought was given to formally declaring war on the USSR, but, as one State Department memo put it, given the primary objective of U.S. policy since the end of World War II and the belief that the United States did not possess the resources to force an unconditional surrender, this was something to be done "only as a final resort." Arguing that care be taken to localize the conflict, the National Security Council repeated this principle at the beginning of July: "We must always be mindful of the basic objective of the U.S. to maintain the peace of the world. We must be guided by the premise that a general war is not inevitable." NSC 73/4 put it this way: "Our efforts should be urgently directed toward preventing global war from developing and toward increasing our war capabilities."[65]

The logic of a symbolic war was not to impose one's will upon the enemy, but, by committing sufficient military assets, to prevent the enemy from imposing theirs, without at the same time threatening to defeat them. To work, limited war assumed that the enemy's ultimate objectives, unlimited though they might be, did not include a willingness to use unlimited means—else neo-Wilsonianism would have been intellectually futile from the very beginning. As Acheson later recalled, "You must be prepared to use force in such a way as not to involve the use of ultimate force. That's what these West Pointers don't seem to understand . . . If you don't limit it, the world is gone." In the new conception of deterrence, the only possible formula for checking expansion and avoiding global conflict was, "If you want peace, make war—but not all-out war." Partly from fear that popular emotions would get out of hand, Truman avoided having to go to Congress for approval of U.S. action in Korea. In this respect, the enormous growth of the presidential war-making power during the cold war was, paradoxically, an outgrowth of the belief in the need for self-restraint that an emotional Congress could not be depended upon to exercise.[66]

This policy demanded a finely nuanced use of force in which it proved impossible to strike a satisfactory balance. Excessive intervention could trigger a world war, whereas a limited use of force might encourage further adventures and produce demoralization in the West. A few crackpot Wilsonians argued for another world war to eliminate the last roadblock to global harmony, but no one in a responsible policy position was willing to propose full-scale war except as a desperate last resort, which would have signalized the bankruptcy of policy. To Acheson, for example, preventive war would merely bring about "all the troubles that we seek to avoid." If Korea was a symbol, it followed then that the purpose of a limited war was to send messages of credibility to friend, foe, and public in a way that would prevent war and stem expansion. In the absence of normal diplomatic contact, limited war was a functional equivalent of diplomacy, a means of communication rather than compulsion.[67]

All this seems clearer in retrospect than it did at the time. Despite Truman's reassuring pronouncements to the American people that military action was designed to avert World War III, he sensed, even before Communist China's entry into the war, that American intervention risked provoking the very war it was intended to avoid. Mindful of the danger, Truman cautioned others that "what has been done may make it imperative to accept full-out war." In August, Ferdinand Eberstadt had said that "there seems to be no uncertainty whatsoever in the course that things are presently taking we are heading definitely and swiftly towards the Third World War." Even Kennan speculated that the Kremlin might have "come to consider war probable though not desirable" because of reasons of prestige that seemed of minor moment from the other side. According to Acheson, "The profound lesson of Korea is that, contrary to every action preceding, the USSR took a step which risked—however remotely—general war. No other action had done this—not even the Berlin Blockade." The string of military successes following the September landing at Inchon placed such fears in abeyance until the Chinese counterintervention.[68]

The Truman administration's improvisatory and imperfect understanding of the new logic of power was underscored by the contradictions that American policy created for itself in each dimension of the world opinion that intervention was supposed to shore up. The first objective, of course, was to send a clear and unambiguous message to the aggressor. Following the initial determination to go in, the message delivered militarily on the ground would, ideally, stop the aggression and deter future outbreaks. It did not work out that way, however, since there soon emerged an obvious incompatibility between the two fundamental Wilsonian aims of deterring aggression and avoiding another world war. The administration was forced to choose between frustration and punishment, depending on which it deemed the lesser evil. If the Communists were simply checked without being made to pay a heavy price, they might be given an incentive to continue aggressions that could result eventually in cracking Western resolve and replaying the events of the 1930s. On the other hand, a punitive approach might touch off an immediate escalation to world war. The Munich analogy offered no guidance whatsoever in resolving this dilemma, which, in its simplest form, would consume ten more years of policy debate before policymakers finally came down firmly on the antiwar side.

In concrete terms, the choice was between seeking a status quo ante peace or pursuing the Communist forces northward beyond the 38th parallel. The most vigorous argument on behalf of punishing aggression and not merely holding the line was made by John Allison of the Division of Northeast Asian Affairs, who insisted that "a determination that the aggressors should not go unpunished and vigorous, courageous United States leadership to that end should have a salutary effect upon other areas of tension in the world." Derisively calling a status quo ante approach "appeasement," Allison depicted the Policy Planning Staff's hold-the-line approach as "a timid, half-hearted policy designed not to provoke the Soviets to war." Seeking to head off a status quo ante solution, John Foster Dulles argued from the standpoint of deterrence that "if there can be armed aggression under conditions such that failure involves no permanent loss, then that puts a premium on aggression. There must be a penalty to such wrong-doing unless we want to encourage its repetition." Allison agreed. The aggressor "cannot embark upon acts of aggression with the assurance that he takes only a limited risk." He was, however, quite cavalier about the possibility of touching off another world war in the process. "When all legal and moral right is on our side why should we hesitate?" he asked rhetorically.[69]

Remarkably, given the stakes involved, the decision was left to the military, the organization least competent to decide this supremely tricky political question. In deference to the tradition of allowing great discretion to the commander in the field, Douglas MacArthur was permitted to cross the 38th parallel in hot pursuit of the fleeing North Korean forces. As his troops advanced, the specter of escalation marched alongside them. Despite the administration's concern to avoid a military clash with the Soviets that, in Acheson's words, could "well produce an incident with incalculable consequences," the success of the 38th-parallel military decision led to the problem most everyone was anxious to avoid. Upset by Truman's decision to intervene in the Chinese civil war by preventing Mao Zedong's PLA forces from invading Chiang Kai-shek's beleaguered outpost on Taiwan, and alarmed by the American presence on the Yalu border, the Chinese Communists counterattacked massively in October 1950. The powerful wave of euphoria generated by MacArthur's successful landing at Inchon and the subsequent advance north of the 38th parallel broke up quickly on the hard rocks of the Chinese intervention. Though warned from the beginning of the possibility of a Chinese riposte, the administration was taken wholly by surprise and overtaken by a heightened sense of danger when it came. Suddenly, despite all the cautionary notes sounded in policy documents, the danger of global war loomed larger than ever.[70]

All the suppressed anxieties concerning war now bobbed to the surface. With China in the war, the desire to inflict punishment was displaced by fear of a larger war. In November, Acheson said "we were much closer to the danger of general war." He told the Senate committee that "anything can happen anywhere at any time." A National Intelligence Estimate of 15 November concluded, on the assumption that the "ultimate objective" of establishing a Kremlin-controlled Communist world was "immutable and dynamic," that Moscow would continue to probe the West. "There is, and will continue to be, grave danger of war," it said. Various forecasts within the administration were quite pessimistic. At an NSC meeting in late November, Acheson said the Chinese intervention "had moved us very much closer to a general war." China expert O. Edmund Clubb, in December, stated that though war with the USSR need not be inevitable, "it must in the present circumstances be deemed 'probable,' and in the near rather than distant future." Ambassador to Moscow Alan Kirk, in a visit with the president, rated the odds at only 3 to 2 against war.[71]

The raucous Truman-MacArthur controversy that followed the general's publicly stated desire to expand the war by blockading China and bombing staging areas in Manchuria was a test, to be sure, of basic principles of civil-military relations, but the pivotal issue underlying the dispute continued to be the question of whether to punish or merely to frustrate the enemy. Traditional punitive logic argued in favor of MacArthur's suggested course, but the growing Wilsonian recognition that excessive military success would lead to failure meant that the decision could only go against the general as the weight of opinion within the administration shifted in the direction of avoiding all-out war. As Dean Rusk acknowledged a few months later, American sights had been lowered to restoring the status quo ante. "Our public position would still be support for the unification of an independent Korea," he explained, "but we would recognize that the Iron Curtain had come down on the 38th parallel."[72]

The wisdom of settling for the status quo ante had been earned the hard way, but it was not clear whether the administration possessed either the desire or the capability to implement successfully its more restrained version of limited-war strategy. As it happened, the policy of frustrating the enemy also produced so much self-frustration that it led to an ongoing consideration in secret of the very same nuclear options for extending the war the administration had so spectacularly rejected in public. Though Truman had been backed by the JCS demigods at the congressional hearings on MacArthur's dismissal, the idea of war as a symbolic action that eschewed its traditional punitive and coercive role was difficult for many to accept, a reluctance best expressed by MacArthur's assertion that "in war there is no substitute for victory." MacArthur's transgression, it seemed, had been to speak approvingly of the sinful urges that continued to well up irrepressibly within the administration's military libido.

At this point, the symbolic strategy seemed to have backfired not only with the enemy, but domestically also as, for a brief moment, the Chinese Communist assault came close to destroying American credibility where it most counted. The transformed war and the grinding military stalemate that followed raised grave doubts about the continued viability of the administration's strategy. Privately, most officials agreed with Lovett that "things were definitely moving in a desperate way." The precipitous decline in self-confidence was evident in Kennan's warning to Acheson that "bluster or petulance or hysteria" in this hour of misfortune could easily lead to "an irreparable deterioration of our world position—and of our confidence in ourselves." As the Korean War settled into a stalemate in the spring of 1951, a growing sense of frustration set in, leading Truman to blow off steam by bombing—in his diary —the Soviet Union and China.[73]

Shaky, too, was domestic opinion. The public's massive outpouring of support for the ancient general was indicative of its lack of sophisticated understanding of Wilsonian policies, which was quite understandable in light of the administration's own deep uncertainties about what it was doing. As the military lines stabilized and on-again, off-again armistice talks dragged on without visible progress, opinion polls indicated an impatience and lack of resolve that cast serious doubt on the public's commitment to this peculiar kind of internationalism. The public yearned for a settlement, expected the South Koreans and other nations to play a much larger role, and entertained with approval the idea of using the bomb on the peninsula, thereby endorsing simultaneously all the policies that, from the Wilsonian perspective, seemed destined to end in disaster. At the same time, withdrawal was never a serious option, since defeat in Korea seemed bound ultimately to unleash public passions. Responding to the assertion of British ambassador Sir Oliver Franks that the allies were "licked in Korea," Acheson predicted that if a defeat in Korea should jeopardize the gains of the Pacific war, "American opinion would not accept such a situation." When it was already too late, a surge of emotional interventionism would trigger another global conflict. And so, as the war ground on, the trapdoor of public support flew open and Truman's popularity went into free fall.[74]

Lastly, the Korean War threw into disarray the administration's policy of building confidence. By throwing into question the central issue of free world morale, the Far Eastern crisis laid bare the inadequacy of American policy in Europe to this point. Though conceptually wobbly on Korean issues, the administration was firm on the symbolic connection of Korea to European opinion. "We must think about Korea as a world matter," Acheson told the NSC, in arguing that a deepening, full-scale war with China would be "a bottomless pit" that would "bleed us dry." As the JCS told MacArthur, the objective in Korea was to "provide a rallying point around which the spirits and energies of the free world can be mobilized to meet the world-wide threat which the Soviet Union now poses."[75]

Ironically, however, the intervention in Korea, undertaken in part to bolster the morale of Europeans, wound up by frightening them. At a cabinet meeting in mid-July of 1950, Acheson described the situation as "one of gravest danger. It is becoming apparent to the world that we do not have the capabilities to face the threat, and the feeling in Europe is changing from one of elation that the United States has come into the Korean crisis to petrified fright.'' Thus Europe would have to be bolstered more directly and with far greater attention to military power than had been shown in the past. For Acheson, the objective must be to hold on and get out without losing face (the object of the commitment to begin with), ''so that we can get ahead with building up our own strength, and building up the strength of Europe.'' In congressional testimony in February 1951 Marshall, now secretary of defense, said that ''the most important, the greatest factor in the creation of military strength for Western Europe in my opinion is the build up of morale,—of the will to defend,—the determination to fight if that be necessary.''[76]

Because preponderance, however desirable in principle, had never been achieved in practice, Korea pointed up the indispensability to the nation of potent and trustworthy allies. Militarily and strategically, Europe was crucial because, as the service secretaries agreed, ''there is no margin left.'' According to Acheson, one of the biggest lessons of Korea was that it was ''of the greatest importance to have as much unity as you can possibly bring about in the world in dealing with a troublesome situation.'' The result was a series of fateful decisions by the administration to militarize NATO, send American troops to Europe, and rearm West Germany in order to shore up Europe's defenses and reinstil confidence on the Continent. Yet these initiatives would themselves cut many ways psychologically because of the different doubts and fears that they raised among the continentals. Inevitably, this inoculation and repeated booster shots would, in the years to come, produce some of the symptoms of the disease being guarded against.[77]

American policymakers knew that the Korean adventure was disturbing to the Europeans, but they believed that a withdrawal would have had even more serious implications for European resolve. Although there had been some consideration given in the darkest days following the Chinese intervention to withdrawing from Korea, maintaining at least a beachhead was essential in order to give heart to America's European allies, ''in the firming up of Germany and the free people to stand against the aggression of the USSR.'' A beachhead would provide ''a continued symbol of UN determination to resist aggression.'' The Europeans, looking at the matter from their narrower regional frame, had no qualms about questioning what seemed to them an increasingly quixotic adventure in Korea. But the administration opted to grind it out in the belief that the Europeans, who acted out of a traditionally narrow sense of self-interest, were not attuned to the logic of world opinion; indeed, given their mental exhaustion, they were hardly in a position to understand the indispensability of psychological strength to seeing through the cold war.[78]

By this time, the shape of the problems to be faced in the future was at last beginning to become clear. Thus, despite a continuing emphasis on rearmament, Acheson told Churchill in January 1952 that his greatest fear was not a general war in Europe, but "creeping actions taken through satellites in parts of the world which would exhaust the Western powers." As Acheson argued in the consideration of NSC 135/2, it would be necessary to "make it very clear that the United States did not intend to confine its role in defense against aggression to areas which already had satisfactory collective security arrangements." Unlike the old diplomacy of imperialism, in which European and Asian alignments had overlapped only partially, there now existed, as far as Washington was concerned, a global playing field without traditional regional balancing mechanisms, one in which the theoretical strategic primacy of Europe gave way in practice to symbolic universalism. This was a connection that Europeans, with their non-Wilsonian traditions, would never fully understand.[79]

Korea also brought the beginning of an understanding within the policy elite of the kinds of predicaments generated by neo-Wilsonian solutions in a modern context. Korea had settled Korea--and that just barely—while opening up a far greater range of problems in Asia and in Europe. Overall, the results of a symbolic strategy rooted in world opinion left a great deal to be desired. It was not clear in the first place whether the intended message had been understood by the Soviets. A briefing book for the visit of French Prime Minister René Pleven to Washington in January 1951 defined the power relationship as "unsatisfactory" because "it has not been sufficient to deter local aggression in Korea, and unless improved might not be sufficient to deter more general hostilities." Another statement of basic national security policy in 1952 warned that "the developing situation may present a continuing and possibly improved opportunity for Soviet expansion by the techniques of political warfare and local aggression, if the free world permits the fear and threat of general war to paralyze its reaction to such threats." Added to that were uncertainties within the government about the practicality of limited war, anxiety over domestic public support, and deep concern over the mettle of America's allies abroad. With these kinds of conundrums, small wonder that for many observers, within the administration and without, the American rationale in Korea was "completely confusing and baffling."[80]

"Success" in beating back the North Korean invasion and the Chinese Communist challenge, then, merely generated a magnified sense of crisis. Korea confirmed the need, envisioned by NSC 68, for a massive military buildup, but that expansion alone proved insufficient to make containment work. One would think that as a nation augmented its power the need for credibility would diminish, but for the militarily revived America of the 1950s exactly the reverse would be true. Restoring the status quo ante at the 38th parallel had checked the immediate threat, but it also brought to light gaping holes in world opinion and free world "morale" that would have to be patched during the Eisenhower years. The only solution to a lack of credibility was more credibility; the only sure answer to lack of commitment, yet more commitment.

7

EISENHOWER'S SYMBOLIC
COLD WAR

T HE EISENHOWER ADMINISTRATION critique of Truman's conduct
of the cold war was the product of contradictory expectations. Although Eisenhower and his secretary of state, John Foster Dulles,
shared with Truman a Wilsonian definition of the threat facing the United
States and a common understanding of the ultimate objectives of the cold
war, they believed that Truman had gone too far and yet not far enough in
waging the struggle. In its prodigal commitment of U.S. land forces and
acceptance of huge defense-driven budgets, the Truman administration
seemed to be wasting the nation's precious assets in a binge of overmilitariza-
tion. And yet, for all its willingness to expend American life and treasure,
it was, as the equivocal results of the Korean War seemed to make clear,
failing at containment. Given these opposing assumptions, the Eisenhower
administration's cold-war strategy bore a conceptual affinity to modern archi-
tecture: less would have to be more.

For Eisenhower, better results at more tolerable cost could be achieved
by making greater diplomatic use of America's nuclear assets and by shifting
some of the free world's defense burden to America's allies. Looked at from
the domestic angle, this strategic approach appeared to be dictated wholly
by ideological concerns for economy. From an international perspective,
however, it was but another attempt at creating an effective form of neo-
Wilsonian collective security. The only satisfactory way of dealing with crises
that produced quagmires like Korea was, by making deterrence more credible, to prevent them from becoming military tests in the first place. Ideally,
this meant displacing the cold war away from concrete tests of military power
and shifting it firmly into the perceptual realm so that it could be fought
out historically, as a struggle of contrasting ideologies of modernization.
Eisenhower and Dulles would succeed in the short run, but in trying to
implement a new kind of symbolic interventionism that would do more with

less, they also generated new paradoxes that in the end proved unsustainable as a basis for policy.

THE STRUGGLE FOR CIVILIZATION

Though somewhat slow to sign up for service on the good ship *Containment,* by the time he became president, Eisenhower's view of Soviet motivation started where the Truman administration's had left off. He was particularly impressed by Rear Admiral Leslie Stevens's argument that ideology was at the root of Soviet behavior. Overall, he thought Stevens's paper to be brilliant, describing it as a piece that had "few if any equals in current military and political writings." Writing to his brother Milton, Ike gushed with praise. "With minor exceptions it represents my beliefs exactly," he said. "But he states the thing *clearly!*" A 1951 letter to one of his many businessman friends, Edward Bermingham, is typical of Ike's maximalist view of ideology. "Communism, both ruthless in purpose and insidious as to method," he claimed, "is using the traditional Imperialistic designs of Russia and the present physical strength of Asia and Eastern Europe to promote the Communist objective of *world revolution and subsequent domination of all the earth* by the Communistic Party, centering in Moscow." In 1956, his secretary noted that "he starts with the premise that Communism is an ideology that seeks to defeat us by every possible means."[1]

Crucially, however, the iceberg of Soviet fanaticism was exposed to the air of reason at its tip. Writing to his wartime colleague Viscount Field Marshal Bernard Montgomery in May 1956, he argued that the Soviets were unlikely to start a war they were bound to lose, even if the ensuing chaos should expand the prospects for spreading communism. Ike insisted that "the Communists are not early Christian martyrs. The men in the Kremlin are avid for power and ruthlessly ambitious. I cannot see them starting a war merely for the opportunity that such a conflict would offer their successors to spread the doctrine." "Everything," he told his press secretary in 1954, "points to the fact that Russia is not seeking a general war and will not for a long, long time, if ever." Despite his image as an ideological fire-eater, Eisenhower's secretary of state, John Foster Dulles, also believed that Soviet ideology had its limits and that the rules for a common language of power could be worked out. "Most Communists are fanatics," Dulles claimed, "but they operate under the iron discipline of the party, and party leadership is coldly calculating." "Soviet leaders are realists," he had declared in 1948. Dulles also drew "a sharp distinction between Russia and the Communist Party," attributing the cold war to the Communist Mr. Hyde, rather than the gentlemanly Dr. Jekyll of Russian nationalism.[2]

Assuming a desire on both sides to avert a war, Ike saw the cold war as an ideological struggle in which America's main objective was to hold and allow history to do its work. For that reason he decided rather early that the nation should concentrate on "strengthening the economic and social dikes against Soviet communism rather than upon preparing for a possibly eventual, but not yet inevitable, war." He emphasized above all America's "strength of will, her moral, social, and economic strength" as qualities more vital to the struggle than mere military strength. Dulles, too, had been critical of the trend to militarization of American foreign policy, believing that the contest would be decided by economic and social forces. "The challenge, in its present phase," he wrote in 1948, "seems not a militaristic challenge, like that of Hitler, Mussolini, and the Japanese warlords. It is a call to revolution." Pointing up another difference with Hitler's Germany, Dulles told Eisenhower that "one of the most dangerous characteristics of the Soviet Communist movement is that it regards itself as timeless." If the nation's fate were entrusted to the military, they would be "apt to muff it because it is not the kind of responsibility for which they are trained," he insisted. The cold war had to be viewed in broader terms, as "*a challenge to established civilization*" of a kind rarely witnessed in history, a challenge that could, in the last analysis, be surmounted only by maintaining the vitality of one's way of life.[3]

Quite contrary to its campaign rhetoric of "liberation," then, which suggested the possibility of a sudden breakthrough, the new administration had few expectations of imminent transformation in the Soviet or the eastern bloc. Eisenhower agreed in 1954 that "the time of a significant rollback was far in the future." In eastern Europe, Dulles anticipated a slow, evolutionary change to what would later be called, somewhat pejoratively, Finlandization. Dulles saw in Khrushchev's October 1956 denunciation of Stalin "cause for hope, because once again it is demonstrating that liberalizing influences from without and within can bring about peaceful change."[4] In this view, communism would end not with a bang, but with a whimper.

Barring war or a sudden collapse of the West, the cold war was firmly redefined, then, in the sense that Kennan had first understood it: as a historical struggle of social systems that would be decided in the long run. As Dulles told the Senate Foreign Relations Committee in 1953, the administration's policy of economy was the product of "a belief that the danger is going to be with us for what may be still quite a long time and that, therefore, we need to have policies which we can live with for some time rather than policies which would so exhaust us that there would be an internal collapse." Eisenhower now saw the nation "passing through and living on a high plateau of tension that may endure twenty or more years; we do not face a mere 'emergency.' " In a meeting with the legislative leadership in December 1954, Eisenhower told them that "we want a program that can be carried on indefinitely." By 1958, he was predicting that "blood, sweat and tears were necessary for the next 40 years if we want to protect our freedom."[5]

If the cold war was indeed a marathon race between the two social systems, the United States needed to pace itself economically lest it collapse before reaching the finish line. "The real problem," according to the president, "was to devise methods of meeting the Soviet threat and of adopting controls, if necessary, that would not result in our transformation into a garrison state." He accused the NSC of dodging "the essential dilemma" facing the country. "The United States was confronted with a very terrible threat," he agreed, but "the truth of the matter was that we have devised no way of meeting this threat without imposing ever-greater controls on our economy and the freedom of our people." "The great danger," he concluded again, "was that in defending our way of life we would find ourselves resorting to methods that endangered this way of life." "The whole thing," he concluded, "was a paradox which must be faced and not evaded." Dealing with short-term contingencies could not be allowed to undermine the achievement of long-term ends.[6]

The greatest immediate threat would be a repetition of Korea-like crises. Ike and Dulles had supported American intervention in Korea at the outset for fear of the larger consequences of inaction, but as the war dragged on its numerous shortcomings became readily apparent. As Eisenhower later recalled, "At best the prospects in Korea appeared to be for an eventual stalemate; at worst they boded involvement with the Soviet Union and the beginning of World War III," in which case it was believed that the Soviets would overrun Europe in a matter of days. Moreover, the thin UN administrative cloak in Korea could not conceal the fact that the operational body beneath was almost entirely American. Eisenhower complained to his vice-presidential running mate, Richard Nixon, that "America has been compelled in the past to provide most of the weapons and ninety percent of the manpower. This is not a fair distribution of the burden of collective security." More important, he did not see any effective deterrent to a repetition of the Korean attack. "We'll have a dozen Koreas soon if we don't take a firm stand," he argued. From the standpoint of long-term victory in the cold war, Korea seemed a Pyrrhic victory, successful in the narrow sense of containing Communist expansionism while doing nothing effective to deter it.[7]

Further debilitating challenges of this sort would undoubtedly arise. Writing to Bernard Baruch in mid-1952, Ike warned him to "expect a continuance of various kinds of satellite conflicts in certain of our sensitive areas." On board the USS *Helena* following Eisenhower's inspection trip to Korea,

Dulles epitomized for the president-elect the kinds of problems to which the United States could look forward. The Soviet plan, he warned, was "to exhaust our resources and our patience and divide us internally by mounting a series of local actions around the world at times and places of their choosing." If so, it would be folly to sit back complacently "while Soviet Communism completes the encirclement which it has planned in order to isolate us." Therefore the central task of administration policy would be to devise a method of dealing with—better yet, preventing—low-level provocations that threatened to turn into Korea-like bogs. Dulles told the NSC in March 1953 that "there must be no repetition of the fuzzy situation in Korea in the spring of 1950, which constituted an invitation to the Soviets to move against South Korea." As an early policy review summed up, peripheral wars were "uneconomical and weakening."[8]

In order to keep the cold-war struggle purely at the level of modernization, the administration's post-Korea policy would feature new variations on the by now familiar Wilsonian themes of power and opinion: the open resort to atomic diplomacy as a deterrent to local aggression—the notorious "massive retaliation" strategy—and an attempt to reinspirit allies, particularly in western Europe, with the morale necessary to hold their own. For Eisenhower and Dulles nuclear weapons promised to solve the budgetary problem while providing, presumably, an unambiguous and convincing form of deterrence against local aggressions. At the same time, a more effective system of alliances would provide a workable substitute for Wilsonian collective security and further ease the burden on American resources. Both expedients sought to turn the cold war in a symbolic direction: the first, by making deterrence more credible; the second, by nurturing a collective will to self-defense that would be impervious to the kind of disastrous demoralization witnessed in the late 1930s.

The Minimal Role of Massive Retaliation

The administration started out with highly publicized hopes of using its superior nuclear striking power to deter local aggressions. Far more economical than conventional forces and yet incredibly more powerful, the bomb seemed the ultimate symbol of credibility and thus the ideal short-term tool for the administration's long-term needs. By contrast, the Truman administration, although highly sensitive to the psychological importance of possessing the bomb, had shown an aversion to "atomic diplomacy" when it decided to give priority to NSC 68's emphasis on conventional rearmament. Reflecting this point of view, Policy Planning Staff Director Paul Nitze, just prior to the change in administrations, had questioned "whether the U.S. Government will be willing to use the atomic threat or to follow through on it in the event of any Soviet move short of direct atomic attack on the United States.'' Concluding that it would be folly to rely on the deterrent power of weapons it was unwilling to use, Nitze advocated a continuation of the conventional military buildup then in progress. But for the incoming administration, this squeamishness was symptomatic of an extravagant and ineffectual approach to the cold war in which the bomb was a worthless resource, a weapon hidden so securely as to be useless in the event of an emergency. Rather than allow the fear of a general war to paralyze policy, many within the administration, most notably Dulles, hoped to make a diplomatic asset of the bomb. Nuclear weapons could, said Dulles in 1952, ''in the hands of wise statesmen, be made to play a master political role of defenders of the peace.''[9]

On becoming secretary of state, Dulles continued to make his argument whenever he could, even though he admitted privately at one point to West German Chancellor Konrad Adenauer that ''even to contemplate it seems unChristian.'' At an early meeting of the NSC, Dulles discussed the inhibitions on the use of the A-bomb that resulted from setting it in a ''special category.'' He was of the opinion that ''we should try to break down this false distinction.'' A 1953 memo argued that ''the number, diversity and power of atomic weapons, together with their application to tactical situations, make necessary the adoption of a general policy for their use in the event of hostilities.'' Noting the previous reluctance to utilize these weapons, it argued that a public announcement of the willingness to use them ''would have a very salutary effect upon the Russians themselves in further deterring them from initiating hostilities.'' The presumed success of the Eisenhower administration's threat to use the atomic bomb to dislodge the military logjam in Korea contributed to the hope that the bomb would demonstrate its utility as an instrument of policy in other areas as well.[10]

Notwithstanding all the rhetoric invested in ''massive retaliation,'' it became clear soon enough that extraordinary dividends of credibility would not be harvested. Eisenhower was, to be sure, consistent in reassuring the military of his resolve to use nuclear weapons once a general war was inevitable or in progress. Bowing to pressures from the defense establishment, NSC 162/1 of 30 October 1953 declared that ''in the event of hostilities, the United States will consider nuclear weapons to be available for use as other munitions,'' although the actual decisions would be made by the president on a case-by-case basis. Eisenhower repeated this determination to Dulles in July 1954: ''When we talk about power, and massive retaliation, we mean retaliation against an act that to us means irrevocable war.'' He also reassured the NSC that ''he didn't think anyone present here thought that the cost of winning a global war against the Soviet Union was a cost too high to pay,'' especially as the United States was "defending a way of life as well as a territory, a population, or our dollar." If the use of atomic weapons was dictated by national security interests, "he would certainly decide to use them."[11]

However, Eisenhower soon enough saw the paradox of a position in which "a war for the American way of life would be the end of the American way of life." Contemplation of a nuclear holocaust simply brought home in a clear and inescapable way the truth of Wilson's insight that modern war was pointless and underlined the importance of avoiding it in the first place. But the question of all-out nuclear war was, fortunately, a hypothetical issue that begged the more difficult practical question of the nuclear deterrent's usefulness in dealing with lesser provocations that were bound to arise in the course of events. Eisenhower had quickly noted the shortcomings of massive retaliation as a tool against political aggression when it was first proposed by Dulles in 1952, but its utility in dealing with local military aggression was another matter, one that Dulles raised repeatedly during NSC meetings and on other occasions. Eisenhower went so far as to give lip service to Dulles's ideas on the use of the bomb in "local" affairs. At the Bermuda meeting with Winston Churchill in December 1953, Eisenhower argued that "the world was in a rather hysterical condition about the atomic bomb." The next day, he "touched upon his belief that Atomic weapons were now coming to be regarded as a part of conventional armament and that he thought this a sound concept." His most celebrated public comment in this vein came during the Quemoy-Matsu crisis, in which he pronounced atomic munitions as different in degree, and not in kind, and therefore certainly usable in war.[12]

Nevertheless, Eisenhower's thinking on the use of nuclear weapons against "local aggression" turned out to be governed by the same fears as his thinking about their use in general war. Rejecting in practice what he accepted in principle, massive retaliation in brushfire conflicts was never approved as a matter of policy. As Eisenhower told the NSC in October 1953, the JCS "should count on making use of special weapons in the event of a general war. They should not, however, plan to make use of these weapons in minor affairs." Following another Dulles plea that "somehow or other we must manage to remove the taboo from the use of these weapons," Eisenhower pointed out that "there were certain places where you would not be able to use these weapons because if you did it would look as if the U.S. were initiating global war. If, however, we got into a global war, we would certainly use these weapons." That kind of assurance was, for Dulles, no assurance at all, because it meant that the weapons would only be wheeled out to deal with the very situation that Dulles wished them to prevent.[13]

The inhibitions against using nuclear weapons as an instrument of diplomacy were only magnified when allies and world public opinion were taken into account. Apart from the danger that their use might set off a world war in which victory was meaningless, their diplomatic use in deterring the enemy frightened some indispensable allies. The mere testing of nuclear weapons, not to mention talk of their actual employment, alienated overseas opinion. "It is driving our allies away from us," Dulles complained on one occasion about an H-bomb test; "they think we are getting ready for a war of this kind. We could survive but some of them would be obliterated in a few minutes. It could lead them to a policy of neutrality or appeasement." "The simple truth of the matter," Eisenhower noted ruefully in 1953, "was that many people in the European countries believe that global war is much worse than surrender to Communist imperialism." By mid-1954, in discussing fears of atomic war, Dulles noted that "our 'tough policy' was becoming increasingly unpopular throughout the free world . . . The tide is clearly running against us." In a ruminative 1955 conversation with Eisenhower, Dulles feared that nuclear striking power "was apt to be immobilized by moral repugnance. If this happened, the whole structure could collapse." On another occasion, he pointed out that "talk of atomic attack tended to create 'peace-at-any-price people' and might lead to an increase of appeasement sentiment in various countries."[14]

Whatever its other limitations, it was apparent from the beginning that the USSR's rapid development of a nuclear arsenal meant that massive retaliation was, at best, a temporary expedient. As a mere stopgap in what was defined as a long-term struggle, its life span was far too brief for it to play the "master political role" that Dulles envisioned for it. As early as 1953, when the bloated American military establishment was placed on a nuclear diet called the New Look, NSC 162 concluded that "increasing Soviet atomic capability may tend to diminish the deterrent effect of U.S. atomic power against peripheral Soviet aggression." The NSC paper concluded that "as general war becomes more devastating for both sides the threat to resort to it becomes less available as a sanction for local aggression." As their nuclear capability increased, the Soviets were likely to believe that "the aversion of the U.S. and, more especially, of its allies to general war will correspondingly increase," giving the Kremlin "greater freedom to take certain actions, including local military actions, without running substantial risk of general war." With the Soviet launch of Sputnik, the first earth-orbiting satellite, in late 1957, Dulles acknowledged ruefully that "this will affect the so-called balance of power."[15]

Dulles himself realized fairly early that massive retaliation was no diplomatic trump card. As he admitted at a 1954 NSC meeting, the United States did not have "an adequate defense against Communist expansion by means other than war." At one meeting with the president in December 1954, for example, Dulles "raised the question of whether the Defense Department and the JCS were in reality planning to deal adequately with the possible 'little wars'; which might call for punishment related to the degree and the locality of the offense which would not justify a massive retaliation against the Soviet Union itself." Thus, with the era of nuclear abundance already in sight, the outlook for the future was hardly reassuring with regard to what was considered to be the central tactical problem of the cold war. As the Joint Chiefs of Staff predicted, if Soviet policy had been so vigorous during the period of American nuclear preponderance, "the aggressive and irresponsible tactics pursued with success by the Soviets thus far will be only a prelude to the proportions which such tactics will attain once the present superiority of the United States has been neutralized." With the coming of "nuclear plenty," National Security Adviser Robert Cutler argued that the resulting condition of mutual deterrence would "enable the Soviet Union to avoid war and nibble the free world to death piece by piece."[16]

By the last few years of the Eisenhower administration, massive retaliation, never having been given the full breath of life to begin with, was dead in everything except name, though the administration was understandably reluctant to say so publicly for fear of lessening whatever residual deterrent effect it might possess. But its obsolescence was apparent from Dulles's complaint to Eisenhower in 1958 that the U.S. strategic concept "too much invoked massive nuclear attack in the event of a clash anywhere with Soviet nuclear forces." The president agreed that American strategy "did not adequately take account of the possibilities of limited war."[17]

The bomb was the ultimate symbol, not of credibility, but of the limits to the use of power in the modern era. As the purest technological expression of power, the bomb simply took to the nth degree Wilson's understanding of the self-defeating nature of total war. Such utility as it had was rooted in the fact of its possession, as a talisman which granted immunity from nuclear blackmail, but its unimaginably excessive power vitiated its usefulness as an instrument of diplomacy. With willpower viewed as central to credibility, the "massive retaliation" strategy was based, as Ike well understood, on making believable a willingness to use a weapon whose employment was irrational according to the traditional means-ends test, whether applied to general war or to local crises.

The only way, ironically, of enhancing the credibility of atomic diplomacy was to speak with calculated ambiguity on the subject, which certainly kept the enemy guessing but also raised the level of anxiety in the West, all the more so as the time of "nuclear plenty" approached. Used in this way, massive retaliation was a unilateralist option whose effect upon public opinion abroad was the reverse of that intended. With all the difficulties inherent in atomic diplomacy as a power option, the administration was pushed all the more urgently in the direction of a neo-Wilsonian reliance on world opinion. An economical version of containment could be made to work only by reinforcing the morale of allies and by managing crises with that end in view.

EUROPE AND MORALE

Credibility remained useful in dealing with the Communist foe, but its place in the cold war's logic of world opinion placed equal if not greater emphasis on the bolstering of one's friends. Eisenhower's experience during World War II had already attuned him to the indispensability of solidarity among allies. The area in which cohesion and morale needed most badly to be restored as a result of Korea was Europe. "That Western Europe not fall to the Communists was a *sine qua non*," Ike told the NSC in 1953. Europe was important, as Eisenhower argued, "as about the last remaining chance for the survival of Western civilization. Our efforts in the United Nations have been defeated by the vetoes of hostile groups—but in the Atlantic Pact we are not plagued by the hostile groups and are simply trying to work out a way that free countries may band together to protect themselves." Unfortunately, NATO seemed at the time "more an idea or concept than . . . a real organization." Eisenhower worried constantly that "lethargy and inaction in Europe . . . would allow that continent to fall into Soviet hands." It was largely his concern over the severity of the European crisis that led him to give up the presidency of Columbia University in order to assume command of NATO forces in Europe.[18]

Eisenhower's conception of the role of world opinion in dealing with local aggression and preventing demoralization was far more focused than the Truman administration's. He emphasized collective security in a truncated, but nevertheless recognizably Wilsonian, sense. He stressed "the job of welding the whole western world into a unit in which each of the parts is willing to exert its full capabilities in support of a common cause." To him, there was "no acceptable alternative to the establishment of collective security among the countries whose welfare directly affects our own." Writing to his brother Milton, he declared that "the establishment of collective security by cooperation is a *must* for the future of our type of civilization." At a 1954 press conference, Ike emphasized once again the need to find a common will when he reminded the reporters that "it is only through collective security among several nations in which it is possible to establish a political background in which it is possible to defeat communist aggression." As Dulles told journalist James Reston, "We believe in collective security and they do not accept our theory.'' Philosophically, collective security was ''the only posture which was consistent with U.S. national security policy as a whole'' since, without it, the United States would become a garrison state. Thus, what was strategic common sense in the 1950s had been a matter of contention only fifteen years earlier.[19]

The key to collective security was morale, which was for Eisenhower less a military concept than a military man's reformulation of the Wilsonian idea of world opinion. To his diary, he wrote: ''Civilian leaders talk about the state of morale in a given country as if it were a sort of uncontrollable event or phenomenon, like a thunder storm or a cold winter. The soldier leader looks on morale as one of the great factors (the greatest) in all his problems, but also as one about which he can and must *do* something. . . . Materialistic factors are important, but much more is involved here.'' Consequently, upon assuming command of NATO forces in Europe in 1951, he reminded George Marshall, then secretary of defense (who needed no reminding), that ''we must never forget that we are putting together a mechanism that has a terrific morale job to accomplish.'' In his 1952 report as supreme commander, he said, ''Our central problem was one of morale—the spirit of man. All human progress in the military or other fields has its source in the heart of man. No man will fight unless he has something worth fighting for.''[20]

Morale was premised on a common sense of values. ''A union of hearts and minds is the indispensable formula for success,'' he told his diary. ''If this union is not established then we must seek some other alternative to collective security for the free world. Any alternative promises little more than tragic failure.'' He wrote of the ''tremendous task confronting educators in all free countries—the development of a common faith, understanding, and loyalty among all the free peoples.'' Writing to W. Averell Harriman, he argued that ''success depends upon a unification that is built upon a common scale of values, and a common determination to meet the risks cooperatively.'' Europe needed ''greater understanding, greater fervor, greater faith.'' America's job was to provide ''enlightened leadership'' that would ''inspire and sustain confidence.'' Ultimately, ''the rebuilding of the European spirit . . . must be the foundation for European strength.''[21]

American leadership and hegemony were intended to be only temporary, a means to the end of establishing a free-standing European balance. As Ike told an NSC meeting in 1953, ''If Europe would do what it should do, conceivably it could by itself defeat Russia.'' Once European morale had been revived and the Continent placed on a self-sustaining basis, ''the whole problem will have been successfully met.'' With the Europeans organized for self-defense, it might be possible, probably within four to eight years, to reduce the American forces stationed in Europe. Writing to one of his many businessman supporters, Eisenhower argued that "if in ten years, all American troops stationed in Europe for national defense purposes have not been returned to the United States, then the whole project will have failed." He likened such a prospect to the futility of Rome's attempting to garrison all its frontiers.[22]

With the weakness of western Europe thrown into bold relief by the Korean War, the choice of a successor to the old nationalistic European balance of power was finally clarified. There remained only two possible institutional solutions, both of them supranational in character, to the problem of European security: the European Defence Community (EDC) and NATO. NATO, it was becoming clear, had all kinds of weaknesses. As Dulles told the NSC in mid-1953, "There is no denying that NATO is sick at the present time." Reporting to Eisenhower a few months later, Dulles claimed that "the NATO concept is losing its grip" among the European allies. Indeed, NATO as then constituted was a standing reproach to Europe's inability to defend itself by overcoming divisions along national lines. In a meeting with reporters at this time, Dulles said that "it is difficult to look at what is happening in western Europe and NOT to feel a sense of despondency." Psychological debility was accompanied by military incapacity. As Dulles pointed out to the Senate Foreign Relations Committee, NATO was "a splendid superstructure, the foundation of which is extremely unreliable because of the fact that there is no provision whereby the Germans can come in to help defend their own land."[23]

EDC seemed by far the preferable solution because it presupposed the existence of a unified and confident Western will capable of generating credibility in its own right, thereby minimizing the drain on American resources. Fortified by a common European army with German contingents, EDC would be tied together by supranational institutions. The plan, first put forward by the French, had been coolly greeted by the Truman administration, which was put off by all the nationalist barriers to its creation. Eisenhower's initial judgment was also negative, since EDC seemed to include "every kind of obstacle, difficulty, and fantastic notion that misguided humans could put together in one package." But once he began to appreciate the scheme's virtues he became one of its most fervent cheerleaders. For his part, Dulles had long been an advocate of European unity as a solution to age-old continental difficulties. Indeed, his oft-stated conviction that European unity was desirable in its own right, cold war or no, was born of a recognition that the problem of the European balance transcended that of the cold war.[24]

Writing to Harriman in June 1951, Eisenhower foresaw "no real answer for the European problem until there is definitely established a United States of Europe." Given the emergency facing the Continent, this step should be taken in "a single plunge." He argued time and again before running for the presidency that "*we must unite western Europe, including Western Germany,* or there is no logical basis for a long-term, enduring peace for the Western world." A failure to create EDC, he argued, "would be fatal—the nations of the free world can succeed together or fail separately." He was no less enthusiastic about the idea after becoming president. There was, he said in 1954, "no satisfactory alternative to EDC." If Europe failed to unite economically and militarily, the effect would be equivalent to "fighting Communism in handcuffs."[25]

From the American point of view, EDC had the additional virtue, if diligently pursued, of pointing the way to the end of the cold war in Europe. As Eisenhower told an NSC meeting in 1955, western European unity "would solve the peace of the world. A solid power mass in Western Europe would ultimately attract to it all the Soviet satellites, and the threat to peace would disappear." NSC 160/1, taking up this "magnet theory" of cold-war victory, argued that "a united Europe would constitute a counterpoise, but not a menace to the Soviet Union. Once firmly established, it should exert a strong and increasing attraction on eastern Europe, thus weakening the Soviet position there and accelerating Soviet withdrawal from that area." EDC could be an effective magnet because, with only a nominal American presence, there would be no need for a Russian security system in eastern Europe with a magnetic force of its own to repel the West and keep the Continent divided. EDC also seemed the only meaningful way of promoting the fulfillment of the election slogan of "liberation and rollback," while at the same time lessening the threat of war and obviating any need to negotiate what was thought to be a "morally reprehensible" deal on the status quo with the Russians.[26]

Not least, EDC held out promise of resolving the German problem, both in the short term and in the long run, something that NATO seemed incapable of doing. Eisenhower wrote to General Alfred Gruenther in 1954 that "the answer to the European problem will be written in German." It was gospel throughout the 1950s, as one NSC document put it, that the ongoing division of Germany created "a serious element of instability in Europe which must be eliminated before a reliable and enduring basis for European security can be established." Any policy of "double containment" that sought to integrate the Federal Republic of Germany into western Europe without striving to unify the Continent operated within a double bind. In a Europe of two armed camps, efforts at German unification could only produce instability. On the other hand, accepting the status quo of a divided Continent would kill off prospects for reunification, foment instability in West Germany, and compromise Western security. To arguments that EDC would foreclose any possibilities of German reunification, Dulles retorted that he had "never accepted this idea that the EDC and the reunification of Germany are mutually exclusive. Quite the contrary." It was EDC's capacity to stabilize Europe militarily while successfully assimilating West Germany and holding out the meaningful promise of a united country that proved so attractive to Dulles and Eisenhower as a way of providing the "evolutionary change" that was the only safe route to cold-war victory.[27]

EDC, however, presumed the existence of the very will to unity and self-defense whose absence was the source of Europe's problems. Despite warnings beforehand that the French, wary as always of Germany and committed to a nationalist destiny, were likely to reject the scheme, Dulles called such talk "defeatism" and predicted that "the EDC is going to go into effect." Dulles tried everything, including his famous, but empty, threat of an "agonizing reappraisal" of U.S. policy. Likening the alliance to a group of mountain climbers who were roped together, Douglas MacArthur II told French Premier Laniel in April 1954, a few months prior to the fatal vote in the National Assembly, that the United States "was not prepared to die simply because France wished to commit what amounted to suicide." He concluded that "the rest of us must cut the rope and leave her on the ledge."[28]

Despite Eisenhower's attempt "to throw all our weight behind the EDC objective," EDC was torpedoed by the French National Assembly in August 1954. According to James B. Conant, the U.S. high commissioner in Bonn, the French preferred "an emasculated NATO, rather than see the creation of a German national army." Eisenhower, in responding to the failure of EDC, said that "we cannot sit down in black despair and admit defeat." Bent on securing "the orientation of the German Federal Republic to the West by all feasible means," the Americans and the British opted to admit West Germany, with a national army that EDC would have circumvented, into NATO, letting the French know that if this were not done the United States would go along without them. It was by no means certain that the United States could have succeeded in unilaterally getting Germany to rearm, yet the French could not be allowed to have the last word. It was abundantly clear, as Ike said, that "we could get along without France but not without Germany."[29]

In purely military terms, the NATO fall-back solution was, as Dulles admitted, "better than EDC." Yet, from the standpoint of morale it was a severe setback, for it ensured the continuation of the dependency relationship. Though Eisenhower had always resisted the proposals of the budget-cutters to pull U.S. troops out of Europe, he had long maintained that "Europe must, as a whole, provide in the long run for its own defense." The NATO solution meant that the United States would be tied down indefinitely on the

Continent, an area, he complained in 1957, "which because of its population, culture and intellectual level of its people, should now need no help from abroad." The NATO solution demonstrated that the revival of European morale that Eisenhower so greatly desired would not take place in the foreseeable future. Therefore America would have to supply the resolve necessary to maintain the cohesion and spirit of the alliance.[30]

The generation of this credibility demanded more of the United States than ongoing contributions of hardware and troops. While it helped create a military balance on the Continent, the NATO solution also mortgaged American policy to a nationalist German public opinion and its desire for reunification, thereby ruling out the political ratification of military realities. Indeed, any indication that the status quo was acceptable would have been interpreted by the West Germans as a betrayal of their aspirations. Because the Germanization of NATO delayed reunification of Germany at a time when the *Bundesrepublik* was not yet firmly cemented within western Europe, Americans were fearful that latent German nationalism would emerge and disrupt the entire continental defense arrangement. This possibility mandated two simultaneous courses of action: the continued pursuit of German reunification in negotiations with the Russians at a time when realities were making it less likely; and the proffering of constant reassurances to the Germans in symbolic ways of the soundness of Adenauer's pro-Western policy of "reunification through strength." Quite understandably, then, the administration's deepest fear for a Germanized NATO was, in Dulles's words, "that the political foundation for it all will remain wobbly and unstable."[31]

At first, the NATO deal on German rearmament produced optimism about unity. The French believed that the end of EDC meant the end of dreams for a united Germany, but the administration for a time continued to act as if nothing had changed. The "Spirit of Geneva" that resulted from the heads-of-state meeting in July 1955 included the hope that the NATO accords would bring significant concessions from the Soviets on German reunification. In the face of considerable skepticism from his brother, CIA chief Allen Dulles, and the joint chiefs, Dulles allowed himself the luxury of believing that "the Iron Curtain is going to disappear," or at least the fabric of its drapery would become softer, and perceived "a real possibility in the present situation for a rollback of Soviet power." Just prior to the conference itself, Dulles indicated that "the present pace and vitality of the West has put too much strain on them" and suggested that the Soviets might be seeking a breathing spell.[32]

At Geneva, the United States strove mightily to convince the Kremlin leadership that the reunification of Germany within NATO would not be harmful to their security interests. According to the logic of Assistant Secretary of State Livingston Merchant, the NATO accords would have been "totally unobtainable except for the purpose of collective defense." Because Western arrangements were transparently defensive in purpose, they were "as a practical matter incapable of use or domination by a single power." It followed, therefore, that "membership of a united Germany in NATO and WEU could not adversely affect the legitimate security interests of the Soviet Union." In the same vein, Dulles argued that the NATO solution for Germany was "going to protect Russia as much as it protects anybody else against the possible resurgence of German militarism." To the Soviet insistence that the rearmament of West Germany in NATO was hardening the German problem and prolonging the cold war in Europe, the Americans responded with warnings not to overlook the lessons of Versailles. "It was worse than stupid," said Merchant, "on keeping that vital nation divided." Continued division, by allowing German nationalist sentiment to fester, would constitute "a growing risk to the security of Europe." Despite the lack of interest from the Soviet side, Dulles told the NSC after the conference that "we might get unification in the next two years." Writing to Chancellor Adenauer shortly thereafter, he described German reunification as the "touchstone" of American policy and predicted that reunification was "in the air."[33]

Dulles's optimism was given a rude jolt at the follow-up meeting of foreign ministers in November. Although the announcement of the Warsaw Pact in May 1955 indicated that the East-West line was being drawn even more tautly, Dulles went to the meeting convinced, as he told the president, that he would be making "constructive proposals which should dissipate any legitimate Soviet concern about the reunification of Germany and its entry into NATO and WEU." Confounding these expectations, Molotov described the Western proposals as "removed from the realities of life," viz. that two sovereign, and presumably permanent, German states now existed. The creation of the GDR, he claimed, had been "a turning point" in the history of Germany and Europe. At the NSC meeting which tried to pick up the pieces, Under Secretary of State Hoover called this a "devastating speech," while Dulles viewed it as an "utterly cynical" rejection of the position he thought had been agreed at the heads-of-state meeting in July.[34]

As the spirit of Geneva dissipated without any movement on European issues, the United States discovered that the alliance solution had in many ways resulted in an increased burden for the nation. As Dulles said, "Our true objective was to get out of Europe, but we cannot do so for the time being because our presence is necessary to tide Europe over its insecurity." Even if judged on narrowly military grounds, NATO came up short owing to the failure of the Europeans to meet their troop commitments. To redress the military balance, the United States was forced to rely increasingly on tactical nuclear weapons, whose introduction would open a Pandora's box of alliance problems in the 1960s.[35]

More important, the failure to move toward German unity aggravated concerns about the flimsiness of Bonn's allegiance to the West. Adenauer had long been perceived in Washington as "one of the great men of our time," by comparison with whom the French statesmen of the day invariably came off as small-minded. Adenauer may have been, in Ike's words, the West's "ace in the hole," but this reliance on one man was a reflection of the fear that the Federal Republic's Western orientation was superficial, leaving open the possibility that the political mood in Bonn might, following the aged leader's death, shift suddenly and drastically in the direction of neutralism and nationalism and a willingness to abandon NATO in order to deal individually with the Soviets. As Anthony Eden warned, the Russians might wish to delay in the knowledge that Adenauer was already seventy-eight "and that time was on their side." As NATO Commander General Alfred Gruenther wrote in May 1956, "The German situation is an uneasy one, and if the Chancellor should ever start to deteriorate we could be in big trouble there."[36]

Holding the West Germans within the alliance meant not only relying on Adenauer, but keeping alive the theme of "reunification through strength" which justified the Federal Republic's ties to the West as the best route to national unity. Any shattering of belief in the inevitability of reunification, any endorsement of the status quo, could arouse the beast of latent nationalism and provoke a breakaway from the alliance. Thus, apart from the internationalist obligation of maintaining European morale, the Americans were committed to maintaining German morale, with its roots in atavistic nationalism, in order to keep the *Bundesrepublik* within the alliance. The tension between these two goals would compromise the very stability the nation was seeking to provide for Europe. The explosion would come in the Berlin crisis a few years hence.

ASIA AND THE UNITY OF WORLD OPINION

The continuing anxiety about Europe was connected to worries about Asia. With the experience of Korea to guide him, Eisenhower's vision of the cold war was, from the beginning, regionally stereoscopic. "The global struggle is an indivisible whole," he wrote to Bob Lovett in December 1951. "The Cold War everywhere, our effort to create strength in Europe, our fighting in Asia—all these are bound together." Lecturing a group of visiting congressmen at his Paris headquarters in June 1951, he stated that "we can disabuse our minds of another thing that creeps in every once in a while—that there is an East-versus-West factor in this problem which we must resolve before we can proceed. Gentlemen, it is East *and* West. They have effects, one upon the other. Events in each case are not simply isolated, unrelated events." Eisenhower's view of this tight East-West linkage remained constant over time.[37]

Both the successes and the failures of European policy imparted a global cast to Asian problems. The progress made toward creation of a military balance in Europe suggested that the Russians would sublimate their expansionist desires by diverting their attentions elsewhere, particularly to Asia. By conventional standards this would have meant that America's European policy was a success, but not by the logic of the cold war. Worried always about world opinion, a military balance alone seemed insufficient to insulate the Continent from shocks elsewhere, since the continued psychological shakiness of Europe made it vulnerable to the demoralizing effects of Soviet advances in the third world. The EDC fiasco and the equivocal NATO solution in Europe were thus closely connected in the minds of American policymakers to local aggressions, which were defined as "conflicts occurring in less developed areas of the world."[38]

The basic problem was the decline of European spirit and power. As Dulles told the Senate Foreign Relations Committee in 1953, "The dilemma confronting us is that of Allies in Europe who are, in a sense, old, tired, worn out, and almost willing to buy peace in order to have a few more years of rest." The weakest link between Europe and the outer world was France. For Eisenhower, France's problems were emblematic of global difficulties caused by Europe's decline. Dulles told Admiral Radford that "France is creating a vacuum in the world wherever she is." The great question was, in his mind, "who should fill the void left by the collapse of France, particularly in the colonial areas?" In a gloomy conversation with the president in December 1956, Dulles maintained that it was "increasingly difficult to maintain the illusion that Paris was one of the great world powers." The British, though more inclined to follow Washington's lead, seemed also to have lost their resoluteness and their appetite for responsibility. While France was "deteriorating as a great power," the British failed to appreciate "that the danger cannot be met by the means which have conventionally applied against national threats. The UK tends to regard as acceptable some division of the world." The failure to approve the EDC and the willingness to cut unsavory deals with Moscow were diagnosed by Washington as nothing less than symptoms of spiritual disintegration.[39]

What did remain of Europe's pretensions to great-power status was, in Washington's eyes, distinctly unhelpful. In the absence of the common civilizational base that made possible the kind of close association underlying

American policy in Europe, adherence to a common anti-Communist ideology was all the more important to holding the line in Asia. Unfortunately, European colonialism got in the way. In 1957, Eisenhower put it this way: "The spirit of nationalism is stronger than communism; unfortunately, it is also stronger than anticommunism." The heritage of colonialism would have been difficult enough for the West to overcome in any case, but the resistance to decolonization among the European nations further marred the attractiveness of Western liberalism in the third world. Ike agreed with historian Arnold Toynbee that colonialism was "the single most important factor" and believed that it should be "militantly condemned by the colonial powers, especially Britain and France. The attempt should be to transfer a necessity into virtue." Dulles was of the same mind. "We have to be spokesman for those wanting independence or we will be licked," he insisted. Because it allowed the United States to burnish its anticolonial image, the Anglo-French intervention in Egypt in 1956 was, in some ways, beneficial.[40]

Though still willing to expend power in Asia for shortsighted colonial purposes, Europe was not willing to exercise it where it counted, on continental security. In contemplating the "dilemmas" posed by regional alliances within a universalist policy context, Dulles said that "we could achieve an immediate strengthening of our NATO defenses if we were prepared to follow the European theory of alliances. But then we would have to write off everything else in the world." The problem with the traditional European outlook was that "people around the world feel lonely and alone" and for that very reason a failure to react in any region meant that "the thing would spread." Events taking place on the periphery were crucial because, though unimportant in themselves, in global context they spoke volumes about the degree to which America and Europe adhered to the belief system that was central to the entire project of modern foreign policy. Early in the administration, Dulles, summarizing an NSC discussion, noted that "we must hold the present outpost position. There is no place around the orbit of the Soviet world which we can now afford to lose because further losses cannot now be insulated and will inevitably set up a chain reaction."[41]

As Europe's self-absorption suggested, world opinion was not really internationalist, or not sufficiently so. Defeat in the third world seemed likely to devastate European morale, but at the same time European provincialism was hamstringing security efforts elsewhere, even to the point of shying away from American toughness. In response, Dulles could do no better than suggest the inculcation of a better understanding of interdependence. Wilson had believed that democracy would bring a commonality of viewpoint essential to internationalism, but Dulles was discovering that no common definition of threat existed. Indeed, domino thinking by its very nature implied that the parts were unable to act for failure to see the whole. Effective internationalism thus depended not so much on democratization as on the diffusion of the proper global historical frame. In the sincere belief that the United States was acting from an "enlightened view of its own self-interest," Dulles clearly wished that the Europeans would abandon their traditional realist perspective, with its inability to acknowledge anything but self-interest, and learn to do the same.[42]

The exhaustion of the allies, their atavistic attachment to colonialism, and their inability to understand that their future hinged on the effective unity of world opinion were signs that the cold-war version of collective security and world opinion rested on a wobbly foundation. Had Europe felt "secure," Asian problems might have been localized, but continental weakness placed special burdens on the United States in areas where stability had formerly been supplied by the colonial powers. Unfortunately, the politics of Asia, besides being more unsettled than Europe's, were also far less promising for creating collective structures of defense. The absence of even the minimal solidarity found on the Continent made American policy in the region highly susceptible to a unilateralism and brinkmanship that would have an equivocal impact upon the morale it valued so highly.

The first major crisis in Asia came with the failure in the spring of 1954 of the French to hold their position in Indochina against the Communist Vietminh forces. As early as 1951, Eisenhower had declared that there was "a *close relationship*" between Indochina and Europe. He pointed out to Averell Harriman the "inescapable effect of this struggle upon NATO prospects and purposes." In testimony before the Senate Foreign Relations Committee in early 1953, Dulles called the situation in Indochina "even more dangerous in its global aspects than the fighting in Korea." Had the line not been held in Korea, it was believed that the situation could still have been contained. With Indochina, however, it was agreed that "the consequences of loss there could not be localized, but would spread throughout Asia and Europe."[43]

When France threw in the towel and agreed to meet at Geneva with the Communists, the Americans sensed a sudden erosion of will in Europe and in Asia. The French decision to seek peace at any price seemed "as grave as the collapse of 1940." As Ike put it, "Here was developing somewhat of a landslide attitude in favor of 'appeasement' of Communist China." With Indochina coming to a boil just as the saga of the EDC was nearing its sorry climax, there existed the possibility of a compound catastrophe. Should the West be bested, Admiral Radford believed that there would be "a tremendous compulsion on the part of Asians to be on the winning side," as he told British Foreign Minister Eden. This "deplorable" French weakness, Dulles told Radford, meant that "we could lose Europe, Asia, and Africa all at once if we don't watch out."[44]

Although there was talk of Southeast Asia's important raw material resources, traditional strategic considerations were secondary. Dulles acknowledged that "these countries are not really of great significance to us, other than from the point of view of prestige." But talking in terms of prestige, a conventional attribute of national power, was far too narrow a way of stating the problem. Closer to the mark was NSC 162, which had concluded in September 1953 that "the principle of collective security through the United Nations, if it is to continue to survive as a deterrent to continued piecemeal aggression and a promise of an eventual effective world security system, should be upheld even in areas not of vital strategic importance." Prestige rested on the credibility of national power; collective security hinged on the credibility of world opinion.[45]

It was in this context of uncertainty about Western resolve that Eisenhower on 7 April first made mention of the "domino theory." The image of toppling dominoes was metaphorical, but it was only in response to a question at an 11 May press conference that Dulles made clear its roots in collective-security assumptions about the indispensability of a united world opinion:

> The situation in that area, as we found it was that it was subject to the so-called "domino theory"? You mean that if one went, another would go? We are trying to change it so that would not be the case. That is the whole theory of collective security. You generally have a whole series of countries that can be picked up one by one. That is the whole theory of the North Atlantic Treaty. As they come together, then the "domino theory," so-called, ceases to apply. And what we are tying to do is create a situation in SEA where the domino situation in SEA will not apply.

Tumbling dominoes were thus equated with collective insecurity, the solution to which was the formation of a solidary world opinion against aggression.[46]

The key to American policy, as Ike had made clear in a speech delivered on 16 April 1953, was unity in the non-Communist world. At that time he declared that "aggression in Korea and SEA are threats to the whole free community to be met by united action." Although the most spectacular aspect of the crisis was the discussion of the possibility of using nuclear weapons to extricate the French garrison at Dien Bien Phu, a unilateral employment of the bomb was always out of the question. It was clear, moreover, that Congress, with the ink barely dry on the Korean Armistice, was skittish about jumping into yet another Asian thicket. Following a discussion with congressional leaders in April, Dulles noted a unanimous feeling that "we want no more Koreas with the United States furnishing 90% of the manpower." On the other hand, Congress "would be quite prepared to go along with some vigorous action if we were not doing it alone." Recognizing the formidable character of this sentiment, Dulles told legislators that he was "strongly opposed to getting our soldiers bogged down in Asia. Other things we can do are better."[47]

United action envisioned American intervention in Indochina only with the approval and cooperation of the French and British. However, after running into determined British opposition to such a scheme, a frustrated Eisenhower complained that "the Churchill Government was really promoting a second Munich." Unity on the diplomatic front was no less difficult to attain. Hoping initially for a "strong and united" Western stance at Geneva, Dulles resigned himself in short order to expect "exactly nothing" from the conference. The United States had "no diplomatic cards to play," thanks to British trepidations and the failure of united action. He complained dourly to Anthony Eden in April that the West at Geneva presented "a pathetic spectacle of drifting without any agreed policy or purpose." The agreements confirmed Dulles's pessimism. The partition of Indochina seemed a bad bargain because of the likelihood of large-scale infiltration southward by the Communists into South Vietnam. The provisions for all-national elections seemed equally ill-advised, since, as Dulles conceded privately, "if elections were held now the Communists would probably win."[48]

With the military option effectively ruled out by opposition at home and abroad and the Geneva conference going badly, the administration shifted to a policy of damage limitation. Despite its pessimistic conviction that the Communists would most likely soon swallow up the rest of Indochina and then the rest of Southeast Asia, Dulles confessed to a reporter, "We cannot afford to come right out and say that." Vietnam, even Laos and Cambodia, Dulles now told reporters, were "important but by no means essential." The saving grace was that the Vietminh success could be treated not as an evacuation signal but as a warning bell to get the Asian house in order. Putting the best face on events, Dulles speculated that "what has been going on and what is in prospect has a good chance of so arousing and uniting the areas outside of Indochina that it may be possible to insulate largely the consequences of a loss of Indochina, particularly if Laos and Cambodia can be saved and brought into the united defense structure."[49]

Resorting to a highly diluted, almost homeopathic, form of united action, the administration decided to build up "the natives" below the 17th parallel by creating yet another collective security treaty organization, SEATO. In pursuing a regional grouping, Ike made clear to Congress that Dulles's plan was designed "not to enable intervention, but so that it might not be necessary to intervene." The policy was in line with Eisenhower's idea of "getting fine ground forces established, so that we do not have to go to the trouble of transporting troops.'' However, Dulles, an enthusiastic salesman for the pact in public, was privately quite worried about committing the United States ''in an area where we had little control and where the situation was by no means promising.''[50]

Dulles was also concerned about being tied down with allies who might not be as dedicated to collective security as the United States. ''They are more concerned with trying not to annoy the Communists rather than stopping them,'' Dulles grumbled to one of his State Department intimates. In another phone call, he said that ''these fellows are so weak and feeble, one wonders if it is any good to have a treaty with them.'' But appearances counted for much. Despite the arguments of some, like Secretary of Defense Wilson, that the United States should withdraw and that ''these people should be left to stew in their own juice,'' Eisenhower resisted this option, arguing that it would ''lead to a grave situation from the point of view of our national security.'' By domino logic, giving up the region without a fight would only have been an invitation to far more serious difficulties.[51]

Prospects seemed little better within South Vietnam. Dulles lamented the absence of a strong government there and noted that French support of the new premier, Ngo Dinh Diem, was ''only half-hearted.'' But Diem's nationalist energy soon made believers of the Americans. By early 1955, the State Department was writing of a new, non-Communist ''revolutionary spirit'' in South Vietnam and arguing that ''the best and perhaps only chance is to back Diem *unconditionally* on the gamble that he can succeed.'' This was an Adenauer solution, the belief that a strong man could, for a critical period of the cold war, shore up societal weaknesses that under ordinary leadership might produce political catastrophe. Soon enough, Dulles was preaching to others the wisdom of this commitment to one man. ''In that part of the world,'' he told Edgar Faure, ''there was no such thing as a 'coalition' government, but one-man governments.'' Given the new-found vigor in Saigon, it was an easy step to the hope, stated by Assistant Secretary of State Walter Robertson, that American backing ''would have a most revolutionary effect on their thinking and on their courage.'' In any event, by 1957 Dulles was confident enough to report to the cabinet following a SEATO meeting that ''the strength of Vietnam is increasing.'' But this attachment to Diem underscored the point that the United States could only nurture and support morale, not create it.[52]

Having just dodged a bullet in Indochina, the administration was uncomfortably aware of the fact that basic regional problems had not been resolved. After the Indochina crisis had been papered over, Ike told George Humphrey that he was still ''frightened most about Asia . . . Asia to my mind has gotten to be critical and these boys are making a play for it.'' Unlike in Europe, where it was seriously hoping for German unification, the United States was content with the two-China status quo, although it was not politic to admit this publicly for fear of undermining Chiang Kai-shek's regime. There was no ''magnet'' theory at work in the Far East, nor was there any overriding need for Nationalist manpower akin to the need for West German troops in Europe. The United States did not expect the Chinese Communist regime to crumble at any time in the near future, nor did it believe that a Nationalist assault on the mainland would be a wise strategy. At an NSC meeting in 1954, Eisenhower ventured the opinion that ''Chiang's only hope was in a general uprising in China, for which Chiang would be called back, like Napoleon from Elba.'' But Dulles, believing that the Chinese revolution was well entrenched, pointed out that ''there was no evidence that such an uprising would occur.''[53]

Although the People's Republic of China was an ''evil fact,'' the administration was counting on an eventual breakup of the Sino-Soviet alliance, at Chinese initiative, to ease its cold-war burdens. As Dulles said in 1953, ''The Chinese were very proud of their history, and Chinese did not like Russians. In the end, therefore, they would split apart; the problem for us was whether we could play this thing for 25 years.'' In the long run, the administration sought consciously to create a Sino-Soviet split by pushing the Chinese so firmly into the Soviet embrace that they would come to appreciate first-hand the barrenness of marriage with the Russians. Actually, it had little choice but to use the stick, since the carrot of accommodation or appeasement was perforce ruled out. As Eisenhower and Dulles well realized, however, a breakup would require a long-term change in political ecology that was of little relevance to the contemporary political environment.[54]

All told, this indicated that the United States was quite prepared to tolerate an Asian balance, reminiscent of the past, that was decoupled from European politics and based on ''natural'' regional forces. But the PRC's ideological zeal, the nonreversible commitment to Chiang's regime, and overriding cold-war criteria of morale, credibility, and world opinion raised the China problem to the first rank in importance. Thus when PRC forces began bombarding the offshore islands garrisoned by Chiang's troops, the issue immediately began to pose by now familiar symbolic problems for the United States. The legal situation, in which the United States had signed a security treaty to defend a faction in a civil war whose enemies had already been granted recognition by some American allies, was knotty enough, but it paled before the strategic quandaries facing the United States[55]

From a strategic standpoint, the offshore islands were hardly prime real estate. Dulles realized that Quemoy and Matsu ''were somewhat comparable to Berlin, which, as a matter of geography and logic, should be treated as part of the surrounding Soviet zone, but which in fact the free world was prepared to defend." These islands, as Dulles well knew, were "hardly defensible positions . . . relatively remote from the centers of free world interests." Indeed, there was a serious question from the military point of view, as Admiral Radford subsequently acknowledged, "whether even Formosa was essential to the security of the United States."[56]

But conventional strategic thinking seemed irrelevant. According to Radford, "the problem facing the U.S. was rather a psychological one at this juncture." As Dulles told Canadian leaders in Ottawa following his trip to the Far East in March 1955, "This was only partially a military problem. The major factors of morale and psychology were involved." Maps might suggest the prudence of withdrawing, but "maps [did] not show the human elements." In a discussion with Walter Bedell Smith about the possibility of an evacuation in the event of a military assault on the islands, Ike revealed that "my hunch is that once we get tied up in any one of these things our prestige is so completely involved." As a result, Eisenhower vowed "that as far as he was concerned, the United States would never tolerate Formosa and the Pescadores going into unfriendly hands."[57]

Some doubters in the realist tradition, like Secretary of Defense Wilson, complained that American policy in the Far East, especially on the offshore islands, was "a lot of double talk." Others, like Treasury Secretary George Humphrey, failed to understand why, instead of concentrating on areas of vital concern, the United States was committed to fighting for obscure parcels of land. But these critics failed to recognize that American globalism meant abandoning an outdated geographic particularism for a reliance on world opinion that emphasized maintaining a perceptual climate resistant to expansionist threats. After listening to Humphrey and Wilson argue once again for drawing a defensible line based on a concept of vital interest that would redefine Indochina and Formosa as places not worth fighting for, Eisenhower responded warmly with the argument that "the problem of the Soviet Union was a new kind of problem, and the old rules simply didn't apply to our present situation." He remarked that "every locality in the world is a source of irritation in dealing with the Soviets."[58]

The crisis once again brought into play the conflicting dimensions of credibility, especially the choice between avoiding a global collapse and preventing a world war. In the first instance, a failure to take a stand seemed likely to embolden the Chinese Communists and the Russians to make new moves in more vital areas. In an NSC meeting, Eisenhower reminded those present of "Lenin's view that the approach to Europe is through the Far East." The crisis was occurring, after all, simultaneously with the critical aftermath of France's rejection of the European Defense Community, at a time when the credibility of the American NATO commitment was especially vital to the success of U.S. policy on the Continent. In a letter to Churchill, Ike repeated the globalist logic that was already so familiar to the grand old man of the alliance. If the Communists broke out into the Pacific, he warned, "all of us, including the free countries of Europe, would soon be in far worse trouble than we are now."[59]

Second, it was generally agreed, as Dulles pointed out, that the capture of the offshore islands "would have a serious psychological impact on Formosa." While there was widespread agreement within the administration that the offshore islands were worthless—on one occasion Dulles remarked "How fortunate it would be if these islands sank to the bottom of the sea"—a withdrawal, it was believed, would have a catastrophic effect on nationalist morale. As Eisenhower pointed out, "The psychological consequences of abandoning those islands were so serious" that "we probably couldn't hold Formosa if Chiang Kai-shek gives up in despair before Formosa is attacked." Here the United States faced the same paradox that it was encountering in Europe. While it was the policy of the United States to defend areas only where the locals had the will to defend themselves, Dulles admitted that "of course morale on Formosa depended very largely on the United States itself."[60]

While Formosa was not strategically vital, its abandonment could very well lead to a general crumbling of faith among America's allies. A U.S. "disassociation," as Dulles put it, "would raise the question as to whether the U.S. was really prepared to stand anywhere in the East." Having just signed the SEATO pact with a group of countries that Dulles considered to be very shaky, Eisenhower administration officials could not help but believe that the effects of a Formosa disaster would resonate far and wide among weak-kneed nations whose limbs were already vibrating. The result would be "a very serious situation all the way from Tokyo to Saigon." Radford pointed out that "the psychological effect of the loss of Formosa, in Japan and other countries in the Far East, would be terrific." The reverberations would extend ultimately to Europe. In his letter to Churchill, Ike accused the Communists of "attempting to disrupt the solidarity of the free world's intentions." As NSC 5501 argued in January 1955, the lines between East and West were drawn so tightly that "any further Communist territorial gain would have an unfavorable impact within the free world that might be out of all proportion to the strategic or economic significance of the territory lost."[61]

Emblematic of the East-West psychological connection was Dulles's hope that a showdown, if it came, could be delayed until the conclusion of the WEU agreements that made possible West Germany's admission into NATO. He got his wish, but, upon his return from a trip to the Far East in which he found the Red Chinese "exuberant—almost hysterical," he concluded that the situation was so critical that "we may have to demonstrate our position by deeds rather than by words." Dulles told the cabinet that the United States should be prepared for "a quite serious showdown in that part of the world."[62]

If inaction would damage morale and lead to a snowballing deterioration of the Western position, taking on the Chinese seemed no more appealing, since a reliance upon nuclear weapons would mean an almost certain escalation into all-out war. Eisenhower was well aware of this, pointing out to the NSC that "when we talk of general war with Communist China, what we mean is general war with the USSR also." After all, the logic of credibility also applied, in its own way, to the Communist world. The Soviets had a great deal riding on this issue, he believed, since a failure on their part to show adequate resolve on behalf of their ally would mean that "the Soviet empire would quickly fall to pieces." Dulles agreed, pointing to the Korean War as an example in which "one thing leads to another."[63]

War with China would certainly send the Communists an unmistakable message of credibility, but it would also estrange significant segments of world opinion, especially in Europe. According to Dulles, the greatest danger of a war with China was not its military aspect, but "the possibility that it might alienate the allies of the United States and might indeed block all our best-laid plans for Western Europe." Eisenhower was all too conscious, as he wrote to his old friend General Gruenther, of European complaints of American "recklessness, impulsiveness, and immaturity in the foreign field." The British, for example, while agreeing that Formosa must be defended at all costs, saw no point to holding the offshore islands. Following discussions with Eden, Dulles realized that a U.S. involvement in those islands "will put U.S. on weakest grounds with its allies and public opinion generally." War with China "would alienate world opinion and gravely strain our Alliances, both in Europe and with Anzus. This is the more true because it would probably lead to our initiating the use of atomic weapons." With its alliances shattered, the United States could look forward to dealing alone with the Communist danger. The president argued that "we are confronted with an extremely delicate situation, because we could not afford to be isolated from our allies in the world." Thus, paradoxically, while the Western world's will to self-defense rested on the credibility of U.S. power, manifestations of credibility in such situations threatened to subvert that will.[64]

Eisenhower also sensed that arguments based on credibility would sound strange to a public only recently baptized to internationalism less through its own inner conviction than by the conversion of its leaders. In an NSC discussion of the offshore islands crisis, Ike pointed out that because "Quemoy was not really important except psychologically," for that very reason "it would be a big job to explain to the American people the importance of these islands to U.S. national security." He warned the NSC "not for one minute to overlook the effect of such a move on U.S. public opinion. The people of the United States won't go to war for 'captious reasons,' and the Council would do well to remember this." Dulles agreed, but reminded the president that the reasons were, after all, not captious. He admitted that "it was a difficult and novel thing for most people to realize that the will and ability to fight for vital things is really indispensable to the maintenance of world peace." Dulles failed to note, however, that what was vital in the cold war had been defined as nonvital in the past. The difficulty, of course, was that U.S. policy had divorced itself from the readily understandable pursuit of interests in the classical sense in favor of a modernist approach grounded in a novel, and less than fully digested, interpretation of world history.[65]

In brief, the Quemoy-Matsu issue "bristled with difficulties" as the means employed to gain credibility once again threatened to undermine their end. All in all, the Quemoy situation was, for Ike, "a liability." Maintaining credibility in one area would erode it in others; yet refusing to maintain it would itself lead to a catastrophe. Understandably, Dulles worried about "drifting in very dangerous waters without an adequately prepared chart." He put his finger on one aspect of the problem when he noted that "until now, much of our thinking has been in terms of the presumption that a 'declaration of intent' on our part to defend the offshore islands was sufficient to deter an attack, and therefore to effectively achieve their defense." This might "no longer be a valid assumption, and we must therefore think in other terms." But that just landed him on the other horn of the dilemma: the "other terms," taking massive retaliation seriously, were unacceptable. In thinking through the issues, Ike, a man not normally at a loss for words, complained in frustration that "the considerations are so elusive that the matter is difficult to put into writing." Ike's powers of articulation did not fail him. It was just that cold-war logic, with its complex connections between power and opinion, its linkage to a set of internalized historical assumptions, and its paradoxical policy choices, made it difficult to define issues in anything but oversimplified either/or terms.[66]

With the alternatives equally frightening, for a time the only way out of this symbolic commitment seemed to lie in its desymbolization. The objective, Ike decided in April, should be to have Quemoy and Matsu transformed into "outposts rather than strongholds and symbols of prestige" by having the generalissimo withdraw voluntarily from the islands, as he had earlier withdrawn from the more distant Tachen group. Officials like Livingston Merchant in the State Department were also beginning to suggest that "the wise policy is for the United States to disengage Chiang Kai-shek's forces and our prestige from the offshore islands." Following the boss's lead, Dulles insisted that "the islands must not be allowed to become a psychological symbol, as in the case of Dien Bien Phu." A few days later, he suggested that "militarily and politically we and the Chi Nats would be much better off if our national prestige were not even remotely committed to the defense of the coastal islands . . . The lesson of Dien Bien Phu should not be forgotten. Originally conceived to be an outpost of transitory value, it gradually became converted into a symbol, so that all else fell with it. The same mistake should not be repeated in regard to Quemoy and Matsu, [which] may not be defensible except by means which may defeat the larger purpose." Dulles suggested that the withdrawal take place after some token resistance in which "Chiang's prestige and standing would be increased rather than decreased."[67]

But this desire to create a semantic counterpart to the distinction between vital and peripheral strategic interests came to nothing because the United States could not have it both ways, basing its policy on the presumption of a shaky world opinion and then trying to argue that symbolism was not important after all. Consequently, as efforts to sway Chiang to greater flexibility on the islands proved unavailing, the administration could not help but back him. It concluded in April 1955 that the paramount consideration was "to preserve the morale and the desire to fight on the part of the Chinats." In July, a vexed Eisenhower tried to explain to Anthony Eden "the great importance that Chiang attached to these islands as 'symbols' to his own forces." It did not matter in the least that Chiang's adamancy was wrong-headed: "Whether or not we agreed with his reasoning we had to accept the fact of his present position." Betraying Chiang on this issue and forcing him to leave the offshore islands would mean, in Ike's mind, that "the center of Communist irritation would be transferred to Formosa and the Pescadores." And that, in turn, would have started an avalanche of defeatism.[68]

Fortunately, by this time the Red Chinese had eased their assaults on the beleaguered offshore islands and opened exploratory talks with the United States. Dulles hoped these talks would buy some time "to try to build up a world opinion which would compel the Chinese Communists to accept the status quo and not seek to change it by force." The earthquake was over, but a brief aftershock occurred in 1958 as mainland forces resumed bombardment of the offshore islands. In the wake of the launch of *Sputnik*, Dulles "had the feeling that the Communist bloc may now be pushing all around the perimeter to see whether our resolution was weakened by the Soviet possession of nuclear missiles." In August, he cautioned that "the Soviets would carry on a war of nerves and that if they felt we were weakening at any point, they would press vigorously." Once again the administration ran through the same conflicting arguments. It worried about the frightening implications of using nuclear weapons—"the heart of the matter" according to Ike. And it was uncomfortably aware of the ironic consequences of its pursuit of credibility. In a 1958 meeting, Eisenhower "expressed some concern that as much as two-thirds of the world, and 50% of U.S. opinion, opposes the course which we have been following."[69]

In a moment of frustration in September, Ike seemed close to throwing in his hand and renouncing the policy so sedulously adhered to, at least in public, during his tenure. He admitted to Dulles that "our position is unrealistic" and spoke of the possibility of "a package deal for a status quo for a few years to give internal forces a chance. We could get out of that damned place where we are caught." Torn by the intolerable dilemmas that U.S. foreign policy had created for itself, he complained that "we are committed, indeed, overcommitted." But Dulles was more confident this time around of having decoded the logic of Chinese behavior, whose language of power also spoke in subtle symbolic terms. He reassured the president that, having avoided war thus far, they could continue to do so in future. Dulles's thoughts turned back, not only to the earlier crisis, but to the Berlin blockade as a situation in which the Communists were "attempting with force, but with a limitation of that force, to capture Quemoy and Matsu. The same conditions prevailed in the Berlin situation." Citing the "different sense of time" possessed by the Chinese (which, he hoped, was much like his), and sensing no real prospect of an invasion, he put his hope in the future, believing that Formosa would "become more Taiwanese as time goes on and that the new elite will be less interested in going back to the mainland." Had Dulles known what was coming with Berlin, he might not have been so confident of his navigational skills.[70]

BERLIN AGAIN

By the end of 1957, despite the new military muscle in NATO and recent progress toward economic unity, the security of post-*Sputnik* Europe seemed as uncertain as ever. To Paul Nitze, Dulles's complaints "reminded him of some of the problems we were faced with in the fall and winter of 1950 when things were going badly in Korea. We were uncertain in Washington how best to restore the situation and our allies were confused and in doubt." The cause of insecurity resided at the very heart of the newly beefed-up

NATO as the failure to achieve German reunification in the mid-1950s set the stage for a new venting of built-up tensions on the Continent in the latter half of the decade. With German unification on Western terms dead in the water, the German question boiled down to one of lashing the Federal Republic as firmly as possible to Western moorings before the seemingly inevitable hurricane of nationalism swept in. As Dulles put it in an NSC meeting devoted partly to damage control, the United States "must be prepared to do . . . everything it could do effectively to develop the integration of Europe." With the failure of EDC, an American-led NATO had become "the great magnet of free Europe" which would "attract and retain the Federal Republic in integration with the free world." Among other things, he proposed greater participation in nuclear policy among the NATO powers as "one way of keeping alive the morale and spirit of NATO" and thereby cementing the alliance.[71]

It was partly out of the feeling that European policy had not been properly grounded that the issue of German neutralization once again began to throw off sparks in 1957. The debate was kicked off by George Kennan's Reith lectures, broadcast over radio, in which he made public his former in-house proposals for a mutual withdrawal of Soviet and American forces in Germany. These proposals were immediately rejected, not only by administration policymakers but by Democrats like Dean Acheson who were closely identified with existing policy. Ike realized that the ramifications extended beyond Germany, for disengagement and neutralization would mean "the complete destruction of NATO." He believed also that "neutralizing Germany would amount to nothing more than communizing it." At the very least, a neutral Germany would be nationalist. With unhappy memories of the 1922 Rapallo treaty between Germany and Soviet Russia in the background, only a supranational approach seemed workable. Dulles argued that "it was not safe to have a unified Germany in the heart of Europe" without some assured external control, such as its solid integration in western Europe. Dulles insisted that "Germany cannot be sterilized—it is a question of turning it loose or tying it in with other countries . . . the latter is safer." Eisenhower saw no other solution to the German problem than to "build up NATO and Germany within it."[72]

In response to critics like Walter Lippmann, who suggested that American support for the goal of reunification was outdated because it was actually feared by the European allies, Eisenhower expressed astonishment. Thus, when he concluded that "we have got to keep our allies," he was referring to keeping the Germans within the fold. Maintaining the alliance required that the Germans be propitiated, which meant, among other things, continuing to press for unification, the promise of which was thought to be central to their psychic well-being. It meant, too, refusing to recognize the de facto postwar status quo in Europe and kowtowing to that sense of German nationalism that was at bottom the force in Europe that American policy most feared.[73]

The State Department realized full well that the end of movement on reunification would have a demoralizing effect on the Germans, yet it was nevertheless at a loss for new policies. In response to a presidential directive to develop new ideas, Dulles admitted that his department "had not come up with anything new and brilliant." The Soviet adoption of a two-Germanys policy in the mid-1950s meant that the only avenue to German unity was "a thorough re-orientation of Soviet policy toward all the Soviet satellites"; in other words, an end to the cold war. Unhappily, Dulles concluded that "there was clearly no chance of such a re-orientation at the present time." It was with great understatement, therefore, that he told Soviet president Anastas Mikoyan early in 1959, "The German problem was becoming more difficult to resolve."[74]

As the German question lost its fluidity, it gained in volatility. In the fall of 1958, Khrushchev once again made Berlin the center of attention by threatening to sign a peace treaty with the GDR, which would have terminated all Western rights in Berlin. The issue was particularly urgent for the Soviets because Berlin's status as an open city and escape valve for refugees from the East made it impossible for the GDR to build up the critical mass for a self-sustaining socialist economy. Equally vital, perhaps, was Khrushchev's need to get his Eastern house in order to face down what looked to be a nuclearized Federal Republic in the near future. This was no mere reprise of the 1948 crisis, because the stakes were far more serious this time around. Whereas formerly the Soviets had sought readmission to the four-power German game, now they were seeking to close it down altogether, with far-reaching consequences for the future of the cold war. Khrushchev was well aware of the explosiveness of this issue; indeed, one of his notes compared Berlin to "a smoldering fuse that has been connected to a powder keg." Dulles agreed, telling White House Press Secretary James Hagerty that Khrushchev was "pushing the world pretty close to war."[75]

Like Quemoy and Matsu, Berlin was conventionally inconsequential, but its symbolic consecration was an act of political transubstantiation that had given it flesh-and-blood strategic attributes. Dulles noted that "if there is going to be trouble something seems to start in Berlin—almost more than anywhere else it is a barometer." Thus, while the issue seemed to rest on seemingly trivial matters, such as whether Americans would accept the replacement of Red Army troops with East German border guards, these issues were invested with enormous psychological significance. As Ike saw it, "If the matter leads from stamping of cards to other things, all our rights can be gradually lost.'' Dulles told Adenauer that ''I think you must realistically admit that the Soviet initiative has added a new psychological element in terms of expectancies, as well as underlining the delicately poised post-war equilibrium in Central Europe.''[76]

Concessions on Berlin would almost surely harden the status quo of two Germanys and kill any chances for reunification. And that, in turn, would almost certainly mean ''death to Adenauer.'' The old man ''had become very inflexible,'' uncomfortably so to American policymakers eager to find some way out of the Berlin maze, but a successor to Adenauer could conceivably make things far worse. As Llewelyn Thompson put it from Moscow, ''We cannot count on [a] man of Adenauer's wisdom always being in power in Germany, and it seems inevitable that sooner or later a demagogue will yield to temptation and exploit German nationalism for his own ends.'' Thus the administration felt it had no choice but to back him while he was in power and to prolong his reign. In the interest of propping up the shaky morale of its West German ally, the United States continued to define as fundamental its interest in staying in a city it did not need, played to a nationalist sentiment it hoped would one day vanish, and kept up hope in a reunification it did not believe was forthcoming at any time in the near future.[77]

Berlin's symbolic significance went well beyond German opinion, however. The administration also emphasized the city's place, as Dulles put it, ''in the overall world picture.'' As Ambassador to Bonn David Bruce summarized it: ''To yield little is to yield everything . . . What they want is the whole thing. And, in the absence of our unshaken will to plunge, if required, into a nuclear conflict, they are in position at worst to . . . expose us particularly as paper tiger.'' In a talk on Berlin, a favorite topic, Acheson insisted that ''we have to stay because to get out will destroy us all.'' In a televised address on Berlin delivered in March 1959, Eisenhower summarized all the arguments that had been making the rounds privately in administration echelons. Yielding to the Soviets ''would mean the end of all hopes for a Germany under a government of German choosing. It would raise among our friends the most serious doubts about the validity of all the international agreements and commitments we have made with them in every quarter of the globe. One result would be to undermine the mutual confidence upon which our entire system of collective security is founded.'' Using rhetorical shorthand, Eisenhower told some legislators in March 1959 that ''any appeasement means disaster.''[78]

Once again, however, the act of creating solidarity worked at cross purposes by threatening to alienate the allies. The triumph of the NATO solution in the 1950s was premised on western European weakness—not so much of its physical capabilities as its spiritual resources. The parlous state of the

European *spirit* necessitated the constant reassurance of an American presence and American guidance. Speaking Dulles's lines for him, Adenauer reminded the secretary that "the unity and determination of the West is the decisive condition for any success vis-à-vis communism and especially vis-à-vis Soviet Russia." In a phone conversation with Eisenhower, Dulles "stressed how important it was to have world opinion behind him." And yet, as the U.S. ambassador to Moscow, Llewelyn Thompson, had to admit, "Khrushchev, merely by putting his Berlin proposal forward, appears to have succeeded in shaking our confidence in our position, and has gained at least a temporary advantage." The will of the other allies seemed in doubt also during the crisis. Early in 1959, following a trip to the European capitals, Dulles described the allies as being in "disarray." Eisenhower was forced to admit to congressional leaders that the determination of the other allies left much to be desired. For Eisenhower, this was "a situation which could lead to the most damaging results if each of the Western Powers began to act separately."[79]

The British posture, which was soft on the issue of recognizing the East German regime, gave rise to worries about the fate of the alliance and America's entire postwar position. In mid-1959, Ike fumed, "If the British won't stand with us in keeping West Berlin and West Germany secure, then their action essentially leaves us alone to adopt a 'fortress America' posture." Dulles informed his British counterpart, Selwyn Lloyd, that softness meant defeat. He wondered "whether if opinion is as represented, Western Europe is really defensible at all . . . If so far as Western Europe is concerned, the will is lacking, then I fear our entire NATO concept and U.S. participation in it will require drastic review." But here Dulles was once again broaching as an alternative a return to the kind of disastrous isolationism the prevention of which was a basic goal of American foreign policy.[80]

Another major cause for worry appeared with the coming to power in France of General Charles de Gaulle. Although the French stood firm with the Americans on the Berlin crisis, French particularism was perceived to be a problem potentially every bit as serious as that of German nationalism and Britain's arm's-length aloofness from the Continent. Prior to de Gaulle's political resurrection, Eisenhower, who shared the view of most Americans in this regard, described France's postwar years as "a twelve year history of almost unbroken moral, political and military deterioration." He had complained for a long time of France's need for "a strong and inspirational leader"—if not a Joan of Arc, then a new Clemenceau. At first, Eisenhower agreed with CIA director Allen Dulles's view that the general's accession provided "more hope for the future of France than had been visible for a long time." But de Gaulle's emergence only confirmed the truth of the adage about the dangers of getting what one wished for, because his nationalist attempts at building French morale by reviving the nation's faith in its tradition of greatness were quickly perceived as a threat to NATO's cohesion. Having just deflected the general's 1959 suggestion for managing the alliance through a three-power Anglo-French-American directorate, Eisenhower was afraid that "other NATO nations will finally become weary with de Gaulle's attitude and lose enthusiasm for the organization." Early in 1960, he was complaining that de Gaulle seemed to be "singularly blind to the fact that if each nation is going its own way, this automatically destroys NATO."[81]

At times, Foster Dulles sensed that issues like Berlin were the diplomatic equivalent of cosmological singularities, points in which the theoretical calculations of credibility broke down. He was not immune to the loss of meaning resulting from the endless repetition of symbolic formulae that seemed to have no solid referent in tangible interests. In May 1958, prior to the onset of the Berlin crisis, Dulles referred to the necessity of once again going to Berlin and stating that an attack on the city would be considered an attack on the United States. He added that "he did not know whether he himself quite believed this or, indeed, whether his audiences would believe it. But he was going to perform this ritual act." Eisenhower expressed "surprise," and noted that "if we did not respond in this fashion to a Soviet attack on Berlin, we would first lose the city itself and, shortly after, all of Western Europe." If western Europe fell, "the United States would be reduced to the character of a garrison state if it was to survive at all." Dulles, of course, knew this liturgy full well, since he was one of its chief authors. Nevertheless, his temporary confusion at the connection between symbols and reality was mild compared to the incomprehension that Ike attributed to the American people when confronted by the prospect of a war starting over what was, after all, the Soviet determination to sign a peace treaty. The president doubted that "public opinion *pushes* us into war," arguing that it might not "even *follow* us into war" over Berlin.[82]

The Berlin problem was rendered more puzzling by the realization that the Soviet position was "essentially defensive," one designed to get the Americans and their allies to accept the postwar status quo in Germany and Europe. The traditional U.S. insistence on free elections, as Thompson telegrammed from Moscow, was "unrealistic," since "such elections would certainly result in resounding slap in face to them" and would have a "chain reaction effect" throughout the Communist bloc. And the chances for a German settlement in the near future were, as the State Department recognized, "virtually nil." Yet the Americans persisted in championing the civic status quo in Berlin, despite its highly volatile character, for want of anything better to suggest and for fear of the direst consequences in Germany and throughout the world. Eisenhower was fully aware of the inconsistencies of American policy, remarking on one occasion that "the Russians say this is an illogical position. We admit it is illogical, but we will not abandon our rights and responsibilities."[83]

The only possible solution from the American perspective was to buy time, something the Soviets increasingly felt they could not afford to barter. Very early on in the crisis, "Dulles said he didn't think we were going to reach a settlement, but what you can do is patch things up and prevent them from becoming acute-and keep things out of war." New initiatives, as he told Senator Fulbright, would be desirable "only for psychological purposes," i.e., to silence critics of American policy. At a White House meeting in September 1959, Eisenhower expressed a desire "to let the German question rest for three years while we go ahead with actions in other fields, [and] we may find that it has become easier to solve." Christian Herter, who took over at State following Dulles's death from cancer, agreed that the best solution would be "a two-to-three year modus vivendi."[84]

Privately, then, American policymakers were beginning to reconcile themselves to a formalization of the postwar status quo, to an institutionalization of the system of double containment that was premised on the division of Germany and Europe. Publicly, however, seeing no alternative, they persisted in their attempts to impress upon the Soviets the folly of such an approach. Ike told Mikoyan that "the Germans were a strong, virile people and if oppressed could react in a way which we would consider undesirable." Dulles, in a separate conversation, informed the Armenian that "there were good and bad Germans and that the situation that evolved after World War I might evolve again." Livingston Merchant told Frol Kozlov that "in the long run it would be disastrous for everyone if Germany were to be kept divided . . . long-continued division would almost inevitably lead to irresponsible leadership." He was puzzled by the Russian failure to credit "our desire to see Germany reunited while moderate leadership was still available." But this line made little headway with the Soviets.[85]

In the course of Khrushchev's celebrated visit to the United States in September 1959, the nature of the problem was at least clarified. Eisenhower admitted to the Soviet chairman that "the present situation in Berlin is abnormal," but he insisted on standing by the American commitment to the German people. To Khrushchev's contention that this was "unrealistic," Ike admitted that "the Berlin question was a symbolic one, irritating to the Soviets and unpleasant for us." Khrushchev responded that "it would be desirable if we could work out common language," but he reminded the president that they lived ideologically in "two different worlds. If we ignore these realities, then we cannot come to terms." "It would be well to recognize the facts," he continued.[86]

In other words, because symbolic agreement was impossible, the only language available was that of accommodation to geopolitical power realities. Although Eisenhower could not endorse this approach, Khrushchev did agree to remove the deadline for the signature of a peace treaty with the GDR on the understanding that there would be a full-dress summit in Paris the following year. By buying some time, the tête-à-tête between the two leaders managed to insert a few control rods into the hot Berlin pile. There essentially the Berlin opera would rest—with the spectacular fireworks of the aborted 1960 summit in Paris as an intermezzo—until the Kennedy administration took office.

By the end of the Eisenhower years, the administration could congratulate itself on having navigated through eight tense years while avoiding total war and a proliferation of Korea-like quagmires. Measured by the standards by which it had come to power, however, that was hardly cause for revelry, because America had failed to take the offensive. As the second Quemoy crisis was drawing to a close, Ike told Dulles of his belief "that in most respects we were on the defensive. That was true militarily and, in the main, economically in the sense that we were merely trying to hold free world positions against Communist assaults." That the administration had not lived up to its own impossibly high standards was evident from the fact that the 1960 campaign between Nixon and Kennedy, which much to Ike's annoyance was fought to an extraordinary extent on foreign-policy issues, saw the same charges of conservatism and lack of credibility leveled against the Republican party that it had used with great success in 1952.[87]

In retrospect, American foreign policy in the 1950s seems schizoid: moderate and peaceful insofar as it successfully avoided war, yet reckless and volatile as time and again it flirted with disaster. This sense of irenic dread, embodied in the persona of that peace-loving warrior, Eisenhower, was the product of his administration's fundamentally contradictory assumptions. Concerned to make containment effective at reduced cost, the concept of credibility during the Eisenhower years was pushed to the point that huge rents began to emerge in what was supposed to be a seamless fabric of world opinion. World opinion, ideally, would handle local aggressions and provide immunity against demoralization. Yet it never worked that way, since the absence of local resolve required American commitments to preserve morale. Thus, contrary to its desire to encourage local self-defense and resistance to communism, the United States during the Eisenhower years found itself more and more resembling Atlas holding up the world. The more everything seemed to depend on demonstrating nuclear resolve in marginal situations, the more psychological tensions were raised to an almost unbearable pitch. Ironically, despite the desire to send clear messages of reassurance and threat to friends and foes, the pursuit of credibility was plagued from within by near-paralyzing uncertainties.

After having lived life on the edge for eight years, the Eisenhower administration discovered that its drive to restore the West's credibility and the deterrent force of world opinion had created situations where that credibility seemed just as much in doubt as when it had started out. It had come full circle, only now the stakes were far more serious, as the nuclear credibility of both sides was at issue in Berlin. Furthermore, the barometer showed every indication of foul weather ahead. Soviet ideological dynamism was on the rise at the same time that pressure was building on Moscow from fraternal contenders for the mantle of ideological supremacy. Analyzing the meeting of world Communist parties in Moscow held in December 1960, Ambassador Thompson reported that the growing Red Chinese challenge to Soviet ideological dominance portended even more difficult times to come. "Khrushchev's need for success will have increased and his ability [to] make compromises on such questions as Berlin will have diminished," he predicted. During the Eisenhower years the country had weathered some serious storms by resorting to makeshift diplomatic shelters, but it was doubtful whether these would be capable of surviving the hurricane season in world politics that awaited the incoming Kennedy administration.[88]

8

JOHN F. KENNEDY AND THE IMPOSSIBILITY OF REALISM

J FK'S WORLDVIEW made an early debut with the publication of his Harvard senior thesis. In *Why England Slept,* a precocious work even when one takes into account the generous editorial assistance supplied by family friend Arthur Krock, the young Kennedy rejected his father's notorious isolationism by arguing that Britain's handling of Nazi Germany had been "a testing ground." "A defeat of the Allies," he suggested, "may simply be one step towards the ultimate achievement—Germany over the world." He concluded that "what we need is an armed guard that will wake up when the first fire starts or, better yet, one that will not permit a fire to start at all." The need to avoid a transformed global environment in which the United States would be left alone, militarily and ideologically isolated, would inform Kennedy's thinking on foreign policy for the remainder of his life. As a congressman and later as U.S. Senator from Massachusetts, Kennedy would further refine this conceptual raw material and make it the basis of his cold-war policies. His inaugural address, with its call for commitment and sacrifice, made eloquently clear that his tenure as president would be the testing ground of the cold war.[1]

JFK believed he had good reason to speak with urgency. In less pressing circumstances, the administration would have sought, in the words of the State Department's new policy planner, Walt Rostow, "to bind up the northern half of the Free World more closely and begin to link constructively to the south," but these forward-looking goals were overshadowed by the need simply to maintain the West's precarious position. In the eyes of the New Frontiersmen, the continued dynamism and growing appeal of communism as a historical ideology, a Soviet state whose power was unmistakably on the upswing, and the radical politics of the international Communist movement presaged a period of relentless probing of points of weakness in the non-Communist world. And the points of vulnerability were many. In Europe, the NATO bulkhead began to spring leaks, as recurring nightmares about the collapse of the alliance and a German breakaway were stimulated by persistent questions about the reliability of the American deterrent and by the emergence of nationalist resentment of America's imperial role. The chronic instability of Europe only exacerbated concerns about Red advances in the third world, which, far from being interpreted as remote and inconsequential episodes, seemed a way for communism to sneak through to historical ascendancy by way of the strategic backdoor. As a result of these ominous developments, symbolic issues related to the morale of the non-Communist world were elevated to even greater importance in American cold-war strategy.[2]

THE WORLD CRISIS

The New Frontiersmen were virtually unanimous in their conviction that Communist ideology had entered a militant phase. White House staffer Arthur Schlesinger, Jr., put it most clearly. The Kremlin, he said, was driven by an "ineradicable view—a view rooted in its theory of history—that any society based on a system of mixed ownership is inherently evil." For Ambassador Tommy Thompson in Moscow, the "major part" of the difficulty was that the "Soviets interpreted everything in terms of class struggle and saw the world only through Marxist eyes." A typical despatch from Moscow in February 1961 stated that the Soviet leadership had an "almost religious faith in their beliefs and this motivates them to [a] larger extent than generally believed." As for Khrushchev, he was "probably the most pragmatic and least dogmatic of all, but he [was] basically as devout [a] believer as any." In sizing up his opposite number, Kennedy took Khrushchev to be "a tough-minded, articulate, hard-reasoning spokesman for a system in which he was thoroughly versed and in which he thoroughly believed." He was no Stalin domestically, but in foreign affairs the earthy Khrushchev was far more the ideologue and more inclined to take risks than his predecessor.[3]

With the ideological waters still running at flood levels, the ultimate goal of containment remained, in JFK's words, "to establish the conditions of peace necessary for an evolution in the Soviet world toward a more open and thus less repressive society." A "talking paper" for the president's first meeting with de Gaulle declared bluntly that U.S. policy, convinced of the link between internal structure and external behavior, required "an essential change in the character of the Soviet regime." In the atmosphere of anti-Stalinist reform following the Twentieth Party Congress, there were numerous hopeful indications that, however slowly, a transition to democratic modernization was in fact taking place. Calling Communist ideology "outmoded,'' the Moscow embassy characterized the internal evolution of the USSR as "proceeding rapidly," noting in particular that with de-Stalinization "an element of democracy has entered both party and country as a whole."[4]

Unfortunately, there seemed little likelihood that the fruits of containment would ripen any time soon. The Soviet state was gaining rapidly in power and was all too aware of its new muscularity. Khrushchev's boastfulness ("We will bury you") and the recent assertion by a CPSU congress that Soviet society would advance within a generation from socialism to full-fledged communism in the process of overtaking the West were unsettling reminders of this self-confidence. Assuredly, the Soviet economy was undergoing stress from the conflicting demands being placed upon it, but no one was anticipating its collapse, much less the emergence of significant constraints that would require any shrinking of its formidable military establishment. "At some point," the CIA suggested, "economic stringencies could lead the Soviets to explore political ways of reducing the burden of armaments, but present indications do not point in this direction." By the raw measures of industrialization, the Soviet Union could legitimately present itself as a role model for other nations eager to take shortcuts to modernity.[5]

The growing perception of Soviet dynamism provided great cause for worry in an administration much taken with the power of images. The incessant emphasis during the campaign on "vigor" was in part an attempt to capitalize on Kennedy's youth and good looks in a media environment where television imagery had become a major political factor, but the administration's concern with appearances extended far beyond mere electoral considerations. New Frontier policymakers were also highly conscious of the international role of symbolism. Chester Bowles argued that "the most significant instruments of leverage and maneuver have now become the intangibles: prestige, influence, image, and ideology." White House aide Douglass Cater told Kennedy that "the nature of meaningful power has changed in the hydrogen age . . . Meaningful power is more likely to be demonstrated by each side's capacity to marshall ideas and actions which are powerful in their impact." During the campaign Kennedy himself had worried openly about the Soviet Union's "powerful effort to take away from us our prestige and our influence." His subsequent goal of beating the Russians to the moon because he "thought of space primarily in symbolic terms" was but one indication of the prominence accorded to imagery in the cold war.[6]

The decisive impact that symbols and images were thought to have on foreign-policy choices pointed up the continued centrality of world opinion to U.S. policy. In a report on NATO, an aging but still highly esteemed

Dean Acheson pointed out that the purpose of American foreign policy was "to maintain an environment in which free societies can survive and flourish." Looking for a catchy countertheme to the superficially attractive Soviet slogan of "peaceful coexistence," the administration pushed pluralism, or "a world of free choice," framing the issue in terms of a pluralistic versus a monolithic vision of the world. In a notable speech delivered in 1962, Schlesinger argued that "the world civil war of our own day is precisely between those who would reduce the world to one, and those who see the world as many." The ideal finally found its slogan the following year in the phrase "a world made safe for diversity."[7]

The world's choices could be influenced positively, through attraction, or negatively, through fear. Kennedy described this "doubting world" as "now balanced precariously on the wall of indecision between the East and the West." In a campaign speech in Muskegon, Michigan, he pointed to a Gallup poll taken in ten countries, in which respondents were asked which superpower would be first in 1970 militarily and scientifically. Most believed the Russians would take over the lead. "That is what hurts the United States," said Kennedy. "All those people who want to go with the winner turn against us and move in the direction of Moscow and Peiping." On another occasion, JFK remarked that "we don't want people in Africa or Latin America or Asia looking to Moscow or Peiping for hope, for the secret of the future." Campaign oratory carried over into policy deliberations once the administration settled into office. A White House brainstorming session in February 1961 concluded that the United States needed to "change our image. before the world so that it becomes plain that we and not the Soviet Union stand for the future."[8]

America could not afford to let the Soviets define civilization by seizing control of the Zeitgeist on which this pluralistic world depended. "What matters fundamentally," Schlesinger would argue, "is public opinion, not as exclamations, but as preconceptions—and in this sense public opinion changes very slowly." And it was precisely these preconceptions, deeper attitudes as opposed to superficial public relations images, that Kennedy was concerned to influence. He was greatly interested in "combating the idea, so prevalent in the underdeveloped world, that we are withering on the vine while Communism forges ahead." Given Khrushchev's cocksure depiction of communism as riding the crest of history's wave, it was all the more important that the United States project full confidence in the inevitable triumph of its version of the future. "This is no atrophied capitalist society," Kennedy insisted. "We have not 'gone over the hill' of history," he had written in August 1960. In some "ad libbing points" for the Vienna summit with Khrushchev, JFK was encouraged to "repeat the theme of confidence in the West—anti-Spenglerism. The West on the rise. All we have to do is hold together.''[9]

Imagery was important in the short run, too, as the key to preventing a collapse of world opinion through fear of Communist power. The immediate problem facing the United States was of ideologically motivated military threats that could trigger an unstoppable stampede away from the West. As JFK's amanuensis, Theodore Sorensen, put it, ''The real cause of difficulty was the Soviet Union's attempt to impose its system upon others by force.'' Kennedy further amplified these complaints in an interview with Alexei Adzhubei, Khrushchev's son-in-law: ''What we find objectionable is when a system is imposed by a small militant group by subversion, infiltration, and all the rest.'' There was no doubt that such challenges would be forthcoming, since they were a built-in fixture of communism, which, as one analysis put it, ''absolutely needs the world of violent conflict which its theory presupposes; without it there would have to be a kind of spiritual demobilization ending in disintegration and collapse.'' American policy therefore started with the assumption, as one of JFK's briefing papers declared, that ''the first task of Soviet policy is still to amass power and utilize it to advance the process of world transformation.''[10]

In sum, the strength and ideological vigor of the USSR was a barometer of stormy times ahead, and Kennedy had predicted as much during the campaign. ''As long as Mr. Khrushchev is convinced that the balance of world power is shifting his way—as long as he is convinced that time and the course of history is [*sic*] on his side—then no amount of goodwill trips or kitchen debates can compel him to substitute fruitful negotiations for force,'' he said on one occasion. This assessment was not altered once the administration took office. Referring to the previous autumn's meeting of Communist parties, George Kennan, whose views were listened to respectfully by Kennedy, argued that its decisions ''rested on [the] agreed calculation, between Russians and Chinese, that America's world position and influence could effectively be shattered in [the] coming period.'' Writing to Secretary of State Dean Rusk, long-time Soviet expert Charles Bohlen pointed to ''*a genuine confidence in what they term the correlation of forces swinging in their favor throughout the world.*'' Upon his return from the unsuccessful Vienna summit, Kennedy ''repeated his view of the Soviet sense of a change in the power balance'' to the congressional leadership.[11]

Developments in the nuclear arms race also pointed to a sharpening of cold-war competition. While the United States would retain and even extend its lead, JFK nevertheless found himself forced to operate in the nuclear environment that Eisenhower and Dulles had fretted about, one in which massive retaliation was no longer credible. Walter Lippmann recognized quickly that Kennedy was "the first President in history who has had to deal with the old issues and with American commitments in terms of nuclear parity." Despite the administration's belief that "the assumed common desire of both to avoid war" might lead to some agreement on nuclear matters, the mere existence of that desire did little to alleviate the threat to the nation's world position. Anticipating this situation, the New Frontier had adopted the views of General Maxwell Taylor, who had been a fierce rearguard critic of massive retaliation as army chief of staff during the Eisenhower years. With the publication in 1959 of *An Uncertain Trumpet,* he openly criticized American policy for offering "no alternative other than reciprocal suicide or retreat in the face of the superiority of Soviet conventional forces." The book provided a strategic rationale for reversing Eisenhower's criticism of the Truman administration. By relying excessively on nuclear weapons, Ike had gone too far in the direction of nuclear war while not doing enough to blunt the conventional threats that could prove decisive in the cold war.[12]

Following the Taylor script, JFK mercilessly criticized Eisenhower's policies as penny wise and pound foolish. He pounded away at "the abstraction of a budgetary balance against the lunging physical reality of Communist power" and criticized "our willingness to place fiscal security ahead of national security," when surely the latter overrode the former. In view of the flexibility now sanctioned by Keynesian macroeconomic science, the budgetary constraints demanded by Eisenhower's garrison state phobia seemed singularly misguided. Since "sacrifice," as he defined it, did not include fiscal austerity, Kennedy felt free to increase spending on both a modern nuclear arsenal and on conventional military forces which, it was argued, would supply the appropriate deterrent to Communist provocation at whatever level encountered.[13]

Most of all, "flexible response" signaled a new willingness to engage in the dirty little wars that Eisenhower believed were the Achilles heel of containment. Kennedy had little choice but to make a virtue out of a vice, since he feared that the Soviets, having neutralized the American nuclear deterrent, would now feel free to expand in other ways. In language recalling Kennan's description of Soviet power as a fluid force that sought to fill every available crevice, JFK described the number of potentially disastrous leaks the United States would be called on to plug in the years ahead: "Their missile power will be the shield from behind which they will slowly, but surely, advance—through Sputnik diplomacy, limited brush-fire wars, indirect non-overt aggression, intimidation and subversion, internal revolution, increased prestige or influence, and the vicious blackmail of our allies. The periphery of the Free World will slowly be nibbled away. The balance of power will slowly shift against us." Describing American power as a curve,

NATO Commander Lauris Norstad put the situation a bit differently: "If there is a gap in that curve, that is where we can expect to be hit."[14]

Contrary to the suggestions of some historians that the Kennedy administration was seeking cold-war victory, its overwhelming concern was the less ambitious aim of avoiding the collapse of global morale. JFK's foreign-policy speeches in the 1960 campaign echoed the advice of sages like George Kennan, who advised the candidate of "a serious possibility that the international situation prevailing at the time a new administration takes office may be as calamitous and menacing as was our internal situation at the time when F.D.R. assumed the reins of government." Repeatedly Kennedy suggested that "the balance of world power is slowly shifting to the Soviet Red-Chinese bloc." In a TV debate in Charleston, West Virginia, in May 1960, Kennedy described the moment as "a time of maximum peril." Shortly after taking office, he predicted that "the climax of the struggle with Communism will come—soon."[15]

The sense of looming crisis far outweighed any belief in the possibility of a swift transition to a genuinely peaceful coexistence. On the contrary, with unabated ideological antagonism and built-in Soviet aggressiveness taken as givens, the era of nuclear plenty placed all the more pressure on avoiding world conquest through piecemeal local aggressions that might sap the will to resist. This assessment was confirmed in the course of some grim discussions with Khrushchev in Vienna in early June 1961. In what Kennedy interpreted as the "most ominous" exchange of their first day of talks, the chairman warned the young president that if a country went Communist as a result of the expression of popular will and the two powers intervened, "our interference could set off chain reaction and lead to war." Soviet confidence in the expansion of communism through wars of national liberation, coupled with the attempt to paralyze Western will by pointing up the threat of nuclear war, made correspondingly greater the need to make world opinion resistant to the combined aura of historical inevitability and unstoppable power radiating from the Communist side.[16]

Ultimately, everything boiled down to the image of U.S. constancy and belief in the nation's willingness to see the cold war through to the end without flinching. This was a point that Kennedy spared no effort to get across. At the Vienna summit, he informed Khrushchev in the bluntest terms that "it is strategically important that the world believe the U.S. a serious country whose commitments one could rely on," a message that he made sure to repeat from time to time. In November 1961, for example, he wrote Khrushchev that prestige "was the element of consequence that is really important to us both." But by definition, resolve, in order to be effectively communicated, has to be demonstrated in practice. The result of this need to show resoluteness, driven by the existence of strategic issues carried over from the Eisenhower years, was a foreign-policy journey filled with unexpected twists and turns.[17]

The Eisenhower administration, by employing the rhetoric of an atomic diplomacy whose utility in the crunch was never fully accepted, had managed to avoid nuclear and conventional showdowns; the Kennedy administration, eschewing a nuclear strategy, was driven by the logic of credibility to deal practically with both. In the process, it was whipsawed by the tensions inherent in the pursuit of the two primary objectives of neo-Wilsonian strategy: preventing global war and avoiding a collapse of world opinion. As the intolerability of further flirtations with nuclear war became a matter of settled conviction in the aftermath of crises in Berlin and Cuba, the pursuit of nuclear accommodation undermined America's credibility within the alliance while contributing to the Communists' confidence that they could, in Bohlen's words, "with impunity, undertake certain actions without incurring a major risk of war." On the face of it, third-world brushfire wars might be no more than the military equivalent of insect bites, but they could easily transmit the fatal contagion of doubt in a perceptual climate where American credibility was under fire and Western morale once again shaky. In the charged ideological atmosphere of the early 1960s, the necessity of nuclear accommodation made conventional confrontation well nigh unavoidable.[18]

BERLIN AND THE CHALLENGE TO CREDIBILITY

Even before settling into office, Kennedy discovered that the situation was more critical than he had supposed. The first unwelcome piece of news came from the departing Eisenhower, who dumped the problems of Laos, Cuba, and Berlin in his lap. Exuding a meretricious decisiveness that belied the tortured doubts he had endured in facing such issues, Ike described Laos as "the cork in the bottle," so vital to the U.S. position that "if it reached the stage where we could not persuade others to act with us, then he would be willing, *as a last desperate hope, to intervene unilaterally.*" Adding to Kennedy's anxieties were the aftereffects of the spectacularly bungled invasion of Castro's Cuba, a local debacle that nevertheless raised the stakes elsewhere. A concerned Rostow told the president that "there is building up a sense of frustration and a perception that we are up against a game we can't handle." The Communist side was predictably heartened by the fiasco at the Bay of Pigs, but in addition, Rostow explained, the Cuban misadventure had "temporarily damaged the grand alliance in all its dimensions."[19]

However worrisome, these events were simply the first flashes of lightning before the storm gathering over Berlin, which remained, in JFK's estimation, "the most difficult and decisive question of all." The future of the city had remained in suspense in the last year of Eisenhower's presidency, as Khrushchev decided to await the changeover in administrations before getting on with the search for a solution acceptable to the USSR. In the interim, the drain of manpower from the GDR had grown even more serious. Meanwhile, with each side locked into its course, no one seemed able to think up a workable way to avoid the coming collision. As Rusk told Adenauer in a visit, "Any negotiations will be very difficult. Since 1948 the margins of compromise have been exhausted. There is very little meat on the bone." Martin Hillenbrand, director of State's Office of German Affairs, in reflecting on the lack of progress since 1958, saw "little reason for thinking that a lasting settlement can be devised."[20]

More so than the Eisenhower administration, Kennedy's people realized that the hard American interest in Berlin was less than compelling by any objective standard. Indeed, if any side had a tangible stake, it was the Soviets. Following the frosty encounter between the president and Khrushchev in Vienna in June, the Russian position was described by JFK as possessing "much superficial attractiveness." The Soviet leader was acting, Kennedy told congressional leaders, "in cold terms of a genuinely vital present interest." State Department hard-liners could continue to trot out the legalistic fiction that "there is in actuality no such country" as East Germany, but administration influentials realized that the Soviet investment in the GDR was too vital to allow a continuation of the civic status quo. Indeed, to perceptive onlookers an understanding of the constraints under which Khrushchev was operating pointed uncannily to the eventual outcome. In March 1961, Thompson wrote presciently from Moscow that "if we expect the Soviets to leave Berlin problem as it is, then we must at least expect East Germans to seal off sector boundary in order to stop what they must consider intolerable continuation refugee flow through Berlin."[21]

A dispassionate appreciation of Soviet raison d'état only underlined the anomalous nature of the American commitment to the status quo in Berlin. Everyone realized that the defense of the city constituted, in Senator Fulbright's words, "a strategic nightmare." Beyond that, high officials also recognized that the official line on solving the Berlin question, a reunification of Germany largely on Western terms, was unrealistic. Not only was it impossible for the Soviets to agree to it, but, as Fulbright reminded the young president, "Western policy on Germany, as officially proclaimed over the last decade, no longer represents the real expectations and practical hopes of Western European governments." One of Bundy's national security aides even ventured to suggest that no one cared very seriously about ending the partition: "What each side wanted was preservation of the *status quo*, although neither was willing to admit it for fear of alienating the Germans.'' Bundy's concurrence was evident from his critique of a paper that spoke of German reunification as a live possibility for the near future. ''We don't believe that,'' he noted to JFK, ''and other nations know we don't.'' This subterranean spring of doubt within the administration found its outlet at the top, as Kennedy himself wondered ''whether really it was to our advantage to press the argument for unification, feeling that our position lacks appeal.''[22]

Berlin was exactly the kind of situation Kennedy wished to avoid—an exposed position with a questionable argument, with nothing to fall back on except nuclear weapons that he did not want to use. Thus, beneath the surface, and in apparent contradiction of its tough campaign rhetoric, the Kennedy administration was beginning to toy seriously with the kind of realistic ''soft'' containment that had been the object of so much criticism in the early 1950s. Recognizing that hard Soviet interests were at issue implied, as Bundy realized, ''that if we think in terms of accommodation, we should be able to avoid a real crisis.'' Privately, he was advising JFK that only allied rights of access to Berlin were fundamental, which implied that the primary desideratum was saving face. Once these were guaranteed, Bundy continued, the United States could consider for further discussion ''such items as the Oder-Neisse line and a de facto acceptance of a divided Germany.''[23]

These were as yet only slivers of doubt in the thickly callused skin of American policy. The subjective neo-Wilsonian arguments on behalf of staying, coupled with a hard line on reunification, easily resisted attempts at penetration by advocates of the case for accommodation. Thus, while Fulbright fully understood that reunification was impossible ''under any conditions now conceivable,'' he realized also that there were ''compelling political reasons why this central fact cannot be explicitly and publicly acknowledged.'' For the same reasons, Bundy, despite the fact that he was in many ways a soft-liner who saw the virtues of realistic accommodation on Berlin and Germany, concluded in the end that Berlin was ''no place for compromise.''[24]

The all too familiar arguments were as persuasive as ever. Given the centrality of Germany in American policy, it was unthinkable to ignore the obdurate Adenauer's feelings on this issue. Henry Kissinger, an influential adviser to the administration, reminded Kennedy that ''[talking] to Adenauer about the wisdom of flexibility in the abstract is like telling a member of Alcoholics Anonymous that one martini before dinner will not hurt him.'' General de Gaulle put in a nutshell the indispensability to the West of a man who acted as a check against his own public. As a cable from Paris reported, ''He has no fears re western Germany as long as Adenauer is alive, but after that who knows.'' According to Kissinger, the repeated traumas of the past half century had produced "an atmosphere of hysteria, a tendency toward unbalanced actions." Germany, he concluded, despite its economic success, remained "a candidate for a nervous breakdown" because deep cultural traits having to do with the "psychological problem of Germany" were still at work.[25]

Though not everyone within the administration would have gone as far as Kissinger on this matter, the majority were in fact not all that far behind. To Rostow, a deal over Germany, or even the suspicion that a tacit deal had been reached, might lead the Germans to feel that "they must look to reunification by their own actions." "Western acceptance of partition would almost certainly reawaken German nationalism," said another analysis. A recognition of the division of Germany would, according to Soviet expert Foy Kohler, "produce a long-run danger of a revival of German nationalism seeking reunification by force." Even those who accepted the reality of partition assumed that official acceptance of a divided Germany "would almost certainly reawaken German nationalism."[26]

Apart from the ongoing need to propitiate the Germans, the subjective argument also took into account the shakiness of America's position in Europe. Although on the face of things Khrushchev appeared to be interested only in stabilizing the postwar status quo in Germany, administration hardliners, led by Acheson, were convinced that his ambitions were more far-reaching. "The central Soviet purpose is to drive us out of Berlin and destroy the European alliance," Acheson claimed. Even if that were not their objective, a Soviet victory in Berlin would be powerfully amplified because, in the State Department's view, Berlin was "the symbol of our determination and ability to prevent further Communist expansion in Europe."[27]

European morale, Washington believed, was quite shaky. As usual, the continental allies were at sixes and sevens in their views of the seriousness of the Berlin question and in their thinking on what should be done about it. In noting this absence of conviction, one research report talked of the alliance as if it were nothing more than a Potemkin village. "There is hope and even some bravado of bluffing it through and holding firm in Berlin," it said, "but when faced with the alternative of nuclear war, evidence indicates firmly that the Europeans are not willing to fight for the defense of West Berlin." Edward R. Murrow, head of the U.S. Information Agency, informed the NSC that the polls in Europe were hardly encouraging. "The problem of morale and purpose in western Europe is more serious than Americans ordinarily believe," he revealed. The polls "showed weakness in European opinion." The State Department concurred. At the height of the crisis, a State Department intelligence report informed the White House of serious cracks in "the most critical sector of world opinion." But just because many Europeans were inclined to appease the Soviets was no argument on behalf of the Americans doing so, inasmuch as concessions would, in all likelihood, lead only to greater pressures on the U.S. position in Europe down the line.[28]

As always, Americans sifted the issues through their globalist sieve, all the more so now that Berlin's importance for the German problem was declining in Washington's eyes. As political scientist Alexander George noted in a RAND Corporation research memo, "A particular diplomatic or limited-war crisis is always but one focal point in the *global* cold war." Rostow reminded Kennedy that an unyielding American stance on Berlin "should be justified not by Berlin but by a general heightening of the danger in the world environment." Specifically, he was concerned to demonstrate that "we are not so obsessed by Berlin that we are going to bug out in Southeast Asia." In firm agreement, Kennedy reminded de Gaulle in July that "while the focus in the struggle against Soviet expansion is certainly now Berlin, this must be evaluated against the background of the world conflict and considered in that light." In his televised speech of 25 July in which he informed the American public of preparations for the impending crisis, Kennedy made a point of emphasizing that the threat to Berlin was "not an isolated problem. The threat is world-wide."[29]

All in all, then, the importance of Berlin could "scarcely be exaggerated," as the State Department put it, because the city had become "the symbol of our determination and our ability to defend the free parts of the world against Communist aggression." Chester Bowles, normally hypersensitive to any hint of Eurocentrism in administration policies, agreed: "Any failure of the United States to defend the right of West Berliners to determine their political system would inevitably undermine the rights of Asians and Africans to determine their own destinies." In stressing the symbolic importance of Berlin, JFK was careful to distinguish between consequential symbolism and empty rhetoric. "The link of West Berlin to the Free World is not a matter of rhetoric," JFK assured Brandt. To ensure that the Soviets made no mistake about the concrete importance attached to this symbol in Washington, the president's brother Robert emphasized "continuously" to the Soviet ambassador "that we would go to war over Berlin." Berlin's symbolic meaning represented the entire system of anti-Communist beliefs, collectively known as world opinion, which was the underpinning for the global policy of containment. The net result, then, local weakness and the desire to avoid a nuclear showdown notwithstanding, was to define Berlin as a fundamental test of willpower.[30]

The crisis as it actually played out was far more equivocal than the showdown scenario suggested. Given the administration's underlying doubts about the conceptual soundness of its German policy and its fear of touching off a nuclear war, showing resolve in this case meant little more than getting through the crisis without appearing to disturb the status quo in Berlin, which accorded closely with what Bundy had in mind by "accommodation." On a legalistic level, the United States succeeded in saving face by managing to reaffirm the rights of the Western allies in the city without chancing a physical confrontation. The most dramatic episode in the crisis, the construction of the wall starting on 13 August, came as a serious blow to the Berliners, who would have to suffer the hardships of artificial separation, and for West Germans, who rightly saw it as a setback to hopes of reunification in the near future. It also had the effect of consolidating the civic status quo and, therefore, of producing an unnegotiated, yet mutually tolerable and well understood, modus vivendi. Khrushchev, despite having resorted to such an ugly way of getting what he wanted, succeeded in peacefully shutting off the refugee spigot, thereby paving the way for the consolidation of the GDR and eastern Europe.[31]

The major direct consequence of the crisis was to push the administration farther in the direction of a far-reaching reversal of its German policy. While Berlin had been temporarily anesthetized, advisers like Averell Harriman believed that a long-lasting cauterization would require at least de facto recognition of the East German regime's existence. "Since Potsdam, I have been satisfied that Germany will be divided for a long time," said Harriman. West German politicians were bound to be upset, "but in the last analysis will have to accept our de facto recognition of the reality of the East German regime." Following the erection of the wall, Washington played for time, hoping that a mutually tolerable status quo had been created, and began actively to contemplate former tabus like acceptance of the Oder-Neisse line, recognition of the GDR, and talks between the two German governments. All of this, NSC staffer Carl Kaysen had argued, would "do no more than accord recognition to present facts."[32]

In mid-1963, during his visit to Europe, JFK gave a fillip to sagging German morale with a resounding address in West Berlin in which he said, ungrammatically, "Ich bin ein Berliner." But this piece of grand cold-war theater only distracted attention from another speech delivered during his visit to the city that more closely reflected his actual desire, which was, in Sorensen's words, that the Germans become "more realistic in accepting a fact which would not and could not be changed by force." Throwing cold water on German aspirations, JFK talked about the need "to face facts as they are, not to involve ourselves in self-deception," while pointing out that reunification would "not be quick and easy." Shortly thereafter, Rusk was much more explicit in a discussion with Soviet Foreign Minister Andrey Gromyko. Over the past two years, "changes had occurred which had taken the fever out of the situation," said Rusk. To be sure, the German problem remained, but it need not become acute "unless, of course, the USSR wanted to make it such." Assuming restraint on both sides, he felt confident that "time was working towards a solution."[33]

This was the closest any administration had come since the end of World War II to acknowledging the acceptability of an approach based frankly on spheres of influence. This new appreciation of the virtues of a divided continent was born of a growing understanding of the ironies of cold-war policy. In September 1963, a month before Adenauer's resignation, Rusk told the anti-Gaullist Foreign Minister Gerhard Schröder that "our experience since the war has indicated that tension has a tendency to lead to a consolidation of the status quo. As we move into a more completely nuclear world, this tendency will increase." The United States remained committed to German reunification, of course, but it was "not likely that we will achieve it through an increase in tension." Adenauer's policy of reunification through strength had been tried and found wanting. The mere flexing of muscles could not produce unification; quite the contrary, the crises that resulted from following a tough line had generated an insatiable demand for credibility that not only drew the lines of division even tighter, but, by making a ticking time bomb of Berlin, threatened to undo the quest for security altogether.[34]

Relaxation was becoming thinkable as a result of a sea change then under way in German public opinion on reunification. In the past, realistic accommodation had been ruled out because, by abandoning the diplomatic search for reunification which had provided Adenauer's major argument for the Federal Republic's attachment to the West, it threatened to conjure up the evil spirit of German nationalism. But in this case, even though the United States came out of the crisis convinced that the Soviets had "produced a heavy impact in West German morale," the demon of German nationalism never did materialize. The quiet after the storm may have had something to do with this. Schröder pointed out that a constant crisis atmosphere had the effect of keeping the unification question open and in the public eye. With a relaxation of tension, he said hopefully, "people might have a tendency to forget about the problem of reunification."[35]

Far more therapeutic than forgetfulness, a painful but realistic understanding that imminent reunification was a will-o'-the-wisp had begun to take root within the Federal Republic, most notably among the heretofore staunchly nationalist Social Democrats. Following Kennedy's visit to Germany in the summer of 1963, the State Department ventured the conclusion that the West German population had "become progressively more convinced that reunification is not likely to be accomplished within the foreseeable future." A research report of August 1963 suggested that West Germans as a whole now saw no alternative to their present reliance on the United States and, finally daring to put an optimistic spin on the future, concluded that it had "become more than ever improbable that Adenauer's departure would lead to any significant shift" in policy. The erosion of the myth of imminent reunification thus opened up the prospect of formalizing a postwar status quo, sought avidly by the Soviets since the mid-1950s, which until recently would have been defined as appeasement.[36]

Although this change of sentiment was an indication that the Berlin Wall was well on the way to becoming, in Anton DePorte's words, "that ultimate symbol of the status quo," the administration would have to pay a heavy price in the coin of credibility in Europe and elsewhere for its circumspection during the crisis and for its subsequent deemphasis of reunification. It is a commonplace that alliances begin to come apart as the threat that brought them together begins to recede, and such a loosening did in fact take place in post-Berlin Europe, in the postures of both America and the alliance. From the American point of view, however, there was nothing normal or reassuring about the process. Quite the contrary, the new self-confidence and assertiveness on the continent, as Rostow recognized, "could take forms disruptive of the common interest." The alliance seemed to be fraying out of a false sense of security, traceable ultimately to a decline of faith in collective solutions and to related doubts about America's credibility, which remained the binding ingredient cementing what otherwise would have been the loose sand of world opinion. Thus the Kennedy administration, which had ambitions at first of implementing a "Grand Design" that would tie an increasingly united and self-confident Europe into a greater Atlantic community, found itself hard-pressed merely to preserve the alliance, much less to improve upon it.[37]

Far from abating, the administration's European headaches grew to migraine intensity as a result of a Gaullist attempt to provide an alternative to Europeans who had long looked to the United States for their salvation, a challenge to American leadership that threatened to have devastating collateral effects upon Germany. American criticism of France in the 1950s had been one long jeremiad on French weakness and indecision. And yet, a revived France proved to be even more nettlesome and obstructionist to American foreign policy in the 1960s. In other circumstances, that revived self-confidence would have been quite welcome, but for the United States it took exactly the wrong nationalist form, as French determination to seek an independent deterrent raised the specter of renewed nationalism in Europe, the collapse of NATO, and ultimately the nightmare of a breakaway *Bundesrepublik* armed with nuclear weapons. Instead of putting the problem of German nationalism on the back burner, then, America's new realism brought it to the forefront of attention in a new and unexpectedly frightening way.

By attending so earnestly to the neo-Wilsonian need to prevent war, the United States created the conditions for undermining the other pillar of cold-war policy, the maintenance of that solidary world opinion without which containment would collapse.

With its grounding in the classical realist tradition, de Gaulle's sense of history differed in fundamental respects from the American internationalist view. The symbol of the French nation to his countrymen, de Gaulle, with his unshakable faith in French greatness and his emphasis on the continuing primacy of nationalism in a "Europe of fatherlands," represented only misguided nationalism to the Americans. For his part, de Gaulle was patronizingly dismissive of the American concern with world opinion. In a revealing conversation with General James Gavin, JFK's first ambassador to Paris, he noted that "the Anglo-Saxon world [was] deeply interested in world opinion." "What is world public opinion?" he asked with unconcealed disdain. The general also derided the American predilection for collective security, questioning America's "curious tendency to wish always to act as a member of some group, whereas a state must have its own policy." He found internationalist logic so inconsistent with the reality of national self-interest, in fact, that he could not bring himself to accept that the United States actually believed in it. That suspicion would be the basis for his contention that it was only an ideological smokescreen behind which the United States advanced its own nationalist agenda.[38]

France and de Gaulle had remained admirably firm throughout the Berlin crisis, but as Berlin began to fade into the background, Paris launched an assault on America's European policy that threatened to undo the NATO alliance and the none-too-stable system of "double containment" that had been so laboriously constructed over the preceding decade. In de Gaulle's eyes, NATO had become an instrument of American domination in Europe that served only to prolong the cold war. Reports from Paris relayed the French view that SHAPE was "an American headquarters that, as a concept, was valid when established but has now been overtaken by changing events." Looking at things from its own nationalist point of view, France attributed to the United States a selfishness that cast into question the integrity of American commitment to internationalism. America's "true policy," de Gaulle suggested, was to "hold power to itself, and prevent the emergence of a significant Europe."[39]

The extent of the general's ambition went far beyond rescuing the French national soul. Indeed, de Gaulle was proposing nothing less than a radically different solution to the problem of the European balance of power. Despite private denials from French diplomats that de Gaulle was bent on creating a European "third force" organized around French leadership, American policymakers failed to be convinced. According to Gavin, regardless of whether or not the United States acceded to the French demand for the creation of a ruling triumvirate for the alliance, de Gaulle would "proceed to organize Europe on his own insofar as he can do so." The objective seemed to be "a strong European power bloc in which France will play the leading role." The French leader, reported Gavin, believed that the United States "should not be mixed up in Western European difficulties and should keep itself apart only bringing its weight to bear in case of necessity."[40]

Presumably, a Europe rid of American influence and revolving instead around Paris would be in a better position to reverse the rapidly congealing division of the continent. The French critique of American hegemony proceeded from the assumption that the United States had become a status quo power in Europe. The American presence, as a memo by Bohlen, Gavin's successor in Paris, put it, was viewed as "a transitory phenomenon," which, if allowed to take root, not only prevented movement but threatened permanently to subordinate the allies. A State Department intelligence memorandum argued that de Gaulle's desire "to build a strong, politically independent Western European bloc around France has the dual aim of making Europe a co-equal ally with the United States in NATO and also of preparing the way for the time, whenever it may come, when the Soviet Union will be disposed to consider a realistic European settlement. At that time, de Gaulle believes, the interests of the European states will best be served if they and not the United States are the Soviet interlocutor." Another report from Paris described de Gaulle as hopeful that his fellow Europeans would "understand that the type of Europe he is proposing is the only one which can stand up to both Russia and the United States and negotiate with the United States, on an equal footing . . . this Europe, as he sees it can only be established once France has regained her power."[41]

Gaullist "realism," from the U.S. perspective, was predicated on historical fantasy: a futuristic mirage and a distorted nostalgia for the past. For onlookers like Bohlen in Paris, de Gaulle was confusing long-term possibilities with short-term necessity, for he was "talking about events which may be a half century off." However noble, the vision of a Europe "from the Atlantic to the Urals" seemed to Americans the stuff of dreams, not diplomacy. The main problem was not the admittedly desirable goal of a united Europe, which would indeed have had the potential to become a "third force" in world affairs; it was the hopeless nationalist methods whereby the French sought to achieve it. In a thoughtful memorandum on the future of NATO which started with the presumption that nationalism was no longer realistic, Acheson argued that "a fundamental reassessment of national interests is needed in light of contemporary facts and interdependence, to replace more limited conceptions of those interests based on an irrelevant past.'' American policy was rightly premised on European unity. As David Bruce put it, European integration was ''an imperative of modern history.'' Crucially, however, what movement toward unity had taken place, it was believed, was primarily the consequence of American leadership in the postwar reconstruction and defense of the Continent. To substitute a Europe of fatherlands was a historically backward step that would reintroduce the disease of nationalism whose symptoms had been suppressed at such great cost and effort.[42]

De Gaulle's traditionalist interpretation of American purpose amounted to a distortion, based on a logic of realistic reductionism, of the hard-won American view of the world. To France, American willingness to accept the postwar status quo meant continued American domination of the Continent with no end in sight for the cold war in Europe. On the assumption that a retraction of Soviet power would be hastened by America's withdrawal and by European independence, French Foreign Minister Maurice Couve de Murville insisted to Rusk that ''the basic French view was that the responsibility for the defense of Europe should be European.'' Whereas de Gaulle saw a marriage of equals, the United States saw itself cast inescapably in the role of paterfamilias. The Americans believed that U.S. hegemony was a product of communal necessity, that it was grounded in fear rather than an overweening power, and that the Continent's continued weakness and instability necessitated an alliance that could be bonded together only by a reassuring American presence. If there was to be a balance of power, JFK believed it would have to be based on NATO, the only institution which could assure security, and that in turn depended on the American commitment, without which Europe would be helpless. America was committed, but commitment had to be reciprocal or else loss of faith in the United States would fracture the alliance.[43]

De Gaulle's critique of American hegemony was closely related to his determination to build an independent nuclear deterrent for France. His desire to join the select club of nuclear powers was partly the product of his indomitable sense of France's greatness. As Schlesinger reported to JFK, it was all ''a psychological matter. De Gaulle sees two categories of nations: superior nations, which have nuclear weapons; and inferior nations, which lack them.'' But, matters of prestige apart, the problem was deeper than that. According to the CIA, de Gaulle perceived NATO as an ''outmoded'' entity that ''no longer offers adequate protection for French interests in the light of changed international power relationships.'' Even as a conventional military mechanism it was deficient, witness the deterioration of French military morale under NATO. Since security in the modern age rested on nuclear deterrence, de Gaulle's nationalist ambitions were fueled also by his conviction that the United States' nuclear deterrent was not credible. American softness on Berlin and the subsequent acceptance of a divided Europe were indicators that Washington's nuclear resolve was not in fact as firm as advertised. This need for accommodation born of the need to avoid all-out war was interpreted as a lack of nerve, which, according to de Gaulle, could be summoned up only by the sacred duty to defend one's nation.[44]

De Gaulle aimed his attack at the point of greatest sensitivity: the willpower and credibility that had been the only antidote to European weakness. He informed Dean Acheson, acting now in the capacity of salesman for the administration's pet policy of flexible response, of his concern that "there could be a nuclear exchange between the Soviet Union and Europe without involving the Soviet Union and the United States." Would an American president risk nuclear incineration to save Bonn or Paris? He thought not. The CIA reported in May 1961 the "widespread belief at the highest levels in Paris that the U.S. would not use its strategic weapons in the event of a Soviet attack on Europe, and there is an even more intense belief that the Soviet Union is operating under this assumption." Shortly thereafter, a cable from Brussels reported a conversation between de Gaulle and Paul Henri Spaak in which the general expressed the "strong and adamant view that the United States would never risk using its strategic nuclear striking power solely for defense of Europe, since this would invite retaliation against American cities."[45]

White House sources might complain that "our emphasis on conventional forces has been distorted to imply a lack of firmness in our nuclear guarantees of Europe," but to no effect. The French pressed the attack on the heart of the U.S. position in Europe and the cold war by arguing that the American nuclear guarantee, enshrined in the doctrine of "first use" of nuclear arms if necessary, was no longer bankable. In the event of a showdown over Berlin, for example, influential French intellectuals argued that NATO would have only three alternatives, "all impossible": to succumb; to fight with conventional weapons, which would mean a rapid Soviet victory; or to launch an atomic war, which would bring "the end of white civilization." This argument was not without its ironies. As Bohlen correctly recalled, "It is no longer as it was several years back—the European fear that American 'irresponsibility' or 'hot headedness' would lead us to premature use of the nuclear weapon, but rather the reverse."[46]

De Gaulle's revisionism raised the possibility of a fundamental reshuffling of the German deck and the system of double containment, for it was widely believed that French possession of a nuclear deterrent would likely stimulate a German appetite for the same. The "key question," according to Rusk, was not France's acquisition of a nuclear delivery capacity, but its "effect on German aspirations and thus on NATO." What if Germany should feel compelled to follow France's example? JFK explained to a visiting Paul Reynaud in April 1961 that "it was not simply a question of France's having a nuclear capability, but the next step would be for Germany to have this capability." Sounding a familiar note, he indicated that "this was dangerous in view of the fact that Adenauer might be leaving the scene some day."[47]

Thus, the French insistence on an independent nuclear deterrent would pose, as Rusk put it, a "very grave threat to allied political cohesion." True, Bonn had forsworn any intention to acquire nuclear arms as a condition of joining NATO. But as a worried Bundy wrote to Raymond Aron in March 1962, "Stronger pledges than this one have been broken before by nations which felt the political pressures for prestige and power." In short, de Gaulle was opening a Pandora's box for the alliance. Rusk cabled the U.S. ambassador in Bonn that French action would "increase risk of war by accident or miscalculation, diminish possibility controlled nuclear response in event of hostilities, raise new obstacles arms control, and pose very grave threat to allied political cohesion. The more rapid and extensive any additional acquisition of these capabilities, the greater will be these dangers."[48]

The president responded sharply to this challenge. He informed the West German ambassador, Wilhelm Grewe, that "the NATO treaty was the legal basis for a U.S. presence in Europe and we could not permit NATO to be dismantled or to have confidence weakened in it." He gave instructions to inform de Gaulle of his "inability to accept the notion that we should stay out of all of Europe's affairs while remaining ready to defend her if war should come." De Gaulle could not have "both our military presence and our diplomatic absence." The general's solution to the problem of American resolve, he insisted, would make matters even worse, since a French-led Europe would make it "most difficult for us to sustain our present guarantee against Soviet aggression."[49]

The crisis in the alliance was overshadowed temporarily in October 1962 with the showdown over the Soviet installation of nuclear-tipped medium-range missiles on the island of Cuba. This was a credibility crisis of the first magnitude, since, unlike previous crises by proxy, it involved a direct confrontation with the Soviets. Although the proximity of Cuba to the United States seemed to set off an almost visceral reaction of the kind traditionally associated with finding an enemy on one's doorstep, the tough American response was conditioned to a large extent by considerations of world opinion. To be sure, there were domestic pressures associated with the crisis. Kennedy would have had the devil to pay at home had he not acted because he had publicly warned the Soviets about installing offensive weapons on the island. But this internal source of pressure in no way deflected the administration from the main line of its policy. JFK had already warned Khrushchev as early as the Vienna meeting that the United States "could not tolerate any action on your part which in a major way disturbed the existing over-all balance of power in the world." As JFK subsequently wrote to Khrushchev, the Soviet gambit in Cuba was "in a broader sense, a dangerous attempt to change the world-wide *status quo.*"[50]

From a strictly military standpoint, Kennedy went along with Defense Secretary Robert McNamara's opinion that "geography doesn't mean that much." For JFK the problem was one of perceptions. He explained afterward that if the missiles had been allowed to remain on the island, "it would have politically changed the balance of power. It would have appeared to, and appearances contribute to reality." Acceptance of a Soviet fait accompli would have had a devastating effect within NATO upon American credibility, it was believed, not to mention worldwide destabilizing effects as a result of a loss of faith in U.S. constancy. Cuba was important, then, because America was playing a psychological game in which the steadiness of America's nerve was being called into question. As McGeorge Bundy subsequently acknowledged, Soviet success "would have been a change more determined by our own perceptions than by those of Khrushchev." Once having taken the measure of the Americans in Cuba, the Soviets were sure to interpret a victory there as a green light for reopening the Berlin issue and for stepping up the pace of challenges in the third world through wars of national liberation.[51]

Ironically, the aftermath of the Cuban missile crisis, despite the widespread perception that it had been a clear American triumph, did not pay the anticipated dividends in European reassurance. Rusk, for example, hoped that American resolve "had removed any illusions they might have entertained as to any US hesitancy in comparable circumstance." However, the crisis was used by de Gaulle to illustrate the inescapability of his nationalist logic. The United States, like any other nation, had demonstrated that it would act only in its own interests, in the event leaving Europe open to "annihilation without representation." Thus far, the United States had shown an aversion to risking war for Berlin, while in Cuba it had demonstrated a willingness to risk war over non-European issues. In both cases, Europe stood to suffer. The United States was simply demonstrating once again that it would go to war, as it had in 1917 and 1941, for reasons sufficient to itself, which would be far too late for France. This kind of reasoning led an exasperated Bundy to complain that "even our final and decisive confrontation in Cuba has been read as a demonstration that while we will not risk our nation for Europe, we will risk Europe to meet a local threat at home . . . The victory of Cuba has increased our stature—but it has also increased the fear that by our local action we might quite literally bring an end to Europe."[52]

The United States had consulted only perfunctorily with its allies, because, as Rusk recalled, "this was an issue primarily between ourselves and the Russians." In any case, there had not been enough time to coordinate a response with the European allies. Bundy explained to Walter Lippmann that "a clear, sharp, well-defined and limited action from the United States Government was hard enough—to get it from two interlocking alliances would have been almost impossible." Nevertheless, pleading an inability to consult, while accepted by de Gaulle as a necessity, played into his argument. Early in 1963, he came out and said it publicly: "The immediate defense, and one can say privileged defense of Europe, and the military participation of the Europeans, which were once basic factors of their strategy, moved by the force of circumstances into second place. We have just witnessed this during the Cuban affair."[53]

Perverse as they sometimes seemed, these arguments could not be ignored. For one thing, de Gaulle's complaint struck a nerve throughout western Europe. Paris reported that de Gaulle "in no wise constitutes [a] voice crying in the wilderness." In addition, although in fundamental disagreement with France's nationalist approach, Americans could not help but be sensitive to de Gaulle's complaint that Europe needed reassurance—coping with European insecurity had, after all, been an abiding problem since the war's end. In response, the United States devised a way of meeting French desires and reducing German nuclear envy as 1962 drew to a close. The scheme called for a multilateral nuclear force (MLF), a NATO-controlled nuclear deterrent, which would preserve the unity of the alliance, provide the Germans with a sense of equality, and resolve nagging doubts about nuclear credibility. There was little doubt from the beginning that the MLF was intended more to provide psychological reassurance than to add to strategic deterrence in Europe. Henry Kissinger explained candidly to Adenauer that the United States "recognized that a political requirement might conceivably exist for a NATO force but it did not think there was a military requirement."[54]

Even as a symbol, however, the MLF was fatally flawed from the beginning because it did not resolve the issue of credibility. The faithful would be allowed to touch the sacred nuclear charm, but it would continue to hang around the neck of its priestly custodian, the United States. Despite much talk of having all the fingers on the trigger, the MLF was supposed to operate on the basis of the principle of unanimity, which meant an American veto. Since this was the only basis on which congressional approval was likely, the reality of American control would remain. Not surprisingly, reports from Paris indicated that de Gaulle found it "extremely difficult to believe that the U.S. is serious about taking Europe in as a partner in nuclear and other major matters." The new scheme was unconvincing even to many Americans. Bohlen, for instance, informed Kennedy that "if we intend to leave presidential authorization for this weapon as is, I believe the multilateral force will soon be exposed as a fraud."[55]

Unfortunately, the formidable Gallic nose for logic sniffed out yet more embarrassing inconsistencies in American nuclear reasoning. For all the talk of its being a nuclear showdown, Cuba, like Berlin, had actually shown a reluctance to go to the brink as both powers had stepped away in horror and relief from the nuclear precipice and compromised on the issues. After Cuba, it was obvious, as one White House memo put it, that "the safety of all depends upon a minimum of decency and reality in communication between Moscow and Washington." Kennedy came out of the episode with renewed hope that some agreements with the Soviets could be negotiated, especially on arms control. The Cuban missile crisis, despite the apparent success, had been above all a sobering episode, one moreover which began to open up new post–cold war vistas in the young president's historical mind, so much so that Sorensen recalled "almost a sense of discovery that he had a major new issue, so to speak, working for him—the issue of peace." Shortly afterward he was writing urgently to Khrushchev, "trying to penetrate our ideological differences in order to find some bridge across the gulf on which we could bring our minds together and find some way in which to protect the peace of the world."[56]

The resulting change in the Kennedy administration's thinking was spelled out in 1963 by French intellectual Jean-Jacques Servan-Schreiber. "The menace of Communism was the absorbing preoccupation of the 1950s," he reported, "but now the present administration was concerned above all with the danger of atomic war, and was highly obsessed by the responsibility of nuclear detonation." If the presumed willingness to go the limit in Cuba had raised such doubts about the American commitment, the subsequent desire of both sides to go on the wagon, which was particularly evident in the denouement of the affair, had even greater implications for the credibility of the nuclear guarantee of Europe. Sorensen recalled being told by a Soviet diplomat: "When the two great powers collide, . . . the other nations of the world are frightened. But when we collaborate, they are terrified." The perception of a growing nuclear entente between the superpowers provided yet another rationale for a European deterrent. Even staunch alliance backers like Raymond Aron were now writing that "the U.S. and Soviet Union have in effect an unwritten agreement, the most stable agreement of the cold war, not to permit the spread of nuclear weapons technology and to avoid any situation which would result in attacks on each other's territory."

Aron concluded that "development of a European nuclear capability is the only practical solution in view of this U.S.-Soviet accord."[57]

Events moved to a climax early in 1963. One startling crescendo came in de Gaulle's famous press conference of 14 January, in which he publicly aired the alliance's dirty linen. In this bravura performance he vetoed Great Britain's application for admission to the Common Market, thus smashing administration hopes, as JFK told André Malraux, that Great Britain's presence in the Common Market "would provide the necessary counterweight to Germany" in the European Community. At the same time, de Gaulle stated his opposition to the very idea of a multilateral force. An even nastier surprise came a week later, when Adenauer flew to Paris for the signing of a Franco-German treaty of reconciliation. With these actions, the rejection of American leadership and the NATO solution, the collapse of the American position in Europe, and the emergence of a Europe of nationalistic, nuclear-armed states, including a western Germany broken loose from its moorings in NATO, seemed suddenly to be more than a theoretical possibility—all seemingly because the lack of American credibility had failed to hold Europe together.[58]

The future of Germany, whose status as ally or potential enemy remained the central problem of American policy in Europe, occasioned the most worry. Though de Gaulle had once told Ambassador Gavin, apparently in the spirit of Franco-German reconciliation, that "France could not exist without Germany," the treaty with the Federal Republic seemed, to American eyes, directed toward pulling Bonn away from NATO's embrace. Alarmed and puzzled at the depth of Franco-American differences, JFK told Couve de Murville that "the treaty really looked to us as though it were something more than the healing of old wounds, but rather as though it were outside of, and directed against, NATO." Voicing one of the administration's nagging fears, Paul Nitze pointed out that the treaty "contains within it the possibility that France and FRG may at some time attempt to negotiate a deal for the reunification of Germany."[59]

Thus the German problem, while beginning to cool off in some ways, was beginning to heat up in others. Relations with Adenauer had soured a good deal in the aftermath of the Berlin affair, in part because JFK had not hit it off with "der Alte," who questioned the young president's cold-war willpower. His brother recalled that JFK "didn't like Adenauer very much," what with the old man's constant griping and the frequent tactless reminders that his relationship with Dulles had been far closer. Nevertheless, everyone realized that Adenauer was an antinationalist German who, in the words of *Washington Post* owner Philip Graham, had been "a stout European—trying to de-fang his own Germans whom he knows and distrusts." Despite his prickliness, he had been indispensable to the alliance. But the old man's time was clearly coming to an end and Americans could not help but think anxious thoughts about what lay ahead for Germany without his reliable hand at the policy tiller. With Germany's course in doubt, French obstreperousness had come at the worst possible time.[60]

In a discussion with Couve, George Ball stated frankly America's deepest fears: "The Germans would never be content with a permanent position of discrimination. Once the *force de frappe* became a reality, the pressures within Germany for a national system would become increasingly difficult to deal with. This would be particularly true of a post-Adenauer Germany where the old Chancellor would no longer serve as a restraining influence and no one could predict the kind of government that might be in power in Germany in a few years." He concluded that "a political Europe capable of making the life and death decisions involved in the management of atomic weapons systems was not going to emerge on the basis of a *Europe des patries.*" On another occasion, he told the French that the United States was "concerned about a revival of the inter-war German psychosis that they are being discriminated against." According to Rusk, the mere prospect of an independent German nuclear program "would shake NATO to its foundations."[61]

A divorce from Washington and quick remarriage with Paris was not very likely in the near term as long as the Federal Republic's need for security was served by NATO, the American deterrent remained credible, and NATO continued to provide reasonable support for German reunification. However, as the Bonn embassy pointed out, "if circumstances were such that Germany considered its long term interests were being neglected by Anglo-American allies, we could thus expect programs for development [of] joint nuclear deterrent." The Germans were not yet questioning American resolve as were the French, but U.S. policymakers were all too ready to believe that they were capable of doing so at any moment. Fueling these suspicions, Adenauer, in a meeting with Lauris Norstad, reminded the general that constant U.S. elections and the changeability of the U.S. political scene made it "extremely difficult for Europeans to depend wholly on [the] U.S. for nuclear weapons or to accept virtually complete control by [the] U.S. of these weapons for the defense of Europe."[62] This was hardly reassuring talk coming from the rock upon which the U.S.-German partnership had been constructed.

Nevertheless, by mid-1963 de Gaulle was successfully isolated and the situation within the alliance temporarily stabilized. The smaller NATO powers in Europe had no desire to follow the general's lead, as it would have required their acceptance of a French hegemony more restrictive than American suzerainty in Europe. Also, the West Germans made efforts to be as reassuring as possible. Former foreign minister Heinrich von Brentano told Rusk and Ball that "only a fool would think of sacrificing anything on the altar of Franco-German reconciliation," especially if it meant abandoning the American connection. He also predicted German support for the MLF on the grounds that it would "help to strengthen NATO and would also have a useful side effect in tending to isolate French nuclear policy." The Germans made good their troth when the Bundestag, in ratifying the French treaty, included a reservation which reaffirmed the primacy of the *Bundesrepublik's* attachment to NATO and the United States. Though the French were still rocking the NATO boat, the refusal of fellow Europeans to add their weight to the rhythmic disturbance meant that there was little danger of capsizing.[63]

The alliance thus bobbed uneasily into the future in heavy seas, having survived for the time being yet another crisis of confidence. Although the crisis was to some extent a consequence of European recovery, and to that extent could be considered an index of continental security, it was not so perceived from Washington, whose alarmed reaction was the product of the tension in American cold-war policy between avoiding war and propping up world opinion. On the bright side of things, the emerging era of nuclear plenty forced the superpowers to acknowledge their common interest in avoiding mutually assured destruction. On the other hand, as interrelated French doubts about the seriousness of the American commitment and its effects upon Europe made clear, this new-found willingness to cooperate in avoiding war proved to be quite dangerous because it corroded the vitals of America's cold-war position. The turn away from nuclear confrontation only unleashed particularist forces that, in the end, would sow chaos in Europe and undermine continental security.

This form of realism, limited to preventing war, merely aggravated the problem of world opinion. It was characteristic of cold-war logic that stability, as judged by traditional realist standards, became a recipe for instability and insecurity when viewed from a neo-Wilsonian perspective. By internationalist logic, accommodation based on fear of nuclear destruction, supremely sensible by a realistic calculus, left the door open to the collapse of world opinion—the hobgoblin of world conquest—as a by-product of demoralization. It was akin to a man throwing away his revolver while a similarly armed criminal did the same, knowing full well that his opponent was adept at other forms of violence and determined to try them out. Thus the turn away from confrontation in Europe not only stirred doubt and dissension within the alliance, it also unsettled the Kennedy administration from a global standpoint by casting an unflattering light on American willpower, prestige, and credibility. As Walt Rostow recalled it, "Laos compounded on

Cuba; and Berlin compounded on Laos. [JFK] felt things were sliding against him, sliding against the free world.''[64]

VIETNAM AS THE WAY OUT

The most intriguing question, and one impossible to answer definitively, is whether Kennedy would have plunged into Vietnam had he lived. Many of the Kennedy loyalists who subsequently broke with the Johnson administration have argued strongly that Kennedy would not have done so. According to Roger Hilsman, who pointed to the small reduction in the number of advisers authorized by Kennedy shortly before his assassination, JFK was ''going in the exact opposite direction that Johnson went, you see.'' Certainly he received enough anti-interventionist advice along the way. Among the many monitory comments in the record, one finds John Kenneth Galbraith, serving as ambassador to India, warning Kennedy about getting involved with ''jungle regimes, where the writ of the government runs only as far as the airport.'' Senator Mike Mansfield told him that the United States was ''too far out on too many costly and shaky limbs in that region and our problem is how to get down from them.''[65] And there were others.

Kennedy himself looked for reasons not to intervene. The exasperating shortcomings of Diem and the Vietnamese, the lack of support from America's allies, the cost in lives and national treasure, the prospect of a Korea-like quagmire, the possibility of escalation—all these reasons and more for holding back occurred to Kennedy and caused him to wonder why an obscure country like Vietnam should be considered so vital to national security. To Walt Rostow, one of the most persistent advocates of an active American intervention from the very beginning (so persistent that, according to Hilsman, JFK derisively called him ''the air marshal'' behind his back), he would ask from time to time: ''Why do we need to hold Southeast Asia? Why can't we get out of there?'' His caution was hard-earned, reinforced by painful memories of his earlier adventures. Sorensen recalled Kennedy remarking on a number of occasions that ''had it not been for the Bay of Pigs, we would have been deeply involved in a war in Southeast Asia.'' All of this seemed to add up to a personal predisposition against going in. When told by George Ball that his policy would lead to a substantial commitment of American troops, he replied: ''George, you're crazier than hell. That just isn't going to happen.''[66]

Further support for the noninterventionist thesis comes from the portrayal of Kennedy as a nonideological pragmatist, which was a common opinion of the man on the part of people who came to know him. Chester Bowles described the approach of the Kennedy people as "an often brilliant pragmatism" that "rarely operated from basic principle." Kennedy was depicted as an unphilosophical person who "liked to deal in hard realities" and talked often in terms of balance of power. Decision making was difficult for him, it has been suggested, because, without "moral impulse or some overwhelming conviction to carry the day for him," he depended on rational technical advice that was quite nuanced and rarely conclusive one way or the other. Thus, the argument goes, as Kennedy's underlying realism began to assert itself, he would have abandoned the threadbare ideological cliches that justified engagement in Vietnam.[67]

Kennedy's realism, when coupled with an underlying Eurocentrism, also seemed to suggest that countries in Southeast Asia were not worth fighting over. Disgruntled liberals like Chester Bowles suspected the administration of being dominated by Europeanists who assumed that if the Continent were secure and stable, policy in the "outlying areas" in rest of the world would pretty much fall into place. According to Bowles, Eurocentrism was shortsighted, because "with the end of colonialism the world was no longer run by Europe and a European balance of power was only part of a policy." Bowles was partly correct. Lacking any clear sense of a vital interest in Southeast Asia—"we couldn't care less, actually" JFK said of Laos—it is clear that he would have preferred to patch up some kind of accommodation there as he had in Laos and later in Berlin. In a November 1961 letter to Khrushchev discussing Laos and Vietnam, for example, he suggested that "both these countries are at a distance from our own countries and can be considered areas in which we ought to find mutual agreement."[68]

And yet, despite a natural reluctance to go in and all the weighty reasons advanced for not doing so, Kennedy's doubts were no different from the puzzlement and exasperation of Eisenhower and Dulles at finding themselves committed to defending out-of-the-way places. While the doubts about symbolic interventionism were familiar, JFK's strategic logic made the connection between events in Europe and Asia even tighter than it had been for his predecessors. The Kennedy administration entered office acutely conscious of a developing shift in the cold-war teeter-totter from West to East. Kennedy had been convinced from the early 1950s that the third world would be the locus of the most intense confrontations in the future. Europe still mattered most, but JFK had spoken during the campaign of "Russia's bid to win Europe to itself by the indirect route of winning the vast outlying raw materials region." At that time, he had described the balance of power as "shifting into the hands of the two-thirds of the world's people who want to share what the one-third has already taken for granted." "If India were to fall, if Latin America turned away, and if the Middle East slid behind the Iron

Curtain,'' he once predicted, "then no amount of missiles, no amount of space satellites or nuclear powered planes or atomic submarines could ever save us.'' As Harriman later put it, "The battle against Communism is in the underdeveloped countries and it's not in Europe.''[69]

Sometimes campaign issues fade out of sight after the transition, but not in this case. Along with Berlin, this issue produced the greatest disagreement at the Vienna summit with Khrushchev. Prior to the meeting, a briefing paper argued that Soviet endorsement of war in former colonial areas would "only lead to more instances of violence and greater danger that hostilities will expand beyond control.'' In their discussion of underdeveloped nations Kennedy warned Khrushchev that the "balance of power could be disturbed if they associated closely with the USSR.'' After Khrushchev refused to back down and told Kennedy to keep his nose out of wars of national liberation or risk starting a larger war, they had nothing more to say to one another. Following his return home from this hair-raising tête-à-tête, Kennedy informed the public in a televised address that "it is clear that this struggle—in this area of the new and poorer nations—will be the continuing crisis of this decade.''[70]

However desirable in principle, there existed no possibility of a realistic accommodation in Southeast Asia in the early 1960s. The source of the strategic challenge was a powerful and presumably fanatical Communist China which, as Sorensen wrote in a year-end summary for 1961, was "the biggest question mark for the future.'' Unlike the Soviets, the Chinese seemed wholly insensitive to the dangers of all-out war and more inclined therefore to run greater risks. According to one State Department analysis of the Chinese, "Their bellicose theoretical argumentation and almost childlike denigration of war in a nuclear age serve as a fundamental point of departure for the more belligerent 'peaceful coexistence' tactics which they urge.'' Because of this radicalism, the looming Sino-Soviet split, something that the United States had been trying to foster for nearly a decade, showed little promise of granting immediate relief. Although the administration continued to believe that a break "would have a profound effect upon Soviet views of the world'' and "might lead, in the long run, to more normal relations with the West,'' there was a recognition, as Sorensen put it, that a split for ideological rather than geopolitical reasons posed "dangers as well as advantages for the West.''[71]

Whatever its long-term benefits, in the short run a split was fueling a competition for primacy in the world Communist movement between the two Red goliaths, a competition likely to be judged by radical standards. Beijing would cause trouble enough in Asia, but as the Moscow embassy realized, the Chinese Communists had "rejuvenated [the] revolutionary posture of

[the] Soviet party.'' Charles Bohlen concluded that the Soviets' way of dealing with their China problem was ''to be more aggressive and Bolshevik in
their actions in the foreign field to avoid being 'outflanked from the left'
by the Chinese.'' Similarly, a CIA task force on the Sino-Soviet split concluded in April 1961 that the Russians would show ''a tendency to follow
a bolder and more assertive course, probably from a desire to accommodate
Chinese views, or, more likely, in an effort to avoid being outflanked on the
'left.' ''[72]

In any case, the differences between the two powers were over means,
not ends, ''over the methods of achieving the goal of becoming masters of
the world'' as Harriman told a French diplomat. In Henry Kissinger's colorful
description of the problem, ''Much of the debate between them has somewhat
of the character of two thieves arguing whether they have to kill you to get
your wallet or whether they can lift your wallet without hitting you over the
head. You lose your wallet either way.'' Bohlen also saw ''very little basis
for any shift in our current policy because of these disputes.'' Instead of
celebrating the end of the myth of Communist unity, the administration concluded that the United States was ''challenged by two totalitarian regimes
which seek to extend their power by a variety of means.'' Reflecting these
glum assessments, in mid-1962 the administration sought to avoid statements
suggesting that the dispute had eliminated or reduced pressures on the free
world. ''A dispute over how best to bury the free world is no cause for
Western rejoicing,'' Kennedy told Congress in January 1963.[73]

In facing up to third-world disturbances, the administration had originally
expected to do so with the strategic luxury of a stabilized Europe. The unexpected turmoil within the alliance and the incessant questioning of American
fidelity, by underscoring the psychological precariousness of what was supposed to be America's unshakable foreign-policy base, simply heightened
American concern with crises on the periphery. As the Gaullist challenge
seemed to prove, the stability of NATO, West Germany's commitment to
the alliance, and its abjuring of an independent nuclear capacity all continued
to depend on the credibility of an American resolve which had been raked
over by a corrosive French skepticism. With nuclear confrontations now out
of the question, that resolve—and, by implication, the nonhegemonic character of American internationalism—could be demonstrated only by a willingness to take on Communist challenges by conventional means in places that
had little obvious cash value to the United States. Had JFK rejected both the
nuclear and the conventional options for dealing with crises, there would
have been nothing to prevent the quick collapse of an already weak and
uncertain world opinion. Far from decreasing the Kennedy administration's

cold-war ardor, the weathering of storms in Europe and Cuba further sharpened its focus on what it had considered all along to be the primary threat, the Communist offensive in the unstable and potentially decisive third world.

The ongoing need to preserve free world morale entailed a willingness to risk another Korea without any possibility of playing the nuclear card, not even in the ambiguous fashion of Eisenhower and Dulles. Although certainly aware of the numerous drawbacks of the Korean quagmire, the Kennedy administration also believed that those disadvantages could, if necessary, be overcome. Public opinion seemed better educated to the gravity of the Communist threat and the need for sacrifice and willpower in meeting it. Unlike in 1952, there was no alternative isolationist worldview waiting in the wings in Kennedy's America at the high noon of the cold war—indeed, such pressure as there was pushed Kennedy toward activism and avoiding the appearance of weakness. The defense establishment was better armed and imbued with a more sophisticated appreciation of limited war that made unlikely the appearance of a new MacArthur. And with the benefit of hindsight and its sense of managerial competence, the Kennedy administration felt better prepared to avoid the kind of adolescent blundering and indecisiveness that had characterized earlier cold-war crises.

The gauntlet would be thrown down by the Communists in any event. According to Rostow, Khrushchev believed "that the techniques he has now adopted will gain victory for communism in the underdeveloped areas, probably without major war." Indeed, the administration generally interpreted "peaceful coexistence" as "a strategy to defeat the West without war." Undoubtedly, Khrushchev was sincere in wishing to avoid provoking a nuclear gunfight with the United States. But as an analysis of one of his important speeches pointed out, this "in no way reflects on his revolutionary zeal in regard to 'national liberation wars' . . . The heightened appreciation of the fertile field that exists for communist maneuvering in the underdeveloped countries is one of the most radical innovations of the post-Stalin era." The administration's view of the basic threat facing it continued to be, as it had been in Eisenhower's time, that "we have more to fear from Communist subversion than from overt aggression."[74]

Rostow and other advisers continued to drive home to Kennedy the gravity of the situation in Vietnam and the implications of its fall. In the aftermath of the Bay of Pigs and Laos, Rostow suggested that Khrushchev had been fortified in his belief that "we do not know how to deal with his tactics and will thrash about ineffectively." Failure in Vietnam would "affect the whole cast of American policy." In a doomsday scenario that Rostow would repeat over the years, the collapse of Vietnam would lead to a loss of

Southeast Asia, stimulate another round of isolationism in American public opinion, trigger a loss of confidence among U.S. allies in Europe, and tempt the Communists to further risk-taking. This sequence of calamities would probably snowball until it was too late to avoid another war. In the end, "a much more dangerous crisis would result, quite possibly a nuclear crisis." He reminded the president that "the New Frontier will be measured in history in part on how that challenge was met. No amount of political jiu-jitsu is going to get us off that hook."[75]

It was not Rostow alone, however, beating the war drums. Kennedy's pragmatism operated from within the guiding framework of the domino theory that had become a metaphor for the neo-Wilsonian worldview underlying the cold war. Berlin and Cuba had been compelling cold-war symbols, after all, and Vietnam was no different. It mattered ultimately because of its global impact on beliefs. Should America lose its resolve, the Communists would be emboldened and the allies disheartened. Kennedy had warned the American Society of Newspaper Editors early in 1961 that "our security may be lost piece by piece, country by country, without the firing of a single missile or the crossing of a single border." Pointing up the centrality of world opinion and morale, he reminded Congress in May 1961 that "it is a contest of will and purpose as well as force and violence—a battle for minds and souls as well as territory." In this struggle, American resolve was the key to maintaining world opinion. "We are the keystone in the arch of freedom," he said in September 1963. "If the United States were to falter, the whole world, in my opinion, would inevitably begin to move toward the Communist bloc." From this perspective, there were no areas strategically more vital than others. In 1961, JFK had admitted that "I don't know where the nonessential areas are." In his final TV interview, he reaffirmed his belief in the domino theory.[76]

While for Eisenhower the nuclear option promised both deliverance and damnation, the kind of internal agonizing that one finds in deliberations about Quemoy and Matsu is absent from New Frontier thinking about intervention in Asia. The balance of consequences between intervention and nonintervention was not so finely poised, being weighted overwhelmingly on the side of predicting calamity if America failed to respond. In reply to Galbraith's accusation of strategic nonsense, the JCS brushed off his critique by stating, as if it were self-evident, that a reversal of policy "could have disastrous effects, not only upon our relationship with South Vietnam, but with the rest of our Asian and other allies as well." Typical were warnings like those periodically emanating from Rusk and McNamara that losing Vietnam would "not only destroy SEATO but would undermine the credibility of American commitments elsewhere.'' The costs of taking the plunge received little mention, by comparison.[77]

Given Kennedy's well-known penchant for sticking to immediate issues, no one knows what he would have done—his brother Robert was quite accurate to say that "well, we'd have faced that when we came to it"—but we do know what his ideological predispositions were. Kennedy's pragmatism would have delayed a decision until the very end, but it must be remembered that pragmatism is not value-free; it operates within and gains its force from a preexisting ideological context that frames ends and suggests the means for achieving them. The Kennedy administration came into power in 1961 informed by a sense of cold-war crisis, convinced that Communist ideology was surging at flood tide, and it came armed also with a well-developed critique of policy, derived from neo-Wilsonian criteria, that corresponded to the internal doubts emerging from the Eisenhower administration in its closing years. According to Rostow, Kennedy was "the instrument for carrying out the consensus built up in the 1950's as men inside and outside the government assessed Eisenhower's errors of omission and commission."[78]

Moreover, the lessons Kennedy learned from his close brushes with disaster in Berlin and Cuba argued in favor of intervention, not against. Cuba had demonstrated the value of local superiority in conventional arms. Berlin had demonstrated the disadvantages of inferiority. Both experiences reinforced the theory of flexible response, while the diplomatic aftereffects of each episode accentuated the problem of credibility. When JFK moved ever so gingerly to cool down the German problem in the interest of avoiding nuclear gun-slinging, even this tentative change of direction in the interest of nuclear realism triggered a disturbing challenge to American credibility that threatened to throw Europe into nationalist, nuclear-armed chaos. By the cold war's unique logic, accommodation was interpreted as an absence of the internationalist resolve that was central to maintaining the alliance and a cohesive world opinion resistant to Communist expansion.

The only justification for disengagement would have been to adopt a form of realpolitik, which, despite Kennedy's occasional use of balance-of-power language, was quite impossible because his realism was not rooted in the classical tradition. JFK's steps toward accommodation and his interventionism are both fully explainable from within the neo-Wilsonian framework. As an adept of the domino theory, where world opinion was the only safeguard against war and world conquest, the meaning of balance of power in Kennedy's usage had been assimilated to cold-war ideology. To be sure, as the shift in German policy after the Berlin crisis demonstrated, Kennedy certainly would have preferred a stable balance in Europe. But Kennedy's response to the ensuing Gaullist challenge made clear that the only kind of balance he and his advisers could envision was an internationalist variant centered on NATO, with Germany as an indispensable ally, held together by confidence in American leadership. This conception assumed both the need for cohesion and the continuing inability of Europe to supply it on its own.

The quest for an arms control agreement with the Soviets and the stabilization of Europe implied only a mutual desire to avoid hot war while continuing the cold, and the resultant family quarrel in NATO highlighted the potentially fatal consequences of taking even so obvious a step. In discussing the possibility of a truly comprehensive détente, Rusk informed Bohlen a few months before Kennedy's assassination that "we have no illusions that any major breakthrough with the Soviet Union is in sight." Despite the signature of the test ban treaty in Moscow in the summer of 1963, it was obvious that the Soviet definition of peaceful coexistence envisaged "continued political, economic, and ideological struggle." But even if regional stability in Europe had been achieved on Kennedy's terms without raising the specter of alliance disintegration, the Chinese revolutionary challenge in Asia would only have accentuated the USSR's competitive posture there and added a military dimension to ever-present American fears of sudden demoralization. The possibility of making another choice in Asia would have required a corresponding willingness by the Communists to elevate power, and a prudent understanding of the outsize risks involved in its employment, above ideology, a conversion experience which was yet nowhere in evidence.[79]

There is no question that Kennedy would have preferred not to intervene in Vietnam. But that preference has to be viewed in light of the unavoidable statesman's duty of having to choose between lesser and greater evils. The real question is not whether Kennedy wanted to go in—he didn't—but whether he had developed a convincing rationale for eschewing intervention apart from the pain that sending American soldiers abroad would cause. Clearly, by the time of his assassination, he had not come close to articulating an alternative to the cold-war outlook that would have justified symbolic disengagement from local conflicts across the globe. It is clear why he did not do so. That kind of changeabout by JFK would have required the reversal of a deeply sedimented worldview, not just the rejection of a superficial metaphor. Not being a realpolitiker, Kennedy could neither dispute, nor justify the acceptance of, the greater evil that domino logic suggested would result from inaction.

In the last analysis, the question of whether or not he would have taken the plunge is irrelevant, except for presentist reasons, for JFK did nothing to convince his successor, Lyndon Johnson, not to follow in his footsteps. Hitherto, the cold-war presidents had, as a result of serious problems encountered in practice, rejected each predecessor's choice of means toward achieving common cold-war ends. By this point in the cold war, alternatives had narrowed to the point that LBJ was not given the luxury of such a choice. The historical issue is not whether or how going in could have been avoided. Rather, the challenge lies in understanding why intervention in Vietnam seemed the only way out of the nation's problems.

9

LYNDON JOHNSON AND THE CRISIS OF WORLD OPINION

I N THE FACE OF A CONTINUED NEED to harness the runaway structural tendencies of modern world politics, the neo-Wilsonian strategy of holding world opinion together underwent its most severe test during the Johnson administration. In Europe, following a brief lull, a renewal of the French mutiny rocked the alliance and reinforced deep anxieties among American policymakers about the future of post-Adenauer Germany. Convinced that the reemergence of European nationalism was related to doubts about the seriousness of America's commitment to defend the continent under conditions of nuclear restraint, policymakers in Washington remained as anxious as ever to demonstrate that the American-led system in Europe was the only viable option. To the untrained eye, western Europe in the 1960s appeared strong and healthy, but in Washington's professional diagnosis it was suffering from a form of political hemophilia in which minor wounds rather than the unlikely trauma of outright Soviet conquest comprised the major threat to its mortality. In order to prevent uncontrolled bleeding of the collective will to resist the Communist challenge, maintaining the credibility of the American commitment to internationalism seemed all the more important.

The dogged pursuit of credibility had always alarmed the foreign audiences that were supposed to be reassured and united by it, and the Vietnam War would be no exception to this pattern. However, this time the entropic effects of U.S. policy reached deep behind the lines of the home front. The dilemma between avoiding war and averting a global failure of nerve, formerly encountered on the international plane and handled with less than complete success, now devolved to the domestic level and threatened to paralyze the very nerve center of world opinion. With the collapse of domestic support for symbolic interventionism, the American public's commitment to internationalism—the extent of its allegiance to the credo underlying credibility—was thrown into question. As policymakers climbed ever higher on the ladder of internationalism only to discover that it could not bear the weight being placed upon it, neo-Wilsonian ideology, always full of inconsistencies, reached the most critical stage of its intellectual journey.

L B J INHERITED Kennedy's problems, commitments, and advisers, but his cold-war outlook was his own, acquired through political osmosis in the course of a long career as a congressman and senator from Texas. By emphasizing "the interdependence of man" and "the civilization of this globe," his postwar internationalism showed an understanding of the ultimate stakes of the cold war and a good layman's command of the neo-Wilsonian strategic vocabulary. He was well versed in the morale-building objective of the Truman Doctrine, noting that "this penetration system by which the Communists are taking over one European government after another to me smacks very much of the Hitler method." And his comments on behalf of the Marshall Plan got to the heart of the internationalist fear of feeble inaction. "One day we will wake up in a world in which the Western hemisphere is a lonely island," he warned, "and all the rest of mankind behind the iron curtain." Were that point to be reached, the Wilsonian military implications of isolation seemed clear enough. It would not be long before "civilization would turn down the short and terrifying dead-end street of atomic warfare." Despite occasional hawkish statements at the time of Korea calling for a showdown with the Soviets, upon reconsideration it became clear to him that the cold war required solutions short of war.[1]

Johnson was especially attuned to the symbolic and psychological side of containment. As Senate majority leader during the 1950s, he supported Eisenhower's credibility policies but went the administration one better by taking the initiative in creating NASA following the Soviet launch of *Sputnik*. NASA was a monument to Johnson's belief in the sizeable annuities that technological preeminence would pay in long-term world opinion. He told Kennedy in April 1961 that "other nations, regardless of their appreciation of our idealistic values, will tend to align themselves with the country which they believe will be the world leader—the winner in the long run. Dramatic accomplishments in space are being increasingly identified as a major indicator of world leadership." As JFK's vice president, Johnson talked the language of credibility and the domino theory as well as anyone. During the Berlin crisis, for example, in which he served as Kennedy's personal representative to the city, Johnson reported that "if we failed to rise to the level of these somber events, all would be lost, for there would be no one who could remove the sense of failure left by our default." His hard-line recommendations on Vietnam were similarly couched in by now unimpeachable domino terms.[2]

Upon assuming the presidency, LBJ confessed that his view of the cold war had been deeply affected by the psychological strain he had experienced during the Cuban missile crisis. Walt Rostow recalled him saying at a staff meeting shortly after Kennedy's assassination: "I want to tell you that one of the deepest things in me is the memory of going to bed at night and not knowing whether there was going to be a nuclear war or not." Making nuclear accommodation his first priority, he told his NSC staffers that "the greatest single requirement is that we find a way to insure the survival of civilization in the nuclear age." On this and related issues, at least, the United States and the Soviets had begun to speak a common diplomatic language under Kennedy, a foreign-policy legacy that LBJ was determined to follow up. At an NSC meeting in December 1963, referring to the nuclear calm that had set in, Johnson remarked that "the basic improvement in the balance of power which had taken place in the last three years is half the explanation for the sense of hope that was developing in President Kennedy's last months." LBJ added pointedly that "he had not become President to give away this advantage."[3]

However, such remarks reflected less a belief in the imminent end of the cold war than a determination to fend off communism in less risky ways. The arrival in 1964 of the bureaucratic Brezhnev regime to replace the impetuous and zealous Khrushchev suggested that Soviet rule was entering the conservative phase of its ideological trajectory in which the concern with self-preservation would outweigh the allure of expansion. Nevertheless, although the ideology was "outdated almost to the point of absurdity," the embassy in Moscow reminded its audience in Washington that "it is the basis on which they hold power." Notwithstanding the forces working for moderation, the fact remained that the Soviet leaders were "hostile to us." So while it was true, as Rostow told the congressional leadership in 1966, that Moscow had "begun to behave more like a nation state and less like a regime intent on world conquest," that was no cause for premature optimism. "There is nothing that has happened over these last three years," he concluded, "which justifies us in believing that if the West is weak and fragmented and fails to maintain integrated defenses, Soviet ambitions will not again be inflamed and the Free World endangered." The confrontation between communism and the free world, Dean Rusk insisted, continued to be "the central, the pervasive crisis of our period of history."[4]

Hegemony and Fear in Europe—Continued

LBJ's decision to devote only a few lines of his memoirs to his dealings with Charles de Gaulle seemed to indicate that he had inherited a continent that was "quite secure," to use Kennedy's public description of the situation a few months before his death. Yet LBJ also admitted that European issues "absorbed much more of my time and attention than most people realized." In the period following Kennedy's assassination, Rostow, in an article entitled "Is NATO Still Necessary?" interpreted the relative quiet in Europe as a sign that the Russian bear was only in hibernation and had not given up foraging in the region. Emphasizing the ongoing need for "effective collective will," he concluded that "our greatest dangers now lie not in the Communist world but in tendencies to fragment our efforts in premature euphoria." And indeed the calm was misleading. By mid-November, 1964, when Ambassador Charles Bohlen was writing to Bundy that "it really looks as though we are headed for genuine confrontation," he was talking about a showdown within the alliance, not with the Soviets. Given the continuing centrality of NATO in America's worldview and the chronic uncertainties about its health, the charge that LBJ was obsessed with Asia was, as Eugene Rostow remarked, "all nonsense." With the administration mindful that it was "essential to have an effective European partner if the U.S. role in the world is to be stabilized for the long term," the Johnson years were in fact an extremely unsettled period during which unresolved problems of French and German nationalism threatened to undo NATO's ligatures.[5]

The brief period of calm meant only that the eye of the Gaullist cyclone was passing over the alliance, with the trailing half of the storm yet to come. Having failed in his earlier efforts to dilute America's exercise of the imperium in Europe, de Gaulle took the alternative tack of seeking to evict the Americans outright by hastening the dissolution of the two rival blocs and promoting a united Europe. In a brief conversation during JFK's funeral, de Gaulle told LBJ in no uncertain terms of his intention "to organize Europe—continental Europe—from an economic point of view and after this is done, perhaps also from the political point of view." LBJ restated politely but firmly the American belief in the continuing need for a strong common defense, but it was clear that de Gaulle would not be dissuaded.[6]

It was not long before the winds once again picked up. In one of his blockbuster press conferences on 4 February 1965, de Gaulle pointed to the seductive prospect of a Europe from the "Atlantic to the Urals." He argued that the six states must succeed "in organizing themselves both politically and in the matter of defense so that the equilibrium of our Continent may become possible." In July 1966, de Gaulle spoke in Bonn of "our Europe:

a Europe which shall find itself little by little, first in detente, then in entente, and finally in cooperation; a Europe which shall once again be whole and in which a whole Germany would again play an essential role. One goes with the other: Europe in its entirety, and Germany in its entirety.'' In short order France extended diplomatic recognition to Red China, announced the intention of building an independent nuclear deterrent or *force de frappe,* and removed French officers from NATO's naval commands.[7]

In March 1966, de Gaulle further shocked the alliance by serving notice of eviction on NATO troops stationed in France and by withdrawing French troops from the alliance command. Shortly thereafter, he left for a trip to the Soviet Union. Indeed, by the following year an intelligence memorandum took seriously the possibility that France would withdraw completely from NATO, despite protestations to the contrary. "There is ample reason to believe," the authors speculated, "that De Gaulle's view of the world situation might lead him to utilize the escape clause which he built into his pledge of loyalty." The Gaullist offensive soon branched out to a critique of America's worldwide role as the French stopped backing SEATO and turned harshly critical of America's involvement in Vietnam. This only underscored what American policymakers well knew: de Gaulle's disavowal of the alliance was the by-product of a fundamental critique of America's *global* policy.[8]

While deliberately muting their public response to these events, policymakers fretted nervously behind closed doors about NATO's future. Unlike the United States, which gave great weight to NATO's long-term role in promoting European integration, de Gaulle seemed to attribute only "a transient if not short-term importance to the Atlantic Alliance." According to the State Department, his logic on this point was quite simple: "The Atlantic Alliance should have the same life span as the threat that called it into existence." Since, in the French view, the cold war in Europe had, to all intents and purposes, come to an end, the alliance ought to be given the quietus. This lack of deep attachment to NATO was confirmed by Premier Georges Pompidou in a Tokyo press conference, in which he expressed surprise that "at the very time when Communist unity is breaking up, there is a desire to establish the same monolithic situation in the Western camp." Absent a compelling Soviet threat, de Gaulle believed that a supranational Europe meant a "Europe under American command" and that supranationalism was nothing more than a code word justifying American imperialism in Europe "forever." The French, he believed, were "the only ones who can say no to the American protectorate."[9]

From the American perspective, de Gaulle's critique involved a false reading of both the system that had guaranteed security and of the dangers still facing Europe should it be abandoned. Moreover, it represented the emergence, however small, of a breach in the dam of containment, which, if left unsealed, could widen into an engulfing deluge. Writing to de Gaulle, LBJ pointed out that NATO, which had emerged in part to meet French needs and at French urging, was still necessary. "Should our collective effort falter and erode the common determination which it reflects," he said, "the foundation of the present stability would be undermined." It seemed doubtful that the new European pattern envisioned by France would be an improvement over the existing system. For example, the main aim of de Gaulle's trip to the Kremlin was, according to the CIA, "to encourage a pattern of bilateral rather than alliance diplomacy between eastern and western Europe." But this decision to "go to Moscow and freewheel with freedom," in Ball's words, was highly worrisome, because it seemed to play into the hands of the Soviet strategy of divide and conquer.[10]

To Americans, de Gaulle, seemingly bent on restoring the traditional, nationalistically rooted balance of power in Europe and incapable of accepting the elementary fact that it had reached an evolutionary dead end, was the personification of an anachronistic European outlook. Vice President Hubert Humphrey accused de Gaulle of seeking "to go back to what I call the period of 1914, the kind of bilateral arrangements that led us through this unbelievable period of turmoil and tension and ultimately destruction from 1914 up through World War II." For Humphrey, all this was but "a return to 19th century balance-of-power foreign policy concepts." In late 1965, a State Department think piece analyzed the problem in similar terms: "The central issue is whether there shall be a collective multilateral system between equal sovereign states employing integration only as needed in the interest of effectiveness, or a system of bilateral power politics involving all the dangers of the turn of the 20th century." Unfortunately, de Gaulle not only spoke for France but was articulating ideas that still appealed strongly to many Europeans. De Gaulle "does reflect and give expression to a certain sentiment not only in France but in free Europe as a whole," said William R. Tyler of State. "Nationalism," warned elder statesman John McCloy, "provoked to some extent by French attitudes, is again emerging in Europe."[11]

De Gaulle's ideas posed a direct challenge to the American conception of internationalism and world public opinion, which was running in another direction entirely. With nationalism posited as the problem, the Americans continued to doubt that the Continent could be organized by Gaullist methods at a time when further progress toward European cohesion and suppression of nationalist impulses seemed called for. De Gaulle's professed commitment to Europe was taken with a large grain of salt, especially as he had in the past ridiculed the possibility of a federated Continent as one in which "there would perhaps be no policy at all." By American lights, the nationalism of French policy did nothing to solve the historical problem of the European balance of power in the only way it could be solved: supranationally, with collective will providing global security. In the absence of genuine political unity, that will could be supplied only through an American-led NATO. According to David Bruce, de Gaulle's French chauvinism was the wrong underlying attitude to hold toward "problems which required the subordination of national interest." All things considered, de Gaulle was far more than a mere nuisance or alliance gadfly. These French "shenanigans," in Bundy's view, seemed to be "calling into question basic arrangements and understandings and going beyond reasonable and legitimate differences in tactics."[12]

By eyeing once again the forbidden fruit of nationalism and balance of power, Europe seemed on the verge of committing a variant of the original sin of American foreign policy: "isolationism." Testifying before Congress in 1965, Rusk pointed to "a certain kind of isolationism among some of those countries who are enjoying relative prosperity, but who have not yet put their full strength into the burdens that need to be carried from the point of view of the free world as a whole." LBJ could understand the historical reasons for "this phase of European isolationism," but, as he told some Reuters correspondents, there was "some danger in Europe of leaving a disproportionate amount of the burden in world affairs to the United States." To Washington, the revival of Europe called for greater burden-sharing within NATO and an expansion of its role, not its elimination. As George Ball put it, America was seeking to devise ways "by which our partners in the Western Alliance can assume a more equitable share of these common world responsibilities." A permanent reliance upon the United States was unhealthy, and not only for the Europeans. Though it made no difference to the world system whether the United States played the role of global Atlas or a more modest leadership role in a system of collective security, the difference between the amount of effort required of the United States in the two cases was enormous.[13]

Johnson's decision to treat de Gaulle with kid gloves reflected in part the conviction—a necessary conviction, given his internationalist logic—that French policy was more a product of personality than raison d'état. Rather than force a demoralizing rupture, LBJ decided to wait France out on the assumption that French policy reflected the idiosyncratic predilections of the man, not the substantive pro-American interests of the French nation. Douglas Dillon predicted that de Gaulle would be succeeded in the near future "by a government more responsive to public opinion, hence more favorable to NATO, United Europe, and the United States." Following his departure

France was "likely to stick to the broadly accepted norms of Western political behavior." Confident of the basic soundness of French political culture, the United States could afford to be more optimistic about France than about post-Adenauer Germany.[14]

The understated approach adopted by Washington also reflected the recognition that France, though important, was not an essential cog in NATO. According to George Ball, who quoted LBJ's salty language, "for the President to get into a 'pissing match' with de Gaulle would only serve to build de Gaulle up and build France up." In the meantime, LBJ intended "to rebuild NATO outside of France as promptly, economically, and effectively as possible." This shift of emphasis suggested an underlying confidence in the soundness of the rest of the alliance. In some ways, the French withdrawal proved to be a blessing in disguise (although, as General Lemnitzer wryly noted, the alliance could ill afford more blessings of this kind). Following a "Tuesday lunch," Rostow expressed the hope that "some European anxiety, if not excessive, could help diminish complacency about European security." In general, this approach jibed with the advice that Eisenhower was giving to Johnson. Ike said that "we should do what we can to move closer to all our allies, particularly including Germany in this situation." This in itself was bound to give de Gaulle "a certain restraint." Otherwise, Eisenhower feared that "strong antagonism and struggles to dominate might once again arise in Western Europe."[15]

But while Germany remained the key to continental security and the basic aim of U.S. policy continued to be "to keep the Germans tied in peacefully," moving closer to Germany was impossible. The other NATO ducklings huddled instinctively under the American mother's warmth, but the United States could no longer be so welcoming to the ungainly and outsized German black swan. Finding itself driven by the compelling logic of nuclear accommodation and by domestic pressures, the United States moved further away from Germany by jettisoning some of the basics of its former German policy. In 1966 and 1967, the United States dropped the multilateral nuclear force project, abandoned any pretense of pushing for unification, and made clear that the stationing of American troops in Germany was not unconditional. To some extent, these moves reflected a growing sense of confidence in the maturity of the German public in the post-Adenauer *Bundesrepublik,* yet at the same time they were made tentatively, with a continued wariness and doubt about the Federal Republic's fidelity to the West. Although LBJ was concerned "not to impose an undue strain on the Germans," he felt he had little choice but to press the relationship, if not to a rupture, to the point that the resulting stresses raised doubts about the strength of the Federal Republic's bonds to the alliance.[16]

For a time, the MLF proposal seemed the best way of dealing with the effect of the Gaullist crisis on Germany's nuclear aspirations. The formula of granting equality in return for Western integration, once a staple of Adenauer's policy, had been a painless way of tranquilizing German nationalism. As Bundy put it in a memo preparing LBJ for a visit of British Prime Minister Harold Wilson in December 1964, the goal of the MLF was to prevent proliferation and to "tie Germany irrevocably to the Western world by giving the Germans the feeling that they are respected first-class members of the Atlantic Alliance." Otherwise, if the United States made no attempt to accommodate Germany's nuclear ambitions, de Gaulle would have been left "a free field."[17]

There were, however, just too many obstacles to the realization of the proposal. Apart from the Rube Goldberg organizational structure of the MLF, congressional insistence on maintaining de facto American control over the alliance's nuclear capability—"the central issue," in Hubert Humphrey's estimation--effectively emptied the proposal of its all-important aura of partnership. Support within the alliance was also problematic. Naturally, the French wanted nothing to do with it, but the British were only lukewarm while the Germans were at best equivocal. The retired Adenauer, in a scorching interview with Kissinger, called the MLF "a fraud in which Germany would be left holding the bag." But the greatest shortcoming of the MLF was that German participation in an alliance deterrent obstructed the conclusion of a nonproliferation treaty (NPT). Intent on pursuing a treaty with the Soviets, by the end of 1964, high administration officials, increasingly convinced that the MLF was "not worth it," were willing to see it "sink out of sight." LBJ accordingly announced in December that the United States would no longer press for its adoption by NATO. The alternative was the creation of a new NATO committee, the Nuclear Planning Group, following whose establishment the United States could negotiate an NPT. Driving home the importance of nuclear accommodation, LBJ told a newsman in 1968 that "nothing could be more important than NPT."[18]

The decision was not easily accepted by administration Atlanticists who were concerned about the effects on the alliance and Germany of pursuing nuclear accommodation with the Soviets. Fearing the disruptive effects of NPT on Germany and NATO, they believed that the priority should be given, as McCloy later put it, to "repair and reinvigoration of the alliance not the inception of a dialogue with the Soviet Union." Rostow, one of the leaders of the resistance, played up the benefits of greater cohesion in world opinion as compared to an only marginally lessened danger of nuclear war. He promoted the MLF as the basis for a strengthened alliance which would permit NATO to "assume a more equitable share of . . . common world responsibilities.'' At one point in mid-1966, Bill Moyers expressed his frustration at this bureaucratic foot-dragging from the "German nuklites," as he called them. "It is unbelievable that these people fight on as they do (like the Japanese on Guam after World War II ended)," he told LBJ, "but they do—and they are effective in putting their views and the old German cause they serve ahead of realistic considerations." Bundy complained that the MLF had become an "obsession."[19]

The echoes on behalf of the MLF continued to reverberate in part because of the conviction that German opinion would not tolerate exclusion from the nuclear club. The embassy in Bonn and the European Bureau in the State Department, for example, continued to argue that "nothing less would satisfy the Germans in the long run." In 1965, an NSC staffer told Bundy that the Germans were looking to a "hardware" solution to the nuclear problem. According to the aide, because of doubt within the Federal Republic about the firmness of American nuclear resolve, the only solution was "some degree of European control." The possibility of a hardware solution of some kind was kept alive because of West Germany's hesitations about the NPT, which was viewed as a bit of superpower complicity at the expense of any nuclear aspirations the Germans might have, not to mention its gloomy implications for reunification. While the NPT and the McNamara solution on consultation won out, LBJ took care to keep his options open because, in his words, "it may be necessary to keep the Germans locked in."[20]

The political turmoil in the Federal Republic in the aftermath of the announcement was also disquieting. The suddenness of LBJ's decision was very embarrassing to Chancellor Ludwig Erhard, but especially to Gerhard Schröder, the one German politician staunchly in favor of the MLF. "We pulled the rug out from under him," Ambassador George McGhee recalled. But the problem ran deeper than mere political embarrassment. Trying to account for why "the Germans behave in a very irrational and immature way," McGhee explained from Bonn that this was part of "their present nature, derived from their basic insecurity and their lack of confidence in themselves and their future." LBJ was always conscious of the underlying problem of German national character. In May 1966, he voiced his uneasiness to Harold Wilson at the "grave danger that the Germans will over time feel that they have been cast adrift. A growing sense of uncertainty and insecurity on their part could lead to a fragmentation of European and Atlantic relations which would be tragic for all of us . . . We cannot risk the danger of a rudderless Germany in the heart of Europe."[21]

Further distancing Washington from Bonn was the administration's decision to stop paying lip service to German reunification. The post-Berlin climate of nuclear accommodation made the Johnson administration reluctant to upset the status quo by continued pandering to the reunificationist sentiment that had made the German issue so volatile in the recent past. "We are for realism in these matters," Bundy advised the president. Not only was reunification patently impossible, it was in some fundamental ways undesirable. As a State Department research memorandum argued, "Reunification would upset the present balance of power within the West European half of the Atlantic system." In the absence of a broader European solution, the smaller continental states, in particular, feared that a reunified German colossus, like the elephant invited to the ball, would trample all the other guests. Unfortunately, despite the sea change in official thinking, reunification remained the official line. Lamenting this element of bad faith in the gap between declaratory and actual policy, Dean Acheson pointed out that "no one in the West, including the Germans, has ever dealt with this frankly, seriously, or apart from oratory." It was especially pointless because, he claimed, "in Germany the sham is recognized."[22]

Just how firmly anchored reunificationist sentiment remained was not entirely clear. The CIA, noting that nuclear realities applied to everyone, suggested hopefully that many Germans had "come to realize that conditions have been fundamentally and irrevocably altered for them by the world strategic situation and the advent of nuclear weapons." But whatever the trend of German sentiment, the United States could no longer afford to play both ends against the middle. American policy, instead of encouraging the West Germans to move in the desired direction of establishing relationships with the East through direct negotiations, was instead promoting continued obduracy. Thus Johnson finally decided to make public the private understanding that the promotion of German unity could no longer be considered a useful route to victory in the cold war. In an October 1966 address, LBJ gave the new approach his imprimatur by insisting that the division of Europe must be resolved peacefully, "healed with the consent of the East European countries and consent of the Soviet Union." Any progress toward reunification would come not through a hard line, but "in the context of a larger, peaceful engagement." Though this step was taken in the belief that German opinion was now ready to face realities, it came at a time when the Germans had still not come to terms with the issue.[23]

In short order, the German connection was further loosened by the question of the future of American troops in Europe, whose continued presence Germans and Europeans had come to take for granted. LBJ was under pressure from a variety of sources to reduce U.S. force levels. With the intervention in Vietnam draining American resources and affecting the balance of payments, McNamara was extremely anxious to economize in Europe. Congress got into the act, too. The Mansfield Amendment, first introduced in

July 1966, began to propose cutbacks in American troops on the Continent. Senator Mike Mansfield, irritated that the United States seemed to be the only government meeting all its NATO commitments, contended that the continued presence of American troops in Europe "was beginning to grate on the nerves of Germans and Europeans." Congress may not have expected complete withdrawal, but LBJ was convinced that it favored substantial cuts in troop levels by a three-to-one margin.[24]

The problem of balancing domestic budgetary demands with the psychological needs of NATO and the West Germans was hardly new, but it became less tractable in the 1960s. Thus far the Germans had been offsetting the balance-of-payments costs incurred from maintaining American divisions in their country, but by the mid-1960s the Erhard government had budgetary problems of its own that made it difficult to satisfy U.S. demands for increased offset contributions. Erhard was in deep trouble on fiscal matters at home—a touchy subject, given previous inflationary disasters in this century—and Ambassador McGhee warned that he had little flexibility on this issue. Too much U.S. pressure might even lead to Erhard's fall, with a less sympathetic government waiting in the wings. With the rupturing of confidence, "Germany and America will tend to drift apart," McGhee predicted. Moreover, this would demonstrate to other Europeans "that we put a low price tag on our military commitment to Europe. In the future Europeans would have little confidence in our assertions." In what followed, McGhee left nothing to the imagination. Germany would reconsider its security policies, the rest of Europe would take a Gaullist turn, the Soviets would adopt a tougher position, and, not least, with such developments "it would be difficult to arrest an increasingly isolationist trend" within the United States.[25]

Following a fence-mending visit by Erhard to Washington, McGhee moderated his gloomy prognosis, but continued to insist that the next six months were "likely to be more troubled than during any previous postwar period." As he later noted, "it looked like the beginning of the end of our strong support for NATO and might lead to further withdrawals and leave Germany defenseless." Further aggravating the situation was the desire of the British government, plagued by fiscal troubles of its own, to make reductions in the Army of the Rhine. If the British withdrew, George Ball feared that "the result would put enormous pressure on the United States to make corresponding withdrawals and a process of unravelling can be started, with critical consequences." McNamara agreed that reducing force structures "may have a traumatic impact in Germany," but he was himself in a box. "Some reductions in US combat power will have to be considered if the problem cannot be solved in any other way," he continued to maintain.[26]

Inevitably, the reduction of the conventional presence would also have an effect on nuclear deterrence. As Eugene Rostow argued, the issue of troop withdrawal "comes down in the end to the credibility of the nuclear deterrent." "The trouble with the damned thing is that the nuclear deterrent doesn't deter," he recalled. "It loses all its credibility if we're not there. That's the paradox of it." Certainly the Germans were drawing connections between the two. Erhard told McCloy that "questions were being asked as to just when the US intended to apply the nuclear riposte and how much of Germany had to be overrun before the riposte would be forthcoming." Given the implications, the possibility of troop reductions without consultation, he insisted, "increased German nervousness and uncertainty." Moreover, a withdrawal would have Continentwide implications for morale. A strong conventional presence, Rusk told Mansfield, "reassures Europeans who might otherwise feel some nervousness about a militarily powerful German neighbor."[27]

Everyone, it seemed, was beginning to get nervous. Johnson's way out was to begin trilateral negotiations with the West Germans and the British. As a reassuring sign to the Germans (and to the State Department) that the United States had not abandoned the old assumptions, he appointed as his special emissary for these talks John McCloy, former high commissioner and one of the chief architects of the policy of tying West Germany firmly to the West. McCloy was no fan of the administration's pursuit of nuclear cooperation with the Soviets, as was evident from his suspicion that "a Soviet-US arrangement is emerging in substitution for the original NATO concept." More so than others, he was quite concerned about "the cohesiveness of NATO and as to European stability if forces were withdrawn from Germany," especially in light of the Gaullist challenge. The situation was made more uncertain still by the end of the Christian Democratic era in Bonn. The fall of the Erhard government, McCloy feared, "could set the Federal Republic adrift in search of new directions."[28]

LBJ insisted on seeing the issue as a "poker game" in which the United States was obligated "to see what the others will put in the pot." He wanted to hold the alliance together, but at the same time hoped to squeeze every possible cent out of the Germans. Claiming to know the German mind from his experience with the German settlement in Fredericksburg, Texas, LBJ claimed that "they are great people; but by God they are stingy as hell." He was a bit irked, too, by the constant German need for reassurance. "If I had a dollar every time I consulted the Germans," he said, "I'd be a millionaire." McCloy warned him that he was playing a dangerous game, that if the alliance collapsed the result would be "going back to the world of dog-eat-dog." But it was always questionable, given resistance inside the Pentagon to McNamara and strong doubts within State about the wisdom of troop cuts, whether LBJ would have gone the limit by withdrawing American troops if his hand had been called.[29]

McCloy's talks with his British and German counterparts were full of references to the portentous implications of their discussions. "More is at stake than questions of force levels in Europe," he informed them. "There is danger that [the] concept of collective security, the keystone of NATO, may be undermined." He was afraid, in particular, of a "reawakening of nationalism in Europe." The response of Kurt Kiesinger, the new chancellor of the coalition government, was hardly encouraging. The very fact that a discussion of this kind had to be held was enough to give rise to the feeling in Germany that "something had 'gone wrong' with the former pattern of good relations between the US and Germany. NATO was in danger of developing into a sort of 'shell with no real spirit left in it.'" Many Germans suspected that the United States had already sold out their interests by making a nonproliferation deal with the Soviets—Kiesinger actually used the word "complicity," whereas Adenauer was reported to have described the NPT as "the Morgenthau Plan squared"—in exchange for Soviet help in Vietnam.[30]

The situation was ultimately resolved by a combination of expedients: a no-gold pledge by the Bundesbank, the purchase of 500 million dollars in bonds, and the avoidance of large-scale troop cuts, aided in part by some imaginative Pentagon basing schemes. Following the conclusion of the deal, one of Johnson's NSC aides reported with some satisfaction that "all in all . . . we have probably avoided what could have become a major crisis in our Atlantic relations." Nevertheless, there was no net addition to alliance cohesion from these talks and some feared that things were going badly awry. Issues like the offset discussions, an assistant secretary of state informed Rusk, "fostered uncertainty abroad and at home about the US commitment in Europe and the fundamental unity of purpose of the three major NATO members, just at a time when De Gaulle was attacking the Alliance." According to Rusk, even modest Soviet gains in Europe constituted "an unacceptable political risk." NATO remained, as Rostow continued to remind the president, "the rock on which all else we do is founded," but events of the mid-1960s had statesmen lying awake at night wondering if that rock was embedded in geologically unstable soil.[31]

In retrospect, some of these disputes seem like domestic spats, noisy perhaps, but hardly threatening to the Atlantic alliance and a fundamentally secure Europe. The Gaullist offensive and the loosening of the bonds with the *Bundesrepublik* were, after all, outgrowths of Europe's recovery and the diminished threat from the USSR after the Berlin crisis. But the perception in Washington of this transitional period was rather different. Europe may have regained its prosperity, but everyone agreed with Acheson that "alone, it is weak, in the sense that it has neither a will nor the power to impose it." If recovery brought with it the revival of nationalism, the consequent slackening of alliance bonds would produce instability in the West, new Soviet thrusts, and eventual disaster for European security.[32]

The United States was racked with doubts during these years about the possibility that this turn toward nationalism and alliance disunity was the result of U.S. policies of accommodation with the Soviets that, although driven by the necessity of exercising nuclear prudence, could be interpreted by others as hegemonism or inconstancy. With a restive France and an unpredictable Germany, the United States placed its hopes for the future in the maturation of a public opinion favorable to internationalism. In the meantime, the only real cure for the disease of particularism was a continued demonstration of American commitment to the larger international cause.

VIETNAM: THE COLD-WAR DILEMMA COMES HOME

As the United States continued nervously to take the temperature of the alliance, the situation in the third world afforded further reasons for apprehension. A CIA National Intelligence Estimate of June 1964 argued that the underdeveloped world was so disorderly that situations were likely to develop which would tend to drag in the great powers. These crises would "engage their prestige to a degree incommensurate with the intrinsic or strategic value of the area itself." Everyone understood that the conditions under which the United States would be engaged in the third world—with timing and location left to Communists operating under the protective canopy of the nuclear umbrella—were not particularly favorable. Therefore the problem in Vietnam had "a special significance for the United States," according to Vice President Humphrey, "because it confronts us with a bold new form of aggression—which could rank in military importance with the discovery of gunpowder."[33]

That such challenges would be forthcoming seemed absolutely certain. Soviet ideology was entering its Thermidorean phase, but not so the Chinese strain. George Ball told the congressional leadership that communism in China was still expansionist because it was "at that raw primitive state—not unlike the state of the Revolution in the Soviet Union in the years after the 1917 revolution." In addition to this ideological thrust, the United States was faced with "the imperial drive of a proud, arrogant, gifted people, who have in the past exercised dominion over the whole of SEA." The events of the cultural revolution in China were described as "fantastic developments" and "wild trouble." The apparent ascendancy of Lin Piao as Mao Zedong's successor, "a thorough Communist, xenophobic in his nationalism, and lacking in true appreciation of the outside world," merely added to American apprehensions about Chinese intentions. Citing one of Lin Piao's speeches, Rusk pointed out that the United States was dealing with leaders "dedicated to a fanatical and bellicose Marxist-Leninist-Maoist doctrine of world revolution." Failing to place such ideological factors center stage would be, as LBJ intimate Abe Fortas once said, "like a production of Hamlet without the prince."[34]

Whatever hopes existed of turning the deepening Sino-Soviet split to American purposes were invariably disappointed. Acting on the presumption that the Soviets were willing to pay a price for the nuclear rapprochement they so clearly desired, the administration sought time and again to have the Soviet Union exert pressure on Hanoi to end its support for the war in the South. But the Moscow connection never materialized because the Soviets were hostages to Chinese radicalism. The Russians had a "more sober view" than Beijing or Hanoi of the risks of American intervention, according to the CIA, but the agency also realized that the Soviets would "probably continue to compete with Peiping for the allegiance of North Vietnam." Explaining the Soviet bind, Ball told Congress that while they did not want a repeat of the Cuba crisis, "at the same time they are members of the Communist club. They are in a competitive situation with the Chinese Communists." As Henry Cabot Lodge, Jr., wrote to Bundy, if the Communists were successful in Vietnam, "it would be interpreted as a vindication of the fanatic Chinese methods over that of the Soviets," in which case the United States could expect to encounter similar challenges "again and again in Asia, Africa, and Latin America."[35]

These gloomy estimates of the limits to Soviet cooperativeness were confirmed as the American intervention deepened in 1965. "The USSR helps when they can," the president told one correspondent, "but I don't think they have the horsepower." But even this was to overstate Soviet helpfulness. Publicly, Moscow criticized the United States for violating the principle of nonintervention in the civil affairs of other states, while privately it did little more than reiterate Hanoi's refusal to guarantee negotiations in return for a halt to bombing of the North. The result, according to Rusk, was that "while the Soviets think they must support Hanoi, they cannot influence its decisions." In its own way, the Sino-Soviet dispute was having the same rigidifying effect on Soviet policy as the disarray within the Western alliance was having on the United States. It was easy enough, in principle, to take the line, as Rusk told Ambassador Anatoly Dobrynin in 1966, that "neither of us should be a satellite of Vietnam," but he realized that the Soviets were as much entrapped by their client state as the U.S. Gulliver was tied down by its own Lilliputians. The unwelcome fact was that conservative ideology could be every bit as threatening as the radical variety. The more Communist ideology became a mask or rationalization for legitimizing Soviet power, the more important it became for the regime to save socialist face in its intramural disputes, lest it be exposed as an ideological paper tiger.[36]

With the socialist states still possessed by ideological demons and with Europe and Asia not wholly secured, the arguments on behalf of intervention followed the pattern of symbolic justification established by preceding administrations. Johnson was acutely conscious of his position in an unbroken chain of presidential commitment. As he reminded some Reuters representatives, American interest in Southeast Asia was "deeply imbedded in our national life, going back to President Franklin Roosevelt's reaction to Japanese takeover of Indo-China." To firm up his ideological authority, he commissioned his aides to come up with a list of presidential pronunciamentos and took pains to keep the domino theory's nominal author, General Eisenhower, consulted and on board. Time and again Johnson asked "if anyone doubted whether it was all worth the effort" and invariably he received a response in domino terms. The object was still to prevent the latter-day acceptance by world opinion of "some Hegelian law of inevitability" that communism was the wave of the future in Asia and elsewhere.[37]

As usual, the argument featured a regional strategic dimension. It was obvious that Vietnam was important to Southeast Asia and more arguably to Asia as a whole—a significant consideration for Johnson, who, more than his predecessors, was convinced of the growing importance of Asia in its own right. But the regionalist justification was never allowed to stand alone. Not content merely to dwell on the importance of specific local interests, policymakers habitually added supplementary internationalist references about the need to avoid isolation. In a good example of this kind of thinking, LBJ had told Kennedy that the alternative to standing fast in Southeast Asia was "to throw in the towel in the area and pull back our defenses to San Francisco and a 'Fortress America' concept." Even as modified, advisers like Harry McPherson were critical of this Asian emphasis, arguing that it was "silly to talk about a rag-tail revolutionary like Ho attacking Hawaii or California." In looking for "a straight argument that our vital interests are involved," McPherson wanted the president to stress that an American defeat would provoke a major regional crisis which could lead to "a Third World War," a rationale more readily understandable in Wilsonian terms.[38]

For all the talk of losing Asia, which was genuine enough, the domino theory was always global, with the United States keeping a nervous eye at all times on the European center. In a real sense, it was believed that the struggle for Europe's future was being waged in the rice paddies of Asia.

Germany, after all, as Dean Rusk later recalled, was "probably the only question on which the Soviet Union and the United States might be drawn into a nuclear war. We're not going to have a nuclear war with the Soviets about polar bears in the Arctic." Bundy, in a speech draft, argued that "we think it clear that success for the free in Vietnam will be success for the freedom of Europe." Conversely, failure in Asia would spell disaster elsewhere. After having talked with various Europeans early in 1965, Rusk told some congressmen that "Europe is watching us in Southeast Asia, particularly the Berliners; and if we pull out of Southeast Asia, what would the rest of the alliances mean, and what would the appetites of the other side amount to?"[39]

The administration attempted time and again to link Vietnam, an obscure symbol, to the defense of the cold war's sacred icon, Berlin. Berlin, the administration believed, effectively epitomized the entirety of American foreign policy. Bill Moyers, in suggesting speech material to Johnson, argued that "once they relate our presence in Vietnam to the defense of liberty in West Berlin, I believe you will find new support for your policies out there." On another occasion, LBJ told congressmen that "the defense of Berlin, right now, is in Vietnam." Drawing the same connection, Attorney General Robert Kennedy declared while in Germany: "If Americans did not stop communism in South Vietnam, how could people believe that they would stop it in Berlin?" As of 1965, morale in West Berlin was high, although former ambassador to Germany James Bryan Conant was quick to warn that "of course, if the Communists were to take over Vietnam, morale would sink rapidly."[40]

Maintaining the allied presence in Berlin had come to stand for the American commitment to defend Europe via the alliance, a commitment that had come into question in the 1960s. For that reason, Charles Bohlen had suggested in 1963 that the United States should "attempt to avoid wherever possible action which would cast doubt upon US determination to defend Europe in the event of war." In a memo to the president, Eugene Rostow reminded LBJ of the importance of Vietnam as a proving ground of American commitment to defend Europe. LBJ's decision to take a stand in Vietnam demonstrated "that we would risk bombs on New York to protect Saigon, and that Moscow would not bomb New York to protect Hanoi." This was, Rostow claimed, "in general aspects, a firm answer to the questions many Europeans, including General De Gaulle, had asked about the future: would we risk war for our allies?" This logic was endorsed by a meeting of a Vietnam panel of outsiders, which included John McCloy and Omar Bradley, held in July 1965. Besides certifying the accuracy of the vision of toppling dominoes in Asia, the panel concluded that "the effect in Europe [of American withdrawal] might also be most serious, and that De Gaulle would find many takers for his argument that the US could not now be counted on to defend Europe.'' Ultimately, a retreat would aggravate both the French and German problems by enhancing de Gaulle's prestige, amplifying European nationalism, and releasing the genie of atomic aspirations.[41]

Unfortunately, U.S. policy could provide reassurance in only a round-about manner. The Vietnam War, like previous cold-war credibility crises, generated resistance to and criticism of American policy that, while preventing defeatism, hardly strengthened alliance morale. Because of widespread criticism from allies and lack of enthusiasm abroad, the administration was painfully self-conscious about having to carry the load almost unilaterally. Occasional efforts by American envoys like Averell Harriman to solicit support for LBJ's Vietnam policy made no dent whatsoever on the ''total and universal lack of comprehension of our Viet-Nam policy'' in Europe. Describing his interview with LBJ after being appointed ambassador to NATO, Harlan Cleveland recalled being urged by the president to '' 'explain to them what we're trying to do there. They don't seem to understand.' ''[42]

The support that was received was tepid at best. The British government, largely at the urging of Laborite Prime Minister Harold Wilson, was rhetorically correct but it resolutely refused to be drawn in. Notwithstanding British membership in SEATO, Wilson fought against continued escalation because of its unfavorable impact on public opinion in Great Britain and the Continent. LBJ, who was quite skeptical of this ''support'' at times, was nevertheless content to count his blessings, because the rest of the Continent was even less well disposed to the American adventure.[43]

The French openly disparaged what de Gaulle viewed as a neocolonial intervention in the internal affairs of the Vietnamese. The general told Bohlen that the United States was ''becoming affected by its own power'' and falling victim to the belief that ''force would solve everything.'' Although he knew full well that the United States would take a dim view of his meddling in the region, in 1966 he went to Phnom Penh and delivered a public broadside against American policy. More ominously, de Gaulle told American diplomats quite frankly that he did not believe the United States could win the war in Vietnam because it was ''rotten country'' militarily. But that was beside the point. It was primarily a ''political and psychological problem,'' he explained, invoking a logic that was the precise opposite of the administration's conception. The more the United States became involved, the more the region's nations would turn against it. Thus, action that Washington interpreted as conclusive proof of manhood indicated to de Gaulle an immature inability to order national priorities. It was frustrating for the administration to see the former charge that the United States would not fight for vital

European interests followed up by the complaint that it was fighting for imaginary Asian stakes, and it was all the more galling to have imperialist motives attributed to it.[44]

According to Harriman, Germany of all the European countries had the "greater understanding of the need to stop aggression." But the Germans were ambivalent, at best; they sensed that the United States was caught in a quagmire while hoping all the while for an American victory because, as Ambassador McGhee recalled, defeat would "decrease our credibility in Western Europe." Erhard played the good soldier by dutifully expressing appreciation for the American effort in Vietnam. "If it was not for the firm US stand there," he told Johnson, "the insecurity, for instance in Berlin, would be much greater. The loyalty of the US to its commitment was a beacon of hope to the Germans and deeply appreciated by them." But Erhard was hardly typical. The retired Adenauer, preferring that the United States stick to its full-time job as Europe's bodyguard and avoid after-hours employment elsewhere, privately called Vietnam "a disaster." Despite assurances from Harriman and others that the United States "was a two-ocean nation and had never permitted its obligations in the Pacific to detract from its concern for Europe," Adenauer warned that "if we kept up our present pace we would lose both Europe and Asia."[45]

In the face of this ambivalence and outright disapproval, the administration could not help but confront the argument that the Vietnam affair, far from demonstrating America's commitment to the defense of Europe and binding together the alliance, was actually sundering it. George Ball, the in-house devil's advocate, tried to use this European concern to his advantage. Arguing from within the cold-war framework and its emphasis on Europe as the area of primary strategic concern, he suggested that the U.S. presence in Vietnam was distorting American policy and hurting the nation's credibility. Only half-humorously, he once drew a map of a small United States and an enormous Vietnam just off the coast, telling Rusk, "This is your map of the world." Seeing no reason to keep a vague treaty commitment to SEATO that other signatories refused to honor, he suggested that U.S. action should "not be judged in juridical terms but in terms of its effect on the credibility of our commitments throughout the world." Since it was obvious that the American image in Europe was being damaged, the United States should withdraw and repair the damage done to the alliance.[46]

While the administration was certainly concerned by the lack of enthusiasm for American policy on the Continent, its estimates of European opinion were always judged by the standard of avoiding the worst case: appeasement. Had collective security been truly collective—something that would have required not only a self-assured and united Europe but also a Continent that shared the internationalist vision of the United States—the United States could have afforded to retreat into the background. But, as things stood, without an American spine for support, the nervous system of world opinion could not function effectively. For the time being, European criticism of American interventionism was far preferable to the defeatism that seemed sure to follow on the heels of an American withdrawal. As Dean Acheson wrote to Lucius Clay following the Berlin crisis: "It is better to have the followers desert the leader, than to have the leader follow the followers."[47]

Some of the European disaffection with Vietnam, LBJ felt, was traceable to the usual leftist antiamericanism, but he recognized that the problem was broader than that, with opposition deeply embedded even in constituencies normally favorable to the United States. The administration attributed the hostility to deficient historical understanding and an inability to appreciate the psychological imperatives for maintaining credibility in the cold war. As Rusk put it, "With the isolationist view in Western Europe they just didn't want to see any problem like the Vietnam problem on their plate." By traditional foreign-policy standards, where security was a function of distance, it was to be expected, in the words of a White House memo, that "those who are more remote and less able to act will find it more difficult to recognize the threat of Communist aggression in Vietnam."[48]

Ideologues who feel that they have a lock on truth characteristically attribute some form of "false consciousness" to those who fail to see things their way. Clearly, Americans thought they grasped the historical logic of the world system in its wholeness, whereas the Europeans, in thinking only of their immediate security, had only a partial consciousness and failed to understand their true interests. European complaints about Vietnam were ignored because they were made from outside the American worldview and thus for the wrong reasons: self-interest and traditional realpolitik. Weakness and vestigial nationalist mentalities meant, in Rostow's estimation, that the United States was "up against an attitude of mind which, in effect, prefers that we take losses in the free world rather than the risks of sharp confrontation." Despite an appeal to the NATO powers to lend a hand, the Western European powers had not yet grown into the responsibilities of world leadership, it was said.[49]

On the other hand, if the United States withdrew, de Gaulle would undoubtedly have been the first to say, "Ah, you see, you cannot rely upon the Americans under a security treaty." In that event, French prestige would be enhanced, European nationalism strengthened, and atomic ambitions correspondingly heightened. Caught between the devil and the deep blue sea, the only way for the United States to avoid criticism was to ensure a successful outcome in Vietnam. As a CIA paper summarized it in 1964, "World reactions would hinge fairly directly on success of US sanctions; if they halted Communist expansion . . . US firmness would be retrospectively admired, as in the Cuban missile crisis showdown; if they ended in failure and retreat, US 'maturity' and world leadership would again be questioned.''[50]

Nevertheless, for all its dismissiveness, the administration was quite sensitive to criticism on this score, primarily because of the effect it had on domestic opinion. In responding to congressional complaints, LBJ argued that ''we're trying to get all of them in there we can, but we are the great power in the world and most of our friends [have] got as many problems as we have and maybe more.'' But privately, the president was clearly nettled and realized that, unlike in Korea, ''we have few allies really helping us.'' ''Are we the sole defenders of freedom in the world?'' he wondered at one crucial meeting—without, however, coming to grips with the circular logic of post–World War II internationalism in which America intervened on behalf of a world opinion that was not only incapable of defending itself but increasingly apprehensive, if not downright hostile, at the thought of the United States doing so.[51]

If European opinion was a continuing disappointment, LBJ took some comfort in being able to argue, at least at first, that practically all the Asian leaders were ''in deep sympathy with us.'' Unlike the distant Europeans, they were close enough to the problem to see it as a direct threat. Johnson asserted that ''a great many governments in Asia and elsewhere understand fully that their security would be in danger if we were to fail to frustrate the purposeful aggression of Hanoi.'' Unfortunately, for whatever reason—fear of antagonizing China while allowing the United States to handle the burden or simply a lack of immediate concern for their security—regional support was quite hard to come by. The lone in-house critic of Vietnam policy of any weight, Under Secretary of State George Ball, pointed out the embarrassing situation in which, ''without exception,'' America's SEATO partners ''viewed the situation in South Vietnam as not calling a treaty into play.''[52]

Privately, the administration received reports from the CIA that the Southeast Asian countries were ''permeated'' with the views of American dissidents. ''The countries don't want the war to go on,'' LBJ complained despondently in January 1966. ''They really want unilateral disarmament.'' In Japan, a functioning democracy where heavy public criticism prevented the government from taking a forthright stand in support of American policy, Rusk insisted that ''the Japanese Government's view has clearly been that it is important for us to succeed in Southeast Asia.'' But that was small consolation, since Japan was seen as ''the most rootless country in the world'' and itself in need of bolstering up. The situation did not improve with time. Writing about his mid-summer 1967 trip to the Far East, Clark Clifford recalled: "It was strikingly apparent to me that the other troop-contributing countries no longer showed our degree of concern about the war in South Viet Nam."[53]

After a meeting of the "Wise Men," an informal group of influentials from whom LBJ occasionally sought counsel, a frustrated Paul Hoffman in 1965 asked: "Hasn't the time come when all nations that covertly support us come out in the open and let the world know that they approve?" Europe's disaffection could be chalked up to remoteness and lack of internationalist vision, but that was not so easily done in the case of Asian nations who chose not to help out. To explain the absence of vocal Asian support, the administration suggested that, because of domestic constraints, "the representatives of these countries might not feel free to express their true opinions concerning United States policy." Rusk replied rather lamely that "the difference between the public view and the private statements of these world leaders is enormous." But that simply suggested that the weakness of world opinion, implicit in the falling dominoes analogy, was once again the justification for going in and staying.[54]

The support that was provided was hardly satisfactory. Reminded that Japanese Prime Minister Eisaku Sato had risked much politically to visit South Vietnam, LBJ responded "but what I'm interested in is bodies." For nations that did contribute troops, like New Zealand and Australia, the despatch of only token contingents was justified by the plea that domestic constraints prevented them from making greater contributions. In the case of the South Koreans, who made a more substantial contribution of manpower, the administration was forced, despite public denials of reciprocity, to offer "sweeteners" by promising to increase military and other forms of aid. The Filipinos, too, exacted a heavy price for a modest contribution. Hubert Humphrey, following a visit to the Philippines, tried to put the best face on the matter by noting, with no apparent embarrassment, that "they didn't ask for all the things that I read about in the newspapers." The importance of allied troops was gratefully acknowledged in all cases, but the contributions hardly seemed in the spirit of things. One can hear the sarcasm in Bundy's rhetorical question: "Who pays the bills?"[55]

The state of morale was no better with America's client state, the Republic of Vietnam. Following the line laid down in the past, the administration defined its mission as stiffening the local will to resist. "The fundamental contest is in South Vietnam and will, in the end, have to be settled by the South Vietnamese," said Bundy in a congressional briefing. There was no lack of information concerning the shortcomings of the Saigon regimes or their inability to generate popular support for the war. Optimism always prevailed, however. "Do the South Vietnamese wish to save themselves?"

McNamara asked rhetorically. He pointed to high ARVN casualty rates as proof that they did. But even the obvious absence of such a will would not have been decisive, since cold-war logic assumed that it was lacking in the first place. The American military presence was intended to nurture in the Vietnamese mind the logic, in Ambassador Lodge's words, "If the Americans can commit themselves, then I can commit myself."[56]

The psychological balance sheet with the immediate enemy in Vietnam, the government in Hanoi, was even worse. Since South Vietnam was weak, this, it was clear, was the more important relationship. "A great deal depends upon what is centrally and really in the mind of Hanoi," Rusk told congressmen. While in the South the overriding goal was to create morale, in the North it was to destroy it. As Lodge reminded the president, "We do not need to define 'victory' and then go ahead and achieve it 100 percent. If it becomes generally believed that we are going to win . . . all else will be a mopping up." The language of power was intended to make Hanoi understand American determination and change course accordingly—"show their bottom before we show ours," in LBJ's dorsal imagery. Before long, however, it became clear that the North Vietnamese were bent on beating the United States at its own game by fighting a war of opinion. This strategy was subsequently confirmed by North Vietnamese hero General Vo Nguyen Giap. "Above all," he recalled, "we wanted to project the war into the homes of America's families, because we knew that most of them had nothing against us." By 1967, the administration had concluded that the Communists had given up any thoughts of military victory: "Their thoughts are focussed on using military power to achieve the most favorable possible political result—with their eyes on the will and political capacity of the people of the U.S."[57]

As the tug-of-war with Hanoi came to be defined in terms of staying power, it became clear that the decisive battle for public opinion would be fought on the domestic front. Worrying about the problem of sustaining a "partial mobilization" for a lengthy period of time, White House aide Douglass Cater warned Johnson that "the Home Front (private sector) is a real front line." Given the need to impress Hanoi with American determination, the enormous external consequences of even marginal internal dissent became evident. Analysts agreed that "people like Lippmann, Morgenthau, Fulbright and marching students do great damage by creating false hopes in unfriendly breasts." "The only basic weakness we have is that our adversary believes that he can win the war in Washington instead of Vietnam," Johnson told some congressmen early in 1967.[58]

The escalation took place slowly, against the advice of those, like Eisenhower, who would have preferred to jump in with both feet and end it quickly. This gradualness was intended in part to avoid the larger conflict that American policy was no longer prepared to run major risks of provoking. LBJ was greatly concerned to keep the USSR and China out of the direct line of action. As he told one newspaperman: "If you throw your weight in all at once, you almost force Russia to help, whereas if you wear them down slowly, you may avoid World War III. We try to do this carefully and discreetly." In an interview with Clair McKelway of the *New Yorker,* he stressed that "we've got to be wise enough and cautious enough not to provoke China and Russia into World War III." In response to a sailor's question as to why the United States was not hitting the enemy harder, LBJ responded: "They have two big brothers that have more weight and people than I have. They are very dangerous. If the whole family jumps on me—I have all I can say grace over now . . . We are not trying to make this a wider war."[59]

But there is little doubt that a creeping escalation was also a device for managing a problematic domestic opinion. The Kennedy administration had enjoyed overwhelming domestic support for nuclear confrontations, a support which was, fairly or not, denied Johnson in the limited war now being fought in part to avoid further nuclear showdowns. The incremental approach grew out of the realization that the war was a battle of national wills in which there could not be, in the nature of things, a decisive military victory in the traditional sense. In internal documents, the importance of sticking it out over the long haul was repeatedly stressed, with nary a doubt that the conflict was open-ended. "At its very best the struggle in Vietnam will be long," Bundy told the president in February 1965. Bundy was thinking in terms of ten years, while some administration advisers had a "twilight war" of twenty years in mind, including the possibility of several Vietnam-type wars being fought at one time. As in arm wrestling, "victory" could come quickly, but only after a long period of attrition in which little seemed to be happening.[60]

The administration fretted from the beginning that the public was not likely to stand for a stalemated conflict. Writing from Saigon, Lodge complained accurately, but irrelevantly, that the U.S. public accepted highway fatalities "more easily than it does casualties on the battlefield." One could wave off the warning of an antiwar senator like Wayne Morse that "it would be a very serious mistake to think the American people would support a stalemated war in Vietnam for a period long enough to force the Communists into negotiating." Less easily dismissed were the admonitions of presidential confidants like Clark Clifford, who predicted gloomily in a meeting at Camp David that "if we don't win, it is a catastrophe. If we lose 50,000 plus [troops] it will ruin us. Five years, billions of dollars, 50,000 men, it is not for us.'' Even in Korea, where the United States had been able to operate under the legitimizing mantle of collective security and to get out with the threat of nuclear action, the public had grown quite restive. Despite this cautionary example—and it *was* on everyone's mind—the logic of the cold war left no other choice but to go into Vietnam with open eyes. Caught between the need to make the commitment and the domestic consequences of making it open-ended, it seemed necessary to downplay the war as long as possible. That is why, in part, Bundy spoke in 1965 of the need to "reconcile the need for a clear decision within the Government with a need to avoid excessive public noise.''[61]

Understandably enough, the administration relied heavily upon the Munich analogy and memories of the 1930s to make its case. Rusk was the most persistent analogizer, as typified by his reminder to some congressmen that ''it was only ten years from Manchuria to Pearl Harbor, only a year and a half from Munich to the outbreak of World War II.'' Communist ideology provided a modern wrinkle in terms of inner motivation, but the problem, stripped to its external structural essentials, remained expansionist regimes in a volatile world where power balances had been destroyed. If left unchallenged, said Rusk, ''these appetites that we have known in the past . . . would continue to feed until they had to be met under circumstances of greater danger, greater catastrophe, and greater disadvantage for the free world.'' These arguments always proved convincing to Johnson. For instance, at a meeting in which an increase in troop levels to 200,000 was taken up, he concluded that ''the lesson of Hitler and Mussolini is clear. I can see five years from now a chain of events far more dangerous to our country.''[62]

Not everyone agreed, however. The administration was knocked off balance by a growing chorus of critics who believed that the Munich analogy was misleading. Foremost among the early dissidents was Senator J. William Fulbright, who accused the administration of being ''severely, if not uniquely, afflicted with a habit of policy making by analogy'' which was ''a substitute for thinking and a misuse of history.'' This accusation of oversimplification would henceforth become the stock in trade of cold-war critics. It was, however, an ironic charge to direct against Wilsonian internationalism, which had always been thought to require a high level of education and sophistication about foreign affairs. Indeed, the administration considered suggestions that it was making policy on the basis of historical memory to be simplistic in their own right. The Munich analogy and domino metaphor were unquestionably too simple, but the truth was that internationalist logic was so complex that a degree of tropic reductionism was inevitable. The administration was caught between the need for transparency, which opened it to criticism on grounds of oversimplification, and its conviction that the real explanation lay "among the vast complexities of world power and American responsibility—the teachings of history and the command of the future," an explanation which was so deeply sedimented in a worldview that it was difficult to articulate and whose complexities made it difficult for the American public to understand.[63]

At issue, for the administration, were not historical memory or making policy by analogy, but the fundamental lessons of history that pointed to the emergence of novel structural problems in international society. Thus Rusk enjoined his listeners not to focus on analogies and metaphors while he continued to insist that a fixation with the historical uniqueness of each crisis drained the twentieth century of its meaning. To him, the events of the 1930s did indeed have validity as "laboratory experiments in the anatomy and physiology of aggression." In responding to Fulbright, LBJ tried to appeal to the senator's own internationalism by arguing that the analogy involved "the broader issue of how inaction would affect the overall balance of security in the world," a world in which modern communications and weaponry had "made this planet a small political community." Johnson tried to point out that Vietnam was rooted in a larger worldview that undergirded all of American foreign policy, the basic assumptions of which were congenial to many of the leading critics. Moreover, the rationale for going into Vietnam was specifically tied to a logic of containment worked out under novel conditions of nuclear plenty. Reminding his tormentors of cold-war crises only recently endured and surmounted with overwhelming public support, the president insisted that "we do learn from the past—including the *recent* past."[64]

The pre-Munich Wilsonian roots of the domino theory were quite clear from its concern with the potentially calamitous effect on world opinion if America failed to keep its word. Following the pattern established by previous cold-war crises, Vietnam had little value in itself except as a way of maintaining the symbolic universe indispensable to containment. While the failure of American policy in Vietnam may have been due to lack of local knowledge, the rationale for intervention did not require anthropological insight because the Vietnam War was never really "about" Vietnam. There was no immediate strategic threat to American interests, as Rostow readily admitted in a draft letter to the commander in chief of the VFW: "The danger is not now, strictly speaking, a military danger, so long as our military strength and the cohesion of our alliances are maintained."[65]

But, as argued above, the 1960s were a period of great insecurity about

NATO's and Germany's future. If the dike of world opinion should break, as Eugene Rostow argued, "a great wave of cumulative change in the direction of political influence could generate a sense of panic that could lead men over the brink once more." "The world, the country, and the Vietnamese would have alarming reactions if we got out," claimed Rusk. Typical was McNamara's 1964 memo to Johnson in which he warned the president not only of "the impact of a Communist South Vietnam in Asia, but in the rest of the world, where the South Vietnam conflict is regarded as a test case of U.S. capacity to help a nation meet a Communist 'war of liberation.'" In a congressional briefing on Vietnam, Bundy eschewed any mechanical domino analogy of conquest by military force, describing instead "a situation of life and hope for one country after another, not only there, but in many other continents." "The shape of the world will change," predicted Paul Nitze, should the United States fail to stop the North Vietnamese and the Vietcong.[66]

This debate never moved beyond cliches because, by attacking the Munich analogy as the basis of the domino theory, the critics of Vietnam were training their sights on superficialities rather than on the underlying historical presuppositions of the neo-Wilsonian worldview, many of which they happened to share. The implication was that the past was being used and abused as a rationalization for special interests who were using an indiscriminate anticommunism to advance their own agendas, all the while ignoring the real historical roots of American foreign policy. Yet the suggestion that the critics had some larger truth was incorrect. The war's critics could offer the alternative of withdrawal, but they offered no alternative worldview as a basis from which to do so. The debate never moved beyond the surface because that would have required both sides to question their underlying—and quite similar—ideological presuppositions. Such questioning was impossible because the beliefs in question were foundational, and could no more readily be called up for examination than a tree can be uprooted for inspection. That kind of questioning could occur only in times of great crisis, when the roots were already being ripped up.[67] And Vietnam was not that kind of crisis.

The opposition that began to take shape was in part the result of the maturation of a postwar baby-boom generation that did not have as part of its mental baggage the historical memory of the 1930s and subsequent events as a way of automatically intuiting the strategic significance of Vietnam. Further tending to cut young people off from mainstream values was a modernization process that created a distinctive and alienated youth subculture. Contributing, too, to public skepticism was a waning of the McCarthyite mentality of the late 1940s and a revival of the liberal anti–cold war dissent that had been shut down in the early years of the cold war. But demography, modernization, and shifting ideological currents only exacerbated what the administration believed to be a far more serious problem. The particularism of its critics, especially their nominalist views of race and culture, convinced the administration that isolationism as a cultural trait in the mass public had not been eliminated.[68]

There was a good deal of talk early on about educating the American people, of offering the "true" complex explanations instead of simplified rhetoric, in the belief that public disaffection, in Lodge's words, "does not reflect deep conviction but a superficial impulse based on inadequate information." But it was not long before LBJ himself was giving vent to fundamental doubts. "Are we starting something that in 2-3 years we can't finish?" he asked in July 1965. When assured by advisers that the American people basically supported the commitment, LBJ, well aware of how ephemeral opinion polls could be, responded: "But if you make a commitment to jump off a building, and you find out how high it is, you may withdraw the commitment." In a discussion of a bombing pause in December 1965, LBJ concluded that "they are right: the weakest chink in our armor is public opinion. Our people won't stand firm—and will bring down the Government." "I've always known we're on thin ice," LBJ lamented in early 1966 in commenting on the "frantic attitude" on the part of some congressmen and senators. As time went on, Johnson tried to look at it philosophically, laying the blame partly on his shortcomings as a communicator, but looking also to history for vindication by recalling the domestic trials of past presidents in difficult foreign-policy situations.[69]

All these forebodings were manifestations of the ultimate Pyrrhonic doubt: that American cold-war internationalism, the "credo" behind credibility, had been erected on a shaky foundation. LBJ liked to talk about the United States remaining true to its national character—"our nation is strongest when it's truest to itself," he told some congressmen in the White House rose garden—but there was a nagging suspicion that that character was not as staunch as it was publicly said to be. "A refusal by many Americans to see the enemy as the enemy," as LBJ told some foreign journalists, was "a reflection of broader and deeper attitudes." In a discussion of one of the bombing pauses, Rusk pointed to "the underlying question of the American people," who, he argued, were "isolationists at heart." In a private briefing of *Washington Post* columnist Chalmers Roberts, LBJ indicated that "we have a substantial portion of people in this country who are isolationists." He complained to Abba Eban of Israel that "the Congress is becoming increasingly independent and isolationist." The lessons of the past had, it seemed, been accepted by the nation's foreign-policy elites but had never been sedimented in American mass culture. The absence of national solidarity on Vietnam was interpreted as an inability on the part of Americans to make strategic judgments on the basis of sophisticated historical analyses.[70]

In debating the consequences of nonintervention in 1964, Lodge had argued that as a result "many voices would arise in America urging us to wash our hands of the world." But now that the country was in, it appeared that the result would be the same. Time and again the administration rehearsed the nightmare scenario of an isolationist revival and its ultimate consequences. Asked by LBJ to spell out the results for a group of Australian broadcasters, Rostow gave a typical summary (paraphrased here by a third party; direct quotations are so indicated):

> *LBJ to Rostow:* What do you think would happen if we pulled out of Vietnam?
> *Rostow:* The U.S. would suffer an immediate and profound political crisis—"the worst of this century." We would be divided by a bitter and prolonged debate, which the forces of "a powerful isolationism" would win.
> *LBJ:* They would say our character had worn out?
> *Rostow:* Yes. And while we were divided and preoccupied by debate, the USSR and China would seize dangerous initiatives. NATO "could never hold up."
> *LBJ:* What about out there?
> *Rostow:* Leadership in Laos, Cambodia, and Thailand "would cave in." They would be compelled to "make deals with China." Concessions would be made "as a matter of political agreement" because no one nation or leader would have the power to withstand Communist pressure. All deals would be made on China's terms. [After describing Japan going nuclear and rising tensions with the USSR, he continues] Looking ahead, the world could return to a cycle of Big Power struggles. A weakened and divided America would be powerless to modify or check the cycle. At worst, America could recover from an isolationist spasm only to be pulled back into wider and more grievous international conflicts, possibly a larger war.
> *LBJ:* In five years could they take Laos, Cambodia, Burma, Thailand, the Philippines and Malaysia?
> *Rostow:* There's no doubt of it. There's no power to stop them.[71]

Isolationism was the administration's bogeyman, but it was not the real problem. The lack of public enthusiasm for Vietnam had less to do with the fundamentals of the cold war, which an isolationist surge would certainly have called into question, than with the way in which containment was being applied. The public continued to support NATO, the rapid construction of a massive nuclear arsenal, and the national security state. Moreover, public support for Vietnam, high at the outset, never did fall below a majority. That this support began to erode only as the indeterminate character of the intervention became apparent suggests that the falling out with the administration was over means, not ends. The issues involved, moreover, were not new, since the turmoil at home was the product of a dilemma, inherent in neo-Wilsonian ideology, that had been faced and finessed repeatedly by previous administrations in their cold-war diplomacy but which was now playing itself out in the domestic theater of public opinion.

The quandary most often associated with Johnson's conduct of the war has been the "guns and butter" dilemma in which he sought to prevent his Great Society from being smothered by full-fledged concentration on Vietnam. A policy of guns and butter, besides being difficult to pull off economically, was impossible to implement psychologically, given its simultaneous encouragement of patriotism and unchecked consumerism, yet Johnson tried to have his cake and eat it. "We are a country which was built by pioneers who had a rifle in one hand and an axe in the other," he said, implying that the nation could continue to wield both. While the guns-versus-butter choice suggests that LBJ's ordeal was the result of trying to have it both ways, one can arrive at a better understanding of the kind of crisis of cold-war internationalism provoked by Vietnam if one sees the administration's domestic dilemma in terms of the impossibility of having it *either* way in fighting the war. For LBJ, neither all-out warmaking nor a sustained incremental involvement was possible. Every cold-war president had been forced to choose between the two neo-Wilsonian goals of avoiding global war, on the one hand, and averting the collapse of global morale, on the other, and Johnson was no exception. That problem, and not the desire to preserve the Great Society, provided the fundamental reason for entering the war on low throttle.[72]

The domino theory had a horizontal dimension, but avoiding the rapid vertical ascent to war had always been more important. Although Johnson on one occasion voiced the wish that "my people were as solid in support of my soldiers as Ho's people are solid in support for his troops," if he had stopped to think about his statement, he would surely have modified it. Johnson was wishfully equating a nationalist willingness to fight and die on the part of the North Vietnamese with the quite different kind of popular commitment that he would have needed to fight the war on his terms. Support for internationalism could only be of a peculiar kind: an unstable blend of neo-Wilsonian logic and self-limiting patriotism. Wilsonianism may originally have tapped crusading energies, but in the era of nuclear plenty it had become an intellectualized doctrine requiring that emotions be kept in check.

Symbolic wars, by definition, were not about the kinds of tangible and emotional interests one feels in one's bones. Not only was it necessary to reason oneself into fighting, this internationalism required an understanding of the dilemma attending the dangers of all-out war on the one hand and the psychological dangers of inaction on the other.[73]

The avoidance of nuclear war had produced a need for credibility to prevent a collapse of world opinion, but that credibility itself depended on public willingness to support an internationalist logic so nuanced that the deep ideological conviction necessary for the willing sacrifice of human life could not be manufactured. That kind of internationalism may have been enough to support a high-tech war of impersonal killing, but not the brutal, close-in combat required by search-and-destroy tactics. Quite clearly the war's opponents did not take the administration's version of the calamitous effects of withdrawal seriously enough to warrant sacrificing life on behalf of dubious abstractions. The government was unable to make a persuasive case for a unilateral internationalism to a growing segment of the public unconvinced of the limitless ambitions of communism, of the psychological weakness of the free world, or of the global relevance of the Vietnamese situation. To a growing contingent of critics, nationalism and anticolonialism, neither of which was germane to the global issues of the cold war, seemed more prominent than global Communist ambition in explaining events in Vietnam, which were in turn partly consequences of the cold-war division of the country.

Assuming that it could have been produced, even a pure, rational internationalism would probably have been insufficient. De Gaulle was right: there had to be a connection between nationalist feeling and making war with conviction. American internationalism in the twentieth century had typically required a patriotic catalyst, whether Pearl Harbor in 1941, the submarine issue in 1917, or the nativist anticommunism of the early cold war that, whatever its undesirable effects upon civil liberties, provided an emotional underpinning of strong public support for the cold war. Following the Gulf of Tonkin incident's miserable failure to provide such a nationalist detonator, the administration quite consciously sought to rein in nationalist passion for fear of its excesses. Patriotic fervor, while necessary in measured quantities, worked counter to neo-Wilsonianism with its emphasis on the importance of symbolic issues and its complex, even paradoxical, sense of the role of power in the modern world.

That the Johnson administration fully understood the self-imposed restraints of limited war and its delicate psychological requirements was evident from the care it took from the outset not to stir up the American public to a crusade. The president was self-consciously "quite careful not to get the country on an anti-communist binge because it tears up what we have achieved with the USSR." He could, in private congressional briefings, rail against extremists, the Left, and "the bastards who find patriotism a dirty word," but he realized that to go public with such emotions would be to risk losing control of them—and of the policy of incremental pressure being applied in Vietnam.[74]

Moyers warned LBJ that "it would be a serious mistake to talk about 'victory' in Vietnam for fear of frustrating the public. LBJ also opposed declaring war—"Definitely no. No, you might bring in China and Russia"—and he was reluctant for that reason to stir up patriotic emotions that could not be controlled. "There's too much power in the world to let the American people become too mad," recalled Rusk. The notes from one meeting reported that "the President said today we have no songs, no parades, no bond drives, etc., and he said we can't win the war otherwise." This repression of nationalist passion only made the policy of suffering a thousand cuts in Vietnam even more difficult to explain. All this suggests that the major domestic threat came from the nationalist right, the "Great Beast" whose inability to understand internationalist logic could push matters rapidly out of control.[75]

LBJ's fears of nationalist extremism were evident from the way he analyzed the implications of the bombing pauses that punctuated the war. Ostensibly designed to get negotiations going, these pauses were as George Ball recalled, "foredoomed efforts, because we weren't prepared to make any real concessions." McNamara admitted as much at a White House meeting when he described the first bombing pause at the end of 1965 as "a propaganda effort," entered into primarily to satisfy domestic and foreign critics who insisted that the United States was not doing enough to encourage negotiations. But LBJ also felt that the pauses would provide ammunition to hawks by making the administration look like "weak sisters." Bundy told LBJ that "the whole American Right is likely to be tempted by the argument that just at the moment of trial we are weakening in our support of our men in Vietnam." According to Ball, LBJ's logic was "if I go through a long bombing pause and nothing happens, then the pressures to escalate are going to be almost irresistible."[76]

By 1967, LBJ realized that he had boxed himself in with his "no win" policy. "If history indicts us for Vietnam," he told one newsman, "I think it will be for fighting a war without trying to stir up patriotism." He agreed with Eisenhower's lament that patriotism seemed to have gone out of fashion, but at the same time a nationalist, MacArthur-like solution to the war would have violated the internationalist logic by which it was entered into and fought. This did not stop him from fuming, on occasion, about the alleged role of American Communists in causing the public's growing alienation. But in talking with some China experts early in 1968, he came back to his original understanding: "We must carry on an endurance contest in Vietnam in such a way as not to lead to inflexibility."[77]

Just as there was no avoiding Vietnam, there seemed no way out of the domestic dilemma. So, while 1968 was filled with dramatic events, there was no comparably dramatic change in Johnson's policy. The Tet offensive, despite heavy losses to the Vietcong, came as a shock to an American public accustomed to hearing official optimism from Washington. Soon afterward General William Westmoreland requested 200,000 additional troops, a request which, had it been honored, would have escalated the American commitment beyond control. Shortly thereafter, Johnson announced his intention not to run again for the presidency in the hope of producing negotiations. Yet he was unprepared to change course in Vietnam, notwithstanding massive desertions from cold-war experts and former advisers like McGeorge Bundy who were now arguing that "there is no force on earth that can hold the American people to more years of the same." But LBJ, the domestic populist turned believer in virtual representation in foreign affairs, refused to admit the error of his policies and continued to stress to his advisers that "so long as he was President the United States was not going to abandon its commitments, or surrender."[78]

Even after the North Vietnamese finally agreed to meet in Paris, the administration refused to change its fundamental position on Vietnam. Bombing halts were debated as earnestly as they had been in 1965 and 1966. On the ground, the war was as bloody as ever while the negotiators remained deadlocked in Paris over symbolic issues. Their inability to agree on the shape of the negotiating table indicated that the contest was still framed in terms of a battle of wills, with the side that gave way on the table presumably willing to give way on all else. By approaching the Paris talks in this fashion, the administration nodded to mounting domestic pressure against the war, but without major modification of its ideological position. As long as Communist expansionist ideology was in the saddle, the United States could not afford to give in.

In Europe, the situation was somewhat better, thanks ironically to the Soviet-led invasion of Czechoslovakia by Warsaw Pact forces. The brutal crushing of the "Prague spring" and its aspirations of creating a socialism with a human face was an unwelcome sign that the cold war was still in force. Although clearly this was a measure of bloc discipline not aimed at western Europe, LBJ opined that "there is danger in aggression anywhere," while Rusk believed that "this shows they hold the US in contempt." On the bright side, however, Soviet brutality served to reinvigorate the alliance by rekindling the kind of fear that had led to NATO's formation. As the *New York Times* correspondent put it, de Gaulle's concept of foreign policy had been "shaken if not destroyed by the Soviet intervention in Czechoslovakia." Returning from a meeting of NATO's nuclear planning group, Defense Secretary Clifford announced that the meeting he had just attended "was the best that had ever been held." Pointing to German plans to expand their military budget, "he believed that the Czech crisis had saved a dangerous situation." Nevertheless, the Europeans, as Clifford made clear, did not want a return to the cold war. "They want detente," he informed LBJ.[79]

By the end of the Johnson years, the neo-Wilsonian strategy of containment was at an impasse. In South Vietnam, the nation was doing little to create an indigenous will to resist. In taking on North Vietnam, the United States became engaged in a long-term struggle of will, a war of attrition that emphasized ability to endure pain under ambiguous circumstances. In Europe, the 1960s were a decade of revived nationalism and continuing uneasiness over the solidity of the cold-war solution to the German question. The result was that world opinion was on the verge of being effectively reduced to American opinion, a far cry from the original Wilsonian conception of a "community of power." But even American opinion was at odds with itself as the domestic foreign-policy consensus, the lifeblood of the credo in credibility, appeared to be falling apart.

As long as Washington remained convinced, in Rostow's phrase, that the United States was "the world's margin of safety," there seemed no alternative to interventionism in what appeared to be, for the time being at any rate, an isolationist world of nations with shortsighted views of their interests. That being the case, a temporary estrangement from world opinion and a willingness to withstand the buffeting of domestic storms certainly seemed preferable to the dangers of structural isolation. Whatever the derelictions of the rest of the world, the problem, after all, in 1919 and 1938 had been American inaction, and policymakers were convinced that America could not afford once again to "break the heart of the world."

This conflict between ideology and popular resistance to its requirements certainly had the potential to become a crisis of the first order if the country had been allowed to sink further into the quagmire, but it was not allowed to reach that point. The transiency of the Vietnam trauma and the essential solidity of the neo-Wilsonian worldview would be confirmed by the subsequent stabilization of containment. Richard Nixon and Henry Kissinger would have a good deal to do with that, but even more consequential in making détente a possibility was the waning of Communist ideology in the People's Republic of China and an end to fears of German nationalism run amok. That, finally, would bring about détente in Europe and a balance in Asia, something akin to the global stability that policymakers had long pined for. And that would enable the cold war to enter its concluding phase as a battle of modernizations.

CONCLUSION

THE ARRIVAL OF DÉTENTE in the early 1970s finally inserted some diplomatic control rods into a dangerously hot radioactive pile. As Communist ideology lost its intensity, as American allies became more tractable, and as the United States extricated itself from the Vietnam debacle, the temperature of the international reactor dropped quickly from the danger level of the 1960s. Thanks to this ideological cooling down, threats of nuclear and conventional warfare dwindled in Asia and Europe and the need to demonstrate the credibility of American power in the free world diminished. Even the United States' aversion to Vietnam turned out to be only an allergy and not a crippling disease of internationalism. Taken together, these changes brought temporary solutions to the entire bundle of neo-Wilsonian problems and finally transformed the cold war from an "imaginary war" into a contest of competing systems of modernization.[1]

In Europe, the developments came quite rapidly and unexpectedly. The French electorate's refusal to renew de Gaulle's mandate in the wake of the May 1968 riots and demonstrations brought to power the more tractable Georges Pompidou, no less a Gaullist in principle, but in practice a man who possessed neither the will nor the resourcefulness necessary to attempt an organization of Europe along Gaullist lines. The attenuation of Franco-American discord was complemented by the emergence of significant areas of agreement. In their views on Germany, on Great Britain's admission to the Common Market, and on Nixon's new Vietnam policy, France was substantially in accord with the United States. Understandably, for two countries whose relationship had always been rather edgy, what passed for a love feast was not destined to last. By 1974, tensions once again flared and some of the old accusations of hegemonism and aspirations for continental leadership resurfaced. But in a Europe where détente and *Ostpolitik* had settled in, French nationalism was no longer the threat it had been and the mutual recriminations lacked the explosive possibilities of the preceding decade's quarrels.[2]

Simultaneously, the foreign policy of the Federal Republic underwent an enormous change, allaying fears that German nationalism might become the wrecking ball of the new house of Europe. Under the leadership of Willy Brandt, Bonn finally accepted a fact that had become increasingly obvious since the Berlin Wall crisis: unification, rather than being accomplished in short order through diplomatic methods, would have to await the verdict of history in the form of an end to the cold war. Brandt understood that West Germany, if it were to avoid swimming against a powerful historical tide, would have to accept the political status quo and focus instead on socioeconomic policies that would promote the long-term collapse of communism in the GDR.

Translated into diplomacy, the product was *Ostpolitik,* a new Eastern policy put into place by a series of dramatic treaties that normalized relations between West Germany and its former antagonists. In 1970, a German-Soviet treaty of friendship renounced the use of force and agreed to recognize the legitimacy of all post–World War II borders in Europe. In the Polish-German treaty signed at the same time, the *Bundesrepublik* specifically repudiated any irredentist desires for the former Reich's Eastern territories. In November 1972, a Basic Treaty between East and West Germany provided for mutual recognition and outlined terms for commercial and cultural contacts between the two Germanys.

Although *Ostpolitik* proceeded in the face of lingering fears that Brandt's policy might detach West Germany from the alliance, it went smoothly enough to allow the process of superpower détente to continue until its formalization in the 1972 Moscow accords. Meeting in the Kremlin, Nixon and Brezhnev signed a Strategic Arms Limitation Treaty and framed it with a set of principles in which both parties agreed to avoid confrontations, forswore attempts at unilateral advantage, and renounced claims to special rights or advantages in world affairs. As if to underline the end of the quarter century of tension that had racked the Continent, in 1972 the four occupying powers concluded a treaty that regularized the status of Berlin. With the sanctification of the status quo, there was no longer much to fear in Europe, either within the alliance or without, which meant that the frailty of European opinion, would not be the major source of unsettlement in U.S. policy that it had been in the past. That it was thought necessary by Nixon and Kissinger to declare 1973 as a "Year of Europe" in U.S. foreign policy is an indication of the extent to which the Continent, once an obsessive concern of policymakers, was allowed to recede into the background.

At the same time, Nixon sought to stop the political bleeding from Vietnam, an open wound that was generating an unprecedented degree of domestic protest. Early in his administration, he confessed to Dean Acheson that while he had been an early backer of the intervention, he now believed that "we had been wrong."[3] Fully aware of the political folly of continuing on the course charted by LBJ, Nixon began to Vietnamize the war on the ground while progressively reducing the number of U.S. combat troops in the country, all the while escalating the air war in an attempt to force Hanoi to the bargaining table. This "negotiating track"—actually the stick in a carrot-and-stick approach—included the secret bombing of North Vietnamese bases in Cambodia, a stepped-up air campaign against the North, and, finally, the risky gambit of mining the approaches to Haiphong harbor early in 1972, just prior to the Moscow summit.

Nixon's policy received an indispensable boost when the People's Republic of China finally quit its role as ideological provocateur and evinced a new-found willingness to do business on the basis of power realities rather than doctrinal ambitions. Following the chaotic cultural revolution, the PRC's ideological pendulum had begun to swing away from Maoist radicalism in both domestic and foreign policy. Jolted into action by border clashes with Soviet forces in Manchuria in 1968, the PRC suddenly showed a willingness to change the status of the Sino-Soviet dispute from a fraternal disagreement within the socialist bloc to a power political struggle. With the ideological winds no longer blowing outward, this new preference for dealing on a realistic basis allowed Kissinger to conduct secret talks with the Chinese leadership that made possible Nixon's visit to Beijing in February 1972. The main achievement of the journey, the Shanghai communiqué, committed both sides to opposing regional "hegemony" and to the pursuit of an eventual "normalization" of relations. This visit, by starting what Nixon called "a civilized discourse" between the two countries, promised to eliminate the conventional threats that had threatened to sprout like mushrooms in the shadows cast by the nuclear stalemate.[4] It also emboldened Nixon to put more pressure on the North Vietnamese to force an agreement.

As the ground war ebbed, the resultant decline in combat casualties and draft calls allowed Nixon handily to win re-election in 1972 against the dovish Democrat George McGovern. Early in 1973, following a renewed campaign of aerial bombardment, the administration finally signed the Paris accords with Hanoi which provided for the full withdrawal of U.S. forces and an end to the air war in return for the release of American prisoners of war. With the fall of Saigon in 1975 following a renewed North Vietnamese offensive, the Indochina war entered a new phase. Initially, the trend of events seemed to confirm the more ominous domino forecasts as North Vietnamese forces dominated Laos and swept victoriously into Cambodia following a disagreement with the fanatically nationalist Khmer Rouge Communist regime. That was the end of Vietnamese expansionism, however. As the myth of ideological fraternity exploded, it became clear that Vietnam, a traditional Chinese enemy and a ward of the Soviet Union, would no longer receive China's support. When the PRC exerted military pressure on Vietnam's northern border in February 1979, Vietnamese expansionism was being halted by what American policymakers, not so long ago, were convinced did not exist: a regional balance of power.

These dramatic changes in Europe and Asia seemed to confirm the Nixon administration's contention that the postwar period had ended and that "the whole pattern of international politics was changing."[5] A metamorphosis of the post–World War II pattern was indeed under way, but it was less revolutionary than the heralds of a world-historical moment made it out to be. Viewed from a longer perspective, these changes in the cold war were only adjustments to the structural situation, originally ushered in by the First World War, that was still very much in existence. The disappearance of the old national-based European balance of power, the historical obsolescence of the warfare system among major powers, and the possibility of a global ideological dominion—these were as relevant to détente as they had been to the cold war. Détente promised only a relaxation of tensions stemming from these fundamental causes rather than an end to the underlying problems of structure and ideology. Thus détente was not so much a supersession of ideology as a diplomatic acknowledgment of its limits.

The way in which the remainder of the cold war was conducted made clear that the changes ushered in by détente were subjective and not structural. The emergence of a stable global balance denoted only a modus vivendi that was based not so much on the formation of an objective balance of power as on an inability of both East and West to sustain the ideological fervor that would have been necessary to a continued prosecution of the cold war in the still vulnerable extremities of the world system. In the USSR, a trend toward nuclear caution and bureaucratic conservatism blunted whatever impulse the regime had toward adventurism; in China, the fiasco of the cultural revolution and ominous disagreements with the USSR prompted the regime to reconsider its hostile stance toward the United States; and in America, the insistent application of neo-Wilsonian logic to crises on the periphery produced domestic discord which, had it not been short-circuited by détente, might have drastically altered the American stance toward world affairs. Détente, according to one analyst, was "a means of coping with and compensating for the loss of American will at a time when there were few other options available."[6] But if the danger and America's capacity to deal with it had been reduced, this only meant that the reliance on world opinion, formerly manifest, had now become latent.

Nixon and Kissinger delighted in purveying the perception that they were foreign-policy realists. Yet there would be no reversion to classical realpolitik because they continued to insist, as had their predecessors, on the indispensability of credibility lest the United States become, in Nixon's words, a "pitiful giant." Protestations of realism notwithstanding, the abandonment of Vietnam remained unthinkable from the standpoint of world opinion because of "the damage that would be done to other nations' confidence in our reliability."[7] In the case of the Angolan civil war, where the same rationale was put forth, one observer thought Kissinger's histrionic description of the global danger resulting from a Communist victory sounded like "a parody of Dean Rusk's verbal excesses on Vietnam."[8]

The limited sweep of détente was evident from the major foreign-policy declaration of this era, the Nixon Doctrine. By stating a determination to put into practice a primary responsibility for local self-defense that had always been desired in principle, it amounted to only a minor emendation of the still regnant Wilsonian outlook. On balance, Nixonian realism was hardly a repudiation of cold-war strategy or neo-Wilsonian assumptions in favor of classical realpolitik. Instead, this new prudence on the periphery was intended to assure the continued support of the policy elites and the public for the cold war's central features.

Because détente represented only an attenuation of ideology, it could only lessen the dangers of the cold war without hoping to address their root causes. Not surprisingly, then, when Americans discovered after the limits of U.S.-Soviet cooperation had been reached that ideology still mattered, the palmy days of détente quickly gave way to blustery reassertions of hostility between the two systems. These differences resurfaced quickly enough in a number of issues carried over and revived from the preceding decades. Despite the existence of caps on the number of launchers allowed each side, the state of the nuclear balance generated fears among skeptics that a Soviet superiority in "throw weight" could be used to blackmail the West in crisis situations. The Western alliance continued to experience episodes of fractiousness, particularly with the debate, begun in the late 1970s, over emplacement in Europe of new intermediate-range nuclear missiles. And succeeding administrations continued to express concern at Communist advances in the underdeveloped world in places like Ethiopia, Angola, and Yemen.

But just as the promise of détente's arrival was oversold, the perils accompanying its departure were exaggerated. Because it was rooted in the understanding that modern structural circumstances made aggressive cold-war policies too dangerous, détente possessed an underlying solidity that survived the rekindling of the ideological fires of the U.S.-Soviet relationship. Thus, while the "second cold war" displayed many of the concerns that plagued the first, its threats and crises did not carry the same symbolic resonance or the consequential implications of prior confrontations. The Soviet incursion into Afghanistan in December 1979, as risky a military gambit as attempted by Moscow in the postwar years, elicited only weak Western protests in the form of a boycott of the 1980 Moscow Olympic games (along with a barely disguised determination to arm the anti-Soviet Afghan rebels). Even in the chilliest phase of the Reagan administration's dealings with the "evil empire," the temperature of relations never dropped to the frigid levels of the first cold war.

The cold war ended with a whimper, and not with the bang that Kennan had feared in the 1940s, because world opinion was no longer at stake. Because the feedback linkages had been severed from the formerly wavering vital segments of world opinion, the symbolic crises of Cold War II failed to touch off the kinds of alarms that would have called out the fire department a few years earlier. Detached from the world opinion that in the past would have amplified them to global significance, these crises were largely localized and thereby reduced in importance. With the waning of ideology, it was not so much power politics as the politics of modernization that took over. Like the Congress of Vienna in 1814, attempts at conservative restoration were foredoomed; at most, détente provided a period of stability that allowed the new ideological forces to work themselves out in a relatively peaceful way.

IT HAS BEEN ARGUED that "every rational construction, whether mathematical or rhetorical, when carried through to its 'logical' conclusion, contradicts itself."[9] American cold-war policy was from the beginning contradictory because it was based on the paradoxical need to speak a language of power at a historical moment when time-honored resorts to power were no longer conceivable and when diplomatic discourse across the ideological barricades was impossible. The ruthlessly logical determination to safeguard world opinion by resorting to symbolic interventionism in areas that were, by realistic standards, strategically negligible had always frightened those segments of world opinion it was supposed to reassure. It foundered badly in the 1960s when it began to undermine its foundation in American public opinion.

And yet, despite claims by some that American policy was "unrealistic," that it was based on illusions, and that the threats to the nation were exaggerated, by any pragmatic definition, one must admit that it worked.[10] The truth, says Richard Rorty, is something that helps us get what we want, which American policy certainly managed to do, and not entirely by good fortune. That it did so in a paradoxical fashion is not necessarily to its discredit since any ideology, once put to the test of experience, is bound to generate paradoxes and inconsistencies. Moreover, the crisis of neo-Wilsonianism occurred only at its ideological fringes. Since its central tenets were never brought into question, it was never in danger of being "hollowed out" at the core like its Communist opposite number.[11]

Actually, American cold-war policy, because it incorporated a modernist sensibility, was quite realistic in a sense that eluded exponents of realism, power politics, and interest theories generally. The struggle for world opinion, although it seemed at first sight to reflect an idealistic neo-Hegelian belief in a world spirit, was actually predicated on the belief that such controlling ideas were products of logical fantasy. Wilson and his successors recognized that there was no Cunning of Reason to guarantee automatically the progressive outcome of conflict situations; indeed, they suspected that the supposed rationality behind the balance-of-power concept was phony, a hypostatized extrahuman law of international relations that presumed to regulate the behavior of states and to assure some sort of harmony. In their realization that history was not part of some meta-narrative, that technology and interdependence had made possible civilization's self-destruction as well as its onward march, and that the liberal sensibility in the twentieth century had suffered enormous shocks to its self-confidence, American policymakers cast off their old historicist baggage and sought to take history in hand. They went further still in the direction of modernity by pushing policy in a symbolic direction that, by realizing the futility of using unbounded power to resolve situations, eventually allowed common values to emerge and to predominate.

The ideology might have been largely Americocentric to begin with, but it was not solipsistic. While Wilsonianism was to a degree culture-bound, it also made room for the assimilation of consensual truths regarding the course of modern world history. The cold war at the outset may have resembled the old story about the blind men and the elephant, each touching different portions of the animal's physiognomy and identifying it as something else. But as it continued, it turned into another kind of story that goes beyond the usual stopping point. If we take it a bit further and presume that the men were allowed to communicate, one could reasonably expect them to agree, after some discussion, that they were all touching an elephant. Thus, after a time, did the cold war's ideological blind men arrive at a consensus on their elephant. The ideology contained within itself the possibility for genuine communication, and therefore of self-transformation, that enabled the construction of an indispensable modicum of mutual understanding among the main contestants of the cold war. This openness to understanding was facilitated by the paradoxical quality of neo-Wilsonianism, which brought with it a built-in sense of limits. Unable to push hell-bent in any direction without running into self-defeating difficulties, the ideology could not take itself absolutely seriously, which is perhaps another sign of the inroads made by modernist doubt.

With the collapse of communism and the Soviet Union in 1990, the end of the cold war brought the United States to the close of an ideological and historical cycle. It had come full circle in the course of seventy-five years to an updated version of the pre-Wilsonian world in which the civilized great powers were envisioned as partners cooperating in maintaining law and order throughout the globe and spreading civilization. Viewed from this century-long perspective, Wilsonianism was only a temporary project, an incredibly bumpy detour in which the industrialized core of the world struggled to avoid self-destruction before rejoining the main road of internationalist civilization. That road, the one being paved by intensified commercial and cultural interaction, once again lies unclearly ahead. Like Woodrow Wilson earlier in the century, we are asking questions for which as yet there are no answers.

Victories in real life, like triumphs in athletic contests, provide only a temporary closure to a relentlessly problematic existence that immediately throws forth new challenges as soon as old problems are overcome. Dean Acheson was well aware of that truth when he ventured long ago to predict what the end of the cold war would be like:

> There is not one more river to cross; there are countless problems stretching, into the future . . . Twice before in our history we thought we had come to the ultimate problem . . . So [beyond the cold war] . . . there stretch further problems, problems of dealing with the awakened masses of Africa, problems of dealing with the dwindling supplies of the world and our recklessness in running through them, problems of bringing the very basic knowledge to people which they have to have to keep alive. And we must manage our problems with the Soviet Union so prudently that we do not as great empires have in the past, deal with one great issue only to find ourselves weak, exhausted and powerless to deal with problems which we have not identified but which lie beyond the immediate horizon.[12]

The cold war has been viewed by some as an interlude following which the world's nations would resume their old power political habits. But it was clear to Acheson that, because of modernity, there could be no return to the ways of the past.

Rather than experiencing the end of history or the revival of traditional norms, the United States and the world were simply resuming a civilizational journey started long ago. The kinds of problems mentioned by Acheson, and others not yet envisioned, faced the ideologically spent Soviet Union and United States as they peered into the murky future of the post–cold war era. Like Wilson in the first decade of this century, policymakers anxiously awaited events to clarify and crystallize thought. Whether or not it would take another disaster on the order of the Great War to provide that sort of crystallization, as it had for Wilson, is not for historians to contemplate, but it is likely, the world being what it is, that a conception of civilization alone will not suffice to see the world through. Needed instead is a new synthesis of civilization, power, and world opinion.

ABBREVIATIONS USED
FREQUENTLY IN THE NOTES

AF	Administration File, AWF, DDEPL
AWF	Ann Whitman File, DDEPL
"The Bible"	Compendium of Hoover materials, HHPL
CF	Confidential File
CFF	Country File, France
CFG	Country File, Germany
DAP	Dean Acheson Papers, HSTPL
DAP: MC	Dean Acheson Papers, Memoranda of Conversation, HSTPL
DAP: Yale	Dean Acheson Papers, Sterling Memorial Library, Yale University
DDEPL	Dwight D. Eisenhower Presidential Library, Abiline, KS
DH	Dulles-Herter Series, EP, DDEPL
DS	Diary Series
EP	Dwight D. Eisenhower Papers, DDEPL
FBP	Family, Business, Personal, FDRL
FCC	Family Correspondence, Children, FDRL
FDR: FA	Edgar Nixon et al., *Franklin D. Roosevelt and Foreign Affairs* (vols. 1-3, Cambridge, MA, 1968; vols. 4, New York, 1979)
FDR: PL	Elliott Roosevelt, ed., *Franklin D. Roosevelt: His Personal Letters* (New York, 1950)
FDRL	Franklin D. Roosevelt Presidential Library, Hyde Park, NY
FRUS	*Foreign Relations of the United States*
GCM	General Correspondence and Memoranda Series, JFDP
HHP	Herbert Hoover Papers, HHPL
HHP: C	Commerce, HHP, HHPL
HHPL	Herbert Hoover Presidential Library, West Branch, IA

HSTPL	Harry S. Truman Presidential Library, Independence, MO
JFDP	John Foster Dulles Papers, Mudd Library, Princeton University
JFKPL	John F. Kennedy Presidential Library, Boston, MA
LBJPL	Lyndon B. Johnson Presidential Library, Austin, TX
LHH	Lou Henry Hoover Papers, HHPL
MC	Memoranda of Conversation, JFDP
NIE	National Intelligence Estimate
NS	Name Series, AWF, DDEPL
NSC	National Security Council
NSC- Trilateral	History of the National Security Council, LBJPL
NSF	National Security File
OF	Official File
OH	Oral History (unless noted otherwise, from the presidential library relevant to the chapter where cited)
OSS	Office of the Staff Secretary
PC	Pre-Commerce, HHP, HHPL
PDDE	Louis Galambos, ed., *The Papers of Dwight D. Eisenhower* (Baltimore, 1978)
POF	President's Office Files, JFKPL
PP	Pre-Presidential Papers, DDEPL and JFKPL
PPP	*Public Papers of the Presidents* (Washington, DC, various years)
PPWW- Baker	Ray Stannard Baker, ed., *The Public Papers of Woodrow Wilson* (New York, 1970)
PSF	President's Secretary's File
PWW	Arthur Link, ed., *The Papers of Woodrow Wilson* (Princeton, 1966)
SDPPS	Anna Kasten Nelson, ed., *The State Department Policy Planning Staff Papers, 1947–1949* (New York, 1983)
SS	Subject Series, JFDP
TCM	Telephone Conversations Memoranda, JFDP
WHM	White House Memoranda Series, JFDP

NOTES

Introduction

1. Dean Acheson, panel discussion with George C. Marshall and Francis Russell, 4 June 1947, Dean Acheson Papers, Sterling Memorial Library, Yale University [hereafter DAP: Yale], series 3, box 47.

2. The word "modernization" does not appear in the 1937 edition of *The Encyclopedia of the Social Sciences*. It first shows up in the *International Encyclopedia of the Social Sciences* (New York, 1968), pp. 386–408. For a few seminal treatments of modernization, see Cyril E. Black, *The Dynamics of Modernization* (New York, 1966); Marion J. Levy, Jr., *Modernization and the Structure of Society* (Princeton, 1966); Shmuel Eisenstadt, *Modernization: Protest and Change* (Englewood Cliffs, NJ, 1966); Talcott Parsons, *The Evolution of Societies* (Englewood Cliffs, NJ, 1977). Alfred Weber, "Fundamentals of Culture Sociology," in Talcott Parsons et al., eds., *Theories of Society: Foundations of Modern Sociological Theory* (New York, 1961), vol. 2, still provides an indispensable point of departure for thinking about the relationship between civilizational processes and cultural transformations. For works dealing specifically with modernization and the study of international relations, none of which were very helpful, I am afraid, for this study, see J. P. Nettl and Roland Robertson, *International Systems and the Modernization of Societies: The Formation of National Goals and Attitudes* (London, 1968), especially pp. 129–86; and Edward L. Morse, *Modernization and the Transformation of International Relations* (New York, 1976).

3. Sociology as a discipline was only getting under way at this time, while modernization as a successor concept to civilization would not be fully articulated until the 1950s. Although many would no doubt disagree, I would maintain that the modernization concept was simply a cleaned-up version of civilization, the main differences being dehistoricization, a much greater degree of conceptual differentiation and refinement, and a none-too-successful attempt at value neutrality by sweeping progress, democracy, and westernization under the rug.

4. Robert Hughes, *The Shock of the New* (New York, 1981).

5. Walter Lippmann, *Drift and Mastery* (Englewood Cliffs, NJ, 1961), p. 151.

6. Alasdair MacIntyre, *After Virtue: A Study in Moral Theory* (Notre Dame, IN, 1981), p. 25.

7. Paul Ricoeur, *Lectures on Ideology and Utopia* (New York, 1986), p. 198.

8. Anthony Giddens, *The Nation-State and Violence* (Berkeley, 1985), pp. 31–35.

9. For a good example of the sense of international possibility born of this sense of radical historical discontinuity, see George S. Morison, *The New Epoch as Developed by the Manufacture of Power* (Boston, 1903), pp. 55–60. However, operating from a discontinuist frame does not necessarily ensure that international relations will be treated in an unconventional way. For example, see R. A. Buchanan, *History and Industrial Civilization* (New York, 1979), pp. 122–34.

10. Samuel P. Huntington, "The Change to Change," *International Politics* (April 1971): 283–322.

11. David Levin, *Forms of Uncertainty: Essays in Historical Criticism* (Charlottesville, 1992), pp. 36, 55–56.

12. As a rather extreme expression of the modern outlook has it: "cultural change may be expected to continue accelerating, compared to rates of genetic evolution. This divergence, I believe, will make it increasingly difficult to interpret current human behavior in terms of history." Richard D. Alexander, *Darwinism and Human Affairs* (Seattle, 1979), pp. 77–78. This argument that there are no lessons to be learned from the past does not mean, however, that historical understanding is outmoded. After all, Alexander's observation is itself a product of historical insight.

13. Not completely different, however. As we shall see, even in the new environment, statesmen afflicted by linguistic lag would continue to make reference to the balance of power. For a useful analysis of the limitations and uses of balance-of-power thinking in explaining policy, see William Curti Wohlforth, *The Elusive Balance* (Ithaca, NY, 1993), pp. 293–307.

14. I would agree that the idea of world opinion is highly problematic, yet at the same time casual dismissals of the concept fail to explain why so obvious an illusion should have had such a powerful hold on Americans—including tough-minded cold warriors. Although this work, which focuses on world opinion as part of American ideology, is not the place to argue the issue in detail, the point is worth making nevertheless: it stands to reason as a matter of logic that something like a world opinion *must* exist as a mental counterpart to the structural realities in the world. At a minimum, it may exist only in an additive sense as the sum total of a chaotic pluralism; under a balance-of-power regime, it would consist of shared understandings concerning rules of the game; it could also include common conceptions of global history and civilizational destinies. The extreme communitarian possibility would be a global culture. For Hegelians, it could be a world spirit. My point here is simply that if one talks of a global structure or civilization, one must talk also of global consciousness, in whatever form.

15. Kenneth Burke, *Attitudes Toward History,* 3d ed. (Berkeley, 1984), pp. 3–44. Hans-Georg Gadamer's *Truth and Method,* trans. Garrett Barden and John Cumming (New York, 1975), is the philosophical work most responsible for promoting the now

widely held view that human beings, in trying to understand the world, are engaged in hermeneutic interpretation as a first-order activity.

16. Sally Falk Moore, "Epilogue: Uncertainties in Situations, Indeterminacies in Culture," in *Symbol and Politics in Communal Ideology,* ed. Sally Falk Moore and Barbara G. Meyerhoff (Ithaca, 1975), p. 219.

17. Michael Fry, ed., *History, the White House and the Kremlin: Statesmen as Historians* (London, 1991), p. 2. This insight accords quite well with the Weberian approach to ideology and its emphasis on the role of "evaluative ideas" in reconstructing "the empirically given." See Lawrence A. Scaff, *Fleeing the Iron Cage: Culture, Politics, and Modernity in the Thought of Max Weber* (Berkeley, 1989), p. 77.

18. David Carr, "Narrative and the Real World: An Argument for Continuity," *History and Theory* 25 (1986): 125. In *Time, Narrative, and History* (Bloomington, IN, 1986), p. 9, Carr argues that "narrative structure pervades our very experience of time and social existence, independently of our contemplating the past as historians."

19. I should note here that the interpretive historical approach employed by these statesmen is in essence no different from the hermeneutic approach that I am using to study them. Just as they rejected traditional criteria of power and interest, my conceptual standpoint in this work departs from the objectivist approaches to the study of foreign policy that have dominated the field of diplomatic history. My general ideas on these points and my critique of traditional interest-derived approaches have been spelled out in an essay, "Interests and Discourse in Diplomatic History," *Diplomatic History* 13 (Spring 1989): 135–61, so there is no need to belabor them here. If we use Gerald Coombs's tripartite division of the profession in *Nationalist, Realist, and Radical: Three Views of American Diplomacy* (New York, 1972), I would put myself squarely in the nationalist pigeonhole. (Better yet is the trichotomy offered by an anonymous reader of this manuscript: power, political economy, and ideology/ culture.) But while hermeneutics presupposes a degree of sympathetic understanding between the historian and his object of study, a melding that Hans-Georg Gadamer called a "fusion of horizons" *(Horizontverschmelzung),* my approach is not particularly celebratory or apologetic. By the same token, it is not critical in the prosecutorial way that many works, informed by different paradigms, can be.

20. George Lakoff and Mark Johnson, *Metaphors We Live By* (Chicago, 1980), p. 14.

21. Max Black, "More About Metaphor," in Andrew Ortony, ed., *Metaphor and Thought* (New York, 1979), p. 31. Another view of metaphor sees it as "the linguistic means by which we bring together and fuse into a unity diverse thoughts and thereby re-form our perceptions of the world." See Eva Feder Kittay, *Metaphor: Its Cognitive Force and Linguistic Structure* (Oxford, 1987), p. 6.

22. John Lewis Gaddis, "Toward the Post–Cold War World," *Foreign Affairs* (Spring 1991): 120.

23. See, e.g., the argument of Douglas J. Macdonald in "The Truman Administration and Global Responsibilities: The Birth of the Falling Domino Principle," in *Dominoes and Bandwagons: Strategic Beliefs and Great Power Competition in the Eurasian Rimland*, ed. Robert Jervis and Jack Snyder (New York, 1991), pp. 112–44, that the domino principle was born in the Truman years.

24. Ernest May, "The Nature of Foreign Policy: The Calculated and the Axiomatic," *Daedalus* 91 (Fall 1962): 653–67. More properly, it is a history of *paradigms* or intellectual scaffoldings. "Axioms" suggests a timelessness and universality that the underlying assumptions in question did not possess. On this distinction, see Stephen Toulmin, *Cosmopolis* (New York, 1990), p. 116. Robert Beisner, *From the Old Diplomacy to the New, 1865–1900* (Arlington Heights, IL, 1975), is one of the few works in diplomatic history to take up the idea of paradigm shifts elaborated by Thomas Kuhn's *The Structure of Scientific Revolutions* (Chicago, 1970). My qualified disagreement with May's view that cold-war decisions are explainable by axioms that are learned a posteriori, through experience, will be taken up in chapter 7.

25. Martin Seliger, *Ideology and Politics* (New York, 1976); Rosa Mayreder, *Der typische Verlauf sozialer Bewegungen* (Vienna, 1917); Theodore J. Lowi, *The Politics of Disorder* (New York, 1971), pp. 32–51; Charles Tilly, *Big Structures, Large Processes, Huge Comparisons* (New York, 1984); Alexander Gerschenkron, *Continuity in History and Other Essays* (Cambridge, MA, 1968). But see also Bertrand Russell, *Power: A New Social Analysis* (New York, 1962), p. 57: "Organizations that have a long career of power pass, as a rule, through three phases: first, that of fanatical but not traditional belief, leading to conquest; then, that of general acquiescence in the new power which rapidly becomes traditional; and finally that in which power, being now used against those who reject tradition, has again become naked." A number of other sociological works bear insights into the generally conservative trajectories of ideologies as a result of their institutionalization, among them Robert Michels's concept of the "iron law of oligarchy" in *Political Parties* (New York, 1968); and Max Weber's "the routinization of charisma," in *Economy and Society*, ed. Guenther Roth and Klaus Wittich (Berkeley, 1978), pp. 246–54.

26. This book follows the general argument of John Lewis Gaddis, *The Long Peace: Inquiries into the History of the Cold War* (New York, 1987); and John Mueller, *Retreat from Doomsday: the Obsolescence of Major War* (New York, 1989), which is to say that it sees American foreign policy in the post–World War II period largely as a success story, although it follows its own peculiar logic and argument.

CHAPTER 1

1. Virginia Woolf, "Mr. Bennett and Mrs. Brown," in *The Captain's Death Bed and Other Essays* (New York, 1956), p. 96.

2. My use of the term "modernity" is intended to encompass both sociological modernization and cultural modernism. Modernism has no standard definition, although the following are among its most obvious features: a move away from realistic representation in art and sculpture; the abandonment of tonality in music; the growing

acceptance of relativity and indeterminacy in science; the rejection of traditional and organically situated architectural form; the questioning of objectivism in philosophy; the related interest in language and the growing understanding that it was in large measure nonreferential. The modernity of American foreign policy, which featured a shift away from realism and objectivism in favor of abstract interpretation, blends well with these cultural trends. However, sociology must be given its due. Unlike some extreme exponents of modernism, I do not believe that political symbols can be wholly independent of external reality or that they are causally determinative. On this point, see Robert Pranger, *Action, Symbolism, and Order: The Existential Dimension of Politics in Modern Citizenship* (Nashville, TN, 1968), p. 138.

For a good discussion of definitions, see Mike Featherstone, *Consumer Culture and Postmodernism* (London, 1991), pp. 1–12. For models of modernism, see Norman F. Cantor, *Twentieth-Century Culture: Modernism to Deconstruction* (New York, 1988), pp. 35–41; and Matei Calinescu, *Five Faces of Modernity: Modernism, Avant-Garde, Decadence, Kitsch, Postmodernism* (Durham, 1987). On the reorientation of cultural forms during this period, see Stephen Kern, *The Culture of Space and Time, 1890–1918* (Cambridge, MA, 1983); and Donald M. Lowe, *History of Bourgeois Perception* (Chicago, 1982).

3. Bradford Perkins, *The Great Rapprochement: England and the United States, 1895–1914* (New York, 1968); John Lewis Gaddis, *Russia, the Soviet Union, and the United States* (New York, 1978), pp. 27–56; Edward Zabriskie, *American-Russian Rivalry in the Far East: A Study in Diplomacy and Power Politics* (Westport, CT, 1976); Akira Iriye, *Pacific Estrangement* (Cambridge, MA, 1972); Charles Neu, *Troubled Encounter: The United States and Japan* (New York, 1975); Holger Herwig, *Politics of Frustration: The United States in German Naval Planning 1889–1941* (Boston, 1976), pp. 13–109; Manfred Jonas, *The United States and Germany: A Diplomatic History* (Ithaca, 1984), pp. 35–64; Akira Iriye, *Across the Pacific: An Inner History of American East-Asian Relations* (New York, 1967), pp. 111–30.

4. Burke, *Attitudes Toward History,* pp. 3–44.

5. Howard K. Beale, *Theodore Roosevelt and the Rise of America to World Power* (New York, 1970), p. 383. See also the similar judgments of Robert Osgood, *Ideals and Self-Interest in America's Foreign Relations* (Chicago, 1953), pp. 67, 85; Frederick Marks, *Velvet on Iron: The Diplomacy of Theodore Roosevelt* (Lincoln, NE, 1979); William C. Widenor, *Henry Cabot Lodge and the Search for an American Foreign Policy* (Berkeley, CA, 1980), p. 164; John Morton Blum, *The Republican Roosevelt* (New York, 1974), p. 126; and Charles E. Neu, "1906–1913," in *American–East Asian Relations: A Survey,* ed. Ernest R. May and James C. Thomson, Jr. (Cambridge, MA, 1972), p. 160. Even Richard Collin's revisionist cultural interpretation asserts that "Roosevelt clearly believed in the balance of power concept." Richard Collin, *Theodore Roosevelt, Culture, Diplomacy, and Expansion* (Baton Rouge, LA, 1985), p. 101.

6. Elihu Root, "Roosevelt's Conduct of Foreign affairs," in *The Works of Theodore Roosevelt,* national edition, ed. Hermann Hagedorn (New York, 1925) 16: xiii, xx. Lewis Einstein, *Roosevelt: His Mind in Action* (Boston, 1930), p. 31.

7. TR to Henry Cabot Lodge, 4 December 1902, *An Autobiography* (New York, 1919), p. 241; TR to Frederick Scott Oliver, 9 August 1906, in *The Letters of Theodore Roosevelt*, ed. Elting E. Morison (Cambridge, MA, 1951) 5: 351.

8. Fritz Stern, *The Varieties of History* (New York, 1972), p. 18, suggests that history was to the nineteenth century what ideology would be for the twentieth.

9. Alexis de Tocqueville, *Democracy in America*, trans. Henry Reeve (New Rochelle, NY, 1966) 2: 158; TR, "History as Literature," *Works*, 12: 7; TR to John St. Loe Strachey, 22 February 1907, *Letters*, 5: 596; TR, "Social Evolution," *Works*, 1: 223.

10. TR, "The World Movement," *Works*, 12: 71. TR, "Biological Analogies in History," *Works*, 12: 37. For the fin-de-siècle beginning of the end of the myth of two worlds, see David Noble, *The End of American History* (Minneapolis, 1985), p. 4.

11. TR, "The World Movement," *Works*, 12: 79; TR to Alfred Thayer Mahan, 13 December 1897, *Letters*, 1: 741; David H. Burton, *Theodore Roosevelt: Confident Imperialist* (Philadelphia, 1969), pp. 63ff.

12. TR to Cecil Spring Rice, 5 August 1896, *Letters*, 1: 554.

13. See Theodore von Laue, *The World Revolution of Westernization* (New York, 1987), p. 36.

14. Herbert Croly, *The Promise of American Life* (Indianapolis, 1965), p. 311. For the traditional view of imperialism as an outgrowth and extension of European politics in which global modernization was not factored into statesmen's calculations, see William L. Langer, *The Diplomacy of Imperialism* (New York, 1972), p. 96. On the civilizing function of imperialism for Roosevelt, see Frank Ninkovich, "Theodore Roosevelt: Civilization as Ideology," *Diplomatic History* 10 (Summer 1986): 221–45.

15. Paul Reinsch, *World Politics at the End of the Nineteenth Century* (New York, 1908), p. 254; Croly, *The Promise of American Life*, pp. 311–12. A view of imperialism from the "broader perspective of world history" informs the more recent interpretation of Geoffrey Barraclough, *An Introduction to Contemporary History* (New York, 1967), pp. 107–8ff.

16. TR, "National Duties," *Works*, 13: 478.

17. TR to Joseph James Walsh, 23 February 1909, *Letters*, 6: 1535; TR, "National Life and Character," *Works*, 13: 216; TR to Henry Fairfield Osborn, 21 December 1908, *Works*, 6: 1435; William Henry Harbaugh, *Power and Responsibility* (New York, 1961), p. 99.

The post facto enthronement of Darwinism as a political ideology in the United States was performed by Richard Hofstadter, *Social Darwinism in American Thought* (Philadelphia, 1944). On Roosevelt's alleged Darwinism, see among others, Blum, *The Republican Roosevelt*, p. 25; Perkins, *The Great Rapprochement*, p. 104; Peter Conn, *The Divided Mind: Ideology and Imagination in America, 1898–1917* (New York, 1983), p. 9. For a revisionist work that squarely denies the existence at any time of a Social Darwinist consensus within the United States, see Robert C. Bannister, *Social Darwinism: Science and Myth in Anglo-American Social Thought* (Philadelphia, 1979), pp. 11–13, 33. Peter J. Bowler, *The Eclipse of Darwinism: Anti-Darwinian Evolution Theories in the Decade around 1900* (Baltimore, 1975), p. 75, sees the 1890s as "the heyday of the new Lamarckian optimism." George Stocking, *Race, Culture, and Evolution: Essays in the History of Anthropology* (New York, 1968), p. 256, is especially good on the cultural bias of Lamarckism and its double-edged possibilities. For a corrective that nevertheless stresses the racial side of TR's Lamarckianism, see Thomas G. Dyer, *Theodore Roosevelt and the Idea of Race* (Baton Rouge, LA, 1980), pp. 21–24. If the mechanism of biological evolution is Darwinian while that of cultural transmission is essentially Lamarckian, by the standards of his time—and ours as well— Roosevelt was a believer in cultural evolution. Indeed, culture and civilization meant pretty much the same thing during his day.

18. Thomas F. Gossett, *Race: The History of an Idea in America* (Dallas, TX, 1963), p. 63. For views that emphasize race at the expense of culture, see Michael Hunt, *Ideology and U.S. Foreign Policy* (New Haven, 1987), pp. 46–91; George W. Shepherd, Jr., *The Study of Race in American Foreign Policy* (Denver, CO, 1970), p. 3; Rubin Francis Weston, *Racism in U.S. Imperialism: The Influence of Racial Assumptions on U.S. Foreign Policy 1893–1946* (Columbia, SC, 1972), p. 35.

19. TR to Henry Fairfield Osborn, 21 December 1908, *Letters*, 6: 1435.

20. TR to Alfred Thayer Mahan, 11 December 1897, *Letters*, 1: 741. Roosevelt also tried to make imperialism palatable by suggesting, in sophistical fashion, that it was a natural outgrowth of America's continental expansion (a point hotly contested by an aging generation of anti-imperialists precisely on the basis of conservative historical arguments) and that it was consistent with the Federalist foreign-policy tradition to which he paid profuse public homage. See Robert Beisner, *Twelve Against Empire: The Anti-Imperialists 1898–1900* (New York, 1971), pp. 220–22.

21. TR, paper delivered before the American Sociological Congress, 31 December 1914, in William H. Harbaugh, ed., *The Writings of Theodore Roosevelt* (Indianapolis, IN, 1967), p. 357.

22. TR to Henry White, 12 August 1906, *Letters*, 5: 359. See also Croly, *The Promise of American Life*, p. 261; TR to Carl Schurz, 8 September 1905, *Letters*, 5: 17; TR, *Presidential Addresses and State Papers* (New York, 1970) 2: 174. On the power differential resulting from the industrialization of warfare, see Daniel R. Headrick, *The Tools of Empire: Technology and European Imperialism in the Nineteenth Century* (New York, 1981).

23. TR to John Davis Long, 23 June and 30 September 1897, *Letters*, 1: 631, 695; TR to editors of the *Harvard Crimson*, 2 June 1896, *Letters*, 1: 505; TR, "Washington's Maxim," *Works*, 13: 192; TR to James Clarkson, 22 April 1893, *Letters*, 1: 313.

24. TR to Albert Shaw, 26 December 1902, *Letters*, 3: 397; TR, "The Monroe Doctrine," *Works*, 13: 169; TR to William Astor Chandler, 23 December 1897, *Letters*, 1: 746; TR to Mahan, 3 May 1897, *Letters*, 1: 607–8; Richard Hofstadter, *The Paranoid Style in American Politics and Other Essays* (New York, 1967), p. 178.

25. Croly, *The Promise of American Life,* p. 297.

26. TR to William Sheffield Cowles, 11 February 1896, *Letters,* 1: 512; TR to Spring Rice, 24 July 1905, *Letters,* 3: 1286; TR, "The Monroe Doctrine," *Works,* 13: 168.

27. TR, "The Monroe Doctrine," *Works,* 13: 172.

28. Richard D. Challener, *Admirals, Generals, and American Foreign Policy 1898–1914* (Princeton, NJ, 1973), pp. 17–18; TR to Hermann Speck von Sternberg, 11 October 1901, *Letters,* 3: 172; TR to Root, 2 June 1904, *Letters,* 4: 811.

29. TR to Spring Rice, 20 July 1900, *Letters,* 2: 1359; TR to George Ferdinand Becker, 8 July 1901, *Letters,* 3: 112; TR to Spring Rice, 2 January 1900, *Letters,* 2: 1128; TR to Spring Rice, 5 August 1896, *Letters,* 1: 555; TR, "The Awakening of China," *Works,* 16: 286–87.

30. TR to Lodge, 16 June 1905, *Lodge-Roosevelt Correspondence: Selections from the Correspondence of Theodore Roosevelt and Henry Cabot Lodge, 1884–1918* (New York, 1925), p. 153; TR to George Otto Trevelyan, 12 September 1905, *Letters,* 5: 22.

31. TR to John Hay, 26 July 1904, *Letters,* 4: 865; TR to Spring Rice, 1 July 1907, *Letters,* 5: 698.

32. TR to Spring Rice, 19 March 1904, *Letters,* 4: 760; Roosevelt, "National Life and Character," *Works,* 13: 214.

33. TR to Spring Rice, 27 December 1904, *Letters,* 4: 1085, 1087.

34. TR to William Howard Taft, 31 May 1905, *Letters,* 4: 1198; TR to Strachey, 21 December 1906, *Letters,* 5: 532; TR to Sir Edward Grey, 18 December 1906, *Letters,* 5: 528; TR to Kentaro Kaneko, 23 August 1905, *Letters,* 5: 4; TR to Andrew D. White, 2 November 1914, *Letters,* 8: 827; TR to Root, 14 September 1905, *Letters,* 5: 26. See also TR to George Kennan, 15 October 1905, *Letters,* 5: 57. Raymond A. Esthus, *Theodore Roosevelt and Japan* (Seattle, WA, 1966), p. 76.

35. TR, "Expansion and Peace," *Works,* 13: 335–36; TR to Whitelaw Reid, 7 August 1906, *Letters,* 5: 348; Address of 5 May 1910 in Harbaugh, *The Writings of Theodore Roosevelt,* pp. 371–74.

36. TR to Spring Rice, 13 August 1897, *Letters,* 1: 645, 647; TR to Strachey, 22 February 1907, *Letters,* 5: 596.

37. TR to Root, 29 January 1900, *Letters,* 2: 1151. See Beale, *Theodore Roosevelt and the Rise to World Power,* p. 382, for Roosevelt's contention that, should Britain fail to do so, "the United States would be obliged to step in, at least temporarily, in order to restore the balance of power in Europe." Apart from the fact that it is totally out of character, the source is second-hand, from a conversation allegedly reported word-for-word (*wortlich*) in Hermann von Eckardstein, *Lebenserrinerungen und politischen Denkwürdigkeiten,* vol. 3, *Die Isolierung Deutschlands* (Leipzig, 1921), p. 175.

38. TR to Spring Rice, 27 December 1904, *Letters,* 4: 1084; Raymond Esthus, *Theodore Roosevelt and the International Rivalries* (Waltham, MA, 1970), pp. 2–3.

39. TR to Jacob Gould Schurman, 25 July 1904, *Letters,* 3: 865; TR to Andrew D. White, 2 November 1914, *Letters,* 8: 827.

40. TR to Strachey, 22 February 1915, *Letters,* 8: 903; TR to Sir Edward Grey, 22 January 1915, *Letters,* 8: 876; TR to Spring Rice, 18 February 1915, *Letters,* 8: 891; TR to Raymond Robins, 3 June 1915, *Letters,* 8: 928. William Harbaugh, "Theodore Roosevelt," in Warren F. Kuehl, *Biographical Dictionary of Internationalists* (Westport, CT, 1983), p. 633, emphasizes TR's "instinct for *Realpolitik*" during the war. By contrast, John Milton Cooper, Jr., *The Warrior and the Priest* (Cambridge, MA, 1983), pp. 276–86, comes closer to the mark in stressing TR's wartime internationalism.

41. TR, "An International Posse Comitatus," *New York Times,* 29 November 1914.

42. TR to Arthur Lee, 22 August 1914, *Letters,* 7: 813; TR to James Bryce, 31 March 1915, *Letters,* 8: 918.

43. Cannon quoted in Donald F. Anderson, *William Howard Taft* (Ithaca, NY, 1973), p. 201.

44. According to Widenor, *Lodge,* p. 149, Roosevelt's "highly personal solution" to modern American foreign policy was "attested to by the fact that it did not survive him."

45. Taft speech, "McKinley and Expansion," 29 January 1908, Papers of William Howard Taft, Library of Congress (microfilm edition) [hereafter Taft Papers]; Address by Taft, "McKinley and Expansion," 29 January 1908, Taft Papers; Knox speech to National Civic Federation, 11 December 1911, Philander Knox Papers, Library of Congress Manuscript Division, box 45.

46. John P. Campbell, "Taft, Roosevelt, and the Arbitration Treaties of 1911," *Journal of American History* 53 (1966): 296. The old Spencerian distinction would find its way into numerous twentieth-century definitions of modernization, as for example in Harold Lasswell's contention that "*unrestricted* pursuit of power is not an acceptable component of a developed national state." See Harold Lasswell, "The Policy Sciences of Development," *World Politics* 17 (January 1965): 292.

47. Toast and address by Taft to Japanese commissioners and the nearly identical toast by Knox to Japanese commercial commissioners, 15 November 1909, Taft Papers. Cf. the comment found in *Journal of Commerce and Commercial Bulletin,* 24 May 1911, Knox Papers: "Seeing that international politics today turns chiefly on questions of trade, diplomacy is necessarily compelled to be commercial in its aims and methods."

48. From a 1912 speech of Willard Straight, quoted in Henry Pringle, *The Life and Times of William Howard Taft* (New York, 1939), pp. 682–83.

49. Lippmann, *Drift and Mastery,* p. 97.

50. Knox speech draft [1911?], Knox Papers, box 45; Knox to Huntington Wilson, 20 May 1910, Knox Papers, box 28.

51. Knox speeches of 11 December 1909, 21 September 1912, and 11 December

1909, all in Knox Papers. See also Akira Iriye, *From Nationalism to Internationalism* (London, 1977), p. 214.

52. Knox speech, "International Unity," 11 December 1909, Knox Papers.

53. Address by Taft, delivered before the Society for Judicial Settlement of International Disputes, Cincinnati, 7 November 1911, Taft Papers; Taft, address to New Haven Republican Club, February 7, 1908, Taft Papers. Joseph Schumpeter, "The Sociology of Imperialism," in *Imperialism and Social Classes: Two Essays* (New York, 1955), pp. 64–65.

54. Taft speech, 2 May 1910, Knox Papers, letterbook no. 10. Quotation from Max Weber's *Wirtschaft und Gesellschaft*, p. 31, as cited in Talcott Parsons, *The Structure of Social Action* (New York, 1949), p. 654.

55. Address by Huntington Wilson, 4 May 1911, Knox Papers, letterbook no. 14; Knox speech, 19 January 1912, Knox Papers, box 46; "Rough Notes on Honduras Loan," February 1911, Knox Papers, letterbook no. 13; Knox, "The Spirit and Purpose of American Diplomacy," 15 June 1910, Knox Papers, box 45. Dollar diplomacy also pointed to the future, as attested to by the periodic bouts of concern for Latin American development shown by American diplomacy for the remainder of the century.

56. Taft Papers. Taft message to Congress, 3 December 1912, Taft Papers.

57. As quoted in V. I. Lenin, *Imperialism: The Highest Stage of Capitalism* (New York, 1939), p. 117.

58. Taft to Thomas F. Millard, 13 April 1909, Taft Papers; Knox to Senator Fred Hale, 28 July 1909, Taft Papers; Knox to Senator Hale of Committee of Appropriations, 28 July 1909, Taft Papers.

59. Charles Morris, *Man and His Ancestors* (New York, 1900), p. 194, as quoted in John S. Haller, Jr., *Outcasts from Evolution: Scientific Attitudes of Racial Inferiority* (Urbana, IL, 1971), p. 152.

60. Taft, Shanghai speech, 7 October 1907, Taft Papers; Taft address, "Christian Missions and Civilization," at Carnegie Hall, April 1908, Taft Papers.

61. Knox to H. M. Hoyt, 8 October 1909, Knox Papers; Knox speech, 11 December 1909, Knox Papers, box 45.

62. Knox Papers, scrapbooks, box 61.

63. Memo, "The Chinese Loan," 30 September 1909, Knox Papers, letterbook no. 7; Bound mimeo, "Chinese Railway and Currency Loans" [1909], ibid.; Knox speech, undelivered, probably 1910, Knox Papers.

64. Knox speech, undelivered, probably 1910. Knox Papers.

65. Undated memo by W. E. Smith, Taft Papers; Knox to W. W. Rockhill, 9 November 1909, Knox Papers, box 42.

66. Rockhill to Knox, 24 January 1910, Knox Papers, box 42.

67. Knox to Taft, 19 December 1910, Taft Papers; TR to Taft, 22 December 1910, Taft Papers.

68. TR to Knox, 8 February 1909, TR, *Letters*, 6: 1514; Taft speech defending Knox [May 1910], Knox Papers.

69. Suggested reply to TR's letter of 22 December 1910, Taft Papers.

70. William Reynolds Braisted, *The United States Navy in the Pacific 1909–1922* (Austin, TX, 1971), pp. 10–12, 34. Memo by RSM (Miller?), 19 September 1910, Knox Papers, letterbook no. 11; Taft, address to Lowell Board of Trade, 19 February 1908, Taft Papers; Taft to James Bronson Reynolds, 10 September 1907, Taft Papers; Knox speech, Asiatic Association, New York City, 25 April 1911, Knox Papers, box 45.

71. Memo by Knox, 23 August 1909, Knox Papers, box 27; Knox to Taft, 26 August 1909, Knox Papers, box 26; Taft to TR, 17 January 1911, Taft Papers. Taft to TR, 22 March 1911, Taft Papers. Michael Hunt in *The Making of a Special Relationship* (New York, 1983), p. 212, suggests that the administration refused to rule out "an eventual appeal to arms." For an opposing view that minimizes American interests, see Warren Cohen, *America's Response to China* (New York, 1980), p. 84.

72. Memorandum by Einstein, "The New American Policy in China" [October 1911?], Knox Papers, letterbook no. 15.

73. Einstein to Knox, 17 October 1910, Knox Papers, letterbook no. 11; J. E. Bashford to Taft, 8 May 1911, Knox Papers, letterbook no. 14. The logic was impeccable, but it failed to foresee the emergence in the 1920s of an aggressive Chinese nationalism which, while lacking the power to force the Japanese out, was nevertheless aggressive enough to frighten the Japanese into consolidating their position.

74. As late as September 1910, the Department failed to anticipate "any serious uprising in China in the near future." Huntington Wilson to Secretary of the Navy, 15 September 1910, Knox Papers, box 43.

75. Knox speeches, "The Chinese Republic" [1912?], Knox Papers, box 46.

76. *Washington Post,* 12 February 1913; Memo, R. S. Miller to Knox, 19 June 1911, Knox Papers, box 10; Draft of a letter from Knox to N. W. Bishop, 26 February 1913, Taft Papers. In what proved to be a remarkably poor bit of forecasting, Miller predicted that "as the years go on, [it] will become as famous and as much honored in diplomatic history as is the 'Open Door' policy proclaimed by Mr. Hay."

77. Memo in Knox Papers, letterbook no. 20; Essay by Einstein, "The Chinese Revolution and American Policy," May 1912, Knox Papers, letterbook no. 18. See also Einstein, "The Future of the American Foreign Service," May 1912, in ibid.

78. Akira Iriye, *After Imperialism: The Search for a New Order in The Far East, 1921–1933* (New York, 1969), p. 14.

79. E. James Hindman, "The General Arbitration Treaties of William Howard Taft," *Historian* 36 (November 1973): 552–65. A good example of this widespread belief among historians in Taft's inconsistency is found in Thomas H. Buckley and Edwin B. Strong, Jr., *American Foreign and National Security Policies, 1914–1945* (Knoxville, TN, 1987), p. 5: "It is one of the paradoxes of American history that

Americans, during the late nineteenth century and after, were more willing to cooperate with the political goals of the European powers in East Asia, where American interests were minor, than in Europe, where American interests were major."

80. Taft, address of 15 April 1911, Taft Papers.

81. Andrew Carnegie to Knox, 28 March 1911, Knox Papers, letterbook no. 14.

82. Taft address of 11 and 15 August 1911, Taft Papers. Taft found a sympathetic comrade across the Atlantic in the figure of the British Foreign Secretary, Sir Edward Grey, who concurred in the lunacy of militarism in the modern age. "The great nations of the world are in bondage . . . to their armies and navies," he told Parliament, "[and] all the time they have been in bondage to this expenditure, the prison door has been locked on the inside." *Parliamentary Debates,* 13 March 1911, p. 1998.

83. Taft to Charlie Taft, 3 August 1911, Taft Papers. Grey also hoped that once the force of example had come into play, it "would have a real effect upon expenditures on armaments and the 'morale' of international politics." See Grey to James Bryce, enclosure Bryce to Knox, 12 April 1911, Knox Papers, letterbook no. 14; William Howard Taft, *The United States and Peace* (New York, 1914), p. 128.

84. Speech by Knox before the International Peace and Arbitration League, 6 May 1909, Taft Papers.

85. *Parliamentary Debates,* 13 March 1911, p. 1976.

86. According to Taft, this provision was not intended to take away the Senate's constitutional powers. "Nobody with any sense ever thought it was." Taft to Horace Taft, 13 January 1912, Taft Papers. Knox insisted that "the decision of the commission does not bind the Senate. It binds the executive." Knox notes, no. 14, Knox Papers.

87. Taft to Knox, 18 December 1913, Knox Papers.

CHAPTER 2

1. George Kennan, *American Diplomacy 1900–1950* (Chicago, 1951), p. 64.

2. In assessing Wilson's intellectual legacy, scholars tend to divide over the question of whether Wilson was an idealist or an ideological interventionist. Those who view him as a visionary tend to believe that he had little lasting impact, albeit from contrasting normative points of view. John Milton Cooper, Jr., in *The Warrior and the Priest,* p. 356, argues that, as a practical matter, Wilson was irrelevant except as "an example to be shunned," while realists like George F. Kennan in *American Diplomacy 1900–1950* and Robert E. Osgood in *Ideals and Self-Interest in America's Foreign Relations* (Chicago, 1953) believed that a revival of his idealism would prove dangerous to American policy, hoping all the while that the United States had outgrown it. In contrast, Wilson's biographer, Arthur Link, in *Woodrow Wilson: Revolution, War, and Peace* (Arlington Heights, IL, 1979), p. 128, laments the failure of the great powers to keep alive the faith. He suggests that Wilson's dreams, had they been realized, could have prevented the Second World War and the cold war, but

that is to make Wilson a prophet without honor. This interpretive tradition has most recently been revived by Thomas K. Knock, *To End All Wars: Woodrow Wilson and the Quest for a New World Order* (Princeton, 1992), especially pp. 271–76. Those who do perceive a continuing relevance find it in Wilson's pioneering interventionism. N. Gordon Levin, *Woodrow Wilson and World Politics* (New York, 1968), p. 260, contends that Wilson "established the main drift toward an American liberal globalism" by his opposition to imperialism and Leninism; while Lloyd Gardner, in *A Covenant with Power* (New York, 1984), argues that Wilson intervened in World War I to preserve the legitimacy of a liberal world order threatened by revolution. Lloyd Ambrosius, *Woodrow Wilson and the American Diplomatic Tradition* (New York, 1987), p. 294, draws a straight line from Wilsonian collective security to the intervention in Vietnam. Then there are those who, like Frederick S. Calhoun, *Power and Principle: Armed Intervention in Wilsonian Foreign Policy* (Kent, OH, 1986), p. 265, argue that Wilson continued to set a standard in terms of both force and ideals. Though there is much to be said for both lines of analysis, this chapter leans toward the second approach by suggesting that his enduring legacy is to be found in some neglected but seminal ideas, whose historical modernism have not been given their due, rather than in his outdated policies.

3. Richard Rorty, *Contingency, Irony, Solidarity* (New York, 1989), p. 91.

4. "Democracy and Efficiency" [c. 1 October 1900], in Arthur Link, ed., *The Papers of Woodrow Wilson* (Princeton, 1966–), 12: 18 [hereafter cited as *PWW*]. On Wilson's pre-presidential understanding of foreign policy, see Cooper, *The Warrior and the Priest*, p. 266. The phrase is from Anthony Giddens, *The Consequences of Modernity* (Stanford, CA, 1990), p. 21, who argues that modernity implies a "radical historicity." A standard dating system, a standard global time, and a mapping and exploration of the globe's remaining crevices provided a "unitary past" and present.

5. Croly, *The Promise of American Life*, p. 261; News report of an address in Montclair, NJ [28 January 1904], *PWW* 15: 143; Reinsch, *World Politics*, p. 257; News report of a political address in Plainfield, NJ, "A Chance for the Democrats" [30 October 1909], *PWW* 19: 464.

6. News report of an address to the University Club of St. Louis [29 April 1903], *PWW* 14: 433.

7. Report of a speech on patriotism in Waterbury, CT [14 December 1899], *PWW* 11: 298; Address at Pottstown [25 February 1899], *PWW* 11: 107; News report of an address on Americanism at Oberlin College, 22 March 1906, *PWW* 16: 340.

8. Archibald Cary Coolidge, *The United States as a World Power* (New York, 1908), p. 7; Preface to a historical encyclopedia, "The Significance of American History," 9 September 1901, *PWW* 12: 180; Memorandum, "What Ought We to Do?" [c. 1 August 1898], *PWW* 10: 575.

9. Woodrow Wilson, *A History of the American People*, vol. 5, *Reunion and Nationalization* (New York, 1902), p. 247; "An Historical Commentary and Critique" [January 1901], *PWW* 12: 62; Memorandum for interview [18 December 1895], *PWW* 9: 365; "Democracy and Efficiency" [c. 1 October 1900], *PWW* 12:

18; News report of a lecture on constitutional government, "The Theory of Organization" [2 November 1898], *PWW* 11: 66.

10. Reinsch, *World Politics,* pp. 253–56; Essay, "Education and Democracy" [c. 4 May 1907], *PWW* 17: 134; Enclosure, WW to Vance McCormick, 15 October 1916, *PWW* 38: 462.

11. See notes for after-dinner speeches, 27 June and 11 September 1908, *PWW* 18: 347, 418. For the promise of cosmopolitanism during this period, see D. Steven Blum, *Walter Lippmann: Cosmopolitanism in the Century of Total War* (Ithaca, 1984); and David A. Hollinger, "Ethnic Diversity, Cosmopolitanism, and the Emergence of the American Intelligentsia," *American Quarterly* 27 (1975): 133–51.

12. "The Significance of American History," *PWW* 12: 180; News report of an address at Oberlin College [22 March 1906], *PWW* 16: 341.

13. News report of an address in Montclair, NJ [28 January 1904], *PWW* 15: 143. See further William Leuchtenberg, "Progressivism and Imperialism: The Progressive Movement and American Foreign policy, 1898–1916," *Mississippi Valley Historical Review* 39 (December 1952): 483–504.

14. News report of an address to the University Club of St. Louis [29 April 1903], *PWW* 14: 434; Address, "The Course of American History" [16 May 1895], *PWW* 9: 267.

15. John M. Mulder, *Woodrow Wilson: The Years of Preparation* (Princeton, NJ, 1978), p. 77; Address to the Pittsburgh YMCA, 24 October 1914, *PWW* 31: 226; News report of the annual banquet of the *Daily Princetonian* [23 March 1903], *PWW* 16: 36. On Wilson's affinities with the New Historians, see Arno J. Mayer, "Historical Thought and American Foreign Policy in the Era of the First World War," in *The Historian and the Diplomat,* ed. Francis L. Loewenheim (New York, 1967), pp. 74–78. Cf. James Harvey Robinson, *The New History* (New York, 1965), p. 265: "It is clear that the conscious reformer who appeals to the future is the final product of a progressive order of things."

16. "The Significance of American History," *PWW* 12: 179; Notes for after-dinner speech to the American Philosophical Society [13 April 1905], *PWW* 16: 53.

17. Address at Swarthmore, "The University and the Nation," 15 December 1905, *PWW* 16: 268; "The Significance of American History," *PWW* 12: 184.

18. Newspaper report of a lecture on Americanism in Wilmington, DE [7 December 1900], *PWW* 12: 44; Historical essay, "Politics, 1857–1907" [c. 31 July 1907], *PWW* 17: 309; Address to the annual dinner of the Cleveland Chamber of Commerce, 16 November 1907, *PWW* 17: 498.

19. Interview [11 June 1905], *PWW* 16: 125; Notes for a lecture on patriotism, 10 December 1897, *PWW* 10: 350. Cf. Address, "The Meaning of a Liberal Education" [9 January 1909], *PWW* 18: 594: "The life of the present day is incalculably complex, and so many of its complexities are of recent rise and origin that we haven't yet had time to understand just what they are or to assess the values of the new things that have come into our lives."

20. For representative realist criticisms of Wilson's attitude toward the balance

of power, see Osgood, *Ideals and Self-Interest in America's Foreign Relations,* pp. 174–75; Norman Graebner, *America as a World Power: A Realist Appraisal from Wilson to Reagan* (Wilmington, DE, 1984), p. xix; Levin, *Woodrow Wilson and World Politics,* p. 8; Kennan, *American Diplomacy 1900–1950,* pp. 69–72.

21. See the characterizations by Arthur Link in *Woodrow Wilson: Revolution, War, and Peace,* pp. 12–13; and *Woodrow Wilson and the Progressive Era* (New York, 1954), pp. 81–82; as well as the famous poison-pen sketch by John Maynard Keynes, *The Economic Consequences of the Peace* (New York, 1971), pp. 42ff. The quotation is from Mulder, *Years of Preparation,* p. 129.

22. Address at University of Michigan on patriotism [22 April 1903], *PWW* 14: 419; Diary of Edith Benham, 4 January 1919, *PWW* 54: 62.

23. Ray Stannard Baker, ed., *The Public Papers of Woodrow Wilson* (New York, 1970) [hereafter cited as *PPWW*-Baker], 6: 195; Address at Guildhall, 28 December 1917, *PWW* 53: 532; Newspaper report of a lecture in Lancaster [6 December 1895], *PWW* 9: 375; Meeting of Council of Ten, 30 January 1919, *PWW* 54: 353; Remarks to foreign correspondents, 8 April 1917, *PWW* 47: 287.

24. Quoted in Mulder, *Years of Preparation,* p. 105. My argument on the balance of power as automatic mechanism, historical system, and rule of thumb comes from Morse, *Modernization,* pp. 38–42.

25. Edward Vose Gulick, *Europe's Classical Balance of Power* (Ithaca, NY, 1955), pp. 10–11. On the Chinese tradition, see Adda B. Bozeman, *Politics and Culture in International History* (Princeton, 1960), pp. 133–46.

26. Address in Chicago on preparedness, 31 January 1916, *PWW* 36: 72; Colloquy with members of the American Neutral Conference, 30 August 1916, *PWW* 38: 114. For those contemplating the resemblance to the War of 1812, I would suggest that the two situations were much more different than alike, for the following reasons: (1) the extent of commercial depredation and violation of neutral rights was greater in 1812 than they were in 1914–17; (2) British actions were accorded greater weight or, at most, the depredations of both sides were viewed with equal gravity; (3) in the war of 1812, the United States distanced itself from larger ideological questions, despite British attempts to raise such issues; (4) The United States was fighting a war of existence in 1812, being engaged in a struggle for *recognition* in the Hegelian sense; (5) there existed in 1812 no weapon comparable to the submarine as a threat to civilization and international law; (6) and lastly, the historical sensibility and geopolitical elements of Wilsonian thought that dominate this chapter were nowhere to be found.

27. Annual message to Congress, 8 December 1914, *PWW* 31: 422; Address in Chicago on preparedness, 31 January 1916, *PWW* 36: 71.

28. E. M. House to Wilson, 22 August 1914, *PWW* 30: 432; Extract from the diary of Colonel House, 30 August 1914, *PWW* 30: 462; Spring Rice to Sir Edward Grey, 3 September 1914, in *The Life and Letters of Sir Edward Grey* (Boston, 1937), pp. 355–56; From the diary of Colonel House, 22 September 1915, *PWW* 34: 506.

29. Memo of interview with Wilson by Herbert Bruce Brougham, 14 December

1914, *PWW* 31: 459; Diary of Colonel House, 30 August 1914, *PWW* 30: 462. On Wilson's Anglophilism, see August Heckscher, *Woodrow Wilson* (New York, 1991), p. 434.

30. E. M. House to Walter Hines Page, 4 August 1915, *PWW* 34: 86; House to Wilson, 16 June 1915, *PWW* 33: 406; House to Wilson, 3 February 1916, *PWW* 36: 123; Diary of Colonel House, 11 April 1916, *PWW* 36: 461–62; Robert Lansing to Wilson, 24 August 1915, *PWW* 34: 319; Lansing diary entry, 24 January 1916, quoted in Calhoun, *Power and Principle*, p. 143. See also Levin, *Woodrow Wilson and World Politics*, p. 40; and Daniel M. Smith, *Robert Lansing and American Neutrality 1914–1917* (New York, 1972), p. 60.

31. Hamilton Foley, *Woodrow Wilson's Case for the League of Nations* (New York, 1969), pp. 103–4.

32. Speech at the National Press Club, 15 May 1916, *PWW* 37: 48.

33. Draft of an article by John Reed, based on an interview with Wilson, 30 June 1914, *PWW* 30: 234; Wilson to Edith Bolling Galt, 8 August 1915, *PWW* 34: 140; Prolegomenon to a peace note, 25 November 1916, *PWW* 40: 69.

34. Prolegomenon to a peace note, 25 November 1916, *PWW* 40: 69; Memo of conversation by Thomas Lamont, 4 October 1918, *PWW* 51: 223.

35. Address at Guildhall, 28 December 1918, *PWW* 53: 532; Address in Free Trade Hall, 30 December 1918, *PWW* 53: 550; Diary of William Bullitt, 8 December 1918, *PWW* 53: 352; Address to the Italian Parliament, 3 January 1919, *PWW* 53: 599; Croly, *The Promise of American Life*, p. 312.

36. Second Inaugural Address, 5 March 1917, *PWW* 41: 333; Wilson meeting with clergymen, 19 June 1917, *PWW* 42: 537; Address while homeward bound on the *George Washington*, 4 July 1919, *PWW* 61: 379; Address to Senate, 10 July 1919, *PWW* 61: 436. As late as December 1916, House could see no strategic threat from Germany following the war unless England was defeated. See House to Wilson, 20 December 1916, *PWW* 40: 294.

37. Speech in Los Angeles, 20 September 1919, *PPWW*-Baker 6: 321; Protocol of a plenary session of the peace conference, 25 January 1919, *PWW* 54: 270; Sir Halford Mackinder, *Democratic Ideals and Reality* (1919), p. 30.

38. Remarks to representatives of livestock growers, 13 March 1918, *PWW* 47: 3; Remarks in Paris to the League for the Rights of Man, 28 January 1919, *PWW* 54: 310.

39. Flag Day address, 14 June 1917, *PWW* 42: 501; Address in Buffalo to the American Federation of Labor, 12 November 1917, *PWW* 45: 12, 14; Foley, *Wilson's Case*, pp. 155–56.

40. Address in Baltimore, 6 April 1918, *PWW* 47: 169; Diary of Dr. Grayson, 2 July 1919, *PWW* 61: 370. See also Fritz Fischer, *Germany's Aims in the First World War* (New York, 1967), pp. 60ff.

41. Wilson to John St. Loe Strachey, 5 April 1918, *PWW* 47: 259. Wilson's ambassador in London, Walter Hines Page, felt that Germany would "reduce Europe

to the vassalage of a military autocracy'' and then "overrun the whole world or drench it in blood.'' See Page to Wilson, 24 November 1916, *PWW* 40: 64. For echoes in the views of a talented young progressive, see Walter Lippmann to Hazel Albertson, 25 September 1914, in *Public Philosopher: Selected Letters of Walter Lippmann,* ed. John Morton Blum (New York, 1985), p. 20. A brief survey of public opinion leaders who saw the German threat in similar terms during these years is provided by Osgood, *Ideals and Self-Interest in America's Foreign Relations,* pp. 114–34.

42. Speech in Pueblo, CO, 25 September 1919, *PPWW*-Baker 6: 412; Meeting with clergymen, 19 June 1917, *PWW* 42: 537. This perspective also informs the more modern interpretation of Geoffrey Barraclough, *An Introduction to Contemporary History* (New York, 1967), pp. 107–8ff.

43. See, e.g., T. Harry Williams, *The History of American Wars* (New York, 1981), p. 380, criticizing the National Defense Act of 1916: "It should have been obvious, from even rudimentary planning, that the place to defeat Germany was in Europe, that the United States would have to dispatch a force abroad to fight with allies—while it still had allies. But none of the persons concerned with planning—the President, his advisors, or the General Staff—grasped this conclusion; they assumed that the United States should prepare to act alone in defending against a German attack.'' Well, if it was so obvious, why didn't they see it?

44. *PPWW*-Baker 6: 353. Levin, *Woodrow Wilson and World Politics,* emphasizes Wilson's opposition to imperialism and revolution, but without noting Wilson's epochal sense of system change.

45. Arthur Link, in *The Higher Realism of Woodrow Wilson and Other Essays* (Nashville, 1971), pp. 127–39, also emphasizes the nonidealistic side of Wilson, insofar as Wilson predicted the folly of a balance-of-power approach to resolving the war's issues, but does not discuss Wilson's understanding of the structural transformation taking place in world politics.

46. Address to the Italian Parliament, 3 January 1919, *PWW* 53: 599.

47. Foley, *Wilson's Case,* p. 202; Speech at Denver, CO, 25 September 1919, *PPWW*-Baker 6: 391. Walter Lippmann, in "The Atlantic and America," *Life,* 7 April 1941, 85–92, was only partly correct when he argued in this famous essay that America had been concerned about the European balance in 1917. He failed to realize that, for Wilson at least, this was only a post hoc rationale for intervention and, moreover, that it was premised on the belief that European security on the old terms could not be secured. For the mistaken notion that Wilson was, *malgré lui,* a balance-of-power thinker, see, e.g., Edward Buehrig, *Woodrow Wilson and the Balance of Power* (Bloomington, IN, 1955).

48. Speech at Helena, Montana, 11 September 1919, *PPWW*-Baker 6: 122. Roland N. Stromberg, *Collective Security and American Foreign Policy: From the League of Nations to NATO* (New York, 1963), pp. 22–23, makes the good point that the league was not "an American idea (Wilson's) that had to be rammed down the throats of reluctant Europeans.'' One may infer from this that America had no

monopoly of idealism and, by the same token, that the idea might have possessed some "European," i.e., realistic, elements. Paul Goldstene, *The Collapse of Liberal Empire* (New Haven, CT, 1977), p. 10, suggests, in a remark fully applicable to Wilson, that "far from denying the existence of power, the whole of the liberal tradition is dominated by a fear of it, a fear grounded in an understanding that power is necessary to the realization of the rights it threatens to destroy."

49. William Howard Taft to Newton D. Baker, 6 February 1917, *PWW* 41: 154. Dorothy Jones, *Code of Peace: Ethics and Security in the World of Warlord States* (Chicago, 1991), p. 20, quotes Léon Bourgeois, Wilson's bête noire at Paris, as saying about power balancers and realists: "The result of their calculations and combinations is that it is almost impossible to localize a conflict—the conflict spreads until it takes in the entire civilized world."

50. On this point, see Richard Hofstadter's classic *The Age of Reform* (New York, 1955), p. 201. This sense of looming catastrophe was not simply fanciful speculation on Wilson's part. As pointed out by sociologist Anthony Giddens in *Modernity and Self-Identity: Self and Society in the Late Modern Age* (Stanford, 1991), p. 34, modernity "balances opportunity and potential catastrophe in equal measure." Wilson, I believe, fully appreciated the existence of such a balance.

51. Address at Mount Vernon, 4 July 1918, *PWW* 48: 516; Address at the Metropolitan Opera House, 27 September 1918, *PWW* 51: 127; Press conference, 29 September 1916, *PWW* 50: 745; Interview by Ida M. Tarbell, 3 October 1916, *PWW* 38: 324.

52. Address at the Metropolitan Opera House, 27 September 1918, *PWW* 51: 127; Remarks to the American Bar Association, 20 October 1914, *PWW* 31: 184.

53. Address, "The Variety and Unity of History" [20 September 1904], *PWW* 15: 475; Address to the French Chamber of Deputies, 3 February 1919, *PWW* 54: 466.

54. Foley, *Wilson's Case,* p. 182; Remarks to the New York Press Club, 30 June 1916, *PWW* 37: 334. Cf. per contra, Sondra R. Herman, *Eleven Against War* (Stanford, 1969), pp. 179–216. My use of "mechanical" and "organic" is not to be confused with the terminology employed by Emile Durkheim in his classic work, *The Division of Labor in Society.*

55. Address to the Italian Parliament, 3 January 1919, *PWW* 53: 598; Diary of Colonel House, 30 August 1914, *PWW* 30: 462; Prolegomenon to a peace note, 25 November 1916, *PWW* 40: 69.

56. Address in Free Trade Hall, 30 December 1918, *PWW* 53: 550; Address to the Grand Army of the Republic, 28 September 1915, *PWW* 34: 534; Address and reply, 10 January 1918, *PWW* 45: 561; Address to the Commercial Club of Omaha, 5 October 1916, *PWW* 38: 337; Address at the Metropolitan Opera House, 27 September 1918, *PWW* 51: 127. For Wilson's views on the transformations of political opinion wrought by the Spanish-American War, see Niels Aage Thorsen, *Woodrow Wilson's Political Thought, 1875–1910* (Princeton, 1988), pp. 75–76.

57. Quoted in George C. Osborn, *Woodrow Wilson: The Early Years* (Baton Rouge, 1968), p. 288; Newspaper report of an address, lecture before Sociological Institute [30 October 1894], *PWW* 10: 100; William Diamond, *The Economic Thought of Woodrow Wilson* (Baltimore, 1943), pp. 42–43; Woodrow Wilson, *The State* (Boston, 1890), p. 635; After-dinner remarks, Paris, 9 May 1919, *PWW* 58: 598.

58. Mulder, *Years of Preparation*, p. 250; After-dinner remarks [17 March 1909] *PWW* 19: 106; Address in Atlantic City, 28 December 1909, *PWW* 19: 638.

59. Quoted in Mulder, *Years of Preparation*, p. 103; After-dinner remarks, 2 December 1916, *PWW* 40: 120; Address to the New York City High School Teachers Association, "The Meaning of a Liberal Education" [9 January 1909], *PWW* 18: 594; After-dinner talk, 9 December 1916, *PWW* 40: 120; Address to the Gridiron Club, 8 December 1917, *PWW* 45: 239. On customs and war, see Diamond, *The Economic Thought of Woodrow Wilson*, pp. 39–40; and Wilson, *The State*, pp. 25–27, 480.

60. Quoted in Levin, *Woodrow Wilson and World Politics*, p. 180; Remarks to foreign correspondents, 8 April 1918, *PWW* 47: 287; Foley, *Wilson's Case*, pp. 59, 102, 106–7. Cf. a news report of a political address in Plainfield, NJ, "A Chance for the Democrats" [30 October 1909], *PWW* 19: 464: "We live in an age in which old things are passing away, in which all things are under scrutiny, in which the renaissance of government by opinion and the general interest is as plainly forecast by every sign of the times as it was in the period preceding the French Revolution." See also Walter Bagehot, *Physics and Politics* (London, 1902), p. 155: "We must examine the mode in which national characters can be emancipated from the rule of custom, and can be prepared for the use of choice."

61. Draft of an address to a joint session of Congress [8 February 1918], *PWW* 46: 275; Address at Mount Vernon, 4 July 1918, *PWW* 48: 516.

62. Interview with Henry Noble Hall, 31 October 1916, *PWW* 38: 569; After-dinner remarks, 2 December 1916, *PWW* 40: 120.

63. After-dinner talk, 9 December 1916, *PWW* 40: 194, 195. On the education of public opinion, see Michael Howard, *War and the Liberal Conscience* (New Brunswick, 1977), p. 71. In 1909 Wilson defined a statesman as one who "speaks, not the rumors of the street, but a new principle for a new age; a man in whose ears the voices of the nation do not sound like the accidental and discordant notes that come from the voice of a mob, but concurrent and concordant like the united voices of a chorus, whose many meanings, spoken by melodious tongues, unite in his understanding in a single meaning and reveal to him a single vision, so that he can speak what no man else knows, the common meaning of the common voice." Address in Chicago, "Abraham Lincoln: A Man of the People," 12 February 1909, *PPWW*-Baker 2: 95.

One is reminded of Carlyle's tailor, who cuts a new pattern for a world habituated to that "greatest of all weavers," custom. "Is not the fair fabric of Society itself, with all its royal mantles and pontifical stoles, whereby, from nakedness and dismemberment, we are organized into polities, into nations, and a whole co-operating mankind, the creation, as has here been often irrefragably evinced, of the Tailor alone? —What too are all Poets, and moral teachers, but a species of metaphorical Tailors?'' Thomas Carlyle, *Sartor Resartus* (New York, 1983), p. 218.

64. Remarks celebrating the centennial of the American Bible Society, 7 May 1916, *PWW* 36: 629.

65. Diary of Edith Benham, 4 January 1919, *PWW* 54: 62; Mulder, *Years of Preparation*, p. 65; Address in New York on Christian youth and progress, 20 November 1905, *PWW* 16: 229. Although the exact character of Wilson's rhetorical style will probably continue to elude precise fixing, after a certain point speculation on the phenomenology of Wilsonianism becomes irrelevant because his ideas enter a larger world of textual discourse. See Paul Ricoeur, ''What is a Text?'' in Ricoeur, *Hermeneutics and the Human Sciences,* ed. John B. Thompson (New York, 1981), pp. 147–49. Further evidence that Wilson saw history as noble, useful, and essential to statesmanship comes from an essay ''The Variety and Uses of History,'' written in 1904, in which he wrote: ''We have used the wrong words in speaking of our art and craft . . . [History] is a high calling and should not be belittled. Statesmen are guided and formed by what we write, patriots stimulated, tyrants checked, reform and progress, charity and freedom of belief, the dreams of artists and the fancies of poets, have at once their record and their source with us. We must not suffer ourselves to fall dull and pedantic, must not lose our visions or cease to speak the large words of inspiration and guidance.'' Address in Chicago, ''Abraham Lincoln: A Man of the People,'' 12 February 1909, *PPWW*-Baker 2: 84. In the same address, he referred to Gladstone's ability ''to rule men by those subtle forces of oratory which shape the history of the world and determine the relations of nations to one another'' (p. 85).

66. The term ''idealism'' in its foreign-policy usage has been hopelessly debased by ''realists'' who have used it to describe those who are presumed to be out of touch with the geopolitical facts of life. This label is an ideological one that should be rejected because the epistemological foundations of realism are equally shaky. In any case, the two outlooks usually diverge not in their analyses of the real world, since they are equally adept at pointing out its iniquities, but in their view of how much it is possible to change it. In Wilson's case, idealistic solutions were thought to be necessary as the only way out of an otherwise impossible situation. The difference thus is not so much in estimates of what is, as in views of what ought to be. By this reckoning, Wilson's pursuit of collective security was a minimalist internationalism that proceeded logically and necessarily from his estimate of the cold facts of the matter. Moreover, as we shall see, his estimate passed the test of time and political experience by becoming culturally embedded or sedimented in the form of cold-war axioms. How can this possibly be called ''idealism?''

67. Address at San Diego, California, 19 September 1919, *PPWW*-Baker 6: 291.

68. Wilson had more Hobbes in him than people realized. See Leo Strauss, *Natural Right and History* (Chicago, 1953), pp. 197–98, for the internationalist implications of Hobbesian logic. Of course, Wilson's views are not far removed in this case

from those of Immanuel Kant, who argued that perpetual peace would be the end result of international rivalry and violence. On the open-ended sensibility of Progressive history, see John Higham, *History: The Development of Historical Studies in the United States* (Englewood Cliffs, NJ, 1965), p. 72.

69. "Democracy and Efficiency," *PWW* 12: 6; Address in Cleveland on preparedness, 29 January 1916, *PWW* 36: 42. In 1903, Wilson claimed that a momentous battle was "being fought for existence in the maintenance of ideals, for the deciphering of morals, for the clearing away of doubts and alarms"; quoted in Mulder, *Years of Preparation*, p. 167.

70. Diary of Colonel House, 30 August 1914, *PWW* 30: 462; Address to National School for Women, 1 May 1916, *PWW* 36: 573; Diary of Raymond Fosdick, 11 December 1918, *PWW* 53: 366; Foley, *Wilson's Case*, pp. 16–17; Remarks to members of B'nai B'rith, 28 November 1918, *PWW* 53: 239.

71. Foley, *Wilson's Case*, pp. 22, 23.

72. Notes of Supreme War Council meeting, 17 March 1919, *PWW* 56: 26. A few days later, he expressed similar concerns about Poland's ability to cope with Germany. Ibid., p. 94; Foley, *Wilson's Case*, pp. 160, 161. Wilson certainly agreed to punitive measures against Germany, as argued by Levin, *Woodrow Wilson and World Politics*, pp. 123–25, and demonstrated by Klaus Schwabe, *Woodrow Wilson, Revolutionary Germany, and Peacemaking, 1918–1919* (Chapel Hill, 1985). However, he stopped short of crippling her ability to dominate eastern Europe probably because of his belief that the creation of a traditional balance would have undercut the league by diverting false hopes into power political channels at the expense of the idea of collective security. A viable balance was, in any case, an oxymoron in Wilson's book, because of the certainty of war. The existence of a balance of power for the short term and the league over the long haul could never stay down in Wilson's historically sensitive gullet.

73. Address in St. Paul, MN, 9 September 1919, *PPWW*-Baker 6: 86; Meeting of Council of Four, 15 April 1919, *PWW* 57: 358; Meeting of Council of Four, 18 April 1919, *PWW* 57: 454; Diary of Ray Stannard Baker, 30 April 1919, *PWW* 58: 270.

74. Wilson discussion with U.S. delegation, 3 June 1919, *PWW* 60: 68; Address to the Belgian Parliament, 19 June 1919, *PWW* 61: 18.

75. Speech at Boston, 24 February 1919, in *PPWW*-Baker 5: 437–39; Foley, *Wilson's Case*, pp. 16–17.

76. Letter, Wilson to Lansing, 24 May 1919, *PWW* 59: 470–71; Report of press conference, 20 July 1919, *PWW* 61: 421; *PPWW*-Baker 6: 301.

77. Bernard Baruch to Arthur Krock, 21 May 1956, in John Foster Dulles Papers, Princeton University [hereafter JFDP], White House Memoranda Series [hereafter WHM], box 7; *PPWW*-Baker 6: 412, 415; Metropolitan Opera House Speech, 4 March 1919, *PPWW*-Baker 5: 451.

78. Coolidge to Howard Temperly, 17 January 1920, in *Archibald Cary Coolidge:*

Life and Letters, ed. Harold Jefferson Coolidge and Robert Howard Lord (Freeport, NY, 1971), p. 238.

79. Speech at Reno, Nevada, 22 September 1919, *PPWW*-Baker 6: 330.

CHAPTER 3

1. Quotations from John Wheeler-Bennett, *Disarmament and Security since Locarno* (New York, 1932), p. 25, and Frank Costigliola, *Awkward Dominion: American Political, Economic, and Cultural Relations with Europe, 1919–1933* (Ithaca, 1984), p. 116.

2. Wilson himself was inconsistent on the point. In August 1923, he wrote that "the world has been made safe for democracy," but shortly before his death he said, "The whole field of international relationship is in perilous confusion." See *PPWW*-Baker 6: 538, 541.

3. Karl Polanyi, *The Great Transformation* (New York, 1944). Wilsonian enthusiasm emerged almost at the exact time that modern cultural anthropology, with its emphasis on unique and incommensurable cultures as the basis of human society and understanding, began its move into the mainstream of the social sciences. See Elvin Hatch, *Culture and Morality: The Relativity of Values in Anthropology* (New York, 1983), pp. 35–59.

4. Herbert Hoover, *Memoirs,* vol. 1, *Years of Adventure 1874–1920* (New York, 1951), p. 36; Lou Henry Hoover, undated articles, addresses, and statements on Herbert Hoover, Lou Henry Hoover Papers, Herbert Hoover Presidential Library, West Branch, IA [hereafter LHH]. On Hoover's later reading habits, see "Mr. Hoover as Reader," *Literary Digest,* 22 October 1932; "What Mr. Hoover Reads," *Saturday Evening Post,* 31 August 1929, 42; William Hard, "The Reading of the Candidates," *Bookman,* October 1928, 146.

5. George N. Nash, *The Life of Herbert Hoover,* vol. 1, *The Engineer, 1874–1914* (New York, 1983), p. 63; Hoover, *Memoirs,* 1: 30; Lou Henry Hoover, manuscript articles, addresses, and statements on Herbert Hoover, LHH; Hoover, "Mining and Milling Gold Ores in Western Australia," *Engineering and Mining Journal* 66 (17 December 1898): 752–56. Hoover believed that Eurasians "have added nothing that is good to the world. In fact, all the good that is in both races is absent in the offspring." His Lamarckian views were clearly expressed in his approval of the restrictive Immigration Act of 1924. Hoover defended Japanese exclusion on the basis of the "biological fact" which made "mixture of blood disadvantageous." Since no population, once admitted, could be kept from mixing with native stock, it followed that immigration from Japan ought to be banned. See Hoover to Mark Requa, 21 April 1924, Pre-Commerce Papers, Herbert Hoover Papers, Herbert Hoover Presidential Library, West Branch, IA [hereafter PC-HHPL]. See also George F. Garcia, "Herbert Hoover and the Race Issue," p. 510; and Thomas B. Dressler, "Herbert Hoover, Reluctant Internationalist" (Ph.D. diss., Brown University, 1973), pp. 15–16. Still, given the bi-directional possibilities inherent in Lamarckism, Hoover was no racist; seen in the context of his time he was racially progressive. There is little

cause to doubt the assessment of Lewis Strauss that he was "absolutely color-blind as to race." Lewis Strauss OH, Herbert Hoover Presidential Library, West Branch, IA [hereafter HHPL]. On Hoover's racial attitudes, see Larry Grothaus, "Herbert Hoover and Black Americans," in *Herbert Hoover and the Republican Era* (Boston, 1984), p. 143; George F. Garcia, "Herbert Hoover and the Race Issue," *Annals of Iowa* 44 (Winter 1979): 507–15; and the detailed treatment by Donald J. Lisio, *Hoover, Blacks, and Lily-Whites: A Study of Southern Strategies* (Chapel Hill, NC, 1985), pp. 13, 23, 27, 282.

6. Hoover, *Memoirs*, 1: 98; Ray Lyman Wilbur, "Herbert Hoover: A Personal Sketch," PC-HHPL; Hoover, address at the Engineer's Club of San Francisco, 12 February 1914, PC-HHPL; Hoover to George Bancroft, 1912, reprinted in 29 March 1919 issue of the Denver *Evening News*, PC-HHPL.

7. Hoover, quoted in David Starr Jordan, *The Days of a Man* (Yonkers-on-Hudson, NY, 1922) 2: 334; Hoover to E. D. Adams, 6 June 1915, PC-HHPL; Hoover to H. Foster Bain, 4 August 1914, PC-HHPL; Hoover to Ray Lyman Wilbur, 4 August 1914, PC-HHPL.

8. Jordan, *The Days of a Man*, 2: 644.

9. Hugh Gibson, *A Journal from Our Legation in Belgium* (New York, 1917), p. 273; George H. Nash, *The Life of Herbert Hoover*, vol. 2, *The Humanitarian* (New York, 1988), pp. 193–94.

10. Brand Whitlock, *Belgium: A Personal Narrative* (New York, 1919), pp. 198, 400; Hoover, American Luncheon Club speech, 18 December 1914, PC-HHPL. However, as his wife later recalled, Hoover had "no special, preconceived admiration" for the Belgian people, they being among the few with whom he was unfamiliar. Also, the effort was not nearly as American as propaganda made it appear to be, only five percent of the total funding being contributed by the American people and the rest mainly from Allied subsidies. To protect the exceptionalist image of his country, Hoover fought numerous bureaucratic battles to insure that the CRB continue to be identified as an American effort. See Lou Henry Hoover to Herbert and Allan, July 1932, LHH; Tracy Kittredge, *A History of the C.R.B.* (London, n.d.), p. 101; John S. Phillips to Hoover, 8 November 1915, PC-HHPL; John L. Simpson OH.

11. Hoover to James Gerard, 5 December 1914, in Kittredge, *A History of the C.R.B.;* Hoover to Page, 20 October 1914, PC-HHPL; Victoria French Allen, "The Outside Man," manuscript, Ben Allen Papers, HHPL, p. 165. The CRB also resembled Wilsonian neutrality in its anti-German coloration. As one American veteran of the CRB recalled, "The most pro-German American who arrived in Belgium didn't stay pro-German for long." See Kittredge, *A History of the C.R.B.*, p. 3; John L. Simpson OH; Francis C. Wickes OH.

12. Hoover to E. D. Adams, 6 June 1915, PC-HHPL. Unlike Wilson, who absolved the German people of any wrongdoing, Hoover felt that "this does not apply to a few men at the top but is becoming the ambition of every German of even half intelligence."

13. Telegram preceding HH to WW, 13 May 1915, PC-HHPL.

14. Hoover to E. M. House, 16 August 1915, PC-HHPL; Hoover to Wilson, 3 September 1915, ibid.

15. Hoover to Wilson, 4 April 1917; Hoover to House, 3 February 1917; Hoover to James E. West, 19 April 1917; all in PC-HHPL. In his *Memoirs*, 1: 219, Hoover made it appear as if his position was much farther from Wilson's than it actually was, since at times his strategic rhetoric verged clearly on outright Wilsonianism. See Hoover et al. to Wilson, 4 April 1917, *PWW* 41: 543; and Hoover statement, "German Practices in Belgium," September 1917, compendium of Hoover materials known as "The Bible," HHPL. The differences were there *in parvo,* I believe, having not yet been fully sorted out.

16. Hoover, *The Ordeal of Woodrow Wilson* (New York, 1957), p. 3.

17. Hoover, press statement, 21 March 1919, "The Bible"; Hoover statement, quoted in Hoover, *The Ordeal of Woodrow Wilson,* p. 172. Once the completed draft treaty surfaced in June 1919, Hoover was so taken aback by its harshness that he predicted the Germans would not sign and, even if they did, that the great difference between Germany's capacity to pay and what was expected of it in reparations would discredit the fledgling democratic order in Germany. For Hoover's opposition to the draft treaty, see Leo Eugene Chavez, "Herbert Hoover and Food Relief: An Application of American Ideology" (Ph.D. diss., University of Michigan, 1976), pp. 298–303.

18. Vance McCormick diary, 9 June 1919, p. 99, Herbert Hoover Papers, HHPL [hereafter HHP]; Hoover to Frederick R. Coudert, 2 November 1918, PC-HHPL.

19. Hoover to Wilson, 11 April 1919, PC-HHPL.

20. Hoover statement, *New York Times,* 26 July 1919, "The Bible"; Hoover interview with the *Washington Star,* 18 March 1920, ibid.; Hoover statement, *New York Times,* 28 July 1919, ibid.; Address before the students of Stanford University, 2 October 1919, ibid.

21. Address before the students of Stanford University, 2 October 1919, "The Bible"; Hoover statement, *New York Times,* 19 March 1920, p. 3, ibid. The internationalist strategic logic would not be wholly abandoned even after Hoover stopped supporting the treaty. "Had we not turned the tide of victory to the allies," he argued in 1924, "we would today be living in a world of armed despotisms; we should be forced to support standing armies of millions of men of our own." Hoover, Armistice Day address, 11 November 1924, "The Bible."

22. Hoover, *Memoirs,* 1: 213, 135. Hoover was not alone in his views. Even so internationalist a secretary of state as Charles Evans Hughes believed that the European balance continued actively to function. According to his biographer, Hughes "conceived of the balance of power as an essentially European tradition." Betty Glad, *Charles Evans Hughes and the Illusions of Innocence* (Urbana, IL, 1966), p. 160.

23. Hoover, *The Ordeal of Woodrow Wilson,* p. viii.

24. Hoover to Warren Gregory, 30 March 1920, PC-HHPL; Hoover to Wilson, 5 June 1919, ibid.; Hoover, treaty statement, 9 September 1920, "The Bible."

25. Hoover, "Problems of Our Economic Evolution," address to Stanford University seniors, 22 June 1925, "The Bible"; Hoover, "Ills We Inherit from the War," *Women's Home Companion*, March 1920, ibid.; Hoover to Robert A. Burdette, 29 September 1920, PC-HHPL; Hoover to William Allen White, 13 June 1924, Commerce: HHPL.

26. Hoover, Lincoln Republican Club Address, Grand Rapids, MI, 11 February 1921, "The Bible."

27. Quoted in Charles Beard, *The Idea of National Interest* (New York, 1934), p. 425; Hoover to Judge William A. Glasgow, 12 April 1919, PC-HHPL.

28. Hoover, press release, 15 September 1920, "The Bible"; Hoover, "American Relations with Russia," address before U.S. Section of the International Chamber of Commerce, 15 May 1927, ibid.; Hoover, address at Boston, 15 October 1928, ibid. Hoover has, at the other extreme, been made out by some historians to be an autarchic advocate of "capitalism in one country." See, e.g., Patrick Hearden, "Herbert Hoover and the Dream of Capitalism in One Country," in *Redefining the Past: Essays in Diplomatic History in Honor of William Appleman Williams*, ed. Lloyd C. Gardner (Corvallis, OR, 1986), pp. 143–55.

29. Gary Dean Best, "Herbert Clark Hoover in Transition, 1919–1921" (Ph.D. diss., University of Hawaii, 1973), p. 166; Hoover to Warren Gregory, 30 March 1920, PC-HHPL; Hoover, telegram to the Convention of the Pacific Foreign Trade Committee, 4 March 1926, Commerce: HHPL.

30. Hoover, "Address on Americanism," 29 October 1919, HHP; Hoover, "Memorandum on the Economic Situation," *Annals of the American Academy of Political and Economic Science* 87 (January 1920): 106; Hoover, speech to the American Banking Association, 1 December 1920, "The Bible"; Summary of Hoover memorandum on the economic situation in Europe, 10 July 1919, in *FRUS: The Paris Peace Conference*, 12 vols. (Washington, 1942) 10: 462.

31. Hoover, address to the Commonwealth Club, San Francisco, 13 October 1919, "The Bible"; Hoover, address to the National Shoe and Leather Exposition and Style Show, 12 July 1921, ibid. Although Hoover said on one notable occasion that "we are able in considerable degree to free ourselves of world influences and make a large measure of independent recovery because we are so remarkably self-contained," even partial integration had major implications. He believed that the American standard of living depended on imports, while exports, "the great balance wheel for our production," were "vital to the stabilization of our industries, of price levels, of wages and of employment." William Starr Meyers, ed., *The State Papers and Other Public Writings of Herbert Hoover* (Garden City, NY, 1934), pp. 375–84. On occasion, claims of U.S. self-sufficiency were inflated for international bargaining purposes.

32. Hoover to Wilson 21 June 1919, PC-HHPL; Hoover, memo on "Progress of Bolshevism," 11 April 1919, ibid.; Minutes of AFL executive council meeting, 17 November 1920, ibid. Theda Skocpol, in *States and Social Revolutions* (New York, 1979), has convincingly argued that the major radical revolutions have taken place in premodern agrarian nations.

33. Hoover to Harding, 8 August 1920, PC-HHPL. On Wilson's view of the relation between culture and ideology, see notes of a meeting of Council of Four on 6 June 1919, *PWW* 60: 209. For the charge of naivete, see Eugene P. Trani, "Herbert Hoover and the Russian Revolution, 1917–1921," in *Herbert Hoover: The Great War and Its Aftermath*, ed. Lawrence Gelfand (Iowa City, 1977), pp. 134–35.

34. Hoover to Wilson, 8 March 1919, *PWW* 56: 376; *Hearings before the Committee on Ways and Means*, 12 January 1920, pt. 2 (Washington, 1920); Captain T. C. Gregory, quoted in George W. Hopkins, "The Politics of Food: The United States and Soviet Hungary, March-August 1919," *Mid-America* (October 1973): 269.

35. Hoover statement, 3 January 1919, PC-HHPL; Hoover, "Some Problems in War Adjustment," address to the American Institute of Mining and Metallurgical Engineers, 16 September 1919, "The Bible"; Hoover, "American Relief—and After," *Saturday Evening Post*, 30 April 1921, "The Bible"; Minutes of AFL executive council meeting, 17 November 1920, PC-HHPL; Inaugural address to American Institute of Mining and Metallurgical Engineers, 17 February 1920, "The Bible."

36. Alexander Gumberg to Kenneth Durant, 21 June 1922, Gumberg Papers, HHPL; Hoover statement, "Tenth Anniversary of American Entry into World War I," 6 April 1927, "The Bible"; Hoover, "American Relations with Russia," Address before U.S. Section of the International Chamber of Commerce, 15 May 1927, "The Bible"; Hoover, address at Lafayette-Marne celebration at West Point, 6 September 1920, "The Bible"; Statement given to Newspaper Enterprise Association, 3 June 1920, "The Bible"; Press statement, 25 April 1919, "The Bible."

37. Hoover, *American Individualism* (New York, 1922), p. 3; Hoover, foreword to M. Friedman, *America and the New Era*, "The Bible."

38. Hoover, *American Individualism*, pp. 4–5; Hoover, *The Challenge to Liberty* (New York, 1934), p. 193; Hoover, address at Johns Hopkins University, 23 February 1920, "The Bible."

39. Hoover, *American Individualism*, pp. 50, 57; Hoover, "Some Notes on Industrial Readjustment," *Saturday Evening Post*, 17 December 1919, "The Bible." In an internationalist vein, Hoover also argued on behalf of "individualism in international economic life, just as strongly as I would make a plea for individualism in the life of our own people . . . this system cannot be preserved in domestic life, if it must be abandoned in international life." The unvarnished language here suggests a pure economic individualism, a consumer-driven utopia with no important mediating structures between the individual and the international society in which Hoover was enmeshed. But that would be a serious misreading of Hoover's thinking. See Hoover, address before the National Association of Manufacturers, New York City, 18 May 1921, "The Bible."

40. Hoover, foreword to M. Friedman, *America and the New Era*, "The Bible"; Hoover, memorandum, "Some Economic Problems in the World," December 1919, quoted in Leo Eugene Chavez, "Herbert Hoover and Food Relief" (Ph.D. diss., University of Michigan, 1976); Hoover address before the San Francisco Commercial Club, 9 October 1919, "The Bible."

41. Herbert Hoover, address before the San Francisco Commercial Club, 9 October 1919, "The Bible"; Hoover speech to the American Institute of Mining and Metallurgical Engineers, 16 September 1919, ibid; Hoover, *Memoirs,* 1: 474. For segmentation as the "counterpole" to the creation of a "supersociety by means of functional differentiation," see Karl Otto Hondrich, "World Societies versus Niche Societies: Paradoxes of Unidirectional Evolution," in Hans Haferkamp and Neil J. Smelser, eds., *Social Change and Modernity* (Berkeley, 1992), p. 350.

42. Best, "Herbert Clark Hoover in Transition, 1919–1921," p. 153; Hoover to William Allen White, 13 June 1924, Commerce: HHPL.

43. Hoover to E. D. Adams, 6 June 1915, PC-HHPL; Hoover, *Memoirs,* 1: 479; Hoover, *The Ordeal of Woodrow Wilson,* p. 72.

44. This situation resembles on the international plane what Emile Durkheim had described as the essential problem of modernization in his *The Division of Labor in Society*: the increasing distance between "organic" solidarity, that is, the reticulation of institutions caused by the growing division of labor, and the diminished sense of "mechanical solidarity," the powerful sense of common values found in primitive societies. Put differently, institutional integration on a global scale is not accompanied by a corresponding cultural cohesion.

45. Dr. Edgar E. Robinson OH.

46. Stimson diaries, 3 April 1932, Yale University.

47. Wilbur to Hoover, 26 January 1933, Foreign Affairs File: Far East (Japanese Incident), Official Correspondence, Jan.-Feb. 1933, Presidential: HHPL.

48. Herbert and Lou Henry Hoover to Mr. and Mrs. Ray Lyman Wilbur, 26 June 1899, PC-HHPL; Undated typescript, Subject File, articles, addresses and statements, LHH; Lou Henry Hoover, undated manuscript, LHH; Draft introduction, 17 November 1942, LHH. The exception that proves the rule is Hoover's harsh remark following the Boxer Rebellion that the only way to do business with Asiatics was to "begin your talk with a gun in your hand." Nash, *The Life of Herbert Hoover,* 1: 139.

49. Hoover, *Memoirs,* 1: 67; Hoover, "The Kaiping Mines and Coal Field," *Transactions of the Institution of Mining and Metallurgy* 10 (17 June 1902).

50. Hoover, *Memoirs,* 1: 67, 69, 71–72.

51. Hugh A. Moran OH; Hoover to Theodore Hoover [1899–1900], Theodore Hoover Papers, HHPL.

52. Stimson diaries, 26 January 1932; Hoover, undated extract, in Foreign Affairs (Manchuria Crisis), Presidential: box 1025, HHPL; Hoover, *Memoirs,* 2: 368–70.

53. Stimson diaries, 21 February 1933, and 10 February 1933; Henry L. Stimson, *The Far Eastern Crisis: Recollections and Observations* (New York, 1936), pp. 235, 241.

54. Osgood, *Ideals and Self-Interest in America's Foreign Relations,* pp. 233–34, stresses Stimson's concern for the Open Door and his romantic attachment to a vision of an Americanized China, but he omitted the central point: Stimson's analysis of the problem fundamentally paralleled his own.

55. Memo by Stanley K. Hornbeck, 9 September 1932, in Justus Doenecke, ed., *The Diplomacy of Frustration* (Stanford, CA, 1981), pp. 180–81; James T. Shotwell, *War as an Instrument of National Policy and Its Renunciation in the Pact of Paris* (New York, 1929), p. 86; Stimson diaries, 6 December 1931. One can detect in the guarded statement by President Calvin Coolidge in 1928 that "any nations engaging in war would necessarily be engaged in a course prejudicial to us" a faint rat-tat-tat that would become a booming drumbeat in years to come.

56. Memo by Hornbeck, 21 November 1931, in Doenecke, *The Diplomacy of Frustration*, p. 87.

57. Henry Stimson, "Bases of American Foreign Policy during the Past Four Years," *Foreign Affairs* 11 (April 1933): 383–85. Stimson compared the attack on Shanghai to the German invasion of Belgium in 1914, which, he recalled, had "shocked the whole world." Japan's assault on that city seemed to be "shaping up an issue between the two great themes of civilization and economic methods." Stimson diary, 8 February and 9 March 1932. He also drew a parallel between Hoover's squeamishness and Wilson's hands-off policy, and believed that Hoover might "affront the thoughtful people of the country by not being ahead of the game." Stimson diaries, 20 February and 9 March 1932.

58. Quoted in William Appleman Williams, *Some Presidents from Wilson to Nixon* (New York, 1972), p. 48.

59. Hoover, *Memoirs*, 2: 331; Castle manuscript, Castle Papers, HHPL, p. 116; Undated extract by Hoover, Foreign Affairs (Manchuria Crisis), Presidential: box 1025, HHPL.

60. Hoover, letter to *New York World*, 22 December 1920, "The Bible"; Stimson diaries, 26 January 1932.

61. Castle to Edwin L. Neville, 20 October 1931, Castle Papers, box 9; Stimson diaries, 9 October and 27 November 1931.

62. Stimson dairies, 14 November 1931; Memo by Hornbeck, 14 February 1933, in Doenecke, *The Diplomacy of Frustration*, p. 198.

63. Stimson diaries, 8 February 1932.

64. Stimson diaries, 27 November, 16 October, and 7 November 1931; Stimson, "Bases of American Foreign Policy," p. 394. See also Martin L. Fausold, *The Presidency of Herbert C. Hoover* (Lawrence, KS, 1985), p. 179.

65. Stimson diaries, 18 February 1932.

66. Hoover, Armistice Day Address, 11 November 1930, in Meyers, ed., *The State Papers and Other Public Writings of Herbert Hoover*, p. 417.

67. Hoover, *Memoirs*, 2: 377–78.

CHAPTER 4

1. Robert Dallek, in *Franklin D. Roosevelt and American Foreign Policy, 1932–1945* (New York, 1979), correctly sees FDR as an internationalist who was forced

by domestic pressures to moderate his policies in an isolationist direction. However, the precise nature of his internationalism is inadequately defined. The term "halfway Wilsonian" is, for my purpose, more precise than Daniel Yergin's characterization of FDR as a "renegade Wilsonian" in *Shattered Peace: The Origins of the Cold War and the National Security State* (Boston, 1977), p. 10; or David Reynolds's term "realistic Wilsonian," in *The Creation of the Anglo-American Alliance: A Study in Competitive Co-operation* (Chapel Hill, 1982), p. 261.

2. For early expressions of FDR's thinking on foreign afairs, see FDR to parents, 16 May 1899 and 21 January 1900, and FDR to "Mama," 7 September 1905, all in Family Correspondence, Children [hereafter FCC], box 11, FDRPL. In 1913 he wrote his wife Eleanor of a cruise with Coolidge and others on the Potomac and Chesapeake Bay during which the party "covered every country on the globe" in the course of an absorbing conversation. FDR to Eleanor Roosevelt, 24 July 1913, in *Franklin D. Roosevelt: His Personal Letters*, ed. Elliott Roosevelt (New York, 1950), [hereafter *FDR: PL*] 2: 209.

3. FDR speech in the *Troy Record* (NY), 4 March 1912, Speech File, FDR Papers, Franklin D. Roosevelt Presidential Library, Hyde Park, NY [hereafter FDRL].

4. FDR, speech in New York City, reported in *New York Times*, 5 July 1917, Speech File, FDRL.

5. FDR, speech at Newport, RI, 22 December 1915, Speech File. See also FDR to Eleanor, 1 and 2 August 1914, FCC, box 12, FDRL; Frank Freidel, *Franklin D. Roosevelt: The Apprenticeship* (Boston, 1952), p. 267. "It would be wonderful to be a war President of the United States," he is reported as telling William Castle, as quoted in Ted Morgan, *FDR: A Biography* (New York, 1985), p. 196.

6. Freidel, *Roosevelt: The Apprenticeship*, pp. 260–61; FDR to Eleanor Roosevelt [October 1914], *FDR: PL*, 2: 257; Dallek, *Franklin D. Roosevelt and American Foreign Policy*, p. 9.

7. FDR speech, 9 August 1920, Speech file; FDR, campaign speech, 1920, FDR Papers, box 24, FDRL; FDR speech in Kansas City, 9 October 1920, Speech File; Article for *Harvard Advocate*, October 1920, Family, Business, Personal, FDRL [hereafter FBP].

8. FDR statement in Cincinnati, 17 October 1920, Speech File; Speech at the Harvard Union, 26 February 1920, ibid.

9. FDR to George Marvin, 10 October 1922 and 29 January 1924, FBP, boxes 68 and 104. Typical of this about-face was FDR's newly pacifistic attitude toward Japan, a nation which a decade earlier he had considered a likely future military opponent. See FDR, letter to the editor of the *Baltimore Sun*, 13 August 1923, box 104, FBP; FDR, "The Japs: A Habit of Mind," draft for *Asia Magazine*, July 1923, box 109, FBP; FDR, editorial for the *Daily Telegraph* [Macon, GA], April 1925, FBP; FDR to George Foster Peabody, 26 September 1923, FBP.

10. FDR to Clarence Poe, 19 January 1926, FBP, box 109; Phi Beta Kappa address at Harvard, 17 June 1928, Speech File; Speech at Chicago Democratic luncheon, 10 December 1929, Speech File; FDR, "Whither Bound," 18 May 1926,

FBP, box 109, FDRL. As another example of his functional-structural internation-alism, FDR agreed with a 1934 article, "Civilization and Liberty," written by Ramsay Muir, whose thesis was that a new era of technological advance would provide the basis for the unification of the world into a single economic and political system.

11. FDR to James M. Cox, 8 December 1922, FBP, box 93; FDR to Mrs. J. Malcolm Forbes, 20 August 1928, FBP, box 104; *Beacon Standard* editorials, 1928, FBP, box 109; FDR, "Whither Bound"; FDR, commencement speech, Fordham University, 12 June 1929, Speech File; Speech at Syracuse, NY, 27 September 1926, Speech File.

12. FDR, letter to the editor of the *Baltimore Sun*, 13 August 1923, FBP, box 104; Speech at Chicago Democrat's luncheon, 10 December 1929, Speech File; FDR, "Our Foreign Policy: A Democratic View," *Foreign Affairs* 6 (July 1928): 573–86; FDR to John Spargo, 17 March 1924, FBP, box 67; FDR to Viscount Robert Cecil, 19 August 1930, *FDR: PL*, 3: 142. FDR went so far on one occasion as to declare that "these materialists who assert that all wars are caused by economic and trade rivalries ought to be put in the insane asylum." FDR, editorial for the *Daily Telegraph* [Macon, GA], April 1925, FBP, box 109. At the same time, he was aware that this global process of civilization would lead to "far more difficult problems, such as the effect of the intermingling of races and of the necessity for increasing populations in given areas of the world's surface and of limiting the increase in other races." FDR, Phi Beta Kappa address at Harvard, 17 June 1928, Speech File.

13. Dallek, *Franklin D. Roosevelt and American Foreign Policy*, pp. 29, 57; FDR to Jesse I. Strauss, 13 February 1936, *FDR: PL*, 3: 555; FDR to Colonel House, 16 June 1937, *FDR: PL*, 3: 689. FDR, address at the San Diego Exposition, 2 October 1935, in FDR, *Roosevelt's Foreign Policy, 1933–1941* (New York, 1942), p. 79.

14. Speech by FDR at Woodrow Wilson Foundation dinner, Washington, DC, 28 December 1933, in Edgar Nixon et al., *Franklin D. Roosevelt and Foreign Affairs* (Cambridge, MA, 1969), [hereafter *FDR: FA*] 1: 561; FDR to Robert W. Bingham, 13 November 1933, *FDR: PL*, 2: 370; FDR to William E. Dodd, 13 November 1933, *FDR: FA*, 1: 485.

15. FDR, speech to the Third Annual Women's Conference on Current Problems, New York City, 13 October 1933, *FDR: FA*, 1: 424; FDR to Dodd, 6 January 1936, *FDR: PL*, 3: 543.

16. FDR to John Cudahy, 8 January 1934, *FDR: PL*, 3: 383; Diary entry, 14 September 1937, in *Navigating the Rapids 1918–1971: From the Papers of Adolf A. Berle*, ed. Beatrice Bishop Berle and Travis Beal Jacobs (New York, 1973), p. 135. See FDR to Lord Cecil, 6 April 1937, *FDR: PL*, 3: 672, in which FDR attributes the success of his Good Neighbor Policy to his preachments.

17. FDR to William E. Dodd, 2 December 1935, *FDR: PL*, 3: 530–31; FDR speech at St. Paul, MN, 9 October 1936, *FDR: FA*, 2: 453; FDR to Arthur Sweetser, 9 December 1936, *FDR: FA*, 2: 534.

18. FDR, message to Congress, 3 January 1936, *FDR: FA*, 2: 155; FDR to Nicholas Murray Butler, 8 September 1936, ibid., 2: 413. There is little doubt that

FDR himself was influenced by isolationism. He shared his time's reluctance to go to war merely for the sake of defending narrow economic interests. "If we face the choice of profits or peace, this Nation will answer—this Nation must answer—'we choose peace.'" This assertion, however, failed to take into account a distinction between expansion of special commercial interests and a complete strangulation of American commerce. "Our present civilization," he argued as always, "rests on the basis of an international exchange of commodities." Autarchy produced only declining standards of living and the pressure to expand at the expense of others. FDR speech at Chautauqua, 14 August 1936; and Speech at Buenos Aires, 1 December 1936, in ibid., 2: 379, 519.

19. The great distance between those who wished to cooperate with the League of Nations and Wilson's original view of the centrality of the United States' contribution is evident from the similarity between cooperationist views and a French proposal at the Geneva disarmament conference. This project stipulated that concentric circles of powers would be responsible for security, the innermost and most important of which would be continental powers. The United States, by this logic, would be in an outer circle, and "would cooperate loyally and effectively in applying Article 16 of the Covenant." See Philip Noel-Baker, *The First World Disarmament Conference 1932–1933 and Why It Failed* (New York, 1979), p. 85.

20. FDR to William E. Dodd, 2 December 1935, *FDR: FA*, 2: 102. See the different interpretation in Robert Divine, *The Illusion of Neutrality* (Chicago, 1962), pp. 120–21, who argues that FDR's attitude toward neutrality legislation was governed by his desire as a "realist" to "make the decision between war and peace free from the demands of national honor and the pressure of economic interests." The widespread acceptance of internationalist strategic logic as "realistic" since World War II provides (usually unwitting) testimony to the inroads made by the modernist outlook.

21. FDR to Oswald Garrison Villard, 24 August 1936, *FDR: FA*, 2: 395.

22. For FDR's analysis, see FDR to Joseph Tumulty, 23 December 1937, *FDR: PL*, 3: 736.

23. Charles Beard, *The Devil Theory of War* (New York, 1969), p. 11. Emphasis in the original.

24. FDR to Colonel House, 17 September 1935, *FDR: PL*, 3: 506–7.

25. Manfred Jonas, *Isolationism in America, 1935–1941* (Ithaca, 1966). Of course, internationalists also felt the pull of supra-ideological necessity when it came time to build coalitions. We tend to forget that the phrase "collective security" was coined in the early 1930s by Maxim Litvinoff as the USSR attempted to shape an anti-Fascist coalition in the League of Nations.

26. Joseph P. Kennedy to FDR, 15 May 1940, President's Secretary's File [hereafter PSF]: FDRL, box 5. To be logically correct about it, if internationalism was a species of idealism, so also was isolationism, since it too was rooted in an exceptionalist hypostatization of history.

27. More traditional rhetorically was Secretary of State Cordell Hull's hackneyed

declaration on July 7 that "there could be no serious hostilities anywhere in the world which did not one way or another affect the interests and obligations of this country." Department of State press release, 7 July 1937.

28. FDR to Anthony J. Drexel Biddle, 10 November 1937, *FDR: PL*, 3: 725; FDR to Endicott Peabody, 16 October 1937, ibid., 3: 717.

29. Welles memo to FDR, 6 October 1937, in William Langer and S. Everett Gleason, *The Challenge to Isolation* (Gloucester, MA, 1970), p. 20; Berle diary entry, 13 October 1937, *Navigating the Rapids*, p. 140.

30. FDR to William Phillips, 7 May 1937, *FDR: PL*, 3: 680; FDR to Mussolini, ibid., 3: 700.

31. *FDR: FA*, 5: doc. 1028. FDR certainly agreed with Welles, who told the German ambassador that "in their dealings with Germany during the past twenty years injustices had been committed by other powers which [he] had always hoped would be righted through peaceful and reasonable negotiations." Memorandum by Welles of conversation with Hans Dieckhoff, 14 March 1938, *FDR: FA*, 5: doc. 920A. At the same time, he understood that the United States could engage in economic but not in political appeasement. See Welles memorandum of conversation with Ronald C. Lindsey, 8 March 1938, *FDR: FA*, 5: doc. 899A. For a fuller discussion, see Arnold Offner, *American Appeasement: United States Foreign Policy and Germany, 1933–1938* (Cambridge, MA, 1969).

32. FDR to W. L. Mackenzie King, 11 October 1938, *FDR: FA*, 7: doc. 1344; FDR to Irving Fisher, 3 and 11 October 1933, ibid., 7: docs. 1323 and 1342; FDR to Oswald Garrison Villard, ibid., doc. 1346; FDR to William Phillips, 17 October 1938, ibid., 4: 819.

33. FDR press conference, 15 November 1938, *FDR: FA*, 7: doc. 1409; FDR to Samuel I. Rosenman, 13 November 1940, *FDR: PL*, 2: 1078.

34. FDR message to Congress, 4 January 1939, *FDR: FA*, 8: doc. 1503.

35. Joseph Davies to Harry Hopkins, 18 January 1939, in Davies, *Mission to Moscow* (New York, 1941), p. 433.

36. For the argument that the threat was exaggerated, with the underlying suggestion that FDR's interventionism was motivated by ideological sympathy for Great Britain, see John A. Thompson, "The Exaggeration of American Vulnerability," *Diplomatic History* 16 (Winter 1992): 28–43. However, making policy on the basis of worst-case possibilities would appear to contain a built-in bias toward exaggeration. While a willingness to fight for the balance of power also requires commitment to an abstraction, one can still visualize a direct threat if the balance fails—an invasion of the British Isles from the Scheldt Basin, for example. Internationalist logic finds it difficult to translate its dangers into direct threats—thus the tendency to exaggerate.

37. FDR telegram to Joseph Kennedy, April 1940, quoted in Michael Beschloss, *Kennedy and Roosevelt: The Uneasy Alliance* (New York, 1980), p. 205; Rexford Tugwell, *The Democratic Roosevelt* (Garden City, NY, 1957), p. 484; Bullitt to FDR, 7 December 1937, *FDR: FA*, 9: doc. 1744; FDR press conference, 20 April 1939, *FDR: FA*, 4: doc. 654; FDR to Josiah Bailey, 13 May 1941, *FDR: PL*, 4:

1154; Berle diary, 26 May 1939, in *Navigating the Rapids*, p. 224; FDR to William Allen White, 14 December 1939, *FDR: PL*, 4: 968.

38. FDR to Joseph P. Kennedy, 30 October 1939, *FDR: PL*, 4: 950; FDR memo to James Roosevelt, 20 January 1938, *FDR: FA*, 4: doc. 774; FDR address to Eighth Pan-American Scientific Congress, 10 May 1940, *Roosevelt's Foreign Policy*, p. 234; FDR to Pope Pius XII, 23 December 1939, *Roosevelt's Foreign Policy*, p. 29.

39. FDR press conference, 15 November 1938, *FDR: FA*, 7: doc. 1409; FDR, message to Congress, 4 January 1939, ibid., 8: doc. 1503; FDR press conference, 20 April 1938, ibid., 5: doc. 1031. According to Rexford Tugwell, "The airplane, he was certain, had changed everything" and even threatened to make traditional naval warfare obsolete. Tugwell, *The Democratic Roosevelt*, p. 487.

40. FDR to William Phillips, 6 February 1937, *FDR: PL*, 3: 656; FDR to Arthur Murray, 13 May 1938, ibid., 4: 781–82; Draft of a radio broadcast for FDR by Welles, 29 March 1939, *FDR: FA*, 9: doc 1685a. See also Daniel Lerner, "Modernization," *International Encyclopedia of the Social Sciences* (New York, 1968), vol. 10, p. 389.

41. FDR to Gertrude Ely, 25 March 1939, *FDR: PL*, 4: 872.

42. FDR to Norman Thomas, 14 May 1941, *FDR: PL*, 4: 1159; Memo, FDR to James Roosevelt, 20 January 1938, ibid., 4: 751; FDR speech, 10 June 1941, *Roosevelt's Foreign Policy, 1933–1941*, p. 251.

43. FDR press conference, 8 April 1939, *FDR: FA*, 9: doc. 1710; FDR conference with Senate Military Affairs Committee, 31 January 1939, ibid., 8: doc. 1565.

44. FDR to William Allen White, 14 December 1939, *FDR: PL*, 4: 968; Fireside chat, 29 December 1940, cited in Wayne S. Cole, *Roosevelt and the Isolationists* (Lincoln, NE, 1983), p. 342; John Morton Blum, *Roosevelt and Morgenthau* (Boston, 1970), p. 272.

45. FDR press conference, 31 March 1939, *FDR: FA*, 9: doc. 1691.

46. FDR conference with the Senate Military Affairs Committee, 31 January 1939, *FDR: FA*, 8: doc. 1565. See also the memorandum handed to Bullitt by Otto von Hapsburg which purports to be a record of a conversation between Hitler and his followers in which the führer outlines a final war against the *Dollarjuden*, in PSF: Safe File, Bullitt, FDRL.

47. FDR press conference, 3 February 1939, *FDR: FA*, 8: doc. 1574; FDR to John Cudahy, 4 March 1939, *FDR: PL*, 4: 863.

48. FDR to Nicholas Murray Butler, 4 August 1939, *FDR: FA*, 10: doc. 1965; Draft of a radio broadcast for FDR by Welles, 29 March 1939, in ibid., 9: doc. 1685a; Fireside chat, 3 September 1939, *Roosevelt's Foreign Policy, 1933–1941*, p. 183; FDR press conference, 4 July 1939, *FDR: FA*, 10: doc. 1908. They didn't agree on much, but FDR would have found no fault with Mussolini's 1939 assertion that "there are not in Europe at present problems so big and so active as to justify a war which from a European conflict would naturally become universal." Mussolini, circa May 15, 1939, quoted in E. H. Carr, *The Twenty Years' Crisis* (New York, 1964), p. 84.

49. See, e.g., the telegram of 25 August 1939 by the British ambassador to Berlin, Sir Neville Henderson, *FDR: FA,* 10: doc. 2040a; Gary Dean Best, *Herbert Hoover: The Postpresidential Years* (Stanford, 1983) 1: 181; Charles and Mary Beard, *The Rise of American Civilization,* vol. 2, *The Industrial Era* (New York, 1928), p. 617; FDR press conference, 23 June 1939, *FDR: FA,* 10: doc. 1892.

50. Gaddis Smith, *Dean Acheson* (New York, 1972), p. 14. On the relationship between modernity and risk, see Giddens, *The Consequences of Modernity,* pp. 124–31.

51. FDR press conference, 20 April 1939, *FDR: FA,* 10: doc. 1744; State of the Union Address, 6 January 1941, *Roosevelt's Foreign Policy, 1933–1941,* p. 321; Beschloss, *Kennedy and Roosevelt,* p. 223.

52. FDR conference with the Senate Military Affairs Committee, 31 January 1939, *FDR: FA,* 8: doc. 1565; FDR to Fulton Oursler, 25 June 1941, in Cole, *Roosevelt and the Isolationists,* p. 433; Blum, *Roosevelt and Morgenthau,* p. 236; FDR to Francis B. Sayre, 31 December 1940, *FDR: PL,* 4: 1093.

53. Memo, Joseph P. Kennedy to FDR, 3 March 1939, *FDR: FA,* 9: doc. 1616a.

54. FDR speech to Pan American Union, 14 April 1939, *FDR: FA,* 9: doc. 1716; FDR, Armistice Day Address.

55. FDR, speech at Queens University, Kingston, Ontario, 18 August 1938, *FDR: FA,* 6: doc. 1234; Hull speech to National Press Club, 17 March 1938, Cordell Hull, *Memoirs* (New York, 1948) 1: 577; Robert W. Tucker, "The Purposes of American Power," *Foreign Affairs* 59 (Winter 1980/81): 264. This concern with cultural values helps explain why FDR began attacking continued appeals for appeasement as "views based on materialism." Contrary to later revisionist arguments, FDR saw isolationism as being economically motivated by narrow special interests. See FDR to Samuel I. Rosenman, 13 November 1940, *FDR: PL,* 4: 1078; FDR to John Cudahy, 18 April 1938, *FDR: PL,* 4: 776. In response to those who would argue "yes, but FDR was defending capitalist economic interests in general abroad," I would make three main points: first, the threat was not merely economic; second, whether one emphasizes the chicken or the egg, there is a mutual dependence between free markets and democracy; third, the restructuring of the international division of labor by the totalitarians would have had a profound impact on the American political economy. The revisionist Open Door historians certainly have a point when they suggest that American policymakers were motivated by a belief in an Open World that transcended the immediate desires of specific business interests. However, they fail to realize the vital role that force and power assumed to the maintenance of the system. Those inclined to argue in ironic fashion that the cold war produced a version of the garrison state in the form of the military industrial complex should pause to consider the huge differences between the kind of international system the United States would have encountered in a totalitarian world and the relatively open environment of the post–World War II period.

56. Maurice Matloff, "Prewar Military Plans and Preparations, 1939–1941,"

paper presented at AHA meeting, New York City, 30 December 1950, in Frank Roberts Papers, Harry S. Truman Presidential Library, Independence, MO [hereafter HSTPL]. RAINBOW-5 and ABC-1 were officially adopted only on 14 May 1941. The world situation was so unprecedentedly complex that FDR rejected any possibility of drawing up hard-and-fast plans to meet the situation. On this point, see FDR to Joseph Grew, 29 January 1941, PSF: Confidential File [hereafter CF], box 13, FDRL; Joint Board estimate, 11 September 1941, FDRL, Safe File: box 1. However, the likelihood is that FDR realized rather early that the United States would have to become a belligerent. Whatever the motivation behind the attempt to sell Lend-Lease as "cheap security" and its pandering to the isolationist desire to stay out of the war, it was, by internationalist *logic,* a specious argument. The program made sense only from a traditional balance-of-power approach, as a means of promoting a stalemate in Europe. But, of course, that was precisely the kind of logic that Wilson had first entertained, and then firmly rejected, a generation earlier. The Century Committee was closer to the mark in its understanding of internationalist strategic imperatives. But its position at this time was still on the fringe of internationalism. See Mark Lincoln Chadwin, *The Hawks of World War II* (Chapel Hill, NC, 1968).

57. FDR to George Gallup, 2 October 1942, *FDR: PL,* 4: 1349.

58. Cole, *Roosevelt and the Isolationists,* p. 7; Blum, *Roosevelt and Morgenthau,* p. 587; Memo by Samuel R. Fuller, Jr. [1 October 1938], *FDR: FA,* 7: doc. 1321. Many in the country would have agreed with the financier Thomas Lamont, who was unable "to distinguish between Hitler and the German people. They are all inbred with the same idea of domination. I think it is inborn and bred in the flesh. It dates back at least to the time of Frederick the Great"; quoted in Patrick Hearden, *Roosevelt Confronts Hitler: America's Entry into World War II* (DeKalb, IL, 1987), p. 230. Even in the mid-1930s, at a time when he was still acting on the basis of his 90 percent–10 percent thesis, Roosevelt wondered if the supposedly misled peoples were really peace-loving at heart. Indeed, he sensed that "all is not well at the bottom." See FDR to Arthur Murray, 4 October 1937, *FDR: PL,* 3: 715; and Message to Congress, 3 January 1936, *FDR: FA,* 2: 154. For FDR's childhood misadventure of being arrested four times in a single day in imperial Germany, see William D. Hassett, *Off the Record with FDR, 1942–1945* (New Brunswick, NJ, 1958), p. 200.

59. FDR to William J. Donovan, 7 November 1941, *FDR: PL,* 4: 1234. All of this suggests that FDR's reference at the Casablanca meeting to a distinction between the German people and the Nazi philosophy was made more from political convenience than personal conviction. FDR to Hull, 17 January 1944, ibid., 4: 1504.

60. FDR to Queen Wilhelmina, 26 August 1944, *FDR: PL,* 4: 1535; Blum, *Roosevelt and Morgenthau,* pp. 572, 577.

61. Office of Strategic Services [hereafter OSS] R & A Branch paper, "The Bases of Soviet Foreign Policy," 1 September 1943, Frank Roberts Papers, HSTPL.

62. FDR to Lord Louis Mountbatten, 8 November 1943, *FDR: PL,* 4: 1468.

63. FDR to Henry Morgenthau, 6 December 1934, *FDR: FA,* 2: 306; FDR to

Fred I. Kent, 26 July 1935, ibid., 2: 585. The fading belief in cultural universalism is evident in the fate of the Cultural Relations program set up by the Department of State in 1938. It started out doctrinally committed to a pure and apolitical internationalism, but by war's end it was clear that culture would be subordinated to the government's foreign-policy goals. Culture became an instrument of foreign policy, part of the general trend among modernizing powers to broaden their foreign-policy objectives, rather than a means of transforming foreign policy. For the story, see Frank Ninkovich, *The Diplomacy of Ideas: U.S. Foreign Policy and Cultural Relations, 1938–1950* (New York, 1981).

64. Quoted in George M. Elsey, *Roosevelt and China, The White House Story: The President and U.S. Aid to China—1944* (Wilmington, DE, 1979).

65. FDR to Pope Pius XII, 3 September 1941, *FDR: PL*, 4: 1204–5; FDR to William D. Leahy, 26 June 1941, ibid., 4: 1177.

66. FDR to Joseph Grew, 30 November 1939, *FDR: PL*, 4: 960; John Foster Dulles, memo of conversation with FDR, 26 March 1943, John Foster Dulles Papers, Mudd Library, Princeton University [hereafter JFDP], box 283.

67. FDR to Thomas W. Lamont, 12 November 1942, *FDR: PL*, 4: 1366; W. Averell Harriman and Elie Abel, *Special Envoy to Churchill and Stalin* (New York, 1975), pp. 170, 227. According to a 1943 report from the OSS R & A branch, "That collaboration with the Soviet Union is not out of the question is also indicated by the shift in Soviet theory and practice from an emphasis on world revolution—which in given circumstances is incompatible with friendly relations with other states—to a concern with soviet national security." The report concluded that the Communist faith, "for the present at least, has little practical significance." OSS R & A branch paper, "The Bases of Soviet Foreign Policy," 1 September 1943, Frank Roberts Papers, HSTPL.

68. It is also noteworthy that many viewed "cooperation" as largely an Anglo-Soviet matter in which the United States would act as impartial mediator. As Admiral Leahy put it in a 1944 letter: "So long as Britain and Russia cooperate and collaborate in the interests of peace, there can be no great war in the foreseeable future." But this seems to me to be vestigial thinking left over from the old neutrality frame of mind. And, in any case, it did not address ongoing Wilsonian strategic concerns. Excerpts from Leahy letter, 16 May 1944, PSF: Safe File, box 8, FDRL. See also Fraser Harbutt, *The Iron Curtain: Churchill, America, and the Origins of the Cold War* (New York, 1986).

69. Eleanor Roosevelt, *This I Remember* (New York, 1949), p. 254.

70. Hassett [5 April 1943], *Off the Record with FDR*, p. 166.

71. Dulles, memo of meeting with FDR, [10?] February 1944, JFDP, box 283.

72. FDR to George Norris, 21 September 1943, *FDR: PL*, 4: 1446.

73. In a way, the United Nations was pre-Wilsonian to the degree that it envisioned the kind of cooperative world that Taft had in mind prior to Wilson's encounter with civilizational roadblocks.

74. FDR to William Allen White, 14 December 1939, *FDR: PL,* 4: 967; FDR to Sumner Welles, 19 May 1942, ibid., 4: 1322.

CHAPTER 5

1. Cyril E. Black, "Change as a Condition of Modern Life," in Marvin Weiner, ed., *Modernization: the Dynamics of Growth* (New York, 1966), p. 26.

2. Truman diary, 22 May 1945, in *Off the Record: The Private Papers of Harry S. Truman,* ed. Robert H. Ferrell (New York, 1980), p. 35; HST, speech at Denver, CO, 28 June 1944, Family Affairs, General File, box 17, HSTPL; Margaret Truman, *Harry S. Truman* (New York, 1973), p. 394.

3. Press conference of 8 October 1945, quoted in McGeorge Bundy, *Danger and Survival* (New York, 1988), p. 144; Notes of Truman-Molotov meeting, 23 April 1945, PSF, box 187, HSTPL; Truman diary, 22 May 1945, in Ferrell, *Off the Record,* p. 35. Many years later, Truman still maintained that "the greatest barrier is the language barrier . . . If we had a universal language which everybody could understand there wouldn't be so much misunderstanding." Transcripts to History of the American Presidency, no. 52, HSTPL. Cf. Ralph Waldo Emerson's comment: "underneath their external diversities, all men are of one heart and mind" in "Prudence," *The Complete Works of Emerson,* 12 vols. (New York, 1968) 2: 239.

4. DDE to John Sheldon Doud Eisenhower, 3 March 1946, in *The Papers of Dwight D. Eisenhower,* ed. Louis Galambos (Baltimore, 1978) [hereafter *PDDE*], 7: 882. Historians have made much of the existence of hard and soft approaches to the Soviet Union during this period, but these were less "axioms" than attitudes applicable to any foreign policy issue at most any time. Without specific policy frameworks to guide them, these prearticulate attitudes hardly merit being called axioms.

5. Charles Bohlen and Geroid T. Robinson, "The Capabilities and Intentions of the Soviet Union as Affected by American Policy," December 1945, *Diplomatic History* 1 (Fall 1977): 394; Intelligence Review no. 2, 21 February 1946, George Elsey Papers, box 63, HSTPL; Masaryk is quoted from Dorothy V. Jones, *Code of Peace: Ethics and Security in the World of the Warlord* (Chicago, 1991), p. 108.

6. Joint Strategic Survey Committee report JSC1731/14, 27 February 1947, *PDDE* 8: 1552.

7. Intelligence Reviews, 4 April 1946, "Soviet Policy toward the Western Powers," and [25 April 1946?], "Soviet Foreign Policy in Eastern Europe," Elsey Papers, box 63, HSTPL; Forrestal to Walter Lippmann, 7 January 1946, in *The Forrestal Diaries,* ed. Walter Millis (New York, 1951), p. 128; War Department Intelligence Division booklet, "The Soviet Union" [1946?], PSF: Foreign Affairs File, Russia, box 187. As the rabid anti-Sovietism of many isolationist American diplomats during the 1930s makes clear, anticommunism was not necessarily tied to fears of a strategic danger to the United States. On this point, see Hugh De Santis, *The Diplomacy of Silence* (Chicago, 1980), pp. 45, 74–75.

8. Edward Willett, "Dialectical Materialism and Russian Objectives," 14 January 1946, PSF: Foreign Affairs File, Russia, box 187; Eben Ayers OH, p. 191; David Bell OH, p. 45; Clark Clifford OH, p. 169.

9. On Kennan's alienation, see Anders Stephanson, *Kennan and the Art of Foreign Policy* (Cambridge, MA, 1989), pp. 230–48; and Walter Hixson, *George Kennan: Cold War Iconoclast* (New York, 1989), pp. 7–10.

10. On Kennan's prescriptive vagueness, see Dean Acheson, *Present at the Creation* (New York, 1969), pp. 348, 446; Barton Gellman, *Contending with Kennan: Toward a Philosophy of Power* (New York, 1984), p. 43; Martin Herz, ed., *Decline of the West? George Kennan and His Critics* (Washington, 1978), pp. 98, 114.

11. PPS 23, "Review of Current Trends of U.S. Foreign Policy," 24 December 1948, in *The State Department Policy Planning Staff Papers, 1947–1949,* ed. Anna Kasten Nelson (New York, 1983) [hereafter *SDPPS*] 2: 126.

12. Charles Bohlen, *Witness to History* (New York, 1973), p. 531; Kennan, "Soviet-American Relations Today," address of 12 May 1947, Kennan Papers, Mudd Library, Princeton, box 17.

13. Kennan to James Byrnes, 20 March 1946, U.S. Department of State, *Foreign Relations of the United States* (Washington, DC) [hereafter *FRUS*], *1946,* 7: 721. Kennan's analysis of "national character" may today seem hopelessly impressionistic, but in the 1940s the concept was still thought to possess analytical potential by the social sciences.

14. For more on this point, see Paul Ricoeur, *Lectures on Ideology and Utopia,* ed. George W. Taylor (New York, 1986). Indeed, even Stalin seemed to take a very un-Marxist line on this point when he commented that communizing the Germans made as much sense as saddling up a cow.

15. Kennan lecture, "Where Do We Stand?" 21 December 1949, Kennan Papers, box 17; Kennan talk, "American-Soviet Relations," 29 December 1946, Kennan Papers, box 16. See, e.g., Robert C. Tucker's argument in *Political Culture and Leadership in Soviet Russia: From Lenin to Gorbachev* (New York, 1987), p. 116, to the effect that "what happened in Russia in the 1930s is not only superficially described but actually obscured by the use of a term like 'modernization.' In fact, the nation underwent a reversion to the Russian past in its developmental mode."

16. Discussion meeting report, "The Soviet Way of Thought and Its Effect on Foreign Policy," 7 January 1947, Kennan Papers, box 16; Kennan, "Psychological Background of Soviet Foreign Policy," 31 June 1947, Kennan Papers, box 1; J. G. Merquior, *The Veil and the Mask: Essays on Culture and Ideology* (London, 1979), p. 27.

17. Kennan lecture, "Trust as a Factor in International Relations," 1 October 1946, Kennan Papers, box 16; David Held, *Introduction to Critical Theory: Horkheimer to Habermas* (Berkeley, 1980), p. 107; De Santis, *The Diplomacy of Silence,* p. 213.

18. Kennan lecture, "Formulation of Policy in the USSR," 18 September 1947, Kennan Papers, box 17; Kennan to Walter Lippmann (unsent), 6 April 1948, ibid.;

Charles Bohlen OH, Dwight D. Eisenhower Presidential Library, Abiline, KS [hereafter DDEPL], p. 17.

19. Kennan lecture, "Trust as a Factor in International Relations," Kennan Papers, box 16; Kennan address, "Soviet-American Relations Today," 12 May 1947, Kennan Papers, box 17.

20. "The Soviet Way of Thought and Its Effect on Foreign Policy," Kennan Papers, box 16; Kennan lecture, 1 October 1946, ibid.; Kennan paper, "Russia's International Position at the Close of the War with Germany," May 1945, ibid., box 1. Perhaps a less confusing way of conceptualizing this problem would have been to use Max Weber's distinction between the "ethic of ultimate ends" and the "ethic of responsibility." As explained by Richard Sennett, *The Uses of Disorder: Personal Identity and City Life* (New York, 1970), p. 130, a responsible act "is always impure, always painfully mixed because of diverse motives and desires: an absolute act, on the other hand, is a struggle toward purity of desire and act as well as toward a 'pure' end." The distinction here, then, is between mixed motives and purism, not between realism and ideology.

21. Kennan lecture, "Where Are We Today?", 21 December 1948, Kennan Papers, box 17.

22. The essay, "The Sources of Soviet Conduct," is reprinted in *Foreign Affairs* 65 (Spring 1987): 852–68. The quotation is on p. 862.

23. PPS 38, "United States Objectives with Respect to Russia," 18 August 1948, SDPPS 2: 392, 338; Kennan lecture, "Contemporary Soviet Diplomacy," 22 October 1946, Kennan Papers, box 16. For time span, see Kennan lecture, 17 September 1946, Kennan Papers, box 16; Kennan, "Psychological Background of Soviet Foreign Policy," 31 June 1947, Kennan Papers, box 1.

24. Kennan, "The Soviet Way of Thought and Its Effect on Soviet Foreign Policy," discussion at the Council on Foreign Relations, New York City, 17 January 1947, Kennan Papers, box 16; Kennan lecture, "Russia's National Objectives," 10 April 1947, ibid., box 17; Kennan to Lippmann, 6 April 1948, ibid.; John Lewis Gaddis, *Strategies of Containment* (New York, 1983), p. 47. Kennan's view of the failure of communism was largely a reflection of his reading of Edward Gibbon, whose *Decline and Fall of the Roman Empire* asserted that there was "nothing more contrary to nature than to hold in obedience distant provinces." But the idea that all ideologues would encounter their Thermidor was at that time also in process of being popularized by the historian Crane Brinton's widely read *The Anatomy of Revolution* (New York, 1938).

25. For typologies of this trajectory, see note 24 of the Introduction. Kennan, however, like the conservative economist Joseph Schumpeter, believed that communism was a product of a civilizational malaise within the West and that, if anything, the future tended to lie with socialism. Kennan lecture, "Russian-American Relations," 20 February 1947, Kennan Papers, box 16; Kennan lecture, "American Capitalist Democracy in a Collectivist Environment," 2 May 1947, ibid. See also Kennan to Robert G. Hooker, *FRUS 1949*, 1: 405. The phrase "balance of ideas" is from

Felix Gilbert, "The United States and the European Balance," *Foreign Affairs* 55 (October 1976): 198.

26. Kennan, "Review of Current Trends in U.S. Foreign Policy," 24 February 1948, in *SDPPS* 2: 381; Memo of meeting, 2 March 1950, *FRUS 1950*, 1: 178; Kennan lecture, 17 September 1946, Kennan Papers, box 16; Memo by Kennan, 7 September 1949, *FRUS 1949*, 1: 381; Kennan lecture, "Where Are We Today?", 21 December 1948, Kennan Papers, box 17. Although Kennan could not imagine an internationalist utopia at the end of the journey, others did. From a more liberal perspective it was still possible to hold that, for the time being, Western diplomacy "must utilize the methods of power politics, which alone can be successful in preventing universal conquest so long as opinion remains dominantly national." See Quincy Wright, "The Relations of Universal Culture to Power Politics," in *Conflicts of Power in Modern Culture,* ed. Lyman Bryson, Louis Finkelstein, and R. M. MacIver (New York, 1946).

27. Truman diary entries, 26 July and 7 June 1945, in Ferrell, *Off the Record,* pp. 57, 44; Truman letters of 11 November 1946, 3 and 13 March 1947, in Margaret Truman, *Harry S. Truman,* 353, 391. See also Eben Ayers OH, 2: 373–74; David Lilienthal, *Journals: The Atomic Energy Years, 1945–50* (New York, 1964) 2: 160. Truman's view was not simply based on what one historian has called the analogy of "red Fascism." His understanding of the Soviets was grounded in timeless examples of universal history besides being connected to the Wilsonian framework of contemporary history.

28. Smith to State, 8 January 1947, *FRUS 1947*, 5: 2–3; Clark Clifford OH, p. 374; Address by George C. Marshall, "Problems of European Revival and German and Austrian Peace Settlements," Chicago, 18 November 1947, in *Germany 1947–1949: The Story in Documents* (Washington, DC, 1950), p. 12; Acheson, address to the American Society of Newspaper Editors, 18 April 1947, DAP: Yale, series 3, box 7. Five years and many crises later, Acheson told Winston Churchill that "the heart of the matter was the concern of the regime to maintain itself in power." Memo of Churchill-Truman meeting, 6 January 1952, Dean Acheson Papers, Memoranda of Conversation, HSTPL [hereafter DAP: MC], box 67.

29. Smith to Marshall, 10 May 1948, *FRUS 1948*, 4: 852; Acheson remarks at a panel discussion with George Marshall and Francis Russell, 4 June 1947, DAP: Yale, series 3, box 47; Acheson, National Press Club speech, 12 January 1950, DAP: Yale, series 3, box 47; Francis Russell to Acheson, 27 March 1947, *FRUS 1947*, 4: 547. Marshall, in a conversation with Molotov in the spring of 1948, repeated the same point: the United States "did not oppose communism simply because of its Marxian ideology but purely and simply because we had seen repeated instances of Communist minorities coming into power by illegal means." Marshall to State, 10 May 1948, PSF, HSTPL, box 187.

30. Willett, "Dialectical Materialism and Russian Objectives"; "The Strategy and Tactics of World Communism," Report by the House Committee on Foreign Affairs (Washington, DC, 1948), pp. 28, 49; Hoyt Vandenberg to Truman, 27 September 1946, PSF: Intelligence File, box 249.

31. See, e.g., the characterization in B. Susser, *The Grammar of Modern Ideology* (New York, 1988), p. 11: "An ideology of skepticism is a contradiction in terms. Whatever the intellectual difficulties or perhaps even the theoretical impossibility of the project, ideology needs to exist and it needs to exist in certainty. No society can escape the need to legitimate its distribution of resources, the advantages and deprivations it mandates, the sacrifices it demands, the violence, even the killing, it sanctions. For these ends, only, a self-confident and definitive ideology will do." Or take the following description by Alvin Gouldner: "Ideology is, above all, action-generating thought and as such skepticism is the father of paralysis. 'It inhibits the feeling of conviction so necessary for the high and sacred moments of practice. For practice is politics; and politics is, in the end, killing.' To indulge in doubt, self-consciousness or humility is to undermine resolve and invite indecision." *The Dialectic of Ideology and Technology* (New York, 1976), p. 24.

32. Historicus, "Stalin on Revolution," *Foreign Affairs* 27 (January 1949): 214; Nitze, "Recent Soviet Moves," 8 February 1950, *FRUS 1950*, 1: 1145–46.

33. NSC 68, April 14, 1950, in John Lewis Gaddis and Thomas H. Etzold, *Containment: Documents on American Policy and Strategy, 1945–1950* (New York, 1978), p. 395; Memo by Hare, 5 April 1950, *FRUS 1950*, 1: 221.

34. Truman to Harriman, 12 February 1951, PSF, box 187. Cf. Leszek Kolakowski's comment in *Main Currents of Marxism*, vol. 1, *The Founders* (Oxford, 1978), p. 348: "Marx constantly regarded the historical process from the point of view of the future liberation of mankind, which was the sole touchstone of current events." Cf. also Murray Edelman, *Political Language: Words That Succeed and Words That Fail* (New York, 1977), p. 25: "So far as political beliefs are concerned, the most potent categorizations almost certainly are visions of the future."

35. *FRUS 1952–1954*, 2: 61. For Bohlen's memo of 27 March 1952, see ibid., p. 6; Kennan, "Foreign Aid in the Framework of National Policy," 10 November 1949, Kennan Papers, box 1.

36. Avi Shlaim, *The United States and the Berlin Blockade, 1948–1949* (Berkeley, CA, 1983), p. 52.

37. Memo, Kennan to Acheson, 17 February 1950, *FRUS 1950*, 1: 164. Kennan also did little to generate sympathy for his view that containment began at home when for other policymakers the basic problem was traceable to Soviet intentions. Kennan, "Where Do We Stand?" 21 December 1949, Kennan Papers, box 17.

38. See Kennan's confused resort to a mutually exclusive dualism in his essay "Two Planes of International Reality," in *Realities of American Foreign Policy* (Princeton, 1954), p. 28: "There loomed suddenly before people a world of power realities overwhelming, now, in their significance, a world in which the statistics of military force seemed to constitute the *only* terms in which external reality could be understood and expressed, the *only* language of international dealings . . . Many Americans now became wholly absorbed with power values to a point where they were impatient of any discussion of international affairs that tried to take account of anything else." Kennan could explain the evolution of American policy only in terms

of schizophrenia when, in fact, it was a logical development, as I shall show in the following chapter.

39. Report to the president, 7 April 1950, PSF: Foreign Affairs File; *New York Times,* 19 May 1949, quoted in Shlaim, *The Berlin Crisis,* p. 90.

40. Acheson speech, "An American Attitude toward World Affairs," 28 November 1939, DAP: Yale, series 3, box 46; Memorandum of conversation between Acheson and Rep. Christian Herter, 24 March 1950, *FRUS 1950,* 1: 207; Notes dictated by Acheson, 27 March 1950, DAP: Yale, series 2, box 47.

41. Clark Clifford OH, 88; National Intelligence Estimate no. 3, 15 November 1950, "Soviet Capabilities and Intentions," PSF, box 187.

42. Minutes of Third Meeting of Washington Exploratory Talks on Security, 7 July 1948, *FRUS 1948,* 3: 157; Hoyt Vandenberg to Truman, 27 September 1946, PSF: Intelligence File, box 249. Anders Stephanson's argument that autarchy and expansionism are logically incompatible ignores, I believe, the "real world" basis of judgments by American policymakers.

43. Kennan lecture, "What Is Policy?", 18 December 1947, Kennan Papers, box 17; Kennan address, "Foreign Aid in the Framework of National Policy," 19 November 1949, ibid., box 1; Memorandum of the Fourth Meeting of the Washington Group Participating in the Washington Exploratory Talks on Security, 20 July 1948, *FRUS 1948,* 3: 193; Attachment to memo to Admiral Hill, 7 October 1946, Kennan Papers, box 28.

44. Memo, DDE to JCS, July 1947, *PDDE* 8: 1856; Bohlen to Nitze, 5 April 1950, *FRUS 1950,* 1: 222.

45. Minutes of PPS meeting, 16 December 1949, *FRUS 1949,* 1: 415; Kennan, "What Is Policy?" 18 December 1947, Kennan Papers, box 17; Kennan lecture, "Trust as a Factor in International Relations," Kennan Papers, box 16; Kennan, "Problems of Russian Relations," lecture to the National Resources Board, 14 January 1948, Kennan papers, box 17.

46. JCS memo signed by DDE, 13 March 1947, *PDDE* 8: 1593; quotation from JCS 1731/14, 27 February 1947, ibid., 1552; NSC 73/4, 25 August 1950, *FRUS 1950,* 1: 377.

47. PPS 20, 22 January 1948, in *SDPPS* 2: 78; PPS 4, 23 July 1947, ibid., 1: 31; Kennan lecture, "Contemporary Problems of Foreign Policy," 17 September 1948, Kennan Papers, box 17. Acheson agreed on the general importance of Europe. Ruminating on the likely effect of Europe's possible engulfment by Communist barbarism, he said, "We are in the position of the individual who, for the first time, on the death of a parent, hears in a new way the roaring of the cataract." Undated notes by Acheson prior to a Congressional hearing, *FRUS 1950,* 1: 394.

48. Kennan lecture, "Contemporary Problems of Foreign Policy," 17 September 1948, Kennan Papers, box 17; Kennan, statement to the Senate Armed Services Committee, 8 January 1948, ibid.; Kennan lecture, 1 October 1946, ibid., box 16.

49. PPS 13, Resume of the World Situation, 6 November 1947, *SDPPS* 1: 130; Address by George C. Marshall, "Problems of European Revival and German and

Austrian Peace Settlements,'' Chicago, 18 November 1947, in *Germany 1947–1949*, pp. 10, 12.

50. Memo, Kennan to Marshall, 20 January 1948, *FRUS 1948*, 3: 7.

51. See the brilliant PPS 55 of 7 July 1949, ''Outline: Study of U.S. Stance toward Question of Western European Union,'' *SDPPS* 3: 194; PPS 43, ibid., p. 495; Kennan, ''What Is Policy?'' 18 December 1947, Kennan Papers, box 17. Kennan did have a distinctly strange conception of balance. As British journalist Henry Brandon remembered it, Kennan was intent on ''persuading the Soviet Union that the United States wanted a neutralized Europe which would act as a buffer between them both.'' Henry Brandon, *Special Relationships: A Foreign Correspondent's Memoirs from Roosevelt to Reagan* (New York), p. 42. This kind of Europe was not likely to unite soon with the kind of strength needed to restore a balance in Europe.

52. Kennan lectures, ''Russia's National Objectives,'' 10 April 1947; Kennan, ''Foreign Policy and the Marshall Plan,'' 20 February 1948; Kennan, ''Estimate of the International Situation,'' 8 November 1948. All in Kennan Papers, box 17.

53. Kennan to Lippmann, 6 April 1948, Kennan Papers, box 17; PPS 43, *SDPPS* 3: 495.

54. Memo, Acheson to Truman, 18 May 1949, PSF-NSC meetings, summaries, box 220; U.S. Senate, Committee on Foreign Relations, *Reviews of the World Situation: 1949–1950* (Washington, DC, 1974), p. 114; Memo of conversation, 11 February 1949, DAP: HSTPL, box 64. See also Wilson D. Miscamble, ''Deciding to Divide Germany: American Policymaking in 1949,'' *Diplomacy and Statecraft* 2 (July 1991): 312.

55. Memo of conversation with Senators Connally and Vandenberg, 14 February 1949, DAP: MC.

56. ''Only such a union holds out any hope of restoring the balance of power in Europe without permitting Germany to become again the dominant power.'' Memo, Kennan to Marshall, 20 January 1948, *FRUS 1948*, 3: 7.

57. Memo by Kennan, 24 November 1948, *FRUS 1948*, 3: 285; U.S. Senate, Committee on Foreign Relations, North Atlantic Treaty, Hearings, 1st session, 81st Congress, pt. 1, 27 April–3 May 1949 (Washington, 1949), p. 199.

58. Memo, Kennan to Acheson, 6 January 1950, *FRUS 1950*, 1: 132; PPS 39, ''United States Policy toward China,'' 7 September 1948, *SDPPS* 3: 431–32; PPS 39/2, 25 February 1949, in *SDPPS* 3: 27; Kennan lecture, ''Problems of U.S. Foreign Policy after Moscow,'' 6 May 1947, Kennan Papers, box 17.

59. On this point see Warren I. Cohen, *America's Response to China* (New York, 1980), pp. 220–21, 249; *Reviews of the World Situation: 1949–1950*, 13 January 1950, p. 1844.

60. Memo by Webb of meeting with Truman, 2 June 1949, *FRUS 1949*, 1: 326; CIA ''Review of the World Situation,'' 12 September 1947, Records of the NSC: CIA File, box 1; Clark Clifford OH, p. 253; Memo by George H. Butler, 19 March 1948, *FRUS 1948*, 3: 59.

61. Draft of NSC 48, 25 October 1949, "US Position with Respect to Asia," PSF: NSC Meetings, box 107; *Reviews of the World Situation: 1949–1950,* 10 January 1950, p. 135. Actually, Kennan's desire to deal in "straight power concepts" rather than cultural ideals would have required a far greater degree of involvement than had historically been the case in a region where policy had been predominantly commercial and cultural. See PPS 51, "United States Policy toward Southeast Asia," 19 May 1949, *SDPPS* 3: 39–40.

62. NSC 48/2, draft, 25 October 1949, PSF: NSC meetings, box 207; PPS 50, 22 March 1949, *SDPPS* 3: 29.

63. Memo of conversation with Truman, 28 April 1950, DAP: MC, box 65.

64. For the Europeanist thrust of this transformation, see Gary R. Hess, *The United States' Emergence as a Southeast Asian Power, 1940–1950* (New York, 1987), p. 370.

65. Michael Cox, "Requiem for a Cold War Critic: The Rise and Fall of George F. Kennan, 1946–1950," *Irish Slavonic Studies* 11 (1991): 1–35. Wilson Miscamble, *George F. Kennan and the Making of American Foreign Policy, 1947–1950* (Princeton, 1992), makes a convincing case for Kennan's influence on a variety of important issues during this period, but Kennan himself would have been the first to admit that he failed to sell his cooperationist approach.

CHAPTER 6

1. In one sense, it was not at all unusual that policymakers faced new intellectual quandaries in the early cold war. As Victor Turner suggests in *The Ritual Process: Structure and Anti-Structure* (Chicago, 1972), p. 147, "Any developing structure generates problems of organization and values that provoke redefinition of central concepts." However, the ideological transformation taking place during these years was more drastic than this view suggests. The shift was one between "fundamental" and "operative" ideology, as elaborated by Martin Seliger, *Ideology and Politics* (New York, 1976). The situation was complicated, moreover, by the absence of historical signposts. Cf. Morse, *Modernization,* p. 27: "The contemporary situation is so novel historically that reliance on the continuity of a particular status quo or on historical experience is a rather uncertain guide to statecraft." For further references to the literature on ideological trajectories, see note 24 in the Introduction, above. For an extended argument on ideological transformation, see Frank Ninkovich, "Ideology, the Open Door, and Foreign Policy," *Diplomatic History* 6 (Spring 1982): 185–208.

2. Memo by Admiral William Leahy [July 1946], Elsey Papers, box 63; U.S. delegation, Sofia, to State, 6 February 1946, ibid.; *The Forrestal Diaries,* 7 March 1947, p. 251; Truman speech draft, 17 April 1948, Speech Longhand Note File, PSF.

3. Arthur Schlesinger, *Foreign Affairs* (October 1967), as quoted in Walter Laqueur, *Europe after Hitler* (New York, 1983), p. 129; Myron Taylor, "Further Observations on the Present State of American-Soviet Relations," 31 July 1951, PSF:

Foreign Affairs File, Russia 1949–53; Address by Rear Admiral L. C. Stevens to the National War College, 25 January 1951, Records of the NSC, box 19.

4. To insist that the cold war was about power politics or the balance of power distorts the unique character of the conflict. As Hugh De Santis has argued, "A balance-of-forces alternative was ruled out because it violated American principles, lacked domestic support, and merely postponed an eventual clash under conditions of revived Soviet strength." De Santis, *The Diplomacy of Silence,* p. 173. See also the essay by Arthur M. Schlesinger, Jr., in Lloyd Gardner, Arthur Schlesinger, Jr., and Hans Morgenthau, *The Origins of the Cold War* (Waltham, MA, 1970), pp. 58–59. One indication that realpolitik was not a central concern was the absence of critical response to what, in strictly power-political terms, were enormous blunders committed during World War II in creating power vacuums in Europe and Asia.

5. Michael S. Sherry, *Preparing for the Next War: American Plans for Postwar Defense, 1941–45* (New Haven, CT, 1977), p. 200; Acheson talk before the American Society of Newspaper Editors, 18 April 1947, Joseph Jones Papers, HSTPL, box 1; DDE to John Sheldon Doud, 23 August 1946, *PDDE* 8: 1250; Minutes of the Second Meeting of the Washington Exploratory Talks on Security, 6 July 1948, *FRUS 1948,* 3: 153. According to the Policy Planning Staff in May 1949, "It is very probable that even military victory, because of the nature of modern war, would mean defeat in terms of the welfare of the American people and a preservation of their way of life." Memo by George H. Butler, 31 May 1949, *FRUS 1949,* 1: 321.

6. For Acheson, see e.g., *Reviews of the World Situation 1949–1950,* p. 22; Thomas Etzold, *The Conduct of American Foreign Relations: The Other Side of Diplomacy* (New York, 1977), p. 73.

7. Douglas MacArthur, statement following Japanese surrender, 2 September 1945, PSF: General File f, Douglas MacArthur. MacArthur's attitude toward war is discussed in Howard Schonberger, *Aftermath of War: Americans and the Remaking of Japan, 1945–1952* (Kent, 1989), p. 59. For early postwar views of the UN, see Morrell Heald and Lawrence Kaplan, *Culture and Diplomacy: The American Experience* (Wesport, CT, 1977), pp. 214–41.

8. Memorandum by Acheson of discussion with Prime Minister Nehru, 13 October 1949, DAP, HSTPL, box 64; Alvin Gouldner, "Some Observations on Systematic Theory, 1945–55," in *Sociology in the United States of America,* ed. Hans L. Zetterberg (Paris, 1956), p. 39.

9. As Acheson, one of the strongest advocates on behalf of building situations of strength, put it, "We had to change the environment in which the difficulties were discussed." Memo of conversation, 20 April 1950, DAP: MC, box 65. On first reflection, this conclusion was consistent with the recommendations made by Kennan, who had described the Kremlin leadership as "impervious to logic of reason" but "prepared to recognize *situations,* if not arguments." Consequently, they would not be disposed to take unnecessary risks. But Kennan's conception of what needed to be done was far removed from what other policymakers deemed necessary. And, as I shall argue, situations of strength, however interpreted, were not enough.

10. Frederick S. Dunn, *War and the Minds of Men* (New York, 1971), p. 10. For an essay that emphasizes the psychological dimension of credibility but without exploring its roots in historical interpretation, see Robert J. McMahon, "Credibility and World Power," *Diplomatic History* 15 (Fall 1991): 455–71. My conceptual approach bears only a superficial resemblance to that articulated in Lynn Boyd Hinds and Theodore Otto Windt, Jr., *The Cold War as Rhetoric: The Beginnings, 1945–1950* (New York, 1991). I would agree that the cold war was, to some extent, a rhetorical construct, but its ideological ccontours are too vast to be bounded by a term like "rhetoric." Cold-war ideology was not created de novo between 1945 and 1950, nor, as I shall show, was it frozen after 1950. Not only was the ideological frame of reference historically deeper than Hinds and Windt believe, it was also broader in character, with world-historical concerns that transcended the domestic issues that they emphasize. Finally, the authors ignore the empirical, existential basis of policy: the lessons learned from past experience and the ongoing praxis that is policymaking. For all the apparent novelty of their argument, underneath their view of the cold war as a rhetorical creation that distorted the international realities of the day lies the old interest theory of ideology posing as rhetorical theory. Similar objections apply to my reading of David Campbell, *Writing Security: United States Foreign Policy and the Politics of Identity* (Minneapolis, 1992).

11. Clark Clifford OH, p. 147; George Elsey OH, p. 354.

12. *The Forrestal Diaries*, 15 August 1946, p. 192.

13. PPS 8, 18 September 1947, *SDPPS* 1: 95; Acheson statement to the House Foreign Affairs Committee, 20 March 1947, DAP: Yale, series 3, box 47; "The Greek Aid Program" (Washington, 1947), p. 2. See also the various assessments of the implications of a Communist victory in *FRUS 1947*, 5: 17, 30, 44.

14. Truman Doctrine draft, 3 March 1947, Joseph Jones Papers, box 1; Draft memo of Acheson's White House presentation, 27 February 1947, ibid., box 2; Draft memo of Acheson's presentation at the White House on 27 February 1947, ibid.; Report of the Meeting of the SWNCC Subcommittee on Foreign Policy Information, *FRUS 1947*, 5: 66. The problem was viewed so seriously that the Policy Planning Staff, a few months later, concluded that "the United States should be prepared to make full use of its political, economic, and, if necessary, military power, in such manner as may be found most effective." PPS 14, 11 November 1947, *SDPPS* 1: 138.

15. Marshall to Truman, 27 February 1947, *FRUS 1947*, 5: 61. The previous day, Marshall had told Truman that "similar situations requiring substantial aid from the Government may develop in other areas." Memo, Marshall to Truman, 26 February 1947, *FRUS 1947*, 5: 58. Similarly, a meeting of the secretaries of state, war, and navy on 26 February 1947 "recognized that the Greek and Turkish problems were only part of a critical world situation confronting us today in many democratic countries and that attention must be given to the problem as a whole." Minutes of meeting, 26 February 1947, *FRUS 1947*, 5: 57.

Many, like Theodore Lowi in *The End of Liberalism: Ideology, Policy, and the Crisis of Public Authority* (New York, 1969), pp. 174ff., continue to view this as the classic instance of "oversell" in which the administration felt compelled to resort to exaggerated anti-Communist rhetoric in order to frighten a lethargic Congress into taking the desired action. From this standpoint, anticommunism was used to sell foreign policy much like sex is used to peddle cars, pushing a product not on its merit but by linking it to compelling but irrelevant images that have greater resonance with the consumer. Because Truman's speech was toned down and because it was a rhetorical expression of basic Wilsonian values, it is more usefully viewed as a high moment of speaking seriously about fundamentals. On Truman's sincerity, see John Lewis Gaddis, "The Cold War, the Long Peace, and the Future," *Diplomatic History* 16 (Spring 1992): 236.

Despite charges of rhetorical overkill, the final draft of the address delivered by Truman to Congress on 12 March 1947 was significantly more cautious than earlier drafts that more accurately reflected the fears haunting the policy establishment. Moreover, administration leaders had some quite strong ideas on the subject of deceiving the public. Acheson, for instance, in a June 1946 address appeared to be addressing precisely this issue when he said that "it is evil for shrewd men to play on the minds and loyalties of their fellows as on an instrument." Such an outlook would do serious damage to democracy, "paralyzing the very centers of moral action, until these oceans of cunning words wash through the minds of men like the sea through the empty portholes of a derelict." Acheson, "Random Harvest," 4 June 1946, DAP: Yale, series 3, box 46. Clark Clifford's subsequent reaction to Richard Freeland's charge of deception in *The Truman Doctrine and the Origins of McCarthyism* (New York, 1971) was that "the first syllable of the word starts with the word 'bull.'" Clark Clifford OH, p. 371. This entire dispute seems to me to feed upon the confusion attendant upon reducing ideology to an epiphenomenon of some presumably anterior, and more fundamental, "interests."

16. Memo, "The Drafting of the President's Message of March 12, 1947— Chronology," Joseph Jones Papers, box 1.

17. Clark Clifford, *Counsel to the President: A Memoir* (New York, 1991), p. 140.

18. As one historian has noted, "The Truman Doctrine was primarily an instrument of economic containment in *Europe.*" Robert A. Pollard, *Economic Security and the Origins of the Cold War* (New York, 1985), pp. 127–28. Truman highlighted the emphasis placed on western European opinion when in interviews for his *Memoirs* he pointed out that "the so-called policy of containment was not a policy of containment at all. It was a policy for the *protection* of those free countries that bordered on the Soviet Union." Interviews with Truman, Papers of Harry S. Truman, Post-Presidential, *Memoirs,* box 4, HSTPL. My emphasis.

19. Kennan, "American Foreign Policy and the Marshall Plan," 20 February 1948, Kennan Papers, box 17; Kennan, "Orientation and Comments," 14–28 March 1947, ibid., box 16; Address by George C. Marshall, 5 June 1947, in Schlesinger, ed., *The Dynamics of World Power* (New York, 1983) 1: 53. On this point, see also Gaddis, *Strategies of Containment,* pp. 36–37.

20. Address by Acheson, 21 January 1948, DAP: Yale, series 3, box 47; Imanuel

Wexler, *The Marshall Plan Revisited: The European Recovery Program in Economic Perspective* (Westport, CT, 1983), p. 55; Lawrence S. Kaplan, *The United States and NATO* (Lexington, KY, 1984), p. 43; Larry I. Bland, ed., *George C. Marshall: Interviews and Reminiscences for Forrest C. Pogue* (Lexington, VA, 1991), p. 558.

21. Jerry Philip Rosenberg, "Berlin and Israel 1948: Foreign Policy Decision-Making during the Truman Administration" (Ph.D. diss., University of Illinois, 1974), pp. 139–47; "Consequences of a Breakdown of Four Power Negotiations on Germany," ORE 57–48 28, September 1948, PSF: Intelligence File, CIA Reports, box 255; CIA 8–48, "Review of the World Situation," 19 August 1948, PSF, NSC Meetings, box 204.

22. Memo for the President, 2 April 1948, PSF: NSC meetings, box 220; Memo for the secretary of state, 29 July 1948, "US Public Opinion on the Berlin Situation," PSF: Subject File, Foreign Affairs File, box 171. The NSC declared that "if we move out of Berlin we have lost everything we have been fighting for." Memo for the president, 23 July 1948: PSF, NSC Meetings, box 220.

23. Douglas to Marshall, 26 June 1948, *FRUS 1948*, 2: 925; Clay to Draper, CC5222, 19 July 1948, in Jean Edward Smith, *The Papers of General Lucius D. Clay* (Bloomington, IN, 1974), pp. 745–46; Saltzman to Hooper, 6 August 1948, 740.00119, Control (Germany)/7–2048, National Archives; *FRUS 1948*, 2: 886; Interview with Dean Acheson, 17 February 1955, Truman Papers, Post-Presidential, *Memoirs*, box 1. See also the speech by Admiral E. T. Wooldridge, 22 July 1948, Frank Roberts Papers, HSTPL.

24. Murphy to Marshall, 13 April 1948, *FRUS 1948*, 2: 893; Murphy to Marshall, 26 June 1948, ibid., 919–20; Princeton Seminars, 8–9 July 1953, DAP, HSTPL.

25. Douglass to Lovett, 17 April 1948, *FRUS 1948*, 3: 90; quoted in Ann and John Tusa, *The Berlin Airlift* (New York, 1988), p. 113; Memo by Beam of meeting, 25 June 1948, between Truman, Forrestal, and Royall, *FRUS 1948*, 2: 928.

26. Royall to Stimson, 21 April 1948, quoted in Thomas E. Lifka, *The Concept "Totalitarianism" and American Foreign Policy, 1933–1949* (New York, 1988), p. 701; Truman, *Memoirs*, 2: 149; CIA 8–48, "Review of the World Situation," 19 August 1948, PSF, NSC Meetings, box 204; R. H. Hillenkoeter to Truman, 6 August 1948, PSF: Intelligence File, CIA reports, box 249. Ironically, Western adamancy on continuing the four-power regime in Berlin was probably reassuring to the Russians, whose main grievance was that American actions had put an end to cooperation in Germany. By continuing to insist that four-power control still applied—an argument admittedly intended to bolster their right to stay in Berlin—the Western allies were thereby pointing out to the Russians the desirability of maintaining joint control over all-German questions and avoiding unilateral attempts to resolve them.

27. R. H. Hillenkoeter to Truman, 22 December 1947, PSF: Intelligence File, CIA reports, box 249; Clay, in teleconference TT9341, 10 April 1948, in Smith, *Papers of Lucius Clay*, p. 623; JCS appendix to NSC 24/2, "Possible US Courses of Action in the Event the USSR Reimposes the Berlin Blockade," PSF, NSC Meetings, box 204.

28. Robert D. Murphy, *Diplomat among Warriors* (New York, 1965), pp. 317, 321.

29. For example, British Ambassador Sir Oliver Franks argued that "the internal logic of the Soviet system demands an attempt at world domination, and their first objective would be the eastern side of the North Atlantic." *FRUS 1948*, 3: 153.

30. Theodore Achilles OH, p. 137; NSC 20/4, 23 November 1948, in Gaddis and Etzold, *Containment,* p. 208; Memorandum by the Participants in the Washington Security Talks, 9 September 1948, *FRUS 1948,* 3: 237–45; Douglass to Lovett, 17 April 1948, *FRUS 1948,* 3: 90.

31. Hickerson to Marshall, 8 March 1948, FRUS 1948, 3: 40; Marshall to Truman, 12 March 1948, ibid., p. 49.

32. U.S. Senate, Committee on Foreign Relations, North Atlantic Treaty, Hearings, 1st session, 81st Congress, pt. 1, 27 April–3 May 1949 (Washington, 1949), p. 15; CIA, ORE 69–49, "Relative US Security Interest in the European-Mediterranean Area and the Far East," 14 July 1949, PSF: Intelligence File, CIA reports, box 249. The U.S. alliance with Europe was based on what Acheson called a "natural identity of interests of the North Atlantic powers." Acheson speech draft, 15 March 1949, PSF, Subject File, box 159. Although there were provisions in the treaty for closer cultural cooperation, which Acheson was criticized for neglecting, these struck him as being beside the point. Most of the cultural preconditions of close relations already existed.

33. As Louis Halle would argue a few years later, the threat was from "a new barbarism resulting from the peripheral disintegration of a civilization that has lost some of its vitalizing principle." Louis J. Halle, *Civilization and Foreign Policy* (Westport, CT, 1975), p. 179. British Foreign Minister Ernest Bevin also saw the military equation in civilizational terms, telling the Cabinet in March 1948: "It has really become a matter of the defence of western civilization, or everything will be swamped by the Soviet method of infiltration." In David Dimbleby and David Reynolds, *An Ocean Apart: The Relationship between Britain and America in the Twentieth Century* (New York, 1988), p. 189. Much of the congressional debate over NATO was muddied over by what appeared to be the scholastic issue of whether or not the NATO alliance was consistent with the United Nations. In order to appease Congress, Acheson was willing to go along with one silly senator who argued that the treaty was perfectly consistent with the Monroe Doctrine. Secretary of Defense Louis Johnson even went so far as to deny that the North Atlantic Treaty was a military alliance! United States Senate, Committee on Foreign Relations, North Atlantic Treaty, Hearings, 27 April–3 May 1949. Although hopes in the UN were obviously misplaced, nevertheless the congressional concern with collective security was quite sound insofar as it reflected an intuitive understanding of the basic approach that would be necessary to fight the cold war.

34. Quoted in Chester J. Pach, Jr., *Arming the Free World* (Chapel Hill, NC, 1991), pp. 204–5, 230.

35. Durbrow to Marshall, 1 December 1947, *FRUS 1947,* 4: 626; CIA, ORE

69–49, "Relative US Security Interest in the European-Mediterranean Area and the Far East," 14 July 1949, PSF: Intelligence File, CIA reports, box 249. On global ambitions for NATO, see Acheson to Truman, 5 January 1951, DAP: MC.

36. *Reviews of the World Situation: 1949–1950*, p. 41; Memo, Dulles to Acheson, 18 May 1950, *FRUS 1950*, 1: 315.

37. DOS Press Release no. 161, 18 March 1949, Official File, box 309; Princeton Seminars, 10–11 October 1953, DAP, HSTPL, box 79; United States Senate, Committee on Foreign Relations, North Atlantic Treaty, Hearings, 27 April–3 May 1949 (Washington, 1949), p. 13.

38. CIA, "Review of the World Situation," 12 September 1947, Records of the NSC: CIA File, box 1; DOS OIR Analysis, "Soviet Internal Situation," 1 July 1949, PSF, box 187; Acheson interview, 16 February 1955, Truman Papers, Post-Presidential, *Memoirs*, box 1; Princeton Seminars, 10–11 October 1953, DAP: MC, box 79.

39. NSC 30, 10 September 1948, "United States Policy on Atomic Warfare," PSF: NSC Meetings, box 204; CIA, "Review of the World Situation," 16 November 1949, ibid., box 207; Gaddis, *Strategies of Containment*, p. 92. I agree with Gaddis, except to note that this was nothing really new. What was different was the perception that the tide of opinion was perceived to be running against the United States.

40. Acheson memo of conversation with Baruch, 3 March 1950, *FRUS 1950*, 1: 184; R. H. Hillenkoeter to NSC Executive Secretary, 25 January 1949, PSF: Intelligence File, CIA reports, box 249; Memo of conversation by Acheson, 24 March 1950, *FRUS 1950*, 1: 207–8; Memo, Edward Barrett to James Webb, 6 March 1950, *FRUS 1950*, 1: 186.

41. Princeton Seminars, 10–11 October 1953, DAP, HSTPL, box 79; Ibid., 15–16 May 1954, box 80; Minutes of PPS meeting, 16 December 1949, *FRUS 1949*, 1: 415; Notes dictated 27 March 1950 for possible speech use, DAP: Yale, series 3, box 47.

42. Meeting of advisory committee, 6 June 1950, *FRUS 1950*, 1: 323.

43. Record of Meeting of State-Defense Policy Review Group, 27 February 1950, *FRUS 1950*, 1: 171.

44. Princeton Seminars, 10–11 October 1953, DAP, HSTPL, box 79.

45. Ernest May, "The Nature of Foreign Policy: The Calculated and the Axiomatic," *Daedalus* 91 (Fall 1962): 653–67; Princeton Seminars, 13–14 February 1954, DAP, HSTPL, box 80. See also Ernest May, *"Lessons" of the Past: The Use and Misuse of History in American Foreign Policy* (New York, 1973), pp. 52–86.

46. Truman, *Memoirs*, 2: 333; Acheson to London, transmitting Truman letter, 9 January 1951, *FRUS 1951*, 7: 39; Truman, message to Congress, 19 July 1950, PSF, Historical Files, box 230. Once again, attempts were made to fit events into a universal pattern. As a State Department pamphlet issued in October put it, "This is a very old cleavage. It goes back to the beginnings of human society . . . the old

reactionary ideas of a single doctrine and a single authority [which] expects eventually to impose its doctrine and its authority on all people.'' *Barron's* magazine in June 1950 argued that ''the citizens of Athens, Rome, and Britain would know what we are about. American troops were fighting in Korea in an ancient and honorable task— to stop the barbarian at the gate.'' Quoted in Bruce M. Russett and Elizabeth C. Hanson, *Interest and Ideology: The Foreign Policy Beliefs of American Businessmen* (San Francisco, 1975), pp. 238–39.

47. Sebald to Acheson, 25 June 1950, *FRUS 1950*, 7: 140; Acheson to London for Bevin, 10 July 1950, ibid., p. 347; Kirk to Acheson, 27 June 1950, ibid., p. 199; OIR estimate dated 25 June 1950, ibid., pp. 150, 154. Robert E. Osgood, *Limited War: The Challenge to American Strategy* (Chicago, 1957), p. 178, rehearses many of the rationales for intervening.

48. For the strongest statement of the argument from historical memory, see Goran Rystad, *Prisoners of the Past? The Munich Syndrome and Makers of American Foreign Policy in the Cold War Era* (Lund, 1982), pp. 31–37. For schema theory, see Deborah Welch Larson, *Origins of Containment: A Psychological Explanation* (Princeton, 1985), pp. 51–57, and Yuen Foong Khong, *Analogies at War: Korea, Munich, Dien Bien Phu, and the Vietnam Decisions of 1965* (Princeton, 1993), pp. 3–18ff. Khong, pp. 18 and 190–205, argues that all possible nonanalogical explanations come up short. However, I would suggest that Dwain Mefford, ''The Cuban Missile Crisis Twenty-Five Years Later: The Learning Continues,'' in *History, the White House, and the Kremlin: Statesmen as Historians*, ed. Michael Fry (London, 1991), p. 56, is closer to the truth in arguing that ''the script-based approach is radically incomplete unless mechanisms are specified for acquiring, composing, and restructuring scripts.'' This book's argument is that those mechanisms are to be found in a complex system of historical understanding rather than in historical analogizing.

49. Important here is the historical preunderstanding emphasized by phenomenological philosophers like Hans Georg Gadamer, *Truth and Method* (New York, 1985), pp. 235–53.

50. In philosophical terms, to argue that statesmen associated Korea with Munich is akin to using David Hume's notoriously unsatisfactory empiricist argument that concepts are the result of habit and association alone. See David Hume, *Philosophical Essays Concerning Human Understanding* (New York, 1983), pp. 81–82.

51. Memo of Blair House meeting, 26 June 1950, *FRUS 1950*, 7: 183. An argument for paradigmatic determinism is found in Victor Turner, *Dramas, Fields, and Metaphors: Symbolic Action in Human Society* (Ithaca, 1974), p. 67. Turner maintains that ''where processes are unconditional, undetermined, or unchanneled by explicit customs and rules, my hypothesis would be that the main actors are nevertheless guided by subjective paradigms . . . [which] affect the form, timing, and style of those who have them.'' All well and good, but that still leaves the question of when and how paradigms are formed and transformed.

52. *Reviews of the World Situation: 1949–1950*, p. 398, 370–71.

53. Jessup notes on NSC meeting, 28 November 1950, DAP: MC, box 65.

54. Princeton Seminars, 13 February 1954, DAP, HSTPL, box 77; Memo to Louis Johnson, 1 August 1950, *FRUS 1950*, 1: 353; Memo of Blair House meeting, 25 June 1950, *FRUS 1950*, 7: 158.

55. Remarks by Edwin Pauley to the Senate Armed Services Committee, 3 August 1950, PSF: Historical Files; Korea, box 230. Actually, the Spanish civil war resembled far more closely than Munich the problem faced by the West in Korea inasmuch as it was widely viewed as a test of the West's will to resist fascism. Even so, the parallel is far from exact. Despite a civil war whose contending factions were backed by ideologically hostile outside powers, there had been no occupation or territorial division, no collective security commmitment by the League of Nations, and, from the American perspective, the Spanish civil war could not be evaluated in the kind of black-and-white terms used in Korea.

56. On the ambiguity of the "Yalta system" in Asia, see Akira Iriye, *The Cold War in Asia* (Englewood Cliffs, NJ, 1974).

57. One of the features of modernity, according to sociologist Anthony Giddens, is that events are increasingly "disembedded" from their local contexts and globalized. Giddens, *The Consequences of Modernity*, pp. 21–29.

58. Drew Pearson column, *Washington Post*, 3 July 1950, Elsey Papers, box 58; Kennan memo, "Problems of Far Eastern Policy," 14 January 1948, Kennan Papers, box 17; Memo for the president, 2 April 1948, PSF: NSC Meetings, box 220. For further examples, see May, *"Lessons" of the Past*, pp. 58–65.

59. "In Christianity, for instance, the symbol of the Crucifix or of the Virgin has exercised an enormous evocative power through the centuries because of the way in which these symbols summarize a whole value system, a whole attitude toward life and the universe. Political images do the same thing at a different level." Kenneth Boulding, *The Image: Knowledge in Life and Society* (Ann Arbor, 1977), p. 110.

60. The phrase "political economy of symbolic exchange" is taken from Timothy W. Luke, " 'What's Wrong with Deterrence?': A Semiotic Interpretation of National Security Policy," in James Der Derian and Michael J. Shapiro, eds., *International/Intertextual Relations: Postmodern Readings of World Politics* (Lexington, MA, 1989), p. 223; Hinds and Windt, *The Cold War as Rhetoric*, p. 242. I would agree with Bruce Lincoln here that "no consideration of discourse is complete that does not also take account of force." Bruce Lincoln, *Discourse and the Construction of Society* (New York, 1989), p. 1.

61. Memo of conversation, 10 August 1950, DAP: MC, box 65; memo of 26 June 1950 meeting at Blair House, ibid.; Charles M. Dobbs, *The Unwanted Symbol: American Foreign Policy, the Cold War, and Korea, 1945–1950* (Kent, OH, 1981), p. x; Raymond Aron, *The Imperial Republic* (Englewood Cliffs, NJ, 1974), p. 309.

According to Ananda K. Coomaraswamy, "The references of symbols are to ideas and those of signs to things"; in "Symbols," in *What Is Civilisation? and Other Essays* (Delhi, 1989). For Terry Eagleton, "Ideology is a matter of 'discourse' rather than of 'language'—of certain concrete discursive effects, rather than of signification as such." Eagleton, *Ideology: An Introduction* (London, 1991), p. 223. Yet another way of putting it is to view metaphor as an instance of second-order meaning, whereas literal language would be first-order. Eva Feder Kittay, *Metaphor: Its Cognitive Force and Linguistic Structure* (Oxford, 1987), pp. 120–21. A more radical approach by modernists and postmodernists, following the tradition of Ferdinand de Saussure, would be to argue that the components of any sign, the signifier and the signified, derive their meaning not from external reality but by virtue of their relationship to other signs.

62. Pauley report, 1946, PSF: Historical Files, Korea, box 230; Memo, Webb to Truman, 18 June 1949, PSF: Korean War File, box 243; Ellis O. Briggs OH, DDEPL, p. 61.

63. Kennan lecture, "Where Are We Today?" 21 December 1948, Kennan Papers, box 17. Although the civil war in Greece did foreshadow the emergence, as one writer put it, of "a new kind of war" in which "victory lay in convincing democracy's enemies that they could not win," it hardly crystallized the problems of intervention that Korea brought to the fore. See Howard Jones, *A New Kind of War* (New York, 1989), p. 36.

64. Memo, Dulles to Acheson, 18 May 1950, *FRUS 1950*, 1: 315.

65. Memo by Carlton D. Savage of PPS, 27 July 1950, *FRUS 1950*, 1: 359; NSC 73, 1 July 1950, ibid., p. 331; NSC 73/4, 25 August 1950, PSF, NSC Meetings, box 209. NSC 73/4 argued on behalf of localizing conflicts in Korea and in other regions should they occur because, despite the Communist tenet that war between communism and capitalism was inevitable, Soviet Russia could be induced "to delay action or retreat from local objectives if strongly opposed." NSC 73/4, 25 August 1950, FRUS 1950, 1: 377.

66. Acheson interview, 16 February 1955, Truman Papers, Post-Presidential, *Memoirs*, box 1, HSTPL. Cf. the comment in D. Clayton James and Anne Sharp Wells, *Refighting the Last War in Korea, 1950–1953* (New York, 1993), p. 245, about "the inexplicable communication, neither oral nor written, between implacably hostile camps who signaled restraint to each other." In arguing the case for communicative possibilities during the cold war, one need not go so far as to accept Kenneth Burke's comment that "even so contradictory an alignment as two armies opposed on a battlefield [might] seem like 'cooperation' in the eyes of God." As Talcott Parsons noted at the time, ideological conflict was an indication of an intracivilizational split, a battle of internationalisms that, despite all the antagonistic rhetoric, presupposed a measure of agreement between the two contestants about the limits within which the conflict took place. See Talcott Parsons, "Polarization of the World and International Order," in *Sociological Theory and Modern Society* (New York, 1967), p. 468; and Kenneth Burke, *The Philosophy of Literary Form* (New York, 1957), p. 215.

67. *Reviews of the World Situation: 1949–1950*, 13 January 1950, p. 189.

68. Memo for the president, 29 June 1950, PSF: NSC Meetings, summaries, box 220; Eberstadt to H. Alexander Smith, 16 August 1950, PP: DDEPL, box 37; Memo

by Kennan, 8 August 1950, *FRUS 1950*, 1: 361; Undated notes by Acheson, *FRUS 1950*, 1: 395.

69. Allison to Rusk, 15 July 1950; Dulles to Nitze, 14 July 1950; Memo by Allison, July 24, 1950; all in *FRUS 1950*, 7: 460–61, 394, 387.

70. Memo, Acheson to Truman, 11 September 1950, PSF: Cabinet, box 159. See the memo by Frederick Nolting, summarizing a meeting of 30 June 1950, in *FRUS 1950*, 7: 258, which provides details of Bohlen and Kennan's apprehensions on this score.

71. Jessup notes on NSC meeting, 28 November 1950, DAP: MC, box 65; *Reviews of the World Situation: 1949–1950*, p. 372; Estimate NIE-3, 15 November 1950, *FRUS 1950*, 1: 414; Summary minutes of NSC meeting, 28 November 1950, PSF: Foreign Affairs, Attlee meeting, December 1950; Memo, Clubb to Rusk, 18 December 1950, *FRUS 1950*, 1: 481; Memo of conversation, Kirk and Truman, 19 December 1950, *FRUS 1950*, 1: 484. A CIA analysis concluded grimly, "The USSR is prepared to accept, and may be seeking to precipitate, a general war between the United States and China, despite the inherent risk of global war." CIA intelligence report, November 1950, DAP: MC, box 65.

72. Memo of a DOS-JCS meeting, 13 February 1951, *FRUS 1951*, 7: 175.

73. Telephone conversation, Lovett and Acheson [November 1950?], DAP: MC, box 65; Kennan to Acheson, 4 December 1950, DAP: Yale, series 1, box 17; HST, longhand notes, 27 January 1952.

74. See *The Gallup Poll: Public Opinion 1935–1971* (New York, 1972), pp. 950, 1027, 1044, 1052–53, 1102–4; Memo of conversation with Sir Oliver Franks, 4 December 1950, DAP: MC, box 65.

75. JCS to MacArthur, 13 January 1951, *FRUS 1951*, 7: 77.

76. Memo by Acheson of Cabinet meeting, 14 July 1950, *FRUS 1950*, 1: 345; Summary minutes of NSC meeting, 28 November 1950, PSF: Foreign Affairs, Attlee meeting, December 1950; Statement by George Marshall, 15 February 1951, before Senate Foreign Affairs and Armed Services Committees, Elsey Papers. Truman appeared initially to fear that the greatest danger would be to the Middle East. See Margaret Truman, *Harry S. Truman*, p. 461.

77. Memo to Louis Johnson, 1 August 1950, *FRUS 1950*, 1: 353; *Reviews of the World Situation: 1949–1950*, 9 December 1950, p. 398.

78. NIE special estimate, "International Implications of Maintaining a Beachhead in South Korea," 11 January 1951, *FRUS 1951*, 7: 63. Even so, Truman added quickly that "we can't lose face by drawing out in a hurry." Summary minutes of NSC meeting, 28 November 1950, PSF: Foreign Affairs, Attlee meeting, December 1950.

79. Memo of Truman-Churchill meeting, 6 January 1952, DAP: MC, box 67; Memo of NSC meeting, 24 September 1952, discussing NSC 135/2, *FRUS 1952–1954*, 2: 136–37.

80. DOS briefing book for visit of René Pleven, January 1951, White House

Central Files, CF, box 41, HSTPL; NSC 135/1 annex, "The Bases of Soviet Action," 22 August 1952, *FRUS 1952–1954*, 2: 113; Memo, John K. Emmerson to Rusk, *FRUS 1951*, 7: 28–29.

CHAPTER 7

1. Diary entry [3 March 1951], *PDDE* 12: 90; Marginal notations on Stevens's address, box 55, Dwight D. Eisenhower Papers, DDEPL [hereafter EP]: PP; DDE to Edward John Bermingham, 28 February 1951, *PDDE* 12: 75; Ann Whitman diary, 4 June 1956, Ann Whitman File, DDEPL [hereafter AWF]: DS, box 8. Despite the enthusiastic praise, Eisenhower refused to travel the road of ideological reductionism. Confessing "a state of intellectual confusion when I attempt to regard either of these influences as the master and the other nothing but a tool," he preferred to interpret the Soviet mentality as "an unholy wedding between Russian Imperialism and personal greed for power with the ideological doctrine of Communism." DDE to Admiral Leslie Stevens, 22 February 1951, *PDDE* 12: 61. Ike's confusion on this score continued. To the degree that the Soviets were ideologues, Eisenhower attributed to them a version of ideology that emphasizes self-deception, in this case coming to believe their own lies about the foreign "bogeyman." He felt that the Communists just had to be aware of the superior appeal of freedom and self-government, otherwise "they would find no necessity for pressing onward through bribery, corruption, subversion and threat of force to bring about the downfall of other governments. Did they actually believe in their system, they would have only to wait complacently for time to bring about the changes they seek." DDE to William Paley, 16 January 1956, AWF: NS, box 25.

2. DDE to Viscount Field Marshal Montgomery, 26 May 1956, AWF: NS, box 21; Hagerty, *Diaries*, 13 December 1954, p. 134; Dulles, "Evolution or Revolution," *General Magazine and Historical Chronicle of Pennsylvania* (Summer 1949), JFDP, box 285; Dulles, "The Christian Citizen in a Changing World," Paper delivered to World Council of Churches, First Assembly, Amsterdam, 22 August 1948, JFDP, box 284; James Russell Wiggins, memo of discussion with Dulles, 12 February 1955, JFDP-additional, box 2.

3. DDE to Edgar Eisenhower, 27 February 1956, AWF: NS, box 11; Memo, DDE to JCS, 25 July 1947, *PDDE* 8: 1856; DDE to Swede Hazlett, 19 July 1947, in Robert W. Griffith, ed., *Ike's Letters to a Friend* (Lawrence, KS, 1984); Dulles to DDE, 17 May 1954, JFDP: WHM, box 1; JFD, "Peace with Russia," *Christian Century*, 25 August 1948, JFDP, box 284; Dulles, "Leadership for Peace," *Zion's Herald*, 16 March 1949, JFDP, box 285.

4. NSC minutes, 5 August 1954, *FRUS 1952–1954*, 2: 711; Memo [by Dulles?], 2 April 1956, JFDP: WHM, box 3.

5. Dulles testimony, 17 April 1953, *Executive Sessions of the Senate Foreign Relations Committee (Historical Series)* (Washington, DC, 1977) 5: 315; DDE, "Observations on the American Scene," 16 November 1950, EP: PP, box 125; Minutes of White House meeting with legislative leadership, 13 December 1954, *FRUS 1952–*

1954, 2: 823; Telephone conversation with Dulles, March 26, 1958, AWF: DDE, box 31.

6. NSC minutes, 24 September 1953, *FRUS 1952–1954*, 2: 469. For worries that even a long-term, peaceful cold war might go badly for the United States, see DDE to Dulles, 5 December 1955, JFDP: WHM, box 3; CIA Senior Research Staff on International Communism, "The Present Communist Controversy: Ramifications and Possible Repercussions," 15 July 1956, AWF: Administration File [hereafter AF], box 13; Solarium discussion in NSC, 30 July 1953, *FRUS 1952–1954*, 2: 436; Dulles to C. D. Jackson, 24 August 1954, JFDP: GCM, box 2; Memo of meeting with DDE, 4 November 1958, JFDP: WHM, box 7.

7. Eisenhower, *Mandate for Change, 1953–1956: The White House Years* (Garden City, NY, 1963), p. 14; DDE to Richard M. Nixon, 1 October 1952, *PDDE* 13: 1368; Robert H. Ferrell, *The Eisenhower Diaries* (New York, 1981), 30 June 1950, p. 175.

8. DDE to Bernard Baruch, 30 June 1952, *PDDE* 12: 1263; Summary of JFD remarks, 11 December 1952, SS *Helena* notes, JFDP: SS, box 8; JFD, "How to Take the Offensive for Peace," *Life*, 24 April 1952; NSC minutes, 31 March 1953, *FRUS 1952–1954*, 2: 267; Summary of points made following Solarium presentations, 16 July 1963, *FRUS 1952–1954*, 2: 950. According to one Dulles intimate, Dulles took Korea to be "a vivid example of the kind of misunderstanding and miscalculation that leads to the wrong results." Roderick O'Connor OH, JFDP, p. 105.

9. Memo by Nitze, 12 January 1953, *FRUS 1952–1954*, 2: 203; Memo by JFD, 31 March 1952, EP: PP, box 24.

10. JFD to Adenauer, 11 August 1956, JFDP: GCM, box 2; NSC minutes, 11 February 1953, AWF: NSC series; Undated memo submitted to NSC, JFDP: WHM, box 7. This was more than bluff on Dulles's part. All of Dulles's close associates in the State Department testified to his cold-blooded approach to this issue. In response to one objection to using the bomb, Dulles replied, "What have we got them for?", arguing that a deterrent was "useful only if it was convincing and that if the impression got out that we wouldn't think of using atomic weapons, the deterrent power would be lost." George V. Allen OH, JFDP 2: 32. Douglas MacArthur II recalled that Dulles advocated "very rapid nuclear retaliation in the event of aggression rather than a 'graduated response.' " Douglas MacArthur II OH, JFDP, p. 25.

11. DDE-Dulles conversation, 20 July 1954, AWF: DS, box 2; NSC minutes, 7 October 1953, *FRUS 1952–1954*, 2: 520–21.

12. The problem was summarized by Eisenhower in 1952 in a letter to General Lucius D. Clay. "What should we do if Soviet *political* aggression, as in Czechoslovakia, chips away exposed portions of the free world?" he asked. "Presumably we'd do nothing," he said, concluding that "this is the case where the theory of 'retaliation' falls down." DDE to Lucius Clay, 10 April 1952, EP: PP, box 24. However, American plans stilled called for nuclear preemption in the event that war seemed certain. For Eisenhower's reflections on the meaningless character of nuclear warfare, see NSC minutes, 4 March 1954, and 3 December 1954, *FRUS 1952–1954*, 2: 636 and

806; NSC minutes, 9 February 1956, AWF: AF, box 27; Memos of conversation, 4 and 5 December 1953, JFDP: SS, box 1.

13. NSC minutes, 7 October 1953, *FRUS 1952–1954*, 2: 533.

14. Conversation with Lewis Strauss, JFDP: Telephone Conversations Memoranda, JFDP [hereafter TCM], box 2; NSC minutes, 13 May 1953, and 24 June 1954, *FRUS 1952–1954*, 15: 1016, and 2: 694; Memo of conversation with DDE, 26 December 1955, JFDP: WHM, box 3; NSC minutes, 5 August 1954, *FRUS 1952–1954*, 2: 707. The bandwagon effect was always perceived to cut two ways. Although the use of atomic weapons would be repulsive to the allies, Walter Bedell Smith predicted that, if the weapons were used successfully, "many of our friends who have fallen away would climb back on the victorious bandwagon." Quoted in Rosemary Foot, *A Substitute for Victory* (Ithaca, 1990), p. 212.

15. NSC 162, 30 September 1953, *FRUS 1952–1954*, 2: 494; Appendix A to Guidelines under NSC 162/2 for FY 1956, ibid., p. 727; Dulles to DDE, 17 October 1957, JFDP: GCM, box 1. See also the study of the NSC Planning Board, 14 June 1954, *FRUS 1942–1954*, 2: 658, discussing the logical difficulties of maintaining a policy of massive retaliation against local aggression.

16. NSC minutes, 24 June 1954, *FRUS 1952–1954*, 2: 694; Dulles, memo of meeting with DDE, 22 December 1954, JFDP: WHM, box 1; Memo by JCS to Defense Secretary Wilson, 23 June 1954, *FRUS 1952–1954*, 2: 684; NSC minutes, 24 June 1954, *FRUS 1952–1954*, 2: 689. See also appendix A to Guidelines under NSC 162/2 for FY 1956, *FRUS 1952–1954*, 2: 727.

17. Memo of conversation with DDE, 1 April 1958, JFDP: WHM, box 6. Robert Cutler argued that the only feasible purpose of massive retaliatory power was deterrence and that it was "not effectively usable against, or in reply to, minor aggression." In dealing with limited conflicts, he believed that the American objective should be "to *stabilize* the situation, rather than, by pressing for outright victory, to provoke a hostile response which may through counteractions lead on to general war." Memo by Cutler, 7 April 1958, ibid.

18. NSC minutes, 7 October 1953, *FRUS 1952–1954*, 2: 528; DDE to Swede Hazlett, 1 November 1950, in Griffith, *Ike's Letters to a Friend*, p. 82; DDE to George Marshall, 12 March 1951, EP: PP, 83; NSC minutes, 31 March 1953, *FRUS 1952–54*, 2: 272; George V. Allen OH, pp. 46–47.

19. DDE to Lucius Clay, 26 April 1951, EP: PP, box 24; DDE to George Allen, 18 December 1951, ibid., box 4; DDE to Milton Eisenhower, 20 September 1951, ibid., box 174; DDE press conference transcript, 19 May 1954, JFDP: SS, box 8; Memo of telephone conversation, 30 December 1953, JFDP: TCM, box 2; NSC minutes, 29 April 1954, AWF: NSC Series. As Dulles put it to Adenauer in 1955, "What we are doing is to carry forward into the international field modern principles of security which are today practiced within every civilized nation. Except in the most primitive societies, security is no longer left to individual action. There is collective security . . . the modern and enlightened way of gaining security as against vast aggressive despotisms represented by the Soviet bloc." JFD to Adenauer, 12

December 1955, JFDP: General Correspondence and Memoranda Series [hereafter GCM], box 2. See also Dulles memo, 7 April 1954, JFDP: SS, box 8; memo of DDE conversation with Styles Bridges, 21 May 1957, AWF: DS, box 9.

20. Diary, 10 October 1951, *PDDE* 12: 629; DDE to George Marshall, 12 March 1951, EP: PP, box 80; Annual report of Supreme Commander of NATO, 2 April 1952, Elsey Papers, box 58, HSTPL. As Ike explained to Robert Lovett: "Frequently, all of us become so involved in the material side of our problems—in the importance of equipping and financing—that we sometimes lose sight of the fundamental importance of morale." DDE to Lovett, 25 September 1951, *PDDE* 12: 566.

21. Ferrell, *The Eisenhower Diaries*, 9 April 1951, p. 190; DDE to William Fletcher Russell, 9 March 1951, *PDDE* 12: 109; DDE to W. Averell Harriman, 17 September 1951, EP: PP, box 55; DDE to George Marshall, 3 August 1951, EP: PP, box 80; DDE to Lucius Clay, 16 April 1951, *PDDE* 12: 211; DDE to Edward J. Bermingham, 28 February 1951, EP: PP, box 11.

22. Solarium discussion by NSC, 30 July 1953, *FRUS 1952–1954*, 2: 437; DDE to George Marshall, 15 November 1950, EP: PP, box 80; DDE to Truman, 24 February 1951, EP: PP, box 116; DDE to Edward J. Bermingham, 28 February 1951, EP: PP, box 11. For a contrasting view that sees hegemony as central to America's self-conception, see Thomas McCormick, *America's Half-Century* (Baltimore, 1989). For the short term, at least, Dulles believed that if the "European nations relied upon themselves and the Asians relied upon themselves the United States would be out of both areas, and without the United States as the balance of power, Russia would be in control in both Europe and Asia." In other words, no possibility of endogenous balance existed in those two regions. James Russell Wiggins, memo of conversation with Dulles, 12 February 1955, JFDP-additional, box 2.

23. Memo, Dulles to DDE, 6 September 1953, *FRUS 1952–1954*, 2: 458; Richard Harkness memorandum, 17 August 1953, Harkness Papers, JFDP-additional, box 1; Dulles testimony, 7 January 1954, *Executive Sessions of the Senate Foreign Relations Committee (Historical Series)*, 6: 11.

24. DDE to George Marshall, 3 August 1951, EP: PP, box 80. For a brief account of the EDC episode, see Brian R. Duchin, "The 'Agonizing Reappraisal': Eisenhower, Dulles, and the EDC," *Diplomatic History* 16 (Spring 1992): 201–21.

25. DDE to Harriman, 30 June 1951, *PDDE* 12: 398; DDE to Robert Lovett, 19 December 1951, EP: PP, box 72; DDE to Winston Churchill, 14 December 1951, EP: PP, box 72; DDE to Walter Bedell Smith, 1 February 1952, EP: PP, box 109; NSC minutes, 1 April 1954, AWF: NSC Series; Conversation with Senator Walter George, 7 January 1954, AWF: DS. Even after EDC's defeat, Ike continued to make the case for European unity, e.g., "If Western Europe could find the determination and ability to combine itself effectively into a federation, there would automatically be established a third great power complex in the world, one that by its history and by the character of its civilization would be dedicated to the same basic principles as we are." DDE to Alfred Gruenther, 2 December 1955, AWF: AF, box 16.

26. NSC minutes, 21 November 1955, *FRUS 1955–1957*, 4: 349; NSC 160/1,

"United States Policy with Respect to Germany," 17 August 1953, AWF: NSC Series, Policy Papers Subseries; Memo of conversation, Dulles and Knowland, 30 August 1957, JFDP: GCM, box 1; Dulles to Adenauer, 15 August 1955, JFDP: GCM, box 2; Memo by Richard Harkness, 1 July 1954, JFDP-additional, box 1.

27. DDE to Alfred Gruenther, 2 November 1954, AWF: AF, box 161; Supplement to NSC 160/1, "Statement of Policy toward East Germany," September 1956, AWF: NSC Series, Policy Papers Subseries; Dulles to Adenauer, 23 July 1955, JFDP: SS, box 8; James Russell Wiggins memo of conversation with Dulles, 30 October 1956, JFDP-Additional, box 2.

28. Livingston Merchant OH, JFDP, p. 36; Memo of conversation, Douglas MacArthur II and Prime Minister Laniel, 14 April 1954, JFDP: WHM, box 1. Despite talk of "agonizing reappraisal" and clumsy hints of a revival of isolationism in the United States, Dulles realized, as he privately admitted, that "the Western European powers are very well aware indeed that the United States cannot permit the Soviets to overrun and occupy Western Europe." See NSC minutes, 20 October 1955, AWF: NSC Series.

29. NSC minutes, 18 June 1953, AWF: NSC Series; James B. Conant to Dulles, 13 November 1953, JFDP: SS, box 8; DDE to Walter Bedell Smith, 3 September 1954, AWF: Dulles-Herter Series [hereafter DH], box 3; Working paper by the NSC Planning Board, October 1954, *FRUS 1952–1954*, 2: 750; Dulles, memo of conversation with Adenauer, 16 September 1954, JFDP: SS, box 8; NSC minutes, 24 September 1954, re NSC 5433, "Immediate US Policy toward Europe," AWF: NSC Series; Dulles, memo of conversation with DDE, 14 December 1954, JFDP: WHM, box 1.

30. DDE to Swede Hazlett, 21 June 1951, in Griffith, *Ike's Letters to a Friend*, p. 85; DDE to Paul Hoffman, 8 March 1957, AWF: AF, box 19. The "great loss," as he saw it, was "the failure of the new arrangements to establish the same degree of inter-European parliamentary control as had been contemplated by EDC." NSC minutes, 6 October 1954, AWF: NSC Series. As late as July 1957 he was still anticipating the withdrawal of American forces from Germany. NSC minutes of 1 July 1957, AWF: NSC Series.

31. Dulles to DDE, 24 September 1954, AWF: box 3. If continental unity was not in the cards, German unification seemed an alternate route for reaching the end of the cold war. A "unified, democratic Germany attached to the free world would represent a major step in rolling back the iron curtain and enlarging the basis for an enduring peace in Europe" while "freeing East Germany from Soviet control might have a magnetic effect on the East European satellites." NSC 160/1, "United States Policy with Respect to Germany," 17 August 1953, AWF: NSC Series, Policy Papers Subseries.

32. Telegram, Dulles to DOS, 17 December 1955, *FRUS 1955–1957*, 4: 369. The alliance quid pro quo for admitting a German national army into NATO had been American agreement to a summit conference in Geneva in July 1955. As Dulles put it, the meeting was agreed to "in order to get our allies to consent to the rearmament of Germany. World opinion demanded that the United States participate in these

negotiations with the Communists.'' According to Ike, just prior to the meeting, ''Our free world system depends on the voluntary alignment of our allies—hence world opinion is quite vital.'' NSC minutes, 21 December 1954, *FRUS 1955–1957,* 5: 307; NSC minutes, 19 May 1955, AWF: NSC Series.

33. Minutes of televised cabinet meeting, 25 October 1954, AWF: Cabinet Series, box 4; Merchant, printed recollections of the summit conference, p. 45, Merchant Papers, box 2; Memo by Merchant, undated, at Geneva, Merchant Papers, box 2; NSC minutes, 28 July 1955, AWF: NSC Series; JFD to Adenauer, 15 August 1955, JFDP: GCM, box 2. See, e.g., the Bohlen memorandum dated 23 July 1955 of a conversation between Eisenhower and Marshal Zhukov at Geneva in which Zhukov insisted that ''if there were no Paris agreements and West Germany in NATO, with eastern Germany in the Warsaw Pact it would have been easier to have agreed on Germany, and that these developments had greatly complicated the question.'' JFDP: GCM, box 3. The WEU, a political offshoot of the 1948 Brussels Treaty signed by Britain, France, and the Benelux countries, was expanded in October 1954 by adding West Germany and Italy, and modified by providing for the control of armaments in its member states.

34. Memo of conversation with DDE, 11 October 1955, JFDP: WHM, box 3; Telegram from U.S. delegation to State, 9 November 1955, *FRUS 1955–1957,* 5: 720.

35. NSC minutes, 7 July 1955, AWF: NSC Series. Dulles told an ambassadorial meeting in Paris in 1957 of his suspicion that ''the Western Europeans rather like the protection afforded by the nuclear power of the United States partly because in conventional armaments the greatest dependence of Western Europeans for security against the USSR would automatically be on the West Germans, both because of their geographic position and because of their potential.'' Minutes of ambassadorial meeting, 6 May 1957, *FRUS 1955–1957,* 4: 580.

36. Memo of Dulles-Eisenhower telephone conversation, 4 October 1954, AWF: DDE, DS, box 7; Memo of conversation at Geneva White House, 17 July 1955, EP: OSS, International Trips and Meetings, box 2; Excerpt from a letter by Gruenther, 14 May 1956, JFDP: WHM, box 3.

37. DDE to Lovett, 19 December 1951, EP: PP, box 72; Transcript of DDE briefing, 19 June 1951, ibid., box 92. In 1957, Eisenhower expected ''a very bleak and desperate future'' if the non-Western world turned toward the Soviets. DDE to Kevin McCann, 2 May 1957, AWF: AF, box 25.

38. NSC minutes, 29 May 1957, AWF: NSC Series.

39. *Executive Sessions of the Senate Foreign Relations Committee (Historical Series),* 5: 143; Memo of conversation, Dulles and Radford, 24 March 1954, JFDP: TCM, box 2; NSC minutes, 25 March 1954, AWF: NSC Series; Memo of conversation with DDE, 3 December 1956, JFDP: WHM, box 3; Memo of 16 May 1954, ''United States Foreign Policy,'' JFDP: WHM, box 7; Dulles, ''Think Piece'' drafts, 1956, JFDP: SS, box 7.

40. DDE to Alfred Gruenther, 30 November 1954, AWF: AF, box 16; Telephone

conversation with Congressman Judd, 24 June 1954, JFDP: TCM. Although the Anglo-French intervention in Suez in 1956 had damaged the alliance, it at least had the virtue of validating America's anticolonialist credentials in the eyes of the third world. "For many years," Dulles said, "we have been in the awkward position of trying to ride two horses—our Western allies with their colonial policy, and the nationalism of Southeastern Asia. For the first time, we stand apart from British imperialism." Richard Harkness memo, 31 October 1956, JFDP-additional, box 1.

41. Notes on remarks at NSC meeting, 31 March 1953, JFDP: WHM, box 7.

42. Memo of discussion at DOS, 6 November 1957, JFDP: GCM, box 3; Dulles speech to Rotary International, Washington, DC, 10 June 1954, JFDP: SS, box 8.

43. DDE to Averell Harriman, 20 April 1951, EP: PP, box 85; Dulles testimony, 13 February 1953, *Executive Sessions of the Senate Foreign Relations Committee (Historical Series)*, 5: 139–40; Memo of White House conversation, 24 March 1953, JFDP: WHM, box 1. Dulles recalled telling Ike on board the *Helena* returning from Korea that while Korea was important, "the really important spot is Indochina, because we could lose Korea and probably insulate ourselves against the consequences of that loss; but if Indochina goes, and if South Asia goes, it is extremely hard to insulate ourselves against the consequences of that." *Executive Sessions of the Senate Foreign Relations Committee (Historical Series)*, 6: 168. An NSC analysis of June 1952 already envisioned reverberations that ultimately "would endanger the stability and security of Europe." NSC 124/2, "U.S. Objectives and Courses of Action with Respect to Southeast Asia," 25 June 1952, NSC Series: Policy Papers Subseries.

44. NSC minutes, 13 May 1954, AWF: NSC Series; Memo of conversation with DDE, 24 March 1954, JFDP: WHM, box 1; Memo of conversation, Eden, Dulles, Radford, and Merchant, 26 April 1954, JFDP: SS, box 9; Conversation with Admiral Radford, 24 March 1954, JFDP: TCM, box 2.

45. NSC minutes, 21 December 1954, AWF: NSC Series; *FRUS 1952–1954*, 2: 496.

46. Dulles press conference, 11 May 1954, JFDP: SS, box 8.

47. Memo of Dulles meeting with congressional leaders, 20 April 1954, JFDP: SS, box 9; Dulles and DDE telephone conversation, 3 April 1954, JFDP: TCM, box 10; Conversation with Senator H. Alexander Smith (NJ), JFDP: TCM, box 2. For Eisenhower's strong resistance to unilateralism, see Melanie Billings-Yun, *Decision against War: Eisenhower and Dien Bien Phu, 1954* (New York, 1988), pp. 150–53. In talking of Southeast Asia's importance, a draft address to Congress had Eisenhower insisting, "It must not fall. If it does, it would make a third world war almost inevitable." First preliminary draft, outline of address to a joint session of Congress on Indochina, JFDP: SS, box 8.

48. Memo of conversation with DDE, 19 May 1954, JFDP: WHM, box 1; NSC minutes, 6 April 1954, AWF: NSC Series; Memo of Dulles-Eden conversation, 30 April 1954, JFDP: SS, box 9; Memo of conversation, Dulles with Australian and New Zealand delegations at Geneva, 2 May 1954, JFDP: SS, box 9.

49. Richard Harkness memo, 24 May 1954, JFDP-additional, box 1; Dulles press

conference, 1 May 1954, JFDP: SS, box 8; Dulles meeting with congressional leaders, 5 May 1954, JFDP: SS, box 9.

50. Summary of DDE's talk with Republican leaders, 3 May 1954, JFDP: SS, box 8; DDE-Dulles conversation, 20 July 1954, AWF: DS, box 2; Memo of conversation with DDE, 17 August 1954, JFDP: WHM, box 1.

51. Conversation with Livingston Merchant, 30 August 1954, JFDP: TCM, box 2; Telephone call to Carl McCardle, 31 August 1954, ibid.; NSC minutes, 26 October 1954, AWF: NSC Series.

52. Minutes of cabinet meeting, 19 October 1954, AWF: Cabinet Series, box 4; Unsigned memo, 11 May 1955 [but with Dulles's handwriting as emendations], JFDP: SS, box 9; Dulles memo of conversation with Faure, ibid.; NSC minutes, 7 June 1956, AWF: NSC Series; Minutes of cabinet meeting, 29 March 1957, AWF: Cabinet Series, box 8.

53. DDE telephone conversation with George Humphrey, 20 December 1954, AWF: DDE, DS, box 7; NSC minutes, 12 September 1954, AWF: NSC Series, box 6. On receding hopes for the collapse of Communist China, see James Russell Wiggins, memo of discussion with Dulles, 12 February 1955, JFDP-additional, box 2; and DDE conversation with Senator Knowland, 26 January 1955, AWF: DS, box 4. Even so, the administration would deny suggestions that an acceptance of two Chinas, which of course presumed the continued existence of the PRC, was somehow a realistic accommodation to the status quo. Dulles insisted that communism, far from being the wave of the future, was "a receding wave." Meeting of 28 January 1957, discussion of NSC 5707, "Basic Problems for US Security Arising out of Changes in the World Situation," AWF: NSC Series. Should the Nationalists lose hope for a return to the mainland, the belief was that "the United States would lose the whole show in the Far East." NSC minutes, 2 October 1957, AWF: NSC Series.

54. Dulles testimony, 24 February 1954, *Executive Sessions of the Senate Foreign Relations Committee (Historical Series)*, 6: 158; DDE to Churchill, 14 December 1954, AWF: DDE, DS, box 7.

55. See Akira Iriye, "Dilemmas of American Policy towards Formosa," *China Quarterly* 15 (July-September 1963): 51–55.

56. Memo of conversation between DDE, Dulles, Prime Minister St. Laurent, and Lester Pearson of Canada, 27 March 1956, JFDP: WHM, box 3; suggestions for inclusion in DDE's Formosa speech, 24 January 1955, ibid., box 2. MacArthur's description of Taiwan as an "unsinkable aircraft carrier" was a silly metaphor because the essential characteristics of a carrier are mobility and portability. As Radford subsequently admitted in an oral interview, "You can't say that anything outside of Formosa is essential to the defense of Formosa, in that sense, any more than you could say the Hawaiian Islands are essential to the defense of the continental United States. The answer is that they're not essential." Arthur W. Radford OH, p. 41.

57. Memo of White House meeting, 22 May 1954, JFDP: WHM, box 1; Summary of remarks by JFD at cabinet meeting in Ottawa, Canada, 19 March 1955, AWF:

DH, box 4; Telephone call to Bedell Smith, 6 September 1954, AWF: DDE, DS, box 7; Memo of conference with DDE, 18 October 1954, JFDP: WHM, box 1.

58. NSC minutes, 6 October 1954, AWF: NSC Series; NSC minutes, 21 December 1954, ibid.

59. DDE meeting with Charles Bohlen, 2 December 1954, AWF: DS, box 3; DDE to Churchill, 10 February 1955, AWF: DH, box 3.

60. Minutes of cabinet meeting, 18 February 1955, AWF: Cabinet Series, box 4; NSC minutes, 18 February 1955, and 10 March 1955, AWF: NSC Series.

61. Draft memo on Quemoy and Matsu, 13 September 1954, JFDP: WHM, box 7; NSC minutes, 20 January 1955, AWF: NSC Series. See also Dulles-Radford meeting with congressional leaders, 20 January 1955, JFDP: WHM, box 2; DDE to Churchill, 10 February 1955, AWF: DH, box 3; NSC 5501, "Basic National Security Policy," 7 January 1955, AWF: NSC Series, Policy Papers Subseries.

62. NSC minutes, 10 March 1955, AWF: NSC Series; Minutes of cabinet meeting, 11 March 1955, AWF: Cabinet Series, box 4.

63. NSC minutes, 2 November 1954, AWF: NSC Series.

64. NSC minutes, 28 January 1955, AWF: NSC Series; DDE to Gruenther, 1 February 1955, AWF: AF, box 16; Dulles to State, 25 February 1955, AWF: DH, box 3; Memo by Dulles, 12 September 1954, JFDP: WHM, box 7; Memo by Robert Cutler of a White House meeting on Formosa, 11 March 1955, JFDP: WHM, box 2. At an October 1954 NSC meeting, Dulles complained of a shearing effect: "You can talk all you want of the bad effect on Asia if the United States does not fight to defend these offshore islands, but you say nothing about the bad effect on Europe if we do undertake to fight to hold these islands. Secretary Dulles warned that we would be in this fight in Asia completely alone. Europe could be written off in such a contingency." NSC minutes, 6 October 1954, AWF: NSC Series. Eisenhower summed up the dilemma in early April: "Opinion in the free world appears to back the American determination to assist the ChNats [*sic*] in the defense of the main position, that is, Formosa and the Pescadores. But . . . world opinion most emphatically repudiates outside interference in any Communist attack on Quemoy and the Matsus." DDE to Dulles, 5 April 1955, AWF: DH, box 4. ANZUS is the acronym for the security treaty signed by Australia, New Zealand, and the United States in September 1951.

65. NSC minutes, 12 September 1957 [1954?], AWF: NSC Series; NSC meeting of 2 November 1954, ibid.

66. NSC minutes, 10 March 1955, AWF: NSC Series; Dulles memo of meeting with Ike, 11 March 1955, JFDP: WHM, box 2; Memo of meeting in Dulles's office, 28 March 1955, JFDP: WHM; DDE meeting with Under Secretary Hoover and Admiral Carney, 25 April 1955, AWF: DS, box 5.

67. Memo of conversation with DDE, 4 April 1955, AWF: DS, box 5; Livingston Merchant to Dulles, 6 April 1955, JFDP: WHM, box 2; Memo of meeting in Dulles's

office, 28 March 1955, JFDP: WHM, box 2; Dulles draft re Formosa, 7 April 1955, JFDP: WHM, box 2.

68. Memo of White House meeting, 1 April 1955, JFDP: WHM, box 3; Notes by DDE of a conversation with Anthony Eden, 19 July 1955, AWF: DS, box 6; NSC minutes, 21 December [1954?], AWF: NSC Series.

69. Memo of conversation with DDE, 5 August 1955, JFDP: WHM, box 3; Dulles conversation with DDE, 12 August 1958, ibid., box 7; Dulles meeting with DDE, 3 August 1958, ibid.; Notes of meeting with DDE, 4 September 1958, ibid.; Memo of meeting with DDE, 23 September 1958, ibid. If anything, the situation permitted even less flexibility, since, as Dulles admitted, the offshore islands were "now so complete and integral a part of the defense of Taiwan that it was not to be compared with the fluid situation of three years ago." Meeting of 2 October 1957, AWF: NSC Series.

70. Conversation with DDE, 6 September 1958, JFDP: TCM, box 10; Memo of meeting with DDE, 11 September 1958, JFDP: WHM, box 7; Dulles conversation with Senator Green, 12 October 1958, JFDP: GCM, box 1. In an attempt to provide some consolation, someone sent in the quotation from Thucydides' *The Peloponnesian War* in which Pericles advocated standing firm on the seemingly trivial matter of the Megaran decree. "You are not really going to war for a trifle," said Pericles. "For in the seeming trifle is involved the trial and confirmation of your whole purpose. If you yield to them in a small matter, they will think you are afraid and will immediately dictate some more oppressive condition." In JFDP: WHM, box 7.

71. Memo of group discussion at State Department, 6 November 1957, JFDP: GCM, box 3; NSC minutes, 21 November 1955, *FRUS, 1955–1957,* 5: 805; Meeting of 6 February 1958, AWF: NSC series, box 82.

72. DDE telephone conversation with Dulles, 5 February 1958, AWF: DDE, DS, box 30; Dulles telephone call to DDE, 19 December 1956, JFDP: TCM, box 11; Meeting of 6 February 1958, AWF: NSC Series. This discussion was touched off by an NSC paper which put forward the possibility that American forces might be asked to leave Germany in the near future. Dulles believed that the Soviets would not countenance reunification without at least giving themselves a good shot at communizing the whole country. Minutes of Conference of Chiefs of Mission, 6 May 1957, *FRUS 1955–1957,* 4: 597.

73. DDE telephone conversation with Dulles, 1 April 1958, AWF: DDE, DS, box 31.

74. Meeting of 19 June 1958, AWF: NSC Series; Memo of Dulles-Mikoyan conversation, 16 January 1959, Livingston Merchant Papers, box 3.

75. Marc Trachtenberg, *History and Strategy* (Princeton, NJ, 1991), pp. 191, 231–34; Telephone call from Hagerty, 29 July 1958, JFDP: TCM, box 10.

76. James Russell Wiggins, memo of discussion with Dulles, 18 November 1958, JFDP-additional, box 2; Memo of conference, Dillon, Goodpaster, and DDE with the British Ambassador, 19 June 1959, AWF: DDE, DS, box 42; Dulles to Adenauer, 28 January 1959, EP: OSS, International Series, box 6.

77. Memo of conversation with DDE, 17 March 1959, EP: OSS, International Series, box 6; Memo of conference with DDE, 24 August 1959, Herter, Ike, Murphy, Merchant, Goodpaster, EP: OSS, Subject Series; State Department Subseries, box 3; Thompson from Moscow to State, 9 March 1959, EP: OSS, International Series, box 6.

78. Memo of DDE conference with legislators on Berlin, 6 March 1959, EP: OSS, International Series, box 6; Telegram, Bruce (Bonn) to State, 2 March 1959, ibid; Acheson, notes for a talk at SAIS, 11 December 1958, DAP: Yale, series 4, box 58; DDE televised speech on Berlin, 16 March 1959, EP: OSS, box 6. Adenauer had already notified Dulles, early in the crisis, that "the first Allied concessions will be the last." Adenauer to Dulles, 21 November 1958, EP: OSS, box 6.

79. Adenauer to Dulles, 30 January 1959, AWF: International Series, box 14; DDE-Dulles telephone conversation, AWF: DDE, DS, box 40; Thompson, Moscow, to State, 19 February 1959, EP: OSS, International Series, box 6; Meeting with DDE, 9 February 1959, JFDP: WHM, box 7; Memo of DDE conference with legislators on Berlin, 6 March 1959, EP: OSS, International Series, box 6; Memo of conference between Dillon, Goodpaster, DDE, and the British Ambassador, 19 June 1959, AWF: DDE, DS, box 42.

80. Herter conference with DDE, 25 June 1959, AWF: DDE, DS, box 42; "Thinking Out Loud," memo by Dulles [1959], JFD: WHM, box 7.

81. DDE to Paul Hoffman, 23 June 1958, AWF: AF, box 19; DDE to Douglas Dillon, 6 May 1953, JFDP: SS, box 8; NSC minutes, 3 June 1958, AWF: NSC Series; Memo of conversation, General Lauris Norstad and DDE, 9 June 1959, AWF: DDE, DS, box 42; DDE to Norstad, 11 January 1960, AWF: DS, box 11. See also DDE to Alfred Gruenther, 22 June 1953 and 26 April 1954, AWF: AF, box 166; and Frank Costigliola, *France and the United States: The Cold Alliance since World War II* (New York, 1992), p. 8.

82. NSC minutes, 1 May 1958, AWF: NSC Series. Late in 1957, Dulles had remarked that "if there was an attack anywhere we would move . . . for the cold reason that if we didn't react the thing would spread." Memo of discussion group at DOS, 6 November 1957, JFDP: GCM, box 3. Ike was uncertain whether to "set public opinion right" or downplay the possibility of war. For a time he leaned in the direction of not letting on how serious the situation was perceived to be. In one of his more bizarre ruminations, during one meeting on Berlin he "pointed out the phrase in the Declaration of Independence which stated, as one of human rights, that of pursuit of happiness. The President applied this to the current situation by stating that we should not worry the public unnecessarily. Instead, we should show them courage and confidence." Memo of conference of legislative leaders with DDE on Berlin, 8 March 1959, EP: OSS, International Series, box 6.

83. Thompson from Moscow to State, 9 March 1959, White House Office, OSS, International Series, box 6; Telegram from Thompson in Moscow, 19 February 1959, ibid.; Memo, attachment to Martin Hillenbrand to Foy Kohler, 16 October 1959; DOS memo, 16 April 1959, "Status of Preparations for Foreign Ministers' Confer-

ences,'' on Berlin and Germany, White House Office, OSS, International Series, box 6. Ann Whitman diary, 1 July 1959, AWF: DS, box 10.

84. DDE-Dulles telephone conversation, AWF: DDE, DS, box 40; Memo of conversation with J. William Fulbright, 2 February 1959, JFDP: GCM, box 1; Memo of conference with DDE, 25 September 1959, AWF: DDE, DS, box 44; Memo of conference with DDE, 24 August 1959, Herter, Ike, Murphy, Merchant, and Goodpaster, EP: OSS, Subject Series; State Department Subseries, box 3.

85. Memo of Mikoyan-DDE meeting, 17 January 1959, EP: OSS, International Series, box 15; Memo of conversation, Merchant and Frol Kozlov, ibid., box 15; Memo of Dulles-Mikoyan meeting, 16 January 1959, Livingston Merchant Papers, box 3.

86. Memo of conversation, DDE and Khrushchev, 15 September 1959, President's Office Files [hereafter POF], box 126, John F. Kennedy Presidential Library, Boston, MA [hereafter JFKPL]; Memo of DDE-Khrushchev White House meeting, 15 September 1959, AWF: International Series, box 48.

87. Memo of meeting with DDE, 24 October 1958, JFDP: WHM, box 7.

88. Unsigned DOS paper, 9 December 1960, EP: OSS, International Series, box 15.

CHAPTER 8

1. John F. Kennedy, *Why England Slept* (New York, 1961), pp. 217, xxiii, 231.

2. Memo, Walt Rostow to JFK, 21 April 1961, NSF, box 231.

3. Schlesinger speech, 6 January 1962, POF, box 65a, JFKPL; Thompson to State, 24 January 1961, ibid., box 125a; Thompson to State, 2 February 1961, NSF, box 176; JFK, *The Strategy of Peace*, ed. Allan Nevins (New York, 1960), p. 34.

4. JFK statement on Khrushchev's visit, POF, box 125; Talking points for JFK–de Gaulle meeting, 31 May–2 June 1961, POF, box 116a; Telegrams, no. 412 from Moscow, 29 January 1960 [*sic*] and no. 1813, 2 February 1961, POF, box 125a. This loosening up of Soviet society provided gratifying confirmation of containment's foundational belief. In Rostow's view, it showed that ''within the Communist bloc history has not stopped.'' Rostow, draft speech to League of Women Voters, 23 April 1962, Sorensen Papers, JFKPL, box 38.

5. National Intelligence Estimates [hereafter NIE] 11–5–63, ''Soviet Economic Problems,'' 25 March 1963, POF, box 125a; The success of communism was not gauged solely by reference to the USSR. Kennedy also pointed to the ''Great Leap Forward'' of Communist China as an example of the dramatic gestures that ''carry credibility with other nations.'' *Strategy of Peace*, p. 75. This gloomy outlook was only partially offset by a critical understanding of the inefficiencies and strains of the Soviet economy. According to Raymond Aron, the USSR was ''the one country where one knows exactly when the moon-bound cosmonaut will return, but where one cannot know when the housewife who has gone out to buy meat at the corner

shop will return.'' Reply to a TASS questionnaire [late 1961], by Raymond Aron, POF, box 125a.

6. Memo by Bowles, "A Review and Appraisal of Our First Five Months," 5 July 1961, POF, box 78; Douglass Cater to JFK, 9 November 1961, POF, box 28; JFK, speech in Hutchinson, KS, 4 May 1960, PP, box 907; Theodore Sorensen OH, p. 1.

7. Acheson report on NATO, March 1961, NSF, box 220; Schlesinger to Edward R. Murrow, 19 June 1961, ibid., box 327; Schlesinger speech in New Delhi, 15 February 1961, ibid., box 326; Schlesinger to JFK, 19 June 1961, ibid. As Secretary of State Dean Rusk put it, "We do not wish to make the world over in our own image." Rusk testimony before Senate Foreign Relations Committee, 31 May 1961, NSF, box 326.

8. JFK speech, Durham, NH, 7 March 1960, PP, box 907; JFK speech, Muskegon, MI, 5 September 1960, ibid., box 910; JFK speech at Presque Isle, ME, 2 September 1960, ibid.; Notes by Bundy of a discussion on the thinking of the Soviet leadership, 13 February 1961, POF, box 125a.

9. Schlesinger talk at Salzburg, "Public Opinion in the United States and Foreign Policy," 27 August 1963, NSF, box 326; Memo, Robert Komer to Rostow, 12 April 1961, ibid., box 176; JFK, "We Must Climb to the Top," *Life,* 22 August 1960, in PP, box 910, JFKPL; "Ad Libbing Points" for Vienna meeting, undated, POF, box 126. This show of confidence was not without its element of doubt. According to Walt Rostow, Kennedy "really feared we might be in a secular decline like the British." Walt W. Rostow OH, p. 122.

10. Sorensen OH, p. 94; JFK interview with Alexei Adzhubei, 16 November 1961, NSF, box 183; G. F. Hudson, "Soviet Fears of the West," March 1962, POF, box 125a, which Bohlen described as "the best short analysis of Soviet policy" that he had read; Memo, talking points for de Gaulle meeting, 31 May–2 June 1961, POF, box 116a. An influential article that caught the administration's attention argued that the Soviet system's rapid growth in economic, scientific, and military strength would "enable its leaders to devote greater rather than smaller resources and political determination to achieving the worldwide purposes that have been proclaimed in an evolving pattern of interpretation by Lenin and Stalin and now by Khrushchev." Philip Mosely, "Soviet Myths and Realities," *Foreign Affairs* 39 (April 1961): 354. As Acheson pointed out, while the environment was "ecumenical," it became "inimical to freedom if the coercion of some societies by others makes inroads in the acceptance of consent." Acheson report on NATO, March 1961, NSF, box 220.

11. Speech to Democratic rally in Alexandria, VA, 24 August 1960, PP, box 910; Kennan to State, 2 June 1961, POF, box 126; Bohlen to Rusk, 23 March 1961, NSF, box 176 (Bohlen's emphasis); JFK meeting with congressional leadership, 7 June 1961, NSF, boxes 70–71.

12. Lippmann to Sorensen, 1 October 1961, in *Public Philosopher: Selected Letters of Walter Lippmann,* ed. John Morton Blum (New York, 1985), p. 605; Back-

ground paper for Vienna summit, 1 June 1961, POF, box 126; Maxwell Taylor, *An Uncertain Trumpet* (New York, 1959), p. 136.

13. JFK, *Strategy of Peace*, pp. 32, 67, 69.

14. Ibid., p. 65; "Meet the Press" interview with Lauris Norstad, 20 January 1963, POF, box 103.

15. Kennan to Kennedy, 17 August 1960, addendum to Kennan OH; JFK speech to Democratic rally in Alexandria, VA, 24 August 1960, PP, box 910; TV debate in Charleston, WV, 4 May 1960, PP, box 909; JFK, Henry Luce address, New York City, 15 May 1961, POF, box 31.

16. Review of Kennedy-Khrushchev conversation, 3–4 June 1961, POF, box 126.

17. Ibid.; Draft, JFK to Khrushchev, 27 November 1961, POF, box 126.

18. Bohlen to Rusk, 23 March 1961, NSF, box 176.

19. Memo by JFK, 19 January 1961, POF, box 29a; Clark Clifford to JFK, 24 January 1961, ibid., enclosing memo of meeting with Eisenhower on 19 January; Rostow to Rusk, McNamara, and [McCone?], 24 April 1961, POF, box 115; Rostow to JFK, 28 April 1961, NSF, box 231.

20. JFK to Acheson, 14 August 1961, POF, box 27; Memo of conversation, Rusk and Adenauer, 10 August 1961, NSF, box 82; Memo by M. J. Hillenbrand, "The Berlin Problem in 1961," 10 January 1961, NSF, box 81.

21. JFK meeting with congressional leadership, 7 June 1961, NSF, boxes 70–71; Thompson to State, 16 March 1961, POF, box 125a; Memo by Department of State on Berlin, transmitted by Battle to Bundy, 30 May 1961, NSF, box 82. According to Walt Rostow in *The Diffusion of Power, 1957–1972* (New York, 1972), p. 231, Kennedy himself broached the possibility of a wall being built. Honoré M. Catudal, *Kennedy and the Berlin Wall Crisis: A Case Study in U.S. Decision Making* (Berlin, 1980), pp. 216, 229–50, argues strongly that there existed foreknowledge of Khrushchev's intention of building a wall. Some commentators, like Richard Smoke and Alexander George, *Deterrence in American Foreign Policy: Theory and Practice* (New York, 1974), p. 437, go so far as to suggest that the administration signaled their acceptance of a wall to the Soviets in advance. The same argument is made by Michael Beschloss, *The Crisis Years: Kennedy and Khrushchev 1960–1963* (New York, 1991), pp. 277–82.

22. Memo by Fulbright, 7 June 1961, POF, box 116a; Marc Raskin to Bundy, 1 June 1961, NSF, box 81; Memo, Bundy to JFK, 11 August 1961, NSF, box 82; Memo of NSC discussion, 29 June 1961, NSF, box 313.

23. Memo, Bundy to JFK, 29 May 1961, POF, box 126.

24. Memo by Fulbright, 7 June 1961, POF, box 116A; Bundy to JFK, 4 April 1961, NSF, box 81.

25. Cable, 18 February 1961, reporting de Gaulle interview with Cyrus Sulzberger, NSF, boxes 70–71; Memo, Kissinger to JFK, 6 April 1961, POF, box 117. Only a very few iconoclasts, like the young historian Manfred Jonas, dared to assert the opposite: "Who really wants a united Germany? Not even the Germans." Memo

by Manfred Jonas, attachment to Schlesinger to Rostow, 9 September 1961, NSF, box 82.

26. Rostow to Bundy, 16 August 1961, NSF, box 82; Memo, Marc Raskin to Bundy, 1 June 1961, NSF, box 81; Memo, Foy Kohler to Rusk, July 1961, POF, box 117a.

27. Memo by Roger Hilsman, 30 June 1961, "The Berlin Crisis: In What Sense a Test of Will?" NSF, box 81; Memo, Bundy to JFK, 29 May 1961, POF, box 126; Talking points for JFK–de Gaulle meeting, POF, box 116a.

28. Office of Naval Intelligence research note, 18 August 1961, NSF, box 82; NSC minutes, 20 July 1961, NSF, box 82.

29. A. L. George, "Military Power and the Cold War," RAND Corporation research memo RM-2689, 26 December 1960 NSF, box 81; Memo, Rostow to JFK [July 1961?], NSF, box 81; JFK to de Gaulle, 20 July 1961, POF, box 116a.

30. DOS memo on Berlin, transmitted by Battle to Bundy, 30 May 1961, NSF, box 82; Memo, Bowles to JFK, 22 August 1961, ibid.; JFK to Willy Brandt, 18 August 1961, ibid.; Robert F. Kennedy OH, p. 101. As Bobby Kennedy later conceded, an element of personal contest existed between Kennedy and Khrushchev. At the Vienna meeting, according to RFK, "Khrushchev thought he was dealing with a rather weak figure—he was dealing with a young figure who had perhaps no confidence, he was dealing with a weak person because if he wasn't so weak he wouldn't have gone through the Bay of Pigs." RFK OH, p. 93.

31. See Khrushchev's comment to William Benton that "Mr. Kennedy tried to argue with me that we should have a status quo," in notes of conversation with Khrushchev, Benton trip to Moscow, 19–29 May 1964, Security Files, Files of McGeorge Bundy, boxes 15–16, Lyndon B. Johnson Presidential Library, Austin, TX [hereafter LBJPL].

32. Harriman to JFK, 1 September 1961, NSF, box 82; Kaysen memo, 22 August 1961, "Thoughts on Berlin," Schlesinger Papers, box NH–3.

33. Sorensen OH, JFKPL, p. 41; Address at Free University of Berlin, 26 June 1963, *Public Papers of the Presidents: John F. Kennedy, 1961–1963* (Washington, DC, 1964) [hereafter *PPP*], p. 273; Rusk-Gromyko conversation, 2 October 1963, NSF, box 187. As Sorensen recalled, Kennedy also informed Khrushchev and Alexei Adzhubei "that in the case of Berlin and Germany, the status quo should be settled upon, inasmuch as it had some advantages for both sides." Sorensen OH, p. 94.

34. This outright willingness to accept the postwar status quo in Europe was a far cry from Kennedy's hard-line campaign rhetoric, in which he had called for a policy of "vigorous, imaginative effort and continual pressure" to promote change in eastern Europe. See JFK speech in Corvallis, OR, 10 February 1960, PP, box 906.

35. Memo of conversation, JFK, LBJ, and Clay, 5 September 1961, NSF, box 317; Memo of conversation, Rusk and Gerhard Schröder, 20 September 1963, POF, box 117A. JFK informed de Gaulle that "the people of West Berlin are badly shaken by the events of the week." JFK to de Gaulle, 17 August 1961, POF, box 116A.

36. Research memorandum REU-59, 3 August 1963, "West Germany: Political and Economic Prospects," NSF, box 75.

37. Anton DePorte, *Europe between the Superpowers* (New Haven, 1979), p. 176; Memo, Rostow to JFK, 15 May 1961, NSF, boxes 70–71.

38. De Gaulle conversation with Henry Cabot Lodge, 28 November 1961, no. 2810 from Paris, NSF, boxes 70–71; No. 4522 from Paris by Acheson, ibid.

39. Gavin to State, no. 3764, 14 February 1962, NSF, boxes 70–71; Memo of conversation, Rostow and Jean-Claude Winkler of the French Embassy, 29 November 1962, NSF, box 71A. Rusk would later complain that de Gaulle saw U.S. policy as "aimed somehow at the maintenance of U.S. influence or control of Europe." Rusk to Bohlen, 25 September 1963, NSF, boxes 72a–73. For de Gaulle's explanation of his geopolitical logic, see Charles de Gaulle, *Memoirs of Hope: Renewal and Endeavor*, trans. Terence Kilmartin (New York, 1971), pp. 199–202.

40. Gavin to State, no. 973, 21 February 1962, NSF, boxes 70–71; Gavin to State, no. 525, 16 May 1962, ibid. See also notes on luncheon conversation at French embassy, 18 June 1963, NSF, box 72.

41. Memo by Bohlen, 7 August 1963, "Continuing Elements of De Gaulle's Foreign Policy," NSF, box 72A–73; Research memorandum REU-31 from INR, 6 April 1963, NSF, box 72; "Report from Paris," 28 September 1963, included in JFK's weekend reading, NSF, box 72A–73.

42. Bohlen to McGeorge Bundy, 2 March 1963, NSF: Bundy, boxes 15–16, LBJPL; Acheson report on NATO, March 1961, NSF, boxes 217–220, JFKPL; Memo by David Bruce, 9 February 1963, V-P Security File, box 4, LBJPL.

43. Memo of Rusk–Couve de Murville conversation, 8 October 1963, NSF, boxes 72a–73. In contrast to world-system theory's arguments about a psychological desire for hegemony arising reflexively from material forces, as suggested in Thomas McCormick's *America's Half Century*, the phenomenology of hegemony as it is outlined here would appear to be far more equivocal and even uncertain.

44. Schlesinger to JFK, reporting conversation with Pierre Mendès-France, NSF, boxes 70–71; CIA, "Current Intelligence Weekly Summary," 18 May 1961, ibid.

45. Acheson to State, no. 4522, NSF, boxes 70–71; CIA "Current Intelligence Weekly Summary," 18 May 1961, ibid.; McArthur to State, no. 1991, 29 May 1961, ibid.

46. Unsigned [Bundy?] memo to JFK, "The U.S. and DeGaulle," 30 January 1963, POF, box 116a; No. A-251 from Paris, 2 August 1962, reporting an article by Jean-Jacques Servan-Schreiber in *L'Express*, 26 July [1962], NSF, box 71A; Memo, Bohlen to Bundy, 2 March 1963, NSF: Bundy, boxes 15–16, LBJPL.

47. Telegram, Rusk to Stoessel, 5 May 1961, NSF, boxes 70–71, JFKPL; Memo of conversation, JFK and Paul Reynaud, 14 April 1961, ibid.

48. Bundy to Raymond Aron, 24 March 1962, NSF, boxes 70–71; Rusk to Walter Stoessel, no. 4770, 5 May 1961, ibid.

49. Memo of conversation, JFK and Grewe, 19 February 1962, POF, box 116a; JFK to Gavin, 18 May 1962, NSF, boxes 70–71.

50. JFK to Khrushchev, 22 October 1962, NSF, box 184.

51. "Cuban Missile Crisis Meetings, October 13, 1962," transcript, 2: 13, JFKPL; McGeorge Bundy, *Danger and Survival* (New York, 1988), p. 452; Dino A. Brugioni, *Eyeball to Eyeball: The Inside Story of the Cuban Missile Crisis* (New York, 1991), pp. 298, 347–50; William G. Hyland, *The Cold War: Fifty Years of Conflict* (New York, 1991), p. 128. See, e.g., McNamara's comments in James G. Blight and David Welch, *On the Brink: Americans and Soviets Reexamine the Missile Crisis* (New York, 1990), p. 188.

52. Telegram, Secto no. 8, Rusk from Paris, reporting de Gaulle conversation, 13 December 1962, NSF, box 71A; Memo to JFK, 30 January 1963, unsigned [Bundy?], "The US and de Gaulle," POF, box 116A.

53. Quoted in David Dimbleby and David Reynolds, *An Ocean Apart: The Relationship between Britain and America in the Twentieth Century* (New York, 1988), p. 251; Memo, Bundy to [Walter?] Lippmann, 13 November 1962, offering critique of a Paris speech draft, NSF, box 71A; Memo, Bundy to JFK, 14 January 1963, NSF, box 73.

54. Gavin to Secretary of State, no. 86, 6 July 1962, NSF, box 71A; Bonn to State, 18 February 1962, POF, box 117. According to influential syndicated columnist Joseph Alsop, the MLF was "one of those Madison Avenue gestures for which American policymakers have always had a weakness." In NSF, boxes 217–220. That was too uncharitable, however, since some enthusiasts within State saw MLF as a smaller version of the EDC, even though its purpose was to reinforce NATO rather than replace it.

55. Memo of conversation, Rostow and Jean-Claude Winkler of the French embassy, 29 November 1962, NSF, box 71A; Bohlen to State, 16 February 1963, NSF, box 72.

56. Sorensen OH, p. 85, JFKPL; Unsigned memo to JFK [Bundy?], "The U.S. and DeGaulle," 30 January 1963, POF, box 116a; JFK to Khrushchev, 16 November 1961, NSF, box 183. The desire for accommodation predated Cuba, but was accentuated by it. As Chester Bowles recalled, "Kennedy was very anxious to create some bridge with the Soviet Union." Chester Bowles OH, p. 21. During the campaign, Kennedy predicted that the 1960s would be "a decade of negotiation—a decade of conferences and meetings—as the world's great powers work to avoid a war of mutual annihilation." Speech at Portland, OR, 16 May 1960, PP, box 909. He also talked of taking risks to "exploit every opportunity that the dynamics of change in Soviet life may offer, to move toward peace." *Strategy of Peace*, pp. 31–32.

57. Reported in no. 13308 from Paris to USIA, 18 April 1963, NSF, box 72; Theodore C. Sorensen, *The Kennedy Legacy* (New York, 1969), p. 371; No. A-1870 from Paris, 9 April 1962, NSF, boxes 70–71.

58. Memo of conversation, JFK and André Malraux, 14 May 1963, NSF: Bundy, boxes 155–56, LBJPL.

59. Gavin to State, no. 2810, 28 November 1961, NSF, boxes 70–71; JFK interview with Couve de Murville, 7 October 1963, NSF, box 72A–73; Memo by Paul

Nitze, 1 February 1963, "A Basis for Possible Substantive Negotiations with the USSR," NSF, box 180.

60. RFK OH, p. 966; Philip Graham to JFK, 9 February 1963, POF, box 30.

61. George Ball, memo of conversation with Couve de Murville, 25 May 1963, NSF, box 72; Memo of conversation, Ball, Bohlen, Couve de Murville, and Alphand, 8 October 1963, ibid., box 72A–73; Memo, Henry Owen to Bundy, 21 April 1961, ibid., boxes 70–71.

62. Dowling (Bonn) to State, no. 1636, 11 January 1962, NSF, boxes 70–71; Stoessel to State, no. 1406 from Paris, 20 September 1962, ibid., box 71a.

63. Memo of conversation, Rusk, Ball, and Brentano, 22 March 1963, NSF, box 81; Memo of conversation, George McGhee and Heinrich von Brentano, 21 March 1963, ibid.

64. Walt Rostow OH, p. 56.

65. Roger Hilsman OH, p. 21; Galbraith to JFK, 10 May 1961 and 2 March 1962, POF, boxes 29a and 30; Memo, Mike Mansfield to JFK, 1 May 1961, V-P Security Files, box 1, LBJPL.

66. Assistant Secretary of State Frederick Dutton to Wayne Morse, 27 September 1963, Hilsman Papers, box 6; Hilsman OH, p. 21; Rostow OH, p. 83; Sorensen OH, p. 22; George Ball, *The Past Has Another Pattern* (New York, 1982), p. 366. As far back as 1954, when the Eisenhower administration was considering extricating the French from the debacle at Dien Bien Phu, he had remarked in the Senate that "without the wholehearted support of the peoples of the associated states, without a reliable and crusading army with a dependable officer corps, a military victory, even with American support, in that area is difficult if not impossible of achievement." Kennedy Senate speech, "The War in Indochina," 6 April 1954, Sorensen Papers, box 55.

67. Schlesinger to JFK, 30 August 1960, POF, box 32; Chester Bowles OH, pp. 27, 63; James McGregor Burns OH, p. 51. Less charitably, he could also be viewed as an unprincipled political opportunist. One doubter was reported as saying in August 1960 that "it isn't what Kennedy believes that worries me. It's whether he believes anything." Even on such a vital issue as the future of Europe, Charles Bohlen remarked that "you didn't feel he had a very deep conviction as to the form one way or another." Charles Bohlen OH, p. 36.

68. Chester Bowles OH; JFK to Khrushchev, 16 November 1961, NSF, box 183. See also Bowles to JFK, 1 December 1962, POF, box 28, JFKPL. One of his aides recalled him saying about Laos that "our interests out there are—we couldn't care less actually. We would like to see them independent." Michael Forestall OH, JFKPL, p. 38. If it were indeed true, by the terms of traditional geopolitical logic, that the strategic heart of the matter lay in Europe, then the only logical course would have been to revert to a pre–cold war emphasis on promoting development in the third world, in which the major task would be "to affect the course of cultural change in the non-Western areas." Gabriel Almond, *The American People and Foreign Policy* (New York, 1960), p. xxx.

69. W. Averell Harriman OH, p. 100; Robert Kennedy OH, 9: 9; JFK, *Strategy of Peace*, pp. 30, 75; JFK speech at Palo Alto, CA, 12 February 1960, PP, box 906.

70. Scope paper for Vienna summit, 23 May 1961, POF, box 126; Review of Kennedy-Khrushchev conversation at Vienna, 3–4 June 1961, ibid,; JFK speech, 6 June 1961, POF, box 125a.

71. Sorensen memo, "The Kennedy Record in Foreign Affairs, 1961," 29 December 1961, POF, box 66a; Bureau of Intelligence and Research, Report no. 8263, 9 May [1960?], NSF, box 176; Memo by John McCone, "An Appraisal of Soviet Intentions," 5 January 1962, POF, box 125a; Sorensen memo, "Taking the Long View in Foreign Affairs," 8 October 1963, Sorensen Papers, box 34. For a view that sees the United States coming much closer to the Soviets as the result of the Sino-Soviet split, see Gordon H. Chang, *Friends and Enemies: The United States, China, and the Soviet Union, 1948–1972* (Stanford, 1990), especially pp. 217–24, 228–52. As the CIA concluded in 1962, when the dispute was out in the open, "The emergence of a separate Asian Communist Bloc under the leadership of China could have grave implications for U.S. security interests in the Far East because of Peiping's militant and intense anti-Western line." CIA memo, "Sino-Soviet Relations at a New Crisis," 14 January 1963, NSF, box 180, JFKPL. Kennedy had already warned in *Strategy of Peace*, p. 38, that the Chinese Communists "may upset it all as they go through a Stalinist phase."

72. Thompson to State, 2 February 1961, NSF, box 176; Bohlen to Rusk, 23 March 1961, ibid.; Sino-Soviet Task Force, "The Sino-Soviet Dispute and Its Significance," 1 April 1961, ibid.

73. Memo of conversation, Harriman and Hervé Alphand, 21 June 1963, NSF, box 72; Q and A session following Kissinger speech at an air base in Pakistan, 2 February 1962, ibid., box 321; Bohlen to Bundy, 25 May 1962, ibid., box 176; Draft DOD document, Basic National Security Policy, 22 June 1962, ibid., box 290, JFKPL; State of the Union Address, 14 January 1963, *PPP* 1963, p. 17. See the memo by Roger Hilsman, S/P draft, 22 May 1962, Hilsman Papers, box 1, a portion of which states: "Statements and interpretations are to be avoided that suggest that: (a) the dispute has resulted in or is likely to result in a change in basic Communist objectives toward the US and the Free World, (b) the dispute has affected the capability of either the USSR or Communist China to endanger the security of the US, (c) the dispute has eliminated or reduced pressures that the Communist powers are bringing to bear on US interests in various critical areas of the world."

74. Rostow to Bundy, 26 May 1961, POF, box 126; Untitled paper analyzing Khrushchev speech of January 1961, NSF, box 176; Memo, Robert Komer to McGeorge Bundy, 12 January 1961, NSF, box 322.

75. Rostow to Bundy, 6 May 1961, POF, box 126; Rostow to JFK, 11 May 1961, NSF, box 231; Rostow, *Diffusion of Power*, p. 270; Rostow to JFK, 24 November 1961, POF, box 65.

76. Address to ASNE, 20 April 1961, *PPP* 1961, p. 306, as quoted in *The Senator Gravel Edition: The Pentagon Papers* (Boston, [1971]), 2: 802; Remarks by Theodore

J. C. Heavner, 25 August 1963, *Pentagon Papers,* 2: 825; Herbert Parmet, *JFK: The Presidency of John F. Kennedy* (New York, 1968), p. 137; NBC interview with Chet Huntley, 9 September 1963, *Pentagon Papers,* 3: 828. For further expressions of JFK's domino theorizing, see JFK news conference, 17 July 1963, *PPP* 1963, p. 569; Special message to Congress, 25 May 1961, *PPP* 1961, p. 804; JFK remarks in Great Falls, MT, 26 September 1963, *Pentagon Papers,* 2: 829–30.

77. Memo, Lyman Lemnitzer to McNamara, 13 April 1962, *Pentagon Papers,* 2: 672; Quoted in William J. Rust, *Kennedy in Vietnam* (New York, 1985), p. 51.

78. Edwin O. Guthman and Jeffrey Shulman, eds. *Robert Kennedy in His Own Words* (New York, 1988), p. 395; Rostow OH, pp. 150, 53. Rostow was almost certainly correct to believe that "in the back of his mind he knew there would have to be a showdown with the north" and that "in the end—reluctantly and painfully—he accepted what any American President in this period would have accepted; that somehow, you had to hold it." Rostow OH, pp. 87, 83. Rostow was also quite accurate when he suggested that "if you knew the doctrine you could predict quite accurately where he would fetch up on a given problem." On pragmatism and value neutrality, see Christopher Norris, *What's Wrong with Postmodernism* (Baltimore, 1990).

79. Rusk to Bohlen, 16 September 1961, POF, box 116a.

CHAPTER 9

1. Rostow OH, p. 9, LBJPL; Commencement address at Johnson City high schools, 4 June 1946, Statements, box 5, LBJPL; "Peace in This Day Is Not Cheap," *Congressional Record,* 7 May 1947, *Statements,* box 6; LBJ radio address, "America in the World Today," on Texas state network, 25 March 1948, *Statements,* box 6; Remarks on the Marshall Plan, 2 April 1948, *Statements,* box 6; Letter from LBJ to constituents, May 1948, *Statements,* box 6. For further description of his postwar views, see Ronnie Dugger, *The Politician: The Life and Times of Lyndon Johnson* (New York, 1982), pp. 362–71; Robert Dallek, *Lone Star Rising* (New York, 1991), pp. 257, 275, 382–84; Philip Geyelin, *Lyndon B. Johnson and the World* (New York, 1966), p. 13.

2. LBJ to JFK, 28 April 1961, POF, box 30, JFKPL; LBJ to JFK, 21 August 1961, V-P Security File, box 2, LBJPL. Johnson was publicly critical of British and French policy during the Indochina crisis of 1954, deploring a "doctrine which smacks strongly of appeasement and Munich," but he endorsed the decision not to send troops without the support of France and Britain. Quoted in Geyelin, *Lyndon B. Johnson and the World,* p. 31. Johnson believed that technological and political leadership went hand-in-hand. "We've had the leadership of the world because we took the air away from Hitler," he said in 1963. LBJ, Sorensen dictaphone recording, 3 June 1963, Office Files of George Reedy, LBJPL.

3. Walt Rostow OH, p. 71, JFKPL; Summary record of NSC meeting, 5 December 1963, NSF: NSC meetings, box 1, LBJPL; Salinger recapitulation of LBJ's remarks at Department of State, 5 December 1963, News Conference no. 29, in NSF: NSC meetings, box 1, LBJPL. At times LBJ even talked as if the cold war were

over. "The dogmas and the vocabularies of the Cold War were enough for one generation," he said hopefully in 1966. Speech at Arco, ID, 26 August 1966, in James MacGregor Burns, ed., *To Heal and to Build: The Programs of President Lyndon B. Johnson* (New York, 1968), p. 1366.

4. Memo, Thompson (Moscow) to LBJ, 15 July 1966, NSF: Memos, Rostow, box 9; Memo, Rostow to LBJ, 5 July 1966, ibid.; Dean Rusk briefing, 13 January 1965, Congressional Briefings on Vietnam, LBJPL.

5. LBJ, *The Vantage Point: Perspectives of the Presidency 1963–1969* (New York, 1971), p. 306; Walt Rostow, "Is NATO Necessary?" April 1964, NSF: Agency File, boxes 35, 42; Bohlen to Bundy, 5 November 1964, NSF: CF, box 170; Eugene V. Rostow OH, p. 19; Memo, Rostow to LBJ, 9 December 1968, NSF: Country File, France [hereafter CFF], boxes 171, 174. General Goodpaster was reporting that Ike's "most active worries are about NATO." Memo, McGeorge Bundy to LBJ, 14 September 1965, NSF: Memos, Bundy, box 4. Europe, as Walt Rostow recalled, had "settled back to a comfortable interval of relative isolation, fragmentation, and disengagement from world responsibility." Rostow, *The Diffusion of Power*, p. 249.

6. Memo of LBJ–de Gaulle meeting, 25 November 1963, NSF: CF, box 169.

7. Excerpts in NSF: CF, box 170; INR research memorandum, "De Gaulle's Foreign Policy, 1969 Version," 20 December 1968, NSF: CFF, boxes 171, 174.

8. Intelligence Memorandum, "France and the Atlantic Alliance," 6 October 1967, NSF: CFF, boxes 173, 174.

9. INR research memorandum, "De Gaulle's Foreign Policy," 20 April 1964, NS: CF, box 169; Pompidou press conference, April 1964, ibid.; Memo of dinner conversation, Couve de Murville, Rusk, Bohlen, and Thompson, 27 September 1965, ibid., box 172; quotations from Jean-Raymond Tournoux, *La Tragédie du Général*, in memo dated 5 December 1967, ibid., boxes 173, 174. Irritating, too, as Senator Fulbright complained, was de Gaulle's tendency to speak of the "Anglo-Saxons" "as though they were a species beneath notice." Voice of America Press Conference by Fulbright, 30 November 1963, ibid., box 169.

10. LBJ to de Gaulle, 22 March 1966, CF: CO52, box 8; CIA intelligence memo, 20 July 1966, NSF: CFF, box 172; LBJ meeting with foreign-policy advisers, 11 February 1966, Meeting notes, LBJPL, box 1. According to the CIA, the general hoped that his dialogue with Moscow would "lay the groundwork for eventual negotiations on European questions between a French-led Western Europe and the Communist countries of eastern Europe, looking toward their reincorporation into an over-all European framework." CIA special report, "France's Dialogue with the Soviet Union," 21 May 1965, NSF: CFF, box 171.

11. Humphrey interview on "Meet the Press," 13 March 1966, NSF: NF, box 4; Humphrey to LBJ, 19 October 1966, ibid.; DOS Paper, "France and NATO," 25 September 1965, NSF: CFF, box 172; William R. Tyler to Bundy, 12 March 1964, NSF: CFF, box 169; McCloy to LBJ, 21 November 1966, NSF: NSC History, box 50.

12. David K. Bruce OH, p. 8; Bundy to LBJ, 2 March 1965, NSF: CFF, box 171.

13. Congressional Briefings on Vietnam, Dean Rusk, 13 January 1965; LBJ meeting with Reuters representatives, 29 April 1968, Meeting notes, box 3; Draft of Ball speech, 6 February 1965, NSF: Bundy, boxes 15, 16. If Europe were left to its isolationist tendencies, Rusk feared that it "would leave the United States more or less alone as great power in the free world . . . We wanted some help in this role." Dean Rusk OH, 6: 18.

14. Memo by Douglas Dillon, "Some Thoughts on US Policy and Gaullist France," enclosure to Bundy to LBJ, 3 January 1966, NSF: MP, box 66; Memo prepared by Nathan Leites for RAND, "After De Gaulle," August 1965, NSF: CFF, box 176. A successor government, concluded a year-end analysis in 1968, would "probably be more willing to promote European integration and in particular to permit British entry." CIA report, "De Gaulle and the Fifth Republic, 1958–1968," 20 December 1968, NSF: CFF, boxes 171, 174. The operating assumption was, as Rostow suggested to LBJ, that de Gaulle was "increasingly operating a personal rather than governmental foreign policy." Memo, Rostow to LBJ, 28 July 1967, NSF: CFF, boxes 173, 174.

15. George Ball OH, 2: 24; Memo by Rostow, 5 April 1966, NSF: Rostow; Memo of meeting between Goodpaster and DDE, 12 March 1966, NSF: NF, box 3; Memo of Goodpaster-DDE meeting, 14 September 1966, NSF: NF, box 3. For further comments on the whys and wherefores of the soft line toward France, see Bundy to LBJ, 1 December 1963, NSF: MP, box 1; LBJ interview with Reynaud, 25 May 1965, NSF: CFF, boxes 171, 174; LBJ to DDE, 29 April 1967, NSF: NF, box 2; Memo, Hayes Redmon to Moyers, 5 March 1966, Office Files of Bill Moyers, box 7, LBJPL; Draft presidential memo to State and Defense departments, 3 May 1966, NSF: MP, box 7.

16. Bundy to LBJ, 9 December 1964, NSF: MP, Bundy, box 2; Undated message from LBJ to Wilson, CF: CO52, box 8. See also memo of conversation, Rusk and Couve de Murville, 19 February 1965, NSF: CFF, box 171; and LBJ's remark to British Prime Minister Harold Wilson that "what is essential is a stable and healthy Germany that can play a constructive role on the side of the West." LBJ to Wilson, 23 December 1965, CF: CO52, box 8.

17. Bundy to LBJ, 5 December 1964,, NSF: MP, Bundy, box 2; Bundy to JFK, 15 June 1963, ibid.

18. Memo of White House conversation, 19 November 1964, NSF: Bundy, boxes 18, 19; Kissinger memo of conversation, 22 June 1965, ibid., boxes 15, 16; Bundy to Rusk, McNamara, and Ball, 25 November 1964, NSF: MP, box 2; LBJ meeting with Bill Theiss of Hearst Press, 1 July 1968, Meeting notes.

19. Memo, McCloy to LBJ, 12 December 1968, NSF: Rostow; Speech draft by Ball, 6 February 1965, NSF: Bundy, boxes 15, 16; Memo, Moyers to LBJ, 29 July 1966, Moyers Office Files, box 12; Bundy to LBJ, 28 January 1966, NSF: MP, box 6.

20. Unsigned memo, "The Case for a Fresh Start on Atlantic Nuclear Defense," NSF: MP, box 5; Edward K. Hamilton to Bundy, 2 November 1965, NSF: Country File, Germany [hereafter CFG], boxes 181–91; LBJ quoted, October 1966, in Eugene V. Rostow OH, p. 15.

21. George McGhee OH, p. 4; Telegram, McGhee to LBJ, 16 January 1965, NSF: MP, Bundy, box 22; Draft letter to Wilson, 20 May 1966, NSF: MP, box 7. As Henry Kissinger reported to Bundy, "The significance of the MLF in German politics is not that there is a popular demand or a partisan issue but that Erhard and Schroeder at our urging have staked their prestige on it." Kissinger to Bundy, 27 November 1964, NSF: Bundy, boxes 15, 16.

22. Bundy to LBJ, 16 May 1964, NSF: MP, Bundy, box 1; INR research memorandum, "Western Europe Looks at Germany," 6 August 1965, NSF: CFF, boxes 181–91; Memo by Acheson, "Study Needed of U.S. Policy towards Europe," 31 March 1965, NSF: MP, Bundy, box 3. George Ball recalled the United States as being in "a rather false situation, because we were making all these noises about ultimate reunification and so on." George Ball OH, 2: 26. Privately, Bundy maintained that any new proposal on Berlin or on Germany could not now be put forward without seriously offending either the Germans or the Russians. Bundy to LBJ, 13 January 1964, NSF: MP, Bundy, box 1.

23. CIA special memorandum, "Bonn Looks Eastward," 10 October 1964, NSF: CFG, boxes 181–91; LBJ speech, 7 October 1966, *PPP* 1966, p. 1128; McGhee to State, 4 October 1966, NSF: MP, Rostow, boxes 11, 12. According to Zbigniew Brzezinski, this address, which he helped draft, "fundamentally reversed the post-war priorities of the United States and Europe. Until that speech, it was a central tenet of American foreign policy that reunification of Germany was a precondition for better East-West relations." Zbigniew Brzezinski OH, p. 10.

24. Memo of conversation, Eugene Rostow and Mike Mansfield, 9 December 1966, NSF: History of the National Security Council, LBJPL [hereafter NSC-Trilateral], box 51.

25. Cable from McGhee, Bonn, 20 September 1966, NSF: MP, Rostow, box 10.

26. McGhee to State, 4 October 1966, NSF: MP, Rostow, boxes 11, 12; Memo, Ball to McGhee, 8 September 1966, ibid., box 10; Memo, McNamara to LBJ, 19 September 1966, ibid.; George McGhee OH, p. 13.

27. Eugene Rostow OH, p. 10; Telegram, memo of conversation between McCloy and Erhard, 20 October 1966, NSF: NSC-Trilateral, box 50; Memo, Rusk to Mike Mansfield, 21 April 1967, ibid., box 51.

28. Memo, McCloy to LBJ, 23 February 1967, NSF: NSC-Trilateral, box 50; Telegram, memo of trilateral talks of 9 November 1966, ibid.; McCloy to LBJ, 21 November 1966, ibid.

29. Memo of conversation with LBJ, McCloy, Rostow, Bator, 2 March 1967, ibid.

30. Telegrams reporting opening of trilateral talks on 3 March 1967, ibid.; Telegram reporting trilateral talks of 5 March 1967, ibid.; George McGhee OH, p. 13.

31. Memo, Bator to LBJ, 17 March 1967, NSF: NSC-Trilateral, box 50; Leddy to Rusk, 23 August 1966, ibid.; Memo, Rusk to Mansfield, 21 April 1967, ibid., box 51; Rostow to LBJ, 10 June 1966, NSF: MP, box 8.

32. Acheson memo, 31 March 1965, "Study Needed of US Policy towards Europe," NSF: MP, box 3. See DePorte, *Europe between the Super-Powers*, p. 194, for an argument that downplays the seriousness of alliance tensions.

33. "Trends in the World Situation," 9 June 1964, NSF: NIE, boxes 1–5; Draft of HHH address at Michigan State University, 1 June 1965, NSF: NF, box 4.

34. George Ball, Congressional Briefings on Vietnam, 9 February 1965; Harriman to LBJ, 9 September 1966, CF, box 7; Rostow to LBJ, 20 September 1966, NSF: MP, Rostow, box 10; cable from Consul General Rice in Hong Kong, 10 August 1966, NSF: MP, Rostow, box 10; Statement by Rusk, 16 March 1966, *Hearings before the Subcommittee on the Far East and the Pacific of the Committee on Foreign Affairs*, House of Representatives, 89th Congress, 2nd session, pt. 2 (Washington, DC, 1969), p. 528; Luncheon meeting with advisers, 22 March 1968, Meeting notes, box 2.

35. Special NIE, 26 June 1963, "The Impact of the Sino-Soviet Dispute on North Vietnam and Its Policies," NSF: NIE, boxes 1–5; George Ball, Congressional Briefings on Vietnam, 4 March 1965; Lodge memo, 2 March 1964, on "Persistence in Vietnam," NSF: MP, Bundy, box 1; Extract from address by Maxwell Taylor at Rotary Club of New York, 3 February 1966, NSF: NF, box 6. In a 14 September 1964 meeting on Vietnam, Rusk expresssed the hope that "as that split grew more severe, there might be real inhibitions about adventure by Peking and Hanoi in Southeast Asia." NSF: MP, Bundy, box 2. On the implications of the split for the Vietnam war, see Douglas Pike, *Vietnam and the Soviet Union: Anatomy of an Alliance* (Boulder, CO, 1987), pp. 59–67.

36. LBJ meeting with Christopher Sewell, 15 September 1967, Meeting notes, box 3; Memo of conversation, Rusk and Hervé Alphand, 21 May 1965, NSF: CFF, box 171; Rusk interview with Dobrynin, 26 May 1966, CF, box 6; Memo, Thompson in Moscow to LBJ, 15 July 1966, NSF: Memos MP, Rostow, box 9.

37. Rystad, *Prisoners of the Past?*, pp. 62–67; LBJ meeting with Reuters representatives, 29 April 1968, Meeting notes, box 3; Meeting on Vietnam, 14 September 1964, NSF: MP, Bundy, box 2; Lodge memo, 2 March 1964, "Persistence in Vietnam," NSF: MP, Bundy, box 1. Eisenhower's letter to Churchill of 4 April 1954, which pulled out all the stops and predicted domino effects in Australia, Japan, and Europe, was thought to be particularly important. Bundy told Andrew Goodpaster that LBJ and Rusk thought the letter was "a fundamental and defining document in American foreign affairs." Bundy to Goodpaster, 19 August 1965, NSF: NF, box 2.

38. LBJ to JFK, 23 May 1961, V-P Security Files, box 1; McPherson to LBJ, 25 August 1967, McPherson Office Files, box 29. LBJ stressed American concern "for a whole great geographic area," and the need to shield an emerging free Asia from Communist threats. "If we abandon our efforts to keep stability in Asia," he

said on another occasion, "every single nation there will once again be an easy prey for these hungry, yearning Communist appetites." Ultimately, "an Asia so threatened by Communist domination would certainly imperil the security of the United States itself." Statements by LBJ in McPherson Office Files, box 29. For the argument that the concern was primarily regional, but within a cold war context, see Gary R. Hess, *Vietnam and the United States: Origins and Legacy of War* (Boston, 1990), pp. 87, 170.

39. Draft of LBJ V-E Day speech, 1965, NSF: Bundy, boxes 15, 16; Congressional Briefings on Vietnam, 2 March 1965; Dean Rusk OH, 6: 22. Fifteen years after the war ended, Rusk was still hewing to this line: "How we reacted would be looked upon by other governments as a sign as to how we would react under other treaties such as NATO and the Rio Pact . . . the reputation of the United States for fidelity to its security treaties is not just a simple question of face and prestige; its a real pillar of peace in the world." Rusk on station KERA television documentary, "The American Experience: LBJ," New York City, 2 October 1991. Similarly, Eugene Rostow saw "the real meaning of these events if one imagined them occurring in Germany, or in Korea. Would the world be concerned if attempts were made to unify those countries by force? The answer is self-evident." Eugene Rostow to Walt Rostow, 13 September 1966, NSF: MP, box 10.

40. Moyers to LBJ, 9 February 1964, Moyers Office File, box 12; Congressional Briefings on Vietnam, 11 February 1965; David L. DiLeo, *George Ball, Vietnam, and the Rethinking of Containment* (Chapel Hill, 1991), p. 69; Lodge to LBJ, 21 January 1965, NSF: Bundy, boxes 15, 16. At an NSC meeting early in 1965, McGeorge Bundy argued that "in other parts of the world, the effect [of a pullout] would also be very serious, even to the extent of affecting the morale in Berlin." Notes of NSC meeting, 8 February 1965, NSF: NSC meetings file.

41. Bohlen to Rusk, 13 December 1963, NSF: CFF, box 169; Eugene Rostow to Moyers to LBJ, 10 April 1965, ibid., box 171; William P. Bundy memo, 10 July 1965, NSF: Bundy, boxes 18, 19; Memo, Ernest Goldstein to Rostow, 27 September 1967, NSF: CFF, boxes 173, 174.

42. See Henry Fowler to Bundy, 5 April 1965, NSF: Bundy, boxes 15, 16; Harlan Cleveland OH.

43. Bruce to State, 2 June 1966, NSF: MP, box 8.

44. Bohlen to State, 3 June 1965, NSF: CFF, box 171; Memo, Harriman to Rusk, 18 March 1964, ibid., box 169; Memo of de Gaulle–Ball conversation, 5 June 1964, ibid., box 170.

45. Harriman to LBJ, 22 November 1966, "Report of Post-Manila trip," NSF: MP, Rostow, boxes 11, 12; George McGhee OH, pp. 18–19; Memo of conversation, LBJ and Erhard, 26 September 1966, NSF: NSC-Trilateral, box 50; Memo of conversation, Kissinger and Adenauer, 22 June 1965, NSF: Bundy, boxes 15, 16; Harriman to LBJ, 22 November 1966, NSF: MP, Rostow, boxes 11, 12.

46. George Ball OH, 2: 17; Memo by Ball, 23 June 1965, quoted in DiLeo, *George Ball*, p. 69.

47. Acheson to Clay, 4 January 1962, quoted in Trachtenberg, *History and Strategy*, p. 220.

48. Dean Rusk OH, 4: 28; Memo, R. C. Bowman to Rostow, 13 July 1966, NSF: NF, box 1. The CIA reported that "the thinking of even the friendliest of our allies tends to be permeated with the views of Walter Lippmann, Senator Morse, and Senator Fulbright." Memo, Ray Cline to Rostow, 13 April 1966, NSF: MP, Rostow, box 7.

49. Rostow to LBJ, 28 July 1966, NSF: MP, Rostow, box 10.

50. Dean Rusk OH, 4: 28; Ernest Goldstein to Rostow, 27 September 1967, NSF: CFF, boxes 173, 174; CIA Draft SNIE 50–2–64 "Probable Consequences of Certain US Actions with Respect to Vietnam and Laos," 23 May 1964, NSF: Bundy, boxes 18–19.

51. Congressional Briefings on Vietnam, 11 February 1965; Meeting notes, 1 July and 26 June 1965, box 1. At a May 1964 NSC meeting, for example, it was noted that one congressman was "unhappy because he believes that our allies really do not give a damn about Communist aggression in Southeast Asia." NSF: NSC Meetings File, 15 May 1964.

52. Meeting notes, 2 November 1967, box 2; LBJ to John Kenneth Galbraith, 20 June 1966, NSF: MP, box 8; Ball memo, 29 June 1965, *Pentagon Papers*, 4: 610.

53. Memo, Ray Cline to Rostow, 13 April 1966, NSF: MP, box 7; Meeting notes, 22 January 1966, box 1; Congressional Briefings on Vietnam, 9 February and 14 April 1965; Clark Clifford, "A Viet Nam Reappraisal," *Foreign Affairs* 47 (July 1969): 604.

54. Hoffman to Bundy, 1 July 1965, NSF: Bundy, boxes 18, 19; Robert E. Kintner to Leonard Marks, 11 August 1966, CF, box 6; Meeting notes, 2 November 1967, box 2.

55. Meeting notes, luncheon meeting, 24 November 1967, box 2; Rusk to LBJ, 14 October 1966, NSF: MP, Rostow, boxes 11, 12; Congressional Briefings on Vietnam, 24 February 1966. On the disappointing results of the "Many Flags Program," see George McT. Kahin, *Intervention: How American Became Involved in Vietnam* (New York, 1986), pp. 333–36.

56. Congressional Briefings on Vietnam, 9 February 1965 and 4 March 1965; Lodge to LBJ, 12 January 1966, NSF: MP, box 6. Lodge, on the scene in Saigon, noted numerous deficiencies in this regard among the Vietnamese: "instability and unwillingness to set quotas and fulfill them; a lack of American-style community spirit; an unwillingness to be impressed with words and promises; an unwillingness to accept responsibility; a lack of a sense of nationhood; a tendency toward sectarianism—or rather medieval gangsterism; a great deal of bureaucratic incompetence; and an even greater amount of intimidation by assassination, maiming and kidnapping." Somehow, he ended on a note of optimism, citing the good qualities of the people and his belief that they would triumph over their shortcomings. Lodge memo to LBJ, 29 April 1966, NSF: MP, box 7.

57. Congressional Briefings on Vietnam, 13 January 1965; Lodge to LBJ, 9 Au-

gust 1966, NSF: MP, box 9; Meeting notes, 20 January 1966, box 1; Stanley Karnow, "Giap Remembers," *New York Times Magazine,* 24 June 1990, 60; Rostow to LBJ, 30 March 1967, NSF: NF, box 7; John McCone memo, "South Vietnam Situation," 25 November 1963, Meeting notes, box 1. "All western logic would indicate that the NLF/Hanoi should start negotiating now, before they lose even more bargaining counters," said Rostow in late 1966. But Rostow was also "unclear how logical they were, notably in the light of their doctrine of protracted war in which they prided themselves on their ability to sweat it out longer than us." Draft memo, Rostow to LBJ, 20 September 1966, NSF: MP, Rostow, box 10; Rostow to LBJ, 10 September 1966, NSF: MP, Rostow, box 10. Despite criticisms from those who argued that the United States was operating from an invincible cultural ignorance in Vietnam, LBJ was in fact quite sensitive to such considerations. A few days into his presidency, he informed his aides that "he wanted to make it abundantly clear that he did not think we had to reform every Asian into our own image." He agreed with his aide Jack Valenti that the United States did not know enough about the Vietnamese mentality. "Every night I put myself in the shoes of Ho Chi Minh," he told Valenti. "I try to think what he is thinking. I try to feel what he is feeling. It's not easy, because I don't know him. I don't know him or his ancestry or his customs or his beliefs. It is tough, very tough." LBJ on 17 December 1965, in Valenti, *A Very Human President* (New York, 1976), p. 222. It was, in any case, not a matter of understanding an alien culture, but of forcing it to behave as the United States wished.

58. Melvin Small, *Johnson, Nixon, and the Doves* (New Brunswick, NJ, 1988), pp. 106–7; Douglass Cater to Bundy, 28 July 1965, NSF: NF, box 1; Bundy to LBJ, 20 April 1965, NSF: MP, Bundy, box 3; Congressional Briefings on Vietnam, 15 February 1967.

"They regard us as weak," LBJ said on another occasion, "therefore they think they will win." Meeting with congressional leaders, 24 February 1966, Meeting notes, box 1.

59. Meeting notes, 17 October 1967 and 16 February 1968, box 3; Tom Johnson's notes of meetings, 18 February 1968, box 1. As Dean Rusk subsequently explained: "One of the effects of a policy of gradual response was that at no given moment did we ever present Peking or Moscow with enough of a change in the situation to require them to make a major decision based on over-all world wide considerations." Dean Rusk OH, 2: 24. On this point see also Bundy to LBJ, 25 May 1964, NSF: Bundy, boxes 18, 19.

60. Bundy to LBJ, 7 February 1965, NSF: MP, Bundy, box 2.

61. Lodge to LBJ, 6 January 1966, NSF: MP, box 6; Morse to LBJ, June 1965, ibid., box 3; Meeting notes, 25 July 1965, box 1; Bundy memo, 16 February 1965, NSF: MP, Bundy, box 2. See the Congressional Briefings on Vietnam, 18 February 1965, where those present repeatedly say "South Korea" when they mean "South Vietnam."

62. Congressional Briefings on Vietnam, 16 and 25 February 1965; Meeting on Vietnam, 22 July 1965, Meeting notes, box 1.

63. Fulbright speech at Johns Hopkins University, 21 April 1966; Paragraph excised in the draft of LBJ V-E Day speech, NSF: Bundy, boxes 15, 16.

64. LBJ to Fulbright, 25 May 1966, NSF: MP, Rostow. "I have never subscribed to the domino theory," said Rusk; "it's much too esoteric." Dean Rusk news conference, 12 October 1967, *Pentagon Papers*, 4: 681. "We do ourselves no service by insisting that each source of aggression or each instance of aggression is unique." Statement by Rusk, 16 March 1966, *Hearings before the Subcommittee on the Far East*, p. 528. That is not to say that the simplistic domino theory based on historical analogy was not influential. For example, in July 1965 Speaker McCormack "was impressed by the analogy to Hitler. The road to appeasement was a road to war," while Bourke Hickenlooper of Iowa concluded that "anything short of a result that would make a reliable buffer against Communism would be disastrous."

65. Draft letter by Rostow, 24 May 1966, NSF: MP, box 7.

66. Eugene Rostow to Walt Rostow, 13 September 1966, NSF: MP, Rostow, box 10; Meeting notes, 26 June 1965; McNamara to LBJ, 16 March 1964, NSF: NSC Meetings File, box 1; Congressional Briefings on Vietnam, 11 February 1965; Meeting on Vietnam, 22 July 1965, Meeting notes, box 1.

67. Jonathan Schell, for one, has suggested that "the doctrine of credibility . . . was firmly rooted in the modern period." Schell, *The Time of Illusion* (New York, 1976), pp. 9–10. This failure of the liberal critics has been repeated by historians refighting the political battles of the period. Biographers of Fulbright and Ball, looking to give their heroes a distinctive opposing point of view, have painted them as realists, when in fact they were very much neo-Wilsonians in their own right. The need for precisely such an examination of "ideology" is argued in Leslie Gelb and Richard Betts, *The Irony of Vietnam: The System Worked* (Washington, DC, 1979), pp. 362–69. Douglas Walton, in *Slippery Slope Arguments* (Oxford, 1992), pp. 101–5, 280, 282, holds that slippery-slope arguments are not necessarily fallacious. To the contrary, they are "often quite correct and reasonable." The only sure test of their truth is a pragmatic one.

68. From its universalist perspective, the administration suspected that its opponents, many of whom were arguing from the standpoint of cultural relativism, were operating from unworthy motives. For example, LBJ believed that Fulbright was guilty of racial bias when, in urging American withdrawal, he told the president that the Vietnamese were "just not our kind of people." The invidious cultural relativism of some Vietnam opponents is evident from the following interview with Eugene McCarthy in the *New York Times Book Review* of 4 August 1968: "I [interviewer] asked him [McCarthy] the final question about Vietnam: 'How are we going to get out? He said 'Take this down. . . . [T]he time has come for us to say to the Vietnamese, We will take our steel out of the land of thatched huts, we will take our tanks out of the land of the water buffalo, our napalm and flame-throwers out of the land that scarcely knows the use of matches. We will give you back your small and willing women, your rice-paddies and your land.' he smiled. 'That's my platform. It's pretty good, isn't it?' "

Similarly, Johnson complained that columnists James Reston and Walter Lippmann, who argued for allying the country only with people of European civilization, had "no faith in the brown man and no faith in the Asian peoples." For the administration, world opinion was precisely that: supracultural and global. Humphrey, in a speech, declared that "if the principle of collective security is good for Europe . . . it is good for Asia; for the brown and yellow people of Asia and not just the white people of Europe, and I think it is just about time we said so." Whether racial or cultural in origin, these criticisms of administration policy, with their clear tendency to compartmentalize the world, were seen as "another form of isolationism." Eugene Rostow OH, p. 39; LBJ interview, 19 October 1967, Meeting notes, box 3; Valenti, *A Very Human President,* p. 375; Interview with Humphrey on "Meet the Press," 13 March 1966, NSF: NF, box 4; Rostow OH, p. 39.

69. Lodge to LBJ, 25 May 1966, NSF: MP, box 7; Meeting notes, 2 July and 17 December 1965, box 1.

70. Congressional Briefings on Vietnam, 5 August 1964; Meeting with Australian broadcast group, 20 September 1967, Meeting notes, box 3; Meeting in cabinet room, 18 December 1965, Meeting notes, box 1; LBJ interview, 13 October 1967, Tom Johnson's notes of meetings, box 1. Charles Bohlen later suggested that "the United States had really had a very short time to develop a national consciousness as to what world involvement meant." Charles E. Bohlen OH, p. 25. Eugene Rostow defined the problem similarly: "To accept reality when reality conflicts with the historical experience of the country." Rostow OH, p. 7.

71. Memo by Lodge, 2 March 1964, NSF: MP, Bundy, box 1; LBJ meeting with Australian broadcast group, 20 September 1967, Meeting notes, box 3. In retrospect, it seems easy enough to question Rostow's logic. Assuming that a Communist heard and took seriously this scenario, the credibility argument would fall down, since it would be irrational to press issues to the point of a world war. The lessons of the past with regard to avoiding total war were thought, after all, to apply in equal measure for both sides. But of course, it was assumed that the Communists, like the west Europeans, were incapable of appreciating the totality of interests involved.

72. Tom Johnson's notes of meetings, 9 August 1967, box 1.

73. Ibid., 13 October 1967, box 1.

74. Meeting notes, 19 October 1967, box 3; Congressional Briefings on Vietnam, 23 February 1967. The *Pueblo* crisis of 1968 is a good example of the administration passing up an opportunity to lather up public anti-Communist emotion.

75. Moyers to LBJ, 27 December 1965, Office Files of Bill Moyers, box 11; Tom Johnson's notes of meetings, 17 August 1967, box 1; Dean Rusk OH, 1: 42; Meeting notes, 19 August 1967, box 1. See also Walt Rostow OH, p. 77; Eugene Rostow OH, p. 15. In response to a query from a sailor aboard the USS *Constellation* who wondered why the United States was not hitting the North Vietnamese harder, LBJ talked with some embarrassment about the need for restraint and the need to

tolerate dissidents, but he never did provide a direct answer to the question, since that would have required implicitly criticizing the questioner for his blinkered patriotism. See Tom Johnson's notes of meetings, 18 February 1968, box 1.

76. Meeting notes, 18 December 1965, box 1; Ibid., 8 February 1967, box 3; Bundy to LBJ, 4 December 1965, NSF: MP, box 5; George Ball OH, 2: 7. The role of public opinion was explained by LBJ in a letter to Australian prime minister, Sir Robert Menzies. A resumption of bombings and further reinforcement of the south, LBJ argued, could take place "with greater support and understanding than would otherwise have been the case, and with some hope that worldwide support for our total position will be stronger than ever in the past." Draft, LBJ to Menzies, January 1966, NSF: MP, box 6. This slighting of the possibility of negotiations was not an oversight. According to Ball, "Negotiation at that time consisted pretty much of saying to Hanoi, 'Look, let's work out a deal under which you will capitulate.' " George Ball OH, 1: 39.

77. Meeting notes, 19 October 1967, box 3; Ibid., 2 February 1968, box 2.

78. Bundy to LBJ, 15 August 1968, Office Files of the President; Meeting with congressional relations officers, Meeting notes, 27 May 1968.

79. Tom Johnson's notes of meetings, 20 August and 25 November 1968, box 1; Shriver, Paris, to State, 11 October 1968, NSF: CFF, boxes 173, 174; Meeting notes, 14 October 1968.

CONCLUSION

1. Mary Kaldor, *The Imaginary War: Understanding the East-West Conflict* (Oxford, 1990), p. 4. I would question, however, Kaldor's hegemonist contention (p. 25) that imaginary war "presupposes that the fear of an external enemy is used to deal with conflicts *within* the blocs." The fear was real enough.

2. See the brief survey by Pierre Mélandri, "France and the United States," in *NATO after Forty Years,* ed. Lawrence Kaplan et al. (Wilmington, DE, 1990), pp. 67–69.

3. Memo of conversation, Acheson, Nixon, Kissinger, 19 March 1969, DAP: Yale, series 4, box 58.

4. Richard Nixon, *U.S. Foreign Policy for the 1970s: The Emerging Structure of Peace* (Washington, DC, 1972), p. 4.

5. Ibid., p. 1.

6. Mike Bowker and Phil Williams, *Superpower Detente: A Reappraisal* (London, 1988), p. 259.

7. Richard Nixon, *A New Strategy for Peace* (Washington, DC, 1970), p. 63. For Kissinger's strong belief in maintaining credibility as "the underpinning of his policies," see Walter Isaacson, *Kissinger: A Biography* (New York, 1992), pp. 120, 161.

8. Quoted in Robert Schulzinger, *Henry Kissinger: Doctor of Diplomacy* (New York, 1989), p. 223. See also Raymond L. Garthoff, *Detente and Confrontation:*

American-Soviet Relations from Nixon to Reagan (Washington, DC, 1985), pp. 524–25.

9. Stanley Rosen, *Hermeneutics as Politics* (New York, 1987), p. 94. In the 1930s, mathematician Kurt Gödel demonstrated that no finite set of axioms can answer all the questions that it raises.'' See *Scientific American* (December 1992): 22.

10. See, e.g., John A. Thompson, ''The Exaggeration of American Vulnerability,'' *Diplomatic History* 16 (Winter 1992): 28–43.

11. For various pragmatic takes on the instrumentality of truth, see Richard Rorty, *Consequences of Pragmatism* (Minneapolis, MN, 1982), pp. xvii, 16, 193, 205. One could argue with some justice that the realistic and strictly logical—and therefore ''scientific''—approach implied in the critique of containment is actually the more utopian outlook, since existence in the modern world without an ideology of some sort, which includes values, to guide human affairs is inconceivable.

12. Acheson, War College Lecture, 27 August 1951, DAP: Yale, series 3, box 47.

INDEX

A-bomb, 183
ABC–1 conversations, 121
Acheson, Dean, on China, 162; on Germany, 158–59, 286; on global danger, 119, 153; and Greek crisis, 173–74; on ideology, 147, 148, 153, 158–59; and Korea, 189–90, 193, 197, 199–200; on leadership, 296; on local wars, 201; on Marshall Plan, 174; mentioned, xi, 319; and NATO, 182, 257–58, 259; and NSC 68, 184–85; on post–cold war problems, 319; on Soviet A-bomb, 183
Adenauer, Konrad, 208, 250, 262; indispensability of, 219, 235; and JFK, 264–65; on MLF, 284; on nonproliferation treaty, 289; retirement of, 254, 260; on Vietnam, 295
Adler, Selig, 109
Adzhubei, Alexei, 245
Allison, John, 198–97
American Association for International Conciliation, 33
American Peace and Arbitration League, 32
Angola, 316
appeasement, FDR, 295–96

Arabic, 47
Aron, Raymond, 193, 260; on nuclear accommodation, 263–64
Asia, importance of 24, 64, 94, 119, 161–64, 199, 269–72, 273, 292; and Vietnam, 292, 297–98
Attlee, Clement R., 187
Australia, 298
axioms, xvii

Bagehot, Walter, 60
balance of power, in Asia, 191, 226; and Eisenhower, 213–15; and FDR, 113; historical demise of, 46, 54–56; and Hoover, 50, 91; and JFK, 258; and Kennan, 155–60; and LBJ, 281–82; and Theodore Roosevelt, 14–15; and Truman 180–81; and Vietnam, 315; and Woodrow Wilson, 44–56, 63–64
Balkan analogy, 51, 64, 93, 160
Ball, George, on de Gaulle, 282, 283; on Germany, 265; on offset payments, 287; on PRC, 290; on Vietnam, 267, 295, 297, 308; on Vietnam and Europe, 295
Baruch, Bernard, 65, 184
Bashford, J. E., 30
Beard, Charles, 108, 119

Berle, Adolf, 111, 114
Berlin, as symbol, 251–52; and
    Vietnam, 293; 1972 accords, 313
Berlin Crisis (1948), 158, 175–79
Berlin Crisis (1958–61), 232–39, 248–
    53; and LBJ, 277
Berlin Wall, 252
Bermingham, Edward, 204
Black, Max, xvi
Bohlen, Charles, 139; on de Gaulle,
    257, 259, 294; on Khrushchev,
    245; on MLF, 263; on NATO, 279;
    on Sino-Soviet split, 270; on Soviet
    ambitions, 150, 154; on Vietnam
    and Europe, 293, 294
Bourgeois, Léon, 51
Bowles, Chester, 243; on Berlin, 252;
    on Eurocentrism, 268; on JFK,
    267–68
Bradley, Omar, 293–94
Braisted, William, 29
Brandt, Willy, 252, 313
Brentano, Heinrich von, 266
Brezhnev, Leonid, 278, 313
Bruce, David, 235, 282
Brussels Pact, 179
Bryan, William Jennings, 3
Bundy, McGeorge, on Berlin, 250;
    on Cuba and Europe, 261; on
    de Gaulle, 261–62, 282; on Ger-
    many, 260, 286; on Vietnam and
    Europe, 293; on Vietnam, 298,
    300, 301, 309
Burke, Edmund, 58, 59
Butler, Nicholas Murray, 33, 106, 118

Cannon, Joseph G., 17
Carnegie, Andrew, 33
Carnegie Endowment for International
    Peace, 33
Carr, David, xv
Carr, E. H., 167
Castle, William, 94
Castro, Fidel, 248

Cater, Douglass, 243, 298
Cecil, Viscount Robert, 104
Chamberlain, Neville, 187
Charles I, 147
Chiang Kai-shek, 197, 226, 231; and
    FDR 126, 127; morale of, 228; sur-
    vival of, 226
China, and Eisenhower, 226–32; and
    Hoover, 89–96; ideology in PRC,
    269–70, 290–92, 314–15; and The-
    odore Roosevelt, 11–12; and Taft,
    24–32; and Truman, 161–64, 191,
    197–98; and Vietnam, 300, 315
Churchill, Winston, 135, 167, 179,
    201, 209, 224, 228
civilization, xi; and FDR, 101–4, 120;
    and JFK, 244; and LBJ, 277; and
    Stimson, 92–93; and Theodore
    Roosevelt, 4–5, 15–20; and Taft,
    21–23; and Woodrow Wilson, 38,
    41–42
Clausewitz, Karl von, 23, 146, 168,
    194
Clay, Lucius D., 176, 177, 296
Clemenceau, Georges, 236
Cleveland, Grover, 10
Cleveland, Harlan, 294
Clifford, Clark, and Clifford report,
    167–68; and Czech crisis of 1968,
    309–10; on ideology, 147, 153; on
    Truman, 138; and Truman Doc-
    trine, 171; and Vietnam, 297–98;
    on western Europe, 162
Clubb, O. Edmund, 1
cold war, as neo-Wilsonian problem-
    atic, 132, 166–70; as struggle of
    modernizations, 205–7, 317
collective security, 211–12
Common Market, 264, 312
Conant, James B., 146, 216, 293
containment, timetable of, 243
convergence theory, 128
Coolidge, Archibald Cary, 40, 66, 100
Coolidge, Calvin, 81

Couve de Murville, Maurice, 264
credibility, and Cuban missile crisis,
    261; and JFK, 247; and NASA,
    277; and Vietnam, 276; and
    Wilson, 65–66
Croly, Herbert, 6, 10, 39
Cromwell, Oliver, 147
Cuba, 248; Bay of Pigs affair, 248;
    and Europe, 261–63; missile crisis,
    260–62
culture, and FDR, 166; Hoover on,
    85–87; and JFK, 243–44; and LBJ,
    403n
Cutler, Robert, 211
Czechoslovakia, 309

Daladier, Eduard, 187
Daniels, Josephus, 101, 102
Davies, Joseph, 113
Dawes, Charles, 69
De Gaulle, Charles, 252; on Adenauer,
    250; and Berlin, 236, 242; critique
    of U.S., 256–57; and Cuban mis-
    sile crisis, 262; and Common
    Market, 264; departure of, 312–13;
    and LBJ, 278–83; and nationalism,
    256–59, 307; and NATO, 280–82,
    289; and SEATO, 280; and
    Vietnam, 280, 293–94, 296; on
    world opinion, 256
De Porte, Anton, 255
détente, 311–13; limited nature of,
    315–17
Diem, Ngo Dinh, 267
Dien Bien Phu, 223
Dillon, C. Douglas, 282
Dobrynin, Anatoly, 291
Dodd, William E., 105
domino theory, and Berlin, 176–77,
    235; and China, 228–29; and Eisen-
    hower, 222–23; and FDR, 116–21;
    and Herbert Hoover, 92–95; and
    Indochina, 222–23; and JFK,
    251–52, 271–272; and Korea, 187;

and LBJ, 292–94; as metaphor,
    xvi–xvii; and Dean Rusk, 301; and
    Henry Stimson, 92–93; symbolic
    character of, 191–95; and Truman
    administration, 151–64; and
    Vietnam, 271–72, 301–2; and
    Woodrow Wilson, 51–56, 68
Douglas, Lewis, 176
Douglas, William O., 136
Dulles, Allen, 217
Dulles, John Foster, on atomic diplo-
    macy, 208–11; and China policy,
    225–32; on credibility, 237; criti-
    cism of Truman, 203; and EDC
    216; on end of cold war, 205; on
    France, 220, 222–23; and Ger-
    many, 216–18, 234–35, 237–38;
    on Great Britain, 221; on ideology,
    204–5; on Indochina, 222–25; on
    Korea, 197; on local aggression,
    194, 206–7, 210–11; mentioned,
    128, 129, 150, 163; on NATO,
    214, 217–19, 232–33; on North
    Atlantic treaty, 182; and Quemoy-
    Matsu crisis, 226–31; on *Sputnik*,
    231–32; and world opinion, 210,
    227–31
Durbrow, Elbridge, 181

Eban, Abba, 308
Eberstadt, Ferdinand, 196
Eden, Anthony, 219, 229, 231
Einstein, Lewis, 2, 29–31
Eisenhower, Dwight D., 135; and
    Asia, 219–22; and Berlin, 232–40;
    and China, 226–32; cold war
    defined, 205–6; domino theory,
    223–24; and EDC, 214–16; and
    Europe, 212–19; and France, 220,
    236–37; and Germany, 215–19,
    232–34, 237–38; Geneva summit,
    217–19; and ideology, 204–5; and
    Indochina, 222–25; on Korea,
    206–7; massive retaliation, 208–9;

Eisenhower, Dwight D. (*continued*)
on morale, 212–14; on NATO,
213–16; Quemoy-Matsu crisis,
226–32; and Vietnam, 292, 299,
300; on war, 168; and world
opinion, 212–13, 220–21, 228–30,
232, 235–36, 240
Eisenhower, Milton, 212
Elsey, George, 171
Erhard, Ludwig, 285, 287–88, 295
Ethiopia, 112
Etzold, Thomas, 168
Europe, balance of power in, 213,
256–57; and colonial atavism, 221–
22; and Cuban missile crisis, 261–
63; and Czech crisis of 1968,
309–10; and détente, 311–13; geographic particularism of, 221, 255;
and LBJ, 274, 276; nationalism in,
281–82, 290; spiritual decline of,
220, 236; and Theodore Roosevelt,
13–16; weakness of, 289–90; and
Vietnam, 270, 272–73, 292–97,
303
European Defense Community, 214–
19; and Asia, 220, 228; and
German problem, 215

Faure, Edgar, 225
flexible response, 246
Forrestal, James T., 137, 140, 167
Fortas, Abe, 291
Four Power Pact (1922), 69
France, 33, 34; after de Gaulle, 312–
13; and Eisenhower, 220, 236–37;
and JFK, 255–60, 262–64; and
LBJ, 279–83, 294; and NATO,
237; weakness of, 236–37
Franco-German Treaty, 264, 266
Franks, Sir Oliver, 199
Fulbright, J. William, on Berlin, 238,
249, 250; on Munich analogy,
301–2; and racism in Vietnam, 299

Gaddis, John Lewis, xvi, 183–84

Galbraith, John Kenneth, 267, 272
Gavin, James, 256, 257
Geertz, Clifford, xiv
Geneva Conference (1954), 224
Geneva summit (1955), 217
George, Alexander, 252
German Democratic Republic, 249
Germany, 15–16; and Eisenhower,
215–19, 232–39; and FDR, 102,
114–20, 123–125; and Federal
Republic, 217; and Hoover, 73–76;
and JFK, 248–55, 264–66; and
LBJ, 283–90; national character,
285; nationalism in, 251, 254; and
NATO, 255, 293; neutralization of,
157–58, 233–34; and NPT, 285;
and nuclear weapons, 218–19,
259–66, 283–85; offset payments,
287–89; and *Ostpolitik*, 312–13;
and public opinion in, 254–55;
reunification, 254, 285–86; troop
reductions in, 286; and Truman,
157–59, 177–79; and Vietnam,
270, 295; Woodrow Wilson on,
47–48, 51–53, 55, 60, 64–65
Giap, Vo Nguyen, 299
Gladstone, William E., 61
Good Neighbor Policy, 106, 116, 130
Great Britain, and Berlin, 36; and
Common Market, 264, 312; and
Vietnam, 294
Greek crisis (1947), 171–72
Grewe, Wilhelm, 260
Grey, Sir Edward, 34
Gromyko, Andrey, 253
Gruenther, Alfred, 215, 219, 229

Habermas, Jurgen, 62
Hamilton, Alexander, 3, 9, 11
Harding, Warren G., 32, 81
Harriman, W. Averell, 128, 150, 160;
on Asia, 269; on Germany, 253; on
Indochina and NATO, 222; on
Vietnam and Europe, 294, 295
Hay, John, 12, 42

Hegel, G. W. F., xvi, 318
Herter, Christian, 153, 184; on Berlin, 238
Hickerson, John, 179
Hillenbrand, Martin, 249
Hilsman, Roger, 267
historical interpretation, xv–xvi, 147–48, 186–91, 318; and containment, 140–41, 145–46; and Eisenhower, 205–6; and FDR, 100–103, 114–16; and Hoover, 86–89; and JFK, 247; and Korea, 186; and Taft, 21–22; and Theodore Roosevelt, 2–4; in Vietnam, 301–2; and Wilson, 42–44, 61–62, 63, 65
Hitler, Adolf, 147
Hobbes, Thomas, 63
Hoffman, Paul, 298
Hofstadter, Richard, 10
Hoover, Herbert, xiv; Americanism of, 72, 86; and Bolshevism, 83–85; and China, 89–91; and Commission for Relief in Belgium, 73–74; cosmopolitanism of, 71–72; on culture, 85–87; and domino theory, 93–95; economic internationalism of, 80–83; and historical particularism, 86–89; on ideology, 86–87; and Japan, 89; and League of Nations, 77–80, 95; and Paris Peace Conference, 75–77; and world opinion, 95–97; and World War I, 73–75
Hoover, Herbert, Jr., 218
Hoover, Lou Henry, 74, 90
Hornbeck, Stanley K., 92
House, Edward M., 48, 75
Hoyt, H. M., 26
Hull, Cordell, 118, 120, 122, 129
Humphrey, George, 227
Humphrey, Hubert, on de Gaulle, 281; on Vietnam 290
Huntington Wilson, Frances, 22

ideology, 278; and FDR, 127–28; flexibility of in cold war, 318–19; and

Hoover, 83–87; and JFK, 242, 245; Kennan on, 139–44; in People's Republic of China, 269–270, 290–92, 314–15; in USSR, 138–44, 146–51, 204, 205, 242–43, 290–92; waning of, 314, 316–17
imperialism, 6–9, 39–42, 44
Indochina, 222–25; and Great Britain, 224; and Korea, 223
isolationism, in Europe, 296; U.S. and Vietnam, 305, 308; in 1930s, 106–9

James, William, 59
Japan, and FDR, 117; and Hoover, 89; and Theodore Roosevelt, 12–13, 27–29, 33; and Stimson, 92, 95–96; and Taft, 32–34; and Vietnam, 297; and Wilson, 44, 46–47, 49–51, 54–56, 63–64
Jefferson, Thomas, 3, 116
Johnson, Louis, 191–92
Johnson, Lyndon B., and appeasement, 295–97; and Asia, 297–300; on Berlin, 293; and France, 279–83, 294; and Germany, 283–90, 295; and Great Britain, 294; and history, 301–3; and ideology, 290–92; and nuclear accommodation, 278; and public opinion, 300–310; and SEATO, 295; and Vietnam, 290–311; and world opinion, 292–93, 302–3, 305; worldview of, 277–78
Johnson, Mark, xvi
Jonas, Manfred, 108
Jordan, David Starr, 72

Kautsky, Karl, 23
Kaysen, Carl, 253
Kellogg-Briand Pact, 69, 95, 96
Kennan, George F., and balance of power, 155–61; and China, 160–64; and containment, 144–46, 149–

Kennan, George F. (*continued*)
51; on Germany, 157–59, 233; and
Greek crisis, 172; and historical
interpretation, 145–46; on ideology,
139–44; on Khrushchev, 245; and
Korea, 191, 194, 199; on local conflicts, 194; and Marshall Plan, 174;
and neo-Wilsonianism, 151–65; on
neutral rights, 37; and NSC 68,
185; popularity of, 146–49; and
restatement of FDR's cooperationist
outlook, 133–34; on war with
USSR, 155; on world domination,
152–55
Kennedy, John F., and Berlin, 248–
53; and credibility, 247–48; and
Cuban missile crisis, 260–61; and
France, 255–60, 262–64; and Germany, 253–55, 264–66; and ideology, 242–43; and local wars,
246, 268–69, 271; pragmatism of,
267–68, 273; and realpolitik, 266,
274; and Sino-Soviet split, 269–70;
and symbolism, 243–46, 272; and
Vietnam, 267, 272–75; and world
opinion, 266–67; worldview of,
241
Kennedy, Joseph P., 109, 119
Kennedy, Robert, on Vietnam, 273,
293
Khrushchev, Nikita, 234, 236, 278;
and Berlin, 249, 253; and Cuba,
261, 263; on Germany, 238–39; as
ideologue, 242–43, 244, 245; and
Vienna summit, 247; and wars of
national liberation, 269
Kiesinger, Kurt, 289
Kirk, Alan, 198
Kissinger, Henry, on Adenauer, 250;
mentioned, 310; on MLF, 262, 284;
and PRC, 314
Knox, Philander, 21, 22–24, 26–27,
31, 34, 35. *See also* Taft, William
Howard
Korea, South Korea and Vietnam, 298

Kristallnacht, 112, 114
Krock, Arthur, 241

Lakoff, George, xvi
Lamarckism, 7, 8, 72
Laniel, Joseph, 216
Lansing, Robert, 48
Lee, Arthur, 17
Leffler, Melvyn, 169
Lemnitzer, Lyman, 283
Lend-Lease Program, 127
Lenin, V. I., 150
Lin Piao, 290–91
Lippmann, Walter, 145; on Germany,
125, 233; on nuclear parity, 245–
46; progressive outlook, xii, 21;
and Vietnam, 299; on world
opinion, 105
Litvinoff, Maxim, 128
Lloyd, Selwyn, 236
local wars, 246–47
Locke, John, 63
Lodge, Henry Cabot, 34
Lodge, Henry Cabot, Jr., 291, 298,
299, 300, 305
Lovett, Robert, on Berlin crisis, 176;
on Korea, 198; mentioned, 162,
167, 219; on military aid, 181
Lusitania, 47, 74

MacArthur, Douglas, 168, 197
MacArthur, Douglas, II, 216
Machiavelli, Niccolò, 45
MacIntyre, Alasdair, xii
Mackenzie King, W. L., 112
Mackinder, Halford, 51
Madison, James, 39
Mahan, Alfred Thayer, 100
Malraux, André, 264
Manchuria crisis, as antecedent of
Munich analogy, 188
Mannheim, Karl, 142
Mansfield, Mike, on Vietnam, 267,
287
Mansfield Amendment, 286–87

Mao Zedong 162, 197, 290
Marshall, George C., on European balance, 156–57; and Greek crisis, 172; on morale, 200; on NATO, 179, 213; on war with USSR, 155, 167; on world strategy, 152
Masaryk, Jan, 136
massive retaliation, 207–12
Matloff, Maurice, 121
May, Ernest, xvii
McCarthy, Joseph, 163
McCloy, John, 281; on Europe and Vietnam, 293–94; on nonproliferation treaty, 284, 289; and trilateral negotiations, 288–89
McGhee, George, 285, 287, 295
McGovern, George, 314
McKelway, Clair, 300
McNamara, Robert, and Cuba, 261; and offset payments, 287–89, 303; on Vietnam, 272, 298, 308
McPherson, Harry, 292
Merchant, Livingston, 218, 238
metaphor, xvi–xvii, 67
Mikoyan, Anastas, 234, 238
Military Assistance Program, 181
Miller, R. S., 31
modernity, xi–xv, 168, 318; and FDR, 113–16; and Wilson, 43, 51. *See also* civilization; power
Molotov, Vyacheslav, 135, 147
Monroe Doctrine, 9–11, 23–24
Montgomery, Bernard Law, 205
morale, 181; and Chiang Kai-shek, 228; and Eisenhower, 212–13; in Europe, 251–52
Morgenthau, Hans, 299
Morgenthau, Henry, 119, 124
Moyers, Bill, on MLF, 284–85; on Vietnam, 293, 308
Multilateral Force, 262–63, 284–85
Munich analogy, in Korea 186–96; in Vietnam 301–2
Munich crisis, 111, 112–13
Murphy, Robert, 177, 178, 179

Murrow, Edward R., 251
Mussolini, Benito, 111

Napoleon, 147
nationalism, in Europe, 290
NATO, 179–81; and Asia, 220–21; and Czech crisis of 1968, 309–10; and EDC, 214–19; fear of dissolution, 287–89; Kennan on, 158; and Vietnam, 270, 296; weakness of, 212
NEP, 84
Neutrality Acts, 107–9
New Look, 210
New Zealand, 298
Nine-Power Treaty (1922), 96
Nitze, Paul, on atomic diplomacy, 207–8; on Franco-German treaty, 264; on NSC 68, 185; on Soviet ideology, 149
Nixon, Richard, and China, 314; and détente, 313; mentioned, 206, 310; and Vietnam, 313–14
Nixon Doctrine, 316
Nonproliferation treaty, 284
Norstad, Lauris, 247, 265
North Atlantic Treaty, 179–81
NSC 68, 149, 153, 168, 184–86
nuclear parity, 210–11, 245–46
Nuclear Planning Group, 284

Oder-Neisse line, 250, 253
Open Door policy, 11–12, 25–31; Kennan on, 161
Oppenheimer, J. Robert, 185
Ostpolitik, 313

Pach, Chester J., Jr., 181
Peabody, Endicott, 119
Pearl Harbor, 121–22
People's Republic of China. *See* China
Philippines, 5, 91, 298
Phillips, William, 115
Pius XII, 114
Pleven, René, 201

Pompidou, Georges, 280, 312
Potsdam Accords, 136
power, and modernity, 17, 20–21, 23, 49–56, 78, 93–94, 116–19, 166–71, 208–11, 227
pragmatism, 273
prestige, and JFK, 247
public opinion, and Vietnam, 270, 276–77, 300–309

Quarantine Speech, 110
Quemoy-Matsu crisis, 226–31; symbolic aspects of, 230–31

Radford, Arthur, 220, 227
Rainbow Plans, 121
Rapallo treaty, 233
realism, xiv, xv, 45, 114, 164, 170, 266, 318
Reed, John, 49
Reinsch, Paul, 6, 39
reparations, 136
Reston, James, 212
Reynaud, Paul, 260
Ricoeur, Paul, xii, 140
Robertson, Walter, 225
Rockhill, W. W., 27
Roosevelt, Eleanor, 129, 148
Roosevelt, Franklin D., and appeasement, 112–12; and China, 103, 115, 126–27; and civilization, 101–4, 120; and domino theory, 116–21; and Germany, 102, 114–20, 123–35; and historical interpretation, 114–16; and ideology, 127–28; and isolationism, 106; and Theodore Roosevelt, 100–102; and United Nations, 129–31; and USSR, 126–28; and Wilson, 102–4; and world opinion, 104–6, 110–13, 124–40
Roosevelt, Theodore, xvii; and China, 11–13; cosmopolitanism of, 4, 16; and Germany, 14–15; and history,

2–4; and imperialism, 5–6, 8–9; and Japan, 12–13; modernity and tradition of, 16–20; and Monroe Doctrine, 10–11, 14–15; and social Darwinism, 7
Root, Elihu, 2, 13, 164
Rorty, Richard, 38, 317–18
Rostow, Eugene, on Europe, 279; on offset payments, 289; on Vietnam and Europe, 293
Rostow, Walt, on credibility, 248; on de Gaulle, 283; on domino theory, 305; on Europe and Asia, 266–67; on JFK, 273; on LBJ, 278; on NATO, 255, 279; on nonproliferation treaty, 284–85; on North-South divisions, 241; on Vietnam, 270–72, 302; on wars of national liberation, 270; on world leadership, 320
Royall, Kenneth, 178
Rusk, Dean, on Cuba and Europe, 261; on false optimism, 278; on Franco-German treaty, 264; on Germany, 253–54, 260, 265; on Germany and Vietnam, 293; on isolationism in Europe, 296; on isolationism in U.S., 308; on Korea, 198; on Munich analogy, 301–3; on opinion in Asia, 298; on PRC, 291; on Vietnam, 291, 295, 299, 303, 308, 316
Russia, 13, 27–28

SALT I treaty, 313
Sato, Eisaku, 298
Schlesinger, Arthur M., Jr., 167; on ideology, 242; on pluralism, 244; on world opinion, 244
Schröder, Gerhard, 254, 285
Schumpeter, Joseph, 23
Schurman, Jacob Gould, 15
SEATO, 224, 228, 280, 295, 297
Servan-Schreiber, Jean-Jacques, 263

Shotwell, James T., 92
Sino-Japanese War, 110
Sino-Soviet Relations, 96; and
   Vietnam, 269–70, 274, 291–92
Smith, Walter Bedell, 147, 148, 227
social Darwinism, 7, 42
Sorensen, Theodore, 245; on Cuba,
   263; on PRC, 269; on Vietnam,
   267
Spaak, Paul Henri, 259
Spanish-American War, 5
Spargo, John, 104
Spring Rice, Cecil, 14, 48
Sputnik, 231–32
Stalin, Joseph, 129, 136, 147
Sternburg, Speck von, 11
Stevens, Leslie C., 150, 167, 204
Stimson, Henry, and domino theory,
   92–93, 94, 95; and Korea, 131,
   188
Strachey, John St. Loe, 53
Straight, Willard, 21
Sun Yat-sen, 30
symbolism, 170–71; 191–95, 227–31,
   243, 317; and Vietnam, 302, 306–7

Taft, William Howard, 56; and arbitra-
   tion, 32–35; and China, 24–32; and
   imperialism, 24; and Japan, 32–34;
   modernity of, 20–23; and Monroe
   Doctrine, 23–24, 35; and Theodore
   Roosevelt, 20–21, 33
Taylor, Maxwell, 246
Tet offensive, 308
Thomas, Norman, 116
Thompson, Llewelyn, on Berlin, 249;
   on Germany, 235, 237; on Soviet
   ideology, 240
Tito, 162
Tocqueville, Alexis de, 3
Toynbee, Arnold, 221
Trilateral Negotiations, 287–89. *See
   also* Germany
Tripartite Pact (1940), 119, 121

Truman, Harry S., 138; and Berlin,
   178; on cooperation, 134–35; on
   ideology, 146–47; on Korea,
   186–87, 199
Truman Doctrine, 171–74; Wilsonian
   character of, 173–74
Truman-MacArthur controversy, 198
Tugwell, Rexford, 114
Tyler, William R., 281

United Nations Organization, 129–31,
   190
USSR, ideology in, 245, 291–92;
   nuclear accommodation, 248;
   strength of, 243; and Vietnam 291,
   300

Vandenberg, Hoyt, 153
Vienna, Congress of, 317
Vienna summit, 244, 247, 249, 261,
   269
Vietminh, 221
Vietnam, 267–75, 290–309, 313–14,
   316; and Asia, 292; and Berlin,
   273, 293; and credibility, 276; and
   Cuba, 273; and de Gaulle, 293–
   94; and détente, 313–14, 316;
   and domino theory, 301–2; and
   Eisenhower, 292, 300; escalation in, 299–300; and Europe,
   270, 272–73, 292–97, 303; and
   Germany, 295; and historical
   understanding, 301–2; and internationalism, 306–7; and Japan, 297;
   and NATO, 296; and New Zealand,
   298; North Vietnam, 291, 298–99;
   and patriotism, 306–8; and Philippines, 298; and PRC, 290–92, 300;
   and South Korea, 298; as symbolic
   war, 306–7; and U.S. public
   opinion, 300–309; and USSR, 300;
   and world opinion, 270, 272. *See
   also* Indochina

War of 1812, 108
Warsaw Pact, 309
Webb, James E., 162, 193
Weber, Max, 23
Welles, Sumner, 111
Western European Union, 218, 229
Western Union, 179
Westmoreland, William, 308
Wexler, Immanuel, 174
White, Andrew D., 15
Whitlock, Brand, 73
Wilbur, Ray Lyman, 72, 89
Willett, Edward, 137–38, 148
Wilson, Charles, 225
Wilson, Harold, 285, 294
Wilson, Woodrow, xvi; and balance of
   power, 44, 49–50, 52–53; 54–56;
   conservatism of, 58–59; on credi-
   bility, 66–66; and domino theory,
   51–53; and Germany, 47–48, 64;
   and historical interpretation, 42–44;

historical significance of, 37–38,
   61–63, 68; and imperialism, 38–41;
   and metaphor, 67; and Wilsonianism, 67–68; and world opinion,
   56–62
Woodrow Wilson Foundation, 102,
   105
Woolf, Virginia, 1
world opinion, 318; and détente, 316;
   and Eisenhower, 212–13, 220–21,
   228–30, 232, 235–36, 240; and
   FDR, 104–6, 110–13, 129–30;
   and Hoover, 74, 84, 92, 95–97;
   and JFK, 243–45, 251–52, 270,
   272–77; and Taft, 22–23; and
   Truman, 70–71, 172–73, 174,
   176–77, 181–82, 183, 199–200; in
   Vietnam, 303, 318; and Wilson,
   56–66. *See also* morale; credibility

Yemen, 316